Peter Normanton ed   r Comics along
with twenty-eight is   blication From
the Tomb. He is currently writing a series of short biographies for PS
Publication's fifteen-volume Harvey Horrors.

The Mammoth Book of
Slasher
Movies

BY PETER NORMANTON

RUNNING PRESS
PHILADELPHIA · LONDON

Constable & Robinson Ltd
55–56 Russell Square
London WC1B 4HP
www.constablerobinson.com

First published in the UK by Robinson,
an imprint of Constable & Robinson Ltd, 2012

Copyright © Peter Normanton, 2012

The right of Peter Normanton to be identified as the
author of this work has been asserted by him in accordance
with the Copyright, Designs & Patents Act 1988.

A copy of the British Library Cataloguing in Publication
Data is available from the British Library

UK ISBN: 978-1-78033-036-5 (paperback)
UK ISBN: 978-1-78033-041-9 (ebook)

3 5 7 9 10 8 6 4 2

First published in the United States in 2012 by Running Press Book Publishers,
A Member of the Perseus Books Group

Books published by Running Press are available at special discounts for bulk purchases
in the United States by corporations, institutions, and other organizations. For more
information, please contact the Special Markets Department at the Perseus Books Group,
2300 Chestnut Street, Suite 200, Philadelphia, PA 19103, or call (800) 810-4145, ext.
5000, or e-mail special.markets@perseusbooks.com.

US ISBN: 978-0-7624-4596-7
US Library of Congress Control Number: 2011939125

9 8 7 6 5 4 3 2 1
Digit on the right indicates the number of this printing

Running Press Book Publishers
2300 Chestnut Street
Philadelphia, PA 19103-4371

Visit us on the web!
www.runningpress.com

Designed by www.basementpress.com
Printed and bound in the UK

Contents

Introduction:
A Born-Again Slasher

WAY BACK THEN you could scream all you wanted, but it was never going to make them stop, as for an entire decade the doors to the madhouse were thrown open to a plethora of hack and slash killers who were free to slip into school dormitories, college campuses, the woods, shopping malls or for the very unlucky their local neighbourhood. Each was armed with a sharp knife, with bloody murder in mind. There never was a decade quite like the eighties. Whether it was food, drink, fashion, music or film, these years can only be described as unique. And we took it all in, thriving on an excess of cheese (the cheesier the better), no more so than in the insanity of the slasher and splatter cinema that suddenly became so popular. As the newfound video market began to expand, so did the excess and we just couldn't get enough of it.

When we first discussed putting together this compilation of slasher and splatter movies, memories of a Monday evening in the pub way back in that sweltering summer of 1984 came to mind. Quite a few of us were serving our time on Thatcher's ever lengthening dole queues as recession continued to ravage an already declining British industry, so a night in the pub was something of a treat. As the miners fought pitched battles with the police in the grim hope of preserving their livelihood, we were hunting down the video nasties that back then were all the rage. If these films hadn't acquired such notoriety we probably would never have bothered with many of them; in fact more than a fair share of them were just plain boring. But did that stop us? No it certainly didn't. That evening the conversation had drifted from how good Van Halen had been at Castle Donnington and the prospect of a new Rush album to the grisly murders in our favourite slasher movies. Needless to say after a few pints of Burtonwood's finest ale our recollection of the gruesome episodes that had been the driving force behind these films had become a little distorted; who killed who and how was now confused. Ironically, given the content of the tome you now have in your hands, I was the one who started to ridicule this excess, delighting in deliberately muddling the butchery of

Friday the 13th Part II with The Boogeyman and Happy Birthday to Me. After four years of unrelenting blood and guts, we had completely overdosed on this gore-ridden pageant. It seems odd when I look back, but I never went to see the sensation that terrorised the cinema-going public in the latter months of that year, Wes Craven's A Nightmare on Elm Street. The poor dubbing, dodgy acting, along with the screaming scantily clad girls and the endless masked killers had finally numbed my senses, and at that moment I needed something different in life. While my interest in horror movies never entirely waned, the gore-mongering passion that had possessed me during those truculent years of my late teens and early twenties had begun to fade.

In the ensuing years, I was all too frequently found stalking the back streets of Manchester city centre rummaging through boxes of old comic books, in search of more horror. A lasting memory of these shops was the racks of videos, and what a lurid display they were! There were many films on show in these shops to which I had never before been privy, and they looked every bit as deranged as the terrors I had previously been watching. The real nasties of those years, however, were conspicuous by their absence; it would be years before I finally understood why I never had the chance to see a copy of Lucio Fulci's The New York Ripper, and later in these pages if you live in the UK you will discover exactly why. My interest in these kill crazy movies was revitalized soon after I got married, and no it wasn't the sight of my wife hacking into a tender loin of beef; rather, it was Bob Clarke's Black Christmas, which was being given a late night showing on Channel 4. Why I had never seen this film escapes me, but it had me on the edge of my seat. I was hooked all over again and just couldn't get enough of this splatter-filled madness, especially if it was a dubbed Italian feature.

During the conversations that took place at the very beginning of compiling these films there were thoughts about presenting a section on the very worst of the slasher and splatter genre. Let's be honest, if you have watched enough of the films you will have seen plenty of howlers, and as I said earlier in this introduction there has been nothing in the history of film, music or fashion that has ever quite matched the cheese of the eighties. However, once I started to research these films, it became obvious this would have been a little unkind, because many of the people who were involved with these productions were doing it for very little pay and for the most part had neither the cash nor the experience to create another

Halloween or **Night of the Living Dead**. It didn't stop them though and in their own way they have become every much a part of the genre as Messrs Carpenter, Raimi, Romero, Fulci and Argento.

Before I let you tuck into these blood-strewn pages I have to confess this is far from being a comprehensive list of these films. I have managed to squeeze in just over 250 entries into the A–Z reference section, which focus mainly on the golden years of the slasher and splatter excess from the late seventies through until the mid-eighties, with over 500 films included in the accompanying index at the end of this book. At the end of my research, there were well over a thousand movies that were deserving of a mention. If you can't find your own personal favourite, or the film you worked on isn't here, I sincerely apologize. As my research continued, it became obvious there was no way I was going to be able to fit every single film into these pages. With that in mind, I prefer to think of this selection as the good, the bad and the ugly of the slasher and splatter genre.

Finally, I would like to thank all of my family and friends along with my colleagues at work for putting up with all of this gory madness for the past nine months. A special thanks goes to my mate of many years who was in the pub that night (what's new?), Glenn Royds, who took the time to read over and correct so many of these entries, and also to Raoul for alerting me to so many of these amazing movies. Last of all, a big thank you to the love of my life, my wife Mary, who has put up with all of this madness for almost twenty-seven years. I couldn't have written this book without her.

Enough of all that, it's time to sharpen the blades again. 🐾

Peter Normanton
September 26, 2011

Blood on the Walls: An Overview of Sixty Years of Blood and Guts

In the beginning . . .

At around the same time as the first horror movies were being made in France at the very end of the nineteenth century, Le Théâtre du Grand-Guignol opened in Pigalle, not far from the centre of Paris in a building that had once been a chapel. When it opened its doors in 1897, it shocked its audience with a series of presentations of what it termed naturalistic horror shows. Of the theatre's entire programme, the horror stories proved the most popular with their effusion of cleverly conceived gory effects and bloodthirsty finales. This stage show excess would eventually be returned to life in such films as **The Ghastly Ones** (1968), **The Wizard of Gore** (1970) and the inflammatory **The Incredible Torture Show** (1976), but never quite with the theatre's dramatic panache. Much of Hammer's garish portrayal from the late fifties through until the mid-seventies was also attributed to the years of Grand Guignol and countless gorefests in their wake would often be referenced alongside this almost forgotten form of entertainment.

The term splatter was first coined by George A. Romero when he attempted to describe his new film **Dawn of the Dead** (1978). Visceral movies had been shocking their audiences for more than twenty years following Hammer's discovery of the lurid premise that came with Eastmancolor, which proved invaluable as they brought life to their adaptations of some of the classic tales of horror from the distant past. Although these films appear tame when compared to the excess of the current crop, their grisly display was something very new and caused considerable concern for the censors on both sides of the Atlantic. By the mid-sixties, Herschell G. Lewis and William Castle embarked on the work pioneered by Hammer as they streched the boundaries of acceptability even further. Lewis's low-budget films rarely went to mainstream cinemas; their destination was the drive-in theatres of the more rural locales of the United States. Drive-in theatres had started life in New Jersey back in 1932 and by the time Lewis was producing his low-budget exploitation features, they had reached their nadir in popularity. Many of the youngsters who turned up at these outdoor shows couldn't have cared less about the content of the features laid before them – they had other things on their mind – leading to these theatres being labelled passion pits. By the 1970s, many of these drive-in theatres had become associated with the growing market for exploitation films, which were a precursor to the excess of the splatter and slasher movies that began to proliferate horror cinema towards the end of the decade. Sadly, the rise of the video recorder would see the demise of the drive-in cinema. While splatter's evil twin the slasher observed a much slower evolution, Romero's film had already turned splatter into a veritable art form with a plethora of directors soon eager to follow suit.

The slashers, splatter and bloody exploitation of the past fifty years are in cinematic terms relatively new developments. Horror movies have been with us since the dawn of film, but not until Hammer in 1957 did anyone dare venture into the domain of blood and guts. The reasons for this rest to a degree with the limitations of black and white film stock, although Alfred Hitchcock would overcome this with **Psycho** in 1960 as would many of his low-budget successors. Public sensitivity and film censorship, however, were of far greater significance in restraining the development of the more gory aspects of the horror movie and, as we shall now see, the censors eventually came to exert a tight control over the studios and their directors.

Censorship in the United States

Censorship has plagued both filmmakers and cinemagoers since the dawn of the twentieth century. Before the censors began to scrutinize the film industry there were very few horror films on show, the most notable of which were **Le Manoir du Diable** (1896), possibly the first horror film, and **La Caverne Maudite** (1898). Japanese filmmakers had also demonstrated an interest in creating horror movies with **Bake Jizo** (1898) and **Shinin no Sosei** (1898). It wasn't until 1910 that the Edison Studios terrified their audiences with a cinematic version of **Frankenstein**.

While these were early days for the motion picture industry, by 1907 censorship had already become a serious issue in Chicago, although the pressure to introduce local by-laws had nothing to do with the few horror movies that were being made at this time. Their misgivings focused on the nickelodeons that were appearing over the length and breadth of the city. With children slipping away from their parents to frequent these establishments, there was mounting concern as to the suitability of many of the films on show. The city issued an ordinance declaring that all films had to be screened before senior police officers to ensure the appropriateness of their content.

In New York, the newspapers sensationalized an arrest that was made when it was discovered children were shown a film depicting a Chinese opium den, leading to the city's police commissioner withdrawing the licences of over 550 film venues on the Christmas Eve of 1908. A few months later the film industry, which was then based in New York, funded a Board of Censorship to legislate for residents of the city. Other cities and states followed suit, most notably the Los Angeles-based organization The Motion Picture Producers Association, which in its remit looked to defend the industry from attacks on its own morality; this precipitated the industry forming its own national regulatory body in 1916, which became known as the National Association of the Motion Picture Industry. They prescribed a set of thirteen points covering the subjects to be avoided in forthcoming storylines, with no reference to any form of visceral carnage; their design was to prohibit the sexual content in these films. Unfortunately, these early guidelines proved powerless in controlling the subject matter presented in the films of the period. As early as 1916, sex was already a great seller, while any sanguiney excess was appreciably conspicuous by its absence.

At the beginning of the 1920s, it was obvious Hollywood wasn't quite as glossy as its publicists tried to paint it. These were the Roaring Twenties and gossip surrounding certain actors, directors and producers was rife, the most notorious of which was the Roscoe "Fatty" Arbuckle rape and murder scandal, which led to further allegations of Hollywood orgies. The studios had also produced a number of risqué films, with the stag movie **A Free Ride** dating back to 1915, which I hasten to add was never considered for major theatrical release. Twelve months later D. W. Griffith's epic masterpiece **Intolerance** was released, resplendent in the allure of a gathering of delightful young ladies bearing their breasts in the opulent surrounds of an ancient Babylonian temple. Griffith's film also contains the first decapitations and a spear being forcibly driven up through a soldier. Although the Fox Film Corporation's **The Queen of Sheba** directed by

J. Gordon Edwards was lost during the 1930s, a few ageing photographs remain of the provocatively dressed lead actress Betty Blythe. Her attire was somewhat salacious, exposing her breasts to emphasize the film's tagline "The Love Romance of the World's Most Beautiful Woman". Such was the country's unease at the nature of these features, over 100 bills were introduced across the states of America during 1921, each designed to censor an entire range of films. Something had to be done, so the Hollywood studios enlisted Will Harrison Hays Sr., the recent chairman of the Republican National Committee and Postmaster General to improve their tarnished image. During his time as Postmaster General, Hays had overseen the stipulations of the Comstock Act of 1873 barring obscene material from being sent through the post. In 1922, he became the president of Motion Picture Producers and Distributors of America and embarked on the monumental task of trying to clean up his country's film industry.

This wasn't to happen overnight, but by 1924 his team had come up with a set of criteria they termed "The Formula" whereby the studios would have to submit their plots to Hay's public relations committee, which inevitably resulted in many films being rejected. However, not every producer forwarded their ideas to Hays' office. Among those that slipped through the net were: **Ben Hur: A Tale of the Christ** (1925) with its scenes of bare breasted dancing girls tossing flowers into the onlooking crowd, the sensual **Flesh and the Devil** (1926) with its undercurrent of homosexuality, along with the highly successful World War I melodrama, **What Price Glory** (1926). Hays then took measures to create a stronger system of self-regulation by establishing a list of 37 "Don'ts and Be Carefuls", again mainly of a sexual nature. Once more, there was little reference to the bloodthirsty, even though Hollywood was beginning to introduce a growing number of horror movies to theatres across the land, such as **Dr Jekyll And Mr Hyde** (1920), **The Phantom Carriage** (1920), **The Hunchback of Notre Dame** (1923), **Waxworks** (1924), **The Phantom of the Opera** (1925), **The Monster** (1925) and **London After Midnight** (1927). Hays' way of thinking wasn't entirely successful as was attested by the eroticism of Clara Bow's display in **It** (1927) and the first male on male kissing scene in William A. Wellman's tale set in World War I, **Wings** (1927), which went on to win the Academy Award for Best Production. It has been estimated that during this period Hays' staff only managed to review about 20 per cent of the American film industry's total output.

When Hays met with Martin Quigley, the publisher of *Motion Picture Herald* who was also a devout Catholic with connections to the loftier echelons of the Catholic Church, he was presented with a set of principles put together by the influential publisher and a Jesuit priest, Father Daniel Lord. Their effect was to create a code of morality that would govern the whole of the American motion picture industry. With the United States thrown into turmoil in the wake of the stock market crash, the Motion Picture Producers and Distributors of America accepted the stringent provisions of the Production Code in 1930. It would, however, take another four years before the mechanism was finally put into place to allow this legislation to bring an end to the lurid portrayals of the past twenty-five years. The filmmakers did all they could to avoid the Code between 1930 and 1934 as their starlets, among them Joan Crawford, Mae West and Barbara Stanwyck, luxuriated in some of their most enticing roles. The world of film, however, was about to change; from 1934, every feature submitted for cinematic release would require a seal of approval. The Code would remain in place until 1968 when its outdated precepts were superseded by the MPAA system of film rating.

Production Code of the Hays Office

The stipulations of the Production Code have been summarized below to show the three General Principles, followed by the subsequent set of specific restrictions:

1. No picture shall be produced that will lower the moral standards of those who see it. Thus, the sympathy of the audience should never be thrown to the side of crime, wrongdoing, evil or sin.
2. Correct standards of life, subject only to the requirements of drama and entertainment, shall be presented.
3. Law, natural or human, shall not be ridiculed, nor shall sympathy be created for its violation.

The specific restrictions, itemized as "Particular Applications" of these principles, were:

- Nudity and suggestive dances were prohibited.
- The ridicule of religion was forbidden, with ministers of religion not to be represented as comic characters or villains.
- The depiction of illegal drug use was specifically forbidden, along with the use of liquor "when not required by the plot or for proper characterization".

- Any explicit portrayal detailing methods of crime such as safe cracking, arson and smuggling was forbidden.
- References to alleged "sex perversion" (such as homosexuality) and venereal disease were forbidden, as were depictions of childbirth.
- The language section prohibited various words and phrases that could be considered offensive.
- Murder scenes had to be filmed in a way that would discourage real life imitations, and the detail of a vicious killing could not be shown.
- "Revenge in modern times" was not to be justified.
- The sanctity of marriage and the home had to be upheld.
- "Pictures shall not infer that low forms of sexual relationship are the accepted or common thing."
- Adultery and illicit sex, although recognized as sometimes necessary to the plot, could not be explicit or justified and were not supposed to be presented as an attractive option.
- Portrayals of miscegenation were forbidden.
- "Scenes of Passion" were not to be introduced when not essential to the plot.
- "Excessive and lustful kissing" was to be avoided, along with any other treatment that might "stimulate the lower and baser element". A limit of thirty seconds was later insisted by the Hays Office.
- The flag of the United States was to be treated respectfully, and the people and history of other nations were to be presented "fairly".
- "Vulgarity", defined as "low, disgusting, unpleasant, though not necessarily evil, subjects" must be "subject to the dictates of good taste".
- Capital punishment, "third-degree methods", cruelty to children and animals, prostitution and surgical operations were to be handled with similar sensitivity.

The continuance of the Production Code would have impeded the evolution of the more extreme forms of American horror cinema, with cinemagoers being denied the chance to experience the gratuitous splatter from overseas creators such as Dario Argento, Lucio Fulci, Umberto Lenzi, Mario Bava and Ruggero Deodato, along with the exploitation savoured by Jess Franco. When the Code was first introduced few foreign films were ever made available in the United States, although there was one notorious exception, Czech director Gustav Machatý's **Ecstasy** (1933), which was scandalized by Hedy Lamarr's nude swim and ever-so-carefully veiled sexual innuendo. The Hays Office hacked into Machatý's film prior to its limited run in the US, although the unedited version is still believed to have made an appearance in certain art house cinemas of the day.

It soon became obvious that one of the many failings of the Code was its inability to differentiate between age groups. Either a film was granted the coveted seal of approval or it simply didn't see release. Further to this during the 1950s some distributors started to defy the code by bringing in foreign imports and by the 1960s with the appearance of Hammer's stock of horror, Alfred Hitchcock's **Psycho** and the drive-in splatter of Herschell G. Lewis along with William Castle, many of the Code's restrictions needed to be relaxed. These films were now requested to carry an announcement recommending their content was intended for mature audiences.

The current system of Motion Picture Association of America (MPAA) letter ratings was introduced in 1968 permitting filmmakers to determine the nature of their film and then place it for submission to receive an official rating based upon the levels of violence, sexual activity, nudity and profanity. This rating system was based on age, but later clarified and then amended to overcome public confusion.

Censorship in the United Kingdom

Legislation evolved in the United Kingdom in a similar way to its counterpart in the United States. Following The Cinematograph Act of 1909, which required cinemas to attain licences from their local authority on the grounds of both health and safety and the content of the films that were being shown, the British Board of Film Censors (BBFC) was established at the request of the film industry in 1912. This fledgeling industry was already reluctant to the idea of being overseen by either national or local government. Although there were links with the government, particularly during the inter-war period, which warned against articulating controversial political views in films made on these shores, these were for the most part very informal. As with the Hays Office, a system for inspecting potential scripts was introduced, inviting British studios to tender their screenplays prior to shooting. Surprisingly, American films were not treated quite as strictly, which allowed a flow of hard-boiled crime movies into the country, but such portrayals were out of bounds for British filmmakers.

During World War II, political censorship became the responsibility of the Films Division of the Ministry of Information; meaning the BBFC would never again be able to influence the more political aspects of film and television. Their role was now more concerned with on-screen depictions of sex and violence with films being routinely censored seemingly as a means of social control. **Rebel Without a Cause** (1955) was cut to prevent the slightest possibility of teenage upheaval and Ingmar Bergman's **Smiles of a Summer Night** (1955) was edited to remove its openly sexual overtures. As social attitudes became more permissive during the 1960s, the BBFC began to devote their attention to those films that featured graphic sex and violence, which led to the prohibition of **Last House on the Left** (1972) and **The Texas Chain Saw Massacre** (1974). Recent years have seen a relaxation in the Board's approach to the guidelines to keep in line with society's ever-changing outlook, with many films that were banned during the 1970s now beginning to see release.

In 1984, the BBFC became the British Board of Film Classification to reflect another change in its role, following the need to make classification a more significant part of its work. Under the Video Recording Act of 1984, the Board was given the responsibility for the classification of videos for both hire and purchase to view in the home as well as those films shown in cinemas across the country. Local authorities still had the final say over who was eligible to see a particular film in the cinemas in their locality, but this power did not extend to cover video recordings. The Video Recordings Act 1984 followed the moral panic created by the tabloid press between 1982 and 1983, which made the video nasty the scapegoat for so many of the country's ills.

The BBFC were now sanctioned to classify films under an age-rated system making it an offence to supply videos to anyone under the designated age of a specified classification. In the event that a film was refused classification, it was made illegal to put it up for sale or supply anywhere in the country. The BBFC's role was also extended to their being empowered to demand cuts to films to enable a particular age rating, or in more extreme circumstances ensure actual classification. The act did not consider possession to be an offence in itself, but "possession with intent to supply" would be punishable by law. The BBFC would continue to demand cuts to those features that contravened the provisions of the Obscene Publications Act or other such legislation, e.g. the Cinematograph Films (Animals) Act 1937 and the Protection of Children Act 1978.

Hammer Films

Among the foreign imports entering the United States during the 1950s would have been a sensationalistic series of luridly bloodthirsty films produced in Britain, made by an almost unknown company by the name of Hammer. Hammer Film Productions was founded in November 1934 by William Hinds, whose stage name in his heyday had been Will Hammer. After only three years, the company was declared bankrupt following a downturn in the British film industry. However, Exclusive, the distribution arm of the organization, survived the liquidation. This allowed Hammer to rebuild, and between 1947 and 1955 they gained a reputation for producing cheaply made B-grade movies, and then in 1955 released their first horror movie. **The Quatermass Xperiment** was an adaptation of the Nigel Kneale scripted BBC television serial **The Quatermass Experiment**. The film was a resounding success, which prompted a sequel, again adapted from the BBC series and now scripted by Neale, **Quatermass 2** (1957).

That same year the company looked to producing an adaptation of Mary Shelley's Frankenstein from a script submitted by Milton Subotsky, but it proved a little too close to Universal's telling of the **Son of Frankenstein** (1939). Jimmy Sangster was brought in to redraft the original screenplay to avoid litigation with Universal and extend the running time to ninety minutes thus making it admissible for distribution across the UK. The gruesome nature of Sangster's script and Hammer's decision to shoot in full colour duly alarmed the BBFC, who were so concerned with the unseemly nature of this feature they felt they would not even be able to classify the film with an "X" certificate. The script, however, remained almost unchanged and under Terence Fisher's direction Hammer's first Gothic horror went into production. The Eastmancolor elevated the level of gore to an intensity that had never before been experienced in film. **The Curse of Frankenstein** was unashamedly graphic in its bloody display and Fisher extracted every opportunity to allow the camera to linger on each of its gruesome scenes. The film proved to be a huge success both at home and in the US.

After a lengthy agreement with Universal, work began on **Dracula**, although the BBFC were once again far from happy with the excess of blood coursing through the script. Terence Fisher's direction helped to make **Dracula** another resounding success as it smashed box office records on both sides of the Atlantic, with Christopher Lee and Peter Cushing excelling in their respective roles. These two films were to provide the formula for Hammer's productions for the next twenty years and forced the censors to re-evaluate their guidelines.

1960

The year 1960 came out to be one of the most significant in the development of cinematic horror. That year five films were released in different parts of the world which would change the face of horror and, as many commentators had feared, open the floodgates for what would become an unwholesome tide of gore-ridden terror. The films in question were **Psycho, Peeping Tom, Les Yeux Sans Visage, Black Sabbath** and **Jigoku**. While many films had threatened to shock their audiences with their explicit titles such as **Corridors of Blood** (1958), these films challenged their audiences in quite different ways and caused immense problems for the censoring authorities across the western world. The audience reaction, however, was very positive and following the success of **Psycho**, Hollywood began to realize there was money to be made in such explicit violence.

After several years of making low-budget nudie films, the highly educated Herschell G. Lewis used his exploitative formula to make a series of bloodthirsty horror movies that were made specifically for the drive-in cinemas of the south-eastern states of the US. They proved to be immensely successful and very soon other directors began to follow suit. As with the B-movie terrors of the 1950s, these films were shot in a matter of days, quite often using only one take. Their intention was to generate a maximum return as quickly as they possibly could, and to hell with the finer points of acting and production. Lewis would ascend to become the first Godfather of Gore, and as ham-fisted as his films were, they would attract a procession of gore-loving teenagers by the carload. Lewis's **Blood Feast** (1963) is now considered to be the first true splatter movie and was very soon followed by so many more.

Grindhouse and Exploitation

With the relaxation of censorships rules in the US, exploitation cinema began to attract a greater following during the 1960s. These suggestive films had been in existence since the 1920s, but the drive-ins and the former bump 'n' grind striptease theatres that had become the grindhouse cinemas of 42nd Street provided a ready market for these low-budget features. They picked upon the more seamy aspects of cinema and attracted a quite unique following. The films on show in these tawdry picture houses covered a wide range of sub-genres, such as biker movies, drug-related features, blaxploitation, nunsploitation, spaghetti westerns, extremes of violence, an abundance of large boobs and more than a smattering of lurid sex. European movies also began to appear in these cinemas coming in from Italy, France and Spain. Eurosleaze attracted yet another audience and soon followed the gialli and cannibal movies. If the celluloid merchandise was cheap enough, then these cinemas were interested and men such as Jess Franco showed themselves quite capable of delivering the goods, time and time again. The quality of many of these films may have been very poor, but the audiences in these rundown establishments were privy to several films that planted the seeds for a generation of filmmakers when they prepared to let the slasher run amok in mainstream cinemas across America. Two of these films in particular were of immense significance; both directed by Mario Bava, the first of which was **Blood and Black Lace** (1964) followed seven years later by **A Bay of Blood** (1971). Although their European counterparts were so often badly dubbed, these gialli, with their penchant for imaginative murder and enticing femmes, soon garnered an appreciative audience.

Away from the world of cinema, a series of murders committed by the Manson Family in 1969 would have considerable repercussions for the whole of the US. The country was shocked by their vicious disregard for human life and there were serious questions asked about family values, many of which were to remain unanswered. Those films that thrived upon an excess of violence once again fell under public scrutiny, but these features also generated considerable amounts of money as evidenced by the work of the prominent Sam Peckinpah. Former college professor Wes Craven had taken a career change, entering the world of low-budget exploitation and realized that a film unreserved in its level of brutality would indeed shock its audience, but would make a highly lucrative return. The evidence was there in the newspaper headlines; the press thrived on excess and the tabloids sold on the back of it. **The Last House on the Left** (1972) was an audacious venture, but its controversial success inspired films of a similar ilk such as Tobe Hooper's **The Texas Chain Saw Massacre** (1974), which in turn inspired even greater excess, some of which again came from Craven in **The Hills Have Eyes** (1977).

1978

The year 1978 proved to be the next landmark for the horror movie. In its day Bob Clark's giallo-styled shocker **Black Christmas** (1974) failed to set the world of film alight, but its point-of-view camera shots caught the attention of many young filmmakers, one of whom was John Carpenter. Carpenter was already carving a reputation as a low-budget director capable of tapping into audience expectation. His film **Halloween** changed the public's perception of the horror movie and became the catalyst for the decade to come. The terror that emanated from the blade of Michael Myers, followed by the carnage of **Friday the 13th** (1980), was to have an unprecedented impact, and for the next few years these two films inspired an onslaught of knife-wielding maniacal killers. **Halloween** redefined the principles of hack and slash that had emerged in the gialli and acquired an intensity of structure with **Black Christmas**, and then **Friday the 13th** went that one step further making the ruthless slaughter even more imaginative.

In this same year, for the second time in his career, George A. Romero unleashed a horde of rampaging zombies, this time in a shopping mall in Monroeville. This film was **Dawn of the Dead**. The scenes, along with the work of the inventive Tom Savini seen in this film, would send the kids across North America and the UK into a zombie frenzy. They also caught the eye of the Italians, in particular one Lucio Fulci, who in the year that followed moved into making horror movies and let loose his own breed of mindless excess in **Zombie Flesh Eaters**, which has also assumed the name **Zombi 2**, and in his boundless enthusiasm he enlivened the craze for Italian splatter. Did these creatures really represent our societal fears, or were they a reflection of Cold War paranoia, or was it something more sinister? It didn't really matter because the kids came out en masse to view some of the most extreme films ever to see release to the silver screen, and they loved every minute of it. Unfortunately, this gory excess didn't come without problems, for not everyone was quite ready for such a graphic onslaught.

The Golden Age of the Slasher

Between 1980 and 1984, those deranged men and women with a hankering for killing annoying teenagers were freed from the asylum and given licence to use a whole range of imaginative weapons. It was no longer just enough to stab the victim to death or strangle them; no, the kills had to go way beyond this to have any hope of maintaining the audience's interest. With so many of these films coming out each and every month, the writers and directors had to come up with something new, or the kids were going to get bored and move on to something new. With **Friday the 13th** there came a whole raft of summer camp slashers and then there appeared the seasonal slashers who enjoyed their slaughter at Christmas while the lovesick saved it as a Valentine's Day surprise. Those who were young enough carried out their heinous activities at school and the chosen few who wanted to further their education continued their butchery at the college campus. These years would give rise to the stalkers in the backwoods and in the wards and corridors of hospitals; nowhere appeared to be safe. Some of these monstrous individuals were carrying out their butchery to the sound of the disco beat, and now and again you just might hear the cheesy metal of the day. While the nutter with the chainsaw prowled through the dark, close in point-of-view camera shots became the order of the day, as the creators of these films encouraged the audience to empathize, or dare I say cheer for the killer. Along the way a host of red herrings would be thrown in, and a good writer and his director would keep you guessing right until the last and then introduce the twist that would leave you flabbergasted; if all went well the remaining girl would finally make her escape. Promiscuity was invariably punished, as was rank stupidity and bullying; only the good girl ever got to go home. There was a formula, but the creators of these films developed a knack for tossing in something new and for four glorious years we were addicted. The slasher never quite went away and if he had thought about slipping off back to the asylum, Wes Craven hauled him back again for a new generation in 1996 with **Scream**.

The 1980s also saw the expansion of the movie franchise. It had already happened in the 1960s with Hammer's monster movies, but when **Alien**, **Halloween**, **Friday the 13**[th], **A Nightmare on Elm Street** and George Romero's **"Dead"** series appeared they became gargantuan money-making extravaganzas which spawned film upon film, as well as video games, toys and comic books.

However, amidst all of this blood-splattered insanity there was a dark cloud forming on the horizon . . .

The Video Nasties Campaign

Towards the end of the 1970s and on into the early 1980s, home video suddenly became very popular. At the time there was no specific legislation covering the material that could be played in the family home, although the Obscene Publications Act of 1959 could still be invoked when necessary. The arrival of home video created a loophole in the existing legislation in that distributors were not legally obligated to submit video material to the BBFC. The public, especially younger viewers, could now get hold of a wide range of material, some of which was incredibly lurid. This included certain extreme horror movies, which in many cases had previously been drastically cut at the time of their original submission to the BBFC to ensure release to the country's cinemas.

It didn't take long before the press caught wind of this emerging phenomenon. The *Sunday People* appear to have been the first to pick upon this proliferation of gruesome films in a spread they ran in December 1981, which is thought to have been the first time the provocative term "video nasties" was used. Several months later, on May 7, 1982, the *Daily Star* returned to this emotive theme, claiming that children were being exposed to "some of the most horrific and violent films ever made" and those scurrilous video distributors had found a way to bypass the BBFC's authority. A few weeks later in an incendiary article, the *Sunday Times* on May 23 alluded to the threat of high street horror invading our homes. Its report described the activities at a video trade fair in Manchester and referred to the violent material that was on offer. With the country seriously affected by increasing unemployment and a downturn in the economy, as well as having endured rioting only a year before, these blood-curdling horror movies suddenly found themselves the scapegoat for the combined failings of society, the authorities and national politicians. Twelve months later, on June 30, 1983, the *Daily Mail* embarked on their campaign, running an article with the headline "Rape of our children's minds" and continued only a day later with "Ban video sadism now". The situation deteriorated when on August 4, 1983, the *Daily Mail* printed yet another article this time entitled "Taken over", making claims that a child had been possessed by one of these evil videos. The effect was such that the media were able to provoke a moral panic, which within a short space of time became almost hysterical, and in due course the newspaper business increased their sales. Their reports never considered the possibility that blame might just rest with those parents who had little interest in the material their children were bringing into their homes.

At this point, the legal profession exacerbated the situation when they used several high-profile cases to defend the misdemeanours of certain unsavoury individuals citing their watching of violent videos as the stimulus for their crimes. The advertising for these new-styled videos also became a cause for concern with the full-page advert for **The Driller Killer** (1979) fuelling the campaign still further. The sensationalistic promotions used for **Cannibal Holocaust** (1980) and **SS Experiment Camp** (1976) didn't help their cause either.

Mary Whitehouse of the National Viewers' and Listeners' Association also began to make her thoughts known, using both television and the press in her determination to preserve the nation's culture. She labelled **The Evil Dead** (1981) as the "number one video nasty", although she later admitted to never having seen it, or many of the other titles against which she was campaigning. As history would one day show, she wasn't the only one who had jumped onto the bandwagon not to have savoured the pleasures of **The Beyond** (1981) and **Zombie Flesh Eaters** (1979).

With mounting public pressure, the only piece of legislation that could be used to alleviate the situation was the 1959 Obscene Publications Act, which authorized the police authorities in the seizure of any material that could deprave and corrupt a significant proportion of its intended audience. As head of the obscene publications unit, Peter Kruger was authorized by the Director of Public Prosecutions (DPP) to apply for a warrant. The police now had the power to confiscate any videos they thought were in violation of the act and carry out the necessary prosecutions. There followed a series of raids on video retailers, but precise definition as to what the officers were supposed to be looking for was never drawn up. The raids eventually moved from video rental shops to the wholesalers and the distributors, which included Thorn EMI. All those who were arrested lived in fear of being fined anything up to £20,000 and facing two years in prison.

During a series of trials across the country, seventy-two titles were placed on the offending list with thirty-nine of them being successfully prosecuted, all of which are listed later on (page 491), with the horror-related films referenced in the main part of this book. The DPP didn't find the judicial process to be plain sailing. At the end of the trial at Snaresbrook in which the case against **The Evil Dead** was dismissed in November 1984, the presiding judge was very critical of the DPP and its persistence in bringing charges against the film. Judge Stable went on to award all of the defendant's costs (Palace Pictures), which were in excess of £20,000, against the DPP. This prompted an enraged statement from David Mellor, the Minister of State who at the time was accountable for the criminal justice policy at the Home Office. The government, however, were reluctant to be associated with statutory censorship, so the British Video Association (BVA) alongside the BBFC looked to creating a principled system of self-regulation. However, these efforts became superfluous when Peter Kruger presented a video containing clips from several terrors such as **The Driller Killer, Snuff, I Spit On Your Grave** and **Faces Of Death** to members of the House of Commons and House of Lords, who were visibly shocked. Still plagued by the hysteria in the press, and with a June general election on the horizon, the Conservative government abandoned the idea of self-regulation. They made a promise to the electorate to "respond to the increasing public concern over obscenity and offences against public decency, which often have links with serious crime", and proposed to introduce the necessary legislation.

"The Parliamentary Group Video Inquiry" headed by sociology lecturer Dr Clifford Hill, which examined the viewing habits of the country's children, initially found that more than one in three children under the age of seven had been subjected to one of the listed video nasties. However, subsequent analysis questioned the validity of the inquiry's findings. There were many who spoke out against the inquiry, but the bill to curb the country's video viewing proposed by Graham Bright was gathering support in the Commons. With few MPs prepared to defend the video nasties, the House of Commons passed Bright's bill without a single dissenting vote, and the Video Recordings Act (VRA) of 1984 entered the statute book to become law on September 1, 1985. This new law meant that all video releases after September 1 had to comply with the act and be submitted for classification to the BBFC, bringing the home video market into line with cinema censorship. Those titles that had been released prior to the act had to be withdrawn from sale and similarly submitted to the BBFC within a three-year period. It became a criminal offence to supply any tape without a BBFC certificate, although it was still within the bounds of the law to own them. In addition, supplying "15" or "18" certificated videos to people of a younger age was also made an offence. Films that had been passed uncut for cinema release could be cut for video, and several films already edited for cinema had to endure further cuts prior to being issued to video. The certification process could become very expensive, which meant many distributors withdrew those films they considered would be unlikely to see passed. Other notable horror titles were submitted, resulting in heavy cuts, or in certain cases outright rejection. By December 1985, the panic was at an end, the Video Recordings Act made the DPP's list of video nasties defunct, as it was now illegal to offer any tape for sale without the appropriate certification.

The Video Recording Act forced many smaller independent distributors out of business, as they were obliged to pay exactly the same certification fees to the BBFC as the giants of the industry, and for many of them their entire catalogue was made up of this extreme brand of horror.

Terror for a New Millennium

As with any other form of cinema, horror has continued to evolve. The past ten years have seen the grainy violence of the 1970s and the graphic displays of the 1980s replaced by torture porn, the Oriental lust for snuff movies and the arrival of the French Extreme. While these films have been criticized for their gratuitous content, they are only emulating the stance of their predecessors in pushing back the boundaries of acceptability. In certain instances characterization has been replaced by a dehumanizing mean spirit, but when we look back to the average eighties slasher these were far from being concerned with the development of a likable three-dimensional cast; let's be honest, most of them were brought in for the slaughter. In recent years the butchery has become more pronounced and the teams of special effects experts have worked to keep up with the demand for this excess. Through it all, however, there has been one set of filmmakers who have kept going and refused to give in: the low-budget guys, the men and women who do it for next to nothing and continue to live the dream. A few of them will make it and open doors for more change, but most of them will just do it for personal satisfaction and the need to share their vision. ❧

An A–Z
of Slasher
and
Splatter
Movies

CONTAINED IN THE reviews that follow, there appears a splatter rating. This is based upon the amount and quality of gore contained in each film, some of which may have been hampered by derisory budgets, but remain nonetheless effective.

Would you believe it, a splatter-free movie!

Sorry folks, a little low key, only one or two bloodthirsty scenes.

Maybe just enough blood to keep the gore-monger entertained.

If you want blood, you got it, but your mamma wouldn't like it; an abundance of slicing and dicing, with a steady flow of blood and guts.

Chop, chop, chop! Now they're really beginning to pour on the gore in an utterly deranged crescendo of butchery – the décor's wall-to-wall splatter!

Prepare for the feast, for it's what you've always craved – a symphony of gore made all the more bloody by a cascade of splatter! If they're not already eye-gouging and gut-munching, heads will surely roll.

28 Days Later

📅 YEAR OF RELEASE: 2002		🏭 PRODUCERS: Robert How (line producer), Andrew Macdonald	
⏱ RUNTIME: 113 minutes			
🌐 COUNTRY: UK		⭕ CERTIFICATE: Australia: MA; Canada: 16+ (Québec); Canada: 18A; Ireland: 18; New Zealand: R16; UK: 18; USA: R	
🎬 DIRECTOR: Danny Boyle			
🎬 PRODUCTION COMPANY: DNA Films, British Film Council		💲 BUDGET: $8,000,000	
		🗂 RECEIPTS: $82,700,000	
✎ WRITER: Alex Garland			
🎞 CINEMATOGRAPHER: Anthony Dod Mantle			

CAST: Alex Palmer, Bindu De Stoppani, Jukka Hiltunen, David Schneider, Cillian Murphy, Toby Sedgwick, Naomie Harris, Noah Huntley, Christopher Dunne, Emma Hitching, Alexander Delamere, Kim McGarrity, Brendan Gleeson, Megan Burns, Justin Hackney, Luke Mably, Stuart McQuarrie, Ricci Harnett, Leo Bill, Junior Laniyan, Ray Panthaki, Christopher Eccleston, Sanjay Rambaruth, Marvin Campbell

WHEN DANNY BOYLE and Alex Garland first proposed to revive George Romero's apocalyptic vision it was considered something of a risk, but in keeping with their credentials they introduced something new to an already saturated subgenre. This wasn't just a regurgitation of the ideas of Romero and his contemporaries; in setting their deranged mob amidst the streets of London, they redefined the mindless zombie of the past thirty years and gave these creatures a unique resurrection.

In the chaos of the film's opening scenes, animal rights activists force their way into a highly secret research facility with a view to freeing the captive chimpanzees. Unknown to them the primates have been infected with a virus designed to trigger an uncontrollable rage. Ignoring the pleas of a scientist, the activists, oblivious to the ferocity of the contagion, free the animals. Within seconds, the entire room is thrown into a murderous frenzy. Twenty-eight days later in an abandoned London hospital, Jim (Cillian Murphy) awakens from a coma. In the hope of trying to make sense of what is going on he takes to the streets to find the city is completely empty. His first encounter with the marauding zombie-like infected is very sudden and comes in the tranquil surrounds of a church, where he knows immediately his life is at stake. The meticulously orchestrated tension played out in the church erupts into a frantic chase with the maddened horde hot on his tail. Rescue comes from fellow survivors, Selena (Naomie Harris) and Mark (Noah Huntley), who lead him to a place of relative safety. Jim now learns the horrifying truth. A virus has spread at an alarming rate across the length and breadth of the country transforming everyone in its wake into a psychotic rabble.

Be thankful for everything, for soon there will be nothing . . .

And so followed the collapse of the whole of the British Isles. Theirs becomes a tale of survival, as a small party head north to Manchester, believing the soldiers based there have a serum that will combat the infection. The journey takes them across a country ravaged by the rabid infected, where the general populace do not have access to guns.

When the survivors reach Manchester, they are escorted under armed guard to a fortified mansion commanded by Major Henry West (Christopher Eccleston). They soon learn West's solution to the infection is to leave these deranged creatures to starve. Their situation becomes appreciably graver when they discover the surviving women are to be used to breed a new human race. In the hours before their escape, Sergeant Farrell (Stuart McQuarrie) suggests that Britain could have been quarantined to contain the epidemic within these shores. When Jim later sees the vapour

trail of an aircraft, he starts to believe the sergeant could be right.

The terms "zombie" and the "living-dead" were never used in this film; this rabid breed were something very different, distancing **28 Days Later** from Romero's atrophied minions. Danny Boyle brings a brooding atmosphere to his creation, particularly in the iconic scenes trailing through an abandoned London, originally shot on digital video and filmed during the early hours of the morning. He then injected the necessary action to keep his viewers on the very edge of their seats. Zombie die-hards were be treated to much flesh eating with the infected throwing up blood and the newly contaminated going through a shocking metamorphosis in a mere matter of seconds. The post-catastrophic images of London were vaguely reminiscent of John Wyndham's imagining of **The Day of the Triffids**, first published in 1951, which Garland later revealed as a great source of inspiration.

Danny Boyle's film proved to be a commercial triumph and received numerous awards including Best Horror Film from the US Academy of Science Fiction, Fantasy and Horror Films, Best British Film (Empire Award) and Danny being awarded the Grand Prize of European Fantasy Film in Silver and an International Fantasy Film Award. His film would continue in the sequel **28 Weeks Later** (2007), along with a graphic novel and a series of comic books. In March 2007, while being interviewed by an Irish radio station, Danny admitted to an interest in adding a third film to the series, "28 Months Later".

28 Weeks Later

📅 **YEAR OF RELEASE:** 2007	
⏱ **RUNTIME:** 100 minutes	
🎥 **COUNTRY:** UK/Spain	
🎬 **DIRECTOR:** Juan Carlos Fresnadillo	
🎬 **PRODUCTION COMPANY:** Fox Atomic, DNA Films, UK Film Council	
✎ **WRITERS:** Rowan Joffe (screenplay), Juan Carlos Fresnadillo	
▢ **CINEMATOGRAPHER:** Enrique Chediak	

PRODUCERS: Bernard Bellew (co-producer), Danny Boyle (executive producer), Alex Garland (executive producer), Enrique López Lavigne, Andrew Macdonald, Allon Reich

CERTIFICATE: Australia: MA; Canada: 16+ (Quebec); Canada: 18A (Alberta/British Columbia/Manitoba/Ontario); Ireland: 18 (DVD rating); Ireland: 16; New Zealand: R18; South Africa: 18; UK: 18; USA: R

RECEIPTS: $28,637,507

CAST: Robert Carlyle, Rose Byrne, Jeremy Renner, Harold Perrineau, Catherine McCormack, Idris Elba, Imogen Poots, Mackintosh Muggleton, Amanda Walker, Shahid Ahmed, Garfield Morgan, Emily Beecham, Beans El-Balawi, Meghan Popiel, Stewart Alexander, Philip Bulcock, Chris Ryman, Tristan Tait, William Meredith

THE SEQUEL TO **28 Days Later** brought Juan Carlos Fresnadillo to the director's chair and from the very offset he escalated the tension before throwing in a pulse-pounding sequence of fast-paced action punctuated by the slavering gore of its illustrious predecessor. In what should have been an idyllic countryside location, very close to London, Don (Robert Carlyle), his wife Alice (Catherine McCormack) along with a few survivors have withdrawn to a barricaded farmhouse. Their existence is shattered when droves of the infected besiege the house. Don panics and in the chaos is unable to save Alice as he tries to find a means of escape. Consumed with fear he takes flight, leaving behind him a scene of utter carnage and his wife about to be consumed by the rabid mob.

It is now twenty-eight weeks since the viral outbreak that almost wiped out the entire population of Great Britain. London has been declared safe with the infected believed to have died of starvation. Those who survived now make their return under the heavily armed surveillance of the American military. Don, now a caretaker, is reunited with his children, Tammy and her younger brother Andy. Although they ask about their mother, he finds it impossible to be completely honest about her final moments. Locked away in a sanitized compound on the Isle of Dogs, the children think only of their mother and, in a bid to rediscover their past, they slip away scurrying through the wreckage of the streets they once knew. When they locate their house, it is in a terrible state, but in the disarray they find some old family photographs. As they prepare to leave, Andy makes a startling discovery: his mother is still alive.

As they leave the house, they are sighted by US soldiers, who escort them back to the safety of the compound. Here Alice is tested and declared infected, but she exhibits an unusual immunity to its more ravaging effects. In the hope of being reunited with his wife and expressing his overwhelming remorse, Don bypasses the internal security. As he holds her in his arms, their kiss damns him for his abandonment and the contamination once again begins to spread. The immediate butchery of his beloved wife reveals him as the most savage of this new breed. The rabid Don will rip his way through the entire compound on a course that will lead him to his own children. The grainy epilogue chases through the darkness as the infected stream forth from the Paris Métro Trocadéro station before the Eiffel Tower, the distorted focus alluding to the catastrophe to come.

Week twenty-eight: no escape.

While the tone was darker than that of its precursor, **28 Weeks Later** was released to enormous critical acclaim, with Fresnadillo praised for his unusually skilled craft. Amidst the despairing scenes of devastation, and the threat of the blood-foaming infected, can be heard the dissident voice of protest. This undercurrent cleverly subverts the blood-craving zombie to the post 9/11 psychosis; ambiguity surrounds the American military presence, their policies being depicted as aggressively insensitive and foolishly complacent. The vision is bleak, with napalm ripping from the skies, the innocent caught in torrents of bullets and streets littered with the remains of the dead and discarded debris. Whether it's the terror of a confined crowd thrown to the mercy of Carlyle's foaming rage or survivors stumbling through the pitch black of an underground station, the combination of impending doom and surging violence makes this a singularly disturbing cinematic experience. 🐾

30 Days of Night

 YEAR OF RELEASE: 2007

 RUNTIME: 113 minutes

 COUNTRY: USA

DIRECTOR: David Slade

 PRODUCTION COMPANY: Ghost House Pictures, Columbia Pictures, Dark Horse Entertainment, 30 Days of Night

 WRITERS: Steve Niles, Stuart Beattie, Brian Nelson

CINEMATOGRAPHER: Jo Willems

PRODUCERS: Ted Adams (co-producer), Joseph Drake (executive producer), Aubrey Henderson (executive producer), Nathan Kahane (executive producer), Sam Raimi, Mike Richardson (executive producer), Chloe Smith (co-producer), Robert G. Tapert

CERTIFICATE: Australia: MA (re-rating on appeal) Australia: R (original rating) Canada: 13+ (Quebec) Canada: 18A (Alberta/British Columbia/Manitoba/Ontario) Ireland: 16 Ireland: 18 (DVD rating) New Zealand: R16 UK: 15 (original rating) UK: 18 (DVD rating) USA: R

BUDGET: $32,000,000

RECEIPTS: $39,568,996

CAST: Josh Hartnett, Melissa George, Danny Huston, Ben Foster, Mark Boone Junior, Mark Rendall, Amber Sainsbury, Manu Bennett, Megan Franich, Joel Tobeck, Elizabeth Hawthorne, Nathaniel Lees, Craig Hall, Chic Littlewood, Peter Feeney, Min Windle

A MAN IS SEEN walking through the desolation of a snow-bound landscape; in the background is the darkened boat from which he has just stepped. His path takes him to the distant settlement of Barrow, Alaska, the northernmost town in the United States, almost eighty miles from the nearest outpost. Once the sun has set in the deepest winter of this northerly region, it won't appear over the horizon for another thirty days. This darkened world is the ideal setting for a band of ruthless vampires, who have made their way across the ice and snow towards this isolated locale, ready to feed their bloodlust on an unsuspecting population. At first the kills are slow and intermittent, but the residents can feel something is wrong and all too soon they begin to fall to these sadistic predators, who take an unseemly delight in tracking down and tearing into their prey. Only a small group of survivors remain, each of whom looks to the local sheriff, Eben Oleson (Josh Hartnett) and his wife Stella (Melissa George) to save them from thus unrelenting malfeasance. It will be days before the light of day pours over this beleaguered town, to force their tormentors into hibernation.

30 Days of Night began life as a comic book series published by IDW during 2002, written by Steve Niles and lavishly illustrated by Ben Templesmith. It was a sharp departure from the romanticized vampire lore of the period, which readily returned to the vampire breed of the Hammer years and Mario Bava's **Black Sabbath** (1963). David Slade's film remained true to Niles' original concept, retaining the sense of isolation and then hurling the inhabitants of this remote town into a completely hopeless situation as these evil creatures ransacked the streets and houses, ruthlessly stalking their prey. The audience were never privy to the thoughts and personalities of the vampire horde; they only ever knew that this was a vicious and cunning influx, with a single-minded desire to satiate its unholy craving. Their discourse was guttural, conversing in a dialect that made them appear all the more inhuman.

They're coming!

With this film only a few minutes old, the violence ascended to an immediate intensity that continued to the terror of the finale, which included a series of incisive decapitations and the regular splatter of blood strewn across the snow. The cinematography in this world without light worked to tremendous effect, using close-up visuals to enhance the suspense and never allowing the audience to forget the intention of this and Niles' original: nobody gets out alive. ✦

555

📅	YEAR OF RELEASE: 1988	✏️ WRITER: Roy Koz	
🕐	RUNTIME: 90 minutes	🎞️ CINEMATOGRAPHER: Lamar "Larry" Bloodworth	
🎬	COUNTRY: USA		
🎥	DIRECTOR: Wally Koz	⚰️ PRODUCERS: Linda Koz (associate producer), Roy Koz (associate producer), Wally Koz	
🎬	PRODUCTION COMPANY: King Video Productions		

CAST: Mara Lynn Bastian, Charles Fuller, Bob Grabill, Scott Hermes, Greg Kerouac, Greg Neilson, B. K. Smith

AN ELDERLY MAN is seen meandering across a seemingly deserted beach as the sun fades into the horizon. This blissful scene is shattered by the grisly antics of a psychopathic hippy. When he stumbles upon a young couple making love he removes the head of the young man and then rapes and butchers his girlfriend. This slasher is infinitely more depraved than your everyday psychopath; he has a hankering for necrophilia and very soon we learn the rape was committed after the girl's death. As terror begins to sweep across the town other young lovers fall before the maniac's blade, each of the female corpses enduring the same indignity as the first. The killer's modus operandi reveals a connection with another series of killings; they follow an identical pattern occurring in the fifth month of the year, for five consecutive nights once every five years. The brusque detectives are now on the case, openly arguing with a female journalist, as they track down their only suspect, a war veteran in a safari shirt. False leads come and go as the boobs and gore intensify the sleaze in this exploitative shocker. As 555 draws to an end, the killer is wracked by a bizarre sequence of flashbacks, each of which repeats so much of the footage already seen in this film.

Wally Koz's family-produced bargain basement slasher was shot on one-inch video tape in Chicago's Ukrainian Village. After being disappointed by so many slapdash horror movies, Koz was convinced that with very little money he could come up with something of far greater worth. He had absolutely no experience as a filmmaker, but such minor trivialities were not going to get in his way. He envisioned distributing this film himself before progressing to new features; sadly, this wasn't to be. For these ninety minutes, however, he revealed the lengths to which independent film productions were prepared to go in the hope of mustering an audience. 555 was unabashed in its excessive indulgence of misogynistic sleaze and gore, so much so it was never going to be endorsed by the MPAA. They did everything they could to seize every copy in the hope of denying potential viewers its graphic content. Their vigilance put an end to Koz's dreams and made his film a rarity for VHS collectors across the globe. It came as a great surprise to Koz when his film received a review in the pages of *Variety* and for a video of this degenerate ilk garnered a reasonably favourable review. This was one of the very few occasions that *Variety* ever cast their eyes over such a despicable feature.

The cheap gore typically managed to hold the film together and included two memorable moments of cinematic splatter. When one unfortunate has his fingers scythed, his screams are never heard as his head is almost immediately

Caution: Viewing may cause severe damage to your brain cells!

removed. For a film blighted by such meagre funding, this scene remains the source of much discussion among those gore mongers whose endeavours have succeeded in tracing this video. If this wasn't enough, a machete was driven into a victim's throat, probably using the remainder of the film's budget.

However, Wally Koz knew how to save a little bit of money, as he used the same pre-recorded scream for every one of the female victim's murders. For sure it was low-budget exploitation, but no one could deny the Koz family's boundless enthusiasm. 🐾

A Bay of Blood

31 YEAR OF RELEASE: 1971		PHOTOGRAPHERS: Mario Bava, Antonio Rinaldi	

RUNTIME: 84 minutes

COUNTRY: Italy

DIRECTOR: Mario Bava

PRODUCTION COMPANY: Nuova Linea Cinematografica

WRITERS: Franco Barberi (story), Mario Bava (screenplay)

PHOTOGRAPHERS: Mario Bava, Antonio Rinaldi

PRODUCER: Giuseppe Zaccarellio

CERTIFICATE: Australia: R; Canada: 13+ (Quebec); Canada: R (Ontario); New Zealand: R16 (original rating: 1972); UK: 18 (uncut version, re-rating); UK: 18 (re-rating: 1994, cut); UK: (Banned) (1984–94); UK: X; USA: R

CAST: Claudine Auger, Luigi Pistilli, Claudio Camaso, Anna Maria Rosati, Chris Avram, Leopoldo Trieste, Laura Betti, Brigitte Skay, Isa Miranda, Paola Montenero, Guido Boccaccini, Roberto Bonanni, Giovanni Nuvoletti

ORIGINALLY RELEASED AS **Reazione a Catena** and also known as **Ecologia del delitto, Bloodbath, Carnage, Twitch of the Death Nerve** and **Last House on the Left II** in the United States, **A Bay of Blood** is considered one of Mario Bava's finest works. Its significance in slasher folklore cannot be underestimated for this minor masterpiece is now acknowledged as being the precursor

to **Friday the 13th** (1980) and the generation that followed. The story struggled with an incoherent plot that was sacrificed for the madness of the movie's predilection for murder, as those at the centre of this tale attempted to dispose of anyone who stood in their way of a family inheritance.

Locked away in her remote mansion overlooking an inland bay, Countess Federica (Isa Miranda) wheels herself through the forlorn shadows. Dwelling on the rain pouring against her window, she fails to notice the presence of her scheming husband Filippo Donati (Giovanni Nuvoletti), who slips a noose around her neck before kicking her from her wheelchair. Ailed by her weakened legs, the countess is unable to stand and the rope around her neck becomes ever tighter as it strangles the last breath from her body. However, Filippo immediately gets his just deserves at the hands of a mysterious killer hidden behind a curtain, who then drags his body away. The discovery of a suicide note, stolen from the countess's diary, satisfies the police that she has taken her own life, but Filippo's death goes strangely unnoticed. So follows the arrival of other relatives and family members, each prepared to do whatever it takes to secure the family inheritance.

The introduction of an almost inconsequential sub-plot was the key feature that would acquire Bava's movie its interminable reputation. The bloody developments observed in this episode were to provide the dynamics for the evolution of the slasher genre that began with John Carpenter's **Halloween** (1978), before descending into the mayhem of the 1980s. Unbeknown to them, the murderous family are joined at the bay by a group of excitable teenagers. Wanting nothing more than a little bit of adolescent fun, they have broken into a vacant cottage on the estate, hoping to find some alcoholic relief and a take-it-easy with their stash of dope. There are teenage kicks aplenty until

one of the group, Brunhilda, decides to go swimming in the bay and runs in with the badly decomposed body of Filippo Donati. In shock, she stumbles through woodland to the cottage to tell the others of her grisly find. However, she is chased and attacked by an unidentified maniac wielding a deathly machete. It doesn't take long before he has her in his clutches and his weapon is buried into her throat. Then it's the turn of one of the boys. Robert opens the front door of the cottage to be confronted by the machete; he takes it full in the face. The killer, whose guise is still obscured, has only just started to get going. He lays his hands on a fisherman's spear and impales the two remaining teenagers, Denise and Duke, who are in bed enjoying their last moments of passion.

This wasn't the finale for this murderous spree, for the family inheritance was still very much at stake. The body count would rise to thirteen, making **A Bay of Blood** Bava's most violent of the twenty-three films he directed. This graphic display, particularly the senseless murders of the teenagers in what appeared to be an idyllic backwater, would leave a legacy to inspire an entire generation of horror cinema. The impact of these grisly killings was such that they would be repeated again and again as the slasher and splatter phenomenon ascended to unparalleled popularity less than a decade later. The first two instalments of the **Friday the 13th** franchise would make ample use of Bava's ingenuity, particularly in **Friday the 13th II** (1981) when both the machete to the face and the impaled lovers were fondly rehashed. On its release in 1971, the reaction to what was just another low-budget movie was anything but flattering, leaving one of the leading horror actors of the day, Christopher Lee, aghast at its content. The critics' disgust was the grindhouse theatres' and drive-ins' manna; they were eager to retain it on their itinerary for the next few years under its American title **Twitch of the Death Nerve**.

While Mario Bava suffered under the critics' wrath, one man on his crew was acclaimed for his exertions,

Terror flows deep! You may not walk away from this one!

Carlo Rambaldi. He was brought in as the special effects man and assigned with the task of designing the make-up for the bloody death scenes. The 1971 Avoriaz Film Festival jurors awarded the film the Best Makeup and Special Effects Award, and in that same year, he went on to earn a "Special Mention" Award at the prestigious Sitges Festival. His career then took off, leading to work on **King Kong** (1976), **Close Encounters of the Third Kind** (1977), **Alien** (1979), **E.T. The Extra-Terrestrial** (1982) and **Dune** (1984).

A Blade in the Dark

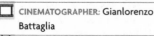
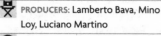

YEAR OF RELEASE: 1983		**CINEMATOGRAPHER:** Gianlorenzo Battaglia	
RUNTIME: 110 minutes		**PRODUCERS:** Lamberto Bava, Mino Loy, Luciano Martino	
COUNTRY: Italy			
DIRECTOR: Lamberto Bava		**CERTIFICATE:** Canada: 13+ (Quebec); Canada: (Banned) (Ontario); Canada: R (Manitoba); UK: 18; USA: Unrated	
PRODUCTION COMPANY: National Cinematografica, Nuova Dania Cinematografica			
WRITERS: Elisa Briganti, Dardano Sacchetti			

CAST: Andrea Occhipinti, Anny Papa, Fabiola Toledo, Michele Soavi, Valeria Cavalli, Stanko Molnar, Lara Lamberti

BRUNO (ANDREA OCCHIPINTI) has rented a huge villa in a quiet rural locale somewhere in Tuscany, to help him get into the right frame of mind to produce the ominous score for Laura's (Fabiola Toledo) forthcoming horror movie. Prior to his arrival the villa had been rented to a woman by the name of Linda, who had apparently departed in rather uncertain circumstances. Soon after meeting his neighbour Katia (Valeria Cavalli), who is still unsettled by Linda's sudden disappearance, she is attacked and killed by a giallo-styled assassin. In the days that follow, Bruno discovers traces of blood around the villa and then finds Katia's diary, which reveals she has learned the enigmatic Linda was concealing a terrifying secret. When his girlfriend Julia (Lara Lamberti) arrives, Bruno seeks to investigate the strange disappearances, but other women visiting the house also go missing, one in a brutal bathroom scene that would attract a considerable amount of controversy. Each new murder seems to echo those committed in the script of Laura's new film. When Anne (Anny Papa) turns up to collect the completed score, she finds herself trapped in the villa with Bruno and Julia, and a killer hiding in the darkness.

Shot in just two weeks and originally

When the lights go out, the knife goes in.

intended as an extended television drama, Lamberto Bava's stylish film was a late entry to the once popular giallo, but gained acceptance from a new audience owing to its narrative that adopted the now fashionable American slasher. Although his feature wasn't entirely original, Bava carefully constructed a mystery around his killer, leaving few clues as to the motive for this brutal spree, while racking up the tension with a series of shadow-laden stalk sequences leading to some explicit kills that exhibited a graphic relish for the depiction of sharpened knives penetrating human flesh. **A Blade in the Dark** was Bava's second appearance in the directorial chair, following his well received dalliance with necrophilia in **Macabre** (1980), and revealed a man whose intense portrayal was highly influenced by the grand master of Italian terror, the esteemed Dario Argento. The viciousness exhibited in the bathroom murder was never going to be acceptable to the BBFC, who insisted on one minute and fifty seconds of cuts to this scene and further edits to some of the more bloodthirsty episodes before the film could be released to video in 1987. For Lamberto Bava, these were early days in what would be a long and successful career in the director's chair. 🔪

A Night to Dismember

YEAR OF RELEASE: 1983	 **WRITER:** Judy J. Kushner
RUNTIME: 69 minutes	**CINEMATOGRAPHER:** C. Davis Smith
COUNTRY: USA	**PRODUCERS:** Larry Marinelli
DIRECTOR: Doris Wishman	(associate producer), Doris Wishman
PRODUCTION COMPANY: Juri Productions	

CAST: Samantha Fox, Diane Cummins, Saul Meth, Miriam Meth, William Szarka, Chris Smith, Dee Cummins, Larry Hunter, Mary Lomay, Rita Rogers, Nina Stengel, Frankie Sabat, Alexandria Cass, Rob DeRosa, Heather Sabat

A YOUNG WOMAN, VICKI Kent (American porn actress Samantha Fox), has been released from a mental institution after the inexplicable murder of two boys. While these murders occurred, members of her family were busily killing other relatives. A sister is butchered in the bathtub followed by an impalement on an axe. It doesn't take long before an aunt is killed in the privacy of her garden by an assassin in the employ of her husband. The guilt-stricken husband confesses to his crime and bows out by hanging himself. This entire succession of murders takes place in the mere matter of minutes the film has been on screen.

Vicki's resentful brother and sister have already embarked on a scheme to drive her to the very edge of madness in the hope that she will once again be committed. They lure her into a darkened bathroom, where they fondle her breasts and smear her body in blood, which is noticeably conspicuous by its absence when she escapes screaming to her bedroom. This is only the beginning; they won't relent until Vicky is hauled away in a straight jacket. Their ploy continues with the most bizarre episode in their grand plan: the brother disguises himself as a zombie and chases Vicki through the woods. If this wasn't enough, her so called boyfriend Frankie is involved with her sister and has another willing girl at his behest, who isn't averse to a good old soft core styled romp. The erotica continues with Vicky's sensuous hallucinations, shots of lovers' bodies writhing over superimposed images of crashing waves set against a dreamy psychedelic vista. These intense images are countered by Vicki's sister's dreams, which are more in keeping with the film's title; a knife is shown in close up repeatedly stabbed into her throat, head and upper body. Frankie doesn't dream his death; he really does get to die, hacked to death by a cleaver.

The self-taught independent filmmaker Doris Wishman was 67 years old when she became aware of the trend for slasher movies and looked to producing her own entry to the genre. She had made a reputation in the early 1960s with eight nudist films, of which her science fiction nudist **Nude on the Moon** (1961) remains the most famous. Often referred to as the female Ed Wood she moved on to sexploitation movies in the mid-sixties and filmed **A Night to Dismember** in 1979. Its release was delayed until 1983 due to a catastrophe at Movielab, where the film was sent

Doris Wishman's cult classic ...

for processing. With thirty-four minutes of the original footage having been destroyed, Doris attempted to reassemble the film using a noire styled narration from Tim O'Malley, the detective assigned to investigate the murders. His words were a vain effort to explain the proceedings, which had become hopelessly confused due to entire sequences having gone missing; hence the puzzling introductory three minutes. Although she had very little funding at her disposal, Doris wasn't averse to throwing in the gore; a dummy was seen to fall before a machete, an eyeball was gouged and we got to see a mutilated body in the freezer. The effects were cheap, the storyline almost impossible to follow and the acting wouldn't have made it to the village hall theatrical society, but this obscurity made it to video in 1989 and finally to DVD in 2001.

A Nightmare on Elm Street

YEAR OF RELEASE: 1984	WRITER: Wes Craven	
RUNTIME: 91 minutes	CINEMATOGRAPHY: Jacques Haitkin	
COUNTRY: USA	PRODUCERS: John Burrows (associate producer), Stanley Dudelson (executive producer), Sara Risher (co-producer), Robert Shaye, Joseph Wolf (executive producer)	
DIRECTOR: Wes Craven		
PRODUCTION COMPANY: New Line Cinema, Media Home Entertainment, Smart Egg Pictures		

CERTIFICATE: Australia: R (original rating); Australia: MA (2005 re-rating); Canada: 13+ (Quebec) (2009); Canada: 14A (Alberta) (2010); Canada: R (Manitoba/Ontario); Ireland: 18; New Zealand: R16 (DVD rating); UK: 18; USA: R

BUDGET: $1,800,000

RECEIPTS: $26,319,961

CAST: John Saxon, Ronee Blakley, Heather Langenkamp, Amanda Wyss, Jsu Garcia, Johnny Depp, Charles Fleischer, Joseph Whipp, Robert Englund, Lin Shaye, Joe Unger, Mimi Craven, Jack Shea, Ed Call, Sandy Lipton

IN THE LEAFY suburb of Elm Street, Springwood, Ohio, Tina Gray (Amanda Wyss) can't escape the nightmares that plague her sleeping hours. Night after night, she cowers in a darkened boiler room, stalked by a hideously disfigured phantasm whose fingers on his right hand have been shaped into razor-sharp knives. On this night, she falls into his clutches and he seizes the opportunity to tear into her clothes. She awakens screaming and finds her nightdress has been ripped, just as it had in her dream. The following day she discovers her friends are haunted by the same torment. That night Nancy (Heather Langenkamp) and her boyfriend Glen Lantz (Johnny Depp) spend the night with Tina, in the hope it will ease her anxiety. When Tina's boyfriend Rod Lane (Nick Corri) turns up, he escorts his young girlfriend to her mother's bedroom, where they are soon entwined in one another's arms. When she falls asleep, Tina is once again beset by the nightmare, only this time she is captured by the killer. Her struggle awakens Rod, who watches aghast as blood pours from his girlfriend's body, which is repeatedly lacerated by invisible knives. In a scene that continues to disturb, the unseen entity forces her up the wall and onto the ceiling, from where she drops to her death. Rod is the only person on the scene and understandably finds himself accused of her murder.

Nancy's nightmares begin to take on an increasingly violent edge. From the confinement of his cell, Rod tells of what happened that night and reveals he too is a victim of these unsettling dreams. Although she finds it impossible to explain why, Nancy is convinced that the slasher in her dreams is responsible for Tina's death. Unable to stay awake she falls into a fitful sleep and sees the mystery figure entering Rod's cell. It is only later she learns the teenager was found in there, hanging from the rafters. To everyone except Nancy, it looks as if Rod has taken his own life and now she is roused from the torment of her dreamworld, clinging to the killer's shabby hat.

Her mother now begins to disclose a dark secret from her past. The owner of the hat, we learn, was a miscreant by the name of Fred Krueger (Robert Englund). He took the lives of over twenty children more than ten years ago. As punishment, the parents of his victims burned him alive in the same secluded boiler room visited in the teenagers' nightmares. Once she has finished her tale, Nancy's mother holds Krueger's razor-like glove aloft, soothing her daughter by insisting he can't hurt anyone anymore. Nancy, with her boyfriend Glen, sets out to put an end to Krueger's schemes, for they know they may never sleep safely again. Glen soon becomes drowsy; as he falls into unconsciousness he is dragged down into his bed and then his body is discharged as a mass of blood and guts. Nancy, however, has succeeded in drawing Krueger from his world; he now stands in the reality of her room. After setting the child murderer on fire, she locks him in the basement, only to find, all too soon, he has broken free. His fiery treads lead to her mother's bedroom where Nancy and her father catch the unstoppable Krueger smothering her mother in flames. Her body is severely burned and her charred remains are seen to wither away. Nancy finally destroys Krueger by turning her back on him, thus rendering him powerless. As she leaves the horrors of her mother's bedroom, she prays those who have fallen to his evil machinations can be returned to life.

If Nancy doesn't wake up screaming she won't wake up at all . . .

The following morning in an epilogue that was producer Bob Shea's idea rather than Craven's, Nancy's prayers are answered, as she is driven to school with Glen and her friends. However, just when you think everything is hunky dory Krueger appears: he's not finished yet. He puts his foot on the gas and drives away with the screaming Nancy, her mother being dragged through the door window by his bladed hand.

By 1984, the golden age of the slasher was almost at an end, with much of the recent crop of entries amounting to little more than worn out cliché. Inspired by reports of people dying in their sleep, Wes Craven delivered this unexpected and highly original take on what had become tired narrative, combining a fastidious plot with crucial fright-filled shenanigans and true to the slasher ilk made imaginative use of a plethora of gut-wrenching gore effects. He had pitched the idea to several studios, including The Walt Disney Company and Paramount Pictures, but each in turn rejected his concept for quite different reasons. Finally, New Line Cinema agreed to take on the film, which marked a diversification in their approach, having up until then acted solely as a film distributor.

The diabolical Fred Krueger, who revelled in an unwholesome mix of murder and mirth, proved to be one of the most memorable villains in cinematic horror. His comedic dialogue would never lessen the terror of his cruel intent, although this in due course was watered down as the sequels ensued and Fred became Freddy. Under Craven's careful direction the audience grew to like these suburban teenagers, as they had with Carpenter's cast from **Halloween**, a bonding which had been largely absent from so many slasher movies of the last few years. Among the endearing cast was a young Johnny Depp, who behind the scenes was very shy and unsure of himself and in this his first role gave only the slightest impression of the talent that would one day follow. The story focused on Depp and his friends rather than the ominous presence of Kreuger; this was their story, not his. The inevitable expansion of the franchise would bring Freddie Kreuger to centre stage, but this would regrettably detract from the true menace in his depraved make up.

Dreams were very much in vogue in 1984 with Paramount having already released **Dreamscape** and the slasher craze had previously been tormented by **Nightmares in a Damaged Brain** (1981), **The Slayer** (1982) and **Blood Song** (1982). However, in his use of the murky shots to engender the impression of dream, Craven broke the rules. He went on to interpose the same technique as his characters awoke, distorting the boundaries between reality and their nightmare world. In this reinterpretation, this was no longer only a dream. The recurrent theme of teenage sexual promiscuity, however, was again invoked, with the perpetrators' falling before the slasher's blade; their loss of innocence was summarily followed by an end to their life.

The film was an almost instant commercial success, making a return on its entire budget during its first week of opening. Eager to reap the rewards there then came, **A Nightmare on Elm Street 2: Freddy's Revenge** (1985), **A Nightmare on Elm Street 3: Dream Warriors** (1987), **A Nightmare on Elm Street 4: The Dream Master** (1988), **A Nightmare on Elm Street 5: The Dream Child** (1989), **Freddy's Dead: The Final Nightmare** (1991), **Wes Craven's New Nightmare** (1994), **Freddy vs. Jason** (2003) and the remake **A Nightmare on Elm Street** (2010).

A Taste of Blood

📅	YEAR OF RELEASE: 1967	🖊️ WRITER: Donald Stanford	
🕐	RUNTIME: 117 minutes	🎞️ CINEMATOGRAPHER: Andy Romanoff	
🎥	COUNTRY: USA	⏳ PRODUCERS: Herschell Gordon Lewis, Sidney J. Reich (executive producer)	
🎥	DIRECTOR: Herschell Gordon Lewis		
🎬	PRODUCTION COMPANY: Creative Film Enterprises Inc.	⭕ CERTIFICATE: UK: 15; USA: Unrated	
		💲 BUDGET: $65,000	

CAST: Bill Rogers, Elizabeth Wilkinson, William Kerwin, Lawrence Tobin, Ted Schell, Otto Schlessinger, Eleanor Vaill, Gail Janis, Herschell Gordon Lewis, Judy Waterberry, Dolores Carlos, Roy Collodi, Karl Stoeber

LUCRATIVE ENTREPRENEUR JOHN Stone (Bill Rogers) receives a parcel, within which he finds two heart-shaped bottles of brandy bequeathed by his recently deceased relative, Baron Khron of Moldavia. The Baron he learns was a descendant of Count Dracula. A note accompanying the parcel insists that Stone toast the deceased Baron; in another six months, he will receive further instructions. As the months go by Stone's wife Helene (Elizabeth Wilkinson) becomes increasingly concerned with a series of subtle changes to his disposition. He is now unusually cold and takes to sleeping during the day and working through the night; furthermore his appearance has also endured a strange transformation. The brandy, which Stone has enjoyed these few months past, has been prepared from the blood of the fabled count; he has now assumed the ancient calling of his family birthright.

Six months later, the vampire Stone receives word to come to London, charging him to lay claim to the estate at Carfax in Purfleet. Reports abound of the murders of Philip Harker, Dr Wayne Seward, and Lord Gold, each

A ghastly tale drenched with gouts of blood spurting from the writhing victims of a madman's lust!

horribly staked through the heart. Dr Howard Helsing (Otto Schlessinger) is certain he will be next, for he knows Stone is mercilessly avenging Dracula's slaughter. He enlists the aid of Helene's former boyfriend Hank. Fearing Stone will turn his wife into a vampire, Hank willingly joins forces with Helsing. Stone, however, has already learned Helsing has taken Helene into his confidence; using his vampiric powers he throws her into a hypnotic trance, convincing her that Helsing is intent on his murder. Before he departs, he places his wife under his control and then savours a portion of her blood. When later taken in for questioning he escapes to suckle on his wife's neck for a second time. Now in an even deeper trance, Helene drives away, with Hank, Helsing and a detective in pursuit. They follow her to an abandoned mansion, where Stone is finally trapped, and as the sun rises over the horizon they stake him through the heart.

Also known by the name **The Secret of Dr Alucard**, Herschell G. Lewis's feature was a marked departure from his previous efforts. While considerably longer in running time to the "Blood Trilogy", by comparison it was somewhat slower paced and offered significantly less in the way of gore. However, it was a worthy attempt to create a horror movie as opposed to the exploitative sensationalism upon which he had built his reputation in the wake of Alfred Hitchcock's groundbreaking **Psycho** (1960). Bill Rogers and William Kerwin turned in some reasonably decent performances, which afforded their roles the kind of authority that had been absent from Lewis's previous efforts. As with many films of the period, **A Taste of Blood** was marred by its night-for-day shots, with the backdrop to the London docklands resembling the Miami skyline.

Absurd

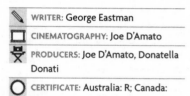

31 YEAR OF RELEASE: 1981		WRITER: George Eastman	
RUNTIME: 96 minutes		CINEMATOGRAPHY: Joe D'Amato	
COUNTRY: Italy		PRODUCERS: Joe D'Amato, Donatella Donati	
DIRECTOR: Joe D'Amato			
PRODUCTION COMPANY: Filmirage, Metaxa Corporation		CERTIFICATE: Australia: R; Canada: (Banned) (Ontario); UK: X	

CAST: George Eastman, Annie Belle, Charles Borromel, Katya Berger, Kasimir Berger, Hanja Kochansky, Ian Danby, Ted Rusoff, Edmund Purdom

FROM THE HIGHLY prolific Joe D'Amato (born Aristide Massaccesi), and originally entitled **Rosso Sangue**, **Absurd** has also gone by the name **Anthropophagous 2**. As with so many of the exploitation features of this era, this unofficial sequel has nothing to do with the gory excess of **Anthropophagous**, which had seen release only a year before. To add to the confusion, this piece of deranged Italian splatter has subsequently been entitled **Horrible** and **The Grim Reaper 2**.

In a nameless American town, actually shot in Italy, a bedraggled stranger (George Eastman) frantically tries to escape a chasing priest (Edmund Purdom). In his desperate attempt to scale a tall gate, he loses his balance and as he falls is disembowelled by the protruding railings. As he reels away, his torn intestines are revealed with an abundance of blood spilling from his body; surely he is about to die. Nursing these near fatal wounds, he is rushed to the hospital, where the doctors stare in disbelief, amazed at his seemingly impossible powers of recuperation. When the priest arrives, he is taken to one side by the investigating police detective, Sergeant Engleman (Charles Borromel). The priest warns the detective that the man in surgery, Mikos Stenopolis, is a homicidal lunatic transformed by a biochemical experiment to be nigh on indestructible. The only way to kill him, the priest explains, is to "destroy the cerebral mass". After the shock of seeing him bolt upright on the operating table, the unspeaking madman escapes. His menacing presence accentuates the sense of dread in the moments before he drives a surgical screwdriver directly through the cranium of a young nurse and then ploughs an industrial band saw into the head of an orderly, with graphically bloody results. As the psychotic Mikos takes to the darkened streets, the blood inevitably begins to flow.

While attacking a motorcyclist he is struck by a hit-and-run driver, which turns out to be a Dr Bennett and his wife, who have left their two children at home with their babysitter. Their daughter Katia is confined to bed, paralyzed by a severe spinal problem, while her fearful younger brother can't shake the thought that the "Bogeyman" is out to get him. When Mikos forces his way into the family home, he traces the babysitter, severely batters her, runs her head into a lighted oven and then slowly burns it. As with **Anthropophagous**, D'Amato had the camera dwell at length on these scenes, bolstering his standing with the gore-mongers, while enraging the censors.

Now assuming the role of the elder sibling, Katia sends her brother for help then struggles from her bed ready to defend herself. D'Amato then delivers the unexpected; in a close up shot, he has Katia take a set of drawing compasses and repeatedly stab Mikos in the eyes. Now blinded, the infuriated killer staggers through the house trying to seize hold of his crippled assailant. This suspense-filled scene provides a fitting climax as the disabled Katia writhes to avoid the thrashing killer, before decapitating him and destroying "the cerebral mass".

D'Amato had been eager to emulate and then improve on the success of his previous film **Anthropophagous: The Beast**, and from the opening frames of his new film went straight for the jugular as he hurled an entire catalogue of graphic outrage at his expectant audience. While hopelessly limited by the constraints of an inadequate budget, he was still able to deliver the American-styled slasher, with script writer George Eatman, whose real name was Luigi Montefiori, engaging just enough narrative to allow the psychopath to stray between a series of set pieces as he killed off a predominantly youthful supporting cast. On its release, **Absurd** was heavily criticized for its similarities to John Carpenter's **Halloween** (1978), particularly the staging of the babysitter and the children placed in her care who became imperilled by a hushed and almost indestructible killer. It was, however, far more bloodthirsty than **Halloween**, which led to it being included on the Director of Public

Prosecution's list of video nasties in November 1983, and was one of thirty-nine titles to be successfully prosecuted under the Obscene Publications Act of 1959 during 1984. This video version had been released with two minutes and twenty-three seconds of edits in the August of 1983. A quarter of a century later it was issued in its original form in France, now entitled **Horrible**, but it is yet to be resubmitted for release to the BBFC.

Aenigma

📅 YEAR OF RELEASE: 1987		✎ WRITER: Lucio Fulci	
🕐 RUNTIME: 90 minutes		🎞 CINEMATOGRAPHY: Luigi Ciccarese	
🌐 COUNTRY: Italy/Yugoslavia		🎬 PRODUCERS: Boro Banjac, Walter Brandi, Ettore Spagnuolo	
🎥 DIRECTOR: Lucio Fulci			
🎬 PRODUCTION COMPANY: A.M. Trading International S.r.l., Sutjeska Film		◯ CERTIFICATE: UK: 15 (re-rating 2003); UK: 18 (original rating); USA: Unrated	

CAST: Jared Martin, Lara Lamberti, Ulli Reinthaler, Sophie d'Aulan, Jennifer Naud, Riccardo, Acerbi, Kathi Wise, Milijana Zirojevic, Dragan Bjelogrlic, Ljiljana Blagojevic, Franciska Spahic, Dusica Zegarac, Zorica Lesic, Rade Colovic

I N THE DORMITORY of an exclusive girls' boarding school located in New England, Kathy (Milijana Zirojevic) busily readies herself for a date, surrounded by a dubious gathering of friends and posters of those desirable heartthrobs of the day, Sylvester Stallone and Tom Cruise. Hours later while parked at a secluded spot with gym teacher Fred Vernon, she enjoys the heat of some back seat fervour, unaware her leering schoolmates can see everything that is going on. When Kathy realizes she has been set up, she takes off in floods of tears, only to be knocked down by an oncoming car. Lying comatose in a hospital bed, she begins to exact her revenge. A new girl has just arrived at the school, Eva Gordon (Lara Naszinsky); she's the kind of girl who likes to be popular with the boys and very soon will become Kathy's unwitting pawn. Having been given Kathy's old room, Eva falls under the comatose girl's vengeful grasp. With Eva now firmly in her control, Kathy embarks on her course of grim retribution by killing her smug gym teacher. Then she prepares for her tormentors, the girls who put in her hospital, hunting them down one by one like lambs to the slaughter. Fulci is typically creative with the death by snails sequence, where one of the girls, in a series of close-up shots, is literally smothered as she lies in her bed; a decapitation ensues with numerous gratuitous stabbings and a strange dreamlike sex scene, which takes a rather grisly turn.

> **All her enemies will be eliminated ... but first they will suffer!**

While the cinematography has been highly praised, this remains one of Lucio Fulci's less known films and for many fails to live up to the bloodthirsty genius he so wilfully splattered across the silver screen only a few years before. **Aenigma** was completed as the craze for Italian horror movies was drawing to an end, and by comparison to those more renowned features is appreciably reserved in its glee for blood and guts. Instead, Fulci attempted to create his own version of **Suspiria** (1977), choosing to develop a stylized atmosphere of menace in the closeted world of the boarding school dormitory. The framework for the film bears similarities to the slasher of the preceding years rather than Italian splatter, at a time when the genre bordered on mediocrity. As with his previous works, there are inconsistencies in the narrative, the maid's glowing eyes are never explained and the relationship with Eva's doctor proves an unsatisfying subplot. Aspects of the **Carrie** (1976) storyline are also in evidence, as the humiliated teenager metes out her cruel reprisal, but in this instance, this would not become Fulci's saviour.

After Death

📅 YEAR OF RELEASE: 1989	✏️ WRITERS: Rossella Drudi (screenplay), Rossella Drudi (story)
🕐 RUNTIME: 90 minutes	
🌐 COUNTRY: Italy	🎞️ CINEMATOGRAPHER: Luigi Ciccarese
🎥 DIRECTOR: Claudio Fragasso	⚗️ PRODUCERS: Franco Gaudenzi, Bruno Mattei (executive producer)
🎬 PRODUCTION COMPANY: Flora Film	
	⭕ CERTIFICATE: Canada: 16+ (Quebec); UK: 18; USA: Unrated

CAST: Jeff Stryker, Candice Daly, Massimo Vanni, Jim Gaines, Don Wilson, Adrianne Joseph, Jim Moss, Nick Nicholson

IN THE DEPTHS of a cave on a faraway island, researchers are about to bear down on a native voodoo ritual. During the ensuing melee, the voodoo priest (James Sampson) is killed as he conspires to open the Third Gate of Hell, all in the hope of giving life to his recently deceased daughter. In the throes of death, he invokes a curse from the ancient "Book of the Dead", whose incantation reaches across the entire island to return the dead to life. Within minutes, four people's faces are torn asunder and bloody carnage ensues. As a family chase through the mist of the forest trying to escape this insanity, they are confronted by a freshly resurrected zombie. Within seconds, the father's neck is savagely gorged and the mother is taken down and eaten alive. Only their young daughter Jenny (Candice Daly) manages to escape, protected by her mother's amulet.

Many years later, Jenny returns with a friend and a group of mercenaries. She is intent on learning the circumstances that led to the death of her parents and seek to become free of the island's curse. As their boat draws into shore, the engine cuts out leaving the party marooned. In a change of scene, three backpackers are observed exploring the same island; they wander into the cave where the high priest and his followers had previously been killed. One of them, Chuck (Jeff Stryker), opens "The Book of the Dead" and accidentally revives the spell that once again resurrects the dead. Only Chuck makes it from the cave; soon after both he and the mercenaries are heavily embroiled with this new wave of the walking dead. Those who fall to this unusually animated horde undergo an all too familiar transmutation to join the ranks of those who have already become zombies, as Jenny and Chuck desperately fight on in the hope of survival. They know the only way to end the curse is to seal the gateway that leads to Hell, so the two of them trek back to the cave. As they explore the cavern, Jenny comes upon a mirror that reveals the flesh melting from her face and, in an exquisitely executed close up, her eyeball is plucked from its socket. As this terrifying transformation takes place, Stryker has to confront the mindless zombies and falls as one of them repeatedly thrusts its hand into his stomach, leaving him to an agonizing death. Before the credits begin to roll, the camera turns its attention to Jenny, whose face has now completely disintegrated to reveal she too is now one of this atrophied breed.

After Death or **Oltre La Morte** was another part in the obsession for Italian zombies, and saw release in the United States as **Zombie 4: After Death** and here in the United Kingdom as **Zombie Flesh Eaters 3**. These titles are typically confusing, as the film bears no narrative connection with either series. Claudio Fragasso, under the pseudonym Clyde Anderson, returned from **Zombi 3** (1988) to direct this low-budget shocker with its implausible plot but distinctive splatter of blood and guts. His film proved a little too dependent on the gore factor, and when to his disdain it was censored, it was robbed of a considerable part of its intended impact. However, its fast pace and succinct editing combined with the handmade zombie effects succeeded in producing a movie that appealed to the bloodthirsty and invited much discussion as to the interpretation of its ambiguous denouement. The statuesque Jeff Stryker, credited as Chuck Peyton, had already starred in a plethora of gay and bisexual pornographic features and would go on to make many more. Fragasso would continue to direct low-budget ventures, which the following year would see him work on the haunted house feature **La Casa** 5 and the film denigrated as one of the worst of all time, **Troll 2**.

Aftermath

📅 YEAR OF RELEASE: 1994	✏️ WRITER: Nacho Cerdà
🕐 RUNTIME: 30 minutes	🎞️ CINEMATOGRAPHER: Christopher Baffa
🌐 COUNTRY: Spain	🎭 PRODUCERS: Nacho Cerdà, Joseph Maar (executive producer)
🎥 DIRECTOR: Nacho Cerdà	
🎬 PRODUCTION COMPANY: Waken Productions	⚙️ CERTIFICATE: USA: Not Rated

CAST: Xevi Collellmir, Jordi Tarrida, Ángel Tarris, Pep Tosar

WITH HIS COLLEAGUES having left for the night, the partially disguised mortician (Pep Tsor) is left alone in the morgue with only the bodies of the recently deceased as company. An autopsy is explicitly detailed; then this troubled employee begins to fondle the corpses. One corpse in particular attracts his attention, that of a young woman who has just been brought in following her death in the impact of a car crash. He tears off her clothes, then slices open her body, becoming aroused as her raw flesh is exposed before savouring his necrophilic lust by climbing astride her lacerated cadaver while taking pictures with an automated camera. Discarding his mask, he then leaves for the evening with his snap shots and the heart he has removed to feed to his dog.

There was no dialogue to Nacho Cerdà's compelling thirty-minute portrayal of sex and mutilation, only a score of beguiling classical music, placing this film among the more disturbing realms of art house cinema. While there was a beauty to the serenity of the music that was facilitated by Christopher Baffa's smooth-flowing camera work, this proves to be a sickening experience, which will live on with the audience long after the lights have gone down. The sense of realism observed in Cerdà's short feature sought to unsettle, surpassing both Johan Vandewoestijne's **Lucker the Necrophagous** (1986) and Jörg Buttgereit's **Nekromantik** (1987) in taking the act of necrophilia further than any director before him. While this wasn't a film made specifically to titillate the gore-mongers, Cerdà consulted with both students and teachers of pathology to ensure he treated his subject matter with the utmost respect and then let the blood flow. During the planning stages, **Aftermath** was to have run to over two hours, expanding the number of autopsies and allowing for considerably more sex. With very little money at his disposal, the director was forced to reduce the scale of his venture and shot the film in only eight days. **Aftermath** was followed by another horror short in 1998, **Genesis**; it would be 2006 before he progressed onto his long-awaited first full-length feature, which came to the cinema screens as **The Abandoned** (2006). This ghostly portrayal would observe a similar beauty in its use of both photography and musical backdrop, but preferred suggestion as its means to frightening its audience to the graphic display that was featured throughout this film. Christopher Baffa's work didn't go unrecognized; he worked on the shelved **Fantastic Four** movie of that year before embarking on a lucrative career behind the camera in television.

Alien

📅 YEAR OF RELEASE: 1979	
🕐 RUNTIME: 119 minutes	
🌐 COUNTRY: USA/UK	
🎥 DIRECTOR: Ridley Scott	
🎬 PRODUCTION COMPANY: 20th Century Fox, Brandywine Productions	
✎ WRITERS: Dan O'Bannon, Ronald Shusett	
🎞 CINEMATOGRAPHER: Derek Vanlint	

PRODUCERS: Gordon Carroll, David Giler, Walter Hill, Ivor Powell (associate producer), Ronald Shusett (executive producer)

CERTIFICATE: Australia: M; Canada: R (Manitoba/Nova Scotia/Ontario, original rating); Ireland: 18; New Zealand: M (re-release); New Zealand: R16 (original rating); UK: 15 (director's cut); UK: 18 (video rating, 1987); UK: X (original rating); USA: R

💲 BUDGET: $11,000,000

🗐 RECEIPTS: $185,000,000

CAST: Tom Skerritt, Sigourney Weaver, Veronica Cartwright, Harry Dean Stanton, John Hurt, Ian Holm, Yaphet Kotto, Bolaji Badejo, Helen Horton

THE COMMERCIAL SPACESHIP *Nostromo* travels through the darkness of space on its return voyage to Earth, with its crew of seven resting in suspended animation. An unknown transmission forces the ship's computer to awaken the crew and then following the instructions of their corporate employers they land on the planetoid on which the signal has been traced. On the surface of the planetoid, the decaying hull of an alien vessel can be seen, and within, the landing party, led by Kane (John Hurt), discover the long-dead pilot, a huge alien life form whose ribs seem to have exploded. As the team make their way around the derelict ship, Ripley (Sigourney Weaver) determines the transmission is actually a warning. Meanwhile, on board the alien ship the exploratory team descend into an enormous chamber laden with a cargo of strange eggs. As Kane examines the cargo, a creature bursts from the egg and envelopes his face. His colleagues' efforts to remove the creature prove unsuccessful until it detaches of its own will and then dies.

At first Kane seems to be fine, but as the crew enjoy a meal before returning to deep sleep he begins a series of uncontrollable convulsions while sitting at the table and then, in one of the most astonishing scenes in cinematic history, a creature erupts from his chest. Kane's upper body is only ever briefly seen; it has been completely ripped apart and the creature scurries away to hide somewhere in the bowels of the *Nostromo*. If they are to survive and return to Earth the crew must hunt down this alien entity, but this will become far more than a game of cat and mouse as Ripley has to fight for her life and overcome this predatory killer to become the final girl in what has been described as a science fiction slasher.

In space, no one can hear you scream.

Dan O'Bannon had written the screenplay for **Alien** while he was still only a student. In his time at the University of Southern California, he also collaborated with John Carpenter and concept artist Ron Cobb to make the cult science fiction movie **Dark Star** (1974). As a long-time fan of science fiction and horror he has always been keen to share his numerous sources of inspiration. These included **The Thing from Another World** (1951), later adapted by John Carpenter, **Forbidden Planet** (1956), **Planet of the Vampires** (1965), Clifford D. Simak's tale "Junkyard"

(1953), a tale of a chamber full of eggs, in addition to EC Comics' infamous line of science fiction and horror titles, a series of comics similarly inspired by many writers of their day. His script became considerably more intense when he discovered the disturbing work of the dark surrealist H. R. Giger, and the creature began to assume a more terrifying magnificence. When Ridley Scott agreed to take on this film, he could see the horror permeating O'Bannon's script, and conceived a very claustrophobic ill-lit design, which made formidable use of the camera's lens to give the project an entirely new dimension. Through the eerie half-light, he would orchestrate the tension just as the slashers would in the not too distant future – the hunter becoming the hunted as this alien being ripped into the cast.

The man behind John Hurt's chest-bursting scene was Roger Dicken, a special effects man whose early career brought him to the studio of Gerry Anderson and the cult television series **Thunderbirds** before moving on to Stanley Kubrick's **2001: A Space Odyssey** (1968). When the alien exploded onto the set, no one knew quite how it was going to happen, thus the terror that wracked each actor's face was very much real. The design team would include Ron Cobb and science fiction illustrator Chris Foss, both of whom O'Bannon had worked with on **Dark Star**, and just for a few days French comic book artist Jean Giraud, otherwise known as Moebius, was brought in to work on the space suite designs, which were then completed by British writer and designer John Mollo.

Alien went on to become an immensely influential film, spawning several imitators including the following year's controversial **Contamination** and many years later the Gothic space terror **Event Horizon** (1997). The film's success led to three sequel **Aliens** (1986), **Alien 3** (1992) and Jean-Pierre Jeunet's **Alien: Resurrection** (1997) along with **Alien vs. Predator** (2004) and **Aliens vs. Predator: Requiem** (2007). Heavy Metal would publish an adaptation of the film in 1979 and Dark Horse would continue the franchise with their **Alien** series with a story arc that began in 1988. Video games and toys continue to follow. ❧

Alone in the Dark

YEAR OF RELEASE: 1982	**PRODUCTION COMPANY:** Masada Productions, New Line Cinema
RUNTIME: 92 minutes	
COUNTRY: USA	**WRITERS:** Jack Sholder (story), Robert Shaye (story)
DIRECTOR: Jack Sholder	

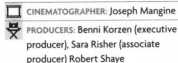

CINEMATOGRAPHER: Joseph Mangine

PRODUCERS: Benni Korzen (executive producer), Sara Risher (associate producer) Robert Shaye

CERTIFICATE: Australia: M; Canada: (Banned) (Ontario); Canada: R (Ontario – Re-rated 1992); UK: 18; USA: R

CAST: Jack Palance, Donald Pleasence, Martin Landau, Dwight Schultz, Erland van Lidth, Deborah Hedwall, Lee Taylor-Allan, Phillip Clark, Elizabeth Ward, Brent Jennings, Gordon Watkins, Carol Levy, Keith Reddin, Annie Korzen, Lin Shaye

DR DAN POTTER (Dwight Schultz) arrives at Dr Leo Bain's (Donald Pleasance) Haven psychiatric institute to take up a new position. Pleasance's role as Dr Bain is redolent of his character Dr Sam Loomis from John Carpenter's **Halloween** (1978), but in this part he is just as crazy as the patients by whom he is surrounded, or as he prefers to call them, "voyagers". He keeps the most dangerous inmates secured behind an electrically activated security mechanism up on the third floor; his forward thinking has seen fit to dispense with the iron bars found in facilities of a more conventional nature. Only a single guard remains on watch. Among the deranged third floor patients are the paranoid former Korean prisoner of war Frank Hawkes, (Jack Palance) and apocalyptic pyromaniac preacher Byron Sutcliff (Martin Landau), who believes himself to be the messenger of God. An overweight child molester Ronald "Fatty" Elster (Erland Van Lidth) and homicidal maniac John "Bleeder" Skaggs (Phillip Clark), whose nose bleeds as he goes in for the kill and refuses to show his face until very late in the film are also

detained on the same floor. Hawkes convinces the others they must kill Dr Potter, rambling as to how he murdered his predecessor and in time will do the same to them.

As he lingers in Dr Potter's office, Ronald Elster thumbs through the doctor's mail. There he finds the doctor's address and a photograph of his daughter. That same night the power supply fails across the entire city. On the third floor of the institute Preacher insists it is he who made the lights go out, which allows him and his psychotic brethren the chance to escape. As looters ransack a nearby shopping centre, the four inmates don new clothes and arm themselves with a crossbow, knives, a pitchfork, an axe and set of handguns. With a tip of the hat to **Friday the 13th** (1980), the "Bleeder" adorns himself in a hockey mask. Leaving a trail of slaughter, the four men head towards the doctor's house, where his daughter is home alone.

Alone in the Dark was Jack Sholder's directorial debut, and one of the first films to come from New Line Cinema. He had at his disposal a first rate cast, whose ability transcended so many of its contemporaries and added a distinct edge to the proceedings. Their maniac performances would make up for the shortcomings in the area of gore. Sadly for Sholder his film's release went almost unnoticed, with his efforts written off as yet another in an ever-lengthening line of slasher movies. However, there was an underlying intelligence to this film, one not always observed among its grisly cohorts. In an ambitious piece of scripting, Sholder used a set of theories advocated by Scottish psychiatrist Ronald David Laing, who recognized a bridge between mental dysfunction and existential philosophy, postulating on the difficulties of the psychotic to adapt to an already psychotic world. For the first half hour Dwight Schultz, prior to his later acceptance to the **A-Team**, and Donald Pleasance discuss in detail such

Too frightened to breathe . . .

aspects of psychiatry and the treatment of these mentally distressed people. Interestingly their dialogue was never used as an attempt to excuse the violent actions of his homicidal cast.

The storytelling coupled a mounting suspense with the exact degree of violence slasher fans had come to expect, although Palance was adamant in his refusal to carry out one of the killings staged in the original screenplay, considering it gratuitous and failing to add to his on-screen persona. Tom Savini boosted the film's credentials, being drafted in for the make-up in a hallucinatory zombie sequence. A wicked sense of dark humour prevailed throughout, in what in its time was an unusual take on a gang of psychos escaping the asylum. The film was briefly banned in the UK, but was excused from the damning list of video nasties.

American Nightmare

📅	YEAR OF RELEASE:	1983
🕐	RUNTIME:	88 minutes
🌐	COUNTRY:	Canada
🎥	DIRECTOR:	Don McBrearty
🎬	PRODUCTION COMPANY:	Manesco Films
✏️	WRITERS:	Steven Blake, John Gault

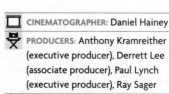

🎞️	CINEMATOGRAPHER:	Daniel Hainey
🎥	PRODUCERS:	Anthony Kramreither (executive producer), Derrett Lee (associate producer), Paul Lynch (executive producer), Ray Sager
⭕	CERTIFICATE:	Australia: M; Canada: R (Ontario); USA: R
💲	BUDGET:	$200,000

CAST: Lawrence Day, Lora Staley, Neil Dainard, Lenore Zann, Claudia Udy, Page Fletcher, Michael Ironside, Larry Aubrey, Michael Copeman, Bunty Webb, Tom Harvey, Paul Bradley, Peter Lavender, Martin Doyle, Don MacQuarrie

A PHONE RINGS AND a surly voice snaps at a young woman telling her to get out, the videotapes that have come into the caller's possession have absolutely nothing on them. When he hangs up, a young prostitute is seen languishing in a hotel bedroom, a bundle of dollars lying at her side. Her client appears from the bathroom wearing only a towel; having carefully washed his hands, he rolls on a pair of latex gloves. The prostitute is eager to convey her heightened sense of arousal and assures her punter everything will be just fine. She is a little premature, for without a word of warning, the man uncovers a sharpened razor and then slits her throat.

In a scenario somewhat reminiscent of Paul Schrader's film **Hardcore** (1979), the son of a prominent businessman Eric (Lawrence Day) uses the return address on a letter in an attempt to find his missing sister, Isabelle. When he locates her apartment, he is introduced to Dolly (Larry Aubrey) a transvestite, who professes it has been days since he/she has seen the sister, he/she knows as Tonya. Eric's investigations reveal his sister has been working as an exotic dancer in a number of sleazy clubs and has fallen into prostitution. Together with his newfound friend, dancer Louise (Lora Staley) and a detective (Michael Ironside), Eric

begins to search for his sister coursing deeper into the sordid underbelly of this downbeat inner-city landscape. As they venture further into this squalid world of murder, blackmail, incest and lurid sex, the hookers, exotic dancers and other shady residents of this tawdry locale are being butchered by a modern-day Jack the Ripper.

Filmed in Toronto during 1981 and then shelved for a couple of years, **American Nightmare** walked the seamier streets of New York City. Don McBrearty's was a change of pace to the run-of-the-mill teenage slasher that had become so much a part of the horror cinema of the day, owing its origins to the exploitation of the grindhouse fleapits with its lurid intimation of sex, lies and videotape. Drawing inspiration from the vicarious Italian gialli, McBrearty presented his audience with a gloved killer whose motivation remained obscured until the finale of what proved to be an intriguing murder mystery. As in many gialli, the police were portrayed as being hopelessly incompetent, leaving it to the hero to hunt down the psychotic killer. Disappointingly, the murders were not as graphic as those staged by their Italian counterparts, nor given the subject matter could they be described as unduly misogynistic. The grim setting, however, was comparable to the urban filth of **The Driller Killer** (1979), **Maniac** (1980) and **The New York Ripper** (1982) but the darkened shots made the erotica appear so very unattractive, which meant it never quite matched its counterparts' potency for sleaze.

The title **American Nightmare** would surface again in Jon Keeyes' unrelated call-in show slasher of 2002 and the well-received documentary starring Wes Craven and George A. Romero examining the many extreme horror movies of the 1970s produced in 2000.

American Psycho

 YEAR OF RELEASE: 2000

 RUNTIME: 102 minutes

 COUNTRY: USA

 DIRECTOR: Mary Harron

 PRODUCTION COMPANY: Am Psycho Productions, Edward R. Pressman Film, Lions Gate Films, Muse Productions, P.P.S. Films, Quadra Entertainment, Universal Pictures

 WRITERS: Bret Easton Ellis (novel), Mary Harron, Guinevere Turner (screenplay)

 CINEMATOGRAPHER: Andrzej Sekula

PRODUCERS: Ernie Barbarash, Alessandro Camon, Joseph Drake (executive producer), Christian Halsey Solomon, Chris Hanley, Victoria Hirst (line producer), Gretchen McGowan (line producer), Michael Paseornek (executive producer), Edward R. Pressman, Jeff Sackman (executive producer), Clifford Streit (co-producer), Rob Weiss (co-producer)

 CERTIFICATE: Australia: R; Canada: 18A; Canada: 16+ (Quebec); Ireland: 18; New Zealand: R18; UK: 18; USA: NC-17 (original cut); USA: R; USA: Unrated (uncut DVD version)

 BUDGET: $8,000,000

RECEIPTS: $34,266,564

CAST: Christian Bale, Justin Theroux, Josh Lucas, Bill Sage, Chloë Sevigny, Reese Witherspoon, Samantha Mathis, Matt Ross, Jared Leto, Willem Dafoe, Cara Seymour, Guinevere Turner, Stephen Bogaert, Monika Meier, Reg E. Cathey, Blair Williams, Marie Dame, Kelley Harron, Patricia Gage, Krista Sutton

FAR AWAY FROM the murders and executions of the grime-ridden streets of **The Driller Killer** (1979), **Maniac** (1980) and **American Nightmare** (1983) was the superficial world of Patrick Bateman (Christian

Bale), a deeply troubled Wall Street broker whose life of mergers and acquisitions has bestowed upon him the trappings of an incredibly rich and successful life. However, his good looks and polished lifestyle conceal a familiar dark secret, one that links him to the murderous individuals who had been prowling New York's downtrodden locales more than a decade past; Patrick is a psychotic monster with a craving for blood and violence. Over the phone, he confesses to having murdered more than twenty people, dispatched in a variety of ways: chainsaw, stabbings, gunshots and sinking his teeth into his lovers during sex. His everyday routine is overly obsessed with the finest detail of perfection, which expands beyond his predilection for banal popular culture to the brutal sex and killing he savours with his countless victims. The blood flows almost unabated, but as the ambiguous finale alludes, is this grisly excess locked solely in Patrick's twisted mind?

American Psycho was Mary Harron's second time in the directorial chair. Some might have said that on this occasion she had been presented with a poison chalice, for Bret Easton Ellis's allegory of the vagaries of corporate capitalism had caused uproar on its initial publication in 1991. Her script remained true to the original, using virtually every line from what had already been distinguished as a highly accomplished literary assault on the absurdities of the self-interested yuppie lifestyle of the 1980s. While Harron deftly harnessed the misogynistic portrayal expressed in Ellis's novel, she wasn't afraid to engage his attack on the perversity of the American dream. The result was a thought-provoking film that succeeded in intriguing the more discerning quarters of its audience rather than engendering revulsion, with Christian Bale excelling in his role as one of modern cinema's most complex monsters. However, Harron was forced to remove several minutes of footage from the final cut, most of it of a sexual nature, to ensure a cinematic release. This of course would have served to claw back the money of those who had shrewdly invested in the project. When her film debuted at the Sundance Film Festival the audience was divided, but on its theatrical release it garnered a far more positive reception. A direct to video **American Psycho 2** was made in 2002, directed by Morgan J. Freeman, which had little in common with the original. 🐾

> **I think my mask of sanity is about to slip.**

Amsterdamned

31 YEAR OF RELEASE: 1988		CINEMATOGRAPHER: Marc Felperlaan
RUNTIME: 105 minutes		PRODUCERS: Laurens Geels, Dick Maas
COUNTRY: Netherlands		CERTIFICATE: Australia: M;
DIRECTOR: Dick Maas		Netherlands: 16 (re-rating);
PRODUCTION COMPANY: First Floor Features		Netherlands: 12; UK: 18 (cut); UK: 15 (re-rating, 2009, uncut); USA: R
WRITER: Dick Maas		

CAST: Huub Stapel, Monique van de Ven, Serge-Henri Valcke, Tanneke Hartzuiker, Wim Zomer, Hidde Maas, Lou Landré, Tatum Dagelet, Edwin Bakker, Door van Boeckel, Barbara Martijn, Pieter Lutz, Simone Ettekoven, Koos van der Knaap, Pieter Loef

USING A SERIES of creepy point-of-view shots, Marc Felperlaan takes his camera underwater to trail a predatory killer around the canals of the darkened city of Amsterdam. Armed with a cleaver taken from a Chinese restaurant he tracks down his first victim, the easiest of targets in such a city, a lady of the night. She never has a chance as he stealthily seizes upon her and thrusts the stolen knife deep into her flesh. He then drags her corpse into the water leaving behind a pool of blood. Her mutilated body is found the morning after, suspended upside down from a bridge.

Detective Eric Visser arrives on the scene with his partner, Vermeer, as a down-and-out woman is questioned about the horrific events of the previous night. She claims she saw a monster crawl from the water and kill the prostitute. The clues suggest a diver is skulking through the canals of this beautiful city. That night, a couple of environmental researchers are observed taking water samples from a chemical plant. They never get to see the morning light, both killed and again dragged below the water. Visser steps up his enquiries and meets the love interest in this film, Laura, a museum guide along with Martin Ruysdael, a former diver. The killings continue, even though a suspect who worked at the chemical plant is taken into custody. The tone changes following the death of one of the investigating officers as an action-packed James Bond-esque speedboat chase ensues between Visser and the killer. Eric pursues the assailant to a sewer only to be wounded in the shoulder by a harpoon. Just as you think he's finished he shoots the killer's masked face before coming round in a hospital bed. The finger seems to point to Martin Ruysdael, but is there a damning connection with the chemical plant?

The city is murder.

With **De Lift** (1983) Dick Maas had shown he was capable of delivering an unsettling horror story set against a modern-day urban backdrop; five years later with the big budget **Amsterdamned** he singlehandedly created the Dutch giallo. True to the guile of Italian masters of this once popular genre, he intertwined a series of twists into his narrative with the darkest of humour, grisly death scenes and outrageous action. While his film may have seemed to be trying to be so many different things, it was never confused; rather, it glided with a fluidity that was symptomatic of an emerging talent. Setting his story in a city famed for its historic splendour, he presented an Amsterdam few have ever seen, one immersed in gloom that concealed a dark secret. In 1988 his movie was the third highest selling motion picture at the American Film Market, although it was dubbed in English for the video version. Maas continues to write and direct and, over twenty years later, remains the Netherland's most commercially successful director. 🖤

And Then There Were None

📅	YEAR OF RELEASE: 1945	✏️ WRITER: Dudley Nichols	
🕐	RUNTIME: 97 minutes	🎞️ CINEMATOGRAPHER: Lucien N. Andriot	
🎥	COUNTRY: USA	🎬 PRODUCERS: René Clair, Leo C. Popkin, Harry M. Popkin	
🎥	DIRECTOR: René Clair		
🎬	PRODUCTION COMPANY: René Clair Productions	⭕ CERTIFICATE: Australia: PG; Canada: PG (Ontario); UK: U (2002); USA: Approved	

CAST: Barry Fitzgerald, Walter Huston, Louis Hayward, Roland Young, June Duprez, Mischa Auer, C. Aubrey Smith, Judith Anderson, Richard Haydn, Queenie Leonard, Harry Thurston

RENÉ CLAIR'S MOVIE was based not on the novel *Ten Little Niggers* (soon after changed to *And Then There Were None* because of the disparaging inference in the word "nigger") by Agatha Christie, but on the play she later wrote in 1943. The identity of the murderer remained the same in both versions, but the outcome as to who survives the murderer's plot was somewhat different.

In his film of 1945 ten people, eight guests and two servants, are invited for a long weekend on an island somewhere off the coast of Devon. Although guests of the mysterious Mr and Mrs U. N. Owen, none of them has ever actually met. It is only after dinner, when their host speaks to them through a gramophone recording, that they learn why they have been invited to this remote island. They are each accused of being responsible for the death of another person or persons. As punishment, they will go to meet their maker before the weekend is out. There is no way of escaping the island, leaving the gathering with a killer in their midst, and each of them with the seeming aptitude for murder.

While searching the island for "Mr Owen" they begin to compare stories, but their camaraderie won't put an end to the death toll, or stop the ten Indian boy statues from disappearing one by one from the centrepiece in the house. Each person with whom the group grow suspicious becomes the next to meet their demise, thus narrowing the list of suspects. Sound familiar? Axe wounds, knives, a hypodermic syringe, falling masonry, all making for a splatter fan's

delight, but remember this was 1945; there were to be no pools of blood or the severing of arteries. In the end it comes down to just two, the apparent hero and heroine of the piece, Lombard and Vera. Each of course suspects the other, but even they can't deny a mutual attraction. Although they are in accord, accepting that neither was ever guilty, Vera still steals away with a gun and shoots Lombard as they stand on the beach. Surely it can't be true – the delectable Vera the mass murderess? It is, however, nothing more than a ruse, a ploy to reveal the identity of the true killer, the man who would see Vera hang for her crimes. She walks up from the beach, only to discover a hangman's noose has already been prepared for her. Judge Quincannon, who sentenced an innocent man to death, reclines in a chair, very much alive after supposedly falling victim to a gunshot wound to the head. As the film reaches its climax, his contemptible machinations are exposed. In his eyes, they are all guilty, for they considered themselves beyond the law. He is their judge and jury; having executed the entire party he would then prepare to commit suicide with a glass of poison. The eventual arrival of the police would find Vera alone with nine dead bodies and an inevitable death sentence hanging over her head. Lombard now appears to enter the scene, though it turns out he is only a friend of Lombard's, and as the film comes to an end, the judge falls dead and he takes her into his arms.

Agatha Christie's novel would become a bestseller, now totalling over 100 million sales, making it the world's biggest selling mystery and one of the most-printed books in history. René Clair's adaptation was also very successful, although not quite on the same scale, but his film provided so many elements for those writers and directors who would one day give rise to the slasher phenomenon. While there was no gore on display, nor the grisly aftermath of the death, the key ingredients were set in place: a madman with a mind for brutal murder, knives, axes, the hapless victims, a beautiful but isolated setting and the heroine we so wanted to survive this madness. The sensibilities of the audience of the day would have no doubt been shocked by this unrelenting onslaught. So much so, it was banned in Finland soon after its release, being the first of many such movies to be subjected to prohibition in this seemingly quiet corner of Scandinavia; that was until Tommi Lepola and Tero Molin's snuff-based slasher **Skeleton Crew** (2009).

Angustia

YEAR OF RELEASE: 1987

RUNTIME: 86 minutes

COUNTRY: Spain

DIRECTOR: Bigas Luna

PRODUCTION COMPANY: Luna Films, Pepón Coromina, Samba P.C.

WRITERS: Bigas Luna (screenplay), Michael Berlin (dialogue)

CINEMATOGRAPHER: Josep M. Civit

PRODUCERS: George Ayoub (executive producer), Andreu Coromina, Pepón Coromina, Norm Hill (video producer), Xavier Visa (associate producer)

CERTIFICATE: Australia: R; Canada: 16+ (Quebec); UK: 18; USA: R

BUDGET: $228,789

CAST: Zelda Rubinstein, Michael Lerner, Talia Paul, Àngel Jové, Clara Pastor, Isabel García Lorca, Nat Baker, Edward Ledden, Gustavo Gili, Antonio Regueiro, Joaquín Ribas, Janet Porter, Patrice Manget, Merche Gascón, Jose M. Chucarro

THE MYOPIC JOHN Pressman's (Michael Lerner) time as an optician's assistant has come to an unceremonious end; dejected, he returns home to break the terrible news to his domineering mother. In truth, he has no one to blame but himself; his mother Alice (Zelda Rubinstein), however, doesn't quite see it this way. To her addled way of thinking, her darling child is a well-respected optician; although nothing could be further from the truth. She vents her rage by hypnotizing her incompetent son and then sends him out with his set of surgical tools to seek revenge on the woman responsible for his dismissal. The unfortunate woman's death fails to satiate his mother's psychotic tendencies, forcing Pressman to seek out more victims. Once he has slain his prey, he takes his scalpel and gouges the eyes from their sockets, before carefully secreting them away. He then returns to his mother who proudly places these trophies among her bizarre collection of eyeballs. She is convinced they hold the key to restoring her son's deteriorating sight.

The film suddenly takes an unexpected turn and the audience realize they have just witnessed a complex showing of a movie within a movie, with Alice and John starring as the lead roles in the macabre presentation "The Mommy". This terrifying film is part of a matinee performance being shown in a cinema somewhere in Los Angeles. Such a grisly showing so early in the day might seem a little farfetched, but George A. Romero's **Night of the Living Dead** (1968) infamously premiered as a matinee, which traumatized many of its young audience. Sitting in this cinema is a pair of teenage girls, the feisty Linda and her friend Patty, who is of a somewhat delicate disposition. They become distracted when they

The eyes of the city are mine.

realize one of their fellow horror buffs (Àngel Jové) is getting a little too involved with Pressman's gruesome undertaking. His oafish figure is now seen entering a similar theatre armed once again with his surgical implements. As Harry O. Hoyt's silent masterpiece **The Lost World** (1925) plays to a captive audience, he once again plies his foul trade, hacking into the onlookers while coolly detaching their eyes to return them to his insane mother's ever-growing collection. His cruel savagery proves the catalyst for the darkened figure reclining amidst the Los Angeles audience; he now displays a pistol, which he fires into the crowd with a relish that echoes the on-screen slaughter.

Shot in Barcelona, Bigas Luna's obscure **Angustia** or **Anguish** crafted a cleverly juxtaposed tale, which in the course of its narration related not one but two stories that came to immerse the surreal with a brutally violent reality. Although Luna had a little in the way of funds, his team laboured to create a convincing Californian backdrop using only a few sets, and then in one of the most original slasher movies of the past thirty-five years he manipulated the minds of his assembled audience. Lamberto Bava in his acclaimed **Demons** (1985) had made use of a similar idea, allowing the illusion of film to conspire with the real world, but Luna ventured further as he schemed to unhinge his audience's perception, which would leave them as disoriented as the myopic John Pressman. His feature was a deftly choreographed exposition of anguish and terror, as his cast fought for survival in the darkened claustrophobia of this Los Angeles auditorium. The impact of **Angustia** has never altered; it remains a stark and uncompromising movie. The tide of blood that flowed unabated through each tale coupled with its ever-rising body count would have those with a delectation for the more sanguinary, slavering on the very edge of their seat.

Antropophagus

📅	**YEAR OF RELEASE:** 1980	📷	**CINEMATOGRAPHY:** Enrico Biribicchi
🕐	**RUNTIME:** 90 minutes	🎞	**PRODUCERS:** Joe D'Amato, George Eastman, Edward L. Montoro (executive **PRODUCER:** Film Ventures International), Oscar Santaniello
🌐	**COUNTRY:** USA		
🎥	**DIRECTOR:** Joe D'Amato		
🎬	**PRODUCTION COMPANY:** Filmirage, Produzioni Cinematografiche Massaccesi (PCM) International	⭕	**CERTIFICATE:** Australia: R; Canada: R; UK: 18 (heavily cut); UK: (Banned) (1984–2002); USA: R (heavily cut); USA: Unrated (uncut)
✏	**WRITERS:** Joe D'Amato, George Eastman		

CAST: Tisa Farrow, Saverio Vallone, Serena Grandi, Margaret Mazzantini, Mark Bodin, Bob Larsen, Rubina Rey, Simone Baker, Mark Logan, George Eastman, Zora Kerova

HAVING TAKEN AN excursion to a remote Greek island, two of them in hope of meeting up with their French friends, a party of tourists become stranded when their boat drifts out to sea. The group are forced to seek help in a nearby village, but as they search the deserted streets, their mood turns to one of apprehension. With darkness now set to draw in, members of the party decide to stay at the house owned by Julie's (Tisa Farrow) friends, who the viewers already know to be dead. Hidden away in the house the group find the French couple's blind daughter. She is beside herself and knows nothing of the whereabouts of the islanders, but jabbers about a man whose body reeks of blood. The remaining members of the group continue in their search for signs of life and come upon a mysterious woman in black, who warns them to leave the village.

As they continue in their exploration of the island, the boat party slowly begin to disappear, falling prey to a terrifyingly misshapen man. A journal discovered in an abandoned mansion tells of a family who many years before were shipwrecked on the island. The father was driven to eat the flesh and blood of his dead kin and in his all-consuming despair fell into madness. Now completely deranged, he turns to killing the island's inhabitants, feeding his newfound cannibal lust after dragging his victims into the shadows of the island's catacombs. In the claustrophobia of the beast's darkened lair the audience are privy to the film's most notorious scene when he grasps a pregnant woman by the throat. During this frenzied strangulation, he tears the unborn child from her womb, and then, in full view of the camera, voraciously feeds upon its flesh. When this scene was first shown, it caused considerable dismay, so much so that D'Amato was later probed as to whether he had actually extracted a human foetus from the mother's womb. With almost the entire group now dead, one of the survivors finally overpowers the cannibalistic maniac by driving a pickaxe into his stomach.

It's not fear that tears you apart ... it's him!

As the creature falls to the floor, he is once again overwhelmed by bloodlust, but this time he is aroused by his own flesh and as the camera's lens frames his ruptured stomach he begins to devour his intestines.

Joe D'Amato's new terror, following the success of **Buio Omega** (1979), was essentially a bloodthirsty piece of exploitation whose subsequent reissues would go on to acquire a plethora of titles, among them **Anthropophagous**, **Anthropophagous: The Beast**, **The Grim Reaper**, **Anthropophagus: The Grim Reaper**, **Man Eater** and **The Savage Island**. While bereft of any true artistic merit, those horror fans who had only recently been led astray by the gore of Romero, Fulci and Argento, were only too eager to get to see the excess that was already being spoken of in this new offering. The film's early pacing has been criticized for being overly measured, but it has also been suggested this gave the air of impending dread the chance to build before the monstrous figure of George Eastman revealed his disfigured face. The violence that ensued was then swift and merciless as he ripped into the throat of an unsuspecting victim before seizing the face of his quarry and dragging it through a hole in the mansion's crumbling ceiling.

An uncut version of **Anthropophagous: The Beast** made it to video in the United Kingdom in February 1983.

However, the severity of its content was such that it attracted the attention of the Director of Public Prosecutions, who duly labelled it as a video nasty, which led to it being prosecuted under the Obscene Publications Act in 1984. The furore came largely as a result of the infamous foetus-eating scene and as the BBC News reported there were accusations that it was a snuff movie.

D'Amato's film is still only available in the UK in its cut form, under the title **The Grim Reaper**. Almost twenty years after the original release first terrorized cinema screens, German low-budget cult director Andreas Schnaas produced an extreme re-telling as **Anthropophagous 2000** (1999) to a somewhat mixed critical response.

April Fool's Day

YEAR OF RELEASE: 1986

RUNTIME: 89 minutes

COUNTRY: USA

DIRECTOR: Fred Walton

PRODUCTION COMPANY: Paramount Pictures, Hometown Films, TCTM

WRITER: Danilo Bach

CINEMATOGRAPHER: Charles Minsky

PRODUCERS: Frank Mancuso Jr.

CERTIFICATE: Australia: M; Canada: 13+ (Quebec); UK: 18 (original rating); UK: 18 (video rating, 1986); UK: 15 (video re-rating, 2002); USA: R

BUDGET: $5,000,000

RECEIPTS: $12,947,763

CAST: Jay Baker, Pat Barlow, Lloyd Berry, Deborah Foreman, Deborah Goodrich, Tom Heaton, Mike Nomad, Ken Olandt, Griffin O'Neal, Leah Pinsent, Clayton Rohner, Amy Steel, Thomas F. Wilson

WEALTHY COLLEGE STUDENT Muffy St John (Deborah Foreman) has invited a group of her friends to stay at her parent's island home for an extended weekend of frivolity. Their arrival on the ferry on the day before April Fool's Day is caught on a home video, conferring the film a strangely sinister introductory sequence. Very soon, the friends are involved in a whole series of amusing pranks. Their stay, however, is marred by the disappearance of one of the guests, and Kit (Amy Steel) remains convinced she caught a fleeting glimpse of his dead body. When the group try to make contact with the police, they learn the lines are down and the ferryman won't be returning to the island for another few days. It isn't long before other members of the party go missing and Muffy's behaviour becomes a cause for concern. When Nikki (Deborah Goodrich) and young Harvey (Jay Baker) trek into the woods to draw water from a well, Nikki drops her flashlight. She descends into the well to retrieve the light and finds the lifeless corpses of her three friends.

Director Fred Walton returned to make his second slasher movie following his debut as a writer and director seven years before on **When a Stranger Calls** (1979). This would be the beginning of a long stream of directorial ventures, which would keep him on film sets well into the next decade. The executives at Paramount Pictures regarded Walton's project as an opportunity to revive the bloodthirsty phenomenon, for which they had been instrumental six years before with **Friday the 13th**. Following the success of **A Nightmare on Elm Street** (1984), the genre had fallen into a downward spiral of self-parody with **Friday the 13th Part V: A New Beginning** (1985) momentarily bringing one of the studio's largest franchises to a grinding halt. Producer Frank Mancuso Jr. wanted to revitalize the slasher movie and when he was approached by Danilo Bach, fresh from his success on **Beverley Hills Cop** (1984), he was very keen to give it a go.

Childish pranks turn into a bloody battle for survival!

The script would adhere to a formula that had become accepted practice, reintroducing the holiday theme, throwing in the obligatory red herrings, toying with incredulous plot twists and revealing secrets at every turn before chasing through the house to dispose of virtually the entire cast. Bach, however, delivered a surprise ending, which in slasher circles still has many people talking. The mood for much of the early part of the film is naturally light, with good-natured antics abounding on a scene-to-scene basis. Slasher devotees, however, have always despaired of its unsatisfactory level of gore, which, coupled with its late entry to the field, probably led to it being almost instantly forgotten. The island setting, along with the unsettling revelations and continual disappearances have prompted innumerable comparisons with Agatha Christie's "Ten Little Indians", and more specifically René Clair's **And Then There Were None** (1945), an adaptation of Christie's play. To their credit Frank Mancuso Jr.'s team captured the very essence of the slasher phenomena, but at the box office it was just a few years too late and maybe displayed a little too much intelligence. Following its release to DVD more than twenty years later, **April Fool's Day** has finally found an appreciative audience and in turn justified Paramount's faith. 🔥

At Midnight I'll Take Your Soul

YEAR OF RELEASE: 1964	WRITER: José Mojica Marins
RUNTIME: 84 minutes	CINEMATOGRAPHER: Giorgio Attili
COUNTRY: Brazil	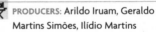 PRODUCERS: Arildo Iruam, Geraldo
DIRECTOR: José Mojica Marins	Martins Simões, Ilídio Martins
PRODUCTION COMPANY: Indústria	Simões
Cinematográfica Apolo	

CAST: José Mojica Marins, Magda Mei, Nivaldo Lima, Valéria Vasquez, Ilídio Martins Simões, Arildo Iruam, Genésio de Carvalho, Vânia Rangel, Graveto, Robinson Aielo, Avelino Morais, Luana, Leandro Vieira, Antônio Marins, Mário Lima

IN AN ANONYMOUS Brazilian town, Zé do Caixão (Coffin Joe, played by José Mojica Marins) considers only the perfect woman could ever bear him a child worthy of his bloodline. The Nietzschean Coffin Joe is the town's bullying undertaker and is disparaging of the townsfolk's fervent Catholicism. His only concern is the need to maintain the "continuity of the blood". Sadly, his wife Lenita (Valeria Vasquez) cannot bear children, so Coffin Joe begins to look elsewhere. To further his pursuit he first murders his wife as the locals enjoy a religious festival, binding her up and leaving her to confront a poisonous spider. When her body is later discovered, the police have absolutely nothing to link him with the murder, leaving Coffin Joe free to continue in his quest. Fulfilling the predictions of a local

gypsy (Eucaris Moraes) he brutally murders his best friend, Antonio (Nivaldo Lima), leaving his grieving girlfriend Terezinha (Magda Mei) ripe for seduction. In his efforts to win her heart, he buys her a canary and then, blinded by lust during the course of their conversation, he becomes a little too amorous. When Terezinha rejects his advances, Coffin Joe attacks and rapes her. Terezinha curses him, vowing to kill herself then return to drag his soul to hell. He retorts with a sneer, but the next day she is found suspended with a rope around her neck in the living room of her home. Coffin Joe's activities haven't gone unnoticed; the town's doctor, Dr Rudolfo, now has his suspicions. When he becomes aware of the doctor's reservations, he decides to pay him a visit. Soon after his arrival, he sets about the fearful doctor, finally gouging out his eyes with his long fingernails before setting his body alight.

Some days later on the Day of the Dead celebrations, Coffin Joe encounters the beautiful young Marta. He is certain she is the woman who will bear his children. In the late evening, he takes her home, only to be confronted by the gypsy who foresaw the deaths of Antonio and Terezinha. She warns the murderous undertaker his soul is already forfeit to the spirits of those he has murdered and Satan himself will come for him when the clock strikes midnight. Soon after leaving Marta in the company of her relatives, he is beset by the same ghostly figures of which the gypsy had foretold. In fear he turns and runs for his life, little realizing he has stumbled upon the vault where both Antonio and Terezinha lie buried. As his mind frantically races, he forces open their coffins in the hope of finding they are still dead. Their eyes stare back at him from within their darkened tomb as maggots immerse their wasted faces. Coffin Joe's terrified screams can be heard away in the town. When the locals enter the vault, they find his horribly disfigured body with his eyes left opened wide to the world just like those he murdered. In the distance, the toll of a bell can be heard, ringing out the stroke of midnight.

Originally shot in thirteen days in 1963, **At Midnight I'll Take Your Soul**, (**À Meia-Noite Levarei Sua Alma**) lays claim to being Brazil's first horror movie. This marks the first instalment of Jose Mojica Marins' existential "Coffin Joe trilogy", to be followed by **This Night I'll Possess Your Corpse** (1967), and **Embodiment of Evil** (2008). There were also three other entries to the Coffin Joe mythos, **The Strange World of Coffin Joe** (1968), **The Awakening of the Beast (O Despertar da Besta)** (1969), banned in Brazil for twenty years owing to its treatment of drugs, prostitution and police corruption, and **Hallucinations of a Deranged Mind (Delirios de um Anormal)** (1978). Marins' creation has been considered as a precursor to the leering psychopath Freddy Kreuger and, in a similar way to his treacherous heir, would go on to become a celebrity figure, making it to the stage, screen and national television before going on to comic books. Marins not only wrote and directed the film; when he couldn't find an actor who could take his creation seriously, he assumed the role himself, using an expressionistic style that harked back to the villains of the earliest days of cinema. With a pitiful budget, an amateur cast and only one studio in which all but a few of the scenes were shot, he put together a gruesome feature that was an unrepentant challenge to his country's Catholicism. His film was shot in black and white, but after half a century, many of the darkened scenes are no longer entirely black. While this feature may have been shot in monochrome, it didn't detract from the viciousness presented in certain scenes, with the intensity of the eye gouging coming fifteen years before Fulci's predilection for this dehumanizing brutality. Later in his career, he would be forced to move into pornography when he produced the highly controversial yet lucrative **24 Hours of Explicit Sex** (1985). As a cult phenomenon Marins is revered and his contribution to the world of horror should never be underestimated.

Audition

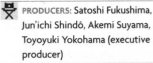

📅	YEAR OF RELEASE: 2000	🎞	CINEMATOGRAPHER: Hideo Yamamoto
🕐	RUNTIME: 115 minutes		
🎦	COUNTRY: South Korea/Japan	🏺	PRODUCERS: Satoshi Fukushima, Jun'ichi Shindô, Akemi Suyama, Toyoyuki Yokohama (executive producer)
🎥	DIRECTOR: Takashi Miike		
🎬	PRODUCTION COMPANY: AFDF, Creators Company Connection, Omega Project		
		🔘	CERTIFICATE: Australia: R; Canada: 18+ (Quebec); Canada: R; Ireland: 18; New Zealand: R18; UK: 18; USA: R (cut); USA: Unrated
✏️	WRITER: Ryû Murakami (novel), Daisuke Tengan (screenplay)		

CAST: Ryo Ishibashi, Eihi Shiina, Tetsu Sawaki, Jun Kunimura, Renji Ishibashi, Miyuki Matsuda, Toshie Negishi, Ren Ohsugi, Shigeru Saiki, Ken Mitsuishi, Yuriko Hiro'oka, Fumiyo Kohinata, Misato Nakamura, Yuuto Arima, Ayaka Izumi

AFTER MANY YEARS of loyalty to the memory of his deceased wife, television producer Shigeharu Aoyama (Ryo Ishibashi) contemplates finding someone to share his life. He speaks of his loneliness to his friend Yasuhisha Yoshikawa (Jun Kunimura), a fellow producer, who devises a hoax audition for a film with the intention of finding Aoyama a new wife. Yoshikawa puts together a plethora of résumés and asks his forlorn friend to choose thirty women to attend the audition. Prior to the big day, Aoyama becomes smitten by one girl in particular, Asami Yamazaki (Eihi Shiina), a shy young woman dressed in virginal white. Yoshikawa finds her a little unnerving, but relents, knowing his long-time friend is completely besotted. Aoyama finds himself drawn closer to the girl, even though there are unanswered questions about some of her former acquaintances who are no longer to be heard from. When their relationship becomes strained, Aoyama decides to call Asami; her apartment appears empty, but her figure can be seen sitting by the telephone with a large canvas bag towards the rear of the room. When the phone rings, the canvas bag begins to violently twitch. The unfeeling inflection in Asami's smile chills the viewer to the bone; Yoshikawa's initial assessment of the girl would appear to have been correct. There is now a change in tone to **Audition**, as it becomes Asami's account of the trauma she faced at the hands of an uncaring older man but it does not excuse one of the most excruciating scenes ever to be committed to celluloid.

She always gets a part.

Audition was but one of five films directed by the inexhaustible Takashi Miike during the year 2000, which for him was nothing out of the ordinary. When compared to so much of his immense catalogue of films this is by far one of his most challenging creations, bearing a narrative energy rarely seen in the horror genre. For much of the early part of his film, both he and writers Ryû Murakami and Daisuke Tengan almost convinced their audience this was a whimsical romancing; only Yoshikawa's sense of apprehension ever suggested

anything different. The last forty minutes proved to be some of the most unsettling in the director's accomplished career, thanks to the writing of novelist Ryû Murakami and the disturbingly surreal screenplay of Daisuke Tengan, which Miike admits to having toned down. It has been insinuated that this is a feminist revenge story, but there are layers of subtext to this film, which continue to confound so many horror devotees; yet equally the violence in the finale has distanced the admirers of more cerebral cinema. The ambiguity surrounding the final third of the film raises questions as to whether this is truly Asami's tale or Aoyama's guilt-laden dreams for what he considers the betrayal of his deceased wife coupled with his treatment of Asami during the fake audition. The finale, however, remains one of the most graphic portrayals observed in horror cinema, largely due to the audience's empathic bond with the distraught Aoyama. ❦

Basket Case

📅 YEAR OF RELEASE: 1982	✏️ WRITER: Frank Henenlotter
🕐 RUNTIME: 91 minutes	🎬 CINEMATOGRAPHER: Bruce Torbet
🎥 COUNTRY: USA	🎞️ PRODUCERS: Arnold H. Bruck (executive producer), Edgar Ievins
🎬 DIRECTOR: Frank Henenlotter	
	⭕ CERTIFICATE: Australia: R; New Zealand: R16; UK: 18; USA: R
PRODUCTION COMPANY: Basket Case Productions	
	💲 BUDGET: $35,000

CAST: Kevin Van Hentenryck, Terri Susan Smith, Beverly Bonner, Robert Vogel, Diana Browne, Lloyd Pace, Bill Freeman, Joe Clarke, Ruth Neuman, Richard Pierce, Sean McCabe, Dorothy Strongin, Ilze Balodis, Kerry Buff, Tom Robinson

A SEEMINGLY ORDINARY YOUNG man from the sticks, Duane Bradley (Kevin Van Hentenryck), arrives in New York City and takes residence in a seedy Times Square hotel. In his possession is a large wicker basket hiding a hideous secret. Hidden within is his grotesque parasitic half-aborted Siamese twin, Belial, whose deformities are such that few people would ever consider him human. Belial resembles a twisted lump of gristle, armed with a pair of claws, yet retains a chillingly human face.

In a flashback sequence, we learn their mother died tragically in childbirth and consequently their father grew to despise them. Still embittered by the death of his wife and afflicted by the shame he feels for the freak-show to which he unwittingly gave life, he is driven to have the twins surgically separated. This would give Duane a chance of a normal life, but neither brother wants to endure this operation. Their father refuses to listen; instead he turns to three doctors of dubious repute. Not even they consider Belial to be human. When the procedure has been completed, he is declared dead. He then suffers the indignity of being disposed with the rubbish. However,

The tenant in room seven is very small, very twisted and very mad.

he is far from being dead; and now he wants revenge.

After killing their father, the twins are raised by a kindly aunt until her death a few years later. This is where we join the film; the twins are in New York, now with telepathic abilities, seeking unholy retribution against the three doctors responsible for separating them. So follow three days of slaughter, each falling victim to Belial's cruel claws. Belial's final killing is a girl for whom Duane has fallen, leading to the finale, hanging from the window of their hotel room, before they finally fall. The quality of the gore may have been appallingly low in budget, but it was vicious and there was plenty of it.

When stripped down, the shoestring budget comedy horror **Basket Case** was a tragic tale of brotherly love and the jealousy that comes with it. Since its release to video, it has gone on to acquire a miraculous cult following which belies its diminutive status and is now considered a classic of exploitation cinema. Under Frank Henenlotter's inventive direction, his story took advantage of the discomfort people find with human deformity and shifts from the plain ridiculous to grindhouse grim, scoured in neon reds and blues, making the sleazy surroundings dirtier and all the more grungy. Belial was a remarkable piece of design; while ludicrous in appearance, Henenlotter's stop-motion gore succeeded in evoking an unexpected degree of threat. **Basket Case** was later known as **House of Freaks** and was to inspire a couple of sequels, **Basket Case 2** (1990) and **Basket Case 3: The Progeny** (1991), both directed by Frank Henenlotter.

Battle Royale

 YEAR OF RELEASE: 2000

 RUNTIME: 114 minutes

COUNTRY: Japan

DIRECTOR: Kinji Fukasaku

PRODUCTION COMPANY: Battle Royale Production Committee, Fukasaku-gumi, GAGA, Kobi Co., M Associates, MF Pictures, Nippon Shuppan Hanbai (Nippan) K.K., Toei Company, WoWow

WRITERS: Koushun Takami (novel), Kenta Fukasaku

 CINEMATOGRAPHER: Katsumi Yanagijima

PRODUCERS: Kenta Fukasaku, Kinji Fukasaku, Kimio Kataoka, Chie Kobayashi, Toshio Nabeshima, Masumi Okada

 CERTIFICATE: Australia: R; Canada: 18A (Alberta); Canada: 18+ (Quebec); Canada: R; Hong Kong: III; Ireland: 18; New Zealand: R18; UK: 18

BUDGET: $4,500,000

CAST: Tatsuya Fujiwara, Aki Maeda, Tarô Yamamoto, Takeshi Kitano, Chiaki Kuriyama, Sôsuke Takaoka, Takashi Tsukamoto, Yukihiro Kotani, Eri Ishikawa, Sayaka Kamiya, Aki Inoue, Takayo Mimura, Yutaka Shimada, Ren Matsuzawa, Hirohito Honda

AT THE DAWN of the twenty-second century, Japan has fallen into social and economic turmoil. With unemployment spiralling out of control, Japanese youth begin to rebel and turn their back on school. The government's reaction is to pass legislation designed to terrify the country into a semblance of order and so comes the draconian edict they call the BR Act. Its stipulations result in a group of forty-two students from a Japanese high school being ordered to compete in a new reality television show. They are each given a bag which contains a randomly selected weapon and some food and water. After collecting their bag, they are then sent to an isolated island to kill one another in a bizarre game that in three days' time will leave only one survivor. An electronic collar fitted with explosives ensures that each of the students complies with the rules; any defiance means instant death. While Shuya, Noriko, and Kawada try to escape the island, their psychotic classmates begin to play this bloodthirsty game.

Veteran Japanese director Kinji Fukasaku's **Battle Royale** was based on the controversial novel written by former reporter Koushun Takami. Although his book went on to become a bestseller in his homeland, its violent content led to its expulsion from the literary competition for which it had been intended. The judges were unable to see beyond the obvious excess in Takami's thought-provoking work and failed to recognize the meaninglessness in his brutal portrayal. Sadly, for Kinji Fukasaku this would be his final film, having directed over sixty movies in an impressive career spanning forty years. When **Battle Royale** was being prepared for its Japanese release, Fukasaku insisted that its bloody display laced with the darkest of humour should be open for teenagers over the age of fifteen; he was resolute in his insistence that this age group should be aware of the damage they were causing across the country.

Forty-two students; three days; one survivor; no rules.

The censors, however, were unhappy with its excess, fearing it trivialized youth violence, and would only make it available to the over-eighteens; there was also the fear this film could be the catalyst that stirred up riots among an already troubled Japanese youth. Fukasaku was incensed; he went away to produce an edited version so that a younger audience could become aware of the message contained in his film. He managed to convince the censors and the movie opened to audiences of fifteen and over, although many observers consider the edited version to be more brutal than the original. Due to its contentious nature, **Battle Royale**'s critical reception across Japan was somewhat mixed and following the Columbine High School killings of 1999 Fukasaku's film had a troubled time in the United States. However, its success at the Japanese box office was to produce a sequel in 2003, **Battle Royale II: Requiem**. Fukasaku would shoot only one scene before his death; it was left to his son Kenta, who had written both screenplays, to bring this follow-up to fruition.

The Beyond

YEAR OF RELEASE: 1981	 DIRECTOR: Lucio Fulci
RUNTIME: 87 minutes	PRODUCTION COMPANY: Fulvia Film
COUNTRY: Italy	WRITER: Dardano Sacchetti

CINEMATOGRAPHER: Sergio Salvati

PRODUCERS: Fabrizio De Angelis

CERTIFICATE: Australia: R; Canada: 16+ (Quebec); New Zealand: R16; UK: 18 (re-rating: 1987, cut); UK (re-rating: 2001, uncut); UK: (Banned) (1984–7); UK: X (original rating: 1981, cut); USA: R (heavily cut); USA: Unrated (uncut); USA: X (original rating)

 BUDGET: $400,000

CAST: Catriona MacColl, David Warbeck, Cinzia Monreale, Antoine Saint-John, Veronica Lazar, Anthony Flees, Giovanni De Nava, Al Cliver, Michele Mirabella, Gianpaolo Saccarola, Maria Pia Marsala, Laura De Marchi

MORE THAN HALF a century ago in the year 1927, in scenes reminiscent of the classic Universal horror movies of the 1930s and 1940s, torch-wielding villagers descend on the Louisiana home of a painter named Schweick (Antoine Saint-John), a man who had stepped too far into the darkness. They force him down into the depths of the cellar, where he warns them that the house was constructed over one of the seven gateways to hell, and claims only he has the power to save them. The mob refuse to listen to him, and in a graphic scenes that had already become a trademark of Lucio Fulci's cinematic work, they chain him up and take a whip to his body before impaling his arms and legs in an excruciating crucifixion.

Over half a century later, a New Yorker, Liza Merril (Catriona MacColl), inherits the same house, and prepares to refurbish the old place. As the build gets under way, there is a series of inexplicable occurrences. A painter falls to his death, another man suffers a broken neck and then a plumber uncovers Schweick's atrophied corpse hidden behind a wall in the cellar. He may have met his death over fifty years before, but Schweick is still intent on revenge and is brutal in his gouging of the plumber's eyes. Lisa is later advised by a blind woman, by the name of Emily (Sarah Keller), she must leave this accursed house. This same woman was also seen during the film's prelude, in what was an appreciably Lovecraftian series of frames. Dr John McCabe (David Warbeck) and his assistant Dr Harris (Al Cliver) are baffled as they examine the two corpses found in the cellar. At the same time, McCabe finds himself attracted to Lisa and tries to help her in understanding these mystifying events. They soon have to come to terms with the shattering fact that the gateway to hell lies beneath the house and it has been thrown open to allow the dead to walk the Earth. A mob of zombies, in truth no more than half a dozen in what was a comparatively low budget presentation, are seen lurching towards the bewildered couple, calling for them to dart down one of the hospital's many stairwells only to stumble into the basement of the hotel. Still hoping to escape this seeming hallucination, they climb through a hole in the wall, only to become lost on the shadowed plains of Hell, blighted by the knowledge they will never find their way home.

Lucio Fulci's E Tu Vivrai Nel Terrore – L'aldilà has also been released as the disappointingly abridged Seven Doors of Death and marked the closing instalment in his zombie quartet, preceded by Zombi 2, also known as Zombie Flesh Eaters (1979), City of the Living Dead (1980) and House by the Cemetery (1981). It is also acknowledged as the finale to his unofficial Gates of Hell series, heralded by City of the Living Dead and House by the Cemetery. Make-up man Giannetto De Rossi overcame the derisory budget to create an impressive series of effects that shocked the audience and ultimately accentuated the brutality in a feature that would have repercussions across the globe. The cast had their eyeballs gouged, were subjected to impalement, had their tongues ripped out, their heads blown off, and as in all Italian splatter movies of note gasped as their throats were duly severed. It contained the excess that fans of the genre craved and was enhanced by the surreal

photography of Sergio Salvati, who observed a perception for the Gothic and enhanced the apocalyptic milieu with a succession of haunting images; yet when required he remained crisp and made extraordinary use of zoom focusing to exacerbate the shocks.

In his quest to make an "Absolute Film" where image and sound transcend the movie's individual elements, Fulci adopted a nonlinear structure to his narrative, causing absolute frustration for the casual viewer. The plot at times appeared devoid of logic and was open in its defiance of convention, yet its visual splendour continues to beguile.

Ideas once espoused by Antonin Artoud along with the writings of H. P. Lovecraft were to have a major influence on this feature; indeed Artoud's controversial approach was evident in so much of Fulci's work from these years. As founder of "The Theatre of Cruelty", Artoud had looked to "Restore to the theatre a passionate and convulsive conception of life, and it is in this sense of violent rigour and extreme condensation of scenic elements that the cruelty on which it is based on must be understood". Fulci looked to use these ideas and succeeded in his damning vision that lay beyond the Gates of Hell.

His extreme visualization of violence again attracted the regulatory encumbrance of the censors. In the

> **The seven dreaded gateways to hell are concealed in seven cursed places … And from the day the gates of hell are opened, the dead will walk the earth.**

United Sates, his film was heavily toned down and issued as **Seven Doors of Death**. On its release to cinemas in the United Kingdom, it was edited by one minute and thirty-nine seconds, removing much of the film's excess. Only eighteen months after its release to video, its explicit content had **The Beyond** pilloried as a video nasty in November 1983. It was later removed from the offending register in April 1985 but wasn't to find distribution in its unedited form until 2002. Fulci has been the target of much criticism, but the influence of this movie can be seen in Sam Raimi's exploits with **The Evil Dead** (1983) and it was also to have a bearing on images seen in both **Hellraiser** (1987) and **Dellamorte Dellamore** (1996).

The Bird with the Crystal Plumage

📅	YEAR OF RELEASE: 1970	🎞️	CINEMATOGRAPHER: Vittorio Storaro
⏱️	RUNTIME: 98 minutes		PRODUCERS: Salvatore Argento, Artur Brauner (executive producer)
🌐	COUNTRY: Italy/Germany		
🎥	DIRECTOR: Dario Argento	⭕	CERTIFICATE: Australia: M; Ireland: 18; UK: 15 (DVD rating); UK: 18 (re-rating, 1986); UK: X (cut, original rating); USA: R
🎬	PRODUCTION COMPANY: Central Cinema Company Film (CCC), Glazier, Seda Spettacoli		
✏️	WRITER: Dario Argento, Fredric Brown	💲	BUDGET: $500,000
		🗄️	RECEIPTS: $1,000,000

CAST: Tony Musante, Suzy Kendall, Enrico Maria Salerno, Eva Renzi, Umberto Raho, Renato Romano, Giuseppe Castellano, Mario Adorf, Pino Patti, Gildo Di Marco, Rosita Torosh, Omar Bonaro, Fulvio Mingozzi

SAM DALMAS (TONY Musante), an American writer working in Rome with his girlfriend Giulia (Suzy Kendall), witnesses the attempted murder of Monica Ranieri (Eva Renzi), the wife of a gallery owner, by a black-gloved assailant wearing a raincoat. Trapped between two automatic glass doors, Sam is unable to come to her aid and can only watch in horror as the villain makes his escape. The investigating officers are forced to take possession of Sam's passport, believing he holds a piece of information that is key to leading them to the arrest of the man they suspect of several other murders in the city. Although Monica survived the attack, Sam can't get the events of that night out of his mind and it is no surprise when both he and his girlfriend become pawns in the killer's deadly game.

All the screaming in the world won't help!

When he receives a telephone call from the assassin he picks upon a particular sound, which turns out to be the cry of a rare species they call "The Bird with Crystal Plumage". There is only one such bird in Rome and that resides in the city zoo. As Argento toys with his audience, the police go through the usual list of deviant suspects while Sam, who is living on the edge of his nerves, continues his investigation, culminating in a taut chase through a darkened building.

The Bird with the Crystal Plumage marked Dario Argento's ascent to the director's chair, after penning several thrillers along with a number of war films and a spaghetti western. The inspiration for his movie, which would establish the stylistic elements of the giallo for the next decade, had taken shape in Fredric Brown's novel *The Screaming Mimi*, written in 1949. Brown's mystery tale had already been directed by Gerd Oswald for its Hollywood release as **Screaming Mimi** in 1958, but his feature would never have dared elicit the lurid display and then engage the violence of Argento's film, an undertaking largely financed by his father. Ennio Morricone's ominous score combined with Vittorio Storaro's opulent cinematography that made abundant use of point-of-view stalking both served to overcome the obvious holes in the plot; and Argento engineered the suspense just as Alfred Hitchcock had before him to lead to what in its day was a quite shocking finale. The killer's garb had been seen only a few years before in Mario Bava's seminal **Blood and Black Lace** (1964), as had elements detected in the explicit murder scenes. However, few in his audience would have been aware of this, so dazzled would they have been by the ambition in Argento's stylish technique that would one day become the hallmark for his mastery of the genre. This same audience would not have known there were those involved with the production who had wanted him removed from his position as director very early on in the shoot.

Although **The Bird with the Crystal Plumage** was by no means as gruesome as Argento's later masterpieces, edits of twenty seconds were demanded when it was submitted for release in the United States. Eight seconds were removed from the shots dwelling on the killer ripping the panties off one of the victims and a further twelve seconds were cut from the elevator scene showing a woman having her face slashed with a razor prior to its issue as **The Gallery Murders**. The BBFC approved this American R edit without any further changes and then, finally, after a thirty-year wait Argento fans in both Britain and the US got to see his debut in its uncut form. 🌸

Black Christmas

📅	**YEAR OF RELEASE:** 1974
🕐	**RUNTIME:** 98 minutes
🌐	**COUNTRY:** Canada
🎥	**DIRECTOR:** Bob Clark
🎬	**PRODUCTION COMPANY:** Film Funding Ltd of Canada, Vision IV, Canadian Film Development Corporation (CFDC)
✒	**WRITER:** Roy Moore
🎞	**CINEMATOGRAPHER:** Reginald H. Morris

PRODUCERS: Gerry Arbeid (co-producer), Bob Clark, Findlay Quinn (executive producer), Richard Schouten (associate producer)

CERTIFICATE: Australia: R; Canada: 13+ (Quebec); Canada: A (Ontario); Canada: R (Nova Scotia, original rating); Canada: PA (Manitoba); Canada: 14A (Nova Scotia, re-rating, 2008); UK: X (original rating, passed with cuts); UK: 18 (video rating, 2003); USA: R

BUDGET: $686,000 Canadian

CAST: Olivia Hussey, Keir Dullea, Margot Kidder, John Saxon, Marian Waldman, Andrea Martin, James Edmond, Doug McGrath, Art Hindle, Lynne Griffin, Michael Rapport, Leslie Carlson, Martha Gibson, John Rutter, Robert Warner

CHRISTMAS COMES BUT once a year; for some of these girls, however, it will never come again. A snow-covered college campus introduces the Bob Clark-directed **Black Christmas**, as an indistinct figure peers into the windows of a large sorority house where a Christmas party is being held. In a point-of-view shot, later used to equal effect by John Carpenter in his preface to **Halloween**, the audience is as close to the prowler as they ever could be as he moves from the periphery of the house to ascend a trellis before slipping into the former mansion

through an attic window. Once in the house he clambers down the attic trap door and secretes himself somewhere upstairs, observing the joyous girls from the shadows of the stairway.

The phone calls had initially seemed nothing more than a childish prank, but their tone has changed and while there is excitement at the party, these calls have started to unnerve this ill-fated gathering as they prepare for the festive holiday season. Barbie's (Margot Kidder) invective shrieking down the phone acts only to incite the caller. His response is a calmly delivered death threat, made all the more chilling by the abrupt manner in which he puts down the receiver.

The first victim is the innocent doe of the house, Clare (Lynne Griffin), who after a row with the abrasive Barbie retires to her room. She never gets there. The psychopath deviously lures her with a mocking meow made to sound like the house cat, then suffocates her in plastic wrap, before dragging her body away to conceal in the attic. Hidden away in the attic he sits Clare's lifeless body in a rocking chair adjacent to the window, with the plastic bag still pulled tightly over her head. Just before making his leave he rests a doll in her lap, mumbling the name Agnes. Our killer it would appear has also been traumatized. Downstairs, life goes on with the other girls oblivious to Clare's death. It is only when her father arrives to collect his daughter for the holidays we learn that no one has laid eyes on her since the quarrel with Barbie. It isn't long before a young girl's body is found by a search party investigating another disappearance.

As these grisly events unfold, Jessica Bradford (Olivia Hussey) has to confront a dilemma in her own life, one that will have a major bearing on the outcome of this film. Having discovered she is pregnant she has to seriously consider an abortion, but boyfriend Peter (Keir Dullea), whose behaviour is erratic throughout, is bitterly opposed to any such suggestion. His unhinged temperament makes him an increasingly likely suspect as one by one the girls in the house begin to disappear.

When a sedated Jessica is left alone in the company of a guard, director Clark cunningly deceives the audience, letting them believe his film has reached its climax. The guard, however, is unconscious and those who have been at the centre of this drama are seen taking their leave, convinced the killer has been revealed. A deathly silence comes down on the house, as the attic door begins to open. The camera takes the audience up into the attic where the bodies of both Clare and the housekeeper have remained unnoticed. The killer now descends from the attic and is heard to utter the words "Agnes, it's me, Billy!" Just before the credits begin to role a lone police officer is seen on the front porch as once again the phone begins to ring.

Black Christmas, also briefly known as **Silent Night, Evil Night** on its US theatrical release, was inspired by a series of murders that occurred during the Christmas period in Quebec. For a long time forgotten by so many horror fans, this film bears many of the hallmarks of the slasher frenzy that would sweep across the film industry as the decade drew to a close. These would include a delightful cast of sorority girls, bawdy antics,

Christmas is coming early this year. And it's murder!

sexual tension, dark comedy, an even darker house and a long knife, along with close-in shots that were designed to convey the killer's perspective. Bob Clark succeeded in maintaining the tension, refusing to neither provide an explanation for the killer's motives nor divulge his identity, which in more modern terrors would have resulted in a sequel. He also created a highly ambiguous finale that was to frustrate many of those when they first saw it, again demanding a follow up.

In a similar way to John Carpenter in his seminal movie, Clark chose to avoid an excess of gore, even as his body count continued to grow. Rather, he used the element of tension, and carefully paced the scares through the shadows and goaded with the ominous presence of the killer hidden within. On its release, there were those who considered this a thriller, but the presence of a mysterious killer armed with a sharp knife and a gathering of vulnerable young girls made it worthy of the then popular giallo. Carl Zittrer's score added to this impression of this Italian trend, as he skilfully augmented the sense of perturbation, later explaining that he tied forks, combs and knives to the strings of the piano with a mind to distorting the sound of the keys. The result remains very unsettling. The semblance to the giallo and the lack of blood may have for so many years consigned **Black Christmas** as a mere footnote in the history of the slasher movie. By 1980, the rulebook to the cinematic American slasher had almost been drawn up, but in 1974 makers of such films would have been very much inspired by the giallo of Italian lore. A case in point is the murder of the chaste Clare, who was the first to face the killer's wrath in rather horrific circumstances; such a killing would have been inconceivable in either **Halloween** (1978) or **Friday the 13th** (1980). Meanwhile Jessica, who in both of the these films would have been condemned well before the finale for being sexually active and daring to consider an abortion, made it to the end, although it remains a matter of debate as to whether she actually survived.

While **Black Christmas** now receives generally positive reviews, the critics of the day weren't entirely disposed to this feature, which was seen as being clichéd and exploitative. The cliché at this point can have only been derived from gialli such as Mario Bava's landmark **A Bay of Blood** (1971), because North American cinema had not attempted a film of this ilk and on such a scale. Bob Clark's film went on to be nominated by the Academy of Science Fiction, Fantasy & Horror Films as "Best Horror Film" in 1976, and in the same year in the Edgar Allan Poe Awards received a nomination for "Best Motion Picture". In the Canadian Film Awards for 1975 it won "Best Sound Editing in a Feature" and Margot Kidder picked up the "Best Performance by a Lead Actress". On its release in Britain, the BBFC removed several expletives in addition to sexual references made during the obscene phone call scenes.

A remake directed by Glen Morgan was released on December 25, 2006.

This version was only loosely based on the original, opting for a more graphic portrayal and dwelled on the mystery surrounding Billy, thus removing much of the ambiguity in Bob Clark's creepy finale.

Black Sunday

📅 YEAR OF RELEASE: 1960	🎞 CINEMATOGRAPHER: Mario Bava, Ubaldo Terzano
⏱ RUNTIME: 87 minutes	
🌐 COUNTRY: Italy	🏆 PRODUCERS: Samuel Z. Arkoff (executive producer, US version), Massimo De Rita, Lou Rusoff (producer, US version)
🎥 DIRECTOR: Mario Bava	
🎬 PRODUCTION COMPANY: Alta Vista Productions, Galatea Film, Jolly Film	
✏ WRITERS: Nikolai Gogol, Ennio De Concini (screenplay), Mario Serandrei (screenplay), Mario Bava, Marcello Coscia (screenplay)	⭕ CERTIFICATE: Australia: MA; UK: 15 (1986); UK: (Banned, 1961); USA: Unrated

CAST: Barbara Steele, John Richardson, Andrea Checchi, Ivo Garrani, Arturo Dominici, Enrico Olivieri, Antonio Pierfederici, Tino Bianchi, Clara Bindi, Mario Passante, Renato Terra, Germana Dominici

I N SEVENTEENTH CENTURY Moldavia a beautiful witch, Asa Vajda (Barbara Steele), and her lover Javuto (Arturo Dominici) are sentenced to death by her own brother. As they are hauled to the stake to burn for their sorcerous crimes, Asa swears revenge and curses her brother's lineage. Her fate is sealed by an iron mask lined with sharpened spikes, which is locked firmly over her head and then forcefully hammered into her face. Blood is seen to ooze from the mask.

Two hundred years later on a storm-ridden night, Dr Thomas Kruvajan (Andrea Checchi) and his assistant Dr Andre Gorobec (John Richardson) are observed crossing through this same region when one of the wheels of their carriage shatters. As the coach driver repairs the wheel, the doctors stumble upon the crypt where Asa has been laid to rest. As he attempts to thwart an annoying bat, Kruvajan breaks the panel enshrouding the dead witch's tomb. Curiosity insists he remove the death mask, but as he does some of his blood drips onto Asa's pallid face. Kruvajan has no knowledge of what he has done and returns with his assistant to the carriage. Here they are greeted by Katia (also played by Barbara Steele) who lives with her family in a nearby castle. Gorobec can't help but be enchanted by her ravishing beauty.

In the darkened shadows of the crypt, Asa is seen rising from the dead. She uses her malevolent sorcery to rejuvenate her lover and then makes her way to the castle still owned by Katia's family, with evil in mind. After seducing Kruvajan to her vampiric domain, Asa turns her attention to the beautiful young girl. She believes that if she can drain Katia's blood, she will gain eternal life. Gorborec must now do all he can to save Katia from the vengeful witch's clutches. **La Maschera del Demonio**, also known as **Revenge of the Vampire** and **The Mask of Satan**, was Mario Bava's first credited directorial work and is acknowledged to be one of the most beautifully photographed films in the history of horror cinema. Shot in black and white, Bava conjured with light and shade to create a Gothic masterpiece reminiscent of the Universal horror movies of two decades past. The influence of Italian director Riccardo Freda and the expressionist Fritz Lang were in evidence in so much of this film, and as the horse-drawn carriage pulls up who can deny the homage to F. W. Murnau's **Nosferatu** (1922). While

Stare into these eyes ... discover deep within them the unspeakable terrifying secret of BLACK SUNDAY ... it will paralyze you with fright!

Bava's film does observe a coherent plot, his real interest lay in creating an air of dread and supplementing this with gloomy but captivating visuals. As an admirer of Russian fantasy and horror, he based his feature on the short story "Vij" written by the Ukrainian born Nikolai Vasilievich Gogol in 1865 and later released as the Soviet Union's first horror film in 1967. However, the final screenplay, which endured so many redrafts during filming, owed precious little to the original. Indeed if Hammer hadn't enjoyed success with **The Curse of Frankenstein** (1957) and **Horror of Dracula** (1958) in Italy, Bava may never have had the chance to produce such an atmospheric classic.

Black Sunday also heralded the arrival of sensuous horror icon Barbara Steele, in one of her most memorable roles. While she struggled with the Italian language, the young actress's macabre beauty cast a spell over her audience and would see her rise to assume the role as the dark queen of horror for decades to come. Her introduction to the world of Italian horror came with a scene laced in sexuality, which was rife with more explicit violence and gore than anything so far committed to film. The opening sequence focusing on the iron mask being driven into Steele's face resulted in the film being banned in the UK until 1968. Similarly there were problems in the United States when the distributor AIP had to remove over three minutes of footage detailing the burning "S" being branded into Asa's flesh and the blood spurting from the infamous spiked mask, the eyeball staking of the vampiric Kruvajan, and the flesh peeling from Katia's father's face, all to make the film more acceptable. While Bava's film was only moderately successful in Italy, it generated a huge turnover across Europe and America and received much critical acclaim before going on to influence a generation of horror filmmakers. Tim Burton would use its sublime imagery during the production of **Sleepy Hollow** (1999) and Francis Ford Coppola's **Bram Stoker's Dracula** (1992) also paid homage to several key scenes from Bava's masterpiece.

Blood and Black Lace

📅 YEAR OF RELEASE: 1964	✏️ WRITERS: Marcello Fondato (story), Giuseppe Barilla (collaboration)
🕐 RUNTIME: 88 minutes	
🎯 COUNTRY: Italy, Germany	🎞️ PHOTOGRAPHERS: Ubaldo Turzano, Mario Bava
🎥 DIRECTOR: Mario Bava	
🎬 PRODUCTION COMPANY: Emmepi Cinematografica, Les Productions Georges de Beauregard, Monachia Film	⚗️ PRODUCERS: Alfredo Mirabile, Massimo Patrizi
	⭕ CERTIFICATE: Australia: MA (2009); Canada: 13+ (Quebec); UK: 18; USA: Unrated
	💲 BUDGET: $150,000

CAST: Cameron Mitchell, Eva Bartok, Thomas Reiner, Ariana Gorini, Dante Di Paolo, Mary Arden, Franco Ressel, Claude Dantes, Luciano Pigozzi, Lea Lander, Massimo Righi, Francesca Ungaro, Giuliano Raffaelli, Harriet Medin, Mary Carmen

RELEASED IN ITALY as **Sei Donne Per L'Assassino**, Mario Bava's film opened with a prowling camera homing in on the brutal murder of the gorgeous model Isabella (Francesca Ungaro) in the grounds of a fashionable "haute couture" house in the city of Rome. What followed would bear so many of the hallmarks of the infamous Italian giallo, rather than the Edgar Wallace-styled murder mystery for which the German backers had hoped. Such detective tales had proven very popular, but Bava's film would become recognized as one the earliest and most influential of this uniquely Italian genre. Poor Isabella met her death as a thunderstorm played out a raging drama in the skies over the city. These scenes, laced with the lurid sexuality only recently observed in Hitchcock's **Psycho** (1960), would have you believe the temptation in her beauty provoked this darkened figure who on this occasion was disguised by a mask rather than the customary black leather gloves of the gialli that followed. The case is assigned to the self-assured Inspector Silvestri (Thomas Reiner), who soon uncovers a web of drugs, corruption and blackmail in this seemingly respectable establishment. His investigation very soon draws up a list of likely suspects. Among them are the owner Massimo Morlacchi (Cameron Mitchell), the wealthy Ricardo Morellin (Franco Ressel), who turns out to have been having an affair with Isabella, the dress designer Cesar Lazzarini (Louis Pigot), and Isabella's boyfriend Frank (Dante Di Paolo) an antique shop owner who supplied cocaine to some of the models.

As the events unfold, we learn Isabella was not the victim of a sex-crazed killer; rather, her fate was sealed when she started to detail a series of improprieties at the fashion house in the pages of her diary. The same mysterious figure dressed in black now makes another appearance, this time in the darkened antique shop owned by her former antique dealing drug-peddling boyfriend Frank. On this occasion, the shadowed figure seizes a clawed mallet and strikes at another model, Nicole (Ariana Gorini). Convinced she now has the diary, he hits her squarely across the face. Stunned by the blow she continues to struggle, but alas, to no avail, she falls to become his second victim. And so the torture and murder continues as this sinister figure leaves in his wake an ever-growing body count of scantily clad beautiful young girls, but fails to locate the incriminating diary. In the course of his scurrilous activities, he shows himself to be an expert with a sharpened blade in addition to asphyxiation by pillow, but his most dastardly moment comes when a model's face is forced down onto a scalding furnace.

A fashion house of glamorous models becomes a terror house of blood!

As would have been expected of a time-served cinematographer of such eminence, although Bava never considered himself as such, the balance created between the light and shadow coupled with the distinctive colour filters elevated the photography in this movie, placing it above so much of the highly competent film making of the period. This visual splendour would have his feature lauded as "decorative horror", but there were those, including American International Pictures, who had serious misgivings as to its lurid portrayal and the explicit nature of the murder scenes. Reviews at the time were mixed; it was only when film historians began to re-appraise Bava's work that the significance of **Blood and Black Lace** in the evolution of the giallo was finally recognized.

Blood Cult

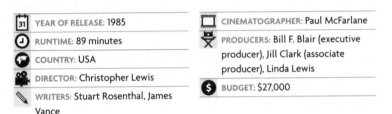

📅 YEAR OF RELEASE: 1985	🎞 CINEMATOGRAPHER: Paul McFarlane
🕐 RUNTIME: 89 minutes	⚙ PRODUCERS: Bill F. Blair (executive producer), Jill Clark (associate producer), Linda Lewis
🎥 COUNTRY: USA	
🎥 DIRECTOR: Christopher Lewis	💲 BUDGET: $27,000
✏ WRITERS: Stuart Rosenthal, James Vance	

CAST: Juli Andelman, Charles Ellis, James Vance, Bennie Lee McGowan, Peter Hart, David Stice, Fred Graves, Bob Duffield, Allison O'Meilia, Christi Beavers, Bryan Gilbreath, Robbie Cobb, Joy Jordan, Mary Dickens, Carolyn Wallace

THE CAMERA DRAWS its focus on a female student showering behind a semi-transparent curtain. As she dries herself, an intruder stealthily makes his way upstairs and then, brandishing a meat cleaver, explodes into the bathroom. In a series of cleverly re-enacted shots made to resemble Herschel G. Lewis's **Blood Feast** (1963), he begins to hack wildly at her exposed body causing a flow of blood to splatter across the room. The poor girl is left for dead as the killer takes off with her severed arm. A prologue then tries to suggest there is an element of truth to this tale, telling of a series

of grisly murders, perpetrated at a mid-western college in the fall of 1985.

The slaughter continues as the killer beats another girl to death with her friend's severed head. The local sheriff now steps in to solve the case, but with the murders beginning to escalate his hopes of succeeding in the forthcoming election seem increasingly remote. The only clue is an amulet found at the scene of each of the murders. Tina, the sheriff's daughter who works as a librarian, traces the amulet to an eighteenth-century coven of witches. Down through the ages this cult has continued in its quest to seek retribution on those who accused its ilk of witchery in 1692. Almost mirroring Lewis's **Blood Feast**, the cult is convinced that with the ritualistic assemblage of the body parts of their victims, their revenge will be complete and a demonic god will arise as their champion.

There is some conjecture as to whether this was the first movie made for the home video market, because John Wintergate's nubile terror **Boarding House** was thought to be the first real shot on video film dating back to 1982, although it did make it into several American cinemas. **Blood Cult** (also known as **Slasher**) has, however, garnered a trashy reputation on being the first of its kind and has since promoted

The first movie made for the home video market. Might just scare you to DEATH!

itself on the auspices of being a bloody slasher. While there was indeed a sanguinary flow to the opening bathroom murder, the remainder of Christopher Lewis's film was unusually devoid of the essential torrent of blood. However, in the film's defence, the production values were appreciably more sophisticated than those of its bloodthirsty contemporaries, although the acting again betrayed the film's amateur status. This was bona fide low-budget filmmaking and while the film stock supplied for Paul McFarlane's camera work was at times grainy, it was to enhance the feature's unwholesome aura and provided more than the occasional moment to savour.

Blood Feast

 YEAR OF RELEASE: 1963

 RUNTIME: 67 minutes

 COUNTRY: USA

 DIRECTOR: Herschell Gordon Lewis

 PRODUCTION COMPANY: Friedman-Lewis Productions

 WRITER: Allison Louis Downe

CINEMATOGRAPHER: Herschell Gordon Lewis

PRODUCERS: David F. Friedman, Stanford S. Kohlberg, Herschell Gordon Lewis

BUDGET: $24,500

RECEIPTS: $4,000,000

CAST: William Kerwin, Mal Arnold, Connie Mason, Lyn Bolton, Scott H. Hall, Christy Foushee, Ashlyn Martin, Astrid Olson, Sandra Sinclair, Gene Courtier, Louise Kamp, Hal Rich, Al Golden

BLOOD FEAST WAS the first part of a collection of films the director's dedicated following have christened "The Blood Trilogy", with **Two Thousand Maniacs!** (1964) and **Color Me Blood Red** (1965) providing the remaining entries in this triumvirate. This is looked upon as the first true splatter movie, rivalled only by Nobuo Nakagawa's **Jigoku**, although there are those who look upon its content as being hopelessly amateurish with few if any redeeming qualities. In its defence, **Blood Feast** was made in only nine days with a hopelessly limited budget.

In a suburban Miami house, an attractive young woman listens to her portable radio, which carries the announcement of yet another murder, one of several in only a matter of days. She turns off the broadcast to enjoy the soothing warmth of her bath, only to be rudely interrupted. At this point in his film Hitchcock conceived the memorable shower scene; Lewis opted for a soap-filled bath with a mind to titillating his audience. The nudity from these shots never made it to the final cut. A greying wild-eyed man suddenly appears in the bathroom and frenziedly stabs the hapless woman through her left eye. As she lies dead, he hacks off her left leg and then makes his escape with it. While not particularly well put together, this level of graphic violence was very new to American cinema; its sole intention

A weird and grisly ancient rite horrendously brought to life . . .

was to shock and that's exactly what it did!

At Fuad Ramses' catering store, a wealthy socialite has requested that Fuad arrange the catering for her daughter Suzette's party. He readily agrees, explaining to his eager client, Mrs Freemont, his intention to present to her guests cuisine that hasn't been prepared in over 5,000 years. The party is only two weeks away, leaving Fuad just enough time to acquire the last of his ingredients. In the storage room to the rear of the premises, he stands before a large gold statue of the "mother of veiled darkness", the goddess Ishtar. He refers to her as being Egyptian, although she is actually of Assyrian and Babylonian origin, but her affiliation with sexuality is quite in keeping with Lewis's lurid design for this film. The diabolical Fuad's scheme is now revealed: he seeks the goddess's resurrection by returning to an ancient blood rite and a concoction made up of the body parts of the dead women. The ensuing atrocities are inflicted on young girls from the surrounding area: a brain is removed from a teenager, a tongue severed from a young wife, and the face sliced from an innocent woman. Each become essential to the consummation of Fuad's diabolical blood feast. The final victim is kidnapped, held hostage in his store and then whipped until the blood flows freely from her back, allowing the evil caterer to gather the final ingredient. Her body is disposed of and later found hacked to pieces by the investigating police.

When his plan to sacrifice Suzette fails, Fuad goes on the run, with the police hot on his tail. There is to be no return for the villain in this piece; he falls to his fate, crushed by a refuse vehicle's compacting blades. The heroic policeman, Pete, Suzette's boyfriend, has the parting line, "he died a fitting end, just like the garbage he was".

The unhinged murderer Fuad Ramses, was described by author Christopher Wayne Curry in his book *A Taste of Blood: The Films Of Herschell Gordon Lewis* as "the original machete-wielding madman", the forerunner to the characters that would slash their way through **Friday the 13th** (1980), **Halloween** (1978) and so many of their ilk of the 1980s. This, coupled with the claim to being the first splatter movie, gives **Blood Feast** a place in the history of the genre, but on its initial release the critics were far from kind. A *Variety* review of May 6, 1964 was venomous, describing the film as a "totally inept shocker", "incredibly crude and unprofessional from start to finish", and "an insult even to the most puerile and salacious of audiences". Lewis's film refused to lie down and die. Jack Weis used his ideas to create a partial remake in New Orleans, **Mardi Gras Massacre** (1978) and the DPP made it immortal by listing it as video nasty in July 1983 following its release to video in May 1982. It remained on the list until the end of the crisis. When it was submitted for its 2001 issue to DVD, cuts were demanded to the scene detailing Fuad's final victim as she was chained and manacled along with her fatal whipping with a cat o' nine tails. Only in 2005 were these edits finally waived.

Blood Song

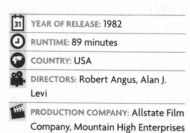

📅 **YEAR OF RELEASE:** 1982		✒️ **WRITERS:** Frank Avianca, James Fargo, George Hart, Alan J. Levi, Lenny Montana, Joseph M. Shink	
⏱️ **RUNTIME:** 89 minutes			
🌐 **COUNTRY:** USA		🎬 **CINEMATOGRAPHER:** Stephen L. Posey	
🎥 **DIRECTORS:** Robert Angus, Alan J. Levi		⚰️ **PRODUCERS:** Frank Avianca, Lenny Montana, Lee Shrout	
🎬 **PRODUCTION COMPANY:** Allstate Film Company, Mountain High Enterprises		🔘 **CERTIFICATE:** Australia: R; UK: 18	

CAST: Donna Wilkes, Richard Jaeckel, Antoinette Bower, William Kirby Cullen, Dane Clark, Lenny Montana, Frankie Avalon

A MIDDLE-AGED MAN returns to his dimly lit home from a business trip and within seconds of him being indoors two shots are fired. He has just walked in to find his wife in bed with another man. Begging forgiveness, he then turns the gun on himself, unaware that a distraught young boy has seen everything that has gone on. As the boy's world falls down around him, he finds solace in his brown flute.

Many years later a patient (Frankie Avalon) is seen escaping from a mental institution; before he takes his leave, he checks he has in his possession a familiar small brown flute. At the same time, a young girl named Marion (Donna Wilkes), who is recovering from a horrific car accident, complains of a recurring nightmare in which a homicidal maniac plays a strange tune on what she can only describe as a mouth instrument; he then carves up several innocent people. Marion fears that these are far more than just dreams; they are a premonition of doom. Her visions also reveal the same murderer planning to bury one of his victims in parkland adjacent to a beach. Those around her think that her abusive father, Frank (Richard Jaeckel), is beginning to affect her mind but elsewhere the escapee, Paul, has buried a hatchet into the face of a driver who offered him a lift in his van. With his flute playing acting as an uncanny overture to his penchant for brutal murder, he then strangles

... the last song you will hear.

his female partner before beginning to stalk Marion, who is somehow linked to him following a blood transfusion.

Blood Song, also released as **Dream Slayer**, is another near-forgotten slasher of the period, which included in its cast former teen idol Frankie Avalon, who gave a credible performance as the menacing mass murderer Paul. Philadelphia-born Avalon was only twelve years old when, trumpet in hand, he first appeared on US television and a decade later after a string of hits went on to make teen-oriented beach comedies. His role in this film was a marked departure from his days as a teenage heartthrob, but revealed an obvious talent in his grim portrayal of this unhinged psychopath. **Blood Song** was also distinguished in being co-produced by former professional wrestler Lenny Montana, who had played Luca Brasi in **The Godfather** (1972), in this, one of his last films.

Robert Angus and Alan J. Levi's film was not the typical slasher, although part of its more intriguing premise placed it in the same camp as Romano Scavolini's **Nightmares in a Damaged Brain** (1981) and J. S. Cardone's often surreal **The Slayer** (1982). While it was not as graphic as much of its ilk, the violence was unduly cruel and its dreamlike qualities would have it one day regarded as a precursor to Wes Craven's **A Nightmare on Elm Street** (1984). 🦇

Blood Tracks

31 YEAR OF RELEASE: 1985		**WRITERS:** Mats-Helge Olsson, Anna Wolf
RUNTIME: 81 minutes		
COUNTRY: Sweden/USA		**CINEMATOGRAPHER:** Hans Dittmer
DIRECTOR: Mats-Helge Olsson		**PRODUCERS:** Tom Sjoberg, George Zecevic (executive producer)
PRODUCTION COMPANY: Smart Egg Pictures		**CERTIFICATE:** UK: 18; Australia: R

CAST: Jeff Harding, Michael Fitzpatrick, Naomi Kaneda, Brad Powell, Peter Merrill, Harriet Robinson, Tina Shaw, Frances Kelly, Karina Lee, Helena Jacks, Lotte Heise, Zin Zan, Chris Lynn, Alex Tyrone, Freddie van Gerber

A QUIET FAMILY WHO reside in a remote area of Sweden suffer at the hands of the drunken father whose bullying behaviour has driven them to the edge of despair. When his abusive behaviour crosses the line, his wife finally comes to the end of her tether and retaliates leaving her husband for dead. The family flee their home, retreating to an abandoned mine high up in the mountains. There they remain in solitude for the next twenty years, and as time goes by they endure an alarming transformation to devolve into grotesquely misshapen savages.

The arrival in the area of the big-haired glam rock band Solid Gold, played by Sweden's eminent glam metal band Easy Action, accompanied by their dubious entourage for the video shoot of their new single "Blood Tracks" brings considerable excitement to this ski resort. However, calamity follows with the first shoot, as an avalanche crashes down the mountainside. Having survived the deluge of ice and snow the video director takes the shoot to the darkened mine shaft and its surrounding buildings, seen at the very beginning of the film. It doesn't take long for the cannibal family to discover there are unwelcome intruders in their domain. Slowly but surely, they hunt these trespassers down amidst the darkness of the disused machinery, dilapidated furnaces and a labyrinth of passages and walkways suspended over a bottomless abyss. There will be no escape as the members of this murderous family make it to the band's ski cabin and drag their victims' bodies back to the mine, keeping some of the women alive for later. At the finale only two survive, rescued by a helicopter as an Easy Action power ballad plays over the bleak landscape. When Kee Marcello of eighties glam metal band Easy Action, and later stadium rockers

Europe, approached Mats-Helge Olsson with a view to producing a film, the director was still sat in a prison cell serving the last few months of a sentence for financial irregularities.

The mountains echoed with the screams of terror.

Upon learning the band had a deal with Warner Bros., B-movie specialist Olsson became very interested and so followed a Swedish heavy metal slasher, strangely reminiscent of Hans Hatwig's all-girl rock blood feast **Blödaren** (1983), which was later packaged as **The Bleeder**. Olsson's film, made on an impossible budget, contained themes previously observed in both **Death Line** (1973) and **The Hills Have Eyes** (1977), which followed the latter in its lust for violent bloodshed. The photography and overall style tried their utmost to appear American, but in so many ways the film failed, appearing awkward with an unappealing assembly of characters

and after so many years of slaughter across the United States and Canada the storyline was now somewhat predictable. However, as his film drew to a close, Olsson created an ambiguity rarely seen in such gorefests, one that would invite many questions and ensure his film would never be forgotten. There was no ambiguity to the make-up and effects, which proved a high point, as did the film's semi nudity, and the killings excelled in being at times quite ingenious. Such was the bloodlust in the original edit, four minutes of gore had to be left on the cutting room floor before the video could see release, although an eighty-five minute print of the film is known to exist. Easy Action broke up in 1986 after making two albums, but, as in so many of these tales of terror, they returned from the dead in 2006.

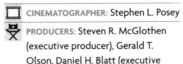

Bloody Birthday

📅 YEAR OF RELEASE: 1981	🎞 CINEMATOGRAPHER: Stephen L. Posey
⏱ RUNTIME: 85 minutes	🏆 PRODUCERS: Steven R. McGlothen (executive producer), Gerald T. Olson, Daniel H. Blatt (executive producer), Max Rosenberg (executive producer)
🌐 COUNTRY: USA	
🎥 DIRECTOR: Ed Hunt	
🎬 PRODUCTION COMPANY: Judica Productions	
✎ WRITER: Ed Hunt	⭕ CERTIFICATE: Australia: R; UK: 18; USA: R

CAST: Lori Lethin, Melinda Cordell, Julie Brown, Joe Penny, Bert Kramer, K. C. Martel, Elizabeth Hoy, Billy Jayne, Andy Freeman, Susan Strasberg, José Ferrer, Ben Marley, Erica Hope, Ellen Geer, Daniel Currie

AS THEY FOOL around among the gravestones a couple of high-spirited teenagers soon become rather amorous. Feeling certain it will be safer to continue their aroused display away from prying eyes, they climb down into a recently dug grave. The boy's lust, however, is cut short when he is beaten to death with a shovel and his girlfriend is then strangled with a skipping rope.

In 1970 in the small town of Meadowvale, California, as the moon eclipsed the sun, throwing the world into temporary darkness, three babies were born. This solar conjunction obscured the planet Saturn, the astrological body holding sway over human emotion. Because of the eclipse, the three children came into this world as a group of uncaring souls, devoid of emotion. Ten Years later, the kids (Billy Jayne, Elizabeth Hoy and Andy Freeman) embark on a violent killing spree, which sends shock waves through this sleepy backwater. Their innocent appearance means the townsfolk never suspect them until it is too late. Those who stand in their way are summarily slaughtered, beginning with their father, bludgeoned to death with a baseball bat, then their

The nightmare begins with the kids next door.

schoolteacher, gunned down, and finally they take on the local police. They also demonstrate a fascination for prying on naked teenagers, soon after disposing of them. However, a young boy and his astrology obsessed older sister (Lori Lethin) soon discover their crimes, only to become the new targets of this evil brood. As the body count mounts, the police authorities become increasingly certain a psychotic killer is stalking the town. Following the denouement only the daughter evades arrest; as her mother drives her away to a new life, she promises faithfully to be a good girl. However, as the credits begin to roll the camera frames her latest victim, a murdered truck driver.

This low-budget obscurity would have been forgotten if it had not attracted the attention of the killer kids' fraternity, predating **Children of the Corn** (1984) and standing alongside the superior **Village of the Damned** (1960), **Children of the Damned** (1964) and **The Bad Seed** (1956). It traded the habitual visceral excess for some rather disturbing images, as the unwholesome triplets wilfully engaged in an assortment of weaponry. Their murderous ingenuity was such that they were able to make use of virtually anything they laid their hands on, including in their arsenal a sprinkling of rat poison smeared over the icing of a cake. Their activities were then dutifully recorded in a macabre scrapbook, bequeathing an odious testament to their merciless accomplishments.

The murderous endeavours of these psychotic cherubs went much further than the misdeeds of the killer kids that had come before them, thus ensuring Ed Hunt's **Bloody Birthday** would disconcert its viewers for decades to come.

Bloody Moon

📅 YEAR OF RELEASE: 1981	✒ WRITER: Erich Tomek
⏱ RUNTIME: 90 minutes	🎞 CINEMATOGRAPHER: Juan Soler
🌐 COUNTRY: West Germany	🎬 PRODUCERS: Wolf C. Hartwig, Otto Retzer (executive producer)
🎥 DIRECTOR: Jesus Franco	
🎬 PRODUCTION COMPANY: Lisa-Film, Metro Film, Rapid Film	⭕ CERTIFICATE: UK: X (original rating); UK: 18
	💲 BUDGET: ESP 23,130,776 (Spain)

CAST: Olivia Pascal, Christoph Moosbrugger, Nadja Gerganoff, Alexander Waechter, Jasmin Losensky, Corinna Drews, Ann-Beate Engelke, Peter Exacoustos, Antonia García, Beatriz Sancho Nieto, María Rubio, Otto Retzer, Jesus Franco

MIGUEL'S (ALEXANDER WAECHTER) life has been consistently blighted by his severely disfigured face. He doesn't help himself when he disguises himself with a Mickey Mouse mask and attempts to have sex with a girl who mistakes him for her boyfriend. The rejected Miguel is thrown into an uncontrollable rage, which results in him repeatedly stabbing her with a pair of scissors. This unsavoury episode is skilfully guided through the eyes of the mask, using one of the highly favoured traits of the slasher years, the close-up point-of-view camera. After his trial, Miguel is locked away for a five-year period of detention in a mental institution, to be eventually released into the care of his sister, Manuela (Nadja Gerganoff). His doctor, however, like many before him, has grave reservations as to his mental state.

Assisted by her wheelchair-bound mother, Manuela runs an isolated boarding school for young women that specializes in foreign languages. As

Miguel becomes fascinated with the delightful Angela, intrigue surrounds a power struggle over the ownership of the school. An element of sleaze is then introduced as we learn Miguel and Manuela became involved in an incestuous relationship five years ago. Miguel has designs to resume their affair, which is revealed in several dubious moments of erotica. It was this clandestine relationship that led to his breakdown and could only continue "if we could get rid of everyone". Very soon, death stalks the school corridors as these desirable young girls fall to a maniac killer and Angela is thrown into a fight for her life. Before the curtain falls on **Bloody Moon**, she would have to face the sight of her friends' bodies laid around her chalet as the killer crept stealthily through the shadows.

That prolific master of exploitation Jesus Franco, a director with over 190 films to his credit, couldn't resist sampling some of the success enjoyed by **Halloween** (1978) and **Friday the 13th** (1980). **Bloody Moon** was released in Spain as **Colegialas Violadas**, which literally translates as the emotive **Raped Schoolgirls**, and would have faced an inevitable backlash as it tried to get past the censors in virtually any country in the world. His film copied elements from one of the earliest slasher movies, Mario Bava's **A Bay of Blood** (1971), particularly the killing of the vulnerable woman in the wheelchair. This came prior to the killer moving without relent through the female cast, thrusting a knife up behind a woman to show it protruding through her breast, then burning one of his victims, before resorting to a screwdriver stabbing and strangulation by metal tongs. Franco capped it all with the infamous decapitation using a circular saw, while a seemingly willing girl was tied to a concrete block. The beheading on the concrete block inspired the German title for this feature **Die Säge Des Todes** or **The Saw Of Death**. On this outing, Franco replaced his customary sleaze with an excess of graphic gore, but in between the kills his movie struggled to maintain any sense of pace.

On its cinematic release in the UK, a minute and thirty-eight seconds were removed from the scene showing the girl's decapitation with the circular saw along with the blood-stained breasts shown earlier in the film. Its subsequent release to video would see it banned as a video nasty in July 1983 for another two years when the furore finally acquiesced. Further cuts were demanded for its reissue in 1993, which included the murder by scissors, two stabbings being merged into one, with the gory close-up removed, deletions to the knife protruding through the girl's breast as well as the subsequent flow of blood, the snake decapitation and the saw decapitation scene, which was completely removed. These cuts did untold damage to what should have been a tawdry piece of exploitation, making the release of 1993 an unsatisfactory addition to the genre. Finally, in 2008 the film was made available to the British public without these encroaching edits. 🍂

Boarding House

31 YEAR OF RELEASE: 1982	✎ WRITER: John Wintergate
⏱ RUNTIME: 98 minutes	▭ CINEMATOGRAPHER: Jan Lucas, Obee Ray
⊙ COUNTRY: USA	
🎥 DIRECTOR: John Wintergate	☗ PRODUCERS: Peter Baahlu, Elliot Van Koghbe (assistant producer)
🎬 PRODUCTION COMPANY: Blustarr	
	◯ CERTIFICATE: USA: R

CAST: John Wintergate, Kalassu, Lindsay Freeman, Joel Riordan, Brian Bruderlin, Selma Kora, Tracy O'Brian, Mary McKinley, Rosane Woods, Cindy Williamson

THE INTRODUCTION TO John Wintergate's film goes straight for the jugular, revealing bloody murder in The Hoffman House. While one chap is pushed into a swimming pool, another unravels his own intestines and then a shady figure in giallo-styled black gloves drives a woman to hang herself. Each murderous scene is alternated with a computer-styled screen that discloses every person who has entered this remote ranch house since 1972 has met with a gruesome end. The next people to sign on the dotted line for this cursed house are a telekinetic fellow and a gang of shapely young girls. Once they settle in the girls are plagued by unsettling nightmares and then fall victim to the black-gloved killer. The body count peaks during the pool party and leads to

Where the rent won't kill you, but something else will!

the final scene placing the killer and two survivors in stand-off telekinetic battle, somewhat reminiscent of a Sergio Leone spaghetti western.

Wintergate's weird offering is one of the contenders for the first shot on video horror movie, although its detractors are critical of its theatrical release on New York's 42nd Street and its run in the drive-in cinemas, making **Sledgehammer** (1983) or **Blood Cult** (1985) more likely candidates, neither of which saw distribution to the big screen. **Boarding House**, or **Boardinghouse** or **Housegeist** or **Bad Force** as it has been known, is also a nominee for being one of the trashiest horror videos of all time. While Wintergate attempted a new angle on the slasher craze with his out-of-body killer, the script, the acting, the editing and the sound were atrocious. With its cast of scantily clad young ladies and hopeless editing it resembled a porn movie throwing in an abundance of trashy gore just for good measure. Yet for all of its lack of technical merit it still has its fans. The possessed refrigerator madly hurling food at the girls still raises many a smile; although you don't have to look too closely to catch sight of the arm stretching out of the fridge.

The Boogeyman

📅 YEAR OF RELEASE: 1980	⚰️ PRODUCERS: Gillian Gordon, Ulli Lommel, Wolf Schmidt, Terrell Tannen
🕐 RUNTIME: 82 minutes	
🌎 COUNTRY: USA	🏅 CERTIFICATE: Australia: R; UK: X (original rating: 1980); UK: (Banned) (1984–92); UK: 18 (re-rating: 1992, cut); UK 18 (re-rating: 2000, uncut); USA: R
🎥 DIRECTOR: Ulli Lommel	
🎬 PRODUCTION COMPANY: Jerry Gross Organization	
✏️ WRITERS: Ulli Lommel, David Herscell	
🎞️ CINEMATOGRAPHER: Jochen Breitenstein	💲 BUDGET: $300,000
	💷 RECEIPTS: $35,000,000

CAST: Suzanna Love, Ron James, John Carradine, Nicholas Love, Raymond Boyden, Felicite Morgan, Bill Rayburn, Llewelyn Thomas, Jay Wright, Natasha Schiano

WHEN WILLY AND Lacey are caught as they spy on their mother and her lover, they are immediately punished. Willy is gagged and then tied to his bed, but his sister manages to set him free. Intent on revenge, the young boy takes the kitchen knife from his sister and sets off towards his mother's bedroom. He confronts his mother's abusive lover before the mirror in her bedroom and stabs him to death.

The film moves forward to see Lacey now married with her own young son, having been brought up with her brother on a farm owned by their aunt and uncle. Such was Willy's trauma that he has never uttered a word since the night of the murder. When Lacey receives a letter from their dying mother, so begin her nightmares of being bound to a bed and threatened by an unseen figure wielding a knife. Her husband has become very concerned, so much so he accompanies her to a psychiatrist before taking his wife to visit the house in which she once lived. While in the house, Lacey catches sight of a reflection that resembles her mother's former lover staring at her from the same mirror in the bedroom where he was stabbed all those years before. Terrified, she loses control and smashes the mirror with a chair. Her husband's concern turns to embarrassment as he offers to take the mirror away to be repaired. A piece, however, is left behind and the three children who now live there are murdered as a mysterious presence stalks the house.

Back at the farm, Willy has become so fearful of mirrors he has taken to blacking them out; only in the last few days, he almost strangled a young girl after catching sight of the reflection of his face. When he comes upon the broken shards of a mirror, a pitchfork rises from the ground and almost impales him. The shattered mirror now begins to exact its revenge engaging an array of scissors, knives and the offending pitchfork in a series of point-of-view shots that as early as 1980 had already become essential to the slasher trope. When a fragment of the mirror becomes wedged over Lacey's eye, she falls prey to the possession of the evil spirit that was once her mother's hateful lover. His vengeful wrath now threatens her family, and only when their priest removes the shard and hurls it into water, where it bursts into flames, can they be sure that they are safe. The remaining pieces are then tossed into

a well, each consumed by fire. One fragment, however, lies hidden on the ground, its reddened glow leaving the story open to a potential sequel.

Ulli Lommel's script was undoubtedly inspired by the work of John Carpenter on **Halloween**, drawing upon his use of point-of-view photography, the synthesized score and the silent killer whose face was obscured for so much of what transpired on screen. As **The Boogeyman** hacked its way to a climax there was also a tip of the hat to the supernatural horror of a few years before, **The Exorcist** (1973), as the priest called upon his faith to rid the world of this recently resurrected evil.

The great seller for Lommel's film would be the novel threat created by the mirrored reflections; its reputation was very soon enhanced when word spread of the grisly nature coursing through its stream of killings. With very little money at his disposal, Lommel knew he had to deliver and so he did with a series of gory death scenes, which worked to lure his audience at a time when the slasher craze was beginning to seize American youth by the throat. A few years later this would draw the attention of the BBFC, who included the film among its video nasties in October 1983, two years after its release to video. It was later removed from the felonious list in July 1985 and was only considered fit to be reissued in 1992, when three minutes of cuts were carried out to Lacey's harrowing

The most terrifying nightmare of childhood is about to return!

nightmare sequence along with those shots tracing the blood trickling down the breasts of the girl who had stabbed herself with the scissors. It would be another eight years before it was finally made available in its uncut form. A sequel followed in 1983, **Boogeyman 2**, which, due to its flashbacks to the original film, also incurred the wrath of the BBFC, with the less offensive **Return of The Boogeyman** being produced in 1994.

Braindead

📅	YEAR OF RELEASE: 1992	🎦	CINEMATOGRAPHER: Murray Milne
🕐	RUNTIME: 104 minutes	🎬	PRODUCERS: Jim Booth, Jamie Selkirk (associate producer).
🌐	COUNTRY: New Zealand		
🎥	DIRECTOR: Peter Jackson	⭕	CERTIFICATE: Australia: R; Canada: 18+ (Quebec); Canada: 16+ (Quebec); Canada: R; New Zealand: R16; UK: 18; USA: Unrated; USA: R (heavily cut)
🎬	PRODUCTION COMPANY: WingNut Films, New Zealand Film Commission, Avalon/NFU Studios		
✒️	WRITER: Stephen Sinclair		
		💲	BUDGET: $3,000,000

CAST: Timothy Balme, Diana Peñalver, Elizabeth Moody, Ian Watkin, Brenda Kendall, Stuart Devenie, Jed Brophy, Stephen Papps, Murray Keane, Glenis Levestam, Lewis Rowe, Elizabeth Mulfaxe, Harry Sinclair, Davina Whitehouse, Silvio Famularo

HAVING NARROWLY ESCAPED the natives on the homage to **King Kong**, Skull Island, an explorer returns an infected Sumatran Rat-Monkey to the Wellington Zoo, New Zealand. Soon after, Lionel Cosgrove (Timothy Balme) takes the girl of his dreams, the local shopkeeper's lovely daughter Paquita (Diana Peñalver), for a cosy day out to the same zoo to see, among many other things, the Sumatran Rat-Monkey. Unfortunately, his overbearing Psycho-esque mother, who is very disapproving of Paquita, has followed them on their romantic escape. While snooping on her son, she gets too close to the monkey and once bitten begins to turn into a voracious zombie. Lionel manages to overcome his horror and as the dutiful son vows to take care of her. However, even though she is prescribed with a veterinary anaesthetic, it proves impossible to keep her under control and his mother begins to rip into the flesh of their neighbours, who in turn become unquenchable zombies.

While Paquita remains unaware of Mrs Cosgrove's deteriorating condition, Lionel keeps her and her zombie accomplices sedated in the cellar of their huge suburban home. This doesn't last long; his mother makes a bid to escape, only to be knocked down by a tram. After the funeral, Lionel makes his way to the graveyard knowing he still has to administer her medication, but is set upon by a gang of thugs. Without the sedative, his mother is free to rise and is once again overwhelmed by the needs of her zombified condition. When she erupts from the grave, the Reverend McGruder is one of her first victims and it becomes obvious he has salacious intentions for the zombie nurse, with a bit of zombie sex in the offering. In no time at all they have a zombie baby, and so the bloodthirsty plague continues until Lionel's house is bursting with this rampaging epidemic.

The rot has set in . . .

When Lionel's avaricious Uncle Les (Ian Watkin) discovers the madness in the cellar, he uses this as a way of forcing his young nephew to relinquish his inheritance. The well-intentioned Lionel now accepts he must kill the deranged infestation thriving beneath the house, so he begrudgingly poisons them. As he sets about burying the zombie corpses, Uncle Les and his friends arrive for the housewarming.

However, in a fitting twist, the poison turns out to be an animal stimulant, and in preparation for the outrageous finale the zombies are already enthusiastically emerging to join the party. Lionel and Paquita find themselves besieged by droves of these putrescent creatures until the doting son reveals the lawnmower and an orgiastic splatterfest of decapitation, severed limbs and disembowelment follows with the zombies being ruthlessly annihilated. Not quite – Lionel's mother has survived to metamorphose into a reflection of her true self, a perverse Oedipal monster fixed on subsuming her once pathetic son. In a confrontation on the roof of the house, she squeezes him back into the depths of her repellent womb only to be subjected to his rebirth as he hacks his way to freedom. As she plummets into the blazing house, both Lionel and Paquita escape, covered from head to toe in gore.

Following the success of his low-budget comedic science fiction horror **Bad Taste** (1987), Peter Jackson returned with a hideously dark comedy **Braindead**, released as **Dead Alive** in the United States owing to a film of the same name being released in 1990 starring Bill Pullman and Bill Paxton. On this occasion, he gleefully followed in the gore-soaked footsteps of **Dawn of the Dead**, **The Evil Dead** and **Re-Animator**. While the censors in both the UK and Australia were a little more appreciative of this visceral humour, many countries recoiled at was has been acknowledged as one of the bloodiest horror comedies ever made. The early parts of this film set in 1957 present a homely setting, alluding to a hopeless love affair, until Jackson splatters the screen in his first wave of gore before completely immersing the entire set in a cascade of never ending entrails. **Braindead** is believed to hold the record for most blood spilled in a film with 300 litres bucketed on for the finale. Jackson's techniques proved almost flawless and awards deservedly followed throughout 1992 and 1993, before he went on to even greater success.

Burial Ground

📅	YEAR OF RELEASE: 1981		🎞	CINEMATOGRAPHER: Gianfranco Maioletti
🕐	RUNTIME: 85 minutes			
🌍	COUNTRY: Italy		⏳	PRODUCER: Gabriele Crisanti
🎥	DIRECTOR: Andrea Bianchi		⭕	CERTIFICATE: Australia: R; Canada: 16+ (Quebec); Canada: 18+ (Quebec); New Zealand: R16; UK: 18; USA: Unrated
🎬	PRODUCTION COMPANY: Esteban Cinematografica			
✎	WRITER: Piero Regnoli			

CAST: Karin Well, Gianluigi Chirizzi, Simone Mattioli, Antonella Antinori, Roberto Caporali, Peter Bark, Claudio Zucchet, Anna Valente, Raimondo Barbieri, Mariangela Giordano

ON ITS ORIGINAL release in Italy, **Burial Ground** went to the theatres as **Le Notti del Terrore** and began with a Professor Ayres as he studied an ancient crypt close to a cemetery. As he hacks away at one of the walls, an evil force is mysteriously set free. With nothing by way of an explanation, a skeletal creature lunges forward heading straight towards him and within seconds several more of these hideous creatures arise from the grave. The chase is all too quick and their quarry brought to slaughter. Unbeknown to them, their cannibalistic urges will soon be satiated by a group of socialites, each with precious little depth to their personalities, who are about to arrive for a weekend of fun and frolicking at a nearby mansion.

When two of the group, George and Evelyn, come upon the artefacts previously unearthed by Ayres, several bulbs explode in the house, a portent of the horror to come. Zombies now lumber from the caves into the surrounding countryside. The group become aware of these maleficent creatures when another impassioned couple are disturbed by a zombie rising from the ground. They bid to escape, but George is the first to die, ripped apart and then eagerly devoured. And so the rest are very soon dispensed. The resourceful zombies gather tools from an old shed, before scaling the mansion in a manner that Romero's and Fulci's rotting offspring never could. One bright zombie hurls a knife, which skewers the hand of his victim; decapitation by a garden scythe then silences her screams. The next victim is seized by the hair and impaled on the sharp edges of a window. Among the marauding mob is the now putrescent Professor Ayres, who returns to rip the throat from one of the party, before feasting on his innards. The following morning the zombies, now disguised as monks, savour yet another victim.

Soon after, the three survivors, Mark, Janet and Evelyn, prepare to meet their end trapped in a workshop. Their attempt to escape is thwarted by Evelyn's zombie son, Michael, who has already shocked his mother with his incestuous sexual advances. Michael, as perverse as ever, exposes her breast, then true to his newfound tastes ferociously bites it off. More zombies appear;

When the moon turns red, the dead shall rise!

in the furore Mark's head is forced into a buzz saw and then the recently slaughtered George returns to savour his dead wife's face. His companions satisfy their cannibalistic cravings with the remainder of her squirming body. Janet is the last to die, swamped by the zombies in what will be their final assault. The grainy scenes that bring **Burial Ground** to an end impart a sense of the apocalypse, making the finale all the more dismal and reflected in the closing caption: "The earth shall tremble, graves shall open, they shall come among the living as messengers of death and there shall be the nights of terror."

Andrea Bianchi's **Burial Ground** was also packaged as **Nights of Terror**, **The Zombie Dead**, **Zombie Horror** and is one of the many films to have been released as **Zombie 3**. Along with Umberto Lenzi's **Nightmare City** (1980), it is one of the few zombie movies where the dead appeared to be more intelligent than their warm-blooded counterparts. This was the heyday of splatter and, typically, any rational character development was sacrificed for extra helpings of blood and guts. The death scenes had to be creative to compensate for the flaws in plot, but all too often Bianchi's limited budget made them appear a tad farcical. Scarce resources prompted effects man Prestopino to design a rubber mask to create the decomposed appearance of the zombies, which was how they often appeared on screen. The pace, however, was breathtaking; if the weekenders weren't in the throes of passion they were desperately fighting for their lives. And just when the viewer thinks this tumult couldn't stop, the film comes to an abrupt end. This may disappoint, but also works to consummate the damning air of doom that has imbued so much of this story.

The film is best remembered for the portrayal of the Oedipal young Michael by Peter Bark, an adult dwarf, whose desire for his mother is far more disturbing than the cannibalistic spectacle at the forefront of this film. When **Burial Ground** was made, child labour regulations made it impossible to employ children in such a role. A few years later, the introduction of the Video Recordings Act of 1984 made it impossible to find an uncut version of this film in the UK. When it was released on video it was heavily censored, with a little over ten minutes removed by the distributors and a further three minutes cut by the BBFC. The film was thankfully restored for its 2004 release. ♣

The Burning

📅 YEAR OF RELEASE: 1981	🏆 PRODUCERS: Michael Cohl (executive producer), André Djaoui (executive producer), Dany Ubaud (associate producer), Jean Ubaud (executive producer), Harvey Weinstein
⏱ RUNTIME: 91 minutes	
🌍 COUNTRY: USA	
🎥 DIRECTOR: Tony Maylam	
🎬 PRODUCTION COMPANY: Filmways Pictures, The Cropsy Venture	⭕ CERTIFICATE: Australia: R; Canada: 13+ (Quebec); UK: 18 (re-rating uncut 2002); UK: 18 (re-rating cut 1992); UK: (Banned) (1984–92); UK: X (original rating: 1981) (cut); USA: R
✏ WRITERS: Harvey Weinstein, Tony Maylam, Brad Grey	
🎞 CINEMATOGRAPHER: Harvey Harrison	💲 BUDGET: $1,500,000

CAST: Brian Matthews, Leah Ayres, Brian Backer, Larry Joshua, Jason Alexander Ned Eisenberg, Carrick Glenn, Carolyn Houlihan, Fisher Stevens, Lou David, Shelley Bruce, Sarah Chodoff, Bonnie Deroski, Holly Hunter, Kevin Kendal

LESS THAN TWELVE months after the original camp slasher first appeared in **Friday the 13ᵗʰ**, a new face arrived on the scene courtesy of a group of boys at a summer camp who play a practical joke on Cropsy, the alcoholic caretaker, a ne'er-do-well with a somewhat tarnished reputation. Their prank went horribly wrong and flames accidently engulfed the caretaker's cabin. In the ensuing devastation, he became overwhelmed by the fire and only saved himself by stumbling down a ravine to douse his burning body in the river below.

Five years have passed and Cropsy has been released from hospital, now horrifically disfigured by the burns he sustained on that terrifying night. While his long coat and sunglasses can disguise his lacerations, the madness within rapidly becomes all too apparent. Before revisiting the secluded camp armed with his trusted shears, he vents his rage by viciously carving up a prostitute. What follows is a bloody killing spree, lightened by an abundance of teenage titillation, as the caretaker returns to confront one of the campers whose shenanigans so hideously scarred his body. Sneak scenes allowed glimpses of the desirable young female cast, which were more than matched by the levels of gore, as Cropsy showed himself to be unyielding in his proclivity for slashing throats and whose devilishly sharpened shears took great delight in severing fingers and impaling tender young flesh before their master was unceremoniously struck in the head with an axe.

In trying to find their way into producing films and profit from the burgeoning slasher market, Harvey and Bob Weinstein successfully launched their careers as acclaimed producers of **The Burning**. This was also one of

Gather around the campfire to die!

the first films to come from their newly founded company Miramax Films. Writer Brad Grey also went on to greater things to become the Chairman and CEO of Paramount Pictures. As well as enticing prog rock legend Rick Wakeman to write the score, the Weinsteins managed to tease make-up effects genius Tom Savini away from **Friday the 13th Part 2** to create the unsightly figure of Cropsy. However, the film ran into problems following the storm over the leniency displayed by the MPAA in their assessment of the previous year's **Friday the 13th**. They remained steadfast in their insistence that certain scenes had to be removed before it received an R rating. One of these scenes was the extreme "raft massacre" where Cropsy dismembered five of the teenagers in only a matter of minutes. Similarly, on its release to video in the United Kingdom, **The Burning** was hounded by complications. Following the sanction of a slightly edited version by the BBFC, an uncut version of the film was inexplicably released by Thorn-EMI. The tapes were summarily impounded under the Obscene Publications Act of 1959, and **The Burning** joined many of its deviant contemporaries on the video nasties list. Tom Savini's dexterity on the "raft massacre" proved to be a bone of contention, as was the image of a pair of scissors piercing into a woman's flesh. Vipco later released a version in the early 1990s with only thirty seconds of gore having been left on the cutting room floor. However, by 2001 an uncut version finally went to print. The furore surrounding this film inevitably made it a great favourite among slasher enthusiasts, with much of its popularity attributed to the gifted Tom Savini.

Cabin Fever

 **YEAR OF RELEASE:** 2002		**PRODUCERS:** Evan Astrowsky, Sam Froelich, Jeffrey D. Hoffman (co-executive producer), Susan Jackson (executive producer), Lauren Moews, Eli Roth	
RUNTIME: 93 minutes			
COUNTRY: USA			
DIRECTOR: Eli Roth		**CERTIFICATE:** Australia: MA; Canada: 16+ (Quebec); Canada: 18A; Ireland: 15; UK: 15 USA: R; USA: Unrated (director's cut)	
PRODUCTION COMPANY: Black Sky Entertainment, Deer Path Films, Down Home Entertainment			
WRITERS: Eli Roth, Randy Pearlstein		**BUDGET:** $1,500,000	
CINEMATOGRAPHER: Scott Kevan		**RECEIPTS:** $33,553,394	

CAST: Rider Strong, Jordan Ladd, James DeBello, Cerina Vincent, Joey Kern, Arie Verveen, Robert Harris, Hal Courtney, Matthew Helms, Richard Boone, Tim Parati, Dalton McGuire, Jana Farmer, Dante Walker, Jeff Rendell

WITH THEIR EXAMS over, five college friends, Jeff (Joey Kern), Marcy (Cerina Vincent), Paul (Rider Strong), Karen (Jordan Ladd) and Bert (James DeBello), take an extended weekend break at a cabin deep in the woods. On the way, they call at a local country store for supplies, in a scene evoking memories of the strange folk in The Texas Chain Saw Massacre (1974). As they stock up, the store owner's mentally challenged son bites Paul on the hand, a reminder as to their being a long way from home and this being very different to the world they have just left behind them. Soon after arriving at the cabin, Jeff and Marcy retire to their bedroom for a few hours of uninterrupted passion, while Paul and Karen head to the lake for a swim and the red-neck practical joker of the crew, Bert, goes off alone hunting squirrels. In a horrendous accident, he shoots a man down whose face appears utterly rancid. In shock, Bert shoots at him again before scarpering back to the cabin. Several hours later, the same man turns up at the cabin and in the ensuing melee attempts to drive off in their car, vomiting a copious amount of blood across the windscreen and seats. In the heat of the moment, Paul sets the decomposing man alight, watching in disbelief as the burning figure staggers into the lake before finally breathing his last breath.

Shortly afterwards Karen takes a drink from the lake and very soon begins to feel unwell. It isn't long before ugly looking welts spread across her thighs, forcing her panicking friends to quarantine her in an adjacent shed. Bert we now discover has also been infected. This flesh-eating virus begins to bring about violent changes in each of the group and their underlying frailties begin to come to the fore. In a clever twist the contamination isn't

Terror . . . in the flesh.

symptomatic of their deaths; this comes from elsewhere.

Eli Roth's darkly comedic splatterfest was written in 1995, when horror was in the doldrums awaiting the rejuvenating arrival of Wes Craven's **Scream** (1996). **Cabin Fever** was styled on the liberal excess that had made the horrors of the 1980s so successful; fuelled by an abundance of gore and gratuitous nudity, it also introduced a paranoiac undercurrent seen in so many B-movies from the 1950s. In this, his directorial debut, Roth evoked memories of **The Evil Dead** (1981) in the isolated cabin scenes and gave a sly tip of the hat to George Romero's zombies. It was a bad experience in Iceland when Roth developed a serious skin infection that sowed these infectious seeds, which gave fruition to a highly successful movie. On its theatrical release the response, given the subject matter, was remarkably positive and spawned a **Cabin Fever 2: Spring Fever** in 2009.

Camp Blood

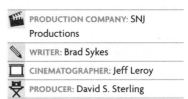

📅 YEAR OF RELEASE: 2000	🎬 PRODUCTION COMPANY: SNJ Productions
⏱ RUNTIME: 73 minutes	
🌐 COUNTRY: USA	✎ WRITER: Brad Sykes
🎥 DIRECTOR: Brad Sykes	🎞 CINEMATOGRAPHER: Jeff Leroy
	🎬 PRODUCER: David S. Sterling

CAST: Jennifer Ritchkoff, Michael Taylor, Tim Young, Betheny Zolt, Courtney Taylor, Joseph Haggerty, Meredith O'Brien, Vinnie Bilancio, Ron Ford, Tim Sullivan, Ivonne Armant, Randy Rice, Shemp Moseley

A COUPLE'S AFTERNOON of bird watching turns to passion in the woods in the vicinity of Camp Blackwood. As they become more fervent, a man adorned in a clown's mask bursts onto the scene, with other ideas on his mind, and very quickly lays them to the slaughter. The film moves on to introduce four campers who have a rendezvous at Camp Blackwood. In a similar way to so many of their predecessors who were trailed by a plethora of killers during the 1980s, they are warned to stay away from the area by an obvious madman, in this case one Bromley Thatcher. Typically, the group refuse to pay any heed to his well-meaning advice and journey on into the woods to be greeted by their female guide, the manly Harris. As the day comes to an end, the teenagers settle down for the night, to awaken next morning to the sight of Harris's charcoaled remains lying on the embers of the camp fire. With their guide now dead the group are at the mercy of the clown, who appears to be

Get ready for a bloody good time!

in league with the unhinged Thatcher. Only Tricia survives the killer clown's insane rampage, but she comes round to find herself seemingly sectioned in a mental institution. After receiving a tranquilizing injection, she begins to hallucinate and in her delirious condition has to face the clown as he cunningly slips into her room.

Brad Sykes' film falls into the category "so bad it's good" as he joined the wave of directors attempting to rejuvenate the passion for the slasher of two decades past. While the acting was in keeping with its B-movie status, his script was often very humorous and captured so much of the golden period that had reached its zenith during the early eighties. Sykes received his first Hi-8 video camera at the age of fifteen and knew his calling was a life in film. Before going on to write and direct the equally no-budget sequels, **Camp Blood 2** (2002) and **Camp Blood 3: Within the Woods** (2005), he turned his attention to the living dead with the **Zombie Chronicles** (2001).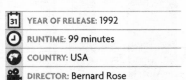

Candyman

📅	YEAR OF RELEASE: 1992	🎬 PRODUCTION COMPANY: PolyGram Filmed Entertainment, Propaganda Films
🕐	RUNTIME: 99 minutes	
🎥	COUNTRY: USA	✏️ WRITERS: Bernard Rose, Clive Barker
📷	DIRECTOR: Bernard Rose	

🎞 CINEMATOGRAPHER: Anthony B. Richmond	⭕ CERTIFICATE: Australia: M; Canada: 13+ (Quebec); Ireland: 18; New Zealand: R16; UK: 18; USA: R
⚏ PRODUCERS: Clive Barker (executive producer), Steve Golin, Gregory Goodman (line producer), Alan Poul, Sigurjon Sighvatsson	💲 BUDGET: $8,000,000
	🖵 RECEIPTS: $25,792,310

CAST: Virginia Madsen, Tony Todd, Xander Berkeley, Kasi Lemmons, Vanessa Williams, DeJuan Guy, Marianna Elliott, Ted Raimi, Ria Pavia, Mark Daniels, Lisa Ann Poggi, Adam Philipson, Eric Edwards, Carolyn Lowery, Barbara Alston

LOOKING TO COMPLETE her college thesis, graduate student Helen Lyle (Virginia Madsen) has become heavily involved in research into urban myth. As she furthers her studies, she comes upon a tale in the locality of the murderous Candyman. According to legend, those who stood before a mirror and chanted his name five times would see the long-dead slave appear before them; however, they would pay for their transgression with their life. That same evening, Helen and her friend Bernadette make light of the story and recite the Candyman's name before the mirror in her bathroom. As they had expected all along, nothing happens.

Eager to broaden her studies she ventures into Chicago's infamous Cabrini–Green housing project. Here, she is told the tale of a child who was only recently gouged and mutilated close by the projects; the locals believe it to have been the work of the Candyman. As she continues to look for more information, Helen is attacked by one of the project's more notorious gang members who, armed with a hook, has assumed the guise

of the Candyman. Although Helen survives the attack and the lowlife is arrested, she begins to hear the echoes of a distant voice that whispers her name. As her sense of unease intensifies, another man approaches her; he also lays claim to being the legendary Candyman. Helen refuses to believe him, but he is resolute in showing her that he is something more than a figure of urban myth. Unable to take anymore, she slumps to the ground only to awaken in the apartment of a woman she had spoken with earlier; there she lies covered in blood, beside a decapitated Rottweiler and then learns the woman's baby has gone missing. Helen is arrested and led away by the police to be later bailed by her husband. The Candyman is now on her trail. He next appears in her apartment and engages his hook to slice open her neck, before slaughtering her friend Bernadette. With no one else having been in the apartment, it looks as if she is the murderous culprit.

With her world slowly beginning to disintegrate, Helen tries to convince her psychologist that the Candyman is very much real, which the urban legend proves by appearing in his office and disembowelling him. Helen knows she has to escape, but when she returns to her apartment, she finds her husband alone with one of his female students. She now has no choice but to return to the projects, for a final showdown with the Candyman.

With the excess of the 1980s teenage slasher phenomenon having burned out some years before, mainstream horror cinema needed something new and original to reinvigorate its flagging premise. This came with Bernard Rose's adaptation of Clive Barker's *The Forbidden*, a short story first published in 1986 that reinvented the centuries-old myth of Bloody Mary. Set amidst the grim reality of Chicago's failed Cabrini-Green housing project, Rose's villain was to take on far greater proportions than the fanciful conjecture of urban myth, in a film that dared to challenge his country's attitudes on inner city racial conflict. This wasn't the horror feature of a decade past aimed solely at a teenage market heading off to the drive-ins; rather, this was a tightly plotted adult movie, which wasn't afraid to deftly pace its narrative flow before delivering the shocks. While Tony

From the chilling imagination of Clive Barker.

Todd's Candyman meted out ample portions of blood and guts, London-born Rose looked to exploit well-healed society's fears of being stranded on the wrong side of town. Poor Helen Lyle would find herself wrongly accused of a series of brutal crimes very much like the heroines of Alfred Hitchcock's films, but she was about to pay the ultimate price for invoking this dread villain of urban myth. The eerie music of Philip Glass and the adept photography of Anthony B. Richmond would ensure this was a film that lived on to haunt its audience long after the closing credits.

While the UK's Channel 4 has been known to show the uncut version of this film, the VHS release of the 1990s and the DVD of 2006 have suffered from the edits insisted on by the MPAA. These include a more graphic shaking of the psychologist where he violently head butts the table prior to the Candyman tearing into his flesh as his hook then emerges from his stomach. The screams at this point were also played down along with the subsequent discharge of blood. This wouldn't prevent a sequel from going into production in 1995 to appear as **Candyman: Farewell to Flesh.**

Cannibal Apocalypse

📅	YEAR OF RELEASE: 1980	✏️ WRITER: Dardano Sacchetti
🕐	RUNTIME: 96 minutes	🎞️ CINEMATOGRAPHER: Fernando Arribas
🐾	COUNTRY: Italy/Spain	🏆 PRODUCERS: Edmondo Amati,
🎥	DIRECTOR: Antonio Margheriti	Maurizio Amati, Sandro Amati
🎬	PRODUCTION COMPANY: Edmondo	⭕ CERTIFICATE: Australia: R; Canada: 18+
	Amati presents, José Frade	(Quebec); Canada: R; UK: (Banned,
	Producciones Cinematográficas S.A.,	original rating); UK: 18 (video rating);
	New Fida	USA: R

CAST: John Saxon, Elizabeth Turner, Giovanni Lombardo Radice, Cinzia De Carolis, Tony King, Wallace Wilkinson, Ramiro Oliveros, John Geroson, May Heatherly, Ronnie Sanders, Vic Perkins, Jere Beery, Joan Riordan, Laura Dean, Lonnie R. Smith

THE VIETNAM WAR had been over for five years, but Norman Hopper (John Saxon) is still being tormented by frightening flashbacks. He is terrorized by the image of a pit holding two of his men who are avidly gorging on the charred body of a Vietnamese woman. When Hopper discovers the pit, he extends his arm to hoist them from their incarceration only to be savaged by Charlie Bukowski (John Morghen), who has been infected with a virulent cannibalistic virus. Hopper then awakens from his nightmare to the sound of the telephone. On the line is Bukowski; he has just been released from a psychiatric clinic and is all too eager to meet up for a drink. Hopper, however, is very aware of his former comrade's predilection and anyway his thoughts are on his young neighbour, Mary (Cinzia De Carolis). As he rolls over to indulge in oral sex, he bites into her tender flesh. The unsuspecting girl is saved by a call from Hopper's concerned wife, who tells of a Vietnam vet who has barricaded himself in a mall. It's Bukowski; he has gone on the rampage and locked himself away in a department store having lost control of his urges and bitten into a woman's neck. As Hopper gets into his car, Mary reveals that she quite enjoyed the bite; hers will be the film's finale once Atlanta has fallen to the insanity of this cannibalistic infestation.

Antonio Margheriti was a veteran of Italian science fiction, action and western films, whose first screenplay had been written as early as 1956. Having worked only a few years before with some of the biggest names in American cinema he now turned to the cannibal craze that had already enjoyed several years of tremendous success in a film, which later went by the names **Invasion of the Flesh Hunters** and **Apocalypse Domani**. Rather than return to the jungles of Fulci and Deodata's features he set his flesh-eating cannibals lose in Atlanta, inviting comparisons with George Romero's **Dawn of the Dead** (1978). His feature was an unusual hybrid, seen to revel in the bloodthirsty excess of the day, and yet evoked concepts that had made both **The Deer Hunter** (1978) and **Apocalypse Now** (1979) such landmarks in the post-Vietnam era. The notion of a contaminating virus was also reminiscent of David Croneburg's **Rabid** (1977) and surfaced twenty years later in Danny Boyle's **28 Days Later** (2002).

There are many gore-mongers who have suggested this film should have

> **POWs in Vietnam ... starved in captivity ... released with a taste for human flesh.**

had more blood and guts, but when effects wizard Giannetto De Rossi was allowed to pour on the blood, he did it in the worst possible taste. As with Umberto Lenzi's **Nightmare City** (1980), a girl was shown having one of her breasts torn off and then greedily devoured, a doctor also had his tongue bitten out, then a mechanic had his thigh clean sliced while Bukowski met his end with the graphic decimation of his stomach, which the intrusive camera so wilfully savoured. As was expected, Margheriti's film was banned in the UK in July 1983 during the Video Nasties scare, only twelve months after it had been made available in its uncut form. This came much to the relief of John Saxon, who was never entirely enamoured with the film's excess. **Cannibal Apocalypse** was finally released in the UK in 2005 with only a two second shot being removed from the sewer shootout, as rats were burned with napalm, contravening the UK's legislation on cruelty to animals.

Cannibal Campout

 YEAR OF RELEASE: 1988

RUNTIME: 89 minutes

 COUNTRY: USA

 DIRECTORS: Tom Fisher, Jon McBride

WRITER: John Rayl

CINEMATOGRAPHER: Tom Fisher

 PRODUCERS: Tom Fisher, Jon McBride, Marshall Peck (associate producer), Joseph Salheb (associate producer)

CAST: Jon McBride, Amy Chludzinski, Christopher A. Granger, Richard Marcus, Gene Robbins, Carrie Lindell, Joseph Salheb, Nancy Sciarra, Ray Angelic, John Farrell

A TEENAGE GIRL JOGS through suburban streets tuned into the sound of some nondescript 1980s synthesized pop music. It doesn't take long before she falls prey to a man wearing a jetfighter's helmet. The prologue, which has nothing to do with what follows, suddenly comes to an abrupt end. In a complete change of direction, four college students are trailed as they travel to a weekend of camping, even though they have been warned to stay away from the area. The group seem to be having so much fun, but one of the girls appears troubled. She has to choose her moment before telling her boyfriend that she is pregnant. Her situation will deteriorate still further when the group make the wrong turn, which leads them straight into the path of three backwoods brothers, one whose face remains obscured by a mask, only to be revealed during the downbeat finale. While the group are understandably wary of the brothers, none of them realizes the clan's true desire is the satisfying of their cannibalistic

craving. As they stalk and abduct the youngsters, we come to learn the reasons for their love of human flesh. From an early age, their mother refused to let them eat either processed or packaged food, because she feared it was preserved with unhealthy chemical products. In its place, she would only recommend the freshest of meat. So follows a weekend of carnage as the four friends are graphically dismembered, disembowelled and then sliced and diced in preparation for the cooking pot.

Jon McBride's shot-to-video movie continued in the tradition established a decade earlier with **The Texas Chain Saw Massacre** (1974) and **The Hills Have Eyes** (1977) and would go on to include **Wrong Turn** (2003). He was one of the many young filmmakers from the period who saw the potential in shooting films to video, overcoming the problems that came with acquiring suitable and affordable film stock. Equipped with his recently purchased camcorder he set out to make his debut feature with only a few hundred dollars and a young cast who were

Friends don't let friends eat friends!

happy to work without pay. McBride's enthusiasm for the project would see him take on some of the writing, as well as directing, acting and then editing twelve hours of footage down to a watchable ninety minutes. At the outset, his film was only going to be viewed by his own close circle of friends, but he succeeded in signing a nationwide distribution deal at a time when small independent films were gaining a following in the increasingly popular video market. Such was his success he returned with the darkly humorous **The Woodchipper Massacre** (1988) at the beginning of a career that has seen his shot-on-video efforts acquire a considerable fan base, especially among aspiring filmmakers.

Cannibal Ferox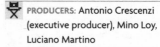

YEAR OF RELEASE: 1981

RUNTIME: 93 minutes

COUNTRY: Italy

DIRECTOR: Umberto Lenzi

PRODUCTION COMPANY: Dania Film, Medusa Produzione, National Cinematografica

WRITER: Umberto Lenzi

CINEMATOGRAPHER: Giovanni Bergamini

PRODUCERS: Antonio Crescenzi (executive producer), Mino Loy, Luciano Martino

CERTIFICATE: Australia: R; Canada: R (Alberta); Canada: 18+ (Quebec); Canada: (Banned) (Ontario); New Zealand: R18 (cut); UK: 18 (re-rating: 2000) (heavily cut); UK: (Banned) (1984–2000); USA: Unrated

CAST: Giovanni Lombardo Radice, Lorraine De Selle, Danilo Mattei, Zora Kerova, Walter Lucchini, Fiamma Maglione, Robert Kerman, John Bartha, Venantino Venantini, "El Indio" Rincon

NEW YORK ANTHROPOLOGY student Gloria along with her brother Rudy and friend Pat journey deep into the Amazon jungle, with Gloria determined to challenge and disprove the tales of tribal cannibalism allegedly being practised in the region. Little do they know, callous drug dealer Mike Lawson and his fugitive accomplice are laying low in the same locale, having escaped the New York mob and criminal charges for murder and drug dealing. Even in this remote spot, the merciless Lawson looks to exploit others, using the natives to mine for emeralds and harvest the coca plant. When the cocaine-crazed villain tortures and kills several natives, among them the chief's daughter, to gratify his sadistic sense of amusement, the tribesman vow revenge and begin to track them down through this tropical forest. As the two men look to escape, they come upon the three students and the group are soon surrounded and then subjected to the most horrific torture by the indigenous warriors, who exhibit a taste for the succulence of human flesh.

Umberto Lenzi's low-budget **Cannibal Ferox** has also gone by the name **Make Them Die Slowly** and in Australia was entitled **Woman From Deep River** to appear as a sequel to one of the director's previous cannibal movies **Sacrifice!** (1972), which had seen release in the Antipodes as **The Man From Deep River**. While **Sacrifice!** can lay claim to being one of the earliest cannibal exploitation films, **Cannibal Ferox** proudly proclaimed to be "The most violent film ever made" and fairly revelled in its supposed ban in thirty-one countries. It will come as no surprise to learn the video release made it to the UK's list of video nasties; the sickening scenes of animal killing, along with the castrations, the slicing of the head and the hooks being driven into Pat's breasts all felt the wrath of

They were cold, sadistic killers who thought they could hide from justice. But now they must face the harsh law of the jungle ...

the BBFC, and to this day Lenzi's film remains heavily cut. **Cannibal Ferox**, which proved to be one of the last cannibal exploitation movies, has a deserved reputation for its gritty edge, and to this effect followed in the footsteps of Ruggero Deodato's **Cannibal Holocaust** (1980) in its use of washed out documentary styled visuals. Its portrayal of the human condition was indeed harrowing, refusing throughout to relent as the degree of violence became all the more acute. The cannibal tribesmen, while presented as an ominous collective with a compulsion for retribution, appear detached, acquiescent adherents to the laws of nature and the claustrophobia of this enclosed jungle terrain. This wasn't the verdant rainforest advocated by those who continue to campaign on behalf of the Amazon Basin; instead the audience were led into an oppressive domain, cleverly contrasted with the police investigation in the harsh urban jungle of New York City. Lenzi's direction in this inner-city terrain works to confuse, giving the impression these scenes have been designed with another film in mind, but viewing his feature as a whole they combine to make this a memorable addition to cannibal cinema. 🍂

Cannibal Holocaust

 YEAR OF RELEASE: 1980

RUNTIME: 95 minutes

COUNTRY: Italy

DIRECTOR: Ruggero Deodato

PRODUCTION COMPANY: F.D. Cinematografica

WRITER: Gianfranco Clerici

CINEMATOGRAPHER: Sergio D'Offizi

PRODUCERS: Franco Di Nunzio, Franco Palaggi

CERTIFICATE: Australia: (Banned) (1984–2005); Australia: R (re-rating: 2005) (uncut); Canada: 16+ (Quebec) (re-rating, uncut) (1984–2001); Canada: R; Ireland: 18 (re-rating: 2006); Ireland: (Banned); New Zealand: (Banned); South Africa: 18; UK: 18 (re-rating heavily cut: 2001); UK: (Banned) (1984–2006); UK: X (self applied: 1981); USA: Open (rating surrendered: 1985); USA: X; USA: Unrated

BUDGET: $100,000

CAST: Robert Kerman, Francesca Ciardi, Perry Pirkanen, Luca Barbareschi, Salvatore Basile, Ricardo Fuentes, Carl Gabriel Yorke, Paolo Paoloni, Lionello Pio Di Savoia, Luigina Rocchi

A TELEVISION PROGRAMME conveys the heightening concern for an American documentary film crew who disappeared months ago while on an expedition to the Amazon rainforest to produce a film on the cannibal tribes of the area. New York anthropologist Professor Harold Monroe (Robert Kerman) now leads a team to learn the fate of Alan Yates (Carl Gabriel Yorke), the director; Faye Daniels (Francesca Ciardi), his girlfriend and script girl; along with their cameramen, Jack Anders (Perry Pirkanen) and Mark Tomaso (Luca Barbareschi). With the help of two local guides, Chaco and his assistant Miguel,

the professor treks to the village of Yacumo. Monroe is aghast when he learns how the unscrupulous documentary team caused nothing but trouble among their people. When he journeys deeper into the rainforest, he encounters the Yanomamö, who eventually lead him to the bones of the missing crew and the surviving reels of film.

On his return to New York City, Monroe is shown Yates' previous documentary, "The Last Road to Hell", and learns how the director staged much of what was seen on the lost reels of film, with the intention of exciting his thrill-seeking audience and bolstering his reputation. The television executives try to overcome the professor's unease, offering him the chance to host the new documentary, which discloses how the crew created this misleading footage while terrorizing the Yacumo village. When they encounter the Yanomamö, the men of the team rape and later impale a native girl, again to add a deceitful substance to the documentary's unsavoury ethic. Soon after, the girl's fellow villagers discover her fate; enraged they begin to track down the crew. Deodato's film now turns; the killing, rape, decapitation and cannibalizing of the crew become its focus, with every grisly detail captured on grainy film by the unprincipled Yates. As the camera falls to the ground, the reel reaches its finale as Yates's bloodied face stares blankly at the camera's lens. Twenty years later, this same image would be repeated for a new audience in the incredibly successful **The Blair Witch Project** (1999). The scenes prove too much for the profiteering television executives and they insist the footage is destroyed. However, we are later informed that the projectionist secretly removed the reels, which he then sold for $250,000.

Cannibal Holocaust is still looked upon as one of the most sickeningly graphic atrocities ever committed to film. The viciousness in its content ensured its ban in many countries yet Ruggero Deodato's film transcended its seemingly exploitative roots to

The mother of all cannibal films.

confer a powerful eulogy on the cruelty inherent to our flawed species. While the film crew were literally torn into shreds and then devoured, with a penis being ripped off, followed by scenes of rape and decapitation, the audience's sympathies lay with the victimized natives, who were to be portrayed as an amusing distraction for a seemingly civilized western audience. This truly was a horror movie, a far cry from so much of the darkly humoured slasher fare that was by then in its ascendancy.

Ultimo Mondo Cannibal or **Last Cannibal World** (1977) had been Deodato's precursor to this shocking episode, which was essentially an action-packed cannibal movie with precious little in the way of gore. His approach to this feature, however, observed a distinct transition, choosing to make use of the documentary filmmaking techniques of Paolo Cavara, Gualtiero Jacopetti and Franco Prosperi. There was a disconcertingly rough edge to the second half of the film, which in a series of powerful scenes revealed only the slightest suggestion of gore rather than the anticipated visceral excess.

Soon after its Italian premiere, **Cannibal Holocaust** was confiscated by a magistrate and Deodato was arrested on charges of obscenity. It was the magistrate's belief the director had produced a vile snuff movie and rumours abounded as to the onscreen killing of some of the actors. Deodato was later cleared, but his film was banned in his home country and then later in the UK. Such was its reputation it faced prohibition across almost the entire globe. The appalling levels of physical and sexual violence were borne out to be highly controversial, as was the unnecessary cruelty displayed towards the animal life featured in the film. This callous disregard had already angered and caused a significant amount of tension among the members of the cast and crew. Furthermore, the unrelenting violence detailed in the grainy documentary sequences, recorded on hand-held cameras, proved a little too realistic for the censoring authorities. In February1982 **Cannibal Holocaust** was released to video in the UK, but by July 1983 its notoriety had ensured it a place among the Director of Public Prosecutions' list of seventy-four videos that proliferated the country without having been certified by the BBFC. The film was successfully prosecuted for obscenity and banned until 2001 when it was passed with an "18" certificate following the extensive editing of the animal cruelty and scenes of sexual violence. Owing to its graphic content, several different versions of **Cannibal Holocaust** have been peddled in various countries with countless edits to the "Last Road to Hell".

Several films have since attempted to pose as **Cannibal Holocaust II**, although an official sequel has never been released and isn't likely to be following a recent breakdown in negotiations between Deodato and potential financiers. Mario Gariazzo's **Schiave Bianche: Violenza en Amazzonia** (1985), also known as **Amazonia: The Catherine Miles Story**, hoped to exploit the movie's infamy when it saw release as **Cannibal Holocaust 2: The Catherine Miles Story**. Antonio Climati's jungle adventure **Natura Contro** (1988), while also going by the name **The Green Inferno**, assumed the title **Cannibal Holocaust II** on its UK release. Bruno Mattei later produced **Mondo Cannibale**, **Cannibal World** in 2003, which was released as **Cannibal Holocaust 2: The Beginning** to an expectant Japanese audience. His film bore an uncanny resemblance in plot to Deodato's original, but lacked the original's abominable groundbreaking impact. Thirty years later, **Cannibal Holocaust** remains a unique moment in the history of cinematic horror.

Cannibal Man

31 YEAR OF RELEASE: 1972		WRITER: Eloy de la Iglesia	
RUNTIME: 98 minutes		CINEMATOGRAPHER: Raúl Artigot	
COUNTRY: Spain		PRODUCERS: Vicente Parra (associate producer), José Truchado	
DIRECTOR: Eloy de la Iglesia			
PRODUCTION COMPANY: Atlas International Film		CERTIFICATE: Canada: 13+ (Quebec); USA: R	

CAST: Vicente Parra, Emma Cohen, Eusebio Poncela, Charly Bravo, Fernando Sánchez Polack, Lola Herrera, Goyo Lebrero, Vicky Lagos, Ismael Merlo, Rafael Hernández, José Franco, Valentín Tornos, Antonio Orengo, Antonio Corencia, Antonio del Real

MARCOS (VINCENTE PARRA) toils amidst the blood and guts of a slaughterhouse as livestock fall to the butcher's knife ready to be carved up and packaged for the shops and markets of his hometown. When he leaves work, he returns to his old whitewashed house in one of the poorer areas of town close to a recently constructed block of flats. While out on a date with his girlfriend Paula (Emma Cohen), the two get a little too passionate on the backseat of a taxi, which annoys the driver. In the ensuing confrontation, the enraged Marcos kills the belligerent taxi driver. The following day Paula insists they should confess his crime to the police. Marcos knows the authorities will never believe his explanation of those tragic events and he does not have the kind of money that can afford a reliable lawyer. Paula persists and threatens to turn him in; unable to curb his anger he slits her throat with a butcher's knife and conceals her body beneath the bed. Soon after Marcos confesses his crimes to his brother Steve, he too insists the police should be informed. Marcos's situation becomes even worse when he once again shows himself incapable of controlling his temper. In the ensuing melee, he bludgeons his own brother to death with a handy wrench. People continue to arrive at his humble abode; first comes his brother's girlfriend, then her father and finally a waitress, none of them ever to be seen again. The bodies are kept hidden in his bedroom, and the odour of decay is disguised by a copious supply of air fresheners. In a rare moment of clarity, Marcos decides to chop his victims into little pieces and take them to the slaughterhouse, where he can then grind them down and mix them with the ordinary supply of meat. As Marcos's world descends into madness, so develops a suggestively homosexual friendship with a curious young man named Nestor (Eusebio Poncela), who spends much of his time walking his dog. From his thirteenth-floor apartment in the flats adjacent to Marcos's house, he has observed the gruesome secret contained within. Maybe he recognizes another social outcast, but for whatever reason he chooses to remain quiet about what he has seen and for once Marcos chooses to spare his life.

When the butcher goes berserk . . .

La **Semana del Asesino**, which translates as "The Week of the Murderer", was entitled **Apartment on the 13th Floor** and was also given the exploitative title of **Cannibal Man** in the hope of arousing more interest when it was released in the UK and North America. The title, however, is somewhat misleading, for there are no scenes of flesh eating evidenced anywhere in this film. Instead, Eloy de la Iglesia's feature is a character study of a seemingly reserved man's struggle in the squalor of his environment and the subsequent anger that so often becomes manifest in such urban decay. It also goes on to reveal how in a single moment a person's life can fall into utter chaos. As a character study, it bears comparison to James McNaughton's equally austere **Henry: Portrait of a Serial Killer** (1986) and is reminiscent of the claustrophobic insanity of Roman Polanski's **Repulsion** (1965). Raul Artigot's grainy cinematography added to the air of despair, which history has shown to be a reflection of a country that thought so little of its poor.

While this wasn't a particularly gory film, with the notable exception of the opening scenes in the slaughterhouse, it still managed to make it to the Director of Public Prosecutions' list of video nasties in July 1983 following its previous release to video in November 1981. It was finally granted an issue to video in 1993, on the understanding three seconds of unpleasantness were removed from the final cut. The relationship between Marcos and Nestor was also considered as being highly provocative and it has been suggested that there was concern among the censors in the UK as to its subtle homoerotic subtext. This wouldn't be the last time Iglesia incorporated a homosexual theme in one of his films, which, in the fiercely Catholic Spain of the day, was considered a challenge to the country's authority.

Cannibal Terror

31 YEAR OF RELEASE: 1981	CINEMATOGRAPHER: Emilio Foriscot
RUNTIME: 93 minutes	PRODUCER: Daniel Lesoeur
COUNTRY: France/Spain	CERTIFICATE: UK: 18 (re-rating: 2003, uncut); UK: (Banned) (1984–2001); USA: Not Rated
DIRECTOR: Alain Deruelle	
PRODUCTION COMPANY: Eurociné	
WRITERS: Julio Pérez Tabernero, H. L. Rostaine	

CAST: Silvia Solar, Pamela Stanford, Olivier Mathot, Gérard Lemaire, Burt Altman, Stan Hamilton, Antoine Fontaine, Antonio Mayans, Michel Laury

THREE PETTY CRIMINALS, Roberto, Lina and Mario, conspire to kidnap the daughter of a rich couple and hold her hostage until they agree to pay their ransom. The police, however, are wise to their scheme and arrive on the scene forcing the villains to take leave of the country with the little girl still their hostage. Their escape leads them to an old friend, Antonio, and his young wife Manuela. While in the jungle, their jeep breaks down and their desirable guide is captured by a cannibal tribe. As she is dragged away, the camera moves in to dwell on her struggling body as it is sliced open and eaten. The kidnappers manage to escape the flesh-hungry tribe and get the jeep back on the road, soon after arriving at Antonio's retreat. The despicable Mario returns his host's hospitality by tying Manuela between two trees and raping her. When Antonio discovers what has happened he lures the kidnappers into the jungle and once he has overpowered them, returns their treachery by binding them to a tree ready for the cannibals to savour fresh meat. Meanwhile, the battered Manuela comes to the aid of the parents of the kidnapped girl, as the cannibal tribesman track them further into their jungle domain.

Deep in the jungle the flesheaters are waiting.

Terreur Cannibale was released just as the boom for cannibal movies was about to implode and included within its running time several sequences from Jess Franco's equally exploitative **Mondo Cannibale** (1980) with rumours abounding that Franco had been brought in to re-film certain scenes. For many years, it was also intimated that Franco had directed this film, but that had fallen to Alain Deruelle. He has never been able to escape the criticism launched at him for his use of so much stock footage, low-budget locales more than likely set in France and a cast of pallid natives, some of whom were overweight, with ever so delicately styled hair. However, there was just enough gore along with a smattering of voyeuristic sex and that provocative title to arouse the interests of the Director of Public Prosecutions in July 1983 following the film's release to video in October 1981. In July 1985, however, **Cannibal Terror**, along with **The Evil Dead**, **Inferno** and **Dead and Buried** would win a case at Snaresbrook Crown Court leading to their removal from the DPP's list of banned videos. It was finally passed without cuts by the BBFC in 2003. ❦

Cat in the Brain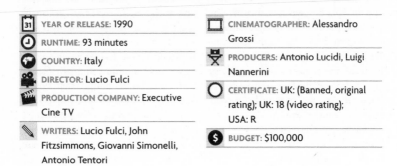

31 YEAR OF RELEASE: 1990	**CINEMATOGRAPHER:** Alessandro Grossi
RUNTIME: 93 minutes	**PRODUCERS:** Antonio Lucidi, Luigi Nannerini
COUNTRY: Italy	
DIRECTOR: Lucio Fulci	**CERTIFICATE:** UK: (Banned, original rating); UK: 18 (video rating); USA: R
PRODUCTION COMPANY: Executive Cine TV	
WRITERS: Lucio Fulci, John Fitzsimmons, Giovanni Simonelli, Antonio Tentori	**BUDGET:** $100,000

CAST: Lucio Fulci, David L. Thompson, Malisa Longo, Shilett Angel, Jeoffrey Kennedy, Paola Cozzo

IN AN INVENTIVE turn that would demand hours of work in post-production, Lucio Fulci plays a tormented version of himself. After years of gory filmmaking, we are witness to his descent into complete and utter madness. His psychiatric consultant, with a mind to murder his own adulterous wife, is far from sympathetic, taking the director back to relive the sadistic depravity of his and several other directors' bloodthirsty films. Tormented by these terrifying visions of rape and butchery, each cut and spliced from a variety of graphic horror movies, Fulci fears he has to be the skulking psychopath in the raincoat as his sense of reality swirls into a visceral kaleidoscope of hallucinatory carnage. As his fragile state of mind deteriorates still further, he alludes to a cat eating away into his brains.

Cat in the Brain, which in Italy was known as **Un Gatto Nel Cervello**, and later entitled **Nightmare Concert** and **I Volti del Terrore**, was a film created for only the most ardent of Fulci's fans. With only a tenuous plot, he and editor Vincenzo Tomassi cut and juxtaposed a variety of extremely gory horror clips to create a grisly pastiche from his most notorious cinematic years. These films would include Fulci's **Touch of Death** (1988) and **Il Fantasma di Sodoma** (1988), along with five films he was brought in to oversee, Mario Bianchi's **The Murder Secret** (1988), Andrea Bianchi's **Massacre** (1989), Leandro Lucchetti's **Bloody Psycho** (1989), Giovanni Simonelli's **Hansel and Gretel** (1989) and Enzo Milioni's **Luna di Sangue** (1989). This unrelenting tide of torturous blood and guts was in many ways a homage to his own achievements, but also dropped a cynical wink to those experts who would have you believe that on-screen violence was precipitant for the atrocities in the world around us. Almost every character in this film was there for the slaughter, whether it was by chainsaw, hatchet or knife. Such was the intensity of the continuous flow of blood, it was almost impossible for the censors to cut, except in Germany where twenty minutes of footage was removed.

When the film was submitted to the BBFC for video release in February 1999, it was rejected because it contained so many sequences detailing unacceptable levels of violence committed against women, which were often sexual in nature. There was a relish apparent in this violence, with the women in certain instances seemingly enjoying their plight. While the BBFC considered the possibility of cutting certain frames, it concluded that the excessive quantity of violence made such an endeavour ultimately fruitless, as it would be unlikely to change the general tone presented in Fulci's film. However, four years later the Board unleashed **Cat in the Brain** on the British public as an "18" uncut. In 2009, Fulci enthusiasts in the United States finally had the chance to see this film just as the Master of Gore had intended. 🦇

Child's Play

📅	YEAR OF RELEASE: 1988
🕐	RUNTIME: 87 minutes
🌐	COUNTRY: USA
🎥	DIRECTOR: Tom Holland
🎬	PRODUCTION COMPANY: United Artists
✒	WRITER: Don Mancini
🎞	CINEMATOGRAPHER: Bill Butler
⏳	PRODUCERS: Elliot Geisinger (co-executive producer), David Kirschner, Laura Moskowitz (associate producer), Barrie M. Osborne (executive producer)
⭕	CERTIFICATE: Australia: M; Canada: 13+ (Quebec); Canada: 14A; Ireland: 18; New Zealand: R16; UK: 15 (uncut) (2005); UK: 15 (cut, 1989); UK: 15; USA: R
💲	BUDGET: $9,000,000
🖥	RECEIPTS: $176,000,000

CAST: Catherine Hicks, Chris Sarandon, Alex Vincent, Brad Dourif, Dinah Manoff, Tommy Swerdlow, Jack Colvin, Neil Giuntoli, Juan Ramírez, Alan Wilder, Richard Baird, Raymond Oliver, Aaron Osborne, Tyler Hard, Ted Liss

CHARLES LEE RAY (Brad Dourif), also known as the Lake Shore Strangler, chases through Chicago's night-time streets, his serial killing ways about to be brought to an end by the gun of Mike Norris (Chris Sarandon). Just before he dies he manages to break into a toyshop and chants a mystical incantation. Huge dark clouds engulf the sky as his evil soul is transferred into the lifeless body of a child's doll. In the same city, Karen Barclay (Catherine Hicks) struggles as a single parent, working on a jewellery counter in a busy department store, to maintain the apartment where she lives with her six-year-old son Andy (Alex Vincent). He can't get enough of the children's television show "Good Guys", and yearns for a Good Guy doll. When he opens his birthday presents and can't find the doll of his dreams,

This doll is a killer.

his disappointment is all too obvious. Karen will do anything to put a smile on her son's face and manages to buy one of the dolls from a peddler for only $30. However, this turns out to be the same doll that was possessed by the monstrous Charlie Lee Ray, who now goes by the name Chucky. Chucky remains lifeless for much of the film, but his blank unfeeling stares are enough to raise a sense of alarm. When he embarks on his bloodshed he uses the stealth and cunning of Charlie Lee Ray to ensure his victims can't slip away. Who would ever suspect a child's toy?

Tom Holland's creepy direction was to surprise the world of horror cinema. With a contrived premise that offered very little flexibility, he created a gripping horror movie with an imaginatively orchestrated air of suspense, much the way Wes Craven had only four years before in **A Nightmare on Elm Street**. Chucky's point-of-view shots kept the audience guessing, but the shocks soon followed as the levels of violence became ever more intense. Holland didn't resort to the more commonplace annoying teenagers and gratuitous sex; instead he cleverly lured his audience and then applied the shock treatment. Maybe he was lucky in that such dolls such as the Cabbage Patch Kids were very much in vogue at that time, or maybe Holland was just born to direct impossible horror movies. His record speaks for itself – he directed **Fright Night** (1985) and has entries in HBO's **Tales from the Crypt** and the **Masters of Horror** series. The final shot of an open door was a portent to the sequels to come, **Child's Play 2** (1990), **Child's Play 3** (1991) – which was surrounded by controversy during the trial of the murder of young Jamie Bulger when the video was found at the house of Jon Venables – **Bride of Chucky** (1998) and **Seed of Chucky** (2004). It was then announced that a darker retelling of this film was scheduled for a release in December 2011. The

Chucky character was also an ideal design for comic books and so followed Innovation Publishing's adaptation of **Child's Play 2** in 1990 along with an ongoing series that commenced a year later, which sadly only ran to five issues. Chucky fans had no need to worry; an adaptation of **Child's Play 3** soon went to press. It wasn't until 2007, when Devil's Due Publishing obtained the licence that the malevolent doll finally returned to comic books. Almost twenty years later Charles Band picked upon this theme to give the world the dubious pleasure of the **Gingerdead Man** (2005), which was followed by a surprising sequel in 2008.

Chopping Mall

 YEAR OF RELEASE: 1986

 RUNTIME: 77 minutes

 COUNTRY: USA

 DIRECTOR: Jim Wynorski

 PRODUCTION COMPANY: Concorde Pictures, Trinity Pictures

WRITERS: Steve Mitchell, Jim Wynorski

 CINEMATOGRAPHER: Tom Richmond

PRODUCERS: Julie Corman, Roger Corman (executive producer), Ginny Nugent (associate producer), Charles Skouras III (associate producer)

CERTIFICATE: Australia: M; Canada: 13+ (Quebec); Canada: R (Ontario); UK: 18; USA: R

BUDGET: $800,000

CAST: Kelli Maroney, Tony O'Dell, Russell Todd, Karrie Emerson, Barbara Crampton, Nick Segal, John Terlesky, Suzee Slater, Paul Bartel, Mary Woronov, Dick Miller, Gerrit Graham, Mel Welles, Angela Aames, Paul Coufos

WITH THE GOLDEN years of the slasher at an end, **Chopping Mall** was released to cash in on the increasingly popular video market. The title proved misleading as a group of teenage mall employees attempted to conceal themselves in the store in preparation for a late night party. It could have been an ideal setting for a slasher movie, but this isn't quite what it appears. The automated security system malfunctions

... they slash their prices – and their customers!

and then goes wild. One by one the three robots try to exterminate the intruders, giving out very little in the way of gore. A suggested title for the film was "Killbots", which would have been far more appropriate.

Christmas Evil

YEAR OF RELEASE: 1980		**CINEMATOGRAPHER:** Ricardo Aronovich	
RUNTIME: 100 minutes		**PRODUCERS:** Pete Kameron, Burt Kleiner, Michael A. Levine (associate producer)	
COUNTRY: USA			
DIRECTOR: Lewis Jackson			
PRODUCTION COMPANY: Edward R. Pressman Film		**CERTIFICATE:** UK: 18; USA: R	
WRITER: Lewis Jackson		**BUDGET:** $750,000	

CAST: Brandon Maggart, Jeffrey DeMunn, Dianne Hull, Andy Fenwick, Brian Neville, Joe Jamrog, Wally Moran, Gus Salud, Ellen McElduff, Brian Hartigan, Peter Neuman, Lance Holcomb, Elizabeth Ridge, Chris Browning, Tyrone Holmes

ON THE CHRISTMAS Eve of 1947, Harry sees his mother being fondled by Santa Claus, who, unbeknown to his young eyes, is actually his father. Unfortunately, this episode of yuletide passion has a traumatic effect upon their son, which becomes manifest thirty-three years later.

Harry (Brandon Maggart) now works hard making toys at the Jolly Dreams toy factory. His home life is a little strange, for he sees himself as Santa Claus and is keen to instil his love for this seasonal jolly giant on all of his colleagues at the factory. From a rooftop vantage, he watches the children to see those who have

been good and those who have been bad, recording his observations in a book that he keeps safely tucked away. However, while he works hard, he comes to realize his colleagues have little regard for him. He is laughed at when he tries to get them to give their unwanted toys to a local children's home. Their laughter triggers his downward spiral; in his mind he really is Santa Claus and he is about to give them all a Christmas they will never forget. Secreted away in his workshop beneath his home, he begins to create toy soldiers armed with swords and axes. He returns to the factory, taking the toys to give to the children, and soon after follows the slaughter with the most graphic murders of the film coming at midnight mass. As Harry's night of slaughter runs out of control, an angry mob carrying flaming torches sets out to find him and chases him through the streets in scenes vaguely reminiscent of Universal's **Frankenstein** features.

Christmas Evil was released as **You Better Watch Out** and on one of its dubious later releases became known as **Terror in Toyland**. It pre-dates the more successful **Silent Night, Deadly Night** (1984) and follows both **Black Christmas** (1974) and **Halloween** (1978) in setting a mass murderer on the loose during a holiday celebration. While **Silent Night, Deadly Night** invited condemnation, Lewis Jackson's obscure film had a somewhat low-key reception. However, it went on to acquire cult status, and was accepted as being an essential part of the seasonal fare. This was in part due to the presence of character actor Brandon Maggart and the film's subversive comedic streak, which included the slapstick being-stuck-in-the-chimney routine, imagining his van is being pulled by reindeer and a police identity line-up of the most scurrilous looking Santas you are ever likely to see. This feature, however, can be looked upon as a psychological study of a man whose obsession becomes so twisted he can't help but lose his mind. Jackson's aim was to make a horror movie, and while it wasn't to adhere to all of the emerging slasher precepts, its violence was graphic, particularly the attack outside the midnight mass where he gouges the eye of one of his victims with a toy soldier and then turns, administering a few machete blows to the head. The title was changed to **Christmas Evil** without Jackson's knowledge; he has since acquired the rights to his film and future releases will go by the original name **You Better Watch Out**.

> **Better watch out . . . Better not cry . . . Or you may DIE!**

City of the Living Dead

📅 YEAR OF RELEASE: 1980	🎬 PRODUCTION COMPANY: Dania Film, Medusa Distribuzione, National Cinematografica
⏱ RUNTIME: 93 minutes	
🌐 COUNTRY: Italy	✎ WRITERS: Lucio Fulci, Dardano Sacchetti
🎥 DIRECTOR: Lucio Fulci	

CINEMATOGRAPHY: Sergio Salvati

PRODUCERS: Lucio Fulci, Giovanni Masini, Robert E. Warner (executive producer), Robert E. Warner (producer: USA)

CERTIFICATE: Australia: R; Canada: 16+ (Quebec); New Zealand: R16; UK: X (original rating: 1981, cut); UK: 18 (re-rating: 1986 cut) (re-rating: 2001 uncut); USA: Unrated

CAST: Christopher George, Catriona MacColl, Carlo De Mejo, Antonella Interlenghi, Giovanni Lombardo Radice, Daniela Doria, Fabrizio Jovine, Luca Venantini, Michele Soavi, Venantino Venantini, Enzo D'Ausilio, Adelaide Aste, Luciano Rossi, Robert Sampson, Janet Agren

I N THE H. P. Lovecraft-inspired haven of Dunwich, New England, a priest Father William Thomas (Fabrizio Jovine) hangs himself in the grounds of the parish cemetery. Although the reasons for what follows are never satisfactorily explained, his suicide throws open the gates of hell. The dead now rise from the earth to end their eternal slumber; the ghoulish priest seen among the first of this unholy horde. The zombies now emerge from the cemetery and begin to scour the town, ripping out their victims' brains and biting into the flesh of all who stand in their way.

Somewhere in New York City, a terrified psychic Mary Woodhouse (Catriona MacColl) collapses and dies during a séance. In death, she experiences a vision of the priest's suicide and the horror that follows. As the police begin their enquiries, another psychic who was present at the séance weeps uncontrollably about the opening of the gates of hell. Peter Bell (Christopher George), an investigative journalist, learns of this strange incident and intent upon furthering his research

goes to visit Mary's grave. As he stands by her unburied coffin, he is shocked when he hears her desperate cries for help. Using a pickaxe, he breaks through the coffin lid in a bid to rescue her, narrowly avoiding hacking her to pieces. She recalls the vision of the priest's death, and the unleashing of a dark force from the very pits of hell. At her insistence, Peter takes her to Dunwich, knowing they must find the remains of the priest before All Saints Day because if he were to arise, the dead will inevitably walk among the living and feed on their flesh. When they eventually reach the town of Dunwich they find the horror has already swept the entire town.

Paura Nella Citta Dei Morti Viventi, also known as **City of the Living Dead** and the **Gates of Hell**, saw Lucio Fulci once again resurrect the dead as he attempted to capture the bloody excess of the previous year's **Zombie Flesh Eaters**, which had seen release in parts of Europe as **Zombi 2**. For the duration of these ninety-three minutes, he succeeded in intensifying the brutality in the imagery from his previous effort and to his credit also

124

created a suitably eerie milieu that was redolent of the works of H. P. Lovecraft, something few filmmakers have ever managed to achieve. This would be the first of three films that witnessed the opening of the gateway to hell. It would be followed by The Beyond (1981), which featured a hotel built over a similarly abstract construct, and then there came the terror lying beneath The House by the Cemetery (1981). City of the Living Dead was also considered the second film in what has been labelled his zombie quartet that began with the Zombie Flesh Eaters and concluded with the two previously mentioned terrors from 1981. On this occasion, Fulci observed a more coherent linear approach to his storytelling than was evidenced twelve months later in The Beyond. To the outsider, however, it resembled a series of disparate episodes, each of which were held together using a wafer-thin premise. Fulci's vision was such he wanted his films to be viewed as a whole, rather than a separate series of unrelated incidents made up of actors, dialogue, scenery, lighting and sound. Viewed in this light, his approach become somewhat easier to understand.

When his cast arrived in Dunwich, they were greeted by the disquiet of a series of Gothic sets immersed in a mist-bound locale that threatened to erupt into hideous violence. Amidst the murk, he created a creepy air of suspense as the dead were briefly caught by the camera's

From the bowels of the earth they came to collect the living . . .

eye and then simply vanished. Gino De Rossi's gore effects were to become the source of much discussion, with a considerable amount of attention being placed on an offending drill as it was bored deep into a victim's face. Further excess would follow with an array of worm-ridden carcasses, eyes that bled, intestines seen to vomit before the camera's gaze and heads brutally torn open to expose the luscious sight of the human brain. Fulci's films had been guilty of greater atrocities, but City of the Living Dead was immediately classified as an "X" when it went for cinematic release in the UK. The BBFC were not entirely enamoured with the drill scene and as a result it was cut from the original release. Further editing came when it was issued to video with cuts to the vomiting scenes and unsightly brain removal. Fulci's second splatterfest wouldn't be seen in it all of its bloodthirsty glory in the UK until the unedited release of 2001. Even though the entire movie was now available, the finale continued to arouse much debate. It has always been considered that the evil priest and his supernatural zombies were all too easily defeated, making many wonder if the director's meagre funding had just run out or was it possible some of the footage had been lost during the editing process. Unlike the two films that followed in the gateway to hell trilogy, the denouement failed to satisfy and begged many questions. 🌿

Cold Prey

📅 **YEAR OF RELEASE:** 2006	
🕐 **RUNTIME:** 97 minutes	
🌐 **COUNTRY:** Norway	
🎥 **DIRECTOR:** Roar Uthaug	
🎬 **PRODUCTION COMPANY:** Fantefilm	
✒ **WRITERS:** Thomas Moldestad, Roar Uthaug, Martin Sundland, Jan Eirik Langoen, Magne Lyngner	

🎞 **CINEMATOGRAPHER:** Daniel Voldheim

🎬 **PRODUCERS:** Axel Helgeland (executive producer), Jan Eirik Langoen (line producer), Magne Lyngner, Thomas Løberg (associate producer), Guttorm Petterson (co-producer), Martin Sundland

⭕ **CERTIFICATE:** Australia: MA; UK: 15; USA: Not Rated

CAST: Ingrid Bolsø Berdal, Rolf Kristian Larsen, Tomas Alf Larsen, Endre Martin Midtstigen, Viktoria Winge, Rune Melby, Erik Skjeggedal, Tonie Lunde, Hallvard Holmen

SNOW FALLS ONTO a struggling scar-faced teenager, as an obscured felon attempts to bury him alive. The newspaper headlines, which date back to 1975, are obsessed with the authorities' efforts to find the boy and his assailant, alas to no avail. Thirty years later a group of amiable young friends are on their way to the same region, Jotunheimen, with the prospect of a few days' snowboarding on the slopes. En route, Young Morten (Rolf Kristian Larsen) accidently breaks his leg, forcing the party to seek shelter overnight in an abandoned mountain hotel. They very quickly discover the phones have been out of action for many years, so any immediate chance of rescue is out of the question. While exploring the isolated hotel they learn it was closed to the public in 1975 when the proprietors' son went missing in the surrounding mountains. Eirik (Tomas Alf Larsen) then sets off to get help, but he doesn't get far for there is a pickaxe-wielding psychopath prowling the grounds and the kids are soon to be his quarry. They don't know it yet, but the Mountain Man is Norway's answer to Michael Myers.

Fritt Vilt was highly derivative of the North American slasher movies of the early 1980s and while it didn't bring anything new to the concept it was the premiere for a fine young director in the guise of Roar Uthaug, whose work was introduced to a far wider audience than he had at first anticipated. Four years before, he had graduated from the Norwegian Film School, and looked set for a career in commercials and music videos. This was his first time in the director's chair on a major production and he began his story very slowly, creating a likeable cast of characters before delivering them to this atmospheric setting, which oozed an unsettling aura of suspense. Such was his precise direction he was able to bring something new to the clichés of over twenty years past and gave the world his resourceful heroine, Jannicke, played by the talented Ingrid Bolsø Berdal. Praise was also lauded on this film thanks to the fluid cinematography of Daniel Voldheim, which savoured these stunning northerly landscapes before turning its attention to the claustrophobic shadows

Prepare for your final descent.

of the deserted hotel. The hotel contained an affectionate wink to Stanley Kubrick's telling of Stephen King's **The Shining** (1980), when one of the couples chooses room 217 for their stay, a portent of doom if ever there was one.

True to the slasher craze of the 1980s, this success was followed by a couple of sequels, **Cold Prey 2: Resurrection** was released in 2008 with Jannicke awakening in a hospital bed, while the latest sequel **Cold Prey 3** (2010) returned to a series of grisly events in the 1980s. This film also paved the way for another Norwegian modern-day slasher, Patrik Syversen's **Manhunt (Rovdyr)** in 2008.

Color Me Blood Red

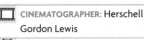

 YEAR OF RELEASE: 1965

 RUNTIME: 79 minutes

COUNTRY: USA

DIRECTOR: Herschell Gordon Lewis

 PRODUCTION COMPANY: Box Office Spectaculars

 WRITER: Herschell Gordon Lewis

CINEMATOGRAPHER: Herschell Gordon Lewis

PRODUCERS: David F. Friedman

CERTIFICATE: Australia: R; New Zealand: R16; UK: 18; USA: Unrated

BUDGET: $50,000

CAST: Gordon Oas-Heim (Don Joseph), Candi Conder, Elyn Warner, Pat Lee, Jerome Eden, Scott H. Hall, Jim Jaekel, Iris Marshall, William Harris, Cathy Collins

WHILE **Color Me Blood Red** was completed in early 1964, it sat on the shelf for over a year as producer David F. Friedman went through the lengthy process of terminating his business relationship with director Herschell Gordon Lewis. When it finally did appear, its low-budget production values saw it recognized as a fitting conclusion to the "Blood Trilogy". B-movie enthusiasts of the period would very quickly observe an obvious parallel with Roger Corman's **Bucket of Blood** (1959), although the acting was never the match of its predecessor.

Don Joseph, or Gordon Oas-Heim, takes the lead role as Adam Sorg, a frustrated painter unable to interest the public in the purchase of his work. After having his efforts sneered at during a local exhibition at the Farnsworth Galleries, he returns to his studio in search of inspiration. When his model Gigi accidentally cuts herself and her blood drips onto the canvas, he finds the revelation for which he has been searching, resulting in an uncontrollable frenzy at the easel. Gigi squeezes every bit of blood she can muster, but it is never going to be enough. It is not long before Sorg has to slice into his own fingers to set loose fresh pigment. He needs to complete the painting he has promised, but realizes it will be impossible to maintain this approach, so he returns to his original supply. Without so

much as a word of warning, he stabs Gigi in the face and turns her bloody head into a brush to put the finishing touches to his painting. Having buried Gigi's body, Sorg takes his masterpiece to display in the gallery. Commercial considerations are now of little import; he seeks the praise of the critics to give him the inspiration to pursue this new medium in the confines of his studio. Potential buyers petition to make their acquisition, but Sorg refuses to sell. He is now fuelled with a passion to create, but he needs to secure another source of this unique pigment. The slaughter now begins as he sets about the murder of other models to achieve his artistic lust.

Lewis heightened the gore factor in his film when Sorg took to the opportunistic stalking of a young couple, before engaging a spear to stab the man, Norman, through the chest. Sorg subdues his screaming girlfriend Betty and steals her away. He is next seen standing before his bloodstrewn canvas. Having exhausted his palette he enters the next room, where Betsy's dead body is tied to a wall, her intestines hanging from her bleeding stomach. Lewis exacts every last morsel from this scene; he has Sorg squeeze more blood from the disembowelled girl before he returns to complete his insane masterpiece. The next day the bloodthirsty artist takes his creation to the gallery and once again refuses to sell. Instead, Sorg storms out of the gallery, failing to realize his

A blood-splattered study in the macabre!

painting is still wet. Herschell G. Lewis's cult following regard **Color Me Blood Red** as the least imaginative of his gory trilogy, lacking the spontaneity that had heralded **Blood Feast** (1963) and revealing little of the excess that had shocked with **Two Thousand Maniacs!** (1964). Sadly, there was nothing new on show and far too much padding was in evidence, particularly the tiresome beach party antics of the local teenagers. The gore-mongers of the day would have still drooled over the shots detailing Betty's ruptured intestines; such hideous scenes at this time were something of a novelty in American cinema. During the making of this movie, Lewis and Friedman considered making a fourth "Blood" film, entitled **Suburban Roulette**. Friedman, however, thought better of it, certain that the "super blood and gore" film market was at saturation point. He took the decision to abandon the series, leaving it to remain in the annals of cinematic horror as a bloody trilogy.

Communion

📅 YEAR OF RELEASE: 1976	🏭 PRODUCERS: Marc G. Greenberg (associate producer), Richard K. Rosenberg, Alfred Sole (executive producer)
🕐 RUNTIME: 98 minutes	
🌐 COUNTRY: USA	
🎥 DIRECTOR: Alfred Sole	⭕ CERTIFICATE: Australia: R (DVD rating); UK: 18; USA: R
🎬 PRODUCTION COMPANY: Harristown Funding	
✏️ WRITERS: Rosemary Ritvo, Alfred Sole	💲 BUDGET: $340,000

CAST: Linda Miller, Mildred Clinton, Paula E. Sheppard, Niles McMaster, Jane Lowry, Rudolph Willrich, Michael Hardstark, Alphonso DeNoble, Gary Allen, Brooke Shields, Louisa Horton, Tom Signorelli, Lillian Roth, Patrick Gorman, Kathy Rich

SET IN A rain-swept New Jersey of 1963, the withdrawn twelve-year-old Alice Spages (Paula E. Sheppard) lives with her mother, Catherine (Linda Miller) and younger sister, Karen (Brooke Shields). Their lives are enveloped by the influential Catholic church with Karen making preparations for her first holy communion. Alice is obviously jealous of her sister and cruelly torments her, stealing her doll before locking her away while wearing a transparent mask. As Karen puts on her white veil and readies herself for her communion, she is strangled in the church by a figure who wears a child's yellow raincoat and a mask identical to that worn by her spiteful sister. Alice then takes her place wearing her sister's veil, which she maintains she picked up from the floor. She soon becomes the prime suspect in the murder of her sister. Can this emotionally disturbed child really be a killer? Maybe not, for as she retreats to her basement shrine surrounded by an assortment of curious paraphernalia, a figure is seen stalking the hallways of her apartment building.

If you survive this night . . . nothing will scare you again.

Alfred Sole's little-known slasher was released a couple of years later as **Alice Sweet Alice**, the title by which it is more commonly known, and in 1981 as **Holy Terror**. This stylish movie would have remained in relative obscurity if it hadn't been for an appearance by Brooke Shields, who two years later attracted controversy in Louis Malle's **Pretty Baby** (1978) and then opened a few eyes in **Blue Lagoon** (1980). With Columbia Pictures having reneged on their interest in distributing this independently made

movie, Allied Artists stepped into the frame. They demanded a change to the title's religious theme, fearing it would affect the public's perception of the film's content and ultimately hinder its prospects at the box office.

The change in title would not alter the observations being made of the Catholic Church in a modern-day inner city environment, but in its deliberation on the loss of innocence and the ensuing deep-rooted remorse, **Communion** had an unusual affiliation with Nicholas Roeg's **Don't Look Now** (1972). Sole, however, ventured considerably further in his narrative; he moved to challenge and question the notion of clerical celibacy. His use of the child's plastic raincoat would again evoke memories of Roeg's seminal tragedy, although the mask that was often found in the gialli of the day actually predated John Carpenter's creation for **Halloween** by two years. *Communion*, the novel written by Frank Lauria, was released in conjunction with the film through Bantam Books.

Contamination

	YEAR OF RELEASE: 1980			**PRODUCTION COMPANY:** Alex Cinematografica, Barthonia Film, Lisa-Film
	RUNTIME: 95 minutes			
	COUNTRY: Italy/West Germany			**WRITERS:** Luigi Cozzi, Erich Tomek
	DIRECTOR: Luigi Cozzi			

CINEMATOGRAPHER: Giuseppe Pinori	CERTIFICATE: Australia: R; Canada: 13+
PRODUCERS: Claudio Mancini, Ugo Valenti (associate producer)	(Quebec); Canada: R (Ontario); UK: 18 (original 1980s video release); UK: (Banned) (1984–2004); UK: 15 (video rating, 2004); USA: R

CAST: Ian McCulloch, Louise Marleau, Marino Masé, Siegfried Rauch, Gisela Hahn, Carlo De Mejo, Carlo Monni

AN ABANDONED SHIP is observed drifting into New York harbour. When it is boarded by Lt. Tony Aris (Marino Mase) and his team of officers, thousands of containers of coffee are discovered, each concealing strange green pods. Shock after shock follows as the decimated remains of the former crew are uncovered below decks. They have fallen prey to this clutch of outlandish eggs, for when the temperature begins to rise they start to hum and then detonate, releasing a toxic liquid which, if it makes contact with the human body, consequently causes it to explode.

Colonel Stella Holmes (Louise Marleau) has been assigned to the case and it isn't long before she determines a link between the appearance of the deadly pods and the recent catastrophic mission to Mars. On the journey through space one of the astronauts disappeared without trace while the other, Commander Hubbard (Ian McCulloch), suffered a nervous breakdown on his return and

You can feel them in your blood!

hit the bottle. The indomitable Holmes has to convince Hubbard to help her to ensure the toxic cargo is returned to Manhattan; only then can she successfully continue her investigation. Their findings lead them on a trail to a coffee plantation in Colombia. Here they locate the missing astronaut from the flight to Mars is alive. Unknown to them his mind, however, is no longer his own; he has been infiltrated by an evil spider-like alien they call Cyclops. This monstrous creature's intent is to swallow the world with its lethal eggs and, as it has done on other worlds, annihilate life across the entire planet.

Contamination, which has also been packaged as **Alien Contamination**, **Contamination: Alien on Earth**, Toxic Spawn, **Contaminazione**, and **Alien 2**, was Luigi Cozzi's follow-up to his Italian box office hit **Starcrash** (1978). In the wake of this success he was keen to become involved with another science fiction venture and very soon found himself directing the first of many features to be inspired by Ridley Scott's **Alien** (1979). The pitiful budget meant that this was to be kept on Earth, and filming was completed over a five-week period, working between Rome, New York City, Florida and Colombia. Sadly, even with its eerie Goblin soundtrack, Cozzi's film did not fare very well on its Italian release, but as with so many of its contemporaries, it was to acquire a quite particular notoriety. As limited as the budget was, Cozzi delivered a series of graphic slow-motion effects to quite literally explode his cast before the camera's lens and their bloody remains spill forth over the set. This visceral excess saw the video cited in the UK as yet another video nasty in October 1983, with the film consigned to the list until January 1985.

When it was released to video by ViP and then European Creative Films, two minutes and forty seconds of cuts had to be made to guarantee it a place on the video shops' shelves. These were earmarked for the opening sequence, where a dead man's decomposing body was found in a cupboard, along with the graphic blast of several men after tampering with the alien pods as well as facial explosions and lingering shots of exploding human guts. There were further cuts to numerous gory explosions seen later in the film and finally the devouring of a man's head by the alien queen. As the years rolled by, attitudes changed and in 2004 the BBFC passed the Anchor Bay DVD as "15" uncut.

As Cozzi's film hit the Italian big screen, Ciro Ippolito released another unauthorized low-budget sequel to Ridley Scott's terrifying masterpiece, **Alien 2 – On Earth or Sulla Terra**. The claustrophobia of the Nostromo was replaced by a pot-holing descent into deep caves in California. Both Cozzi and Ippolito would continue to write and direct for many years to come, carving out highly successful careers in Italian film and television.

Creep

YEAR OF RELEASE: 2004	**PRODUCERS:** Julie Baines, Alexandra Ferguson (line producer), Martin Hagemann (co-producer), Barry Hanson (co-producer), Robert Jones (executive producer), Kai Künnemann (co-producer), Jason Newmark
RUNTIME: 85 minutes	
COUNTRY: UK	
DIRECTOR: Christopher Smith	
PRODUCTION COMPANY: UK Film Council, Filmstiftung Nordrhein-Westfalen, Dan Films, Zero Film GmbH	**CERTIFICATE:** Australia: R; Canada: 13+ (Quebec); Canada: 14A (Ontario); Canada: 18A (Manitoba); Ireland: 18; New Zealand: R18; UK: 18; USA: R (cut)
WRITER: Christopher Smith	
CINEMATOGRAPHER: Danny Cohen	**RECEIPTS:** £1,728,375 (UK 2005)

CAST: Vas Blackwood, Ken Campbell, Kathryn Gilfeather, Franka Potente, Grant Ibbs, Joe Anderson, Jeremy Sheffield, Sean De Vrind, Ian Duncan, Debora Weston, Emily Gilchrist, Craig Fackrell, Elizabeth McKechnie, Kelly Scott, Strapper appears as Ray the Dog

AS THEY GO about their daily routine in the upkeep of the London sewage system, two operatives, Arthur (Ken Campbell) and George (Vas Blackwood), uncover a tunnel they haven't previously encountered. Their exploration of this dark passageway brings them face to face with a deathly flesh-eating abomination.

Heading home late one night after a party, Kate (Franka Potente), a repellant London socialite, falls asleep on the platform while waiting for the last train. She awakens to find herself trapped in the bowels of the London underground, with all the exits firmly locked until early morning. By chance, a deserted train making its return to the depot draws up at the platform. She boards one of the carriages and meets the overly fixated Guy (Jeremy Sheffield) seen earlier at the party; she becomes the object of his desire before his thoughts turn to rape. During the attack, the creature from the film's opening scenes makes a return and drags him away, having already butchered the driver. Thus begins a nightmarish ordeal in the disorientating claustrophobia of these dimly lit tunnels, as Kate and a young homeless couple are stalked by a malfeasance with an instinct for vicious slaughter. Her path takes her deeper into the warren and on into the sewage system, where she discovers an abandoned subterranean surgery. Only then does she realize the nature of the beast.

The comparatively low-budget **Creep** has been compared to another British shocker from the past, the almost forgotten cannibal killer **Death Line** (1972), which made a similar descent into the London Underground. Christopher Smith confessed he had no knowledge of this almost forgotten precursor at the time of his shoot; rather, he referred to the underground scenes from **An American Werewolf in London** (1981) as his source of inspiration. Like many other regular passengers on the London Underground, Smith had been frustrated by the experience of being stranded in one of the system's many tunnels for an overly long period and having to endure the sweat-ridden irritation of not knowing what was going on; not surprisingly for a man of his integrity this stimulated an idea. While he may not have mustered the hefty backing of the American studios, Smith wasn't remiss when it came to serving up the grisly mayhem by the bucket load in a tense and well-paced splatterfest that harked back to the Italian predilection for gore during the late 1970s and on into the 1980s. The ruthlessly determined and selfish figure of Kate didn't have the vulnerable qualities of the final girl of two decades past; her bourgeois tendencies made it very difficult to applaud her efforts as she sought to escape the creature that wanted so badly to savour her flesh.

As **Creep** progressed, the audience's sympathy turned to the cannibalistic villain of the piece, poor Craig, who just couldn't help himself.

The Curse of Frankenstein

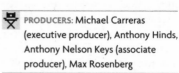

📅	YEAR OF RELEASE: 1957	🎬	PRODUCERS: Michael Carreras (executive producer), Anthony Hinds, Anthony Nelson Keys (associate producer), Max Rosenberg
🕐	RUNTIME: 82 minutes		
🌐	COUNTRY: UK		
🎥	DIRECTOR: Terence Fisher	⭕	CERTIFICATE: Australia: M; Canada: PG (Ontario); UK: 12 (video re-rating); UK: 15 (video rating) (1989); UK: X (original rating) (2003); USA: Approved
🎞	PRODUCTION COMPANY: Hammer Film Productions		
✏️	WRITERS: Jimmy Sangster, Mary Shelley		
🎞	CINEMATOGRAPHER: Jack Asher	💲	BUDGET: £65,000
		🗂	RECEIPTS: $7,000,000

CAST: Peter Cushing, Hazel Court, Robert Urquhart, Christopher Lee, Melvyn Hayes, Valerie Gaunt, Paul Hardtmuth, Noel Hood, Fred Johnson, Claude Kingston, Alex Gallier, Michael Mulcaster, Andrew Leigh, Ann Blake, Sally Walsh

CHARGED WITH MURDER, Baron Victor Frankenstein (Peter Cushing) awaits the guillotine. From the confines of his prison cell, he tells a priest the story of how he created life from reconstituted dead bodies and how his creation escaped to commit the crimes of which he has been accused. For years, the Baron dedicated himself to studying under his teacher and friend Paul Krempe (Robert Urquhart). Their time together in the laboratory seems to be the orphaned Baron's only reason for living. As they further their endeavours, their experimentation miraculously returns a dead dog to life. Victor's obsession demands they build on this success with a view to creating human life. Krempe refuses to become involved with such a heinous scheme and warns of the dangers of tampering with the forces of nature. Although he is opposed to his former protégé's macabre designs, he stays on in the house to protect

Victor's fiancée Elizabeth (Hazel Court), in what appears to be little more than an arranged marriage. Victor is oblivious to Elizabeth's needs; he thinks only of his compulsive research and the nurturing of his abominable child, a victim of the gallows pole, who now lies incarcerated in a fluid-filled tank. He later acquires the hands and then the eyes just before turning on the electricity to breathe life into his bizarre creation (Christopher Lee). The creature's brain, however, has been damaged and very soon it will break free to doom its surrogate father.

The experienced Terence Fisher was given the creative freedom to reinterpret this classic, and he took considerable care to ensure the details in set design and costumes were appropriate for this celebrated Gothic-styled tragedy. **Curse of Frankenstein** was Hammer's first venture into pure horror although the studio's **Quatermass Xperiment** (1955) had contained more than a smattering of terror. It was also the first Hammer movie to be shot in colour, making ample use of the lurid capabilities of Eastmancolor, and more significantly was the first terror-based pairing of one of the genre's most renowned duos, Christopher Lee and Peter Cushing. Surprisingly Lee was only considered for the role when Bernard Bresslaw's agent demanded a little more than Hammer could afford. This film, along with their masterpiece of the following

All new and never dared before!

year, **The Horror of Dracula**, was to define the company's way of thinking for their forthcoming excursions into horror, which continued for almost twenty years. Its ever so tepid application of gore was but the beginning of the genre's predilection for sanguinary excess, although in its day it was to upset many of the critics as the public flocked by the thousand to savour its gruesome pageant.

Universal had already threatened to sue Hammer if they were seen to imitate the make-up first used on Boris Karloff's monster, so it was left to Phil Leakey to create something no one had before seen. His skill coupled with Lee's portrayal made the monster every bit as terrifying as it had been at Universal and in the eyes of many of Mary Shelley's ardent enthusiasts, his design was far closer to the description alluded to in the original novel of 1818. Leakey, however, was never happy with his work, being denied both the time and budget to create the impression for which he would have hoped and ultimately been remembered. This wouldn't prevent Hammer's Frankenstein creation from returning for another six outings in, **The Revenge of Frankenstein** (1958), **The Evil of Frankenstein** (1964), **Frankenstein Created Woman** (1967), **Frankenstein Must Be Destroyed** (1969), **The Horror of Frankenstein** (1970) and **Frankenstein and the Monster from Hell** (1973). 🦇

Curtains

📅	YEAR OF RELEASE: 1983	🎞	CINEMATOGRAPHER: Robert Paynter
🕐	RUNTIME: 89 minutes	⏳	PRODUCERS: Peter R. Simpson, Richard Simpson (executive producer)
⭐	COUNTRY: Canada		
🎬	DIRECTOR: Richard Ciupka	⭕	CERTIFICATE: Australia: M; UK: 18; USA: R
🎥	PRODUCTION COMPANY: Simcom Limited, Curtains Productions		
✒	WRITER: Robert Guza Jr.	💲	BUDGET: $700,000 Canadian

CAST: John Vernon, Samantha Eggar, Linda Thorson, Anne Ditchburn, Lynne Griffin, Sandee Currie, Lesleh Donaldson, Deborah Burgess, Michael Wincott, Maury Chaykin, Joann McIntyre, Calvin Butler, Kate Lynch, Booth Savage, William Marshall

AFTER BRINGING DIRECTOR Jonathan Stryker (John Vernon) the rights to his new film, "Audra", Samantha Sherwood (Samantha Eggar) assumes she will be given the lead role. Audra was a dangerously psychotic woman and the only way for a method actress of Samantha's calibre to become immersed in this woman's hopelessly deranged character is to appear insane and be committed to an asylum. While confined to the sanatorium her performance becomes a little too convincing and Stryker takes the decision to leave her there. He now has to find a new Audra and auditions six young women in the privacy of his remote New England mansion. One of these women tempts fate and openly admits she would be prepared to kill for her part in this film.

Miles away from this secluded location Samantha has managed to escape her self-imposed incarceration, and arrives at the manse just as a crone-masked killer embarks upon the slaughter of these young hopefuls.

Following the success of **Prom Night** (1980) the Canada-based production team of Peter and Richard Simpson went straight into production with former cameraman Belgium-born Richard Ciupka, now promoted to directorial duties, to make a film that drifted into near obscurity before achieving a quite unique cult following. To say **Curtains** had a problematic production is an understatement. A few weeks into the shoot, the original lead actress, Celine Lamez, was fired when she refused to appear in a full frontal nude scene. Her scenes then had to be repeated, using her understudy Linda Thornson, thus adding to the film's spiralling expenses. Once the shoot had been completed, many scenes were heavily edited leaving gaping holes in what should have been a reasonably linear plot. Meanwhile the backers were becoming increasingly concerned with Ciupka's ability as a director, which led to him walking away from the film and Peter Simpson completing the second part of the shoot. Three years later **Curtains** was finally ready for release, but made very little impression on a market which by then was completely saturated by the slasher phenomenon. However, in keeping with the terrors of these years, this film refused to remain buried and acquired a more accepting audience when issued to video.

The VHS phenomenon of the 1980s certainly helped in bringing this film to a new audience, but this would have only ever worked if it had followed

Behind every curtain, someone is watching … something is waiting!

the now established conventions of the slasher trope. It achieved this by creating an unsettling milieu became immersed in this murderous episode, principally in the form of an old house, which on many occasions has provided a fitting backdrop. **Curtains** could also boast one of the more memorable kills of the slasher years, the 'skate and slash' of Christie (Lesleh Donaldson) as she joyfully skated in the early morning to an eighties tune, only to discover a strange looking doll buried under the snow. It was then the killer engaged his pursuit, in a series of expertly choreographed chase scenes. This was almost matched by the final kill in the shadows of the claustrophobic prop room that ensured so much of the film's eerie premise was brought to a climactic finale. Ciupka would put this film behind him as he continued his career behind the camera and returned to the director's chair at the beginning of the 1990s ✤

Dawn of the Dead

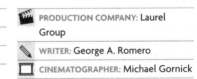

📅 YEAR OF RELEASE: 1978	🎬 PRODUCTION COMPANY: Laurel Group
🕐 RUNTIME: 126 minutes	✏️ WRITER: George A. Romero
🌐 COUNTRY: Italy, USA	
🎥 DIRECTOR: George A. Romero	🎞️ CINEMATOGRAPHER: Michael Gornick

PRODUCERS: Claudio Argento (associate producer), Alfredo Cuomo (associate producer), Richard P. Rubinstein, Donna Siegel (associate producer)

 CERTIFICATE: Australia: R; Canada: 13+ (Quebec) (2004); Canada: R (Manitoba/Ontario); Canada: 18+ (Quebec) (Original rating); Ireland: 18; New Zealand: R16 (DVD rating); UK: 18 (video rating, 1987); UK: X (original rating, cut); USA: X (original rating); USA: Open (rating surrendered, 1983); USA: Unrated (theatrical rating, rating surrendered)

 BUDGET: $650,000

 RECEIPTS: $55,000,000

CAST: David Emge, Ken Foree, Scott H. Reiniger, Gaylen Ross, David Crawford, David Early, Richard France, Howard Smith, Daniel Dietrich, Fred Baker, James A. Baffico, Rod Stouffer, Jese Del Gre, Clayton McKinnon, John Rice

HYSTERIA AND DISBELIEF engulf a television station as it reports on the zombie apocalypse that has now spiralled out of control. While a scientific expert fails to offer an explanation as to why this catastrophe is sweeping the globe, he carries a warning that even those walking dead recognized as friends and family can no longer be considered so; they are all abominations with but one craving – the pleasure of human flesh.

Two national guards, a reporter and her pilot boyfriend flee the besieged city of Philadelphia on board a helicopter. They land at a deserted shopping mall where they look to seek refuge, first slaying the zombies who have made their way into the complex and then by obstructing the large glass doors at the entry with vehicles. As they fight to clear the mall one of the national guards is bitten by the contaminated breed; it won't be long before he takes his place among this mindless herd.

After making this shopper's paradise their own, the four settle in to their new life, but all too soon they realize that while they are safe from a society in collapse, they are little more than prisoners. The gravity of their situation is compounded by the revelation that Francine is pregnant and then a gang of bikers explode into the mall. They break down the doors, allowing droves of zombies to run amok in the halls and corridors of this huge shopping complex. As the bikers ride around the stores taking an insane pleasure in gunning down the zombies, a gun battle ensues with the team. The pilot takes a shot to the arm before being attacked by zombies in an elevator. The zombies then turn on the bike gang, who make a hasty retreat leaving the mall besieged by this deranged infestation. Only Francine the reporter and Peter, one of the national guards, make it to the roof to take a helicopter on into a country that has fallen into madness.

George A. Romero's **Dawn of the Dead**, which is also known as **Zombi** and **Zombie: Dawn of the Dead**, marked the second instalment in his Living Dead series. The zombie outbreak that plagued **Night of the Living Dead** (1968) has now spread across the world; the original cast of characters, however, never gain a mention. Romero had hoped to produce a more ambitious sequel to his cult phenomenon of 1968, but his subsequent films hadn't been particularly successful, which made it difficult to finance the extravagant venture he had envisaged at a time when zombie movies were not in vogue. The idea had come in 1974, when Romero was invited to visit the Monroeville Mall. It had started as a joke, the idea that someone could survive in the mall should a catastrophe befall the country, but what had been intended as meaningless banter inspired Romero, who began to write the screenplay for what would become **Dawn of the Dead**. Unable to secure US funding, Dario Argento, who was an acknowledged admirer of **Night of the Living Dead**, announced he was willing to assist Romero in his project in exchange for international

distribution rights. Argento had only recently acquired an international reputation with the loaded **Deep Red** (1975) and **Suspiria** (1977).

With its savage depiction of flesh eating, dismemberment and exploding heads, **Dawn of the Dead** on its 1979 US release was without doubt the goriest film to have come out of America. Tom Savini's sanguinary effects were to set the standard for a new generation of visceral zombie movies and ensured he would never be out of work, although much of his subsequent efforts were to endure heavy censorship on both sides of the Atlantic. Romero's script was laced with dark humour and, as with his previous films, notably **Night of the Living Dead** and **The Crazies** (1973), he induced an undercurrent of social commentary which didn't get in the way of the requisite chomp of the zombie horde. While in the mall, he presented a vision of a pleasure-seeking America unaware that complete social collapse was a stone's throw from its own doors. Beneath the seeming lustre, there was a country ignorant to the ravages of corporate consumerism, one that had already forgotten the political strife of the decade before.

> **In 1968, George Romero brought us *Night of the Living Dead*. It became the classic horror film of its time. Now, George Romero brings us the most intensely shocking motion picture experience for all time.**

The film was premiered in Italy in the September of 1978 as **Zombi: L'alba dei Morti Viventi**, nine months prior to its release in the US. Romero's splatterfest captured the imagination of the Italian public and proved to be a turning point for Lucio Fulci, who looked to direct a so-called sequel, **Zombie 2**, better known as **Zombie Flesh Eaters** (1979) and **Zombie**. His film was also immensely popular and paved the way for some of the most memorable horror movies of the next few years. On its eventual American release the reviews were largely accepting of **Dawn of the Dead**'s excessive gore and its receipts at the box office secured Romero's career. He returned with the first of his official sequels with **Day of the Dead** (1985), and twenty years later came **Land of the Dead** (2005), **Diary of the Dead** (2007) and **Survival of the Dead** (2009). **Dawn of the Dead** was remade in 2004. A television show loosely based on the films is still in the planning stages. 🍁

Day of the Dead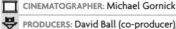

 YEAR OF RELEASE: 1985

 RUNTIME: 102 minutes

 COUNTRY: USA

 DIRECTOR: George A. Romero

 PRODUCTION COMPANY: Dead Films Inc., Laurel Entertainment Inc., Laurel-Day Inc.

 WRITER: George A. Romero

CINEMATOGRAPHER: Michael Gornick

PRODUCERS: David Ball (co-producer), Salah M. Hassanein, Ed Lammi, Richard P. Rubinstein

 CERTIFICATE: Australia: R; Canada: 18+ (Quebec) (video rating, 1998); Canada: (Banned) (Nova Scotia/ Ontario) (uncut version); Canada: R (Ontario) (cut); Canada: R (Manitoba); Canada: 14A (Ontario) (Re-rated 2008); Ireland: 18; UK: 18 (video re-rating) (1997); UK: 18 (original rating, cut); UK: 18 (video rating) (1986, cut); USA: Unrated

 BUDGET: $3,500,000

RECEIPTS: $34,000,000

CAST: Lori Cardille, Terry Alexander, Joseph Pilato, Jarlath Conroy, Anthony Dileo Jr., Richard Liberty, Sherman Howard, Gary Howard Klar, Ralph Marrero, John Amplas, Phillip G. Kellams, Taso N. Stavrakis, Gregory Nicotero, Don Brockett, William Cameron

THE FINAL PART of George A. Romero's trilogy opens with a group of people searching for survivors in the devastated streets of Fort Myers, Florida. Their efforts go unrewarded, attracting instead an unwelcome gathering of zombies. Frustrated, they make their return to an underground silo where we learn they are assigned to a military backed scientific detachment researching the zombie epidemic. The tension between the scientists and the military has been mounting for some time as their supplies have slowly diminished and little progress has been observed in the experiments on the zombie specimens held captive in the bunker's maze of underground tunnels.

Dr Logan, the facility's head scientist, borders on insanity. He has been surreptitiously using dead soldiers in his research and remains steadfast in his belief that the zombies can be calmed and trained. If his experiments were ever discovered, he would be executed. This, however, does not deter him; he appears almost oblivious to the threat that surrounds him. In his laboratory, he keeps his prize specimen, Bub, a seemingly docile zombie who has exhibited a menial recognition of his past. The herded zombies, however, remain as dangerous as ever and it is no surprise when they break free of their restraints, and begin ripping and biting into the soldiers and one of the scientists. Rhodes, the military head of the base, is furious with this turn of events and declares the operation is to be terminated and the zombie specimens

The darkest day of horror the world has ever known.

destroyed. Logan can't stop himself; he is soon after found feeding human flesh to Bub and Rhodes makes the grisly discovery in the freezer of the remains of his soldiers. As the audience always knew, Logan would one day have to pay the price for his gruesome experimentation. It isn't long before the zombies have completely overrun the caves as the military fall into chaos and Bub exacts his revenge on Rhodes for the killing of Logan. Those who survive manage to make it to a helicopter only to be confronted by another marauding band of zombies. Just when the audience is convinced that the apocalypse has consumed the heroes of the piece, Romero proves himself benign as he bestows upon his surviving cast an optimistic epilogue with the heroine of the story, Sarah, awakening on a beautiful beach, with the helicopter in the distance. Close by, her fellow survivors enjoy the surf as she crosses off another day on her calendar.

George A. Romero was offered seven million dollars to turn his latest script into another full-length film; in return it was insisted he make an R-rated film suitable for release to the corporate cinema chains that had become commonplace across the United States. Romero declined. He was adamant his grisly feature could only ever appear as an Unrated film;

anything less would have been a compromise. The investors were all too aware that if they agreed to Romero's demands, his proposal would receive only a very limited release that would make it difficult to see a healthy return on their investment. The budget was subsequently halved. This made it impossible for Romero to produce the film he had so carefully planned. He was forced to re-write and scale down his script, although elements would surface twenty years later in **Land of the Dead** (2005). On its eventual release, the cinema-going public overlooked his film; at that time it was but one of many horror movies, most of them being "R" rated, which included **Re-Animator, Fright Night**, and **Return of the Living Dead**. Those who did see **Day of the Dead** were unsettled by it dark premise and cast of unsympathetic characters. The film was indeed grim, but unlike its precursors in the trilogy it did offer the faintest glimmer of hope at the finale.

The social commentary permeating **Dawn of the Dead** was largely forgotten, although Romero had hoped to demonstrate how a lack of communication could result in chaos and collapse. Pandemonium ran rife, and once again droves of zombies were set loose with Tom Savini's team, creating some of the most realistic splatter scenes of their career. Bodies were ripped apart and the zombies looked more disgusting than ever before with an array of bite marks and atrophied faces. A direct-to-DVD prequel set in 1968, written and directed by Ana Clavell, was released in 2005, entitled **Day of the Dead 2: Contagium**. A remake of **Day of the Dead** was also issued directly to DVD in 2008, although it only used a few elements of the original, principally the underground silo. 🖤

Dead and Buried

📅 YEAR OF RELEASE: 1981		🎥 CINEMATOGRAPHER: Steven Poster
🕐 RUNTIME: 94 minutes		🎬 PRODUCERS: Robert Fentress, Michael I. Rachmil (associate producer), Ronald Shusett, Richard R. St. Johns (executive producer)
🌐 COUNTRY: USA		
🎥 DIRECTOR: Gary Sherman		
🎬 PRODUCTION COMPANY: Barclays Mercantile Industrial Finance		⭕ CERTIFICATE: Australia: R; Canada: 13+ (Quebec); UK: 18; USA: R
✏️ WRITERS: Jeff Millar, Alex Stern, Ronald Shusett, Dan O'Bannon		💲 BUDGET: $3,000,000

THE HORRIFIC BURNING of a photographer, by a gang of locals in broad daylight, acts as the prelude to the macabre carryings on in the quiet coastal town of Potter's Bluff. Shortly afterwards the same photographer is seen happily working away at the town's petrol station, as if he hadn't a care in the world. Sheriff Gillis (James Farentino) becomes suspicious when other people travelling through this picturesque resort start to go missing and then inexplicably turn up alive. With the help of the town's eccentric coroner, Dobbs (Jack Albertson), the sheriff tries to discover who is behind these senseless killings. His efforts, however, have no effect on the murderers, as they feed their excitement by photographing the deaths of their victims. Gillis is also beginning to have major concerns about the odd behaviour of his wife, Janet.

The unsettling nature of these deaths becomes all the more apparent when Gillis accidentally collides with someone as he is called out to deal with yet another attack. As he gets out of his squad car to examine the scene, he is shocked to find

It will take your breath away . . . all of it.

a severed arm enmeshed in the front grill, which will not stop twitching. In the resulting confusion the man he has just knocked over attacks him then retrieves his dismembered arm before taking off into the night. Dobbs later reveals the severed arm had come from someone who had to have been dead for more than four weeks. The sheriff is dumbfounded but his enquiries soon reveal his coroner to have a shady past; he was dismissed from his job many years before for carrying out a series of unauthorized autopsies. Dobbs then reveals his theory on reanimation and we learn the truth about the townsfolk of this idyllic locale.

Eight years after directing **Death Line** (1973), Gary Sherman returned with his eerie zombie movie **Dead and Buried**, which included the names of **Alien**'s Dan O'Bannon and Ronald Shusett among its writers. A surreal ambience pervaded his atmospheric direction as this ill-lit, fogbound coastal haven slowly began to evoke a cloying sense of claustrophobia while a deranged mob revelled in the slaughter of those who innocently set foot in this town. The pacing was often dreamlike, but this was punctured by a series of horrific and closely observed murders, including a hacking by fish hooks, burning by acid and death by embalming, each cleverly handled by special effects man Stan Winston. Stan had already acquired a formidable reputation having designed the Wookie costumes for the **Star Wars Holiday Special** (1978) and would go on to ply his craft on **Aliens** (1986), **Edward Scissorhands** (1990), the **Terminator** series (1984–2009) and **Jurassic Park** (1997) among many, many others. **Willy Wonka**'s (1971) kindly Jack Albertson took on a morbidly eccentric role as the town's coroner and mortician, with a predilection for syringes. The young Lisa Marie, prior to her appearances in **Mars Attacks** (1996) and **Sleepy Hollow** (1999), played one of her earliest roles, and among the rampaging townsfolk, Robert Englund was also to be found, three years before he was set loose in **A Nightmare on Elm Street** (1984).

Gary Sherman had assembled a very respectable team, but **Dead and Buried** could have drifted into almost obscurity if it hadn't been for the public outcry in the UK during the early 1980s, when the video nasty became the scourge of the country. On its low-key UK release in 1981, the film was given an "X" certificate, and at that time remained uncut. This was altered when it was released to video and then lambasted as a shameful video nasty in November 1983, before being dropped from the list in January 1985. When it was presented to the BBFC for release to video in 1990, thirty seconds of cuts were required before it could be passed as an "18". On its return to the cutting room the attack and burning of the photographer by a mob of zombies was edited, as was the deletion of a hypodermic syringe being plunged into the photographer's eye and the bludgeoning of a hitchhiker with a rock. Finally, in 1999 Sherman's film was passed by the BBFC to appear as it had on its cinematic release and, as with many other features of the period, this unusual zombie feature went on to attain its own cult following. ❦

The Dead Next Door

📅 YEAR OF RELEASE: 1989	🎬 CINEMATOGRAPHER: Michael Tolochko
🕐 RUNTIME: 84 minutes	🎬 PRODUCERS: Sam Raimi, J. R. Bookwalter, Jolie Jackunas (line producer), Scott P. Plummer (co-producer), Michael Todd (associate producer)
🌍 COUNTRY: USA	
🎥 DIRECTOR: J. R. Bookwalter	
✏️ WRITER: J. R. Bookwalter	
	💲 BUDGET: $75,000 (estimated)

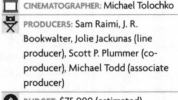

CAST: Pete Ferry, Bogdan Pecic, Michael Grossi Mercer, Jolie Jackunas, Robert Kokai, Floyd Ewing Jr., Roger Graham, Maria Markovic, Jon Killough, Scott Spiegel, Jeff Welch, Michael Todd, J. R. Bookwalter, Jennifer Mullen, Joe Wedlake

A SCIENTIST AND his daughter cower in mortal terror; he is about to pay the greatest price for his heinous experimentation in resurrecting the dead. In the town of Akron, Ohio, zombies are then seen overrunning a video store with one of the corpses shuffling up to the counter intent on taking a copy of **Dawn of the Dead.**

A few years later, that one foolish act has placed humanity in a desperate fight for survival as they battle the ever-growing zombie multitude. The Zombie Squad, an elite tactical team, has been trained by the government to put an end to these putrescent creatures, but even as they slaughter the mindless enemy, one of the team suffers a bite from a zombie's decapitated head as it lies on the floor. Unfortunately a cure for this virulent contamination is yet to be discovered. The Squad's brief is to move on and return to the source of the contagion in Akron, Ohio. Once they arrive, they disperse to retrieve the documents left by the scientist whose experiments unleashed this deathly host. Their examination of the area uncovers a zealous religious cult, a group committed to the new dominion of the zombie. In a turn so very reminiscent of **Dawn of the Dead,** the brethren reveal they will sacrifice the living to satiate the zombies'

craving for warm flesh. The cult, led by Reverend Jones, is fervent in the belief that it is God's will that the dead have arisen to punish the whole of mankind for their misdeeds. However, it soon comes to light that the Reverend's son was savaged by a zombie, and now takes his place among the shambling throng. The Zombie Squad are left to counter the serious threat posed by the cult and stave off the relentless tide of zombies as they race against time to locate the scientist's notes.

The Dead Next Door is the perfect example of how a youngster with an enthusiasm for filmmaking can get his work out there alongside the best, as long as he has belief and can capture the imagination of a man like Sam Raimi. Sam had enough faith in J. R. Bookwalter to finance this feature with his fee from **Evil Dead II.** Bookwalter's labour of love has its detractors; the Super 8-mm film certainly doesn't help, nor does some of the acting, and Bruce's Campbell's dubbing of two of the protagonists' voices has raised more than a few eyebrows. It should be remembered that this feature was shot when the man in the director's chair was only nineteen years old, with precious little experience in professional film production, and he had to wait another four years before his endeavour released to video. The volunteers in Akron provided their services for free during the shoot as well as post production. The film recalled the years of fan-film production as evidenced by the characters' names, Raimi, Carpenter, King, Savini and Romero. At the heart of Bookwalter's film was a craving for blood and guts and the application of gore was surprisingly effective, with decapitations and disembowelments aplenty, as were the zombies, which exhibited some rather ingenious design. Sam Raimi's faith was vindicated for this was only the beginning for the dedicated Bookwalter, who has since gone on to a highly successful career in directing and film production.

Dead Snow

YEAR OF RELEASE: 2009	 CINEMATOGRAPHER: Matthew Weston

 RUNTIME: 91 minutes

COUNTRY: Norway

 DIRECTOR: Tommy Wirkola

PRODUCTION COMPANY: Euforia Film, Barentsfilm AS, FilmCamp, Miho Film, News On Request (NOR), Yellow Bastard Production, Zwart Arbeid

WRITERS: Tommy Wirkola, Stig Frode Henriksen

CINEMATOGRAPHER: Matthew Weston

PRODUCERS: Tomas Evjen, Jan-Erik Gammleng (supervising producer), Espen Horn (executive producer), Ingrid Lill Høgtun (supervising producer), Kjetil Omberg (executive producer), Terje Stroemstad, Harald Zwart (executive producer)

CERTIFICATE: Australia: R; Canada: 14A (Manitoba); Canada: 18A (British Columbia/Ontario); New Zealand: R16; UK: 18

CAST: Vegar Hoel, Stig Frode Henriksen, Charlotte Frogner, Lasse Valdal, Evy Kasseth Røsten, Jeppe Laursen, Jenny Skavlan, Ane Dahl Torp, Bjørn Sundquist, Ørjan Gamst

A FRIGHTENED WOMAN chases through the snow-covered woods only to be trapped and graphically devoured by Nazi Zombies. Oblivious to this gruesome tragedy a group of medical students travel to this snow-laden retreat intent on a long Easter weekend of fun, fun, fun, not to mention the obligatory tumble between the sheets. Their cabin is located high up in the snow-bound mountains, far from the prying eyes of civilization and a perfect setting for something to go disastrously wrong. The youngsters don't share these concerns; they are here to enjoy themselves, unwinding with snowball fights and speeding around on a motor sled. As they take delight in their short vacation, a mysterious hiker arrives and tells the group of the region's bloody past and the years of Nazi occupation. When they later uncovered a box of Nazi gold, this is the moment when the film takes a far darker course. Over sixty-five years ago the Nazis occupied the area, and prior to leaving for the Fatherland they slaughtered the local populace and looted their homes; as the tide of war changed some of them never made it home and eventually perished in the snow, taking their ill-gotten gold with them. However, in making their discovery, the students awaken the dead and the Nazis arise from their frozen burial ground, still attired in full military regalia. Death hasn't cured this silent troupe of Schutzstaffel zombies; they march towards the hapless revellers with one thing in mind. Only the strongest will survive as the students attempt to escape their bloodthirsty onslaught.

While the storyline is somewhat basic, **Død Snø** engages virtually every aspect of the zombie and splatter films

Ein!
Zwei!
Die!

of twenty years past to magnificent effect. The influences are all too apparent, but instead of just copying the likes of Messrs Romero, Raimi and Jackson, Tommy Wirkola pays homage to their sanguinary accomplishment and then throws in something of his own. He takes great care to balance the humour and horror in his film before ripping out intestines, severing heads, gouging out eyes, splattering brains as well as indulging in some penis munching. Per Steinar Hoftun, Shino Kotani and Steinar Kaarstein were each deservedly lauded for their exceptional work, which was hampered by the cold and, as ever, limitations with the budget. While the Norwegian heavy metal soundtrack ground away, the effects team used over 450 litres of fake blood as the Nazi menace returned from its icy grave. Their presence would garner mixed reviews from the critics at home but across the globe **Dead Snow** made such an impact a sequel is now in preparation.

Death Line

YEAR OF RELEASE: 1973	**WRITERS:** Ceri Jones (screenplay), Gary Sherman (original story)
RUNTIME: 87 minutes	**CINEMATOGRAPHER:** Alex Thomson
COUNTRY: UK	**PRODUCERS:** Paul Maslansky
DIRECTOR: Gary Sherman	**CERTIFICATE:** Canada: R; UK: 18 (video rating) (1989) (uncut); UK: X (original rating) (cut); USA: R; USA: Unrated (DVD rating)
PRODUCTION COMPANY: Harbor Ventures K-L Productions	

CAST: Donald Pleasence, Norman Rossington, David Ladd, Sharon Gurney, Hugh Armstrong, June Turner, Clive Swift, James Cossins, Heather Stoney, Hugh Dickson, Jack Woolgar, Ron Pember, Colin McCormack, Gary Winkler, James Culliford

A PROMINENT CIVIL SERVANT is observed furtively pursuing his predilection for sleaze amidst Soho's seedy back streets. A young couple, the antagonistic Alex (David Ladd) and his pretty girlfriend Patricia Wilson (Sharon Gurney) soon after find him unconscious on the steps of a tube station. When they return with a policeman his body has disappeared. Such a senior figure just can't go missing on the streets of London and the acerbic Inspector Calhoun (Donald Pleasence) and Detective Sergeant Rogers are soon on the case. This isn't the first disappearance in the area and very soon Gary Sherman's picture observes a change to its tenor to become far more than another murder mystery.

Towards the end of the nineteenth century, eight men and four women were buried when a tunnel collapsed during the excavation of the London Underground. They were able to survive by eating the dead and reproduced offspring in the grimness of this dank subterranean world. Deep in the labyrinthine tunnels, hidden away from the city's daily commuters,

> **Beneath modern London lives a tribe of once humans. Neither men nor women ... they are the raw meat of the human race!**

the last of the descendants (Hugh Armstrong) weeps over his love's (June Turner) deathbed. In an uninterrupted shot, his grisly lair is exposed, revealing dismembered body parts strewn across the floor and partially eaten corpses suspended from the wall. With the death of his love, the cannibalistic creature returns to the surface to find a new mate and in his search abducts Patricia. A frantic Alex makes Calhoun aware of her capture and then ventures into the warren of tunnels to rescue his girl. Meanwhile, Calhoun and Inspector Richardson (Clive Swift) continue in their search for the missing civil servant's body. Their investigations take them into a part of the underground not seen in over seventy years.

Gary Sherman's forgotten gem is essentially one of human survival, and has also gone by the name **Raw Meat**. In his debut as a director, this quirky low-budget feature encapsulated much of the feel of the London of the early 1970s, with its groovy gear and often grimy backstreet locales, before descending into the bowels of the earth.

In these darkened tunnels, his team created an oppressive domain and in their day the effects they created were considered utterly repulsive, at least for a British audience. Donald Pleasence fairly revelled in his role using the acid tongued wit of the police inspector to his own advantage in scenes that were alleged to have been adlibbed. It was Hugh Armstrong's heartfelt portrayal of the cannibalistic monster from below though that went on to garner the viewer's attention. The gruesome scene in his bloody lair was forgotten when the tragedy surrounding his plague-ridden existence was revealed. While the audience was never left in any doubt as to his vicious nature, his motivation was never one of pleasure; rather, it was instinctive, allowing him only ever to survive on a day-to-day basis. The audience were forced to consider who the monster truly was. The esteemed figure of Christopher Lee also made a cameo appearance as an MI5 agent, who is certain the missing civil servant had more to answer for than drooling over Soho's peep shows.

Death Proof

 YEAR OF RELEASE: 2007

 RUNTIME: 114 minutes

 COUNTRY: USA

 DIRECTOR: Quentin Tarantino

 PRODUCTION COMPANY: Dimension Films, Troublemaker Studios, Rodriguez International Pictures, The Weinstein Company

 WRITER: Quentin Tarantino

 CINEMATOGRAPHER: Quentin Tarantino

PRODUCERS: Elizabeth Avellan, Shannon McIntosh (executive producer), Robert Rodriguez, Pilar Savone (associate producer), Bill Scott (line producer), James W. Skotchdopole (line producer), Erica Steinberg, Quentin Tarantino, Bob Weinstein (executive producer), Harvey Weinstein (executive producer)

 CERTIFICATE: Australia: MA; Canada: 18A (Canadian Home Video rating); Canada: 13+ (Quebec); Ireland: 18; New Zealand: R16; South Africa: 16LV; USA: R; USA: Not Rated (extended version)

CAST: Kurt Russell, Zoë Bell, Rosario Dawson, Vanessa Ferlito, Sydney Tamiia Poitier, Tracie Thoms, Rose McGowan, Jordan Ladd, Mary Elizabeth Winstead, Quentin Tarantino, Marcy Harriell, Eli Roth, Omar Doom

IN A BAR in Austin, Texas, four vapid girls meet for a drink and look to score some weed. As their conversation becomes more boisterous, Julia announces that earlier in the day she appeared on the radio, offering a free lap dance from another of the gang, Arlene; all the lucky fellow has to do is address her as "Butterfly", offer her a drink, and recite a verse from a poem. In the shadows lurks a sadistic mind, veteran "Stuntman" Mike (Kurt Russell), who has the girls firmly in his sights. He follows Julia's instructions from the radio show and charms his way to a dance. As the girls leave the bar, one of their acquaintances, Pam (Rose McGowan), accepts a lift home from the stuntman. As he drives Pam off in his death proof Chevy Nova, the audience knows he intends to kill her and very soon so does she. When he slams the brakes on in his stunt car, her head is smashed straight into the dashboard. He takes off and on a quiet road finally comes upon the girl's car. Calculatingly he puts his foot down and as he picks up speed hits them head on, killing all four women, but never offers an explanation. Only Texas Ranger Earl McGraw is certain that Mike is the culprit, but he has no evidence with which to prove his suspicions.

Fourteen months later, Mike turns up in Lebanon, Tennessee, now with a Dodge Charger at his behest. Three similarly tasteless girls, who

A white-hot juggernaut at 200 miles per hour!

have caught the attention of the cold-hearted Mike, are on their way to the airport to collect stuntwoman Zoë Bell. She is hell bent on test-driving a Dodge Challenger and playing a game they call "Ship's Mast", where she rides on the bonnet of the car with only leather belts to hold onto, while one of the girls drives the vehicle at speed. The girls are having a fun time, until Mike turns up and rear ends the Challenger when it has seriously kicked into gear. As the cars chase at speed Zoë holds on for dear life until she is hurled from the bonnet. In the ensuing fracas, one of the girls wounds Mike with her gun as he exits his car and as he makes his getaway, the girls vow to exact their revenge. When they catch up with him, their onslaught is vicious; they drag him from his car and rain blow after blow to his head until he falls to the floor unconscious. After the credits, Abernathy kicks Mike to the head one more time and just for good measure crushes his skull.

This wasn't the first time in his career Quentin Tarantino had divided his audience as on this occasion he attempted to create a retro homage to the exploitation cinema of three decades past. Fans of these movies would have understood the awkward switch in caption at the beginning of his film, swapping from "Quentin Tarantino's Thunderbolt", to the crude title card announcing "Death Proof" along with the appalling errors in continuity, the poor film stock and the jumpy editing. He referenced several car chase classics from the past, among them **Vanishing Point** (1971), **Two-Lane Blacktop** (1971) and **Dirty Mary, Crazy Larry** (1974), each providing his film with a sense of perspective, but his critics persisted in giving him a hard-earned lambasting. They poured scorn on the meaningless dialogue, which seemed to slow the movie down, forgetting the fact that exploitation cinema was characterized by these often uneventful sequences. At the box office, **Death Proof** struggled, proving just how difficult it is to recreate the grindhouse of the past and revealing how modern cinemagoers have little appreciation of this sleazy low-budget phenomenon.

Death Screams

📅 YEAR OF RELEASE: 1982	✏️ WRITER: Paul C. Elliott
🕐 RUNTIME: 88 minutes	🎬 CINEMATOGRAPHER: Darrell Cathcart
🌎 COUNTRY: USA	⚱️ PRODUCERS: Ernest Bouskos, Charles Ison
🎥 DIRECTOR: David Nelson	
🎬 PRODUCTION COMPANY: ABA Productions	⭕ CERTIFICATE: UK: 18; USA: R

CAST: Susan Kiger, Martin Tucker, William T. Hicks, Jennifer Chase, Jody Kay, John Kohler, Andrea Savio, Curt Rector, Josh Gamble, Hanns Manship, Helene Tryon, Mary Fran Lyman, Monica Boston, Mike Brown, Sharon Alley

DAVID NELSON'S ENTRY to the slasher mayhem of the early 1980s also went by the names of **House of Death** and **Night Screams**. As with so much of its ilk it offered nothing new to the genre, but it was a fitting example as to how the formulaic slasher had very quickly become embedded into the psyche of the American horror film industry. Nelson's film adopted the modus operandi from the very opening scene, set late at night with a couple in the full throes of passion, this time draped over a motorcycle. The fun and games are interrupted as a train rolls by on the bridge above them and before you know it, their lustful embrace is no more, their dead bodies hurled into the river.

And so it continues in a vein with which you will be completely familiar. In a long sequence of frequently creepy scenes, the locals make merry at the closing night of carnival in Shelby, North Carolina. While this is in full swing, several high school seniors decide to spend the night down by the river, excitedly anticipating their new lives at college. They are an easily recognizable crowd, the protagonists who regularly turn up in these films, the nubile teen queens one of whom was a former Playboy Playmate of the year (Susan Kiger), the loud-mouthed party animals and the quiet girl of the piece. And as teenagers do, although some of them look a little older than teenagers, they are keen to party. They might have reconsidered their late night jaunt if anyone in the area had reported the fatal events from a few nights before, but nobody did. The gang have to make the obligatory trip to the cemetery and deliver a series of one-liners and jokes you will have heard before, but they probably contained an element of originality back in 1982.

Hidden amidst the carnival revellers lurks the shadowy figure of the person responsible for the murder of the love-makers by the river. This troubled individual appears scarred by a trauma

The last scream you hear ... is your own!

from the distant past, the memories of which have once again come to the surface. Garbed in blood-stained black, the killer follows the group as they amble towards the riverside, taking in the cemetery. Here he reveals a taste for the machete, which really comes to the fore when the kids enter the so-called death house, for all of twelve minutes at the end of the film. The gore fan does get to savour a couple of decapitations, a disembowelment on the stairs, a hack to the throat and one girl after being viciously attacked finds herself the unfortunate recipient of an arrow wound. In shock she stumbles onto an abandoned carousel, which surprise, surprise begins to move; with nowhere to run she is suffocated as a plastic bag is pulled over her head.

There's more nudity than gore, but Nelson's film will appeal to those enthusiasts who relish the machete murder. To his credit his portrayal of small town life with the killer hiding in the shadows is suitably eerie and he builds on this to create some effective shots of the dark mist-enshrouded woods and the timeworn cemetery. 🩸

Deep Red

📅 YEAR OF RELEASE: 1975		🎥 COUNTRY: Italy	
🕐 RUNTIME: 126 minutes		🎬 DIRECTOR: Dario Argento	

PRODUCTION COMPANY: Rizzoli Film, Seda Spettacoli

WRITERS: Dario Argento, Bernardino Zapponi (screenplay)

CINEMATOGRAPHER: Luigi Kuveiller

PRODUCERS: Claudio Argento

(executive producer), Salvatore Argento

CERTIFICATE: Australia: R; Canada: 13+ (Quebec); Canada: 18+ (Quebec) (Original rating); UK: 18; USA: X (original rating); USA: R; USA: Unrated (director's cut)

CAST: David Hemmings, Daria Nicolodi, Gabriele Lavia, Macha Méril, Eros Pagni, Giuliana Calandra, Piero Mazzinghi, Glauco Mauri, Clara Calamai, Aldo Bonamano, Liana Del Balzo, Vittorio Fanfoni, Dante Fioretti, Geraldine Hooper, Jacopo Mariani, Furio Meniconi, Fulvio Mingozzi, Lorenzo Piani, Salvatore Puntillo, Piero Vida, Nicoletta Elmi, Dario Argento, Salvatore Baccaro, Bruno Di Luia, Attilio Dottesio, Tom Felleghy, Glauco Onorato, Franco Vaccaro

THE TUNE TO a nursery rhyme haunts the opening sequence as two darkened figures tussle with a knife, with one of them suffering fatal injuries. This simple score will serve for the duration as the killer's calling card as Argento's film follows murder upon bloody murder. Having witnessed the killing of Helga Ulmann (Macha Méril), a psychic who had picked upon the murderous intentions of someone sitting in her audience, piano teacher Marcus Daly (David Hemmings) sets out to bring them to justice. Minor details will have a bearing on later events, but Daly never quite grasps this, convinced the killer's face hides among the pictures adorning the walls of the victim's home. However, the clue doesn't fall into place and when Detective Giordani arrives on the scene he is unable to identify the offending visage.

When Daly later discusses the tune with a psychiatrist friend, the analyst hypothesizes on an association with a harrowing event from the killer's past. Using this information Daly continues with his investigation, tracing the music to a novel, "House of the Screaming Child", written by Amanda Righetti (Giuliana Calandra), which makes reference to a murder. Minutes before he makes her acquaintance, Righetti is stabbed by the silent assassin and then drowned in a bath of scalding water. As she dies, she manages to scribe a message in the condensation on the wall of the steamy bathroom. As she had hoped, Daly finds the message, but how could the killer have known he was on his way to see her? It is almost as if he is being shadowed. Undeterred he lays his hands on a photograph of the novel's haunted house to further his quest in determining the whereabouts of this mysterious domicile. We soon learn the house has been deserted for more than twenty years. As he rummages through the rooms he comes upon a young child's drawing of a little boy standing over a dead man, a blood-stained knife held firmly in his hand. The picture contains a vital clue, but the murders won't stop until Daly finally confronts this psychologically disturbed killer.

Dario Argento's film was first released in Italy as **Profondo Rosso**, and would later acquire the name **The Deep Red Hatchet Murders**. This landmark giallo is considered by many to rate alongside **Suspiria** as his finest masterpiece. In its day, it was looked upon as an engrossing murder mystery, enthralling in its use of Gothic visuals, while engaging with an abundance of ingenious set pieces each brought to life by skilful cinematography and an atmosphere augmented by the outlandish discord of the Goblin music score. However, even though Argento unnerved his audience, disturbing them in often baroque settings, and

> **The maker of "SUSPIRIA" now takes you on a journey through the macabre, the bizarre ... the unnatural.**

encouraging his well-chosen supporting cast to heighten the degree of perturbation, his work was dismissed by critics as being a disjointed mess. His detractors failed to comprehend the elaborate nature of his approach to both violence and suspense. Throughout this feature, he demonstrated an acute precision in building his audience's sense of anticipation and then delighted in the cruelty of the kill. True to the giallo he drew out the murder scenes, relishing Righetti's scalding and the psychiatrist's brutal beating, culminating in his being stabbed by the customary long-bladed knife. The splatter fan would lick his lips as throats were lacerated and teeth collided with solid marble, but he would also be conferred an intriguing narrative with intricate twists and turns. 🩸

Delirium

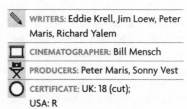

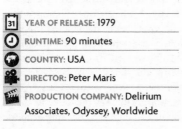

📅	**YEAR OF RELEASE:** 1979		✏️	**WRITERS:** Eddie Krell, Jim Loew, Peter Maris, Richard Yalem
🕐	**RUNTIME:** 90 minutes			
🎬	**COUNTRY:** USA		🎞️	**CINEMATOGRAPHER:** Bill Mensch
🎥	**DIRECTOR:** Peter Maris		⏳	**PRODUCERS:** Peter Maris, Sonny Vest
🎬	**PRODUCTION COMPANY:** Delirium Associates, Odyssey, Worldwide		⭕	**CERTIFICATE:** UK: 18 (cut); USA: R

CAST: Turk Cekovsky, Debi Chaney, Terry TenBroek, Barron Winchester, Bob Winters, Garrett Bergfeld, Nick Panouzis, Harry Gorsuch, Chris Chronopolis, Lloyd Schattyn, Jack Garvey, Mike Kalist, Myron Kozman, Pat Knapko, Letty Garris, Charlotte Littrel

TWO MEN ARE seen hurling a corpse into the Mississippi River. They return to their car and drive away into the night. Elsewhere in St Louis, Susan Narcross (Debi Chaney) arrives home from an evening out to find her roommate Jenny Thompson (Pat Knapko) impaled to a door with a spear. Jenny had brought back a rather creepy looking fellow to the apartment for sex, but he was unable to overcome his impotency and when taunted stabbed her to death. Detectives Sergeant Paul Dollinger (Nick Panouzis) and Larry Mead (Terry Ten Broeck) are handed the case and their interview with Susan reveals her friend had dated a man named Charlie (Turk Chekovsky), who had been in the girls' office earlier in the day looking for a job. As the detectives try to find their man, Charlie has stolen a car and picked up a long-legged hitchhiker (Letty Garris). When they arrive at the beach, she decides to take a swim in the sea. Charlie has other things on his mind; he follows her into the surf and throttles her. As he continues on his journey, he meets a young farm girl who seems to enjoy flirting with him. Her enticing behaviour is rewarded with a pitchfork through the neck. The scene is then set for the slaughter of a woman in her bath, but he ends up stabbing her delivery boy. While working at her office, pretty Susan uncovers a link between the psychopathic Charlie, a Vietnam vet, her

boss Andrews and a secret organization of vigilantes who have served in Vietnam and are intent on bringing their own kind of justice down on those who would disobey the law.

Delirium was one of the first slasher movies to follow in the wake of John Carpenter's **Halloween** (1978) and would have received greater accolade if it had not been such a confusing hybrid. The first half of the movie reveals Charlie as an unnerving killer, a man who evokes fear, but the story-line completely threw its audience to become a post-Vietnam action thriller. The early scenes in this film were bitterly misogynistic with themes reminiscent of the following year's **Maniac** and **Don't Go in the House**, but the change in pace halfway through the proceedings made it likeable to a poor man's **Star Chamber** (1983). Peter Maris made graphic use of his killings almost a year before **Friday the 13th**, but because of his film's confused script and poor production it was forgotten and never credited for its explicit display. The sexualized murder and gore were to attract the attention of the British authorities, as was the bizarre use of the tune "Approaching Menace" written by Neil Richardson and used in the long-running quiz *Mastermind*, when it was released to video in July 1982. The vicious misogyny placed it on the DPP's list of video nasties in the November of

1983; it wasn't removed until May 1985. It was later released to video in 1987 as **Psycho Puppet** with a wide range of cuts, and as a piece of weird cinema is yet to see official release to DVD. While **Delirium** is regarded as a failure, Maris would continue in a fruitful career as a low-budget film director.

Dellamorte Dellamore

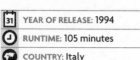

📅 YEAR OF RELEASE: 1994	
🕐 RUNTIME: 105 minutes	
🌐 COUNTRY: Italy	
🎥 DIRECTOR: Michele Soavi	
🎬 PRODUCTION COMPANY: Audiofilm, Bibo Productions, Canal+, Eurimages, K.G. Productions, Silvio Berlusconi Communications, Urania Film	
✏️ WRITERS: Gianni Romoli, Tiziano Sclavi (novel)	

📷 CINEMATOGRAPHER: Mauro Marchetti	
🎭 PRODUCERS: Conchita Airoldi, Heinz Bibo, Tilde Corsi, Dino Di Dionisio, Gianni Romoli, Michele Soavi	
⭕ CERTIFICATE: Australia: MA; Canada: 13+ (Quebec); Canada: 18 (Nova Scotia); Canada: R (Manitoba); UK: 18; USA: R	
💲 BUDGET: $4,000,000	

CAST: Rupert Everett, François Hadji-Lazaro, Anna Falchi, Mickey Knox, Fabiana Formica, Clive Riche, Katja Anton, Barbara Cupisti, Anton Alexander, Pietro Genuardi, Patrizia Punzo, Stefano Masciarelli, Vito Passeri, Alessandro Zamattio, Marijn Koopman

THE CAMERA ZOOMS from within a skull to bring the focus onto a man who is chatting ever so politely on the telephone. As the conversation unfolds, a knock comes to the door and thus enters a zombie. Ever so calmly, the man picks up his gun and places a bullet into the creature's head. The conversation resumes as the camera pans onto the adjacent cemetery.

The man on the phone is Francesco Dellamorte (Rupert Everett), the caretaker of Buffalora's cemetery, a town with little appreciation for this man and his work. The townsfolk have a cruel habit of teasing him about the lack of love in his life. Every night, with his mute assistant Gnaghi (Francois Hadji-Lazaro) at his side, he disposes of the living dead who inexplicably climb from the grave seven days after their burial. Francesco's isolated lifestyle does have its moments; he falls in love with many women (each played by Anna Falchi) but his passionate affairs never seem to end particularly well. The first of his loves is recently widowed and still has a voracious appetite for sex. When her dead husband comes back from the grave, the dastardly fellow ends her life in a fit of jealous rage. Dellamorte mourns her death but she is later consigned to his cemetery, before the seven days are over, so she very soon makes her return. This causes much concern for the cemetery's keeper. Then there follows the mayor's personal assistant, with a rather cynical take on politicians, and the amorous college girl. Surrounded by such intensity, Dellamorte is driven to the point of madness. In his deranged state, he threatens those who had once made fun of him; but someone beyond the cemetery is murdering the people of this town.

On its release in the United States, this film was known as **Cemetery Man** and sadly failed to attract much attention. However, in subsequent years it was to garner a cult following on both sides of the Atlantic thanks to Gianni Romoli's episodic interpretation of an Italian comic book series and Michele Soavi's enigmatic

Zombies, guns and sex, OH MY!!!

direction. His vision breathes a life into the screen, freely fashioning wide angles and then engaging a precision in detail engendered by the expert use of slow motion. Soavi had been a strong protégé of the celebrated Dario Argento, but regrettably would only direct four films before retiring and becoming distanced from the film industry. In this his final film, he reflected on life and death invoking an unlikely blend of horror, comedy and romance. He also brought out the best in the aspiring Rupert Everett, a name not normally associated with horror, but who nonetheless portrayed a man bordering on madness with a tenebrous sense of wit.

Another name coupled with Dario Argento was also at work in this film: special effects man Sergio Stivaletti. He was assigned to create the mist that loomed over the graves, making this a suitably atmospheric locale, and then went on to produce the gore and an assemblage of zombies who truly looked as if they had spent seven days buried beneath the ground. **Dellamorte Dellamore** is a unique deliberation on life and death, one that transcends this frequently grisly genre.

Demons

 YEAR OF RELEASE: 1985

 RUNTIME: 88 minutes

COUNTRY: Italy

 DIRECTOR: Lamberto Bava

 PRODUCTION COMPANY: DACFILM Rome

WRITERS: Dardano Sacchetti (story), Dario Argento

CINEMATOGRAPHER: Gianlorenzo Battaglia

PRODUCER: Dario Argento

CERTIFICATE: Australia: R; Canada: R; Canada: 16+ (Quebec); New Zealand: R18; UK: 18; USA: Unrated

BUDGET: $1,800,000

CAST: Urbano Barberini, Natasha Hovey, Karl Zinny, Fiore Argento, Paola Cozzo, Fabiola Toledo, Nicoletta Elmi, Stelio Candelli, Nicole Tessier, Geretta Geretta, Bobby Rhodes, Guido Baldi, Bettina Ciampolini, Giuseppe Mauro Cruciano, Sally Day

ON THE BERLIN subway, a young student Cheryl (Natasha Hovey) tries to evade a mysterious pursuer disguised in a demonic mask, who to her surprise offers her tickets for the reopening of the ageing Metropol cinema. She talks one of her friends into going along, even though she has no idea as to what to expect on the night. While they stand in the excited crowd they meet George (Urbano Barberini) and Ken (Karl Zinny) and decide it might be a good idea to tag along with them. As they hang around in the lobby, a woman is observed trying on a mask similar to that seen in the film's introductory sequence; it leaves a series of scratches on her face. When the assembled throng finally get in to see the film, it opens with the camera panning over an eerie graveyard where Nostradamus was said to have been laid to rest. The on-screen terror becomes increasingly disturbing as a demonic species violently rip and tear into their defenceless quarry, stripping them of their humanity to transform them into murderous beasts. The woman who was cut by the mask leaves her friend to the film's grisly excess, while she exits to the bathroom. The scratches on her face has started to worry her; as she examines herself in the mirror, festering pus explodes and she is thrown into a tumultuous transformation. When she leaves the bathroom, she is no longer human, having been turned into one of the onscreen demons. The creature makes her way to her seat and then savages her friend. Within minutes, her brutalized companion endures the same transmutation to emerge as one of the demon spawn and sets about the slaughter of the screaming crowd. Those who can escape dash to the exits, only to find they have been bricked up. As the massacre turns into a splatter frenzy, the demonic infestation spreads on through the cinema and out into the streets of Berlin, leaving the youngsters to fight for their lives.

Their evil becomes an orgy of bloodshed.

With the triumph of **Dawn of the Dead**, Dario Argento and Lamberto Bava were eager for further success in the United States. Their film **Demons** was to epitomize so much of the cheesy teenage culture of the 1980s but did have a rock soundtrack that included music from the big names of the day – Saxon, Accept, Mötley Crüe, Billy Idol and Rick Springfield. Their songs played out to a diabolically amusing horror movie riding on the most meagre of plots, whose sole purpose rested on having another set of zombie-like creatures run wild and swell the gore factor of this already bloodthirsty decade. The mystery man from the beginning of the film was played by Argento's protégé Michele Soavi, who would soon rise as a director to complete his masterpiece **Dellamorte Dellamore** (1994). The idea of the film within a film would take a different turn a couple of years later when Bigas Luna's almost forgotten **Angustia** saw a preposterously limited release. Argento and Bava's film proved popular to the point where a sequel was released the following year, **Dèmoni 2 L'Incubo Ritorna** also known as **Demons 2**. A confusing series of unofficial sequels flooded the market during the years that followed to take advantage of the franchise: **La Casa Dell'Orco** or **The Ogre House** or **Demons III: The Ogre** (1988); Soavi's own **La Chiesa**, **The Church**, **Demons 3** (1989) and Umberto Lenzi's **Dèmoni 3** (1991) also known as **Black Demons**. Then came Soavi's **La Setta** or **The Schism** or **Demons 4, The Devil's Daughter** (1991); the remake of Mario Bava's **Black Sunday** (1960) entitled **La Maschera del Demonio**, **The Mask of the Demon** or **Demons 5: The Devil's Veil** (1989) and **Il Gatto Nero**, **The Black Cat** or **Demons 6: De Profundis / From The Deep** (1989).

Der Weg nach Eden

YEAR OF RELEASE: 1995		**WRITER:** Robert-Adrian Pejo
RUNTIME: 80 minutes		**CINEMATOGRAPHER:** Wolfgang Lehner
COUNTRY: Austria		**PRODUCERS:** Michael Seeber, Heinz Stussak
DIRECTOR: Robert-Adrian Pejo		
PRODUCTION COMPANY: Prisma Film		

ROBERT-ADRIAN PEJO'S **The Road to Eden** wasn't going to need endless sessions on the casting couch, but its unsettling content may well have been inspired by Nacho Cerda's **Aftermath** (1994). His documentary was an elegy to those who have passed from us and revealed the procedures that take place in the time immediately after death. In a similar way to

Aftermath, a mortician steps into the spotlight; this time, however, he will examine real corpses and will observe a solemn respect for those laid before him. Janos Keserü is a senior dissector and mortician in Budapest; death has been at his side since childhood for his father was dedicated to the same profession and from him he learned the intricacies of vivisecting a body and putting it back together again ready for the family funeral. The law in Hungary stipulates the cause of death be determined for everyone who dies. This entails that every corpse is very carefully dissected. While Pejo filmed Keserü`s routine in an impassive manner, the images detailing the removal of the brain and the deep incisions into the torso are far more gruesome than those we have relished in this selection of splatter movies. In these eighty minutes, we come to acquire both knowledge and respect for Keserü and his sombre trade; sadly, this record of his work is a rarity, and is only available on VHS with distribution limited to Germany.

Deranged

31 YEAR OF RELEASE: 1974	WRITER: Alan Ormsby
RUNTIME: 82 minutes	CINEMATOGRAPHER: Jack McGowan
COUNTRY: Canada/USA	PRODUCERS: Peter James (executive producer), Tom Karr, Bob Clark
DIRECTORS: Jeff Gillen, Alan Ormsby	
PRODUCTION COMPANY: Karr International Pictures	BUDGET: $200,000

CAST: Roberts Blossom, Cosette Lee, Leslie Carlson, Robert Warner, Marcia Diamond, Brian Smeagle, Arlene Gillen, Robert McHeady, Marian Waldman, Jack Mather, Micki Moore, Pat Orr

BY 1974, THERE had been insane killers by the drove cutting and hacking their way through so many almost forgotten celluloid features, but this was the first film to try to tell the true story of Ed Gein, the man whose traumatized life story provided the inspiration for Alfred Hitchcock's **Psycho** (1960). Ezra Cobb is a hopelessly damaged individual who continues to look after his domineering mother somewhere in the American Midwest. His mother's religious fanaticism has turned to become mean and spiteful, exhibiting an unhealthy contempt for women. Even though he is subjected to her bitter cruelty on a daily basis, his mother remains the font in his downtrodden life.

When she passes away, Ezra is inconsolable yet even in death he can still hear her voice whispering through the rooms of the family homestead. It has been a year since his mother died, but his condition has already become delusional. Such is his deranged state he exhumes her body and returns her to the comfort of their home; for Ezra things are now just the way they used to be. The sound of her voice seems ever stronger as his cold gaze becomes all the more distant. He takes to digging up other corpses, lovingly restoring and embalming them, before sitting them at his mother's side. He also borrows another leaf from Gein's book, using them as internal decor and then develops a taste for cannibalism.

It doesn't take long before his pursuits turn to hunting down live victims, in the hope of appeasing his mother's endless scolding. As he relaxes in this newfound perverse domesticity, his neighbours introduce him to a woman whose husband has recently passed away. In a darkly comedic episode, she attempts to seduce him and then pays the price. So follows the barmaid, who is tied to a chair and entertained at a dinner table attended by rotting corpses in a scene akin to

Pretty Sally Mae died a very unnatural death ... But the worst hasn't happened to her yet! DERANGED ... confessions of a necrophile!

that same year's **The Texas Chain Saw Massacre**. The distraught barmaid is then privy to the sight of Ezra garbed in the skin of a dead woman, seventeen years before **The Silence of the Lambs**.

Having raised the money to produce **Deranged** from promoting concerts for bands such as Led Zeppelin, Tom Karr immediately ran into difficulties. Bob Clarke, the director of **Black Christmas** (1974), declined the offer to assume the director's chair fearing the subject matter in Alan Ormsby's script was just too disturbing. On its American release, the distributors were shameless in their exploitation of this disturbing feature, renaming Jeff Gillen and Ormsby's low-budget feature **Deranged: The Confessions of a Necrophile**. While **In the Light of the Moon** (2000) was a more accurate portrayal of Gein's life, **Deranged** was appreciably darker, conveying a far more chilling sense of unhinged realism. It was never to be described as a particularly gory movie, although its kills are still acknowledged to have been well observed, and while it was immediately overshadowed by the visceral power of Tobe Hooper's seminal movie, it set the tone for the generation to come.

This was one of special effects artist Tom Savini's earliest assignments and coupled with Jack McGowan's cinematography that melded the depth in the shadows with muted lighting they helped to form an unsettling portrait. Together with his director, McGowan was able to create a suitably creepy atmosphere and when required he captured the desperation that came with the frantic chase scenes. It was, of course, Roberts Blossom who brought the man at the centre of this film to life. He produced a genuinely credible portrayal of an unstable mind with a capacity for both intense brutality and heartfelt pathos. Following its release to the drive-in cinemas in 1974, **Deranged** disappeared almost without trace with the negative feared to have been lost. It was later recovered in Florida, but wasn't completely restored which meant much of Savini's gory effects were omitted until the 1990s. In 2007, a Thirtieth Anniversary Collector's Edition was released in Germany; unfortunately the US version had to remove a brain-scooping scene to receive its R rating.

The Devil Hunter

YEAR OF RELEASE: 1980	**WRITERS:** Julián Esteban, Jesus Franco
RUNTIME: 102 minutes	
COUNTRY: Spain, France, West Germany	**CINEMATOGRAPHER:** Juan Soler
	PRODUCERS: Julián Esteban, Daniel Lesoeur (associate producer), Karl Spiehs (co-producer)
DIRECTOR: Jesus Franco	
PRODUCTION COMPANY: Eurociné, J.E. Films (Julián Esteban Films), Lisa-Film	**CERTIFICATE:** UK: (Banned); UK: 18 (uncut); USA: Not Rated

CAST: Ursula Buchfellner, Al Cliver, Antonio Mayans, Antonio de Cabo, Burt Altman, Gisela Hahn, Muriel Montossé, Werner Pochath, Melo Costa, Aline Mess, Claude Boisson

LAURA CRAWFORD'S CAREER as an actress/model is rudely interrupted by a gang of kidnappers as she prepares for her latest role in South America. They steal her away into the jungle and demand a huge ransom. To ensure she doesn't escape, the nubile Laura is guarded by a totem pole-styled monster who calls himself "The Devil". She is forced to endure an unholy amount of degrading torment at the hands of the monster before the gang get their ransom, and then has to watch as bound maidens are offered to the beast, one of whom he greedily devours very early on in the film. Finally Peter Weston (Al Cliver), the devil hunter, assisted by his Vietnam vet friend, fly by helicopter into the heat of the jungle to stage a rescue.

Hunted, raped and tormented out of her mind ...

Jesus Franco returned for another piece of Eurotrash in a film whose original title **Sexo Cannibal** left little to the imagination. For almost the first half hour, the rushed script made very little sense, but Franco's eye was set on exploiting the sleaze and capitalizing on the cannibal craze, which was still in its prime. The gore was by no means as intense as that splattered across its contemporaries, with the obvious exception of the labia eating scene, but the nudity of the dancing natives and the two female leads gave the sleaze-mongers a peak at the bare flesh they so badly craved. The scenes of violence were rife with the brutality that had

become intrinsic to these features, while the locations were unusually stunning and indeed added to any sense of atmosphere. The pacing, however, was typically tedious and hampered further still by unnecessary sub-plots. Franco was obviously keen to get his shoot completed as quickly as he could, to allow him to move onto his next money-making venture, because there are numerous errors in continuity and Al Cliver actually took an impromptu tumble. For Franco fans such clangers were nothing new, and it wasn't surprising when this film, also known as **The Man Hunter** and **Mandingo Manhunter**, attracted the concerns of the DPP, although it had been around for almost three years when it was added to the Video Nasties list in August 1984. Franco's film was to become one of the collectable DPP39s but modern audiences can now view his lurid contrivance without cuts.

The Devil's Rejects

YEAR OF RELEASE: 2005	
RUNTIME: 107 minutes	
COUNTRY: USA/Germany	
DIRECTOR: Rob Zombie	
PRODUCTION COMPANY: Lions Gate Films, Cinerenta Medienbeteiligungs	

KG, Cinelamda Internationale Filmproduktionsgesellschaft mbH & Co. 1 Beteiligungs-KG (as Cinelamda), Devil's Rejects Inc., Entache Entertainment, Firm Films, Creep Entertainment International, Spectacle Entertainment Group

 WRITER: Rob Zombie

CINEMATOGRAPHER: Phil Parmet

PRODUCERS: Peter Block (executive producer), Michael Burns (executive producer), Mike Elliott, Ali Forman (associate producer), Andy Gould, Marco Mehlitz, Brent Morris (co-producer), Michael Ohoven, Guy Oseary (executive producer), Michael Paseornek (executive producer), Julie Yorn (executive producer), Rob Zombie

CERTIFICATE: Australia: MA; Canada: 18+ (Quebec); Canada: 18A (British Columbia/Ontario); Canada: R (Alberta/Manitoba/Nova Scotia); Canada: R (Ontario) (unrated version); Ireland: 18; New Zealand: R18; UK: 18; USA: Unrated (DVD version); USA: NC-17 (original rating); USA: R

BUDGET: $7,000,000

RECEIPTS: $19,390,029

CAST: Sid Haig, Bill Moseley, Sheri Moon Zombie, William Forsythe, Ken Foree, Matthew McGrory, Leslie Easterbrook, Geoffrey Lewis, Priscilla Barnes, Dave Sheridan, Kate Norby

MONTHS AFTER THE carnage of **House of 1000 Corpses**, Texas Sheriff John Quincey Wydell (William Forsythe) and a band of State Troopers besiege the psychopathic Firefly family. Mother Firefly (Leslie Easterbrook) is captured, while Otis (Bill Moseley) and Baby (Sheri Moon) manage to escape and soon after kill a nurse and then drive away in her car. They head to a rundown motel in the desert where they sadistically torture and murder two members of a band. Baby's father, Captain Spaulding (Sid Haig), turns up at the motel and then scenes of degradation follow, with rape and murder followed by more murder as the family leave their calling card smeared in blood on the motel room's wall "The Devil's Rejects".

Wydell has learned that Mother Firefly murdered his brother. In his dreams, Wydell's brother demands he seek revenge, and when he awakens the now psychotic sheriff butchers Mother Firefly. He then tracks down the remaining Fireflies, locating them to a brothel owned by Captain Spaulding's brother, Charlie (Ken Foree). Assisted by a couple of mean bounty hunters known as the "Unholy Two", the sheriff captures the surviving family members and tortures them, nailing Otis's hands to a chair and stapling crime scene photographs to his and Baby's stomach.

He turns to Captain Spaulding and beats him before taking a cattle prod to both him and Otis. He then leaves the house ablaze and takes an axe to Charlie. Tiny, who had gone missing in the

Death walks behind. Hell waits ahead.

siege at the beginning of the film, turns up to break Wydell's neck and save his low-life family. He is left behind as Otis, Baby and Spaulding leave in Charlie's car, only for them to be gunned down as they drive into a police barricade.

Rob Zombie's sequel to the excess of his **House of 1000 Corpses** (2003), returned to the year of 1978 as his Manson family-styled sadists continued to revel in their life of wilful depravity. On this outing, Rob took the time to build on the characters that he had introduced two years before and was to succeed in fleshing the Firefly family with a set of personalities as well as creating a degree of motive, albeit despicably twisted. He was quick to defend the sickening scenes in his film, insisting his intent was never to glorify violence nor was there a desire to see the audience cheer the bad guys. However, in the movie's closing scenes the villains

of the piece are portrayed as anti-heroes as they are martyred in a blaze of glory to the sound of Lynyrd Skynyrd's iconic "Free Bird". If there was a glow amidst the audience, maybe they should have remembered that these were the same degenerates who had savoured every single moment of humiliation they inflicted in the motel rooms, culminating in murder and rape during a sequence of events very reminiscent of the Manson inspired **Last House on the Left** (1972). In a similar way to Wes Craven's problematic film, Rob showed how even the most law abiding could be dragged down to the abominable levels of the Firefly family. When **The Devil's Rejects** was submitted to the MPAA, the censors were far from happy with the scenes in the motel, forcing two minutes of unpleasantness to be removed prior to its theatrical release. This was later restored for the DVD. ✷

Diary of a Serial Killer

📅	YEAR OF RELEASE: 1995	✎	WRITER: Philip Cheng Chung Tai
⏲	RUNTIME: 84 minutes	▭	CINEMATOGRAPHER: Cheung Man Po
🎥	COUNTRY: Hong Kong	⚱	PRODUCER: Peter Chan Chiu Miu
🎬	DIRECTOR: Otto Chan Juk Tiu	◯	CERTIFICATE: Australia: R; Hong Kong: III
🎞	PRODUCTION COMPANY: Skylark Films		

CAST: Kwok-Pong Chan, Farini Cheung, Ka-Kui Ho, Kenny Ho, Siu Ling Wong, Yuk-Mui Yeung, Timothy Zao

ALTHOUGH LAU SHU-BILL (Chan Kwok-Bong) appears to be an ordinary fellow, he is an insatiable sex addict. His wife does her best to arouse his desires but her efforts appear hollow and uninspired. Frustrated he turns to the shady streets of Hong Kong. When he takes a girl back to a hotel room, Lau turns to violence and strangles her in the shower. Murder follows upon grisly murder as Lau justifies his homicidal activities as a favour to each of these girls, providing them the chance to reincarnate from the misery of their worthless existence. On several occasions, he is nearly apprehended, but the incompetence of the police and his wife and sister's unawareness of his sadistic nature allow him to continue in his perverse deliverance. When he falls in love with one of his potential victims, he makes his last mistake and finds himself hauled away to a prison cell, from where his story is told in a series of flashbacks.

Otto Chan's film **Diary of a Serial Killer** was based on Li Wenxian's reign of terror in Guangzhao's Wong Po village between 1991 and 1996. Over this five-year period he raped and murdered thirteen women, most of whom were prostitutes. He later told the arresting officers he wanted revenge for a prostitute who had swindled him. Chan allows his unsavoury tale to unfold by way of the flashback narrative used to similar effect by Danny Lee in **Dr Lamb** (1992) and Herman Yau in **The Untold Story** (1993). It was little more than an exploitative piece of cinema, which borrowed liberally from **Dr Lamb** in its portrayal of Lau's rape and mutilation; it would be these gratuitous scenes that would eventually afford this film a Category III rating. The Hong Kong comic book-styled excess had dead bodies spurting reservoirs of blood even though they had lain dead for several days and then sickened its audience with the severing of one of his deceased victim's vaginas. The sleazy direction would demand the camera's lens linger over every girl in the film, as each of them stripped naked before the sexual violence and torture escalated to bloody murder. Cheung Man Po's photography, however, captured the essence of Chan's movie in being at times menacing and then in his use of lighting created a suitably unnerving atmosphere, yet during the film's one moment of love-making a gentle eroticism was clearly observed. Having shocked for almost the entirety of its duration, the image of the doll shown during **Diary of a Serial Killer**'s closing moments sought once more to disturb, returning unsettling memories of William Lustig's **Maniac** (1980).

Don't Answer the Phone

31 YEAR OF RELEASE: 1980   ⏱ RUNTIME: 94 minutes

COUNTRY: USA

DIRECTOR: Robert Hammer

PRODUCTION COMPANY: Scorpion

WRITERS: Michael D. Castle, Robert Hammer

CINEMATOGRAPHER: James L. Carter

PRODUCERS: Michael D. Castle, Robert Hammer, Michael Towers (executive producer)

CAST: James Westmoreland, Ben Frank, Flo Lawrence, Nicholas Worth, Denise Galik, Stan Haze, Gary Allen, Michael D. Castle, Pamela Jean Bryant, Ted Chapman, Chris Wallace, Dale Kalberg, Deborah Leah Land, Tom Lasswell, Mike Levine

IN THE SQUALID world of the late seventies–early eighties sleazy misogyny, Vietnam vet Kirk Smith Beefy (Nicholas Worth) takes the excess to the next level as an impotent maniac, consumed by a psychotic hatred of women. When he's not pumping iron he's photographing scantily clad young ladies and selling the shots to a slime ball publisher, who fits perfectly with **Don't Answer the Phone**'s seedy premise. Kirk is a deeply troubled man, still tormented by the years of abuse he endured at the hands of his bullying father. Alone in his apartment he continues to engage in a vitriolic dialogue with his long-deceased persecutor. These brief episodes are intended to provide an insight to this hulking man's murderous spree before he sets out to kill those women of Los Angeles he believes need a lesson in morality. His first victim is a young nurse whom he strangles and rapes and as his depraved vendetta spreads, he begins to rant over the phone in a mock Mexican accent to a talk show psychiatrist, Dr Gale (Flo Garrish). These phone calls come to a climax when Kirk strangles a prostitute while he forces her to talk

live on air with Dr Gale. The broadcast turns to one of uncontrollable screaming across the radio waves of the entire city as Kirk tightens his deathly grip around her throat. At first the police refuse to believe the psychiatrist's claims; they are more inclined to take their enquiries to one of the city's rundown brothels, where they delight in intimidating its deviant clientele. Kirk slips up when he leaves some of his candid snapshots on the scene of one of his many grisly crimes. Detective Worth finally takes his man down in a slow-motion sequence leaving Kirk for dead in a blood-tinged pool, and who will ever forget the film's closing line "Adios, creep!"?

Don't Answer the Phone started life as **The Hollywood Strangler**, adopting a similarly catchy title to the previously successful horrors **Don't Look in the Basement** (1973), **Don't Ride on Late Night Trains** (1975) and **Don't Go in the House** (1980). This was to be former photographer Robert Hammer's only appearance in the director's chair, as he placed his own particular stamp on the depraved world of exploitative cinema. While this was an early and highly competent entry in the use of hand-held camera filming, there was no effort made to gloss over what was a trashy piece of cinematic misogyny, slavering in its relentless portrayal of sex and violence. Its market was the grindhouse strips of hardcore sleaze and the ever-growing home video market. As with that year's **Maniac** and **He Knows You're Alone,** Hammer departed from the emerging slasher trope, leaving his audience in no doubt as to the identity of his rapist killer, who was played with a chilling menace by Nicholas Worth. Worth's lengthy career also saw regular appearances in **Star Trek Deep Space Nine** and **Star Trek Voyager,** along with providing his voice for The Reaper in **The Hills Have Eyes II** (1985). What followed was an uncompromising violent display targeted at his female cast, who were nearly all damaged by drug addiction, physical abuse or the threat of suicide. Rather than revelling in an excess of gore, his film derived its cruel pleasure in lingering over its semi-naked female victims struggling and squirming as the murderer strangled the very life out of them.

The rights to Michael Curtis's book *Nightline* were purchased in the making of this film for only $2,500. Curtis's book was a fictionalized account of the Hillside Strangler murders committed by the psychotic Kenneth Bianchi and his cousin Angelo Buono between 1977 and 1978. Shortly afterwards another murderous pair, Lawrence

> **RUN – if you must. HIDE – if you can. SCREAM . . . but he'll know you're alone!**

Bittaker with Roy Norris, who had photographed over 500 pictures of girls taken along the Pacific Coast Highway, went on a similar murderous spree. The details of their crimes were infinitely worse than anything detailed in Hammer's film. While Hammer has many pleasant memories in the making of his feature, the trauma of trying to find a distribution deal resulted in a swift change of career; he moved into finance, but admits he could very easily be persuaded to return to make another film. Fans of this film still prefer the original US VHS edition as the latest issue to DVD has suffered at the hands of a set of butchering censors. The original version released to cinemas in the UK was only reduced by around a minute when submitted to the BBFC, with edits demanded to three specific episodes. These include the tying-up of a woman prior to her murder, and her nightdress being ripped open. The shots of her breasts being burned with candle wax were not included in the original submission. The cuts to this release continued with the strangulation of the model, which was heavily edited, along with the removal of the shot of the killer placing a coin in her stocking. Finally, the murder of another prostitute was also missing a similar shot of a coin. This was later reinstated in 2005, but the previously mentioned cuts had been lost and only slightly marred the film's final restoration. ✒

Don't Go in the House

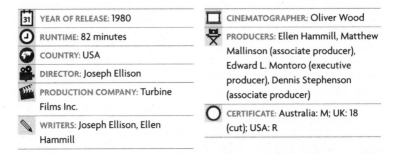

📅 YEAR OF RELEASE: 1980	🎞 CINEMATOGRAPHER: Oliver Wood
🕐 RUNTIME: 82 minutes	⚱ PRODUCERS: Ellen Hammill, Matthew Mallinson (associate producer), Edward L. Montoro (executive producer), Dennis Stephenson (associate producer)
🌐 COUNTRY: USA	
🎥 DIRECTOR: Joseph Ellison	
🎬 PRODUCTION COMPANY: Turbine Films Inc.	
✏ WRITERS: Joseph Ellison, Ellen Hammill	🔵 CERTIFICATE: Australia: M; UK: 18 (cut); USA: R

CAST: Dan Grimaldi, Robert Osth, Ruth Dardick, Charles Bonet, Bill Ricci, Dennis Hunt, John Hedberg, Johanna Brushay, Darcy Shean, Mary Ann Chin, Lois Verkimeps, Susan Smith, Jim Donnegan, Claudia Folts, Denise Woods

Don't Go in the House was dismissed when it first came to the cinemas and was yet another slasher of the period to lay forgotten until its short-lived release to video. Director Joseph Ellison had broken the rules with his entry to these years of mayhem, frustrating his audience with a conspicuous lack of blood and guts. To add to its problems this was also an independent production, reliant on a similarly small independent distribution company by the name of FVI. Unfortunately, they didn't do a particularly good job in their promotion of this film, and as a result many potential cinema-goers were oblivious of its existence.

Donald Kohler (Dan Grimaldi) stands transfixed at the incinerator plant where he works, morbidly fascinated by the sight of a colleague catching fire. As a child, his arm was seriously burned by his domineering mother as punishment for a minor misdemeanour. Years later, now a grown man, he arrives home from work to discover his mother lying dead in her chair. The voices in his head insist it's party time! And so, after years of being downtrodden, Donny cuts loose, turning up that crazy disco sound and bouncing on the furniture. Donny, however, is beginning to lose his grip on reality as the whispers and echoes around his head assume control of his faculties. Picking up a young lady, he takes her home to meet his mother. She is the first of many, each of them blondes and brunettes, much like his tyrannical mother. Once inside the house he strips them, liberally douses their trussed bodies in petrol and then in quite graphic shots incinerates them with a flame-thrower while locked away in a homemade steel-plated room. Donny's calm demeanour, coupled with the silence as he looks on, emphasizes the true horror of what has just happened. In a deranged display echoing **Psycho** (1960) and **Deranged** (1974), he dresses their charred bodies in his mother's clothes and settles them in her bedroom, where in the shadows

he finds time for quiet conversation. Suspicions are aroused when he dons a disco suit and soon after, taking to the dance floor, sets light to his date's hair.

Ellison's film was by no means a classic of the genre, but it was a compelling account of the final stages of a complete psychological breakdown. The allusions to mental illness would cause much heated debate when the film went to video release, but the gore-mongers of 1980 felt cheated – too much in the way of disco and an absence of bloody carnage.

Don't Go in the Woods Alone

31	**YEAR OF RELEASE:** 1981		**CINEMATOGRAPHER:** Hank Zinman
🕐	**RUNTIME:** 82 minutes		**PRODUCERS:** James Bryan, Roberto Gomez, Suzette Gomez, William Stockdale (associate producer)
🎬	**COUNTRY:** USA		
🎥	**DIRECTOR:** James Bryan		
✎	**WRITER:** Garth Eliassen	◯	**CERTIFICATE:** Australia: R; UK: 18; USA: R

CAST: Jack McClelland, Mary Gail Artz, Angie Brown, Ken Carter, David Barth, Larry Roupe, Amy Martell, Tom Drury, Laura Trefts, Alma Ramas, Carolyn Braza, Frank Millen, McCormick Dalten, Cecilia Fannon, Dale Angell

A WOMAN IS SEEN chasing through the woods; she plunges into a stream and then disappears. Soon after, she is recorded as yet another missing person. A shift in scene introduces four young campers, Craig, Peter, Ingrid and Joanie, trekking through this vast

wilderness in search of a weekend of fun-filled adventure. As they hike through the woods, someone armed with a sharp spike has set about the slaughter of the other visitors to the area. Very soon, they will face the same nightmare as they encounter a dense part of the forest that becomes appreciably darker with each passing step. With the sense of isolation becoming more obvious, something appears in the shadows brandishing a machete and carves up young Craig. The rest of the group flee into the forest with the maniac murderer in close pursuit.

James Bryan's film has been placed among the worst films in the genre and yet it has still managed to acquire something of a cult reputation. The story was highly derivative of the previous year's **Just Before Dawn** but on this occasion failed to offer the obligatory twist to the closing proceedings. Further to this, the acting left much to be desired along with a predictable plot beset by just too many gaping holes. The killer was given little in the way of background

> **Everyone has nightmares about the ugliest way to die.**

and the dubious make-up job certainly didn't do him any favours. However, for all of its failings **Don't Go in the Woods Alone** contained a series of expertly crafted shocks in addition to a collection of grisly kill scenes which led to an appallingly gruesome finale. While some of the photography gave away the fact Hank Zinman was still learning his trade, the tracking across this mountainous terrain certainly made up for this failing, being pleasant on the eye yet providing an ever so threatening backdrop. The film was released to video in the early 1980s, and may have passed unnoticed if it hadn't made it to the UK's list of video nasties before being banned under the stipulations of the Video Recordings Act. Up until its uncut release in 2007, it was considered a video rarity.

Don't Go Near the Park

📅 YEAR OF RELEASE: 1981	✏️ WRITERS: Linwood Chase, Lawrence D. Foldes
🕐 RUNTIME: 80 minutes	🎞️ CINEMATOGRAPHER: William DeDiego
🐷 COUNTRY: USA	
🎥 DIRECTOR: Lawrence D. Foldes	⚱️ PRODUCERS: George Foldes (executive producer), Lawrence D. Foldes
🎬 PRODUCTION COMPANY: Star Cinema	⭕ CERTIFICATE: Australia: R; Canada: (Banned) (Ontario); UK: 18; USA: R

CAST: Aldo Ray, Meeno Peluce, Tamara Taylor, Barbara Bain, Robert Gribbin, Linnea Quigley, Chris Riley, Lara Morann, Earl Statler, Cambra Foldes, K. L. Garber, David Ariniello, Steven Lovy, Janet Giglio, Doug White, Steven Leider

TWELVE THOUSAND YEARS ago, tribe members Gar (Crackers Phinn) and Tra (Barbara Bain) were banished for ritually cannibalizing their kinsmen's children in the hope of gaining eternal youth. Before they were set free, the ageing queen of the tribe cursed them to walk the earth for all eternity; the only way that they can retain their youth is to continue to consume human flesh. After a long line of killing sprees lasting nigh on one hundred and twenty centuries, Gar leaves the Los Angeles park that he and Tra have made their home, and in a very short space of time finds an apartment, meets and marries an attractive young lady (Linnea Quigley,) who gives birth to their daughter Bondi (Tamara Taylor). When she becomes a teenager, Bondi runs away from home. No longer able to endure the instability of her family life, she falls into the hands of a gang of rapists, in what are the most disturbing scenes of the film. When she escapes, thanks to her father's magic amulet, she joins two other runaways who by a strange coincidence live with the sister of the cave dwellers. Bondi now learns she is to be sacrificed and then devoured to allow Gar and Tra preserve their eternal

It's the last place you'll ever play!

life. When their plan is discovered zombie-like creatures rise from the earth and Gar and Tra acquire laser beam eyes in what will be the build up to the final showdown.

Lawrence David Foldes had only just turned twenty when he directed this rather ambitious film, so maybe his lack of experience can be forgiven. **Don't Go Near the Park**, which has also gone by the names **Curse of the Living Dead**, **Nightstalker** and **Sanctuary for Evil**, was a very amateur-looking production, blighted by unconvincing make-up, inadequate use of lighting and acting on a par with so many of these exploitative ventures. The storyline defied belief in its lack of coherence and culminated in a finale that its audience would never have been able to predict. The title of the film was evocative of two other reasonably successful exploitation features, **Don't Go in the House** (1980) and **Don't Look in the Basement** (1972); unfortunately, it did not begin to compare. Fans of horror scream queen Linnea Quigley will be delighted to see one of her earlier scantily clad appearances, in a career that continues to this very day. For Foldes this would be his skeleton in the closet as he moved on to new projects and gained experience that took him on to far greater things. While the gore effects were not particularly convincing, their excess, which focused on lacerated stomachs and their entrails being torn from them, gave the film an element of lasting notoriety. These scenes of course meant that when Foldes' film found its way into the UK in 1983 it was registered as a video nasty in the November of that year, not to be removed from the offending list until July 1985. It would be over twenty years before it would be seen in its entirety, following its release to DVD in 2006 in what had become, if only for a while, a more tolerant Britain.

Don't Look in the Basement

 YEAR OF RELEASE: 1973

 RUNTIME: 89 minutes

 COUNTRY: USA

 DIRECTOR: S. F. Brownrigg

 PRODUCTION COMPANY: Camera 2 Productions, Century Films

 WRITER: Tim Pope

 CINEMATOGRAPHER: Robert B. Alcott

 PRODUCERS: S. F. Brownrigg, Walter L. Krusz (executive producer)

 CERTIFICATE: Australia: R; UK: X (1977); UK: 15 (DVD rating); USA: R

CAST: Bill McGhee, Jessie Lee Fulton, Robert Dracup, Harryette Warren, Michael Harvey, Jessie Kirby, Hugh Feagin, Betty Chandler, Camilla Carr, Gene Ross, Annabelle Weenick, Rosie Holotik, Rhea MacAdams

CHARLOTTE BEALE (ROSIE Holotik) leaves her position as a hospital supervisor to join a secluded private mental institution, headed by a Dr Stevens. His approach to therapy is somewhat radical in that he allows the psychologically disturbed to confront their inner demons and hopefully cure themselves. Before she arrives to take up her new role, Dr Stevens is murdered. The strict Dr Geraldine Masters (Annabelle Weenick) attempts to calm the patients with the help of Sam (Bill McGhee), a lobotomized giant whose mind is that of a child, manifested by his fixation for chocolate ice-lollies. When she arrives, her welcome from Dr Masters isn't the most cordial and she learns she will be sharing her accommodation with the inmates. To make matters worse her skimpy nurse's outfit also leaves nothing to the imagination. As she sleeps at night, the patients can be heard roaming freely around her bed. Among them are the nymphomaniac Allysson, who also has homicidal tendencies; Harriet, a woman haunted by the death of her child in a horrendous accident; the Sergeant who blames himself for the death of his platoon; Judge Cameron, a man with delusions of power and an unsettling predilection for an assortment of axes; and Danny whose insanity triggers the murders that follow. Each of them begins to test her sanity, pushing her to the brink in the hallways and confined stairways that lead to secreted passageways and other hidden parts of this institution. Nurse Beal comes to realize there is something seriously wrong here, but what will she find on her one visit to the basement?

The day the insane took over the asylum!

Sherald Brownrigg's low-budget exploitation shocker was originally entitled **The Forgotten**, and has also gone by the name **Death Ward 13**, but **Don't Look in the Basement** proved a little more apt on its release to the drive-ins. This well-plotted film cleverly escalated the atmosphere, thriving on the air of obsessive madness, using unusually well-lit scenes whose starkness conspired to unsettle the viewer. The film wasn't exceptionally gory, largely because the slaughterhouse entrails Brownrigg had hoped to use started to rot due to the heat on the set. The stench was to prove a little too much for the cast and crew. Maybe it was the stench, but this piece of exploitation was cited as a video nasty in the August of 1984 as word spread of its release to video some eighteen months before in February 1983. It was removed from the list in December 1985 and released uncut in 2005. Although this version is unavoidably grainy, it couldn't disguise the gorgeous former Playboy Playmate, Rosie Holotik, who made it to that magazine's cover in April 1972.

Don't Open Till Christmas

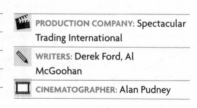

📅 **YEAR OF RELEASE:** 1984		🎬 **PRODUCTION COMPANY:** Spectacular Trading International	
🕐 **RUNTIME:** 86 minutes			
🌐 **COUNTRY:** UK		✏️ **WRITERS:** Derek Ford, Al McGoohan	
🎥 **DIRECTOR:** Edmund Purdom		🎞️ **CINEMATOGRAPHER:** Alan Pudney	

PRODUCERS: Stephen Minasian, Dick Randall

CERTIFICATE: Australia: R; UK: 18; USA: R

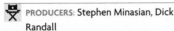

CAST: Edmund Purdom, Alan Lake, Belinda Mayne, Mark Jones, Gerry Sundquist, Kelly Baker, Kevin Lloyd, Wendy Danvers, Nicholas Donnelly, Pat Astley, Laurence Harrington, Ken Halliwell, Ray Marioni, Wilfred Corlett, Ricky Kennedy

IN A LONDON backstreet, a parked car reveals a man dressed as Santa Claus (John Ashton) getting rather aroused with a female acquaintance (Maria Eldridge). Before he can consummate his passion, he realizes someone is prying on them and gets out of the vehicle, preparing for a confrontation. It never happens, for as he turns to face the offending peeping tom he immediately falls to the ground, the victim of an unidentified killer's blade. His female companion is the next to confront the assassin's sharpened implement. Shortly afterwards with a fancy dress party in full swing, another Santa (Laurence Harrington) is killed by a spear when it is driven through his head. The brooding Chief Inspector Harris (Edmund Purdom) and Sergeant Powell (Mark Jones) are immediately assigned to the investigation, but they are baffled by the lack of evidence.

The murders continue as an aspiring newspaper reporter, Giles (Alan Lake), begins to take an unhealthy interest in the case. While he follows his own line of enquiry, Gerry (Kevin Lloyd), a porn magazine photographer, focuses his lens on a model named Sharon (Pat Astley) posing in nothing but a Santa robe, thigh high boots and skimpy panties. When the police spot the titillating shoot, the pair is forced to make their escape into the London night. The terrified Sharon stumbles into a darkened alleyway only to be set upon by the killer, who wastes little time in slashing a razor across her exposed breasts. However, she manages to survive, only to be arrested for indecent exposure. Sometime later, in a sleazy strip club another Santa (Wilfred Corlett) engages a stripper (Kelly Baker) hidden away in the privacy of a booth. Before she can settle to her routine, he is butchered before her very eyes. We eventually learn that as a child the killer witnessed his father dressed as Santa canoodling with a party guest, before murdering his mother.

This sleazy mix of murder and gory splatter epitomized Dick Randall's low-budget approach to exploitative filmmaking, yet at the outset there were high hopes that it would be a lucrative successor to his chainsaw terror, **Pieces** (1982). Sadly, **Don't Open Till Christmas** turned out to be a problematic endeavour, running to almost two years in production. Lead actor Edmund Purdom and former sex film director Derek Ford, the film's writer, both resigned from the director's chair leaving the film's editor and former sex cinema owner Ray Selfe to bring this troubled feature to completion, but even he was unable to retain any sense of coherent narrative. The quality of the acting once again begged many questions, but the gore factor more than made up for these shortcomings, as the male victims were roasted, gouged, shot, stabbed, speared and, in a grimy toilet scene, castrated. In the repressed

> ... t'was the night before Christmas, and all through the house, not a creature was stirring ... they were all dead!

Britain of 1985, such a scene was only going to add to the film's difficult history and before it could be released in any format, it was subject to a substantial amount of editing, as was the scene involving the scantily clad Pat Astley. For all of its failings Randall's film was an intriguing glimpse of the sordid underbelly that the authorities in the UK tried to keep hidden from public view, but for those that so desired it was there ready to be found.

The Dorm that Dripped Blood

📅 YEAR OF RELEASE: 1982	✏️ WRITERS: Stephen Carpenter, Stacey Giachino
🕐 RUNTIME: 84 minutes	
🎬 COUNTRY: USA	📷 CINEMATOGRAPHER: Stephen Carpenter
🎥 DIRECTOR: Stephen Carpenter, Jeffrey Obrow	
	⚰️ PRODUCER: Jeffrey Obrow
	⭕ CERTIFICATE: UK: 18; USA: R
	💲 BUDGET: $90,000

CAST: Laurie Lapinski, Stephen Sachs, David Snow, Pamela Holland, Dennis Ely, Woody Roll, Daphne Zuniga, Jake Jones, Robert Frederick, Chris Morrill, Chandre, Billy Criswell, Richard Cowgill, Kay Beth, Jimmy Betz

THE AGEING DORMITORY, Morgan Meadows Hall, has been condemned and is being made ready for the bulldozers. Joanne Murray (Laura Lapinski) and her friends have the unenviable task of removing the desks, beds and other paraphernalia over the Christmas holiday period. One of the girls, Debbie (Daphne Zuniga), learns her grandmother is ill and has to return home with her parents. However, before they leave the school Debbie's head is crushed off-screen by a car and her parents are seen to die at the hands of a mysterious killer, all of which takes place in less than thirty seconds. The next day the crazy looking John Hemmit (Woody Roll) is spotted loitering around the school premises. Soon after Bobby Lee Tremble (Dennis Ely) arrives, claiming to be interested in buying the old desks, but his attention seems drawn towards Joanne. As night falls, caretaker (Jake Jones) comes face to face with the prowler and gets a drill to the back of his head, in what is without doubt the goriest scene in the movie. The friends become seriously concerned when both the power and the phone lines are cut off. One by one, they are hunted down in the darkness leading to an intense climax that carries a surprise of its own.

The name **The Dorm that Dripped Blood** still evokes memories of Amicus's memorable portmanteau terrors made between 1964 and 1973, but this was another standard slasher movie, which

A crash course in terror!

crammed in virtually every cliché known to this strain of eighties-styled horror movie. Stephen Carpenter and Jeffrey Obrow's Death Dorm college project was hopelessly underfinanced, culminating in the low-budget production values that have come to typify the genre. However, their efforts were rewarded when it was granted a limited theatrical release, albeit with much editing by the distributor. Carpenter and Obrow's concerns with the budget and a lacklustre plot meant much of the earlier part of the film was spent exploring the basement with flashlights, after they had immediately grabbed the audience's attention with a quite brutal series of murders. The slaughter would eventually resume with the head in the pressure cooker that has since been used on both the lurid cover to the video and the 2003 DVD release, and the body count would rise to a lofty ten before the killer's identity was finally revealed. The shadows and point-of-view killer shots certainly worked to raise the tension, as did Chris Young's atmospheric score that would see him embark upon an incredibly successful career. Carpenter and Obrow would continue to nurture their writing and directorial skills to produce the more successful **The Power** (1984) and then **The Kindred** (1987). The diminutive student backing and limited cinematic release would make **The Dorm that Dripped Blood** one of the more obscure entries from the period, but its notoriety was guaranteed when it was prosecuted by the DPP to join the list of offensive video nasties in October 1983 following its release to video in June 1982. It was removed from the list in September 1985 but ten seconds of cuts to the drilling of the caretaker have still never been made officially available in the UK.

Dr Giggles

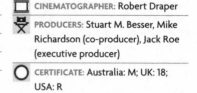

📅	YEAR OF RELEASE: 1992	🎞️	CINEMATOGRAPHER: Robert Draper
🕐	RUNTIME: 95 minutes	⚰️	PRODUCERS: Stuart M. Besser, Mike Richardson (co-producer), Jack Roe (executive producer)
🎯	COUNTRY: USA		
🎥	DIRECTOR: Manny Coto		
🎬	PRODUCTION COMPANY: Dark Horse Entertainment, JVC Entertainment Networks, Largo Entertainment	⭕	CERTIFICATE: Australia: M; UK: 18; USA: R
		💳	RECEIPTS: $8,403,450
✏️	WRITERS: Manny Coto, Graeme Whifler		

CAST: Larry Drake, Holly Marie Combs, Cliff De Young, Glenn Quinn, Keith Diamond, Richard Bradford, Michelle Johnson, John Vickery, Nancy Fish, Sara Melson, Zoe Trilling, Darin Heames, Deborah Tucker, Doug E. Doug, Denise Barnes

IN THE YEAR 1957 the locals of a quiet suburb in the town of Moorhigh have discovered Dr Rendell's dark secret – that he and his son, Evan Jr., nicknamed "Dr Giggles" owing to his hideous laugh, have been ripping out the hearts of their patients in a macabre attempt to return the doctor's dead wife to life. The townspeople take it on themselves to put an end to the doctor's heinous practice and Evan Jr. is carted off to the asylum.

Thirty-five years later Evan Jr. (Larry Drake) escapes the institution in which he has spent nearly his entire life. In his bid for freedom, he performs a heart removal in front of the inmates, and then continues on his way to avenge the trauma inflicted by his hometown, just like Michael Myers before him. The Rendell family home is now dilapidated, having been deserted these thirty-five years past. With revenge in mind, the nervously giggling Rendell Jr. now assumes his father's position and takes up residence in the abandoned house.

Teenager Jennifer (Holly Marie Combs) is ailed by an undiagnosed heart condition and her life has just gone even further downhill: her father, Tom (Cliff De Young), has moved his girlfriend Tamara (Michelle Johnson) into their home. With the school term now at an end Jennifer and her boyfriend Max (Glenn Quinn), along with a group of friends, seek out some teenage kicks at the Rendell house, not realizing Jr. is back in town. For them it's now too late; true to the slasher trope of the 1980s Rendell takes the group out one by one, this time using an array of medical instruments, each of which are only ever used once, surely in the interests of hygiene, and then begins his house calls, saving Jennifer for his final piece of surgery. The gore certainly splatters across the screen, with shredded flesh ripped and torn by this vile assemblage of implements, and in the spirit of Freddie Kreuger a mocking repartee of jokes accompanies each gruesome murder. The darkly comedic carnage brings death by blood pressure cuff, bladed thermometer, suffocation in the form of bandaging, castration, poisoning, lethal injections and a bizarre rotating drill inserted into the nasal cavity. Rendell Jr.'s imaginative quest for revenge knows no bounds.

With **Dr Giggles**, Manny Coto produced a mean-spirited film reminiscent of the formulaic excess of the early eighties frenzy for slashers, but his proliferation of wickedly humorous one-liners insisted it was not to be taken too seriously. The film was unapologetic in acknowledging its grisly predecessors, again and again it has to be said, with Larry Drake excelling in the lead role as the deranged Rendell Jr. **Dr Giggles** never claimed to be original; rather, it was an unashamed homage to the films that had made the slasher genre so special for so much of the 1980s. A two-issue comic book adaptation of the film ensued, published by Dark Horse Comics, which varied to the version that finally appeared on screen due to it being based on an earlier draft of the script. Queen's Brian May also stepped in to produce the score.

Dr Lamb

📅	YEAR OF RELEASE: 1992	✏️ WRITER: Law Kam Fai	
🕐	RUNTIME: 89 minutes	🎞️ CINEMATOGRAPHER: Kin Fai Miu	
🌐	COUNTRY: Hong Kong	⚱️ PRODUCERS: Danny Lee (executive producer), Parkman Wong	
🎥	DIRECTORS: Danny Lee, Hin Sing "Billy" Tang	⭕ CERTIFICATE: Hong Kong: III	
🎬	PRODUCTION COMPANY: Grand River Film Ltd, Heroes United Films Ltd		

CAST: Danny Lee, Simon Yam, Kent Cheng, Pik Yu Chung, Si Man Hui, Eric Kei, Emily Kwan, Hoi-Shan Lai, Siu-Ming Lau, Julie Lee, Parkman Wong, Siu Ling Wong, Usang Yeong Fang

A GROUP OF CHILDREN are watched as they happily play together, all except one. Lam appears a little withdrawn and bullied by his stepfamily; he also has a tendency to spy upon his parents as they make love and then catches glances of his stepsister as she takes a bath. He grows up to become a disturbed brooding individual, dogged by sexual inadequacy. He drives his taxi through rain-swept nights and then returns to the home of his stepsister to spend a little too much time alone in his room. While Lam and his family continue with their everyday lives, the police are investigating the discovery of a series of horribly disfigured bodies. By chance, a gruesome snapshot is found; then Lam's tale begins to unfold using a sequence of flashbacks from the moment when he is arrested in a photography shop. Lam is another crusader with a message from God to remove the fallen women from the streets of Hong Kong. The scenes depicting his interrogation are brutal as the police extract his grisly confession. Battered and bruised Lam begins to reveal his murderous obsession, which he has seen fit to capture on videotape and in the hundreds of shocking photographs he had hidden away detailing dismemberment, mutilation and necrophilia. As payment for his appalling catalogue of crimes, Lam suffers at the merciless hands of the

authorities and his own stepbrothers and sisters.

Hong Kong's celebrated Danny Lee made his directorial debut in a stylish movie that would have major bearing on the course of the region's burgeoning film industry. His feature was based on a series of murders that terrorized Hong Kong in 1982, perpetrated by the former colony's only convicted serial killer. A technician in a photo lab had processed one of Lam's rolls of film and was shocked to find images of what appeared to be a woman's mutilated breast; this turned out to be one of hundreds of similarly disgusting photographs depicting lacerations, body parts and alleged necrophilia. After several days of violent interrogation taxi driver Lam Gor-Yu admitted to this crime and then continued in his revelations on his murder of three other girls, each of whom he considered "bad and filthy". He attempted to justify his actions by claiming his orders had come from God. He was later sentenced to life-long imprisonment.

Both Lee and his co-director Hin Sing "Billy" Tang worked with their cameraman Kin Fai Miu to fashion a series of haunting flashbacks that were swathed in exaggerated blues and reds to forge a sense of dread in Lam's shadow-laden world and ensured every single frame taken in his room was meticulously considered. There was plenty of blood of guts on show in **Dr Lamb**, but the violence and brutality was nowhere near as excessive as the splatter observed in the following year's **The Untold Story**. This, however, would not save their work from the scrutiny of the Hong Kong censors, who were only prepared to give it a Category III rating when several even more extreme shots were edited. There is, however, a very rare Spanish videotape which is alleged to contain the original uncut version, but its graphic scenes apparently only run to an extra fifteen seconds. Such was the impact of **Dr Lamb**, the flashback structure would be repeated in **The Untold Story** and the team's scenes of rape and mutilation would be copied in Otto Chan Juk Tiu's gore-drenched **Diary of a Serial Killer** (1995). With the demise of the American slasher and Italian splatter, the age of the extreme Hong Kong Category III was now about to dawn.

Dracula

📅 YEAR OF RELEASE: 1958

🕐 RUNTIME: 82 minutes

🎥 COUNTRY: UK

🎬 DIRECTOR: Terence Fisher

🎬 PRODUCTION COMPANY: Hammer Film Productions

✏️ WRITERS: Jimmy Sangster, Bram Stoker

🎞️ CINEMATOGRAPHER: Jack Asher

🎬 PRODUCERS: Michael Carreras (executive producer), Anthony Hinds, Anthony Nelson Keys (associate producer)

⭕ CERTIFICATE: Australia: M; Canada: 13+ (Quebec); UK: 12A (re-rating) (2007); UK: 15 (video rating); UK: X (original rating); USA: Approved

💲 BUDGET: £81,000

CAST: Peter Cushing, Christopher Lee, Michael Gough, Melissa Stribling, Carol Marsh, Olga Dickie, John Van Eyssen, Valerie Gaunt, Janina Faye, Barbara Archer, Charles Lloyd Pack, George Merritt, George Woodbridge, George Benson, Miles Malleson

WHEN JONATHAN HARKER (John Van Eyssen) arrives at the castle of Count Dracula, he comes upon a luscious young woman who claims she is being held prisoner. Before Harker can attend to her needs, the Count makes his first appearance and brusquely ushers the fatigued Harker to his room. In the confinement of his locked chambers, Harker begins to write his journal and we learn he has journeyed to Klausenberg to put an end to the evil Count's reign of terror. In the days that follow, he again encounters the young woman and as she begs for help, her demeanour begins to change. To Harker's shock, she becomes feral and sinks her teeth into his neck just as an enraged Dracula emerges from the shadows, baring his fangs. Soon after awakening the next day, he makes preparations and then armed with a stake he descends into the crypts beneath the castle. There he finds the coffins of Dracula and the temptress that gorged on his neck. He wastes no time in impaling the woman, but is too late to deal with Dracula, for the evil Count has already risen and is ready to defend himself.

In the weeks that follow, Dr Van Helsing makes his way to Klausenberg. There he is presented with Harker's journal and then at the castle discovers his friend has been killed by the Count. He returns to tell Arthur Holmwood and his wife Mina, the brother and sister-in-law of Harker's fiancée Lucy Holmwood. Lucy appears to be ill, but as Dracula descends onto her terrace, we learn she too has fallen to this vampiric curse. Although Van Helsing does all he can to save the girl he knows she now belongs to the Count, giving him no option but to drive a stake through her heart. Van Helsing now has to return to Dracula's castle in an

The chill of the tomb won't leave your blood for hours ... after you come face to face with DRACULA!

effort to trace the Count's coffin, but Mina too has been cursed by his deathly bite. Although Van Helsing and Arthur do all they can to watch over the ailing girl, Dracula enters her room and once again savours her blood. However, the Count knows he must return to the security of his castle before sunrise and in his desperation tries to bury Mina, still barely alive, in the grounds adjacent to the crypts. Thankfully, Van Helsing and Arthur manage to thwart him, leading to a fateful altercation in the castle. When all seems lost, Van Helsing, in one of horror cinema's most iconic moments, drags the curtain open to allow the sunlight to pour into the room; he then uses candlesticks to create a cross and forces Dracula into its glare. There is no hope for the Count as he crumbles into dust and as he does, Mina is seen to recover. As the film comes to an end, Dracula's ashes are blown away in the wind, leaving only his ring to remind us of his wicked reign.

While there were many changes to Bram Stoker's original novel of 1897, Jimmy Sangster created a script that captured the essence of the Dracula myth as it pitted the venerable good against the very personification of evil. Under Terence Fisher's splendid direction both Christopher Lee and Peter Cushing excelled, bringing a menace and charm to their roles as they led to one of Hammer's most memorable finales. Bernard Robinson's set designs enhanced the Gothic milieu, as the mists seen drifting across the graveyards worked to intensify the film's foreboding allure. Along with its predecessor, **The Curse of Frankenstein** (1957), this set the tone for Hammer's success for the next twenty years, combining the Count's bloodthirsty lust with a sexual chemistry never before seen in cinema. **Dracula** was to have a major influence on the exploitation boom of the 1970s, paving the way for the eroticized flow of blood that immersed the extreme cinema of those years. To modern eyes, these bloody scenes appear somewhat tame, but in its day many of these scenes would have been considered unusually shocking.

When the film was released to the theatres of the United States as **Horror of Dracula**, certain scenes had been removed, most notably the onset of the impaled Harker's decomposition, which had already been censored in the UK. A considerable part of Count Dracula's putrefaction as he met his end was also consigned to the cutting room floor, only to be seen by audiences in South East Asia. In the forthcoming years Christopher Lee would return to this role on a further six occasions while Peter Cushing was to play the part of one of the Van Helsing family four more times. Lee had followed in the footsteps of Bela Lugosi, creating a monster for a whole new generation.

The Driller Killer

📅 YEAR OF RELEASE: 1979	
⏱ RUNTIME: 96 minutes	
🎥 COUNTRY: USA	
🎬 DIRECTOR: Abel Ferrara	
🎬 PRODUCTION COMPANY: Navaron Productions	
✎ WRITER: Nicholas St John	
▢ CINEMATOGRAPHERS: Ken Kelsch, James Lemmo	

PRODUCERS: D. A. Metrov (associate producer), Rochelle Weisberg (executive producer)

CERTIFICATE: Australia: MA (re-rating) (uncut); Australia: R; Canada: 13+ (Quebec); Ireland: (Banned); New Zealand: R18; UK: 18 (cut); UK: 18 (video re-rating, uncut, 2002); USA: Unrated

💲 BUDGET: $20,000

CAST: Abel Ferrara, Carolyn Marz, Baybi Day, Harry Schultz, Alan Wynroth, Maria Helhoski, James O'Hara, Richard Howorth, Louis Mascolo, Tommy Santora, Rita Gooding, Chuck Saaf, Gary Cohen, Janet Dailey, Joyce Finney

DIRECTOR ABEL FERRARA assumed the lead role in his film **The Driller Killer**, to give a crude but nonetheless effective performance as Reno Miller, a struggling New York painter. Reno's world is slowly disintegrating and as it collapses, so his sense of frustration begins to intensify. Early in the film, he denies knowing a derelict in a church who it turns out is really his father; his constant sarcasm provokes arguments with all and sundry; he is behind on the rent on his flea-bitten apartment and has bills that he can never pay. In this grimy downtrodden part of Manhattan this man is being pushed to the very edge and his deteriorating state of mind isn't helped by his roommates, Carol (Carolyn Marz) and the drug-addicted Pamela (Baybi Day). They are on show to provide an element of sleazy eroticism, with their sexual proclivity and lesbian frolickery, which was a rare sight for the general cinema-goer in the late 1970s. To make matters worse, just as he is trying to complete his masterpiece a punk rock band moves in nearby. The noise gets louder and louder and Reno's frustration begins to turn to rage. Even as he sleeps, his dreams are plagued by blood-strewn imagery and the deafening sound of drills. When he finally snaps he doesn't take it out on the band; instead he cuts loose, murdering the down and outs in the surrounding area with a recently purchased cordless drill. The first gets it in the chest with Reno gleefully laughing. With the filter on the camera's lens now glazed in scarlet, this night becomes one of slaughter as the vagrants are drilled down one by one. The following day an infuriated Reno bores a derelict's hands into a wall, in a scene of suffering symbolic of a mock crucifixion; he then delivers his victim to eternal salvation. When his painting fails to sell to Dalton, a gay gallery owner, Carol packs her bags and leaves him, condemning Reno to the inescapable maws of insanity. Dressed in black with lips smeared in blood red, an unstable Reno then invites Dalton over to his apartment. Reno's new image is striking but it will be the last Dalton ever gets to see. With Pamela dispatched off screen Reno's drill-crazy trail leads to Carol and her estranged husband for what will be a nail-biting conclusion.

Abel Ferrara's low-budget psycho-drama has been described as "a bargain basement **Taxi Driver**", a sensationalized observation of a man's descent into madness, in essence the victim of a decaying urban landscape very similar to Eloy de la Iglesia's **Cannibal Man** (1972). The budget was such he had to film in his own Union Square apartment and shoot on the surrounding streets. While not regarded as a true slasher picture, the extremes in violence leading to the climactic finale have rarely failed to excite that breed of horror connoisseur seeking an objectionably dark movie, and there is a notable absence of light in these grimy locales. This film makes you aware of the violence contained in this grisly horror, without needing to supply a body count of blood-soaked torsos. The soundtrack was also a blast back to a singular moment in history, the late seventies New York punk scene led by the Ramones, New York Dolls, Television and Patti Smith.

Although well received on its American release in 1979, it was to provoke unprecedented concern in the UK, and was duly hounded by the country's self-appointed moral guardians. This was primarily due to Vipco's advertising campaign, which in 1982 endorsed the shocking image of a man being drilled through the forehead by the Driller Killer. The British public were rarely privy to such graphic imagery and as a result the film was damned by the wrong kind of attention. There were numerous complaints to the Advertising Standards Agency and further opposition in the national press. National outrage backed by the tabloid press was quick to blame **The Driller Killer** and its bloodthirsty ilk for a decline in social values, which was ironically fundamental to Ferrara's original narrative. Few of its persecutors would have ever seen the film, but the attention grabbing sensationalism of the advertising campaign had completely backfired. According to Mike Bor, the Principal Examiner for the British Board of Film Classification: "**The Driller Killer** was almost single-handedly responsible for the Video Recordings Act 1984". The film was listed as a video nasty and banned in the UK. It wasn't until 2002 that this movie was officially released uncut to what by then was a new generation of horror enthusiasts in the UK. ❧

It will shatter you!

Dying Breed

📅 YEAR OF RELEASE: 2008		⚗ PRODUCERS: Michael Boughen, Christopher Mapp, (executive producer), Rod Morris, Matthew Street (executive producer), David Whealy
🕐 RUNTIME: 92 minutes		
🎥 COUNTRY: Australia		
🎬 DIRECTOR: Jody Dwyer		
🎞 PRODUCTION COMPANY: Ambience Entertainment		⭕ CERTIFICATE: Australia: MA; New Zealand: R18; UK: 18; USA: R
✏ WRITERS: Michael Boughen, Jody Dwyer, Rod Morris		💲 BUDGET: AUD $3,000,000 (Australia)
🎞 CINEMATOGRAPHER: Geoffrey Hall		

CAST: Nathan Phillips, Leigh Whannell, Bille Brown, Mirrah Foulkes, Melanie Vallejo, Ken Radley, Elaine Hudson, Sheridan Harvey, Peter Docker, Boris Brkic, Phillip McInnes, Ian "Paddy" McIvor, James Portanier, Sally McDonald

IN THE OPENING sequence of Jody Dwyer's **Dying Breed**, the early nineteenth-century Tasmanian legend Alexander "The Pieman" Pearce escapes his penal colony confinement to seek refuge in the island's forests and turns to cannibalism. Almost two hundred years later four young adventurers arrive on the island, one of whom, Nina, is solely intent on carrying on with the research her sister started prior to her death eight years ago while looking for the last remaining Tasmanian Tiger, a species acknowledged to have become extinct in the first part of the twentieth century. In a similar way to **Wolf Creek** (2005), there are references to missing backpackers and the local inhabitants are just as unsettling. Nina and her companions soon discover that her sister was yet another victim of the cannibalistic inbred descendants of Alexander Pearce. This family will do all that it takes to ensure the survival of their deviant bloodline, resulting in a desperate fight for survival for these young explorers.

First-time film director Dwyer explored the legends from Tasmania's past, and twisted them very subtly

Everybody has different tastes.

for his own purposes. The real Pearce, after being sentenced in Ireland to penal transportation for the theft of six pairs of shoes, had escaped with seven other prisoners and when captured admitted to cannibalizing some of his fellow escapees as a means of survival. The judge refused to believe his grisly tale and he was again imprisoned only to escape with another inmate, whom he also readily consumed. This time he was convicted and was hung in July 1824. His fictional descendants have much in common with the inbred terrors of **Deliverance** (1972), **The Texas Chain Saw Massacre** (1974), **The Hills Have Eyes** (1977) and **Wrong Turn** (2003), with Rebecca (Melanie Vallejo) strung up and savagely dismembered in a way that was reminiscent of Ruggero Deodato's hugely controversial **Cannibal Holocaust** (1980). Dwyer was very assured in his direction, affording his tale a pace and then raising the tension amidst the ominous backdrop of this verdant forest, before delivering the visual torment that has become intrinsic to the modern-day horror movie. The cast would include the already prolific writer and actor of

Saw (2004), Leigh Whannell, as Nina's boyfriend Nat, who true to form made a convincing addition to a film, which was hell-bent on becoming ever more vile as it journeyed deeper into this eerie terrain. The excruciating sequence with the bear trap in the mineshaft compounded by the close-in shots detailing a pickaxe to the head would delight the slavering gore-mongers, but the film's notoriety was ensured when the promotional poster was censored by an Australian company specializing in bus shelter advertising. Its depiction of a half-eaten pie, containing an eyeball and the remains of a finger, was just a little too much for them to stomach.

Eaten Alive

📅	YEAR OF RELEASE: 1977	🏆	PRODUCERS: Alvin L. Fast (co-producer), Larry Huly (associate producer), Robert A. Kanto (associate producer), Mardi Rustam, Mohammed Rustam (executive producer), Samir Rustam (associate producer)
⏱	RUNTIME: 91 minutes		
🎥	COUNTRY: USA		
🎬	DIRECTOR: Tobe Hooper		
🎞	PRODUCTION COMPANY: Mars Productions Corporation		
✏	WRITERS: Alvin L. Fast, Mardi Rustam, Kim Henkel	⭕	CERTIFICATE: Australia: R; New Zealand: R16; UK: 18; USA: R
🎬	CINEMATOGRAPHER: Robert Caramico	💲	BUDGET: $520,000

CAST: Neville Brand, Mel Ferrer, Carolyn Jones, Marilyn Burns, William Finley, Stuart Whitman, Roberta Collins, Kyle Richards, Robert Englund, Crystin Sinclaire, Janus Blythe, Betty Cole, Sig Sakowicz, Ronald W. Davis, Christine Schneider

A DARK, GREEN-TINTED moon hangs over the Louisiana Bayou as Clara Wood (Roberta Collins) wanders the streets after being dismissed from the town's brothel. The downtrodden girl had refused a dubious proposition for sex from a sodomy-loving punter known as Buck (Robert Englund) and now makes her way through the misty swamp to the secluded Starlight Hotel. The place it has to be said has seen better days. When she enters the rundown reception area, she is met by the maniacal owner Judd (Neville Brand) and his pet crocodile languishing in the swamp close to the porch. Judd, we soon learn, has severe difficulties in being able to communicate with ordinary people. When he discovers Clara worked as a prostitute, he flies into a maddened rage and attacks her with a pitchfork before feeding her to the crocodile. It isn't long before an irritable couple and their daughter arrive at the hotel. They have to watch as their pet dog is devoured by the crocodile. So follows Harvey Wood (Mel Ferrer) and his daughter, who are looking for his missing daughter, Clara, the prostitute seen at the beginning of the film. They are accompanied by the local sheriff. Each will eventually meet their fate at the hands of the psychotic Judd and his insatiable pet.

There is little in the way of plot to Tobe Hooper's low-budget follow-up to **The Texas Chain Saw Massacre** (1974); rather, the viewer is presented with a raw and nasty nightmare damned by an overriding sense of inevitability. The cheap sets and swampland mists enhance the unsettling atmosphere in a tale based on the mass murderer Joe Ball, who it

You check in alive ... but check out dead!

is alleged in the 1930s fed over twenty of his female victims to the alligators in his bar. True to its exploitative nature, Hooper's film has been passed off under a variety of different names, including **Death Trap**, **Horror Hotel**, **Horror Hotel Massacre**, **Legend of the Bayou**, **Murder on the Bayou**, **Le Crocodile de la Mort** and **Starlight Slaughter**, and has also been marketed as his lost movie.

In the United Kingdom on its 1978 release, it was censored to make it palatable for a British audience, but managed to get into the country as an uncut video in July 1982. With Mary Whitehouse taking a personal dislike to the movie, it was predictably listed as a video nasty in July 1983, but was later removed in December 1985 following several unsuccessful prosecutions. When it was again released to video in 1992 a total of twenty-five seconds were removed to limit the film's excessive violence.

The Ebola Syndrome

YEAR OF RELEASE: 1996		**WRITER:** Ting Chau
RUNTIME: 98 minutes		**CINEMATOGRAPHER:** Tsui Gok Bing
COUNTRY: Hong Kong		**PRODUCER:** Jing Wong
DIRECTOR: Herman Yau		**CERTIFICATE:** Hong Kong: III
PRODUCTION COMPANY: Jing's Production		

CAST: Anthony Wong Chau-Sang, Yeung Ming Wan, Fui-On Shing, Wong Tsui-ling, Miu-Ying Chan, Meng Lo

KAI (ANTHONY WONG Chau-Sang) is deep into his sex with the boss's wife. When his boss catches him in the act, he is threatened with castration. This doesn't seem to bother Kai; he slaughters his boss and his associates along with his wife and then flees to South Africa. Ten years later, still in his self-imposed exile, he endures a lowly existence as a poorly-paid employee in a Chinese restaurant. While trying to buy meat for the restaurant from a Zulu tribe he rapes an unconscious woman, who we learn is infected with the Ebola virus. His frustrations begin to mount in the restaurant and once again his temper gets the better of him and he murders his boss and his wife after raping her. His sick mind then tries to hide the evidence of his crime; he chops up their dead bodies and turns them into hamburgers, which he offers for sale in the restaurant. The virus begins to spread. As the police dragnet begins to close, he returns to his native Hong Kong and continues in his scurrilous activities. The Ebola epidemic begins to hit the streets of Hong Kong.

The opening sequences to Herman Yau's **The Ebola Syndrome** feature a violent intensity rarely experienced in western cinema; this is gruesome B-movie horror all the way from Hong Kong, inspired by its twisted predecessors **Dr Lamb** (1992) and **The Untold Story** (1993). Although some of the sex is suggestive, the rape scenes are horribly brutal; the enigmatic Kai is at heart one vicious individual. The gore levels are the equal of anything the South East Asian film industry has to offer, which includes a series of highly innovative scenes as bodies are butchered to make hamburgers and eyes are avariciously chewed out of a living head. The depiction of the Ebola virus is probably the most disturbing element in this film; for the infected their lives will become one of unfathomable horror. However, Yau's film, although controversial, manages to play out as a macabre comedy with Anthony Wong shining in his portrayal of the demented Kai.

Edge of the Axe

📅 YEAR OF RELEASE: 1988	🎬 PRODUCTION COMPANY: Galupas Entertainment
🕐 RUNTIME: 91 minutes	
🎥 COUNTRY: Spain/USA	✏️ WRITER: Pablo de Aldebarán
🎥 DIRECTOR: José Ramón Larraz	🎞️ CINEMATOGRAPHER: Tote Trenas
	⏳ PRODUCERS: José Frade, Francisco Lara Polop (executive producer)

CAST: Barton Faulks, Christina Marie Lane, Page Mosely, Fred Holliday, Patty Shepard, Alicia Moro, Jack Taylor, Conrado San Martín, Joy Blackburn, May Heatherly, Elmer Modling, Javier Elorrieta, José Frade, Christina Lane

IN THE REMOTE community of Paddock County, North California, a killer freely stalks the homes of the local female residents, chopping them up with a sharpened axe. When a dead body is discovered in the ceiling of a local tavern, the sheriff dismisses it as suicide. This lax attitude only encourages the killer as he wantonly plies his brutal trade, even during the hours of daylight. One of them of particular note takes place in a car wash, in a violent episode inflicted by a figure whose face remains hidden by a white mask, not unlike that worn by Michael Myers. The sheriff displays little interest in the escalating severity of the murders, still choosing to play their significance down. A series of red herrings are thrown into the proceedings, including the creepy pastor and a newly arrived pianist. The most likely suspect remains young Gerald, who is enamoured by Lilly, the cute heroine of the proceedings. As the body count continues to rise, they take it on themselves to investigate these crimes and are certain they know the killer's identity. Then it becomes their turn as the killer begins to prey upon them. This game of cat and mouse reaches absolute fever pitch when the film comes to the most abrupt of ends, with the killer's identity having only just been very subtly disclosed.

José Ramón Larraz had already carved a reputation with his lesbian **Vampyres** movie in 1975. **Edge of the Axe** continued his association with horror, this time with a modest low-budget slasher, produced when these films had fallen from favour. His direction, while slow between kills, was carried out with gusto, thus affording the attacks an unbearable degree of ferocity and in their wake dissipated an unsettling ambience across an isolated town firmly caught in the grip of fear. The photography shone throughout, savouring the kill and then surprising the audience with some quite beautiful backdrops. The director had a reputation for casting and using the camera's lens to adorn his films with some rather beautiful women; **Edge of the Axe** was no exception. However, contrary to the slasher trope, these girls remained fully clothed, which duly caused howls of derision among the genre's teenage addicts. Visually Larraz's killer was reminiscent of Michael Myers in **Halloween** and as with this psychopath before him prowled though this film with a disturbing air of menace. The BBFC removed a reported twenty-six seconds of footage when they gave it an "18" certificate, making certain murder scenes appear awkward, suggesting individual frames had gone missing; this appears all the more likely when comparing the ease with which the camera flows during the remainder of the film. Over twenty years later conjecture continues as to whether an unedited gory version of **Edge of the Axe** actually does exist.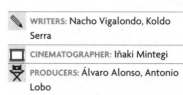

El Tren de la Bruja

📅 YEAR OF RELEASE: 2003	✏️ WRITERS: Nacho Vigalondo, Koldo Serra
🕐 RUNTIME: 18 minutes	
🎥 COUNTRY: Spain	🎞️ CINEMATOGRAPHER: Iñaki Mintegi
🎬 DIRECTOR: Koldo Serra	⏳ PRODUCERS: Álvaro Alonso, Antonio Lobo
🎬 PRODUCTION COMPANY: Arsénico Producciones, Jaleo Films	

CAST: Manolo Solo, Jon Ariño, Héctor Alterio, Nacho Marcos, Santiago Guibert, Jesús Pueyo, Fernando Calvo, Elena Mendiola, Nacho Vigalondo

IN A DARKENED room, an intimidating voice (Hector Alterio) instructs a lone man (Manolo Solo) to sit down and attach himself to an electrically wired chair, which stands in the beam of a single spotlight. His air of confidence gives the impression he is willingly participating in a scientific experiment; this seems all the more likely when his arms begin to bleed and he appears completely unaffected by the flow of blood. However, just beyond the shaft of light he begins to become aware of a build up of indiscernible noise, which as it increases in intensity starts to undermine his self-assurance. As his ordeal persists the resonance becomes more threatening, but the darkness continues to veil its mysterious source. As the fall of the light becomes more focused, his imagination conspires to deceive his mind, yet still he fights to retain his composure. A hand then seizes his shoulder. He turns to be confronted by a masked figure adorned in a butcher's apron and then to his horror realizes a severed finger has been placed on his head. Tearing the wires from his body, he breaks free of the chair.

While all of this has been going on the taunting somewhere in the background has continued without relent. The masked menace now stands astride him; it is obvious something is seriously amiss. In only a matter of minutes, his situation has gone through a drastic change as laughter is heard from an audience obscured by the shadows. The man at the centre of the experiment withdraws to the apparent safety of his chair as a stream of blood drips onto his body. His would-be assailant then uncovers a severed head, and tosses it into his lap. Reeling in terror, he then has a gun forced against his head. In the darkness, a group of excited onlookers steadily count down to zero. At the allotted moment, the gun goes off and the man crumples to the floor. There he lies, dead. Light suddenly floods the room as the camera draws back to reveal it is almost empty. The man in the mask is seen as he is ushered away, his face wracked in self-recriminating torment.

A year after its release the highly original **El Tren de la Bruja**, which has also been passed off as **Spook House**, became the recipient of the Grand Prize for Best European fantasy short film at the Amsterdam Fantastic Film Festival and also gained recognition as the Best Spanish Short at the San Sebastian Horror and Fantasy Film Festival. It

is hard to believe this intense piece of storytelling was completed in only two days. Koldo Serra would eventually move on into a successful career in television, and his film could well have drifted into complete obscurity if it had not been for the impact of Eli Roth's **Hostel** (2005). There are many who believe this short feature provided the inspiration for Roth's blockbuster. Unlike Roth, Serra kept his audience guessing, refusing to make it clear as to whether this was truly an experiment, or, as in **Hostel**, it was really a sinister game of torture and death to entertain those of incomparable affluence. Rather than relying on the graphic nature espoused by its successor, Serra made adept use of light and sound to create a sense of atmosphere and ultimately instil in both his audience and the protagonists on screen a sense of fear. He also had the good fortune to attract an actor of the calibre of Manolo Solo, who in only eighteen minutes endured a remarkable transformation in character.

Evil

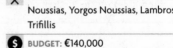

 **YEAR OF RELEASE:** 2005		**WRITER:** Yorgos Noussias	
RUNTIME: 92 minutes		**CINEMATOGRAPHERS:** Claudio Bolivar, Petros Noussias	
COUNTRY: Greece			
DIRECTOR: Yorgos Noussias		**PRODUCERS:** Claudio Bolivar, Petros Noussias, Yorgos Noussias, Lambros Trifillis	
PRODUCTION COMPANY: Ekso Productions			
		BUDGET: €140,000	

CAST: Meletis Georgiadis, Yannis Katsambas, Andreas Kontopoulos, Themis Katz, Pepi Moschovakou, Argiris Thanasoulas, Stavroula Thomopoulou, Mary Tsoni

To Κακό, or **Evil** as it was billed outside its native Greece, was the country's first encounter with the zombie apocalypse. When three construction workers stumble upon a hidden cave, they are attacked by an unseen force that rushes towards them in a sequence, which invites comparison with Sam Raimi's **The Evil Dead** (1981). Although the team manage to escape the cave, none of them can remember what actually happened down there and it is obvious something in their demeanour has changed. As evening falls, the three go their separate ways only to undergo a shocking metamorphosis to rise as zombie-like creatures with an insatiable need to feed upon human flesh, turning their victims within seconds into the walking dead. In a few short days, the entire city of Athens falls to the ensuing carnage, while a few survivors try to escape this mindless bloodthirsty frenzy, leading to a truly dark finale that is rarely observed in American zombie cinema.

Greece just got scary ...

There was some genuine humour observed in this film, some of which was inspired by Peter Jackson's **Braindead** (1992), but it was essentially a brutally violent offering very much in the mould of Danny Boyle's **28 Days Later** (2002). With a hopelessly limited budget, Yorgos Noussias's effects team returned to the seminal **Dawn of the Dead** (1978) in blowing away zombies' heads, and then dishing up decapitations and disembowelments galore as they set out to annihilate anything that lived. His film moved at a fast pace even though the zombies can only shuffle through the Athens streets tracked by inventive camera work and split-screen editing. The cast eagerly embraced their roles, insisting the viewer roots for their escape from this infernal nightmare, but the denouement seeks to disturb, offering a doom-ridden finale. Noussias returned with more backing for a highly praised prequel, **Evil – In the Time of Heroes** (2009), starring Billy Zane, in which many of the actors apparently worked without pay.

The Evil Dead

📅 YEAR OF RELEASE: 1981   🕐 RUNTIME: 85 minutes

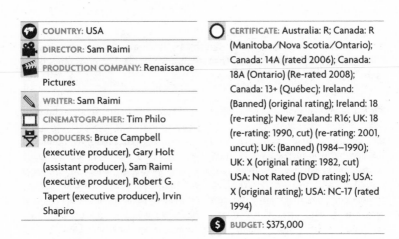

COUNTRY: USA

DIRECTOR: Sam Raimi

PRODUCTION COMPANY: Renaissance Pictures

WRITER: Sam Raimi

CINEMATOGRAPHER: Tim Philo

PRODUCERS: Bruce Campbell (executive producer), Gary Holt (assistant producer), Sam Raimi (executive producer), Robert G. Tapert (executive producer), Irvin Shapiro

CERTIFICATE: Australia: R; Canada: R (Manitoba/Nova Scotia/Ontario); Canada: 14A (rated 2006); Canada: 18A (Ontario) (Re-rated 2008); Canada: 13+ (Québec); Ireland: (Banned) (original rating); Ireland: 18 (re-rating); New Zealand: R16; UK: 18 (re-rating: 1990, cut) (re-rating: 2001, uncut); UK: (Banned) (1984–1990); UK: X (original rating: 1982, cut) USA: Not Rated (DVD rating); USA: X (original rating); USA: NC-17 (rated 1994)

BUDGET: $375,000

CAST: Bruce Campbell, Ellen Sandweiss, Richard DeManincor, Betsy Baker, Theresa Tilly, Philip A. Gillis, Dorothy Tapert, Cheryl Guttridge, Barbara Carey, David Horton, Wendall Thomas, Don Long, Stu Smith, Kurt Rauf, Ted Raimi

THE EVIL DEAD was first introduced as a virtually unknown feature in 1978 entitled **Within the Woods**, created with the purpose of enticing potential investors to fund Sam Raimi's idea for a horror movie. This short film had similarities with the motion picture it later spawned and included among the cast one Bruce Campbell. **The Evil Dead** was Raimi's debut as a director and although its comic book-styled horror proved hugely controversial, he immediately distinguished himself, making an extraordinarily powerful movie with a very restrictive budget.

Five college kids, Ash (Bruce Campbell), his girlfriend Linda (Betsy Baker) and their friends Cheryl (Ellen Sandweiss), Scott (Hal Delrich) and Shelly (Sarah York), spend the night in an isolated mountain cabin set in a deep forest. The cabin is strangely similar to the refuge shown in the classic Norwegian terror of 1958, **Lake of the Dead** (**De Dødes Tjern**), directed by Kåre Bergstrøm. As they make themselves comfortable, they find an ageing tome scribed in hieroglyphics sitting beside a reel-to-reel tape recorder. The tape, recorded by a professor of archaeology, warns of the evil incantations entered in the Sumerian "Book of the Dead", and their power to invoke a malevolent force hidden in the woods. This force has but one desire, to possess and then corrupt those that it encounters. Once the malignancy has taken hold there is only one way it can ever be exorcized, by bodily dismemberment.

The students foolishly take little heed of the professor's warning and all too soon the evil in the woods begins to sweep around the cabin, with Shelly the first to be affected. She is transformed into a murderous crone. Poor Cheryl is then lured into the woods; chasing through the darkness she stumbles and is horrifically tree-raped by a demonically possessed branch. This single incident would in time arouse the wrath of censors across the globe and assure the film's notoriety. It is now the students realize there is no escape; the bridge leading back to town has been torn down. One by one each of them falls foul of this destructive presence, and turns into a deranged abomination. When Linda succumbs to the evil force, Ash can't bring himself to take the chainsaw to her neck, so instead he buries her in the woods. This isn't the best idea he has ever had and when she returns the evil within has become so much more intense. Blasting and chopping, Ash makes it all the way to the shattering finale when he catches sight of "The Book of the Dead" falling into the fire. As the flames destroy the book, its demonic creations are seen to disintegrate. He now staggers to the door, the sole survivor of this frenzied assault. As he gathers his thoughts in the calm of the early morning light, the evil once again rises from the earth. Gathering pace through the woods its malevolence bears down on Ash, who turns to the camera, his face wracked in terror, just before the screen goes black.

Can they be stopped?

Despite the limited resources and the eighteen months of filming, Sam Raimi produced a fast-paced shocker that terrified his audience and ultimately proved a milestone in horror cinema. The outrageous overacting combined with the excessive gore saw this comic book-styled extravaganza push back the boundaries, and all for $375,000. However, by inadvertently challenging the acceptability of such violent excess, Raimi alarmed the distributors and in due course provoked the censors. There were major concerns regarding the misogyny in the tree rape, a scene Raimi has since admitted he regrets. The film's graphic penchant for violence and gore caused many American distributors to stay well away from its excessive premise and not until the Cannes Film Festival did The Evil Dead acquire a distributor. The film was championed by Stephen King but predictably ran into serious difficulties in the UK, even though it was duly recognized for its parody of horror and almost passed uncut, but was then burdened by even more problems in Germany. Its inevitable inclusion on the list of video nasties, with Sam Raimi prepared to defend his film in an English Court of Law, further added to its notoriety and generated an enthusiastic following on the black market. A heavily edited version was later made available in 1992 but in recent years Anchor Bay

Entertainment has been able to release the film unrated.

The film was followed by the sequels, **Evil Dead II** and **Army of** **Darkness**, with a third in the planning for 2013. A stage musical has also been produced along with a comic book adaptation published by Dark Horse.

Evilspeak

📅 YEAR OF RELEASE: 1981		🎞 CINEMATOGRAPHER: Irv Goodnoff
🕐 RUNTIME: 89 minutes		🎬 PRODUCERS: H. Hal Harris (associate producer), Gerald Hopman (associate producer), Sylvio Tabet (executive producer), Sylvio Tabet, Eric Weston
🌐 COUNTRY: USA		
🎥 DIRECTOR: Eric Weston		
🎬 PRODUCTION COMPANY: Leisure Investment Company, Coronet Film		⭕ CERTIFICATE: Australia: R; UK: 18; USA: R
✎ WRITERS: Joseph Garofalo, Eric Weston		💲 BUDGET: $1,000,000

CAST: Clint Howard, R. G. Armstrong, Joseph Cortese, Claude Earl Jones, Haywood Nelson, Don Stark, Charles Tyner, Hamilton Camp, Louie Gravance, Jim Greenleaf, Lynn Hancock, Loren Lester, Kathy McCullen, Lenny Montana, Leonard D'John, Bennett Liss

A GROUP OF SPANISH monks accompanied by well-armed Conquistadors make their way along a southern Californian beach as their cohorts unload crates from the incoming rowboats. Their path takes them to a hooded figure bearing a sword. This man is Lorenzo Esteban, a heretic exiled from his native Spain and excommunicated from the Catholic church who has at his beck and call a fanatical set of followers. He refuses to renounce his pursuit of evil and is soon after seen rousing his frenzied disciples. As their chant rises to an impassioned crescendo, Esteban stands behind a partially clad young woman, raises his sword and brings it down to remove her head, which flies through the air to land, as the scene changes, as a football in the present day of 1981.

In a military academy a game of football is taking place and well-intentioned Stanley Coopersmith (Clint Howard) is about to hand victory to the opposition. This will gain him even more abuse from a bullying gang led by Bubba (Don Stark). Stanley is an easy target, a downtrodden orphan whose clumsy ways have made him an outcast at West Andover Academy. Here he is humiliated by Bubba and his lamebrain associates, and suffers similar torment from the teaching staff, the coach, the colonel, as well as the reverend. As a punishment Stanley is sent to the chapel to clean a darkened cellar; there he finds a book in a secret room that details the Black Mass. The book, written in an age-old language, is revealed to be a journal kept by the evil Esteban. Stanley becomes obsessed with this and the other strange artefacts hidden away in this old room and uses a computer to translate the incantations. In so doing, he unleashes an evil force to take revenge on those who have for such a long time plagued him. Estaban returns to possess Stanley's body and as he once again seizes hold of his sword to inflict a bloodthirsty carnage, a pack of murderous wild boars pour forth from the bowels of the earth. For the last ten minutes of this film, Stanley enjoys his moment only to be damned to an eternity locked in the computer's memory.

Data incomplete ... Human blood required. Thus spake the computer.

This was the beginning of Eric Weston's time in the film and television industry and **Evilspeak** also known as **Evilspeaks** and **Computer Murders**, proved a rather amusing gorefest. While his movie adopts so many of the accepted clichés of the day, following on from the bullying observed in **Carrie** (1976) he introduces a new monster,

a home computer that becomes the villainous tool of the piece. This was at a time long ago when such technology was only just beginning to encroach on our everyday lives. From Joseph Garofalo's script entitled "The Foundling", Eric Weston brought in the possessed computer and then shot his film over a three-week period, in a condemned South Central Los Angeles church, which burned to the ground only three days later.

Clint Howard had already been in film and television for eighteen years when **Evilspeak** went into production, but this was his first major role in a performance that had the audience firmly on his side. His murderous display was the gore-monger's delight and when it was released uncut to video in August 1983 it was eagerly snapped up. However, when the Video Recordings Act entered the statute books its excessive finale coupled with Satanic themes saw it banned as a video nasty in March 1984. It wasn't to see release to video until 1987, when the BBFC insisted on a multitude of edits running to over three and a half minutes, beginning with the prologue's decapitation. There then followed edits to a neck breaking in the basement, the boars' attack in the bathroom and the subsequent devouring of guts, the reverend's nail to the head, Stanley splattering the head of one of his teachers and the boars consuming the students, along with numerous other decapitations. The BBFC's stipulations were to diminish so much of the impact of Weston's original idea; but in 2004, an extended version of the film was released, thankfully restoring every single moment of gore.

Exposé

YEAR OF RELEASE: 1976	**CINEMATOGRAPHERS:** Dennis C. Lewiston, Phil Meheux
RUNTIME: 84 minutes	**PRODUCERS:** Brian Smedley-Aston, Paul Raymond (executive producer)
COUNTRY: UK	
DIRECTOR: James Kenelm Clarke	**CERTIFICATE:** Australia: R; New Zealand: R18; UK: X (original rating); UK: 18 (video rating, cut); USA: X; USA: R (edited for re-rating)
PRODUCTION COMPANY: Norfolk International Pictures	
WRITER: James Kenelm Clarke	**BUDGET:** £50,000

CAST: Udo Kier, Linda Hayden, Fiona Richmond, Patsy Smart, Karl Howman, Vic Armstrong

THE OPENING SCENES reveal a suspiciously paranoid Paul Martin (Udo Keir) putting on a pair of rubber gloves before having sex with his girlfriend Suzanne (Fiona Richmond). Following the success of his first novel, Paul has withdrawn to a quiet house in the Essex countryside in the hope of bringing his next work to completion. His agent needs another bestseller and hires a beautiful secretary, Linda (Linda Hayden), to work with the self-possessed writer. Linda is a highly sexed young woman and, when away from her employer's instruction, is taken to openly masturbating in the fields that surround the house and is seen to have an enflamed lesbian encounter with the statuesque Suzanne. There is, however, something very strange about Linda and it isn't wise to cross her path as two youths discover after they have raped her. As the body count begins to rise, Paul learns to his cost that he has made a huge mistake in bringing the psychotic Linda into his home.

Exposé, which has also assumed the names **Trauma** and **The House on Straw Hill**, played as a psychological thriller and with its profusion of sex and violence was counted as part of that decade's lust for cinematic exploitation. Partly financed by adult entertainment and property mogul Paul Raymond, the publicity surrounding the film promised "Nothing, but nothing, is left to the imagination . . . ", casting British sex queen Fiona Richmond in her first major role. Although her part in the script was secondary to that of Linda Hayden, Richmond's popularity in Raymond's line of top-shelf men's magazines automatically gave her the bigger billing. Hayden, whose acting ability throughout surpassed her colleagues', later distanced herself from the film as she pursued a successful career in the theatre and national television. Her role was reminiscent of Susan George in **Straw Dogs** (1971), with her murderous revenge on the low-life rapists coming two years before Camille Keaton's bloody reprisal in **I Spit on Your Grave** (1978).

She'll take your breath away . . . Your life is next.

The low ceilings were matched only by the diminutive budget, but the house afforded the film a claustrophobic feel, while the miles of open fields evoked a sense of hopeless isolation, allowing director James Kenelm Clarke to focus on the development of his characters and expound his plot by way of a series of highly compelling scenes. By modern standards, the violence appears tame, but the throat slitting, along with the bloody shotgun murders and the slashing of the naked Fiona Richmond in the shower as the blood poured across her breasts, down past her vagina, were a cause for concern among the authorities. On its initial cinematic release, over three minutes were removed from both the sex scenes and stabbings to make it suitable for distribution as an "X"-rated feature. Following the video explosion of the early 1980s, an unedited version made its way into the country around March 1984 only to be almost immediately banned as a video nasty. The current DVD release is still missing fifty-one seconds, with edits to the rape scene, which still contains a suggestion that Linda was seen to be enjoying her ordeal, as well as the blood dripping onto Suzanne's breasts. **Exposé** remains a popular entry for horror enthusiasts on these shores, but it is has been largely neglected across the rest of the world. It is in essence a very British affair, albeit mean-spirited, trying to find a place among the more exotic Euro-exploitation of the mid-1970s.

Eyes of a Stranger

 YEAR OF RELEASE: 1981

 RUNTIME: 84 minutes

COUNTRY: USA

DIRECTOR: Ken Wiederhorn

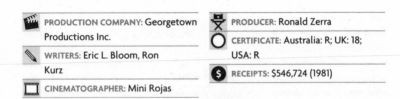

PRODUCTION COMPANY: Georgetown Productions Inc.

WRITERS: Eric L. Bloom, Ron Kurz

CINEMATOGRAPHER: Mini Rojas

PRODUCER: Ronald Zerra

CERTIFICATE: Australia: R; UK: 18; USA: R

RECEIPTS: $546,724 (1981)

CAST: Lauren Tewes, Jennifer Jason Leigh, John DiSanti, Peter DuPre, Gwen Lewis, Kitty Lunn, Timothy Hawkins, Ted Richert, Toni Crabtree, Robert Small, Stella Rivera, Dan Fitzgerald, Jose Baramonde, Luke Halpin, Rhonda Flynn

A MURDEROUS RAPIST stalks the night of Miami in search of the vulnerable, abusing them with sordid telephone calls before dispatching them with an array of oh-so-familiar sharpened weapons. While the calls are not quite as sinister as those that terrorized **Black Christmas** (1974), they still serve as a chilling calling card. A woman's dead body is soon discovered in swampland and then Debbie Ormsley (Gwen Lewis) and her boyfriend Jeff (Timothy Hawkins) are butchered in the privacy of her home. Local news reporter Jane Harris (Lauren Tewes) begins to suspect her neighbour, Stanley Herbert (John DiSanti), whose behaviour has become strangely erratic. The killings continue with Herbert seemingly leaving evidence for Jane to discover. No one will listen to her, and to make matters worse Jane fears for her defenceless younger sister, Tracy (Jennifer Jason Leigh). The child's psychosomatic injuries have left her deaf, blind and mute as a result of her abduction several years before. Jane will discover facets of her own hitherto undisclosed personality before this game of cat and mouse is skilfully drawn to its climactic finale.

The voice on the telephone that all women dreaded.

Eyes of a Stranger would be director Ken Wiederhorn's second horror movie following **Shock Waves** (1977), which only ever saw very limited release; he later returned to frighten his audiences with **Return of the Living Dead Part II** (1988) and seven episodes of **Freddy's Nightmares** between 1989 and 1990. Here, Wiederhorn managed to create a suspense-charged movie very much in the Hitchcock vein containing key elements of the brutality and voyeuristic sleaze that had already enticed the growing army of fans for this kill-crazed cinematic experience. The filming techniques and cleverly staged lighting combined to leave a grimly washed out tone, which reflected his movie's intentionally disreputable character. This was never more so in evidence than when the killer's distorted image was observed pressed up against the glass of the shower prior to Wiederhorn building the tension to deliver his feature's closing scenes. The violence was excessive, particularly during the episode when a woman was attacked and then raped in her own apartment, followed by the blood bath in a lovers' lane washed down with the memorable head in the fish-tank. On its release, much of Tom Savini's expertise was once again censored, which was to dilute so much of the film's vicious impact. The uncut version was recently released in Warner's **Twisted Terror Collection**, giving horror fans the chance to see Wiederhorn and Savini's grand design just as it should have been three decades before. **Eyes of a Stranger** will also be remembered for a young Jennifer Jason Leigh, who in her first major role in film produced a highly credible performance. 🦋

Eyes Without a Face

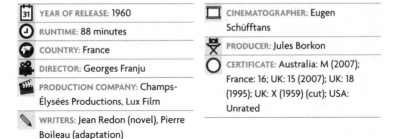

📅 YEAR OF RELEASE: 1960	🎞 CINEMATOGRAPHER: Eugen Schüfftans
🕐 RUNTIME: 88 minutes	
🌐 COUNTRY: France	☠ PRODUCER: Jules Borkon
🎥 DIRECTOR: Georges Franju	⭘ CERTIFICATE: Australia: M (2007); France: 16; UK: 15 (2007); UK: 18 (1995); UK: X (1959) (cut); USA: Unrated
🎬 PRODUCTION COMPANY: Champs-Élysées Productions, Lux Film	
✎ WRITERS: Jean Redon (novel), Pierre Boileau (adaptation)	

CAST: Pierre Brasseur, Alida Valli, Juliette Mayniel, Edith Scob, François Guérin, Alexandre Rignault, Béatrice Altariba, Charles Blavette, Claude Brasseur, Michel Etcheverry, Yvette Etiévant, René Génin, Lucien Hubert, Marcel Pérès

DR GÉNESSIER, TO his friends and associates, is a highly reputable skin graft surgeon; his basement surgery, however, hides a terrible secret. Young girls have also been going missing on the streets of Paris. The culprit it turns out is the doctor's daughter, Louise, who by day works as an assistant at the family clinic. She scours the streets of Paris looking to befriend young girls, before leading them to their macabre fate in the lower echelons of her father's remote mansion. Once the doctor has incapacitated these hapless girls, he surgically removes their facial skin then transplants the tissue onto the face of his other daughter, Christiane. The unfortunate girl has been horribly disfigured in an accident some time before, an incident for which her father was responsible. The scars are so unsightly she is forced to hide herself away in the darkened manse and secrete her injuries behind a white mask. In his search for perfection, the guilt ridden Dr Génessier continues to fail and more young girls soon lose their lives.

Les Yeux Sans Visage represented a first for French cinema; up until this time, no one else in the country had seriously considered making a horror movie. British horror films such as **The Curse of Frankenstein** (1957) and **Horror of Dracula** (1958) had already proved very popular with French filmgoers and in their wake Jules Borkon looked to profit from this recent wave of grisly interest. His director, Georges Franju, was always at odds with those who looked upon his film as little more than a horror movie; his vision, he insisted, was one of "anguish". The abhorrence detailed in each skin graft was reminiscent of the many incarnations of the Frankenstein creation, but the more discerning would have also distinguished a similar pathos between the so-called monster of the Universal years and that of Christiane.

Splatter purists would be disappointed by an appreciable lack of blood in evidence in the doctor's basement; but in its day this would have been far too much for the squeamish French censors. Its premise, however, still worked to disturb and was intensified by the cinematography of Eugene Schüfftans. He was inspired by the darker elements of German expressionism, imparting the Villa Génessier an air of tenebrous despair, with superlative use of light and shadow, to create the impression that this was a prison from which there was no hope of escape. For all of his craft, Schüfftans would be rebuked by French reviewers, who were now drawn to the new wave and tired of what were considered outmoded techniques. Franju, in turn, employed a subtlety to shape a nightmarish air that echoed the truly reprehensible nature of Génessier's misguided toil. Only when necessary did he deign to shock. You can only imagine the dismay felt by his audience as the doctor sliced into the beauteous faces of his many victims. The seeming success of the operation would have momentarily served to assuage this jolt to the senses, only to see the anguish to which Franju referred fracture Christiane's delicate features as they tear apart only weeks after her operation. These scenes ingeniously reflect the cruelty of the Génessier described in Jean Redon's original novel, a trait Franju had to play very carefully so as not to offend the censors in both France and Germany. The result, however, was one of heartbreak for the distraught Christiane, whose tragedy was cast at the very centre of this morbid drama.

On its release, the film suffered almost universal critical rejection. Members of the audience in both France and Edinburgh were witnessed to faint at the abominable scenes in basement surgery, a situation upon which modern-day promoters would now readily seize. Only the London *Observer* was appreciative of its artistic merits. For the American release of 1962, the film was drastically edited. It was conferred the indignity of an English-language dub, and re-titled **The Horror Chamber of Dr Faustus**. Further to this, shots of the grafting process were removed together with a series of minor scenes alluding to Doctor Génessier's humanity, particularly his care for a small child at his clinic. This revised feature was only ever conferred a limited theatrical run, and was given little if any recognition. As the years passed, film historians began to acknowledge the true worth in Franju's film, finally understanding its nuances, and filmmakers of repute such as John Carpenter, Jesús Franco and John Woo would soon attest to its influence. John Carpenter has suggested that **Eyes Without a Face** inspired the idea for the mask worn by Michael Myers in **Halloween** (1978). Several years after the release of his masterpiece, he recollected the film crew "didn't have any money to make a mask. It was originally written the way you see it; in other words, it's a pale mask with human features, almost featureless", very similar to that which disguised the face of the melancholic Christiane.

Eyes Without a Face received a second major theatrical release in September 1986, in conjunction with notable retrospectives at the National Film Theatre in London and the film archive Cinémathèque Française for its fiftieth anniversary in France. As a founder of Cinémathèque Française, the archive celebrated the achievements of Franju by showcasing the director's back catalogue. The film was later released in its original form to American theatres, rather appropriately on October 31, 2003, with its original running time and title fully restored.

Faces of Death

 YEAR OF RELEASE: 1980

 RUNTIME: 105 minutes

 COUNTRY: USA

 DIRECTOR: John Alan Schwartz

 PRODUCTION COMPANY: F.O.D. Productions

 WRITER: John Alan Schwartz

 PRODUCERS: William B. James (executive producer), Herbie Lee (associate producer), Rosilyn T. Scott

CERTIFICATE: Australia: (Banned) (original rating); Australia: R (re-rating) (2007); Australia: R (uncut); New Zealand: (Banned); UK: (Banned); UK: 18 (cut); USA: Not Rated (1984–2003)

BUDGET: $450,000

RECEIPTS: $35,000,000

CAST: Michael Carr, Samuel Berkowitz, Mary Ellen Brighton, Thomas Noguchi

ORIGINALLY PRODUCED FOR the Japanese market, **Faces of Death** was announced as a documentary studying the nature of death; it was in truth little more than a "mockumentary" expanding on the success of Antonio Climati's **Savana Violenta** (1976). Also marketed under the name **The Original Faces of Death**, this feature, narrated by Dr Francis B. Gross (Michael Carr), placed faked deaths alongside shocking real-life footage. Special effects artist Allan A. Apone has since admitted almost 40 per cent of this feature's contents had been feigned; this, however, does not detract from the film's disturbing impact. The images of cattle waiting to have their throats cut as they stand in line in the slaughterhouse along with baby seals being clubbed to death are as unpleasant as they were over thirty years ago. The producer's crowning moment comes with newsreel footage of the fatal accident of a cyclist whose shattered remains were exposed to the

Banned in forty-six countries!

camera's eye. Shots of paramedics were greedily devoured as they retrieved blood clots, brain matter and clumps of hair from the tarmac. Such grisly imagery was broadcasted virtually every night to an audience who had become almost blasé; their seeming immunity to this extreme content had previously provided the catalyst four years before for Tobe Hooper's **The Texas Chain Saw Massacre** (1974). Stock footage went on to record more accidents and airline disasters but much of the film, including the autopsy scenes, executions, the ravages of an alligator and a bear, were staged by the production crew.

John Alan Schwartz's documentary has revelled in its widespread ban spanning more than forty countries. This prohibition was at times only temporary, but it bequeathed **Faces of Death** a welcome notoriety that has continued with each passing year to be its key selling point. Schwartz's feature was a clever exercise in audience manipulation, but it was surprisingly very reasonably produced by a team of experts. While there were objections to the creators' attempt to blur the line between fact and fiction, it was a teenage sensation seeker's delight. Such was its success, **Faces of Death** was succeeded by five sequels, each sadly characterized by increasingly diminishing standards of production.

Fatal Games

 YEAR OF RELEASE: 1984

 RUNTIME: 88 minutes

COUNTRY: USA

DIRECTOR: Michael Elliot

PRODUCTION COMPANY: Impact Films

WRITERS: Rafael Buñuel (screenplay), Michael Elliot (screenplay)

CINEMATOGRAPHER: Alfred Taylor

PRODUCERS: Jonathon Braun (associate producer), Rafael Buñuel (co-producer), William Kroes (executive producer), Christopher Mankiewicz

CERTIFICATE: Australia: R; UK: 18

CAST: Sally Kirkland, Lynn Banashek, Sean Masterson, Michael O'Leary, Teal Roberts, Spice Williams-Crosby, Melissa Prophet, Angela Bennett, Nicholas Love, Lauretta Murphy, Michael Elliot, Christopher Mankiewicz, Ed Call, Mel Klein, Alan Waite

IN THE SAME year as the Los Angeles Olympic Games, Michael Elliot introduced his own version of the Olympiad with **Fatal Games**, which started life as **The Killing Touch**, and later saw release in Holland in a title that captured the magic of that year, **Olympic Nightmare**. There were elements in this film that bore a close resemblance to Herb Freed's **Graduation Day** (1981), but even with the Olympic backdrop Elliot's feature lacked its predecessor's eighties kitsch. The athletes and gymnasts of Falcon Academy of Athletics are lined up to test their physical abilities against other hopefuls for the forthcoming Olympics. Hiding in the background, a typically obscured figure broods obviously contemptuous of this gathering and, for reasons known only to him, decides to put an end to their hopes, on

Someone is stopping the nation's top athletes dead in their tracks

205

this occasion armed with a javelin. His fitting choice of weapon could have made for some interesting kills, indeed the first entry was a huge surprise, but the audience became frustrated as the gore was kept to an absolute minimum. Instead they were presented with that other teenage hankering, female nudity, and there was plenty of it. This nubile excess, however, was counteracted by a storyline that was overly concerned with family values and the sacrifice of relationships as the athletes pursued their goal. There was a long list of suspects that was to keep the viewer guessing, but Elliot's film never quite hit the mark as a credible slasher movie.

Final Exam

📅	YEAR OF RELEASE:	1981
🕐	RUNTIME:	89 minutes
🎥	COUNTRY:	USA
🎬	DIRECTOR:	Jimmy Huston
✒	WRITER:	Jimmy Huston
🎞	CINEMATOGRAPHER:	Darrell Cathcart

PRODUCERS: Carol Bahoric (associate producer), John L. Chambliss (executive producer), Lon Kerr (executive producer), Michael Mahern (executive producer), Myron Meisel

CERTIFICATE: Australia: R; Canada: 13+ (Quebec); UK: 18; USA: R

CAST: Cecile Bagdadi, Joel S. Rice, Ralph Brown, DeAnna Robbins, Sherry Willis-Burch, John Fallon, Terry W. Farren, Timothy L. Raynor, Sam Kilman, Don Hepner, Mary Ellen Withers, Jerry Rushing, Shannon Norfleet, Carol Capka, R.C. Nanney

AS NIGHT DRAWS in over a tranquil lovers' lane, a young couple relish the heat of a few torrid moments in the back of their car. Their fervour lasts for only a few moments, because the girl is sure she can hear something nearby and urges her boyfriend to put the top back over the convertible. Then someone bangs against the car and climbs onto the bonnet before tearing open the roof. In terror, the young man tries to speed away but the figure seizes hold of him and repeatedly thrusts his blade. As the opening credits roll on screen, the girl can be heard hysterically screaming.

It's the end of the year at Lanier College, with most students having left for the holidays and the seniors about to take their final exams. Among them are the very likeable Courtney (Cecile Bagdadi) and her geek friend Radish (Joel S. Rice). Radish has already heard of the lovers' lane murders and revels in repulsing his friends with all of the grisly details. For the best part of an hour the audience come to know the assembled cast and chuckle at their tomfoolery; there are the usual sub-plots and a few misleading shocks before the killing finally begins. The last half hour sees the students being disposed of in a movie that endorses suspense rather than an abundance of blood and guts. The ever-diminishing number of students has Courtney finally pitted against a stalker, who evidences little in the way of motive other than a desire to kill and has nothing to do with the various strings to the plot, other than the fact he gets a kick out of vicious murder.

Some pass the test ... God help the rest!!!

Jimmy Huston overcame a limited budget to nurture a sense of inescapable dread as every shadow became tainted in menace, even when the film appeared to be laughing along during the lull of the first hour. Having augmented the terror, Huston should also be praised for bringing out the best in what was an inexperienced cast. If **Final Exam** was to be criticized it would have been for its uncompromising adherence to so much of the formula that had already come to epitomize these films. For the slasher purists, however, this would inevitably make this film a hidden gem. Huston, like Carpenter before him, kept the tide of blood to a minimum, while his kills proved incisive and at times ingenious.

The Final Terror

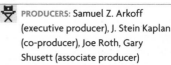

31 YEAR OF RELEASE: 1983		PRODUCERS: Samuel Z. Arkoff (executive producer), J. Stein Kaplan (co-producer), Joe Roth, Gary Shusett (associate producer)
RUNTIME: 82 minutes		
COUNTRY: USA		
DIRECTOR: Andrew Davies		CERTIFICATE: Australia: R; UK: 18; USA: R
WRITER: Jon George		
CINEMATOGRAPHERS: A. Davidescu, Randall Robinson		

CAST: John Friedrich, Adrian Zmed, Ernest Harden Jr., Lewis Smith, Rachel Ward, Daryl Hannah, Akosua Busia, Joe Pantoliano, Mark Metcalf, Cindy Harrell, Irene Sanders, Richard Jacobs, Donna Pinder, Jim Youngs, Lori Butler

AMIDST THE BEAUTIFULLY filmed Californian backwoods, a group of forest rangers, coupled with their girlfriends, enjoy a short camping holiday. As they trek to their camp they pass a mental institution, which stirs a few obvious comments. Later that night while sitting around the fire the head ranger recounts the tale of the family who once lived in these parts and how the uncle, who was the family breadwinner, had raped the daughter. Fearing her family would lose everything, she kept her trauma buried away inside. Her anguish resulted in a complete breakdown and her being admitted to the institution they had come upon earlier in the day. Her mental state was such there was no option but to have the child adopted. Nineteen years later, her child had grown up and when he returned to visit her and then set her free to roam the woods. At this point a member of the group, who has been irritating throughout, becomes disgruntled and leaves the party. Then one by one, in this isolated landscape, the campers begin to disappear, the victim of a killer who can disguise themselves with leaves and moss and blend into the foliage and rock topography. Those who survive unite to take on the evil that has spent the last hour slaughtering their loved ones. At the last, they learn the reality behind the prowler in the woods and

If you go down to the woods today, you're sure of . . .

a few truths about their cantankerous colleague.

Andrew Davies's entry to the slasher years, which also went by the names **The Campsite Murders** and **Forest Primeval**, proved to be something of a disappointment for the hardcore lovers of violence and sleaze. Obviously inspired by the immense success of **Friday the 13th**, with elements of **The Burning**, his film also paid homage to John Boorman's **Deliverance** (1972), placing the cast at the mercy of the enormity of this remote wilderness. Shot in 1981, Davies's movie had to be shelved when a distributor couldn't be found, owing largely to the fact his feature just didn't know what it wanted to be. While sumptuously photographed, it struggled to be a bona fide horror movie, lacking the tension and the degree of violence that had become essential to these years of hack and slash terror. The build up to the finale certainly kept the audience on the edge of their seats, but the film failed to live up to the expectation threatened in the title. **The Final Terror** wasn't released until 1983 when Daryl Hannah and Adrian Zmed had made their ascent to stardom. Soon after, Davies would go on to greater success with **Under Siege** (1992) and **The Fugitive** (1993).

Flesh for Frankenstein

	YEAR OF RELEASE: 1973
	RUNTIME: 95 minutes
	COUNTRY: USA, Italy, France
	DIRECTORS: Paul Morrissey, Antonio Margheriti
	PRODUCTION COMPANY: Compagnia Cinematografica Champion, Braunsberg Productions, Carlo Ponti Cinematografica, Rassam Productions, Yanne et Rassam

	WRITERS: Paul Morrissey, Tonino Guerra, Pat Hackett, Mary Shelley
	CINEMATOGRAPHER: Luigi Kuveiller
	PRODUCERS: Andrew Braunsberg, Louis Peraino, Carlo Ponti, Jean Yanne
	CERTIFICATE: Australia: R; Canada: 18+ (Quebec); New Zealand: R18; UK: 18; USA: X; USA: R (cut, 1975); USA: R (re-release: 1992)
	BUDGET: $450,000

CAST: Joe Dallesandro, Monique van Vooren, Udo Kier, Arno Juerging, Dalila Di Lazzaro, Srdjan Zelenovic, Nicoletta Elmi, Marco Liofredi, Liù Bosisio

UDO KIER OFFERED a perverse interpretation of a Baron Frankenstein who dreams of a proto-Nazi styled super-race returning to his Serbian homeland, a breed that mirrors the god-like deities of ancient Greece. Assisted by his loyal aide Otto, he turns to the hideous crime of stealing corpses to create a beautiful female monster, stitched together from numerous bodies. The time is now ready for him to bequeath her a handsome male partner to serve as her lover and give life to a new race of superior offspring brainwashed into his way of thinking. While the baron enjoys his insane fantasy, his insatiable wife Katherine, who could well be his sister (Monique Van Vooren), takes pleasure in her heated affiliation with the stable-boy, Nicholas (Joe Dallesandro). The husband and wife, or is it brother and sister, also have a strange relationship with their offspring, grooming them to one day stand in their shoes. In Nicholas, the Baron is convinced he has found the perfect brain to guide the statuesque body he has so carefully constructed. When he attempts to remove the head of his wife's lover, he mistakenly decapitates his friend, who appears to be gay. When the Baron performs what will be the final operation on his creature, he has dreams that the bizarre couple will very soon begin to mate, but his experiment soon runs out of control, leading to a ghastly finale. The closing chapter is an unholy bloodbath, which pushes ever further into the realms of depravity.

We dare you to see . . .

The Gothic-styled **Flesh for Frankenstein** and **Blood for Dracula** (1974) were made back-to-back using virtually the same cast and crew with Andy Warhol's name exploited purely to improve the film's marketability. Director Paul Morrissey, a long-time friend of Warhol, created a bizarre parody dripping with blood, incestuous couplings, necrophilia, the visceral splitting of stomachs, impalements, not to mention a huge amount of severed body parts, and while this madness was going on he laced it with sex coupled with a darkly comedic dialogue. In a film that was actually considered mainstream by comparison to his earlier more experimental works, Morrissey used the inspiration of Italian horror movies to stretch the boundaries of American horror cinema, merging an overindulgence of gore with explicit perversity. The photography was strangely colourful, making the on-screen blood and guts resemble an outrageous comic book; and then Morrissey's team made preparations to release their effort in 3-D, ready to pour the grisly excess all over their audience. Conjecture remains as to whether Antonio Margheriti was actually involved with this film, as it has been suggested that his name was only ever used to draw in the Italian audience.

On its release, Morrissey's movie was understandably considered controversial and there was never any doubt that the American censors were going to be alarmed by its extreme profusion of sex and gore. They had no choice but to give it an "X"-rating. Two years later, and with only eight minutes of cuts, it was granted a similar certificate in the UK. The video was released in 1981 as it was originally screened (minus the 3-D effect), and then again in 1983 with just over two minutes of cuts; both were subsequently banned and placed on the DPP's list of video nasties in March 1984. There the film stayed until the panic in the UK had died down. The complete version wasn't to be approved on this side of the Atlantic until 2006, when British horror fans finally got to see Morrissey's insane piece of intemperance.

Forest of Fear

📅 YEAR OF RELEASE: 1980	🎥 DIRECTOR: Charles McCrann
🕐 RUNTIME: 89 minutes	🎬 PRODUCTION COMPANY: CM Productions
🌐 COUNTRY: USA	

WRITER: Charles McCrann

CINEMATOGRAPHER: David Sperling

PRODUCERS: J. William Lee (associate producer), Charles McCrann, Scott Roberts

 CERTIFICATE: Australia: R; UK: (Banned); USA: R

CAST: Charles McCrann, Beverly Shapiro, Dennis Helfend, Kevin Hanlon, Judith Brown, Pat Kellis, Roger Miles, Phillip Garfinkel, Bob Larson, Harriet Miller

A CAR TRAVELS ALONG a dirt track, which winds its way through a dense forest. When the track comes to an end two men (James Hart and John Kuhi) leave the vehicle and begin to trail through the woods. Within minutes, their path brings them to a campsite; as they slowly move in, they are forced to shoot a semi-naked woman with the bullet hitting her in the throat. In the gunfight that follows, they are killed by her hippie associates. The two men were Federal Officers on an assignment to locate a crop of marijuana. Their boss (Paul Haskin) now puts a plan into place to have the entire area sprayed with an experimental herbicide, known as Dromax; his intention is to destroy the illegal crop. Back in the forest, the hippies return to gather their harvest, but as they go about their illegal trade, they become covered in the spray as it rains down from a plane circling overhead. Very soon, they are coughing up blood, their skin turns pale and then they begin their rampage

NOTHING prepared the world for the HORROR . . .

transformed into bloodthirsty mindless zombies. For the duration of the film, this contaminated band will shamble through the woods slaughtering anything that falls their way. Only the forest ranger Tom Cole (Charles McCrann) along with his wife Polly (Beverly Shapiro) and half brother Jay (Philip Garfinkel) can put an end to this carnage, but don't expect a happy ending; this feature takes a rather downbeat turn, one that is very much in keeping with zombie lore of the past four decades.

For his one and only movie, shot in Pennsylvania during 1979, Charles McCrann assumed the role of director as well as writer, in addition to taking a leading role. McCrann also edited and produced his project, which is known alternatively as **Bloodeaters**, **Blood Butchers** and **Toxic Zombies**. This wasn't truly a zombie movie, although Craig Harris's low-budget make-up was very effective; it was, however, an interesting precursor to the backwoods slasher that would soon come to prominence. Over the years, there has been much criticism of the movie's often static photography, even though the point-of-view shots worked to build a degree of tension as the victims chased through the dense forest undergrowth. By comparison to the sensationalistic movies of its time the gore was far from excessive. However, when it was in evidence, the camera seemed to delight in languorously dwelling upon the stump of an arm as it liberally spurted blood and then altered its focus to labour over a knife to the eye, before moving on to a bloodthirsty

bite to the throat. These scenes would be seen as being little more than gratuitous violence and would bring this film to the attention of the DPP after its release to video in November 1982; twelve months later it was banned and has remained so for almost thirty years. McCrann would always remember his efforts with a fondness, often talking of his experiences as he went on to enjoy a very successful career in insurance brokerage. Sadly he too became a victim of mindless violence, losing his life during the 9/11 terrorist attack on the World Trade Center.

Friday the 13ᵗʰ

📅	YEAR OF RELEASE: 1980	⚊	PRODUCERS: Sean S. Cunningham, Alvin Geiler, Stephen Miner
🕐	RUNTIME: 95 minutes		
🎯	COUNTRY: USA	⭕	CERTIFICATE: Australia: R; Canada: R; Canada: 18+ (Quebec); Ireland: 18; New Zealand: R16; UK: 18 (video rating) (1987); UK: X (original rating); USA: Unrated (uncut); USA: X (original rating); USA: R
🎥	DIRECTOR: Sean S. Cunningham		
🎬	PRODUCTION COMPANY: Paramount Pictures, Georgetown Productions Inc., Sean S. Cunningham Films		
✎	WRITER: Victor Miller	💲	BUDGET: $550,000
☐	CINEMATOGRAPHER: Barry Abrams	💱	RECEIPTS: $37,000,000

CAST: Betsy Palmer, Adrienne King, Jeannine Taylor, Robbi Morgan, Kevin Bacon, Harry Crosby, Laurie Bartram, Mark Nelson, Peter Brouwer, Rex Everhart, Ronn Carroll, Ron Millkie, Walt Gorney, Willie Adams, Debra S. Hayes

MANY YEARS AGO in the summer of 1958, two camp counsellors at Camp Crystal Lake slip away from the campfire to steal a few

moments of intimacy. As they undress, an unseen attacker stealthily makes his way towards them with bloody murder in mind. The story then leaps forward twenty-two years to a young woman named Annie (Robbi Morgan) as she enters a small diner hoping to obtain directions to Camp Crystal Lake. Her simple request provokes considerable alarm, and to add to her dismay a strange old timer named Ralph (Walt Gorney) warns that those at the camp are all doomed. As she continues on her journey, she learns how a young boy drowned in Crystal Lake in 1957, only a year before the murders of the counsellors. Soon after, she hitches a ride from another driver, whom the viewer never gets to see, and falls victim to a hunting-knife, as her throat is viciously slashed.

The scene shifts to the camp as the other counsellors, Ned (Mark Nelson), Jack (Kevin Bacon), Bill (Harry Crosby), Marcie (Jeannine Taylor), Alice (Adrienne King) and Brenda (Laurie Bartram) busily work away on the cabins and the camp's facilities. They too receive a visit from old Ralph, who repeats his ill-starred warning. In the distance, the rumble of a violent storm can be heard, presaging the nightmare to come.

The killer, whose face remains shadowed throughout, cunningly seeks to isolate and then murder the counsellors. Ned is lured into a cabin, beckoned by a strange voice. Marcie and Jack later enter the same cabin and enjoy sex in one of the bunks, unaware that Ned's dead body is draped across the upper berth. When Marcie leaves to visit the bathroom Jack is set upon by the killer, who has bided their time beneath the bunk. The murderer forcefully drives an arrow up through

the bed, perforating Jack's throat, leaving him for dead. Marcie meets her end shortly afterwards in the showers, hit full in the face with an axe. The tension becomes unbearably taut as the body count begins to rise. Bill, Alice and Brenda indulge in "strip Monopoly" until Brenda remembers that she has left her cabin windows ajar. As she departs, she is drawn to the archery range, to be confronted by an unseen presence. Steve, the owner, returns with supplies; he too falls prey to the murderer, although he seems familiar with his attacker. Having heard Brenda's screams, Alice and Bill leave the cabin to investigate, only to find a bloody axe in Brenda's bed. The sense of isolation is complete when the phone lines go down and so follow the lights across the camp which plunges it into total darkness.

Bill takes it on himself to check the generator, but fails to return. Alice then flees to the main cabin and tries to hide, but the silence is shattered when Brenda's corpse is hurled through the window. In the aftermath, a car engine is heard and Alice runs out to find a middle-aged woman, who introduces herself as Mrs Voorhees (Betsy Palmer), the mother of the boy who drowned all those years ago and still blames her son Jason's death on the two counsellors whose sexual antics blinded them to his plight in the lake. Mrs Voorhees becomes violent and pulls a large knife on Alice. A lengthy chase ensues with Mrs Voorhees speaking to herself in Jason's voice, evoking memories of twenty years past and the schizophrenia that drove Norman Bates to murder in **Psycho**. Cornered in a storage shed, Alice deals her attacker a shattering blow with a cast iron skillet; Mrs Voorhees drops unconscious, seemingly dead. Alice escapes the shed and takes time to gather herself at the lakeside. She takes a little too much time for the deranged Mrs Voorhees is far from death's door. Rushing from the darkness, she once again brandishes the machete and as the two of them wrestle at the water's edge Alice seizes the blade and decapitates her hysterical attacker. Shocked, the young girl staggers towards a canoe and rows out to the middle of the lake, where she immediately falls into a deep sleep.

The following morning Alice is awoken by several policemen who call to her from the shore. After almost an hour and a half of tension, there would have been sighs of relief around the cinema as Alice prepared to be rescued. None of them, however, could have anticipated the decomposing corpse of the long-dead Jason (Ari Lehman) as it ascended from the lake to launch a vengeful attack and then haul her from the canoe. In her desperation, Alice kicks and struggles to awaken in a hospital bed, where a police officer explains how they pulled her from the lake. When she asks about Jason, the officer informs her they never recovered nor did they see any sign of a boy.

Such was his desire to overcome any potential legal problems with the name **Friday the 13th**, director Sean S. Cunningham advertised his film in international *Variety* magazine without a completed script. Cunningham was no stranger to the shocks of the modern-day horror movie, having previously worked on Wes Craven's notorious **The Last House on the Left** (1972). It was the later success of John Carpenter's **Halloween** (1978) that provided the inspiration for creating this particular feature. As with Mario Bava's **A Bay of Blood** (1971), Cunningham and his writer Victor Miller sacrificed the intricacies of plot development for the grisly excess of an ever-growing body count. To their immense credit, there was more than enough of a story here to make it palatable for the majority of the movie-going public. Further to this, the frenzy witnessed in the ever-increasing body count would make this film the archetype for the slasher fare of the next few years. As he dispatched his victims in a series of excruciating set pieces, Cunningham carried his ace card in the guise of one Tom Savini. Savini had attracted a great deal of attention for his work on **Dawn of the Dead** (1978); it was his creativity and meticulous attention to detail that afforded such a gruesome credibility to these nine-five minutes of slaughter.

The nature of the killings and the accompanying bloody display inevitably made this film one of the most controversial of its day, but this only added to the incredible success of **Friday**

Fridays will never be the same again.

the 13th, and with this Paramount Pictures immediately acquired the worldwide distribution rights and began plans for a sequel. Although the films were never popular with critics, the media franchise is considered as one of the most successful in American cinema. There are now eleven films in the series, comprising **Friday the 13th Part 2** (1981), **Friday the 13th Part III** (1982), **Friday the 13th: The Final Chapter** (1984), **Friday the 13th: A New Beginning** (1985), **Friday the 13th** **Part VI: Jason Lives** (1986), **Friday the 13th Part VII: The New Blood** (1988), **Friday the 13th Part VIII: Jason Takes Manhattan** (1989), **Jason Goes to Hell: The Final Friday** (1993), **Jason X** (2002) and **Freddy vs. Jason** (2003), along with a remake of the original in 2009. A television series would follow with novels, comic books, documentaries, computer games and model kits. It is true to say Jason's hockey mask would go on to become one of the most recognizable images in popular culture.

Frightmare

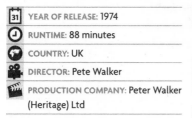

YEAR OF RELEASE: 1974

RUNTIME: 88 minutes

COUNTRY: UK

DIRECTOR: Pete Walker

PRODUCTION COMPANY: Peter Walker (Heritage) Ltd

WRITERS: David McGillivray (screenplay), Pete Walker (original story)

CINEMATOGRAPHER: Peter Jessop

PRODUCERS: Tony Tenser (executive producer), Pete Walker

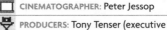 

CERTIFICATE: Australia: R; New Zealand: R16; UK: 18; USA: R

CAST: Rupert Davies, Sheila Keith, Deborah Fairfax, Paul Greenwood, Kim Butcher, Fiona Curzon, Jon Yule, Trisha Mortimer, Pamela Fairbrother, Edward Kalinski, Victor Winding, Anthony Hennessey, Noel Johnson, Michael Sharvell-Martin, Tommy Wright

IN THE OPENING sequence of black-and-white footage recording the events of 1957, Dorothy and Edmund Yates (Sheila Keith and Rupert Davies) are committed to an institution for the criminally insane: Dorothy for hideous acts of murder and cannibalism and her devoted husband for attempting to disguise her grisly crimes. Fifteen years later, they are released, with the authorities satisfied they are once again fit to take their place in society.

With the fragile Dorothy's case now closed, the couple retreat from the world to retire to the solitude of an old farmhouse somewhere in the English countryside.

Edmund soon gains employment as a chauffeur, leaving his wife alone in the cottage, which begins to assume a progressively threatening air. With too much time on her hands, Dorothy's blood lust once again comes to the fore. She plans to satiate her cravings by taking out an advert in a magazine offering tarot readings. Her visitors are the lonely, with no friends or family; as with so many of her ilk her cannibalistic yearning is legitimized by the firm belief she is doing them a favour. The earlier diagnosis now appears somewhat premature; for hidden away in this rather sedate setting, she violates her victims with a series of household implements and then engages a set of power tools that are the match of anything seen in **The Driller Killer** (1979), **The Toolbox Murders** (1978) and **The Texas Chain Saw Massacre** (1974). She is no longer the feeble old dear whom the experts only recently declared sane; this is a manipulative monster with an overwhelming need to bask in her repulsive pleasures. When she returns to a corpse she has hidden away in the barn, Dorothy deploys a power drill to its head as if she had

Dare you see the film that shocked the critics?

spent many years in the trade. As the ensuing visceral discharge drenches her wrinkled face, her expression turns to that of a grinning maniac. Miles away in London, Edmund's daughter from a previous marriage, Jackie (Deborah Fairfax), has her own views on her stepmother's mental condition. She is certain her psychotic relative hasn't been cured and endeavours to convince her boyfriend (Paul Greenwood), who just happens to be an aspiring psychiatrist. Dorothy's deep-rooted problems become more acute when she learns her unruly daughter, Debbie (Kim Butcher), who is supposed to be in Jackie's charge, has inherited her cannibalistic urges.

Pete Walker's controversial descent into cannibalism in the sheltered domain of England's home counties has been described as the UK's answer to that same year's **The Texas Chain Saw Massacre**, principally due to its bleak premise and obdurate attitude towards violence. While it may appear otherwise, this flesh-eating venture was really just another piece of exploitation, with Walker wanting only to shock his audience. The sensation seekers, however, were thwarted in their quest for such gastronomic immoderation, with Walker's film choosing significantly more discussion on the joys of human flesh rather than the extremes they desired. This, however, was 1974; cannibalism was a relatively new phenomenon for cinemas in the UK and even this director, straight off the back of the similarly exploitative, **House of Whipcord** (1974) and a series of stag movies, knew he was going to have to tread very carefully. Although Walker has always denied there was an underlying subtext to his film, he did appear to be questioning the aptitude of the authorities to be able to accurately appraise the nature of a person's sanity and furthermore if it was possible to successfully rehabilitate such individuals. Walker himself had been abandoned as a child and had seen firsthand how those in authority dealt with the unfortunates in their care. **Frightmare** was a typically low-budget feature, but as with so many of these films the cinematography was used to magnificent effect, revealing an intense disquiet with inspired use of interior lighting, which afforded the cottage a suitably inauspicious air. This damning ambience was made all the more perturbing by Sheila Keith's compelling performance as she chopped and changed between the weak and feeble-minded old dear before turning as the situation required to assume her true guise, as that of the calculating psychopath.

Frontier(s)

 YEAR OF RELEASE: 2007

 RUNTIME: 108 minutes

 COUNTRY: France/Switzerland

 DIRECTOR: Xavier Gens

 PRODUCTION COMPANY: Cartel Productions, BR Films, Europa Corp.

 WRITER: Xavier Gens

 CINEMATOGRAPHER: Laurent Barès

 PRODUCERS: Luc Besson (Co-producer), Hubert Brault (executive producer), Eric Garoyan (co-producer), Karim Guellaty (associate producer), Rodolphe Guglielmi (co-producer), Bertrand Ledélézir (co-producer), Noël Muracciole (co-producer), Frederic Ovcaric (co-producer),Teddy Percherancier (co-producer), Laurent Tolleron (producer)

 CERTIFICATE: Australia: R; France: 16; Ireland: 18; New Zealand: R18; UK: 18; USA: NC-17;

BUDGET: $3,000,000

CAST: Karina Testa, Samuel Le Bihan, Estelle Lefébure, Aurélien Wiik, David Saracino, Chems Dahmani, Maud Forget, Amélie Daure, Rosine Favey, Adel Bencherif, Joël Lefrançois, Patrick Ligardes, Jean-Pierre Jorris, Stéphane Jacquot, Christine Culerier

WRITER AND DIRECTOR Xavier Gens felt nothing should be left to the imagination for his film **Frontier(s)**, so be prepared for the excruciation of decapitations, severed limbs, prolonged death scenes and a plethora of torturous implements. The film's creator has little time for the racist right wing that has cast its shadow over modern-day France and there is strong evidence of this reflected in his work. **Frontier(s)** takes itself very seriously, created against the backdrop of real socio-political unrest in Paris, which resulted in rioting between October and November 2005 after the deaths of two young suspects electrocuted in a power substation along with a similar skirmish with the police late in 2007. In his wrath Gens does not feed on the entrails of splatter past; this is a new breed that goes beyond the concept of gratuitous to wallow in the twenty-first century's relish for torture porn.

Protest riots spark across the chaos-ridden city of Paris following the election of a right-wing candidate to the French presidency, driving a group of Muslim teenagers, Alex, Tom, Farid, Sami and his pregnant sister Yasmine, to escape the city and head for Amsterdam with their ill-gotten gains seized during a robbery. However, in the melee, Sami is shot and the group are forced to go their separate ways. As Alex and Yasmine help Sami to the emergency hospital, Tom and Farid hold onto the money and continue to the border.

As they approach the Dutch border, Tom and Farid book into a rooming house. They can't believe their luck when hosts Gilberte and Klaudia offer free accommodation with the bonus of sex with two local girls of dubious repute; it's hardly the best sex ever, but that's not the point. Meanwhile the police have been notified of Sami's gunshot injury, forcing a fearful Yasmine to make a run for it, knowing she must honour her brother's dying wish and keep the unborn child. She takes off with Alex, contacting Tom and Farid and seeking directions to their address. Soon after Tom and Farid have spoken to their friends, they make a chilling discovery. Having escaped the violence of fascist Paris they face an even greater menace: their benevolent hosts are sadistic Nazi cannibals and they are not the first visitors to fall into their foul clutches. As part of his grand design, their deranged patriarch, a former SS officer and Nazi war criminal Le Von Geislerhe, looks upon Yasmine as the means to conceiving a new Aryan master race. Although brutalized, Yasmine has a chance of survival; the men, however, aren't going to make it. They are subjected to various games of dehumanizing torture before they have no choice but to accept their demise, a despairing motif so much employed by recent torture

What are your boundaries?

porn. Alex is cruelly punished by the depraved von Geisler, pliers used to sever his Achilles tendons, while Farid is graphically cooked alive; the blood-curdling carnage ensues with an assault armed with a bow saw.

Initially, von Geisler wishes for Yasmine to enter an unholy matrimony into the family circle to continue the iniquitous bloodline, but when they learn of her pregnancy, she is entrusted to Eva. Eva will be her salvation, in a film that offers just a fragment of hope before the final credits begin to roll. It is Yasmine who they can't break down, a girl who, while drenched in blood, fights doggedly for her life, impaling bodies and lacerating the throats of her merciless captors.

The parallels with **Hostel** and **Motel Hell** are obvious, along with the saw-driven brutality running wild in **The Texas Chain Saw Massacre.**

It is this gratuitous nature which subsequently consigned **Frontier(s)** to very mixed reviews when handed to the critics, unable to reconcile the appalling levels of violence with the underlying message. It was intended to be one of the "8 Films to Die For" at Horrorfest 2007, but the MPAA's deliberations gave it an NC-17 rating, limiting it to ten US theatres unrated for one weekend before being released on DVD only a week later.

Frontier(s)' savage portrayal runs like a compilation for the most hardened gorefiend, with an assemblage of degenerates whose debased characters are beyond redemption, but director Xavier Gens insists there is a purpose to his enfant terrible, as he attempts to demonstrate his opposition to the extreme right that continues to infiltrate French politics.

Frozen Scream

31 YEAR OF RELEASE: 1975		WRITERS: Doug Ferrin, Celeste Hammond, Michael Sonye	
⏱ RUNTIME: 85 minutes			
🌐 COUNTRY: USA		CINEMATOGRAPHER: Roberto A. Quezada	
🎥 DIRECTOR: Frank Roach		PRODUCER: Renee Harmon	

CAST: Renee Harmon, Lynne Kocol, Wolf Muser, Thomas Gowan, Wayne Liebman, Lee James, Sunny Bartholomew, Bill Oliver, Bob Rochelle, Teri Argula

AS THE WAVES crash onto a beach, a superimposed image of Doctor Lil Stanhope (Renee Harmon) appears on screen to deliver a grim monologue. She speaks of how man has dreamed of immortality and his pursuit of eternal life has been devoured by death itself. A young couple's late night swim in the privacy of their pool is interrupted by a hooded figure and for no apparent reason sets about their murder. Shortly afterwards an anxious Ann Gerrard (Lynne Kocol) phones her husband Tom (Wolf Muser) from a phone box just before he is attacked by two hooded men. One of his silent assailants injects him with a serum, but absconds when Ann arrives on the scene. She awakens the next day in a hospital bed insisting her husband has been murdered, but her friend Dr Lil Stanhope assures her that his death was the result of a heart attack.

At the hospital, Detective Kevin McGuire (Thomas Gowan) questions Lil about the disappearance of two of her and Dr Sven Johnson's (Lee James) students, but she claims she has no knowledge of their whereabouts. She later confides in Dr Johnson, revealing her concern about Ann's persistence about her husband's death. Following her discharge, Ann discusses her fears with the detective and when the scheming pair host a Halloween party, she decides to take a sneak peak in the basement. Here she discovers a laboratory and soon learns that Sven plans to murder her. In a bid to escape, she runs headlong into a refrigerated room, which holds the

A real chiller!

frozen bodies of her husband and the missing students. Only when cornered does Sven confess to their crimes and the process used to simulate Tom's apparent death. They had hoped to use a serum to attain life immortal and resurrect the dead to use as their obedient slaves.

Frank Roach and Renee Harmon were community college teachers of acting, whose project wilfully turned a blind eye to obtaining the necessary permits as they filmed around Los Angeles. In terms of production, it stood alongside the works of Edward D. Wood Jnr. with a suspect plot whose focus was cryogenics. Dream sequences were juxtaposed with the narrative flow, as if to distort the timeline, in a film that may well have been forgotten but for the video boom of the 1980s and the intervention of the DPP. The axe murders, one of which shows an offending implement embedded in a victim's skull and the shard of glass to the eye, ensured a ban in the August of 1984 following its release in 1983. It was, however, dropped in the October of 1984, and has only very recently been issued to DVD. Together with its obedient zombie slaves it was the film that refused to lie down and die, as was H. Kingsley Thurber's score, which was later used in **Don't go in the Woods** (1982). 🍁

The Funhouse

YEAR OF RELEASE: 1981	
RUNTIME: 96 minutes	
COUNTRY: USA	
DIRECTOR: Tobe Hooper	
PRODUCTION COMPANY: Mace Neufeld Productions, Universal Pictures	
WRITER: Lawrence Block	
CINEMATOGRAPHER: Andrew Laszlo	

PRODUCERS: Steven Bernhardt, Mark L. Lester (executive producer), Brad Neufeld (associate producer), Mace Neufeld (executive producer), Derek Power

CERTIFICATE: Australia: R; New Zealand: R16; UK: 15 (re-rating); UK: 18 (video rating, 1987); UK: X (original rating); USA: R

RECEIPTS: $7,886,860

CAST: Elizabeth Berridge, Shawn Carson, Jeanne Austin, Jack McDermott, Cooper Huckabee, Largo Woodruff, Miles Chapin, David Carson, Sonia Zomina, Ralph Morino, Kevin Conway, Herb Robins, Mona Agar, Wayne Doba, William Finley

HER FATHER INSISTED she stay away, but Amy Harper (Elizabeth Berridge), together with her new boyfriend Buzz (Cooper Huckabee) and friends Liz (Largo Woodruff) and Richie (Miles Chapin), are drawn to the gaudy allure of the travelling carnival show. Amy's father had every reason to be concerned; only the year before several young girls had been found dead when the fair last visited town. The gang are not put off by these tales; instead, they revel in the excitement of this tawdry excess, riding the rides, taunting the freaks, mingling with various reprobates, and then they fall upon a sleazy circus-styled strip club. Dazzled by the thrill of the fair they fail to realize Amy's younger brother Joey (Shawn Carson) has followed them. Wandering around alone he soon comes to see how scary the carnival really is, and of this group of revellers, only he can see the darkness secreted in its garish pageant.

As the show closes down for the night, Richie stupidly goads the group into spending the night in "The Funhouse". There in the shadows they witness the murder of a prostitute, killed by the unspeaking ride assistant, dressed as the Frankenstein monster. Terrified, the teenagers look to escape, but find themselves locked in the now sinister ride. When the murderer's father, the barker, discovers his crime, the film delivers another shock. In the ensuing struggle, his Frankenstein mask is displaced to unveil a hideously deformed visage, a pallid inhuman freak with sharpened teeth. With the kids reeling from this terrifying sight, the barker immediately senses their prying eyes; he and his son then begin to stalk "The Funhouse" with grisly murder in mind.

Tobe Hooper turned down the chance to work with Steven Spielberg on **E.T. The Ex-Terrestrial (1982)**, having already committed to directing this atmospheric take on the carnival chiller. **The Fun House** gave every impression of the low-budget nostalgia of the 1950s, and then very shrewdly weaved this imagery with the popular slasher trend to reveal Hooper as a now matured director. The opening sequence paid tribute to both **Psycho** and **Halloween** in its suspenseful close-in trailing of the film's heroine. Unlike **The Texas Chain Saw Massacre**, his latest offering wasn't to over indulge with excessive displays of human entrails, although it did concede to the obligatory decapitation along with a drawn-out impalement. Hooper's treatment of the monstrous Gunther

> **Something is alive in the funhouse . . . something that, tonight, will turn the funhouse into a carnival of terror!**

was reminiscent of his chainsaw-crazed predecessor, with the audience being swayed to sympathize with his repulsively misshapen form. This would of course be transformed to sheer terror as he worked his way though this deathly carnival attraction to track down the innocent Amy Berridge after slaughtering her friend Liz.

The film was reasonably well received with John Beal's creepy score gaining universal commendation. Unfortunately, its video release wasn't particularly well timed, coming as the scourge of the video nasty befell the UK. The BBFC proved a little too quick in applying the label video nasty, as it was discovered to have been confused with Roger Watkins' exploitation masterpiece **The Last House on Dead End Street** (1977), which also went by the name **The Fun House**. A novelization of the screenplay was written by Dean Koontz, which, due to delays in the production process, saw publication prior to the film's release.

The Ghastly Ones

YEAR OF RELEASE: 1968	**DIRECTOR:** Andy Milligan
RUNTIME: 81 minutes	**PRODUCTION COMPANY:** ASA Productions
COUNTRY: USA	

WRITERS: Andy Milligan, Hal Sherwood

 PRODUCER: Jerome-Fredric

BUDGET: $10,000

CINEMATOGRAPHER: Andy Milligan

CAST: Veronica Radburn, Maggie Rogers, Hal Borske, Anne Linden, Fib LaBlaque, Carol Vogel, Richard Romanus, Eileen Hayes, Don Williams, Hal Sherwood, Neil Flanagan, Ada McAllister, Robert Adsit

THE PROLOGUE TO Andy Milligan's film, which was set in the latter part of the nineteenth century, follows two lovers whose peaceful stroll is interrupted by Colin (Hal Borske), a retarded hunchback who wastes no time in dispatching the romantic pair. He gouges out the man's eye and turns to the camera holding an object almost the size of a tennis ball. We are then introduced to three sisters and their husbands who have received a letter from the family lawyer, H. Dobbs (Neil Flanagan), requesting they attend a reading of their eccentric late father's will. The reading demands that each couple spend three days in the sinister family home of Crenshaw House, located on a secluded island and bring the "sexual harmony and marital love" that it had never come to know. Only then would the inheritance be settled. The retarded Colin bids the three couples welcome by killing a rabbit before

Mad creatures of the night existing only for sensual sadistic moments of human slaughter!

their eyes and then feasting on its raw innards. Hours later the remains of the rabbit are found smeared across one of the beds with a scrawled message proclaiming "blessed are the meek, for they shall inherit". So follows a series of grisly murders engaging pitchforks and hatchets that result in disembowelment and a decapitated head served at the dinner table as the three-day retreat reveals a dark secret from the sisters' past.

Cult filmmaker Andy Milligan staged his first horror movie, later entitled **Blood Rites**, in his own Victorian home on Staten Island. Fans of trash cinema have for a long time placed his techniques alongside those of Ed Wood; and as with his predecessor, this tortured director's films are distinguished by an inimitable charm. Filmed on a hand-held 16-mm camera, his slasher mystery feature resembled a homemade movie, appearing fifteen years before the shot-on-video phenomenon ascended to popularity. His framing has been the source of much criticism, chopping the heads and limbs off his cast, in addition to leaving members of the crew in shot. The sound was also intermittently muffled and, on other occasions, Milligan's voice could be heard as he strived to keep the proceedings under his control. A closer examination of the gore effects would reveal they were inspired by his theatrical background; unfortunately these enthusiastic efforts were found wanting when transferred to the cinema screen.

At this time there was a growing trend in exploitation cinema to feature forays of gratuitous nudity, but as with so much of this film, it was so badly shot. In conversation some ten years later, Milligan revealed he had used Hostess Sno-Balls to create the infamous eye-gouging episode. This admission came after he had produced a more competent remake of the events recorded in this film, which saw release as **Legacy of Blood** (1978). **The Ghastly Ones** may well have drifted into obscurity, as did most of Milligan's catalogue of films from the period, but when it was released to video in the UK in March 1983 it acquired a newfound notoriety, becoming one of the DPPs video nasties in August 1984 and remaining there until the panic came to an end. 🦇

Girls Nite Out

📅	YEAR OF RELEASE: 1984	🎞️	CINEMATOGRAPHER: Joe Rivers
🕐	RUNTIME: 96 minutes	⚗️	PRODUCERS: Richard Barclay (executive producer), Arthur Ginsberg (associate producer), Anthony N. Gurvis, Kevin Kurgis (executive producer)
🌐	COUNTRY: USA		
🎥	DIRECTOR: Robert Deubel		
🎬	PRODUCTION COMPANY: Concepts Unlimited	⭕	CERTIFICATE: Australia: R; UK: 18; USA: R
✏️	WRITERS: Joe Bolster, Anthony N. Gurvis, Kevin Kurgis, Gil Spencer Jr.		

CAST: Julia Montgomery, James Carroll, Suzanne Barnes, Rutanya Alda, Al McGuire, Lauren-Marie Taylor, David Holbrook, Laura Summer, Mart McChesney, Carrick Glenn, John Didrichsen, Lois Robbins, Mathew Dunn, Susan Pitts, Paul Christie, Gregory Salata, Tony Shultz

AT DEWITT COLLEGE in Ohio, the victorious basketball team are returning to their dormitory rooms in readiness for a night of celebration. One of the victors seeks consolation following a break up with his girlfriend and learns that many years ago another student found his girl had been cheating on him and went berserk, killing her in his ensuing rage. The preparations for the party, however, continue – a party that will build to the excitement of a scavenger hunt. As the students begin to strut their funky stuff, the crazy who killed his roving girlfriend escapes the asylum. With the disco sound echoing around the college, the killer takes on a unique disguise, one never before seen in any slasher movie; he slips into the costume of the basketball team's bear mascot, discarding the fake plastic claws for sharpened knives that were unusually reminiscent of the glove that Fred Kreuger was to brandish later that year. He then begins to stalk the basketball team's cheerleaders, phoning the school radio station whenever he rips out one of his victim's throats. The school's security guard, it is revealed, is the father of the murderer's first victim from all those years ago, but he will be hard pressed to bring this killer to justice.

Robert Deubel's film was originally shot in 1982 under the title **The Scaremaker**, but wasn't to see release until 1984. With the relative success of several other campus slashers such as **Prom Night** (1980), **Final Exam** (1981), **Graduation Day** (1981) and **Night School** (1981), the distributors recognized the potential in the more lurid moniker of **Girls Nite Out**. Deubel's movie was the standard slasher fare of the period, although the bear costume did make for some mild amusement, at least until the killings started and the audience came to realize just how hateful this maniac really was. Although it promised much, **Girls Nite Out** offered little in the way of gore and nudity, but Deubel was no slouch when it came to creating suspense, particularly in the film's final half hour, where it bordered on becoming a detective story, before delivering an unexpected twist. **Girls Nite Out** was saved by its fast-paced direction, coupled with Joe Rivers' ability to engineer the ill-lit shots, which were to facilitate a brooding atmosphere and augment the tension as the movie hacked its way to the finale. ❧

> **It began as a game ...**

Graduation Day

📅 YEAR OF RELEASE: 1981		🎞 WRITERS: Anne Marisse, Herb Freed
🕐 RUNTIME: 96 minutes		
🌐 COUNTRY: USA		✏ CINEMATOGRAPHER: Daniel Yarussi
🎥 DIRECTOR: Herb Freed		⚱ PRODUCERS: David Baughn, Herb Freed, Hal Schwartz (associate producer)

| CERTIFICATE: Australia: R; UK: 18; UK: 15 (DVD rating); USA: R | BUDGET: $250,000 |
| | RECEIPTS: $23,894,000 |

CAST: Christopher George, Patch Mackenzie, E. Danny Murphy, E. J. Peaker, Michael Pataki, Richard Balin, Carmen Argenziano, Beverly Dixon, Virgil Frye, Hal Bokar, Denise Cheshire, Bill Hufsey, Linnea Quigley, Karen Abbott, Vanna White

TO THE LYRICS "everybody wants to be a winner", the Midvale High School athletes go through the motions as the camera juxtaposes between their various excursions before finally coming to rest on Laura Ramstead, whose incredible acceleration pushes her on to victory in the 100-metre dash. Her moment of glory, however, is short lived; she collapses and dies on the spot; Ash her coach (Christopher George) and boyfriend (E. Danny Murphy) race towards the scene but are unable to save her.

Laura's older sister Anne (Patch Mackenzie) arrives home from her Naval detachment, having been invited to collect her sister's award at the school's graduation ceremony. Soon after her appearance, a jogger is murdered by an unidentified figure carrying a switchblade and stopwatch. The slasher convention was now a few years old, and Herb Freed's story adhered to its principles dispatching the remaining members of the track team, one by one, this time at the hands of an assassin garbed in a tracksuit and fencing mask. The image may not have evoked the same level of dread as that of Michael Myers, but this style of mask made a return in John Ottman's **Urban Legends: Final Cut** (2000). The slaughter went on to include the obligatory decapitation, which was not the most convincing episode but was later followed by an inventive slaying using an American football, armed with a protruding sword. The killer was seen to launch the ball from afar and as it descended it ripped into the victim's stomach. In the aftermath of these murders, scarlet lipstick has been left on the face of the victims gathered on a once-proud team photograph. This inference throws suspicion on Anne, who could be using her military training to avenge her sister's unfortunate death.

Former rabbi, Herb Freed had been involved with making adverts for much of the earlier part of his career, but between 1977 and 1981 he turned to making horror movies, principally **Beyond Evil** (1980) and **Haunts** (1977). When

Graduating from high school has never been so deadly . . .

he conceived the idea for **Graduation Day** with writer Anne Marisse, he made use of every element of the slasher trope that was now in vogue. His film is now very much of its time and has become a nostalgic journey for those who were lucky enough to have been there. There was no escape from the roller-disco and the heavy metal sound that excited the youth of these years, and the delightful heroine as ever managed to keep her clothes on, unlike several members of the cast; in addition she also gave the audience some seasoned martial arts moves just for good measure. It worked; Freed's movie captured the imagination of cinema-goers across the whole of the US and it went on to be a huge commercial success. The presence of Christopher George no doubt gave his film a boost and a young Linnea Quigley was also to be found among the cast in what were very early days in a long and successful B-movie career. An ear piercing performance from Vanna White didn't do her career any harm; two years later she went on to host the US version of **Wheel of Fortune**.

The Guard from the Underground

YEAR OF RELEASE: 1992		**PRODUCTION COMPANY:** Nichiei Agency	
RUNTIME: 97 minutes		**WRITER:** Kiyoshi Kurosawa	
COUNTRY: Japan		**BUDGET:** $90,000	
DIRECTOR: Kiyoshi Kurosawa			

CAST: Makiko Kuno, Yutaka Matsushige, Hatsunori Hasegawa, Ren Osugi, Takashi Naito

A FORMER GALLERY CURATOR named Akiko (Makiko Kuno) has secured a position with the prestigious Akebono Corporation. Her new role is to assist and provide advice on its acquisitions of highly valuable artwork, with a view to selling them on at an astronomical profit. When she arrives on her first day, the security guard has no knowledge of the department for which she will be working. To add to her sense of unease, radio broadcasts tell of the escape of the deranged "Sumo Killer", who is standing trial for murder. He had apparently beaten his girlfriend and a fellow wrestler to death. That same day a towering security guard (Yutaka Matsushige) also assumes his new duties with the company; he very quickly reveals his penchant for violence. When she finally does get to her office, Akiko's boss reveals himself as an ill-tempered tyrant, while her immediate colleagues are an awkward set who appear intent upon making her life unnecessarily difficult. Within days, they become the security guard's new targets as he begins to stalk the stairways and corridors of this corporate edifice.

With Akiko locked in a document room and the building's lighting no longer working, the stage is set for a murderous finale.

The Guard from the Underground, which was also entitled **Jigoku No Keibiin** on its release and later went by the name **Security Guard from Hell**, has been described as a fast and cheap homage to the slashers of a decade past. For director Kiyoshi Kurosawa it marked his return to Japanese cinema following four years in the wilderness. Having agreed to create a piece of soft-

**Broken bones . . .
Oozing blood . . .
Sumo killers.**

core pornography, he presented his backers with a philosophical treatise portraying very little in the way of sex. The financiers were far from impressed. This direct-to-video film was his chance to restore the industry's faith in his ability before going on to direct more significant works, which would include **Cure** (1997), **Charisma** (1999), **Pulse** (2001), **Bright Future** (2003) and his internationally acclaimed **Tokyo Sonata** (2008). Here, with very limited funding, he proved himself unusually inventive, creating a series of set pieces amidst these dimly lit corridors and annexes as the killer's indeterminable actions spiralled into abject mindlessness. This isn't a film in any way concerned with the subtleties of character development; rather, its design is to slaughter as many of these corporate types as possible. Strangely, for a movie of its kind the violence is not especially explicit, albeit with one notable exception involving a locker.

Guinea Pig

31 YEAR OF RELEASE: 1985–9	**WRITERS:** Satoru Ogura (story), Hajime Tabe, Kazuhito Kuramoto, Yoshikazu Iwanami
COUNTRY: Japan	
DIRECTOR: Satoru Ogura, Hideshi Hino, Masayuki Kusumi, Hajime Tabe, Kazuhito Kuramoto	**CINEMATOGRAPHER:** Kazuhito Kuramoto
PRODUCTION COMPANY: Sai Enterprise	**PRODUCERS:** Satoru Ogura, Hideshi Hino

CAST: Hiroshi Tamura, Kirara Yûgao, Shinsuke Araki, Ivu, Masahiro Satô, Rie Shibata Keisuke Shinki, Mitsuru Fukikoshi, Kobuhei Hayashiya, Masami Hisamoto, Nezumi Imamura, Ivu, Tamio Kageyama, Natsumi Ogawa, Oto, Pîtâ, Masahiro Satô, Rie Shibata, Naoto Takenaka, Yoshiaki Umegaki, Shigeru Saiki, Mari Somei, Masami Hisamoto, Gô Rijû, Tsuyoshi Toshishige, Toshihiko Hino, Mio Takaki, Tomorowo Taguchi, Yumi Iori, Misuzu

THE CARNAGE ON display in the Guinea Pig or Za Ginipiggu series of short films had regularly been threatened during the grindhouse years of exploitation, but no one ever dared take it quite so far. Over twenty years after they first appeared, these six films are still considered the most excessive movies to see production in Japan. Their relish for agonizing pain and gore recorded between 1985 and 1989 would be instrumental in the rise of the torture porn that has tormented western cinema for the last decade. Their notoriety stemmed from the furore that arose in the wake of the first two features, which forced producer and acclaimed horror manga creator Hideshi Hino and fellow creator Satoru Ogura to prove that no one had been harmed during their making. So shocked was actor Charlie Sheen in 1991, he panicked after watching Flower of Flesh and Blood (1985), believing he had been given a genuine snuff movie. He reported the film to the FBI and then informed the MPAA in the hope of preventing the global export of this sickening series. In the UK, a horror fan who had arranged for a copy of the film to be posted to him from abroad faced jail when he was accused of being in possession of a snuff movie. Only when the true nature of the film was established in a courtroom was his sentence reduced to a £600 fine. The Hino-directed Mermaid in a Manhole (1988) was also found in the huge anime and horror video collection of Japanese child serial killer Tsutomu Miyazaki, when he was arrested in July 1989. The series was once again the focus of much unwanted attention, which would inevitably heighten its infamy, although confusion remained as to whether Miyazaki had been acting out the gratuitous scenes from Flower of Flesh and Blood. Such was the mounting controversy surrounding the series, which had already been considerably toned down, it was forced out of production in its native Japan, although it has now been reissued in the United States to an ever-growing fan base. Miyazaki was eventually executed for his crimes in June 2008 and while the Japanese film industry has produced its fair share of blood and guts in the years following the Guinea Pig series, rarely has it gone to such extremes. This, however, changed with Kôji Shiraishi's Grotesque (2009), which in its unsavoury depiction of the acute sexual torment, humiliation and torture of its male and female victims, stooped to far greater depths than the indulgence so far observed in the recent craze for torture porn. Shiraishi's film offered absolutely nothing by way of narrative or development in character and as such found itself subsequently banned by the BBFC.

The reviled initiation to the **Guinea Pig** series, **Devil's Experiment** (1985), which has also been packaged as **Akumano Jikken** and the excruciatingly appropriate **Unabridged Agony**, along with the second feature **Flower of Flesh and Blood** (1985), or **Chiniku No Hana**, work in a similar way to Shiraishi's **Grotesque**. Each of these cheap-looking productions was devoid of storyline and offered nothing by way of characterization; their creators' sole intent was to shock the viewer into believing they had in their possession a snuff movie, and as we now know they certainly succeeded. There were claims that Hideshi Hino had received a similar video through the post, which acted as the catalyst for the series, but the outcry in Japan was such the films that followed, while extreme, returned to conventional use of plot and introduced fully fleshed characters. The Japanese fascination for the snuff video refused to go away; it surfaced a few years later in **The Evil Dead Trap** (1988), a film that at first glance appeared to jump on Sam Raimi's lucrative bandwagon, and whose depiction of the barbaric practice of eye popping gave Lucio Fulci a run for his money.

Satoru Ogura had become disillusioned with what he saw as being the banal horror of the latter part of the 1970s and early 1980s. **Guinea Pig: The Devil's Experiment** (1985) allowed him

to create his kind of terror and marked the first of the series to see public release. A gang of three men have kidnapped a young woman and then embark on a torturous experiment to see how much pain her body can endure. For the duration of these unbearable forty-three minutes this hapless soul was verbally abused, punched and kicked, clawed, then had one of her fingernails removed before boiling water was poured over her arm. As it began to blister, maggots were forced into the wound and then scattered across her battered body, one of which crawled under her eyelid. The so-called experiment then demanded this unholy trio insert a needle into the poor girl's eye. As the violence and beatings became more protracted, the inevitability of the young girl's fate was all too obvious.

Flower of Flesh and Blood or **Chiniku no Hana** (1985) was inspired by an unmarked parcel that had been sent to Hideshi Hino in the post. It was alleged to have contained an 8-mm film along with fifty-four photographs and a nineteen-page letter explaining the atrocious scenes in the contents of the package. After watching the film, which apparently documented the appalling torture of a woman, he handed this vile subject matter to the police. For less than £20,000, he went on to make this forty-two-minute documentary-styled re-enactment of what he could remember from the tape, which bears a close resemblance to a tale from his own manga series. A man dressed as a samurai (Hiroshi Tamura) uses chloroform on an unsuspecting woman (Kirara Yûgao) in the less populated suburbs of Tokyo and then takes her against her will to his home. She awakens to find herself tied to a bed in a darkened room that, as her eyes begin to focus, reveals the splattered stains of dried blood strewn across its walls. Before he begins to dissect his victim, the sadist stands before the camera and details that which will follow. He then proceeds to butcher her body and adds her body parts to his gruesome collection. Hino's film has been described as horror in its purest form; the youth of Japan certainly loved it, giving it a top ten position among the country's video releases. This video also made it into the hands of American horror journalist Chas Balun, who copied it and introduced it to the underground horror cinema that was already discreetly operating in the United States. These bootlegs soon became treasured collector's items and the **Guinea Pig** series acquired a hush-hush popularity. Hino's ideas have continued to influence other modern creators, surfacing in Argentine Mariano Peralta's controversial **Snuff 102** (2007), which resulted in the director being attacked following a screening at the Mar Der Plata Festival.

Flower of Flesh and Blood was an extreme piece of filmmaking and its success allowed Hino to continue his **Guinea Pig** movies. The series, however, was taken over by JHV, who refused to tolerate a repetition of the public outcry that had followed in the wake of the release of the first two films. Directed by Masayuki Kusumi, **He Never Dies** or **Senritsu! Shinanai Otoko** (1986) ran to forty minutes and with an increased budget finally introduced the vaguest

element of plot and rudimentary characterization. The series, which had established its unrelenting reputation on an almost incomprehensible nihilism, now turned to comedic gore. A heartbroken young man, whose girlfriend has ditched him for one of their smarmy colleagues, is then sacked by his boss. Having also fallen foul of his family, this despairing chap turns to suicide. However, when he slits his wrist he is shocked to see the blood stop flowing and the gash heal. Feeling no pain, he then cuts deeper and soon realizes he is "the man who cannot die". In contrast to the first two entries in the series, this man inflicts pain on his own body and then plans an amusingly elaborate revenge on his former girlfriend and her new lover.

Hideshi Hino returned to direct the fourth short feature in the series, **Mermaid in a Manhole** or **Manhoru no naka no Ningyo** (1988), which had an extended running time of fifty-seven minutes. His tale of a grief-stricken painter (Shigeru Saiki) was based on one of his own manga. Having recently lost his wife, the painter returns to the river he played in as a child only to find it has been turned into a foul-smelling sewer. There he meets the mermaid (Mari Somei) who inspired him all those years ago. She has been stuck in the sewer for so long she has become infected, so he takes her back to his home in the hope of reviving her in the clean water of his bath. As she writhes seductively in the water, her illness soon takes a turn for the worse and the boils on her skin become pus-ridden bloody ruptures. Taking body art to the extreme, the artist uses the discharge from these lacerations to commit her portrait to a peculiar canvas, but her health declines and she eventually dies.

That same year **Guinea Pig** ventured into splatter-drenched science fiction in the Kazuhito Kuramoto directed **Android of Notre Dame** or **Nôtoru Damu no andoroido** (1988), which ran to fifty-one minutes. Kuramoto had already carved a reputation in the Japanese porn industry and on this outing told the disappointing story of a diminutive scientist by the name of Karawaza (Toshihiko Hino) who had struggled to discover the cure for his sister's (Mio Takaki) failing heart. Up until this point, his research had been limited to experimenting with animals, but his endeavours now required a human guinea pig. A phone call from a man named Kato (Tomorowo Taguchi) provides the offer of the body of a recently deceased young girl in return for a substantial sum of money. The body soon turns up in a cardboard box! The experiment is again unsuccessful, despair turns to rage and then he hacks the broken body to pieces; Karawaza knows he needs a fresh corpse. When Kato reveals his true colours, the scientist is forced to escort him to his laboratory and he finally gets his live specimen.

The final tale in the series, **Devil Woman Doctor** or **Pita no akuma no joi-san** (1990), from director Hajime Tabe, whose background was in computer games, amounted to little more than fifty-two minutes of comedic gore sketches. In tone it had more in common with the third **Guinea Pig, He Never Dies** (1986), including in its cast one of Japan's leading transvestites Pîtâ, also known as Shinnosuke Ikehata in the part of the female doctor of the feature's title. She has been assigned to a bizarre surgical enterprise that has been designed to treat only the most extreme cases, which necessitates a regular dosage of mutilation, blood, guts and, true to **Guinea Pig**'s original premise, death. If the first of her patients becomes anxious, his head explodes; her next victim, I mean patient, is plagued by an exploding heart. And so the slapstick would continue in a tale that was as far removed from the series' graphic origins as could be imagined, but it still attracted a huge following. A seventh video **Guinea Pig 7: Slaughter Special** was released in 1991, collecting some of the most gruesome moments from the previous films, but the end alas was nigh.

Halloween

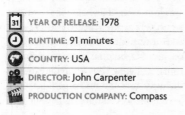

📅	YEAR OF RELEASE: 1978
🕐	RUNTIME: 91 minutes
🌐	COUNTRY: USA
👤	DIRECTOR: John Carpenter
🎬	PRODUCTION COMPANY: Compass

International Pictures, Falcon International Productions

✎ WRITERS: John Carpenter (screenplay), Debra Hill (screenplay)

▭ CINEMATOGRAPHER: Dean Cundey

PRODUCERS: Moustapha Akkad (executive producer), Debra Hill (producer), Kool Marder (associate producer), Irwin Yablans (executive producer), John Carpenter (producer)

 CERTIFICATE: Australia: R; Canada: R; Canada: 13+ (Quebec); Canada: AA (Ontario) (video rating) (1982);

Canada: R (Manitoba) (re-rating) (2003); Canada: R (Manitoba/Ontario) (original rating); Canada: R (Nova Scotia); New Zealand: R16; UK: 18 (video rating); UK: X (original rating); USA: PG-13; USA: R

 BUDGET: $320,000

RECEIPTS: over $176 million

CAST: Donald Pleasence, Jamie Lee Curtis, Nancy Kyes, P. J. Soles, Charles Cyphers, Kyle Richards, Brian Andrews, John Michael Graham, Nancy Stephens, Arthur Malet, Mickey Yablans, Brent Le Page, Adam Hollander, Robert Phalen, Tony Moran

ON HALLOWEEN NIGHT 1963, police were called to a Victorian-styled house in the small town of Haddonfield, Illinois. There they found the body of seventeen-year-old Judith Myers, stabbed to death by her six-year-old brother, who, having returned from trick-or-treating, found her in bed with her boyfriend. The eerily silent child was incarcerated in the Smith's Grove Sanatorium under the care of psychiatrist Sam Loomis (Donald Pleasence), the one person who recognized the evil locked in his soul. After being institutionalized for fifteen years and knowing he faced a life of imprisonment, Michael Myers (Nick Castle) escapes just days before Halloween. Only Loomis knows his patient is heading home to Haddonfield. Soon after his arrival, Michael slips off with a white mask. These impassive features proved an unwitting stroke of genius and bore an uncanny resemblance to the mask that haunted George Franju's **Eyes**

Without a Face (1960). This would in due course make Michael's deadpan presence all the more ominous.

As bookish Laurie Strode (Jamie Lee Curtis), Michael's younger sister, discusses plans for Halloween with her world-wise friends Lynda (P. J. Soles) and Annie (Nancy Kyes-Loomis), she is certain that someone just out of eyeshot is watching her. Unbeknown to her dismissive friends they are also being observed. Later that evening while Laurie babysits across the street, Annie is confronted by Michael, who, without a word of warning, strangles her and then slits her throat. When Lynda appears at the seemingly empty house accompanied by her boyfriend, they seize the opportunity to slip upstairs to the bedroom. This would be their last, for shortly afterwards both are killed by the masked Michael, Lynda as she tries in desperation to call Laurie. Perturbed by Lynda's incoherent telephone call, Laurie crosses the street to the now darkened house. There she discovers the three dead bodies and Judith Myers' tombstone. What follows is a game of life and death as the amoral sadist stalks the innocent heroine of the piece, while Loomis and the Sheriff frantically try to bring him down. The film bows out with a shot of the Myers' house and Michael's heavy breathing, his face still concealed behind his mask. The image carries a warning; Michael Myers is still out there, alive and intent on the kill.

Filmed in only twenty-one days in the spring of 1978, John Carpenter's **Halloween** is a masterpiece of cinematic horror. Carpenter had already directed two acknowledged cult classics with **Dark Star** (1974) and **Assault on Precinct 13** (1976); this time with co-writer Debra Hill he created a film that would assume the mantle as the first in a long line of slasher films, which drew its inspiration from Alfred Hitchcock's time-honoured **Psycho**. Executive Producer Irwin Yablans had aims to make a horror movie to rival **The Exorcist**, and with his business partner, Moustapha Akkad, toyed with the idea of a psychotic killer that stalked babysitters. Based on this, Carpenter and Debra Hill prepared a script they called "The Babysitter Murders". Yablans then suggested using a Halloween backdrop; thereafter the film became **Halloween**.

Carpenter's film both instigated and cleverly re-worked the principles that would become the blueprint for the slasher movies of the next decade. The

The trick is to stay alive!

first-person camera perspective was one of the many hallmarks of this feature and was used to disquieting effect as the silent assassin came to the fore, as he had four years before in **Black Christmas**. These houses weren't the Gothic manses of horrors past; everyday settings were now the norm, and the audience were introduced to the chaste female heroine, who proved invariably more resourceful than her male counterparts. Unlike many of his successors, Carpenter chose restraint in his portrayal of graphic violence, thus embracing Yablans' request "that the audience shouldn't see anything. It should be what they thought they saw that frightens them". To this effect, Carpenter conjured with the light and shadow, deceiving his audience as Michael prowled in the shadows akin to a childhood's monster under the bed.

The film succeeded in garnering a positive response from the audience for which it was intended, with comparatively very little advertising. The impression made by Carpenter's moody, yet unsophisticated score was similar in effect to that of Mike Oldfield's prelude to **The Exorcist** (1973) and Bernard Hermann's strings for the **Psycho** (1960) shower scene and became synonymous with the movie's unsettling premise. The columnists, however, proved more reticent. The movie's detractors regarded Carpenter's ideas as derivative, sourcing too much from Hitchcock, De Palma and Lewton; further there were those who felt it lacked the erudition observed only a few years before in **Carrie** (1976) and **The**

Exorcist. Later analysis questioned the extensive use of the peeping tom-styled roving camera, which aroused fears of the audience identifying with the villain, as it had done before in José Mojica Marins' **Coffin Joe** series and would do again in the **Friday the 13th** franchise as well as **A Nightmare on Elm Street.** There were those commentators who felt the film mirrored the declining moral values of America's youth, inferring an allegorical connotation between sexual awakening and, at the hands of Michael Myers, the death of innocence. Carpenter has always been quick to dismiss such scrutiny.

Halloween was the surrogate to seven sequels, along with a remake in 2007 followed by a 2009 sequel to the remake entitled **Halloween II**, which has no bearing on the original released in 1981, which was the highest grossing horror movie of that particular year. The sequels, with the exception of **Halloween III**, were to continue the legend of Michael Myers but were continually censured owing to their explicit display of violence and gore. A mass-market paperback by Curtis Richards, entitled *Halloween*, was published by Bantam Books in 1979, followed by a video game for the Atari 2600 in 1983, and later a series of comics were published by Chaos Comics in 2000 and, more recently, Devil's Due in 2008.

Happy Birthday to Me

📅 YEAR OF RELEASE: 1981	✎ WRITERS: Timothy Bond, Peter Jobin, John Saxton John Beaird
⏱ RUNTIME: 110 minutes	
🌐 COUNTRY: Canada	🎞 CINEMATOGRAPHER: Miklos Lente
🎥 DIRECTOR: J. Lee Thompson	🎬 PRODUCERS: John Dunning, Stewart Harding, Andre Link
🎬 PRODUCTION COMPANY: Canadian Film Development Corporation (CFDC), Columbia Pictures Corporation, Famous Players, The Birthday Film Company	⭕ CERTIFICATE: Australia: R; Canada: 13+ (Quebec); New Zealand: R 16; UK: X (original rating); UK: 18 (video rating, 1986); UK: 15 (video re-rating, 2004); USA: R
	💲 BUDGET: $3,500,000 Canadian

CAST: Melissa Sue Anderson, Glenn Ford, Lawrence Dane, Sharon Acker, Frances Hyland, Tracey E. Bregman, Jack Blum, Matt Craven, Lenore Zann, David Eisner, Michel-René Labelle, Richard Rebiere, Lesleh Donaldson, Lisa Langlois

VIRGINIA WAINWRIGHT HAS everything going for her; she is young and beautiful, and her fellow classmates would have you believe she is one of Crawford Academy's most popular seniors. She has also earned a place in a rather elite crowd, which includes among its membership some of the most affluent seniors at the school. The self-styled Top Ten gather each evening at the Silent Woman Tavern located somewhere near the Academy. While making her way to the tavern one of the clique, Bernadette O'Hara, is beset by an unknown figure. She manages to repel his attack and while making her escape, seeks help from a student with whom she seems acquainted. Her appeals fall on deaf ears as the unseen student takes a blade to her throat.

The Top Ten spend too much time playing elaborate shenanigans and this night is no different. After dunking a pet mouse in an offended drinker's beer, the group dare one another to hit the accelerator and take their cars over a rising drawbridge. Although the car in which Ginny is forced to travel makes it over the bridge, she vents her anger at being coerced into such a precarious jaunt. She continues on her way home, but unknown to her is followed by someone who enters her bedroom and makes off with her panties. We now learn that Ginny is trying to pick up the pieces of her shattered life after narrowly escaping death as she traversed a similar drawbridge some years

Because of the bizarre nature of this birthday party, pray you're not invited.

before. Ever since the accident, she has had to attend regular therapy sessions, but her memories of the incident remain somewhat vague.

In the days that follow the angry scene at the drawbridge, her over-privileged friends are murdered in a variety of grisly and imaginative ways; two of them seemingly at the hands of the disoriented Ginny. Her confusion is heightened when in a series of flashbacks she recalls the death of her mother and the betrayal by her friends. With only days to go to her eighteenth birthday, Ginny contacts her psychiatrist (Glenn Ford) in the hope of uncovering more of her past. When he insists he can no longer help her, she responds by taking a poker to the back of his head. Several days later her father returns home for her birthday celebrations to find his wife's desecrated grave and the corpses of the butchered Top Ten seated at the family dining table, which looks just as it did four years before on the night of Ginny's betrayal. His daughter then enters, carrying a large cake, quietly murmuring "Happy Birthday". This, however, isn't the finale, far from it, for there will be a series of further twists before J. Lee Thompson brings his film to its shocking climax.

Having already made a whole string of highly successful movies, including **The Guns of Navarone** (1961) and **Cape Fear** (1962), Bristol-born J. Lee Thompson put together this cult slasher, which carefully adhered to the precepts of this lucrative cinematic trend before culminating in one of the most unexpected twists so far ventured by the genre. Thompson was a well-respected director, whose finest work was arguably during the 1950s and early 1960s, with a reputation for working very closely with his cast. In so doing, he got the very best out of his team, placing **Happy Birthday to Me** leagues ahead of so many of its contemporaries. A high level of competence was observed in both the direction and cinematography, with a skilled manipulation of the set's lighting to ensure this feature did more than just chill the spines of its assembled audience. Although his film can boast six rather bizarre killings, including the infamous skirmish with the shish kebab skewer, Ginny's

graphic brain surgery rates as one of the most stomach turning episodes of the entire period.

In the United States, the MPAA called for the editing of certain scenes, but surprisingly the print issued for cinematic release in the UK, along with the 1986 RCA/Columbia video, opted for the gorier footage, which included the weight-lift and shish kebab death scenes. This release also contained a haunting music score, which, for contractual reasons, was replaced with a disco soundtrack for the DVD of 2004. The DVD annoyed fans still further in returning to the edited print first released in the United States in 1981. **Happy Birthday to Me** may not have been very popular with many of the critics, but among horror film regulars this film is one of the essential entries of the period.

Hatchet

31 YEAR OF RELEASE: 2006

RUNTIME: 84 minutes

COUNTRY: USA

DIRECTOR: Adam Green

PRODUCTION COMPANY: ArieScope Pictures, High Seas Entertainment, Radioaktive Film

WRITER: Adam Green

CINEMATOGRAPHER: Will Barratt

PRODUCERS: Scott Altomare, Sarah J. Donohue (line producer), Sarah Elbert, Roman Kindrachuk (executive producer), Andrew Mysko (executive producer), Cory Neal

CERTIFICATE: Australia: R; Ireland: 18; New Zealand: R16; UK: 18; USA: NC-17 (original rating); USA: R (cut)

BUDGET: $1,500,000

CAST: Joel David Moore, Tamara Feldman, Deon Richmond, Kane Hodder, Mercedes McNab, Parry Shen, Joel Murray, Joleigh Fioravanti, Richard Riehle, Patrika Darbo, Robert Englund, Joshua Leonard, Tony Todd

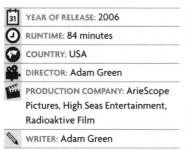

HATCHET WAS ANOTHER attempt to build on the success of **Scream** (1996) and emulate the golden years of the eighties slasher. As they fish in a backwater swamp, two hunters, Sampson (Robert Englund) and his son Ainsley (Joshua Leonard) are slaughtered by a hideous entity. Some miles away in the Mardi Gras celebration of New Orleans, a group of friends set out with an inexperienced guide, Shawn (Parry Shen), on a haunted swamp tour. On the same tour are a couple of topless girls, Misty (Mercedes McNab) and Jenna (Joleigh Fioreavanti) along with their seedy director, Shapiro (Joel Murray).

Soon after entering the swamp, a hobo warns them to stay away from the area, but Shawn continues to take them further into this swampland where they come upon several derelict houses, one of which was home to the deformed Victor Crowley (Kane Hodder). Many years ago young Victor was hidden away by his protective father until, one Halloween, a group of teenagers threw fireworks into their house, which resulted in a huge fire. As his father took a hatchet to the door to save his son, he accidentally killed him as the blade hit him full in the face. Victor's father never recovered and died of a broken heart. Local legend tells of a vengeful spirit that murders all those who enter the swamp. One of the girls sees someone in the trees, and then Shawn crashes the boat leaving the party in this alligator-infested terrain standing before the house of Victor Crowley. Very soon, Victor will continue his vengeful wrath.

Stay out of the swamp.

After making commercials for cable television and fronting the heavy metal band Haddonfield, Adam Green returned to the slasher formula of the 1980s in what was an amusing homage, which saw guest appearances from horror legends Robert Englund and Tony Todd. While there was nothing new in his film, his script threw in the one-liners, contained enough topless shots to delight the male element of his teenage audience and ran at a fast pace as the kills came in ever so typically graphic fashion. **Hatchet 2** appeared in 2010 and followed on from the unsatisfactory finale, which, true to the slasher trope, had left this original outing open for a lucrative sequel.

Haute Tension

YEAR OF RELEASE: 2003		COUNTRY: France	
RUNTIME: 91 minutes		DIRECTOR: Alexandre Aja	

PRODUCTION COMPANY: Alexandre Films, Europa Corp.

WRITERS: Alexandre Aja, Grégory Levasseur

CINEMATOGRAPHER: Maxime Alexandre

PRODUCERS: Alexandre Arcady, Robert Benmussa, Andrei Boncea (executive producer), Inigo Lezzi (line producer), Mehdi Sayah (assistant producer), Luc Besson (co-producer)

CERTIFICATE: Australia: R; Canada: R (Manitoba); Canada: 18A (British Columbia/Ontario); Canada: R (Alberta); Canada: 16+ (Quebec); Ireland: 18; New Zealand: R18; USA: NC-17 (original rating); USA: R (cut); USA: Unrated (DVD rating); USA: R (edited for re-rating); USA: R (edited version)

BUDGET: €2,200,000

RECEIPTS: $3,645,438

CAST: Cécile De France, Maïwenn Le Besco, Philippe Nahon, Franck Khalfoun, Andrei Finti, Oana Pellea, Marco Claudiu Pascu, Jean-Claude de Goros, Bogdan Uritescu, Gabriel Spahiu

FROM THE OUTSET, Alexandre Aja's film had but one desire and that was to shock, initially allowing the camera's lens to dwell upon a girl wearing only a hospital patient's gown whose back has been severely lacerated. We are then thrown into a change of scene, as a fearful young woman chases through a forest to meet with a road where a car's headlights reveal a nasty gash to her stomach. In a matter of minutes the audience have been sufficiently warned. What will happen in the next hour and twenty minutes will take them a lot further than the average horror movie; Aja will go out of his way to sicken using every means at his disposal.

Marie (Cécile de France) and Alex (Maïwenn Le Besco) take their time as they enjoy a leisurely drive to Alex's family home in the country in the hope of getting on with some exam revision. As they continue on their journey, a seedy fellow (Philippe Nahon) is observed reclining in the seat of his truck. His expression is one of perverse delight as he wallows in the heightened ecstasy of fellatio, then soon after discards a severed head from the window of his vehicle before promptly driving away. It is not until much later that the girls arrive home and after the long drive yearn for nothing more than a solid night's sleep. There is already a suggestion Marie has a hankering for Alex, but such thoughts are swept aside when a loud banging comes to the front door. Alex's father hurries downstairs to be confronted by the intimidating figure from the truck and the incisive slash of his razor. He isn't finished yet; once inside the house the killer forces his quarry's head through the slats of the stairway then decapitates him with a bookcase. The girl's mother is then exposed to his murderous rage; her throat is cruelly sliced open to be followed by an effusive splatter of blood.

In desperation, Marie tries to find somewhere to hide as the killer's blade is heard carving into his victim; her hands are later revealed to have been severed.

Cocooned by her earplugs, Alex has remained completely oblivious to the furore that has besieged her home. That is until she awakens and finds the killer's knife poised at her throat. While this is going on Marie attempts to phone for help as Alex's little brother escapes into the fields. The killer, now brandishing a shotgun, follows the child from the house. Marie seizes the opportunity to come to the aid of her friend, but fails as she bids to free her from her chains. Refusing to be deterred she lays hands on her weapon of choice which takes the shape of a razor sharp kitchen knife. The killer continues to work at an alarmingly quick pace and by now has already removed Alex to the rear of his truck. Discreetly, Marie secretes herself at the back of the vehicle and then they set off, eventually stopping at a petrol station, where the silent assassin's bloody spree summarily continues. The petrol assistant takes the full force of an axe, then the forecourt's cameras reveal a strange sight: all is not quite as it at first seemed.

Haute Tension was released as **High Tension** in North America, and when it entered the UK it was given an appropriate release as **Switchblade Romance**. The original American theatrical version was instantly cut by several minutes owing to the film's graphic content. An element of this can be attributed to the welcome return of one of horror's former masters, make-up artist Giannetto De Rossi. Many years before De Rossi had worked under Lucio Fulci, with his last entry in the macabre coming at the height of Italian horror boom on Fulci's own **House by the Cemetery** (1981). While De Rossi once again excelled in his bloody craft, he couldn't take all of the blame for the censor's wrath. From its opening scenes, Aja's film was just too violent for mainstream audiences, exultant in its ferocious intensity, which would continue without relent for the entirety of the excessive proceedings.

As with many of its explicit predecessors, the plot was sacrificed for the purpose of sadistic carnage, but the tension in its claustrophobic embrace held the audience firmly in its grasp. The camera work combined with the fast-paced direction to overwhelm the limitations in narrative and then ten minutes before his tale came to its damning finale Aja revealed he had been hiding something, throwing in an inexplicable twist that tossed the whole film on its head. The denouement observed a commonality with so many facets of modern French cinema and among fans of this specific genre was lauded for the effect in its final delivery. The reviews were understandably mixed, with many critics being appalled by the prolonged brutality; many raised questions about that which transpired at the denouement, while others drew

Hearts will bleed.

unhealthy comparisons with Dean Koontz's novel *Intensity*, first published in 1995. Alexandre Aja, however, had shown that a small French production company could shock even the most bloodthirsty hack and slash enthusiast and produce horror at its most visceral.

He Knows You're Alone

📅	YEAR OF RELEASE: 1980	📷	CINEMATOGRAPHER: Gerald Feil
⏱	RUNTIME: 94 minutes	🎬	PRODUCERS: Joseph Beruh (executive producer), Robert Di Milia (co-producer), Edgar Lansbury (executive producer), George Manasse, Nan Pearlman (co-producer)
🌐	COUNTRY: USA		
🎥	DIRECTOR: Armand Mastroianni		
🎬	PRODUCTION COMPANY: Metro-Goldwyn-Mayer (MGM)	⭕	CERTIFICATE: Australia: R; UK: 18; USA: R
✒	WRITERS: Scott Parker	💲	RECEIPTS: $4,875,436

CAST: Don Scardino, Caitlin O'Heaney, Elizabeth Kemp, Tom Rolfing, Lewis Arlt, Patsy Pease, James Rebhorn, Tom Hanks, Dana Barron, Joseph Leon, Paul Gleason, James Carroll, Brian Byers, Curt Hostetter, Robin Lamont

TWO YOUNG WOMEN are so engrossed by the tension of a slasher movie they fail to take notice of a man who slinks into the seat behind them. The onscreen slaughter is of little interest to him; he seeks his own thrills and, just to prove the point, lurches forward to stab one of them through the back of her seat. The killer (Tom Rolfing) has a homicidal appetite for blushing brides, having murdered his intended some years before when she stood him up at the altar. Ever since he has been trailed by the man she had hoped to marry, policeman Len Gamble (Lewis Arlt).

The stalker turns his attention to young Amy Jensen (Caitlin O'Heaney), whose future husband Phil is away on his stag weekend. Amy and her likeable friends, Joyce and Nancy, are getting together with friends for the excitement of the hen party. The girls may not be about to walk the aisle themselves, but all too soon they become the killer's prey. As she tries to save herself, Amy has to turn to her former boyfriend Marvin (Don Scardino), who now works in the morgue, a locale which provides for a thrilling climax.

Armand Mastroianni's entry to the slasher years rehashed themes already observed in John Carpenter's **Halloween** (1978), but his creepy direction and clever pacing ensured his audience never became bored. The execution of the point-of-view camera shots heightened the menace as Mastroianni worked to disguise the killer's face and, as in **Halloween**, the splatter factor was kept to an absolute minimum, no doubt at the request of MGM. There was thankfully one particular gruesome moment which has lived on with the movie's fans: the chilling sight of a severed head immersed in the depths of a fish tank. The creativity shown in his opening scenes wasn't to go unnoticed; Wes Craven later used it in the introductory sequence to **Scream 2** (1997). The main score, however, was just a little too reminiscent of Carpenter's synthesized theme, but worked to similar effect in evoking the requisite air of suspense. **He Knows You're Alone** also marked the debut for a young Tom Hanks, who gained his very first couple of scenes before marching on to one of cinema's most successful careers.

> **Every girl is frightened the night before her wedding, but this time ... there's good reason!**

Hell Night

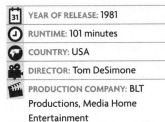

YEAR OF RELEASE: 1981		**WRITER:** Randy Feldman	
RUNTIME: 101 minutes		**CINEMATOGRAPHER:** Mac Ahlberg	
COUNTRY: USA		**PRODUCERS:** Bruce Cohn Curtis, Mark L. Rosen, Chuck Russell (executive producer), Joseph Wolf (executive producer), Irwin Yablans	
DIRECTOR: Tom DeSimone			
PRODUCTION COMPANY: BLT Productions, Media Home Entertainment		**CERTIFICATE:** Australia R; UK: 18; USA: R	

CAST: Linda Blair, Vincent Van Patten, Peter Barton, Kevin Brophy, Jenny Neumann, Suki Goodwin, Jimmy Sturtevant, Hal Ralston, Carey Fox, Ron Gans, Gloria Heilman

AMIDST A COLLEGE'S partying, the president of the Alpha Sigma Rho fraternity commands that four pledges, each attired in fancy dress, stay at Garth Manor until dawn on Hell Night to ensure they fulfil their initiation rites.

As the four students are escorted to the abandoned manse, a story is told of how twelve years before, Raymond Garth murdered his wife and three of their deformed children; legend would have you believe one son managed to survive. In despair, the father later hung himself in the confines of the family home. With this chilling account still fresh in their minds, the pledges begin to settle for the night waiting for dawn in a house that, although deserted for more than a decade, appears remarkably well furnished. They are completely unaware that the other members of the fraternity will attempt to frighten them using some of their own special effects. However, the lofty pranksters are set upon by an unseen figure; one of them is hauled screaming into a trench and then decapitated, another has his neck broken and the president is eventually impaled on a scythe. There is more to the legend than the pledges have been told and very soon they learn there are two killers in their midst. The pace accelerates as the imaginative slaughter continues in the tunnels situated beneath this ageing hall, and true to the slasher trope only the final girl will survive.

Pray for day!

Hell Night took the popular slasher theme of the day and swathed it in the mystery of an ageing haunted house. Tom DeSimone had learned his trade in adult films and in what was only a forty-day shoot he, along with his crew, produced a very creepy episode. His film was immersed in the atmospherics of the autumnal clime and the enormity of the imposing Gothic locale. Such was the allure of this house he didn't need the pools of blood that were already congealing in so many cinemas of the day. The murders for this movie were frequently carried out off screen and were cleverly worked to fuel the audience's anticipation rather than cause frustration. The script then deliberately played down the conventional juvenile sex and nudity of these films, choosing instead to flesh out the characters of the four pledges. Among the novices was Linda Blair, who had been the centre of so much attention following her role in **The Exorcist** (1973). Strangely the two actors who played the killers were never listed in the film's credits; their real names have, for over thirty years, become something of a mystery.

Hellraiser

 YEAR OF RELEASE: 1987

 RUNTIME: 94 minutes

 COUNTRY: UK

DIRECTOR: Clive Barker

PRODUCTION COMPANY: Cinemarque Entertainment BV, Film Futures, Rivdel Films

WRITER: Clive Barker

 CINEMATOGRAPHER: Robin Vidgeon

PRODUCERS: Mark Armstrong (executive producer), Christopher Figg, Selwyn Roberts (associate producer), David Saunders (executive producer), Christopher Webster (executive producer)

 CERTIFICATE: Australia: M (theatrical rating); Australia: R; Canada: 13+ (Quebec); Canada: 18A (Alberta) (re-rating, 2000); Canada: R (Manitoba/Nova Scotia/Ontario); New Zealand: R16; UK: 18; USA: R

 BUDGET: $1,000,000

RECEIPTS: $14,564,027

CAST: Andrew Robinson, Clare Higgins, Ashley Laurence, Sean Chapman, Oliver Smith, Robert Hines, Anthony Allen, Leon Davis, Michael Cassidy, Frank Baker, Kenneth Nelson, Gay Baynes, Niall Buggy, Dave Atkins, Oliver Parker

FRANK COTTON HAS an insatiable lust for life's pleasures, the more bizarre the greater his sense of personal gratification. When he is offered a small puzzle box in an exotic foreign market place, with the promise of pleasure beyond the ken of mortal man, he eagerly accepts. He has no conception of the demonic Cenobites, a sadomasochistic breed that dwell beyond the gates of the box and take a perverse delight in entrapping their victims to render them to an eternity of exquisite pain and torture. Frank disappears without trace and months later leaves his suburban home to his brother Larry and sister-in-law Julia. While Frank was a thrill seeker, his brother lives a quite pedestrian life and his wife is an uncaring woman with little comprehension of life's little pleasures. Her only sense of arousal comes from the memory of her sordid affair with Frank.

Somehow, Frank managed to escape the Cenobites' agonizing clutches, but his body has been ripped and torn beyond recognition. When Larry injures himself and his blood spills onto the attic's wooden floor, Frank is returned to life, but he needs more if he is ever to be completely regenerated. Once she has overcome her disgust, Frank finds a willing ally in the heartless Julia. She uses her guile to attract the men she meets in the pubs and bars of the area and brings them home to the attic space to allow her former lover to feed on their life force. With each new victim, he comes closer to returning to the world of living flesh. However, Julia's erratic behaviour has aroused the suspicion of Larry's daughter, Kirsty. When she ventures into the attic room, she discovers her stepmother's dark secret and only just escapes with her life. As she breaks away from her treacherous uncle, she triggers the puzzle box and sets in motion the elaborate process that opens the gates to the domain of eternal torment and brings her face to face with Pinhead and his debauched cohorts. They see only the smooth flesh of a new victim and prepare to drag her into their darkened world of pain and suffering, but true to the heroines of slasher lore she remains strong in their presence and enters into a bargain to lead them to her uncle in exchange for her life. She now has to use her cunning to avoid her duplicitous stepmother and return Frank to the torment of the puzzle box.

In this, his stunning debut as a director, Clive Barker brought to the silver screen one of his darkest creations, mischievously toying with the more dubious delights of sex and death. In the UK, his film attracted an "X" certificate; the BBFC were appreciably perturbed by this cruel flirtation with sadomasochism. The black leather and fetish wear of the Cenobites was certainly not the customary fare of the average British cinema, even though the more astute would have discerned Barker was narrating a very subtle tale of romance, albeit diabolically macabre. The script was based on his short story *The Hellbound Heart*, an account inspired by a meeting with the English industrial band Coil, who he later hoped would write the score for his film. Among band member Peter

Demon to some. Angel to others.

"Sleazy" Christopherson's collection of pornography were a number of masochistic gay magazines; the images provided the glimmer of an idea for the torturous dominion of the Cenobites. Their vicious display was balanced by a warped surrealism that seeped through the atmosphere of this tale set in an English suburbia inhabited by so many Americans, each of whom, true to Barker's original, revealed themselves as well-rounded characters able to hold the viewer's attention. While nowhere near as gory as so many of its contemporaries, the scenes of Frank's torment were excruciating and served as a reminder of the hedonist's descent into a hell of his own making.

The leather-clad Pinhead would continue to emerge from the sickening horror of the puzzle box, to become a lucrative horror icon and spawn seven sequels **Hellbound: Hellraiser II** (1988), **Hellraiser III: Hell on Earth** (1992), **Hellraiser: Bloodline** (1996), **Hellraiser: Inferno** (2000), **Hellraiser: Hellseeker** (2002), **Hellraiser: Deader** (2005) and **Hellraiser: Hellwood** (2005) along with a series of comics published by Marvel's Epic imprint and later Boom! Studios. 🦇

Henry: Portrait of a Serial Killer

31 YEAR OF RELEASE: 1986	RUNTIME: 83 minutes

COUNTRY: USA

DIRECTOR: John McNaughton

PRODUCTION COMPANY: Maljack Productions

WRITERS: Richard Fire, John McNaughton

CINEMATOGRAPHER: Charlie Lieberman

PRODUCERS: Malik B. Ali (executive producer), Waleed B. Ali (executive producer), Lisa Dedmond, Steven A. Jones, John McNaughton

CERTIFICATE: Australia: R (uncut) (2005); Canada: 18+ (Quebec); Ireland: 18; New Zealand: (Banned) (uncut); New Zealand: R18 (cut); UK: 18; USA: Open (rating surrendered: 1989); USA: X (original rating: 1988)

BUDGET: $111,000

RECEIPTS: $609,939

CAST: Mary Demas, Michael Rooker, Anne Bartoletti, Elizabeth Kaden, Ted Kaden, Denise Sullivan, Anita Ores, Megan Ores, Cheri Jones, Monica Anne O'Malley, Bruce Quist, Erzsebet Sziky, Tracy Arnold, Tom Towles, David Katz

A NAKED WOMAN LIES dead in a field. The camera follows the path of the impassive Henry (Michael Rooker), juxtaposed with images of other murder victims, their terrified screams reverberating to disturb the viewer and prepare them for the unhinged madness that is about to follow. Henry has trailed an unsuspecting woman, watching in the distance as she enters her home.

By day, Henry works as a pest exterminator, sharing an apartment with Otis (Tom Towles) and his sister Becky (Tracy Arnold). Garbed in his work clothes he has little difficulty in entering the homes of his victims and is seen returning to the home of the woman he followed shortly before. Soon after, her dead body is revealed with an electric cable choking her throat; cigarette burns can be seen running down from her neck to her breasts. Otis reveals he met Henry

while serving time in prison; although Henry never talks about it, he killed his mother. However, he eventually does open up to Becky about his mother and her cruelty, although his story is strangely confused. He recalls how she made him dress as a girl, and was then forced to watch her engage in sex with her seedy clientele. Unable to endure further humiliation he claims to have stabbed her and then insists he shot her. Henry's grasp on reality is obviously not all that it should be.

When the two men travel to a seamy part of town and pick up a couple of prostitutes, Henry turns on the women and strangles them before breaking their necks. Initially Otis appears shocked, but he too has killed in the past and the following night they murder a shady trader who deals in stolen electrical goods. Henry stabs him with a soldering iron and then smashes a television set over his head. Otis then takes great pleasure in plugging in the set and electrocuting him. They then help themselves to a video camera, which they use to record the rape and slaughter of an entire family. Later they are seen savouring their grisly activities in their apartment, just as the voyeuristic Mark Lewis had previously done in Michael Powell's **Peeping Tom** (1960), with the sickening Otis taking considerably greater delight in their escapades than his brooding partner.

As the body count continues to rise, the police appear alarmingly ineffectual. Henry believes himself to be clever enough to evade capture as he continually alters his modus operandi and keeps on the move. The film takes a turn when Otis becomes his next victim. Henry walks in on him to find him attempting to strangle Becky, having already raped her. Otis's death is typically brutal and soon after Henry is observed calmly dismembering his former accomplice in the bath, before disposing of his remains in a river. As the psychopath leaves town with Becky, she confesses her love. Henry dispassionately admits to feeling the same way, not that he has any understanding of human emotion – his mother saw to that many years ago. In the harrowing finale, he dumps a suitcase by the side of the road. The camera homes in towards the abandoned case, which is revealed stained in blood. The film ends as it began with the sounds of a desperate struggle and screaming as Henry now

Yeah, I killed my Mama ...

drives away to continue in his life of murderous crime.

The inspiration for Henry came from the confessions of the serial killer Henry Lee Lucas, who admitted to more than 600 murders between 1975 and his arrest in 1983. An investigation undertaken by the Texas Attorney General's office invalidated the vast majority of his claims, leading to Lucas being convicted of eleven murders.

John McNaughton's film based its premise on Lucas's violent fantasies rather than the crimes for which he was actually found guilty. Lucas's appalling childhood never gave him a chance. He murdered his abusive mother in 1960, a violent prostitute who frequently made him watch her while she had sex with clients, and for his matricide he served ten years in prison before eventually being paroled. Following his conviction, he was sentenced to death for the murder of an unidentified female victim known only as "Orange Socks". In 1998 the Governor of Texas, George W. Bush, commuted the sentence to life in prison, three years prior to Lucas dying of heart failure.

McNaughton's disturbing film was shot on 16-mm film in less than a month with a budget that amounted to a meagre $111,000. He kept his costs to a minimum by employing family and friends, with Mary Demas excelling as she played three different murder victims. The diminutive budget afforded the film a bleakness that befitted its sordid nature, with the city of Chicago assuming a depressingly downtrodden guise. Only Gerald Kargl's unrelenting portrayal of the Salzburg serial killer Werner Kniesek, in his controversial debut **Angst** (1983), has ever exceeded McNaughton's psychotic depiction.

The movie's violent content coupled with the producers' concerns over the quality of the final cut meant it would be another four years before McNaughton would see his film released devoid of a rating. Before the film was submitted for classification in the UK, thirty-eight seconds were removed, without his approval. The scene had depicted a half-naked woman sitting on the toilet with a broken bottle lodged in her mouth. The BBFC then insisted a further twenty-four seconds had to be cut from the family massacre, making specific reference to Otis groping the mother's breasts before and after killing her. Only then was this film considered suitable for a cinematic release. Further cuts were ordered when it was later submitted during the 1990s, this time moderating the impact of the murder of the shady salesman and once again the distressing butchery of the family. It wasn't until 2003 that an uncut version of the film was classified for British DVD release. Chuck Parrello was offered the chance to direct a sequel; **Henry: Portrait of a Serial Killer, Part 2** was to continue the slaughter in 1996.

The Hills Have Eyes

📅 YEAR OF RELEASE: 1977	⏳ PRODUCER: Peter Locke
🕐 RUNTIME: 89 minutes	⭕ CERTIFICATE: Australia: R; New Zealand: R18; UK: X (original rating, cut); UK: 18 (cut, 1987); UK: 18; USA: X (original rating); USA: Unrated (DVD version); USA: R
🌐 COUNTRY: USA	
🎥 DIRECTOR: Wes Craven	
✏️ WRITER: Wes Craven	
🎞️ CINEMATOGRAPHER: Eric Saarinen	💲 BUDGET: $230,000
	🧾 RECEIPTS: $25,000,000

CAST: Susan Lanier, Robert Houston, Martin Speer, Dee Wallace, Russ Grieve, John Steadman, James Whitworth, Virginia Vincent, Lance Gordon, Michael Berryman, Janus Blythe, Cordy Clark, Brenda Marinoff, Peter Locke, Flora the Dog

AN OLD MAN (John Steadman) is observed readying himself to leave his home in the desert. As he loads his truck, he gazes out across the arid wasteland as if trying to trace an unseen presence. There is not a soul to be seen, so he continues in his preparations, only to be confronted by a ragged young girl (Janus Blythe). Unable to restrain his annoyance, he chastises her owing to the activities of her kinsfolk. The girl protests, claiming their ambush of a nearby airfield was simply to assuage their hunger. When she pleads with him to take her away, he refuses, knowing she would never survive in the world beyond the desert. A sound in the background interrupts their discourse, prompting the girl to take cover.

Retired detective Big Bob Carter (Russ Grieve) and his family are holidaying in a trailer in the arid vastness of the same desert. When they the stop at an isolated gas station they are advised to keep to the highway. Bob, however, knows best and takes a short cut through a former nuclear test site. There is an air of inevitability leading to the seemingly accidental crash. The damage to the vehicle's axle leaves the family stranded in this unforgiving wilderness. Bob and his son-in-law, Doug (Martin Speer), set out to find help completely unaware that they have been lured into

A nice American family. They didn't want to kill. But they didn't want to die.

a trap by an inbred cannibalistic family eager for human flesh. Wes Craven carefully builds the tension to fever pitch in the hours before nightfall; then the psychotic family begin to close in on their city-dwelling prey. The ensuing slaughter is brutal. If they are to survive, the remaining members of this family will have to match the depravity of their persecutors. As the closing frames fade to red, Doug is seen in close up, still stabbing and kicking the dead body of one of his cannibal assailants, a scene that was cut for its initial release in the UK.

In 1977, Wes Craven revisited the theme of family vengeance, a premise he had used to deliver such a shocking impact five years before in **Last House on the Left**. Although he had resisted several offers to return to such a degree of violence, personal finances left him with no other option. **The Hills Have Eyes** is a gruesome exploitation film so typical of the period, yet Craven's craft went that one step further in creating a cult classic unhinged by a rawness to its intensity and resultant harrowing brutality. His simple narrative drew upon the dubious tale from the sixteenth century of the incestuous Sawney Bean clan, who are alleged to have committed similar atrocities along the coastal pathways of Ballantrae, Ayrshire. He went on to evoke his interest in Greek mythology, attaching such names to the clan as Juno, Pluto, Mercury and Mars, and in a similar way to these epic tales revealed how good and evil could become obscured, with the good having to fall to the ways of evil if only to protect themselves from the encroaching malevolence. The grainy edit and claustrophobia that was evident, even in such an immense landscape, combined to augment the sense of dread, ensuring that this was a film which would live on with those exposed to its savagery.

Before it could be seen in the cinemas, several of the more graphic takes had to be removed with the footage left on the cutting room floor, now believed to have been lost. In the weeks after its release, this low-budget terror proved to be a surprising success, and in the years that followed went on to acquire cult status. After working on **A Nightmare on Elm Street**, Craven was given the chance to direct a sequel in 1985, **The Hills Have Eyes Part II**, although he later disowned it. In 2006, Alexandre Aja directed the remake, with a new telling of **The Hills Have Eyes II** following in 2007 scripted by Craven and his son Jonathon. 🍁

Hospital Massacre

YEAR OF RELEASE: 1982	
RUNTIME: 89 minutes	
COUNTRY: USA	
DIRECTOR: Boaz Davidson	
PRODUCTION COMPANY: Golan-Globus Productions	
WRITERS: Marc Behm (screenplay), Boaz Davidson (story)	

CINEMATOGRAPHER: Nicholas Josef von Sternberg

PRODUCERS: Yoram Globus, Menahem Golan, Geoffrey Rose (executive producer), John Thompson (associate producer), Christopher Pearce (associate producer)

CERTIFICATE: USA: R

CAST: Barbi Benton, Charles Lucia, Jon Van Ness, John Warner Williams, Den Surles, Gloria Jean Morrison, Karen Smith, Michael Frost, Jimmy Stathis, Lanny Duncan, Marian Beeler, Elly Wold, Jonathon Moore, Gay Austin, Bill Errigo

YOUNG HAROLD HAS an innocent crush on Susan, one of the girls in his class, but takes things just a little too far. He just won't stop harassing her, and when she laughs at his Valentine card he completely loses control. Breaking into Susan's house, he takes his rage out on her brother, killing him by breaking his neck with a coat hanger. The last we see of the lovelorn murderer is the image of him running away from the scene in fits of hysterical laughter.

Nineteen years later Susan (Barbi Benton) has married and been divorced. She leaves the new man in her life in the car as she goes into a Los Angeles county hospital for a routine check up. However, events in the hospital take a strange turn. Unbeknown to her a mysterious figure disguised in a surgical mask has placed a set of false test results in her medical file. From that moment on, the staff in the hospital begin to treat her as if she is very seriously ill. They detain her by forcibly restraining her in straps and keep her locked away in private wards while the medics subject her to a series of humiliating examinations. Some of these assessments can only be described as sleazy and are obviously played for effect, as Barbi Benton had been a *Playboy* cover girl some years before. As she endures these often shameful procedures, she is pursued by the maniac in the mask as he stalks the hospital wards, slaughtering anyone who crosses his path with a variety of surgical tools that would inspire **Dr Giggles** when he embarked on his rampage in 1992. Hours later, her boyfriend finally gets out of the car and starts to search the near deserted hospital, only to be decapitated and have his head presented to Susan encased in a box of Valentine's Day

pastry. Shock followed upon shock as **Hospital Massacre** coursed to its climactic finale with the screaming Susan having to come face to face with the man in the surgical mask.

The original working title for Boaz Davison's obscure terror was **Be My Valentine, or Else . . .** which might just have given too much of the game away. Davison returned to the surgical world of **Halloween II** to create another low-budget shocker, in the hope of rehashing its predecessor's premise to produce something the audience would never forget. While college fraternities and sororities had been played to death, the hospital setting had yet to be fully explored. This typically illogical film made a few hours of medical carnage resemble the St Valentine's Day Massacre, using a seasonal day of celebration as the backdrop for yet another slasher's modus operandi. There were countless holes in the script in addition to so many obvious red herrings, but Davison laid on the suspense and kept his viewers chewing away on their fingernails. This wasn't a film that relied upon reels of gore, although there was a worthy axe to the head and an over-sized hypodermic syringe that did its fair share of damage. Much, however, was left to the audience's imagination to guess just what the crazy guy in the mask was really up to. All these years later few enthusiasts remember this film; it's still to see release to DVD, but it certainly did Davison very little harm as he furthered his career and went on to far greater things. ❧

Hostel

 YEAR OF RELEASE: 2005

 RUNTIME: 94 minutes

 COUNTRY: USA

 DIRECTOR: Eli Roth

 PRODUCTION COMPANY: Hostel LLC, International Production Company, Next Entertainment, Raw Nerve

WRITER: Eli Roth

CINEMATOGRAPHER: Milan Chadima

PRODUCERS: Chris Briggs, Mike Fleiss, Daniel S. Frisch (co-producer), Eli Roth, Scott Spiegel (executive producer), Quentin Tarantino (executive producer), Philip Waley (co-producer), Boaz Yakin (executive producer)

 CERTIFICATE: Australia: R; Canada: 18+ (Quebec); Canada: 18A (Alberta/ British Columbia/Manitoba/Nova Scotia/Ontario); Hong Kong: III; New Zealand: R18; South Africa: 16; UK: 18; USA: R

 BUDGET: $4,500,000

 RECEIPTS: $80,578,934

CAST: Jay Hernandez, Derek Richardson, Eythor Gudjonsson, Barbara Nedeljakova, Jan Vlasák, Jana Kaderabkova, Jennifer Lim, Keiko Seiko, Lubomír Bukový, Jana Havlickova, Rick Hoffman, Petr Janis, Takashi Miike, Patrik Zigo, Milda Jedi Havlas

A COUPLE OF AMERICAN tourists, Paxton (Jay Hernandez), a law graduate, and Josh (Derek Richardson), an aspiring writer, and their Icelandic companion (Eythor Gudjonsson), enjoy the highs and erotic pleasures of Amsterdam. For a man of the law, Paxton displays little in the way of morality; ruled by his desire for hedonistic pursuit he experiences everything the city has to offer. They eventually meet up with Alex, who recommends a hostel in Bratislava, a city almost bereft of young men following the ravages of war. If these three men had taken the time to read up on the history of the region they would have known the war had ended some sixty years before and the last invasion of Czechoslovakia had been in August 1968, when the Warsaw Pact had laid siege to the country. Such trivialities are not their concern and they make the journey to Slovakia and quickly find the hostel, where a dubbed version of producer Tarantino's **Pulp Fiction** plays on a portable television in the reception. Alex's story appears to be true, for not long after their arrival a host of young lovelies make themselves readily available. Then the film takes a rather dark turn and the amorous tourists become the exploited. The hostel is a cover for a bizarre organization, where the wealthy exchange huge sums of money to indulge their darkest fantasies. This affluent gathering has moved on to the extremes of sadism and murder, to satiate their burned-out sexual craving. Chainsaws, knives and drills complemented by an acetylene torch are the order of the day as this claustrophobic nightmare begins to engulf the hapless tourists. The finale that takes place in this dungeon-like world becomes one of revenge as Paxton bids to escape from one of the most black-hearted films of its generation.

With the release of **Hostel**, torture porn had come of age. Eli Roth had promised much, and his movie turned out to be a resounding box office success, but in its wake caused utter dismay among his audience. There was a dark sense of inevitability hanging over the last hour of this film, which traumatized its audience, using an effective sequence of agonizing torture scenes in sets that left no doubt as to the cruel fate awaiting those who had been hurled into this remorseless domain. However, he fell into the trap of the slasher movies of twenty years past with the focus of his film resting too heavily on the sadist's torturous lust, forfeiting any conceivable indication

Ten thousand people are killed in America each year. Over 2,000 with firearms. Americans ... they have no imagination!

of character development. As a satire of a world obsessed by the excesses of consumerism, it was reminiscent of George A. Romero's **Dawn of the Dead** (1978); but in its grisly exposition, it was infinitely more brutal. Koldo Serra's acclaimed short **El Tren de la Bruja** (2003), in which a man agrees to be tormented while strapped to a chair in a darkened room, is thought to have inspired Roth's script for his film. Having been inspired by the gore of Lucio Fulci and especially **Alien** (1979), he would in turn go on to influence a succession of films that revelled in the pain and suffering of their victims, but as with **Hostel** they were found equally wanting in their failure to elicit a due sense of empathy. In the months after its release, many people in both Slovakia and the Czech Republic were openly angered by his depiction of the region, but in truth it had never been Roth's intention to cause such offence. His was a film that explored the depths of human depravity and exposed just how little his fellow countrymen knew of the world beyond their borders, hence the trip to war-torn Slovakia. Two years later Roth pandered to a new set of sadists, producing a sequel **Hostel: Part 2**, this time throwing a group of delectable young ladies into this unrelenting world of torment. 🐾

The House by the Cemetery

📅 YEAR OF RELEASE: 1981	
🕐 RUNTIME: 87 minutes	
🎥 COUNTRY: Italy	
🎬 DIRECTOR: Lucio Fulci	
🎬 PRODUCTION COMPANY: Fulvia Film	
✒ WRITERS: Elisa Briganti (story), Lucio Fulci (screenplay)	
🎞 CINEMATOGRAPHER: Sergio Salvati	

PRODUCER: Fabrizio De Angelis

CERTIFICATE: Australia: R; Canada: 16+ (Quebec); UK: 18 (re-rating: 1988, heavily cut) (re-rating: 2001) (cut); UK: (Banned) (1984–8); UK: X (original rating: 1981) (cut); UK: 18 (uncut version, re-rating); USA: Unrated

CAST: Catriona MacColl, Paolo Malco, Ania Pieroni, Giovanni Frezza, Silvia Collatina, Dagmar Lassander, Giovanni De Nava, Daniela Doria, Gianpaolo Saccarola, Carlo De Mejo, Kenneth A. Olsen, Elmer Johnsson, Ranieri Ferrara, Teresa Rossi Passante

RELEASED IN ITALY as **Quella Villa Accanto al Cimitero**, Lucio Fulci's atmospheric tale, partially inspired by the writings of H. P. Lovecraft, begins with the camera's gaze falling on the softness of a naked young woman (Daniela Doria). This doesn't last; soon there will be the customary bucket load of bloodthirsty carnage, as Fulci was enrolled alongside Herschell G. Lewis to become "the Godfather of Gore", in this the final part of the "hell's gate" trilogy. Secreted in a deserted old house the girl dresses after sex and calls out for her lover. She receives no response. She learns why when she stumbles upon his mutilated corpse. The shocks continue when a sharp knife is forcibly thrust through

the back of her head. We are never privy to the killer's identity; all we see is her body being dragged through a doorway leading down to the cellar.

Several months later, Norman and Lucy Boyle (Paolo Malco and Catriona MacColl) with their son Bob (Giovanni Frezzi) prepare for their move to New England. Young Bob cannot take his eyes away from the photograph of a creepy old house, in which he can clearly see a young girl warning him not to go there. When they enter their new, but dilapidated, home the cellar door, observed in the film's opening sequence, has been locked and nailed shut. The following day, flashlight in hand, Norman descends the cellar stairs only to be attacked by a huge bat, which tears into his hand. In an effort to defend himself, he brandishes a knife and vigorously lunges at it. Blood oozes from its body as it dies on the kitchen floor. The gore continues to spill when the property agent, Mrs Gittelson, arrives at the house. The viewer only ever gets to see an emaciated arm that attacks the poor woman with a poker and then into her breasts before frenziedly ripping her neck open.

While trying to find Bob, Anne, the babysitter, ventures into the cellar; but is set upon and graphically decapitated by the still-obscured murderer. The child now appears, only to see Anne's severed head rolling down the metal stairs. That night the boy returns to the cellar. The door slams shut and in the shadows, a glowing pair of eyes can be seen, their gaze refusing to leave the terrified child. Petrified he begins to scream, awakening his mother, and then Norman returns and takes an axe to the cellar door, while Dr Freudstein (Giovanni De Nava) holds Bob's head against its wooden panels, inviting yet another decapitation. Instead, we are treated to a vivid hacking of Freudstein's left hand.

How no one ever discovered the cellar's grisly secret remains one of the films many mysteries. A charnel house containing the mutilated cadavers of his abducted victims is thrown open to the light, littered with surgical apparatus and a blood-stained

Can anyone survive the demented marauding zombies?

pathologist's slab. While there are so many memorable moments in this film, the appearance of Dr Freudstein surely must be its crowning moment, now turned into a putrescent corpse. Using the dismembered body parts of his victims, the deranged surgeon has succeeded in keeping himself alive. His body, however, is disgustingly maggot-ridden; they erupt when Norman drives a surgical knife deep into his stomach. The blow fails to stop him. Enraged he tears out Norman's throat and then turns to the escaping Lucy. He unceremoniously drags her down a metal ladder, battering her head against each of the rungs. Finally, as he splatters her skull into the concrete floor, there is a violent discharge of blood and brains. Only Bob survives. He is saved by Mae, the girl from the picture, who now stands at her mother's side, Mary Freudstein (Teresa Rossi Passante). She leads both Mae and Bob from the house and through the wintry grove on into the netherworld.

An abundance of motifs inspired by many previously successful horror films are in evidence in Fulci's movie, notably **The Shining** (1980), **The Amityville Horror** (1979), **The Haunting** (1963), **The Omen** (1976), **The Exorcist** (1973) and of course the many incarnations of **Frankenstein**. His craft allowed him to instil a creepiness to the house and its grounds, providing enough scares to keep his audience on the very edge of their seats. While the acting may have appeared occasionally wooden, it wasn't to distract from Fulci's vision as he showed himself to be a veritable maestro of splatter, devising a succession of imaginative death scenes in one of his most unsettling features.

House by the Cemetery has endured many difficulties with the BBFC; the cinema version was edited to remove the poker murder and the slashing of Ann's throat. Its release prior to the Video Recordings Act saw the film banned amidst the hysteria of the campaign against video nasties. Although it was to gain official approval in 1988, it was again edited to remove the cinema cuts and had the first stabbing removed, then saw cuts to the bat attack, Norman's throat being torn out, and tracking shots of the mutilated bodies in the basement climax. Over seven minutes were later censored in 1992, making this particular presentation virtually unintelligible. However, the 2001 Vipco DVD issue restored nearly all of the previous edits, with fewer changes to the poker murder and one of the throat cuttings. Although the BBFC were finally prepared to release Fulci's masterpiece without cuts, the film was again prosecuted under the Obscene Publications Act following the discovery of bootleg copies of the uncut version from January 1983. The BBFC once again had little choice but to demand further revisions. Finally, the cuts were waived for the 2009 Arrow DVD.

The House on Sorority Row

YEAR OF RELEASE: 1983	John G. Clark, Robert Maier (line producer), Thomas W. McMahon (executive producer), John Ponchock (executive producer), Alec Rabinowitz (associate producer), Mark Rosman
RUNTIME: 91 minutes	
COUNTRY: USA	
DIRECTOR: Mark Rosman	
PRODUCTION COMPANY: VAE	
WRITERS: Mark Rosman, Bobby Fine	**CERTIFICATE:** Australia: M; UK: 18; USA: R
CINEMATOGRAPHER: Tim Suhrstedt	**BUDGET:** $425,000
PRODUCERS: Ed Beyer (co-producer),	**RECEIPTS:** $10,604,986

CAST: Kate McNeil, Eileen Davidson, Janis Ward, Robin Meloy, Harley Jane Kozak, Jodi Draigie, Ellen Dorsher, Lois Kelso Hunt, Christopher Lawrence, Michael Kuhn, Michael Sergio, Ruth Walsh, Ed Heath, Jean Schertler

MARK ROSMAN'S STORY begins on a stormy night in 1961, as a doctor arrives at a rather sinister-looking house. His patient is the pregnant Dorothy Slater (Lois Kelso Hunt), who is now in the agonizing throes of childbirth. Complications follow and when Mrs Slater comes round the doctor can only offer his condolences. An ominous air of mystery hangs over the trauma of this night; all is not as it seems.

Twenty-two years later, having just graduated, an excited group of sorority sisters are seen packing away their belongings. They start drinking ready to party, discussing boys and anticipating the excitement of their lives ahead. Mrs Slater, now a sorority mother, returns home and an altercation with the intoxicated girls ensues. She is adamant that they must leave the house by morning. Supported by her cane she climbs the stairs to the toy-filled attic; her demeanour would suggest she is on the verge of a complete nervous breakdown. Downstairs the girls are blissfully ignorant of her deteriorating mental condition and prompted by Vicki conspire to avenge her outburst with the assistance of her boyfriend's gun. However, during the course of their charade the weapon goes off leaving the troubled Mrs Slater slumped on the floor, dead. In their distress, the girls try to wrap her body in tarpaulin, hoping to hide it by sinking it to the bottom of the swimming pool. Their callous behaviour has not gone unnoticed; a few hours later someone takes Mrs Slater's robe and then walks away with her trusty cane.

The girls have no choice but to go ahead with their party; any change in their plans just might arouse suspicion. With the celebrations in full swing, an inebriated college boy becomes the killer's first victim as the cane is forcibly rammed through his throat. He crumples to the floor, blood freely spurting from his neck. Then one by one, each of the girls suffers a similar fate.

The uncomplicated plot has offered comparisons to **Friday the 13th**, and in that respect contained very few surprises, even when at the film's claustrophobic finale the heroine breathed a sigh of relief oblivious to the tortured murderer's eyes once again flickering to life. Although it wasn't a runaway success on its theatrical release, **The House on Sorority Row** was to emerge as a cult favourite among the VHS-addicted slasher buffs and went on to attain a quite worthy reputation. It is now considered superior to many of its sorority brothers and sisters, largely due to Richard Band's haunting score and a well presented cast who were tormented in the ever-mounting suspense, along with a suitably gory assemblage of kills. Rosman's interests,

Seven graduates of sorority sisters stalked as they hold a guilty secret.

it turned out, didn't lie with horror, as he later admitted; he used this film to further his career, having previously learned much from working with Brian De Palma. His work didn't go unnoticed, as elements in his tale paved the way for the box office hit of 1997, **I Know What You Did Last Summer**. The film was remade in 2009 under the title **Sorority Row** with **Star Wars** actress Carrie Fisher cast in the role as the housemother. 🔪

The House on the Edge of the Park

📅 YEAR OF RELEASE: 1980		🎞 CINEMATOGRAPHER: Sergio D'Offizi	
🕐 RUNTIME: 91 minutes		⚰ PRODUCERS: Franco Di Nunzio, Franco Palaggi.	
🌐 COUNTRY: Italy			
🎥 DIRECTOR: Ruggero Deodato		⭕ CERTIFICATE: Australia: Refused Classification; Canada: (Banned) (Ontario); Canada: 18+ (Quebec); UK: (Banned) (1984–2002); UK: 18 (heavily cut); USA: Unrated	
🎬 PRODUCTION COMPANY: F. D. Cinematografica			
✎ WRITERS: Gianfranco Clerici, Vincenzo Mannino			

CAST: David Hess, Annie Belle, Christian Borromeo, Giovanni Lombardo Radice, Marie Claude Joseph, Gabriele Di Giulio, Brigitte Petronio, Karoline Mardeck, Lorraine De Selle

PRIOR TO THE opening credits beginning to roll, the thuggish Alex (David Hess) is seen driving around the streets of New York. When an attractive young woman pulls up alongside him, he tails her and then cuts her off. His movements are incisive, giving absolutely no hope as she is raped and then strangled in the back of her car. As he leaves her body, Alex takes a trophy and steals his victim's locket. Shortly after, he meets up with his slow-witted friend Ricky (Giovanni Lombardo Radice); the pair is set for a night of dancing to the New York City disco beat. Their plans change when they come to the aid of an affluent young couple whose car has broken down. Ricky soon traces the fault and they find themselves invited along to a party. Before long, Alex and Ricky are in the company of a set of rather well to do young people, but find themselves belittled for their obvious lack of class. The superiority of this repulsive gathering angers Alex, so much so the ruthless psychopath within him once again comes to the fore and he draws his straight razor. He and his slime ball friend then turn this upmarket party into a night of violence, humiliation and rape. Little do they know a twist awaits them; one their dullard imagining could never have conceived.

Shot over a three-week period for relatively little money, Ruggero Deodato's violent descent into exploitation genre rekindled unsavoury memories of David Hess's brutal portrayal from Wes Craven's Last House on the Left (1972). Under Deodato's direction, Gianfranco Clerici and Vincenzo Mannino's scripting of Hess's character was given considerably more depth than that of Krug Stillo in Last House on the Left, but he remained at heart a psychotic lout whose only means of communication was by way of violence. When Deodato first saw the script he felt strangely unusually uncomfortable; his first impression was that its content was far too violent. However, he translated his unease to heighten the film's psychological impact and engineered some quite remarkable shots to suggest a film befitting a more substantial budget. He then drew upon the unattractive qualities of his well-heeled party-goers,

David Hess, star of "Last House on the Left", is loose again . . .

intimating they may have deserved some of their discomfiture, but when innocent young Cindy (Brigitte Petronio) joined the proceedings the acute distaste in Hess's character was finally laid bare. The House on the Edge of the Park then assumed the hateful guise for which it is still remembered, and not surprisingly was rejected by the BBFC when it was submitted for certification preceding its intended release to cinemas across the country. In the October of 1982, it was made available on video but was only on the shelves until July 1983 when it was cited as a video nasty. It was to remain on the list until the furore came to an end. On its submissions for release in 2002 and 2009, Deodato's film struggled before the UK's censors with eleven minutes and forty-three seconds of cuts demanded to the rape and assault scenes, heavily prescribed edits to the razor-slashing of Cindy and the opening murder scene, along with the removal of shots to a head being slammed onto a table top. In 2006, the BBFC commissioned a group of academics at Aberystwyth University to conduct research into responses to films that contain scenes of sexual violence. The House on the Edge of the Park was one of the films the team were asked to examine and Deodata attended a forum to discuss this in addition to many other of his films that have attracted the censor's scrutiny. Thirty years after the event he remains committed to directing a sequel, still starring both David Hess and Giovanni Lombardo Radice. Across the Atlantic, the USA Media Blasters' release is available without cuts, running to the full ninety-one minutes.

The House that Screamed

📅 **YEAR OF RELEASE:** 1969		✏️ **WRITERS:** Narciso Ibáñez Serrador, Juan Tébar	
🕐 **RUNTIME:** 99 minutes			
🌐 **COUNTRY:** Spain		🎞️ **CINEMATOGRAPHERS:** Manuel Berenguer, Godofredo Pacheco	
🎥 **DIRECTOR:** Narciso Ibáñez Serrador			
🎬 **PRODUCTION COMPANY:** Anabel Films, Anabel Films S. A.		🎟️ **PRODUCERS:** Arturo González, Jose M. Maldonado (assistant producer)	
		💾 **RECEIPTS:** ESP 104,871,715 (Spain)	

CAST: Lilli Palmer, Cristina Galbó, John Moulder-Brown, Mary Maude, Cándida Losada, Tomás Blanco, Maribel Martín, Pauline Challoner, Teresa Hurtado, Conchita Paredes, Víctor Israel, María José Valero, Ana María Pol, Blanca Sendino, Paloma Pagés

YOUNG THERESA (CRISTINA Galbó) arrives at a school run by Madame Forneau (Lilli Palmer) located somewhere in a remote region of southern France. The Madame, she will soon learn, is a strict disciplinarian and although Theresa tries to befriend her adolescent son (John Moulder-Brown), he displays some rather unsettling voyeuristic tendencies. She should be sure to tread very carefully because his domineering mother will not have him mixing with these dubious young women. He spends his days strolling around the perimeter of the school and traversing its labyrinthine passageways waiting for a girl "just like his mother". The girls who have been sent to the school have somewhat chequered pasts, being considered wayward, and there are suggestions of heated lesbianism. While under the Madame's watchful eye, their various transgressions are meted out by an agonizing series of punishments, each of which are captured before the camera's lens. For much of the early part of the film, the pacing appears a little slow, but becomes charged when the girls seemingly begin to escape the school by night. However, murder is afoot in this oppressed manse, and as the girls sleep a silent assassin treads the corridors with slaughter in mind. As the suspense mounts, one of the girls is tracked to a greenhouse in a slow-motion killing that culminates in a climactic finale in the attic.

One by one they will die!

Uruguayan Narciso Ibáñez Serrador's directorial film debut came with **La Residencia**, which outside Spanish-speaking countries was known as **The House that Screamed** or **The Boarding School**. Throughout the early sequences of his film, he was steadfast in observing the development of each character with a view to garnering empathy for every one of these ill-fated young girls. He drew upon the Gothic styling of Mario Bava's past masterpieces and then in his atmospheric moulding of both archetypal and modern terror was to provide the inspiration for Dario Argento when he later conceived his tour de force, **Suspiria** (1977). Juan Piquer Simon would also look to this almost forgotten film when he commenced shooting his gory but much maligned slasher of 1982,

Pieces. There was a subtlety observed in time-served television director Serrador's menace that was enhanced by cinematographer Manuel Berenguer's stealthy camera work. He glided along the corridors and on through the attic spaces to make the audience believe the killer was poised to spring from the shadows at any given moment. While the murder scenes were suitably stylish they couldn't be described as gory; Serrador instead preferred to augment the tension in the magnificence of this Gothic setting. His film was a welcome departure from the Euro-sleaze of the period, tempting with eroticism rather than the visual tease of his European contemporaries. He would take another break from his work in television to direct the cult favourite **Quién Puede Matar a un Niño** (1976) also referred to as **Who Can Kill a Child?**, **Death is Child's Play** and **Island of the Damned**, where possessed children were murdering their elders. 🦋

I Know What You Did Last Summer

 YEAR OF RELEASE: 1997

 RUNTIME: 100 minutes

 COUNTRY: USA

DIRECTOR: Jim Gillespie

PRODUCTION COMPANY: Columbia Pictures Corporation, Mandalay Entertainment, Summer Knowledge LLC

WRITERS: Lois Duncan (novel), Kevin Williamson

CINEMATOGRAPHER: Denis Crossan

PRODUCERS: William S. Beasley (executive producer), Stokely Chaffin, Erik Feig, Neal H. Moritz

CERTIFICATE: Australia: MA; Canada: 14A (Ontario, 2006); Canada: 16+ (Quebec); Canada: AA (Ontario); New Zealand: R16; UK: 15 (video rating) (1998); UK: 18 (original rating); USA: R

BUDGET: $17,000,000

RECEIPTS: $125,586,134

CAST: Jennifer Love Hewitt, Sarah Michelle Gellar, Ryan Phillippe, Freddie Prinze Jr., Bridgette Wilson, Anne Heche, Johnny Galecki, Muse Watson, Stuart Greer, J. Don Ferguson, Deborah Hobart, Mary McMillan, Rasool J'Han

AFTER WINNING A beauty contest, Helen Shivers (Sarah Michelle Gellar) and her friends, Julie James (Jennifer Love Hewitt), Barry William Cox (Ryan Phillippe) and Ray Bronson (Freddie Prinze Jr.), combine their graduation celebration with the fourth of July festivities. In the closeted world of this quiet seaside town, the four friends head off to a party and then as night falls make their way to the beach. Barry, who has had far too much to drink, lets Ray drive his car home, but as they take a bend on a cliff-side road, they knock down and seemingly kill a man walking by the roadside. While they try to work out what to do with the corpse, Julie's friend Max Neurick (Johnny Galecki) arrives, but they manage to convince him that everything is fine so he carries on his way. However, when the four friends try to dump the body, it returns to consciousness and lunges at Helen. They finish him off

This secret is about to kill them all!

and in the hope of safeguarding their futures agree never again to mention the events of this night. A year later, Julie receives a note in the post, containing the words "I know what you did last summer". All is no longer well with the former friends and they each in turn receive a reminder of what occurred that night twelve months before. They now know their precious futures are in jeopardy and someone saw what happened that night; they set out to trace their persecutor, with characteristically alarming consequences.

Following his success in writing Wes Craven's cleverly referenced **Scream** (1996), Kevin Williamson returned with a story loosely based on Lois Duncan's book, *I Know What You Did Last Summer*. While time-served Lois's story was essentially a morality tale, Williamson chose the slasher root and together with director Jim Gillespie was gifted a huge budget to make this film just that little bit special. With its all-star teen cast, this feature offered much for a new generation of slasher fans, but for veterans offered little that could be considered new. British director Gillespie, on his first Hollywood outing, produced a rather beautiful looking movie that even in the politically correct world of the 1990s wasn't afraid to savour a series of fairly gruesome scenes. Although the enthusiasts who had taken so much pleasure in the mass slaughter of the previous decade denigrated Gillespie's film, trashing it as an entertaining mystery, along with **Scream** it had a key role in returning the teen slasher to movie theatres and generated enough excitement to command a sequel, **I Still Know What You Did Last Summer** (1998).

I Saw the Devil

📅 YEAR OF RELEASE: 2010	🎞 CINEMATOGRAPHER: Mogae Lee
⏱ RUNTIME: 141 minutes	🎬 PRODUCERS: Kee-young Cheong, Hyung-cho Il, Hun-you Jeong, Seong-weon Jo, Yeong-shin Kang, Byung-ki Kim, Hyun-woo Kim, Jae-young Kim, Jung-hwa Kim, Kil-soo Kim, Greg Moon, Jae-sik Moon, Bryan Song, Youngjoo Suh
🌐 COUNTRY: South Korea	
🎥 DIRECTOR: Jee-woon Kim	
🎬 PRODUCTION COMPANY: Softbank Ventures, Showbox/Mediaplex, Peppermint & Company, Siz Entertainment	
✒ WRITER: Hoon-jung Park	⭕ CERTIFICATE: Hong Kong: III

CAST: Byung-hun Lee, Min-sik Choi, Gook-hwan Jeon, Ho-jin Jeon, San-ha Oh, Yoon-seo Kim

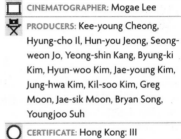

ABEAUTIFUL YOUNG WOMAN is powerless to prevent her abduction at the merciless hands of a psychotic serial killer. He isn't looking for ransom; his needs are purely sadistic as he inflicts a series of agonies on his victim, drawing out the torment as he has done so many times before. In a succession of excruciating shots, he wreaks numerous blows to her head with a hammer and then dismembers her lifeless body. Kyung-chul's (Min-sik Choi) victim was the fiancée of Kim So-Hyun (Byung-hun Lee), an undercover operative with an assassin's instincts; she was also the daughter of the former Chief of Police. The despairing Kim So-Hyun, a man of few words, embarks on the hunt that will lead him to his fiancée's killer and ultimately see him become a vengeful psychopath. It doesn't take long before he locates two potential suspects; repeated beatings, however, reveal they had no involvement in his fiancée's murder. His search eventually reveals the true culprit, the psychotic Kyung-chul. Rather than putting an end to Kyung's worthless life, Kim beats him to a pulp and then gives him the chance to escape. Kim takes a perverse delight in the knowledge he can do this time and time again, for he has forced the killer to swallow a transmitter. He will be able to trace Kyung's every move and now has the opportunity to exact his cruel revenge. The killer will come to know the pain suffered by his victims as Kim dedicates his every waking moment to the miscreant's unending torture, each time allowing his quarry to survive and lick his bloodied wounds, only to repeat the vicious process all over again. Battered and bruised, Kyung's tenuous grip on reality refuses to simply lie down and die; very soon, he turns the tables and strikes back setting the scene for a brutal finale.

Evil lives inside.

The violent confrontation between Kyung-chul and Kim So-Hyun that would have ordinarily climaxed such a film came unusually early in this tale of bloody retribution. Hoon-jung Park's story, however, was more concerned with the dehumanizing nature of revenge and in a noiresque narration revealed the depths to which an honourable man would stoop in the grim hope of relieving his utter desolation. Director Jee-woon Kim, who had already made his mark internationally with the acclaimed **A Tale of Two Sisters** (2003) and **A Bitter Sweet Life** (2005), deliberately used the violence in this ferocious revenge thriller to make his audience experience the most profound discomfort. There was nothing in the slightest way gratifying about this merciless portrayal. Dismemberment, decapitation, jaw breaking, screwdriver attacks, an icepick to the cheek, the severing of an Achilles tendon and a beating to the head with a pipe were just some of the brutal episodes endured by the cast. However, even amidst this unrelenting violence there was a beauty observed in Mogae Lee's cinematography, which became almost simplistic during the gritty fight scenes. Such aesthetic considerations were not to save Kim's film from the scrutiny of the Korea Media Rating Board, which demanded he edit his feature prior to it being approved for its release to cinema, objecting to the violent content as an offence to human dignity. Kim acquiesced for if he had failed to follow their directives his film would have been given a restricted rating, thus forbidding it to be seen in theatres or released on DVD, making it a prospective entry to the less lucrative world of underground cinema. 🐾

I Spit on Your Grave

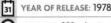

📅	YEAR OF RELEASE: 1978
⏱	RUNTIME: 101 minutes
🎬	COUNTRY: USA
🎥	DIRECTOR: Meir Zarchi
🎞	PRODUCTION COMPANY: Cinemagic Pictures
✏️	WRITER: Meir Zarchi
🎬	CINEMATOGRAPHER: Nouri Haviv
⚖️	PRODUCERS: Meir Zarchi, Joseph Zbeda
⭕	CERTIFICATE: Australia: (Banned) (1997–2004); Australia: R (2004) (uncut); Australia: R (original rating)

(cut); Canada: 14A (Alberta); Canada: (Banned) (Nova Scotia) (original rating); Canada: (Banned) (Ontario); Canada: 16+ (Quebec) (video rating); Canada: 18 (Nova Scotia) (re-rating) (1998); Canada: R (Manitoba); Ireland: (Banned) (2002); New Zealand: (Banned, original rating); New Zealand: R18 (re-rating, 2004); UK: (Banned) (1984–2001); UK: 18 (heavily cut); USA: R (edited for re-rating); USA: Unrated (uncut video version); USA: X (original rating)

💲 BUDGET: $80,000

CAST: Camille Keaton, Eron Tabor, Richard Pace, Anthony Nichols, Gunter Kleemann, Alexis Magnotti, Tammy Zarchi, Terry Zarchi, Traci Ferrante, William Tasgal, Isaac Agami, Ronit Haviv

JENNIFER HILLS (CAMILLE Keaton) drives from her home in New York City to the upstate countryside to write the manuscript for her first novel. She soon settles in the idyllic lakeside cabin that she has rented to pursue her writing. Her arrival in town unfortunately attracts the wrong kind of attention, in the guise of Johnny (Eron Tabor), the local garage owner, and his two friends Stanley (Anthony Nichols) and Andy (Gunter Kleemann). Stanley and Andy trace Jennifer's cabin and begin to cruise by in their speedboat; at night they prowl unseen, taking in as much of the house as they can. A

few days later as Jennifer relaxes on the lake, they surprise her in their speedboat and tow her to shore. The scenes that follow detail Jennifer's graphic rape at the hands of the contemptible trio and Matthew the mentally impaired grocery boy. The dialogue in this prolonged unpleasant sequence, lasting almost half an hour, is almost non-existent. The gang instruct Matthew to complete their dirty work and kill Jennifer, but he is unable to bring himself to do it. He later lies, claiming to have stabbed Jennifer to death.

In the ensuing weeks, Jennifer's mental state becomes impaired as she goes over the events of that terrible day. As she stands in church, she begs forgiveness before vowing to kill the low-lifes who have caused her this pain. She is no longer the happy-go-lucky girl who drove from New York City; the scars this gang of degenerates have inflicted run deep and in her inevitable psychosis she begins to plan her bloody revenge. Turning the tables, she now stalks her violators. The halfwit Matthew is enticed into sex beneath a tree; he fails to see the noose until it is too late. In the soothing comfort of a hot bath, Jennifer then removes the aroused Johnny's genitalia and savours the moments as he bleeds to death. When Stanley and Andy learn that Johnny has gone missing they take their speedboat to Jennifer's cabin, worrying something might have happened to their worthless cohort. Axe in hand, Andy leaves the boat, but Jennifer's guile relieves him of it and she buries it squarely into his back while the drowning Stanley is soon after disembowelled by the boat's propellers. As Andy and Stanley's bodies descend into the lake, the avenged Jennifer is observed with a twisted smile as she speeds away in the boat.

Day of the Woman, now known by its re-release title, **I Spit on Your Grave**, has also gone by the names **I Hate Your Guts** and **The Rape and Revenge of Jennifer Hills**. It remains one of the most controversial films of

After it was all over . . . she waited . . . then she struck back in a way only a woman can!

the twentieth century, inspiring Arthur Jeffreys' **Demented** (1980), before attracting an unofficial restyling in 1985 as **Naked Vengeance**, and then being subject to a remake in 2010. When it was first released in 1978, as **Day of the Woman**, such was the level of violence it had to be considerably toned down to comply with the stipulations made by the Motion Picture Association of America. The film's explicit content forced Zarchi to undertake his own distribution, releasing it on limited runs to rural drive-in theatres. Sadly, for all of his efforts he struggled to make it break even. In 1980 the Jerry Gross Organization, a company associated with several grindhouse movies, including **Zombie Flesh Eaters** (1979), agreed to give the film a wider release. They reinstated many of the cuts and insisted the feature carry a new title, one that matched the notoriety of its unsavoury content, **I Spit on Your Grave**. The poster accompanying the movie's release made Zarchi's efforts resemble one of the countless exploitation features of the period; it would go on to acquire a similar notoriety.

On its new release, the critics condemned the film for its brutal portrayal and outrageous depiction of gang rape. Across the globe, the censors would ban this repackaged feature from their cinemas, uncomfortable with its seeming glorification of violence against women. However, it eventually did find its way into many of these countries, when it was cut to video. This gained Zarchi's film a new audience, which reappraised his film, considering it an indictment of male sexuality, albeit rather heavily handled. It soon became known that Zarchi's need to make this film had come about when he came to the aid of a woman who had been raped in New York. He saw firsthand the trauma that came with such an abhorrent crime and was then horrified by the incompetence of the police authorities. It was never his intention to make an entertaining distraction; indeed the nihilism exhibited in this movie is as far removed from any notion of entertainment as could be imagined. His mistake, however, was to hand it to a company who had made their name in exploitative cinema.

Although the Canadian government initially prohibited showings of Zarchi's film, in the 1990s they allowed each of the provinces to determine whether to permit showings. In the United Kingdom, the film was cited as a video nasty. It remained on the Director of Public Prosecutions' list of banned films until 2001, when provision was made for a heavily censored DVD release, with almost three minutes of the rape scene thankfully consigned to the cutting room floor. 🌸

Ichi the Killer

📅	YEAR OF RELEASE: 2001
🕐	RUNTIME: 129 minutes
🌐	COUNTRY: Japan, Hong Kong, South Korea
🎥	DIRECTOR: Takashi Miike
🎬	PRODUCTION COMPANY: Omega Project, Omega Micott Inc., Emperor Multimedia Group (EMG)
✒️	WRITERS: Hideo Yamamoto (manga), Sakichi Satô (screenplay)
🎞️	CINEMATOGRAPHER: Hideo Yamamoto

PRODUCERS: Yuchul Cho (co-producer), Akiko Funatsu, Toshiki Kimura (associate producer), Sumiji Miyake (executive producer), Dai Miyazaki, Elliot Tong (co-producer), Albert Yeung (executive producer), Toyoyuki Yokohama (executive producer)

CERTIFICATE: Australia: R; Canada: R (Manitoba); Canada: 18+ (Quebec); Ireland: 18 (heavily cut); New Zealand: R18; UK: 18 (cut); USA: R (cut); USA: Unrated

BUDGET: $1,400,000

CAST: Tadanobu Asano, Nao Ohmori, Shinya Tsukamoto, Paulyn Sun, Susumu Terajima, Shun Sugata, Toru Tezuka, Yoshiki Arizono, Kiyohiko Shibukawa, Satoshi Niizuma, Suzuki Matsuo, Jun Kunimura, Hiroyuki Tanaka, Moro Morooka, Hôka Kinoshita

ICHI THE KILLER, which translates as **Killer No. 1** from the original Japanese, became a manga comic book phenomenon soon after its release in 1999, written by the man behind the camera, Hideo Yamamoto. The innovative Takashi Miike boosted its cult status taking this deviant yakuzza war story to considerably greater extremes. While not conceived as a horror movie, given its partiality for gore, it would be impossible to deny it a place in any celebration of the splatter movie.

Set in the disreputable Shinjuku gangland district of Tokyo, the leader of the Anjo gang has seemingly gone missing, taking with him a substantial amount of the gang's money. His number one hit man and sadistic partner, the facially disfigured blonde Kakihara (Tadanobu Asano), is anxious to locate his whereabouts. Suspecting Suzuki, another hit man, knows more about the boss's fate, Kakihara systematically tortures him in the hope of gaining information. He suspends Suzuki from a ceiling, using metal hooks to pierce the man's back, and then thrusts metal yakitori skewers through his body. Still unable to get Suzuki to talk, his predilection for the sadistic commands he pours boiling oil over his victim. Suzuki it turns out is innocent. Kakihara has gone too far, so much so he is subsequently dismissed from the

gang. His severing of the end of his tongue as he departs in an almost masochistic peace offering confirms he is anything but a run-of-the-mill street thug.

Intimating she has clues as to the killer's identity, nightclub hostess Karen (Alien Sun) tells Kakihara where he might be found. However, the pair is oblivious to the fact that a duplicitous gang informer, Jijii (the old man), is the mind behind Anjo's disappearance and has already gathered his own band of assassins, among them the deranged Ichi. The profoundly psychotic Ichi, a man who murdered his own parents, is paradoxically also a quivering wreck. In a further twist to the tale, the cunning Jijii has placed Ichi in a hypnotic state, in which he has been convinced he was the victim of bullying as a child and failed to prevent the rape of a girl who saved him from harm. He now believes he must punish anyone he considers a bully and, to add to his volatility, sexual arousal is invariably a precipitant to bloody murder.

Having assumed control of Anjo's gang, Kakihara searches the streets with a handful of assassins desperate to find his boss. It is not long before word of the enigmatic Ichi and his death-dealing martial arts skills comes to his ear; there is also mention of a set of death-dealing blades concealed in the lining of his boots. While Kakihara goes to

It's been a while since I wanted to despair. Really.

great lengths to hunt down Ichi and the double-dealing Jijii, his nemesis is relentless in his slaughter of this Yakuza. When he learns that Anjo was killed by Ichi, Kakihara's lust for the perverse intensifies; he now begins to nurture a homoerotic attraction for his adversary in a theme reminiscent of Clive Barker's **Hellraiser** (1987). Could this disturbed assassin finally satiate his masochistic craving to bathe in the most exquisite pain imaginable? The answer is delivered during the finale on the rooftops of Shinjuku. In this action-packed clash, Kakihara engages his metal skewers, driving them into Ichi's ears to drown his cries, before seeing the psychotic assassin slice the head from one of the surviving gang members. As the film climaxes Ichi impels one of his razor-bladed boots firmly into the middle of Kakihari's head. Kakihara falls to his death, basking in the perversity of this the greatest feeling

in his entire misbegotten life. However, when Jijii stands over his body, there is no wound to his head; Ichi's assault had been a hallucination. Kakihara had jumped to his death while Ichi fell to his knees in tears.

Modern-day CGI allowed Miike to replicate the cruel extremes of Yamamoto's original manga, now laced with the darkest of humour. The flippant slant to this ultra-violent piece of innovation was recognized by the BBFC, who limited their censorship to a little over three minutes in this sensationalistic over-the-top splatterfest. As a publicity gimmick, vomit bags were handed out to those attending the screenings at the Toronto International Film Festival and the Stockholm International Film Festival screenings of this film. Apparently one person was said to have thrown up and another fainted.

In My Skin

📅	YEAR OF RELEASE: 2002	🎞	CINEMATOGRAPHER: Pierre Barougier
🕐	RUNTIME: 93 minutes	🎬	PRODUCERS: Stéphanie Carreras (associate producer), Laurence Farenc, Alain Rocca (associate producer), Laurent Soregaroli (associate producer)
🐑	COUNTRY: France		
🎥	DIRECTOR: Marina de Van		
🎬	PRODUCTION COMPANY: Lazennec & Associés, Canal+, Centre National de la Cinématographie (CNC)	⭕	CERTIFICATE: Australia: R; Canada: 16+ (Quebec); France: 16; New Zealand: R18; UK: 18; USA: Unrated
✎	WRITER: Marina de Van		

CAST: Marina de Van, Laurent Lucas, Léa Drucker, Thibault de Montalembert, Dominique Reymond, Bernard Alane, Marc Rioufol, François Lamotte, Adrien de Van, Alain Rimoux

ESTHER (MARINA DE Van) may be highly intelligent and rather beautiful, but she also has a very unusual addiction, one that contradicts her professional persona. She may not evince any signs of self-loathing or an aversion for her body, but her life devolves into a nihilistic fixation as she cultivates a chilling predilection for self-mutilation. Her disturbing compulsion begins when she accidentally injures herself. With her leg encased in bandaging it soon begins to itch and she finds it impossible to resist scratching. Consequently her wound splits open, and immediately starts to seep. Tearing and cutting away at her injury she comes to regard her body in a both new and disturbing way, soon losing the sensation in her leg and then becoming distanced from those around her, particularly at work. The self-mutilation continues in a bizarre restaurant scene, where over several glasses of wine she begins to lose control of her body, giving the impression her arm has been severed. As her friends continue in the triviality of their conversation, of which she manages to remain a part, she indulges her desire by picking at her arm under the table with a knife. Her friends and family are completely ignorant of her descent into this obsessive madness, although her boyfriend becomes increasingly anxious as to the bizarre nature of her behaviour. Locking herself away in a hotel room, she photographs her mutilated body and in an act of extraordinary narcissism, derives an almost masturbatory pleasure from her very self. With the masochistic removal of the skin around her face she seals her own destruction, but for her this has become a voyage of unsavoury self-discovery.

The fetishist cannibalizing observed in Marina de Van's **Dans Ma Peau** introduced the French avant-garde to the domain of splatter and in a quite straight forward way raised innumerable questions as to the individual's place in society. The camera never once shied from the unpleasantness; rather, it engaged in the most elegant fashion. In this perfect example of the new wave of the French extreme, the underlying lust of the gore-monger was so exquisitely observed.

The Incredible Torture Show

📅 YEAR OF RELEASE: 1976		✏️ WRITER: Joel M. Reed	
🕐 RUNTIME: 91 minutes		🎞️ CINEMATOGRAPHER: Ron Dorfman	
🌐 COUNTRY: USA		🎬 PRODUCERS: Alan C. Margolin, Joel M. Reed	
🎥 DIRECTOR: Joel M. Reed			

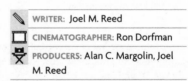

CERTIFICATE: Australia: R; Canada: (Banned) (Nova Scotia/Ontario); Canada: 16+ (Quebec); Canada: R (Manitoba) (re-rating); New Zealand: R18; USA: X (original rating); USA: R (re-rating) (rating surrendered); USA: Unrated

CAST: **Seamus O'Brien, Viju Krem, Niles McMaster, Dan Fauci, Alan Dellay, Ernie Pysher, Luis De Jesus, Helen Thompson, Saiyanidi, Carol Mara, Linda Small, Alphonso DeNoble, Illa Howe**

THE SADISTIC MASTER Sardu (Seamus O'Brien) and his vile midget assistant, Ralphus (Luis De Jesus), front a macabre Grand Guignol-styled S&M theatre in the heart of New York. Before the eyes of an unsuspecting audience, the sardonically witted Sardu acts out a grotesque murderous cabaret to the nightly sound of rapturous applause. On stage the bound girls are subjected to a whole variety of torturous pursuit, including the ever-tightening vice, hacksaws, eye gouging, electrocution to their nipples, darts aimed at a target painted on one girl's backside while another girl bites onto a rope holding a blade that will remove her head if she lets go, as the evil midget canes her backside. Following the flagellation, dismemberment and cannibalism an evil surgeon (Ernie Pysher) molests one of the restrained girls and then drills into her skull before sucking out her brains. Sardu's ardent followers have no idea each performance is for real and that the naked beauties paraded before their lustful gaze are kidnap victims thrown into a bizarre world of white slavery, forced to endure unrelenting torment and finally death.

Sardu becomes enraged when theatre critic Creasy Silo sarcastically refuses to acknowledge the art in his perverse display. Desperate for a positive review he kidnaps the critic and then abducts ballerina Natasha DeNatalie to induct her into his performance and bestow upon his show a much-needed degree of artistic merit. His felonious activities bring Sardu some unwanted attention in the guise of Natasha's boyfriend, Tom Maverick, and the shady Detective Tucci. As they further their search, Sardu's depraved lifestyle is laid bare. In the cellar beneath the theatre, he keeps his naked performers locked away in a cage, only ever seeing release to serve his sick cravings. For the moment, they remain under lock and key as Sardu and Ralphus torture their captives, preparing for their bloodthirsty ballet.

SARDU: he was the creator – the director – the master!

The girls, however, will very soon have their day, as Natalie's boyfriend and the detective get closer to uncovering the appalling secret hidden beneath the theatre.

Fly-fishing fanatic Joel M. Reed's **Bloodsucking Freaks**, which has also seen release as **The Incredible Torture Show** and **Sardu: Master of the Screaming Virgins**, has been repeatedly chastised as a worthless piece of misogynistic trashy grindhouse cinema. Its scenes of humiliation and violence, specifically inflicted on the female cast, aroused the wrath of the feminist group Women Against Pornography. It was a little difficult to take umbrage with them, because this really was low-budget exploitation cinema quite literally stripped bare; Reed freely exchanged any notion of narrative flow, talent for acting and special effects for cheap

gore and the wilful torture of his naked female cast, to make, arguably, one of the worst films of all time. The grainy budget celluloid stock emphasized the movie's sordid nature, yet elevated it to become a classic for fans of exploitation cinema. Its premise and mean-spirited dark humour contained elements of Herschell Gordon Lewis's **The Wizard of Gore** (1970); these combined with Reed's seamy excess to make for an enduring cult favourite, but not surprisingly it has had a highly controversial history. When it was prepared for release, it was unrated and was later given an R-rating when a series of cuts were finally agreed. Reed can't get enough of low-budget filmmaking, still making appearances at horror conventions, and remains determined to bring out a sequel **Bloodsucking Freaks 2: The School.**

Inferno

31 YEAR OF RELEASE: 1980		PRODUCERS: Claudio Argento, Salvatore Argento (executive producer), Guglielmo Garroni (executive producer)	
RUNTIME: 107 minutes			
COUNTRY: Italy			
DIRECTOR: Dario Argento		CERTIFICATE: Australia: R; Canada: 13+ (Quebec); New Zealand: R18; UK: X (cut); UK: 18 (cut); UK: 18 (re-rating, uncut); USA: R	
PRODUCTION COMPANY: Produzioni Intersound			
WRITER: Dario Argento			
CINEMATOGRAPHER: Romano Albani		BUDGET: $3,000,000	

CAST: Leigh McCloskey, Irene Miracle, Eleonora Giorgi, Daria Nicolodi, Sacha Pitoëff, Alida Valli, Veronica Lazar, Gabriele Lavia, Feodor Chaliapin Jr., Leopoldo Mastelloni

IN HER GOTHIC-STYLED New York apartment, the poet Rose Elliot (Irene Miracle) has fallen to the possession of the alarming contents of an ancient text by the name of "The Three Mothers", which she recently purchased from a local antiquarian bookseller. The book tells of three buildings constructed for three mothers, in Rome, New York and Freiburg. The three mothers, Mater Suspiriorum, Mater Lachrymarum and Mater Tenebrarum, are the incarnation of pure evil and conspire to bring forth a world of sorrow and suffering. Their machinations have resulted in a series of bloody murders that have left a trail across Europe to the United States. As Rose delves further into the book, she learns of three keys. She becomes convinced that she lives in one of the buildings described in the pages of this book. When she descends into the cellar to look for this mysterious key, she encounters a flooded chamber and a portrait bearing the words "Mater Tenebrarum". Unknown to her, a shadowed figure watches as she leaves the cellar. Soon after, her brother Mark (Leigh McCloskey), a music student in Rome, receives a letter from his obviously distressed sister begging him to come to New York. As he sets off on his way, he leaves behind the misery and death of a school covertly run by Mater Lachrymarum. When he arrives in New York he discovers his beloved sister has disappeared and very soon learns of her

Come face to face with hell.

death and the murderous power of the three sisters.

Following the success of **Suspiria** (1977), Dario Argento embarked on yet another stylish masterpiece, this time abandoning any notion of linear storytelling to create a series of hauntingly beautiful set pieces. This was to be the second of the trilogy of the three witches, which built further on the inspiration derived from Thomas de Quincey's *Suspiria de Profundis*. It would be almost another thirty years before his trilogy was concluded, when **The Mother of Tears** finally came to cinema screens in 2007. With **Inferno** Argento tried to elucidate the fear in his audience, removing the spoken word from some of his finest scenes as Keith Emerson's organ-based score heightened the tension, most notably in the submerged chamber and the university lecture theatre in Rome. As his audience's sense of trepidation began to escalate, he conjured with the radiance from cleverly hidden sources of light to imbue them with increasingly surreal hues of colour set against the ever-embracing shadow. The effect was to engender an impression of dream, but this was in essence the very darkest of dreams. Mario Bava's son Lamberto worked closely with Argento as his assistant director on this film in the same year as his directorial debut on **Macabre**, but **Inferno** proved so much more grisly. The excess was such the film was listed as a video nasty in August 1984, as the DPP chose to ignore the film's imagery and architectural magnificence, features so rarely seen in horror movies. It was removed from the list in September 1985 and when released to video in 1987 was subject to over four and a half minutes of expurgation. The unedited version was finally sanctioned for issue to DVD in 2010.

The Initiation

 YEAR OF RELEASE: 1984

RUNTIME: 97 minutes

COUNTRY: USA

DIRECTOR: Larry Stewart

PRODUCTION COMPANY: Georgian Bay Productions, Initiation Associates

WRITER: Charles Pratt Jr.

CINEMATOGRAPHER: George Tirl

PRODUCERS: Jock Gaynor (executive producer), Bruce Lansbury (executive producer) Scott Winant

CERTIFICATE: Australia: R; USA: R

CAST: Vera Miles, Daphne Zuniga, Clu Gulager, James Read, Marilyn Kagan, Robert Dowdell, Patti Heider, Frances Peterson, Hunter Tylo, Paula Knowles, Trey Stroud, Peter Malof, Christopher Bradley

FOLLOWING A DREAM-LIKE prelude, Kelly Fairchild (Daphne Zuniga) prepares herself to pledge to the most prominent sorority sisterhood at her college. For many years, however, she has been troubled by the same nightmare: surrounded by an inferno of flames she sees someone falling before a killer's blade. Her secretive mother (Vera Miles) continues to put her bad dreams down to the pressures of being at college. In an effort to rid herself of her nightmares, Kelly eventually agrees to see a college professor who specializes in memory regression.

Meanwhile a deranged inmate has escaped from the town's mental facility; having already murdered his nurse he has secreted himself in a dimly lit shopping mall. Back at the college, Kelly has learned that her pledge entails breaking into the same mall, which is also owned by her father, Dwight (Clu Gulager). Once inside they must steal the security officer's uniform, which for Kelly will be no problem as she

They pledge themselves to be young, stay young ... and die young!

has the keys and knows where the uniforms are stored. Once within this claustrophobic setting the girls are stalked and mercilessly slaughtered by a killer armed with an array of gardening implements and whose guise as ever remains obscured. The killer, we learn, has a strange connection with Kelly's recurring nightmare and she is his intended victim.

Television director Larry Stewart's well-paced film proved to be a more memorable entry in the pantheon of college-themed slashers, following in the path of **Hell Night** (1981) and **House on Sorority Row** (1983). While it was unable to bring anything new to the now established slasher format, its murder scenes were applauded and Stewart revealed his expertise as he heightened the suspense for his film's closing half hour in the point of view cat and mouse chase amidst the isolated corridors of the shopping mall. While the murder scenes were not particularly gory, the teenage audience were compensated by the sight of Daphne Zuniga as she prepared to remove her clothes.

Inside

📅	YEAR OF RELEASE: 2007	⚰️	PRODUCERS: Priscilla Bertin (supervising producer), Vérane Frédiani, Rodolphe Guglielmi (co-producer), Fryderyk Ovcaric (co-producer), Teddy Percherancier (co-producer), Franck Ribière
⏱️	Runtime 83 minutes		
🌐	COUNTRY: France		
🎥	Directors: Alexandre Bustillo, Julien Maury		
🎬	PRODUCTION COMPANY: La Fabrique de Films, BR Films, Canal+, CinéCinéma, Cofinova 3, Soficinéma 3, Uni Etoile 4	⭕	CERTIFICATE: Australia: R (2011); Canada: 16+ (Quebec); Canada: R (Ontario); UK: 18; USA: NC-17 (original rating); USA: R (cut)
✏️	WRITER: Alexandre Bustillo		
🎞️	CINEMATOGRAPHER: Laurent Barès	💲	BUDGET: $3,000,000

CAST: Béatrice Dalle, Alysson Paradis, Nathalie Roussel, François-Régis Marchasson, Jean-Baptiste Tabourin, Dominique Frot, Claude Lulé, Hyam Zaytoun Tahar Rahim, Emmanuel Gue, Ludovic Berthillot

CHRISTMAS EVE SHOULD be a time of celebration, but not for Sarah Scarangelo; she still grieves for her husband Matthieu who was killed in a car crash some months before. Guilt-ridden Sarah had always thought that she and her unborn child were the only ones to survive the wreckage of those tragic moments and now readies for her next day's journey to the hospital. To her surprise, a knock comes on the door. Standing before her is a woman who asks to use the telephone. Unnerved, Sarah refuses, but the woman insists that she knows Sarah and tries to barge her way into the house. Although heavily pregnant, Sarah fends off the incensed woman and makes a phone call to the police. When they arrive there is no sign of the strange woman, but they promise to keep an eye on Sarah in the hours before she goes to the hospital. However, the woman cunningly avoids detection and enters Sarah's house with a mind to ridding her of her unborn child. Terrified and helpless, Sarah locks herself in the confines of the bathroom. The woman remains on the other side of the bathroom door and a night of vicious torment ensues as she viciously slaughters all who try to enter the house and Sarah fights a determined battle to save the life of her unborn baby. The disturbing climax brought the excess endured for the last half hour to a blood soaked finale, which offered little compromise as it continued to jolt its audience and left in its wake a haunting message.

At first glance Alexandre Bustillo's story may appear somewhat simplistic, but under his and fellow director Julien Maury's careful guidance this became one of the most shocking and challenging

films of 2007. Their debut as directors encouraged two amazing performances from their leading ladies Béatrice Dalle and Alysson Paradis in the claustrophobic environment of the three rooms that made up Sarah's home, with most of the filming taking place in the bathroom. This was nothing new in French cinema; Eric Valette's Lovecraft styled horror **Malefique** (2002) picked upon this tradition staging virtually the entire shoot in a single prison cell. The violence witnessed in À L'Intérieur was relentless in its visceral portrayal; its cruel intensity would place Bustillo and Maury's feature firmly among the degenerate wave of the new French extreme, and naturally invited comparisons with the torture porn that had only recently come to the fore. When an effusion of blood was seen to spurt across the walls during the latter part of the film, memories of Dario Argento's excessive climax to **Tenebrae** (1982), subsequently cut in many countries across the globe, were once again brought to mind. À L'Intérieur was elevated to become so much more than torture porn, as the two directors masterfully orchestrated the tension in a disturbing drama that was more dependent on suspense than smearing the screen in gore. Bustillo and Maury's success would see them return in 2011 accompanied by actress Béatrice Dalle for their possessed house terror, **Livid**.

Intruder

COUNTRY: USA

DIRECTOR: Scott Spiegel

🎬	**PRODUCTION COMPANY:** Beyond Infinity, Phantom	🎬	**PRODUCERS:** Lawrence Bender, Douglas Hessler (co-producer), Douglas Scott-Hessler (co-producer), Charles Band (executive producer)
✎	**WRITERS:** Lawrence Bender (story), Scott Spiegel (screenplay)		
🎞	**CINEMATOGRAPHER:** Fernando Argüelles	◯	**Certificate** Australia: R; New Zealand: R16; UK: 18; USA: R
		💲	**BUDGET:** $100,000

Cast Elizabeth Cox, Renée Estevez, Dan Hicks, David Byrnes, Sam Raimi, Eugene Robert Glazer, Billy Marti, Burr Steers, Craig Stark, Ted Raimi, Alvy Moore, Tom Lester, Emil Sitka, Bruce Campbell, Lawrence Bender.

THE OWNERS OF the local convenience store have had to announce to their staff that the shop will be shortly closing down; these are troubled times and in an ever changing world the store is no longer viable. Even though the teenage night shift will soon lose their jobs, they continue as they have been instructed to price down the stock so that it can be sold off at a discount. One of the cashiers, Jennifer (Elizabeth Cox), has become deeply anxious following the release of her ex-boyfriend Craig (David Byrnes), who has been serving time for manslaughter. This bullying hot head has already had an altercation with one of the store managers, Bill (Sam Raimi)) and has made threats to come back and cause more trouble. As the youngsters set to work someone begins butchering them using a typically outrageous modus operandi, which is both gruesome and at the same time highly inventive. The killer makes ample use of the tools made available to him in the domesticity of this local shop, paying specific attention to the meat hooks, a box crushing machine, meat slicer and then an eye is rammed into a spiked letter opener. As the film gathers speed Jennifer finds herself as the final girl just before Spiegel delivers his twist ending, the shock of which momentarily overrides the movie's prolonged periods of teen humour.

A new dimension in terror.

Scott Spiegel's darkly comedic slasher, conceived several years after the genre's golden period, carried so many of the hallmarks that had become synonymous with these grisly features. His directorial debut was fraught with so many of the problems associated with low budget film making, but his innovative approach to camera work and use of lighting ensured his film held the viewer's attention. Scott had been school friends with both Sam Raimi and Bruce Campbell, and had learned his trade working with them on some of their early movies. He then went on to co-write the script for **Evil Dead 2**. Unfortunately, Campbell struggled to help his friend out on this particular film, only managing a cameo appearance owing to his involvement with **Maniac Cop**. The excessive levels of gore unfortunately aroused the interest of the censors and Spiegel's efforts consequently suffered badly in the cutting room. In the UK, the BBFC specified the certificated print could only be released if just over five minutes of the carnage was removed from the final edit. However, a very rare video version is still in existence. This presents the film as Spiegel had originally intended, making it one of the last great slasher movies to come out of the eighties.

Island of Death

📅 YEAR OF RELEASE: 1977	🎞 CINEMATOGRAPHERS: Nikos Gardelis, Nico Mastorakis
🕐 RUNTIME: 108 minutes	
🎦 COUNTRY: Greece	🎥 PRODUCERS: Nico Mastorakis, Nestoras Pavelas
🎬 DIRECTOR: Nico Mastorakis	
🎬 PRODUCTION COMPANY: Omega Pictures	🔘 CERTIFICATE: Australia: R; UK: (Banned) (1984–2002); UK: 18 (cut); UK: 18 (uncut) (2010)
✏ WRITER: Nico Mastorakis	

CAST: Robert Behling, Jane Lyle, Jessica Dublin, Gerard Gonalons, Jannice McConnell, Nikos Tsachiridis, Marios Tartas, Ray Richardson, Efi Bani, Clay Half, Elizabeth Spader, Jeremy Rousseau, Mike Murtagh

A YOUNG BRITISH COUPLE Celia (appearing as Jayne Ryall) and Christopher (Robert Behling) take a holiday on the small Greek island of Mykonos. As they arrive, they appear to be an ordinary innocent couple, until Christopher makes a call to his mother from a call box while enjoying a very heated moment of passion; his mother of course is disgusted. This scene carries a warning: this couple are far from normal; they are a psychotic brother and sister on an unholy mission. Very soon, they are laying the island's perverted inhabitants to the slaughter, all in the name of God. Christopher takes delight in photographing his catalogue of atrocities, including his urination on an older woman, which some observers still insist she actually comes to enjoy. She is then beaten and decapitated with a bulldozer.

The hypocritical couple's victims range from homosexuals, lesbians, a nymphomaniac, a couple of hippies and a policeman, each dispatched in a brutal and unusually imaginative way before the film's twist prior to the credits begin rolling onto the screen.

Nico Mastorakis's film, which also goes by the names **A Craving for Lust**, **Cruel Destination**, **Devils in Mykonos**, **Island of Perversion** and **Psychic Killer 2**, has been described as a classic in the field of exploitation and followed on the back of the 1970s grindhouse boom and the success of **The Texas Chain Saw Massacre** (1974). As a first time director, Mastorakis's aim was to make money; to do so, he was at least going to have to match every other exploitation producer of the period. With this in mind, he made a film that went out to shock, as Tobe Hooper and Wes Craven had before him, using some of the most degrading episodes so far committed to film. While it included many sequences of sex with the delicious Celia regularly removing her clothes, and scenes of

> **The lucky ones simply got their brains blown out.**

rape, one with a goat, its display of nudity was somewhat fleeting. Sex in Mastoraki's movie was invariably a precursor to violence and death, the three essential ingredients to any sleazy exploitation feature of the period. Typically, the acting was poor, but the humour was dark and the photography well staged. When it was first released to cinemas in the UK, almost fourteen minutes of sadistic footage had been removed. Five years later, it was packaged as a video and issued in the November of 1982, when it roused the wrath of the moral crusaders of the day, whose demands insisted it be listed as a video nasty. There was confusion when it was removed from the list having been mistaken with Narciso Ibanez Serrador's film of the same name, only to be returned in October 1985 until the end of the so-called crisis. The film was finally issued uncut to DVD in 2010. These problems with the BBFC wouldn't deter Mastoraki, who went on to acquire a reputation as a highly capable low budget filmmaker. 🔪

The Janitor

🔪 🔪 🔪 🔪

 YEAR OF RELEASE: 2003

 RUNTIME: 92 minutes

 COUNTRY: USA

 DIRECTORS: TJ Nordaker, Andy Signore

 PRODUCTION COMPANY: Clean Kill Productions

WRITER: Andy Signore	
CINEMATOGRAPHER: John Carreon	

PRODUCERS: John Carreon), T. J. Nordaker, Andy Signore, Chip Signore (executive producer), Steve Signore (executive producer.

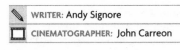

CAST: Andy Signore, Bruce Cronander Crystal LeBard, G. Larry Butler, Skip Pipo, John Carreon, Rachael Ann Bennett, Kelly King, Stephanie Christine Medina, Logan Christopher, Allison Alley, Jerry G. Angelo, Kit Bateman Heather Black, Jason Blackburn

ALTHOUGH LIONEL (ANDY Signore) puts a lot of effort into his janitorial duties for the Generico Corporation, he has become disgruntled by the belittling treatment he receives from the company's staff. When he leaves work, he returns home where he lives with his janitor guru, Cornelius Growbo (Bruce Cronander). Infuriated by the conduct of those who work for the company he embarks on a series of sadistic reprisals aimed at those who refuse to afford him some respect. With the body count now escalating, an FBI agent is placed on the case, but Lionel's rancour drives him on in his retaliatory crusade. The blood bath is brought to a halt when he falls for Hillary (Fiona MacIntyre), a recently widowed colleague. Sadly, for him she decides to leave the company, fearful she will become another of the killer's victims. Her decision is upsetting, but it encourages Lionel to search for work elsewhere.

Evil works the nightshift . . .

Later on while in the pub, he finds himself in the company of a group of gorgeous girls from the Tau Nu Alpha Sorority House who need someone to clean up after their parties and topless slumber gatherings. Lionel eagerly offers to take the job and rushes home to tell Mr Growbo of his change in fortune. Mr Growbo proves not to be such a good friend; he immediately slips off to the Sorority House and takes Lionel's dream job from under his very nose. The embittered Lionel then takes out his anger on a couple of Generico's employees who he discovers having sex in the reception area, but is caught by Willis, the new janitor (John Carreon). Willis, it turns out, is as deranged as Lionel, and wants a piece of the grisly action. The pair of them head to the sorority house to seek out their bloody revenge.

The Janitor was an independent low-budget slasher movie that delivered on both the queasy gore and irreverent comedy. First time directors T. J. Nordaker and Andy Signore never once intended for their film to be taken too seriously, but they deftly picked upon so many of the features that made the slasher comedies of the 1980s so successful and rehashed it for a new generation. The blood and guts flowed freely as did the hot girl action and they even dared to create a graphic parody of the celebrated **Psycho** shower scene. 🔰

Jigoku

📅 YEAR OF RELEASE: 1960	✏️ WRITERS: Nobuo Nakagawa, Ichirô Miyagawa
⏱️ RUNTIME: 101 minutes	
🐗 COUNTRY: Japan	🎬 CINEMATOGRAPHER: Mamoru Morita
🎥 DIRECTOR: Nobuo Nakagawa	⏳ PRODUCERS: Mitsugu Ôkura
🎬 PRODUCTION COMPANY: Shintoho Film Distribution Committee	⭕ CERTIFICATE: Canada: 13+ (Quebec); USA: TV-MA

CAST: Shigeru Amachi, Utako Mitsuya, Yôichi Numata, Hiroshi Hayashi, Jun Ôtomo, Akiko Yamashita, Kiyoko Tsuji, Fumiko Miyata, Torahiko Nakamura, Kimie Tokudaiji, Akiko Ono.

THEOLOGY STUDENT SHIRO Shimuzu (Shigeru Amachi), along with his mysterious friend Tamura (Yoichi Numata), becomes an accessory to a hit-and-run accident, which results in the death of what may have been a Yakuza gangster. His guilt-ridden conscience insists that he give himself up to the police. However, when he tries to go to the authorities his taxi crashes, killing his girlfriend Yukiko (Utako Mitsuya). Shiro's life becomes one of drink and despair and to make things worse he learns that his mother is terminally ill. He sets of, to the nursing home owned by his father, Gozo, in Tenjoen. When he enters the home, it resembles a vision of hell on earth, where, amidst the drunken painters and negligent doctors, he learns the truth about his adulterous father and meets Sachiko, a girl who looks exactly like his dead girlfriend. The distraught young man escapes the insanity of the home and makes his way along a railway line. As he continues his battle with his guilt, he is again confronted by the elusive Tamura, which leads to him being accosted by his dead girlfriend's mother, intent on revenge. Very soon, Shiro will leave our world in a climax that sees the death of virtually all the residents in his father's nursing home; then he faces that which lies beyond the gates of hell in a succession of extreme scenes, the likes of which had never before been seen in cinema across the globe.

281

Director Nobuo Nakagawa, described as the Japanese Alfred Hitchcock, funded much of his film **Jigoku**, which literally translates as "Hell", with his own money. He was then fifty-five years old, and considered a veteran of Japanese cinema, when he created this daunting vision of hell, which entwined the Christian and Buddhist interpretations of eternal damnation. His thinking on this feature turned away from the traditional Japanese ghost stories for which he had previously acquired a very favourable reputation and instead produced a nihilist piece of Grand Guignol that was to provide the firmest of foundations for the excessive Japanese terrors to come. For the first part of his Faust inspired masterpiece he embellished his characters with considerable depth, lamenting on life and death, and then cast them into a surreal depiction of flayed flesh, spikes driven through jaws, torn limbs and disembowelled intestines. The cinematography created the strangest of hues to engender a world of torment that the reproachful Shiro would have to escape. Back in 1960, there was nothing in film that could quite be described as Jigoku's match. It would inspire later remakes in 1979 and 1999, neither of which captured the bizarre premise of the original.

Juan de los Meurtos

📅 YEAR OF RELEASE: 2011	✏️ WRITER: Alejandro Brugués
⏱️ RUNTIME: 100 minutes	🎬 CINEMATOGRAPHER: Carles Gusi
🌐 COUNTRY: Cuba	⚰️ PRODUCERS: Claudia Calviño (executive producer), Inti Herrera (executive producer), Gervasio Iglesias (executive producer)
🎥 DIRECTOR: Alejandro Brugués	
🎬 PRODUCTION COMPANY: La Zanfoña Producciones, Producciones de la 5ta Avenida	💲 BUDGET: $2,700,000

CAST: Andrea Duro, Alexis Díaz de Villegas, Luis Alberto García, Jorge Molina, Blanca Rosa Blanco, Jazz Vilá, Susana Pous, Elsa Camp, Andros Perugorría, Eliecer Ramírez

FORTY-YEAR-OLD JUAN HAS done virtually nothing with his life; his friend Lázaro, an army trained martial arts expert, can say the same thing. As a series of violent attacks pour through the streets of his hometown, the radio reports put the blame on Cuban dissidents paid by the US government. However, Juan and his friends soon realize their attackers are not normal human beings; the venom in their bite has the capacity to turn the victims into violent killers, whose numbers grow by the hour. In true Romero fashion, Juan soon learns the only way to bring them down is to destroy their brains. Our shrewd-minded hero also knows the best way to confront the situation is to turn his back on his socialist past and cash in on the situation. Seeing a window of opportunity his slogan becomes "Juan of the Dead, we kill your beloved ones". Lázaro, along with his children Vladi and Camila, stand at Juan's side ready to help people get rid of the menace that surrounds them . . . all of course for a reasonable price. The zombies are already running out of control, devouring flesh and, as they have in the past, ripping out guts. The people of a ravaged Havana look to leave the island and head out to sea. Juan, however, has no choice but to fight for his homeland, armed with a baseball bat and catapult.

There are suggestions that Alejandro Brugués' gore-strewn action-packed black comedy, **Juan de los Meurtos**, could be Cuba's first feature-length horror film as the government banned the production of horror and fantasy-based films adjudging them to be detrimental to the political leanings and the social programme of the Cuban government. However, one of Brugués' cast and crew, Jorge Molina, wrote and directed **Ferozz: The Wild Red Riding Hood** in 2010, a film steeped in witchcraft and Satanism that contains scenes comparable to the torture porn of more recent cinematic horror. Brugués defied his country's social programme and grew up watching American zombie films, owning a copy of Sam Raimi's **The Evil Dead** (1981), and saw the potential in the hopelessly resigned city of Havana. For fifty years the people of Cuba had lived with the prospect of a war with the United States; instead they face the mindless onslaught of the living dead. This was the zombie movie Brugués, a graduate of Cuba's International School of Film and Television, had hoped to make. With the success of his film **Personal Belongings** (2006) he was able to negotiate enough backing to create a movie that would be considered a blockbuster by Cuban standards, with most of it coming from Spanish financiers and the state-owned Cuban Institute of Cinematographic Industry and Arts. His tight camera angles give the impression of an almost deserted city as the threat drives the populace away into the sea. As his team strove to make the film a success, Brugués

Fifty years after the triumph of the Revolution, a new Revolution is about to begin.

almost ran into trouble with the police when they were summoned by the city's municipal rubbish collectors, who found a zombie's head mixed in with the refuse, which says much for the make-up effects.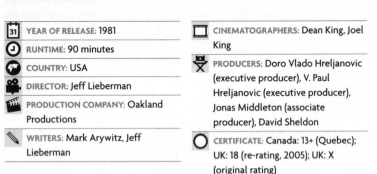

Just Before Dawn

📅 **YEAR OF RELEASE:** 1981	
🕐 **RUNTIME:** 90 minutes	
🎥 **COUNTRY:** USA	
🎬 **DIRECTOR:** Jeff Lieberman	
🎬 **PRODUCTION COMPANY:** Oakland Productions	
✒️ **WRITERS:** Mark Arywitz, Jeff Lieberman	

CINEMATOGRAPHERS: Dean King, Joel King

PRODUCERS: Doro Vlado Hreljanovic (executive producer), V. Paul Hreljanovic (executive producer), Jonas Middleton (associate producer), David Sheldon

CERTIFICATE: Canada: 13+ (Quebec); UK: 18 (re-rating, 2005); UK: X (original rating)

CAST: George Kennedy, Mike Kellin, Chris Lemmon, Gregg Henry, Deborah Benson, Ralph Seymour, Katie Powell, John Hunsaker, Charles Bartlett, Jamie Rose, Hap Oslund, Barbara Spencer

A COUPLE OF HUNTERS come upon an abandoned church in a mountainside forest. When they cross its threshold to explore the interior they are confronted by a machete-wielding man who laughs heartily and then delivers a hack to the groin of one of the men. The other quickly makes his escape.

Five campers, Warren (Gregg Henry) the keep-fit enthusiast, his shy girlfriend Constance (Deborah Benson), Jonathon (Chris Lemmon), the girl-mad party animal, and his desirable girlfriend Megan (Jamie Rose), along with the geek cameraman, Daniel (Ralph Seymour), arrive in the mountains. They have ignored the warnings of forest ranger Roy McLean (George Kennedy) not to continue in the direction in which they are heading. Further along the way they come close to hitting the surviving hunter, who insists they turn round and drive away. Once again they fail to take heed of this sound advice and look instead to set up camp. After an evening of light-hearted revelry they retire, all the while being watched by a presence in the woods. The following morning, they catch sight of a young girl named Merry

Logan (Kati Powell) before she scampers into the forest. Later, as Megan swims naked in a pool, she assumes the hands that stroke her legs beneath the water belong to Jonathon, but he is already drying himself off. Panic immediately sets in, but she manages to swim to safety. There is something amiss in this beautiful spot, but the teenagers do not have the wherewithal to take any notice of the signs around them.

When Jonathon spots Merry and begins to chase her, he is forced to cross a roped bridge overhanging a fast-flowing river. As Merry manages to get further away, Jonathon is struck in the hand by a machete brandished by a malformed man whose incessant laughter makes this episode even more terrifying. The rope bridge breaks, and the youth falls into the turbulence below. In a bid to save himself he begins to climb, only to come face to face with the same man, who kicks him to his death down in the rapids. The killer then tracks down Megan and Daniel, who have found the church seen at the very beginning of the film. Daniel receives a fatal machete blow to the stomach and when Megan escapes into the church she is greeted by what appears to be the same man only to learn, shock of shocks, he is one of identical twins. Her discovery won't save her as he begins to hack her to pieces with his trusted machete, while his deranged brother uses Daniel's camera to commit their activities to film. While searching for the hapless campers the forest ranger Roy comes across Merry's family, a barmy

The nightmare has begun . . .

hillbilly father and a hushed mother who is also her sister. He reveals the homicidal twins are theirs, but they have no love for trespassers and now bear down on Warren and Constance. Constance's sanity is now at stake.

It will come as no surprise to learn Jeff Lieberman regarded John Boorman's **Deliverance** (1972) as being the main influence on his entry to the backwoods slasher genre, borne out by its release in France as **Survivance**. He still considers **Just Before Dawn** to be one of his own personal favourites and while it bears a thematic comparison to **The Hills Have Eyes** (1977), Lieberman maintains he hadn't seen this movie at the time of filming. With so many slasher films gaining theatrical release, his film was just one of many and passed by very quietly. However, with the arrival of the video market it amassed a staunch following, gaining praise for its opulent cinematography, which did so much to capture the magnitude of this eerie locale, yet at the same time imposed a sense of claustrophobia seen in so many memorable horror movies. With an above average cast who were destined to achieve greater things, Lieberman had the chance to concentrate on generating the suspense and intensifying the atmosphere rather than relying solely on the exploitative violence preferred by so many of his contemporaries. Other forest-based blood baths would follow, but few would match the tension in Lieberman's narrative. 🖤

Killer Nun

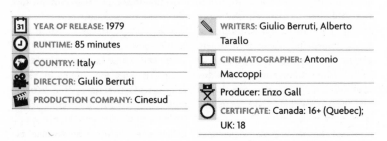

📅 YEAR OF RELEASE: 1979	✏️ WRITERS: Giulio Berruti, Alberto Tarallo
🕐 RUNTIME: 85 minutes	
🎦 COUNTRY: Italy	🎞 CINEMATOGRAPHER: Antonio Maccoppi
🎥 DIRECTOR: Giulio Berruti	
🎬 PRODUCTION COMPANY: Cinesud	⏳ Producer: Enzo Gall
	⭕ CERTIFICATE: Canada: 16+ (Quebec); UK: 18

CAST: Anita Ekberg, Paola Morra, Alida Valli, Massimo Serato, Daniele Dublino, Lou Castel, Joe Dallesandro, Laura Nucci, Alice Gherardi

S ISTER GERTRUDE (ANITA Ekburg) is convalescing following neurosurgery on a brain tumour and feels she needs more time in which to recover, but her Mother Superior foolishly thinks otherwise. When she returns to her duties in the geriatric hospital, she soon becomes addicted to their supply of morphine as she tries to rid herself of the incessant headaches and then her schizophrenia once again begins to come to the fore. In her deranged state, she entices an impressionable young nun, Sister Mathilde (Paola Morra), into a lesbian affair, demanding that her lover wears silk stockings. She then dismisses the hospital's doctor, leaving her free to torment the elderly patients, one of whom has her false teeth shattered by the maddened Gertrude. It isn't long before a series of deaths occurs in the hospital with the deteriorating Gertude as the obvious suspect. She doesn't help her situation when she visits a neighbouring town

and after meeting a young man allows him to stand her up against the wall and take complete advantage of her willing body. Her Mother Superior must now intervene if this madness is to be brought to an end.

Giulio Berruti's **Suor Omicidi**, also entitled **Deadly Habit**, was based on a series of murders and maltreatment in a geriatric home in the town of Wetteren in Flanders, Belgium, towards the end of 1977. Sister Godfrida of the Apostolic Congregation of St Joseph was accused of stealing more than $30,000 dollars from her elderly patients to support her morphine addiction. She also confessed to killing three patients with overdoses of insulin, because they had become difficult during the night, and was allegedly ripping out catheter tubes from bladders. Berruti's film never quite captured the horror of these events in the predominantly Catholic region of Flanders, but it remains an intriguing addition to the nunsploitation phenomenon, which peaked during the 1970s, and whose cinematic origins can be traced back to a Scandinavian silent film **Häxan** (1922). **Killer Nun** is a hybrid of the sleazy nunsploitation cinema of the period and the popular giallo murder mystery, but appears restrained when it is trying to deliver the exploitation demanded of these particular genres. The gore was only ever implied, although the killings were appreciably sadistic, especially the torture with pins and the hypodermics administered to the face. This, coupled with former Miss Sweden Anita Ekberg's strong performance, had Mary Whitehouse denounce Berruti's film as a video nasty and it was banished to the Director of Public Prosecutions' list of objectionable films in August 1984,

only to be dropped in the July of the following year. When **Killer Nun** was submitted for its 1993 release to video, the scene detailing the torture of the old woman, with the close up of a needle piercing her eye and the scalpel lacerating her bandaged flesh, had to be removed. The merits in Giulio Berruti's occasionally stylish direction were ignored, as was Alessandro Alessandroni's compelling score; the DPP could see this was a very sleazy entry in the already bothersome exploitation genre. It would finally gain acceptance before the BBFC when it was presented for release to DVD in 2006. The scenes that had once caused offence now appeared dated and no longer contained their original shock value; as a result the film was finally released uncut.

Killer Party

📅 YEAR OF RELEASE: 1986	🎞️ CINEMATOGRAPHER: John Lindley
🕐 RUNTIME: 91 minutes	🎬 PRODUCERS: Grace Gilroy (associate producer), Marjorie Kalins (coordinating producer), Kenneth Kaufman, Michael Lepiner
🌐 COUNTRY: United States	
🎥 DIRECTOR: William Fruet	
🎬 PRODUCTION COMPANY: Marquis, Polar Entertainment Corporation, Telecom Entertainment Inc.	⭕ CERTIFICATE: Australia: M; UK: 18; USA: R
✏️ WRITER: Barney Cohen	💲 RECEIPTS: $681,337

CAST: Martin Hewitt, Ralph Seymour, Elaine Wilkes, Paul Bartel, Sherry Willis-Burch, Alicia Fleer, Woody Brown, Joanna Johnson, Terri Hawkes, Deborah Hancock, Laura Sherman, Jeff Pustil, Pam Hyatt, Howard Busgang, Jason Warren

A GROUP OF STUDENT friends Phoebe (Elaine Wilkes), Vivia (Sherry Willis-Burch) and Jennifer (Joanna Johnson) are delighted when they gain acceptance into their house sorority. On the night of the initiation, Vivia had played a prank on the sisterhood, which is why she and her friends were so readily accepted. Now she must engage in a similar escapade at a party planned by her sorority sisters for a neighbouring fraternity in an old house, which twenty years before had also been home to a similar fraternity. The sisters cajole their housemother into letting them celebrate in the abandoned house. Before the girls make their way to the house, the housemother decides to pay a visit to ensure it is still safe. In the overgrown garden to the front of the manse she stands over a grave and talks to someone called Allan, explaining why she is allowing the girls to have their party and tells him what happened all those years ago was merely an accident. As she attends to an unsteady banister, a mysterious figure, who is obviously someone of her acquaint, appears before her and bludgeons her to death. The girls remain unaware of this fatal occurrence and begin to decorate the old house for their April Fool's Day party and at the same time prepare some mischief. Poor Jennifer has serious misgivings about the house's dark past, but the party goes ahead. Once the festivities get under way the guests begin to fall foul of the killer seen earlier on the stairs. He stalks the house dressed in a deep-sea diver's suit employing a hammer, a pitchfork, a corkscrew and a guillotine to dispose of his victims. In a twist that sets it apart from so many slashers of the era, an evil spirit sweeps through the house turning Jennifer into a demonic creature, akin to **The Evil Dead**, that crawls around the chandeliers and across the ceilings before it too joins in with the butchery.

Canadian director William Fruett had directed the controversial, but later acclaimed, violent horror **Death Weekend**, which also goes by the name **House by the Lake** (1976). Filming on **Killer Party** is claimed to have started in 1978, but as it neared completion the budget became exhausted and production was ceased until 1984, when it was finally finished only to languish for another two years before receiving a limited theatrical release by MGM. This version was severely edited, removing much of the gore seen in the original cut. The title was also altered from **The April Fools** to **Killer Party** because the distributors were concerned that it could be confused with the darkly comedic **April Fool's Day** released that same year. When it saw release in 1986, the slasher years were almost over and the set pieces appeared clichéd; yet if, as it is claimed, this was originally shot in 1978, it could have been a highly influential movie and bears certain similarities to **Hell Night** (1981). **Killer Party** has become another rarity from the 1980s, and is currently only officially available in the VHS format. ❧

The Last House on the Left

 YEAR OF RELEASE: 1972

 RUNTIME: 84 minutes

 COUNTRY: USA

 DIRECTOR: Wes Craven

 PRODUCTION COMPANY: Lobster Enterprises, Sean S. Cunningham Films, The Night Co.

 WRITER: Wes Craven

CINEMATOGRAPHER: Victor Hurwitz

PRODUCERS: Sean S. Cunningham, Katherine D'Amato (associate producer), Steve Dwork (assistant producer), Steve Miner (assistant producer)

 CERTIFICATE: Australia: Refused Classification (original rating: 1987); Australia: R (re-rating: 2004); Canada: R; Ireland: 18 (cut UK version); New Zealand: R18 (re-rating: 2004); New Zealand: (Banned) (original rating); UK: 18 (re-rating: 2008) (uncut); UK: 18 (re-rating: 2002) (cut); UK: (Banned) (1984–2002); UK: R (original rating: 1974); USA: X (original rating); USA: R (heavily cut); USA: Unrated (uncut)

BUDGET: $90,000

RECEIPTS: $3,100,000

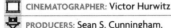

CAST: Sandra Peabody, Lucy Grantham, David Hess, Fred J. Lincoln, Jeramie Rain, Marc Sheffler, Richard Towers, Cynthia Carr, Ada Washington, Marshall Anker, Martin Kove, Ray Edwards

THE INSPIRATION FOR Wes Craven's controversial **The Last House on the Left** goes back to the thirteenth-century Swedish ballad "Töres dotter i Wänge", first adapted for the cinema by Ingmar Bergman for his film **The Virgin Spring** (1960). Bergman soon after received an Academy Award for his achievement as Best Foreign Film. Craven's vicious offspring certainly remains a landmark in its own right, but was adjudged as being cold and dispassionate in its violent portrayal and was never going to be considered for an Academy Award.

During the prologue, we are told the events in this story are based on an incident that actually happened, but conjecture remains as to the truth behind this statement. The Cohen Brothers later made a similar declaration in the preamble to their movie **Fargo** (1996), the impact of which would have a major bearing on the audience reaction to the staging of certain scenes. Craven boldly set out to exaggerate the shocks in what proved to be a very disturbing piece of cinema. On the eve of her seventeenth birthday, Mari Collingwood plans to travel to New York to see the underground band Bloodlust, accompanied by her close friend Phyllis Stone. As she heads off in the family car, a couple of sadistic prison escapees, Krug Stillo, a rapist and serial killer, along with Fred "Weasel" Podowski, a child molester and murderer, are hiding out with their partner Sadie (Jeramie Rain) and Krug's drug-addicted son, Junior Stillo (Marc Sheffler).

After the gig, the two girls try to score some marijuana. Their wayward mission leads them to Junior who makes them an offer of Colombian grass if they will come back to his apartment. Once inside they are overcome by the two escaped criminals and their accomplice Sadie. Phyllis does her best to resist, but is punched in the stomach and brutally raped. The repulsive scene is juxtaposed with the parents of Mari and their preparations for her surprise party.

When morning comes, the girls' ordeal continues as they are imprisoned in the boot of the gang's car and driven away to the countryside, as they journey north to Canada. In a strange twist of fate, their vehicle breaks down in front of Mari's house as the police are following up on the reports of the girls' disappearance. When the gang realize there is no chance of getting the car repaired, they drag the kidnapped girls into the woods and then begins the cruel torture with appalling beatings, urination and forced lesbian sex. After trying to escape, Phyllis is

tracked to a nearby cemetery, where Weasel plunges his knife into her back, shortly before the rest of the gang catch up to continue the merciless assault and then eviscerate her. Moments later, her severed hand is presented to Mari, as she endures the humiliation of having the evil Krug's name carved into her chest before being raped and shot as she attempts to make her escape along a lakeside.

Craven hasn't finished with his audience yet. Having changed their clothes the gang arrive at the Collingwoods' home, introducing themselves as travelling salesmen. In a series of tense scenes, Mari's mother Estelle discovers the gang's involvement with her daughter's disappearance. She and her husband flee the house and scurry into the woods, where they find Mari next to the lake only just alive. The poor girl tells of their ordeal and then dies. The enraged parents carry their daughter's body back to the house as the stimulus behind the violence now shifts from being gratuitous to bloody revenge. Ironically, it was Krug's slaughter at the hands of the incensed chainsaw-wielding Doctor Collingwood which proved to be one of the most sadistic moments in the entire film.

Written by Wes Craven in 1971 as **Night of Vengeance**, the original concept was far more graphic than the film that finally saw completion. Soon after shooting began, the decision was taken to tone down the excess Craven had first envisaged to make for what the production team considered as being a much softer film. While this was going on, their exploitative brainchild went through many name changes, including **Sex Crime of the Century**, **Krug and Company** and **The Men's Room**. The film's infamy was made all the worse as its debut came only a few years after the infamous Manson Family massacre. This series of grisly murders had sent shockwaves across the United States; their ferocity presented an unsettling reflection of a part of the American way of life many would have preferred to have forgotten and raised concerns as to the erosion of family values.

There was nothing new about the idea of a revenge movie, but this was infinitely more vicious than anything that had been seen before and paved the way for films such as **Death Wish** (1974) and the equally contentious **I Spit on Your Grave** (1978). Craven's movie also attracted the attention of the censors, particularly in the United Kingdom. The film was refused a certificate for cinema release by the BBFC in 1974 owing to its sadism and violence. However, when home video arrived in the early 1980s it saw a release with very few cuts. At this time a video did not fall under the jurisdiction of the BBFC, but this loophole in the legislation generated the video nasty scare that began in 1982, backed by the tabloids and culminated in the Video Recordings Act of 1984. The film was now banned, and it took its place on

To avoid fainting, keep repeating "It's only a movie . . . It's only a movie . . . "

the Director of Public Prosecutions' list of inflammatory video nasties. For **The Last House on the Left** the ban remained in place for the remainder of the 1980s and on into the 1990s. Its standing as a video nasty, however, inevitably elevated it to a status of cult notoriety. Blue Underground Limited toured an uncut print around Britain without the consent of the BBFC, with Southampton City Council granting this version their "18" certificate in the hope of overcoming the ongoing problems with the BBFC stance on certification. It was later granted a licence for a one-off showing in Leicester in June 2000, but the BBFC remained steadfast.

The dispute continued with the BBFC winning an appeal in June 2002 made to the Video Appeals Committee (VAC) by video distributor Blue Underground Limited. The BBFC had insisted sixteen seconds of cuts to scenes of sexual violence before the video could be given an "18" certificate. Blue Underground Limited stood their ground refusing to make the cuts, so the BBFC again rejected the video. The distributor then appealed to the VAC, who upheld the BBFC's decision. During the appeal, film critic Mark Kermode was called in as a horror expert to make a case for the film's historical importance. However, after his report, the committee not only upheld the cuts but actually increased them, with the film being granted an "18" certificate with thirty-one seconds of cuts in July 2002. It was released in the UK on DVD in the May of the following year. Those scenes that fell foul of the BBFC were made available as a slideshow extra on the disc; in addition a web-link was provided to a website from where the cut scenes could be viewed. Finally, in March 2008 the BBFC classified the film uncut for video, thirty-six years after it had first been released to American theatres. A year later Rogue Pictures released a remake with Wes Craven as producer, now without the hullabaloo that surrounded the original.

Lisa, Lisa

📅	**YEAR OF RELEASE:** 1974	✏️ **WRITER:** Frederick R. Friedel
🕐	**RUNTIME:** 65 minutes	🎞️ **CINEMATOGRAPHER:** Austin McKinney
🐑	**COUNTRY:** USA	🏆 **PRODUCERS:** Irwin Friedlander (executive producer), J. G. Patterson Jr.
🎥	**DIRECTOR:** Frederick R. Friedel	
	PRODUCTION COMPANY: Frederick Productions, Empire Studios	⭕ **CERTIFICATE:** Australia: R; UK: 18; USA: R

CAST: Leslie Lee, Jack Canon, Ray Green, Frederick R. Friedel, Douglas Powers, Frank Jones, Carol Miller, George J. Monaghan, Smith Hart, Scott Smith, Jeff MacKay, David Hayman, Don Cummins, Jaqueline Pyle, Lynne Bradley

SHARP DRESSED THEY may be, but these three men, Steele (Jack Canon), Lomax (Ray Green) and Billy (Frederick R. Friedel), have murder in mind as they lie in wait to repay a friend's betrayal. When Audrey arrives, accompanied by his gay lover, the gang force a lit cigar into his throat and then Steele and Lomax systematically beat him to death. His lover narrowly escapes via the window but Audrey is left for dead on the floor. Steele and his accomplices then quickly depart the city to avoid police detection, heading into the remote countryside. During the course of their journey, they terrorize an innocent shopkeeper and then force a teenage girl (Carol Miller) to strip before they take aim at the apples placed on her head. Their travels take them to an isolated farmhouse where they find a reclusive girl, Lisa (Leslie Lee), who looks after her wheelchair-bound grandfather (Douglas Powers). Safe in the knowledge that this is an easy number, the hoodlums decide to stay for the night. In the night, Lomax becomes interested in the girl and tries to rape her. To his shock, she pulls a razor from her bedside table and soon graduates to the virtues of a sharpened axe. Although much of the violence takes place off screen, the silent girl makes able use of her axe as she slays each one of her assailants, with blood recurrently splattering across the screen.

At last – total terror!

Shot in only ten days on film that was purchased as surplus stock from filmmakers of more substantial repute, **Lisa, Lisa** became more commonly known as **Axe**, and has also gone by several different aliases including, **California Axe Massacre**, **The Axe Murders**, **California Axe Murders** and the emotive **The Virgin Slaughter**. Frederick Friedel's feature was another low-budget exploitation movie very much in the tradition of **Last House on the Left** (1972), which for many years has been maligned for its awkward camera techniques and flawed storyline. However, the gaps in this account rest with the distributor whose demands meant much of his film was left on the cutting room floor. Their intention was to present a feature for the drive-ins on a bill with two or three other movies; so Friedel had little choice but to cut it down to the bone. This destroyed any attempt at credible characterization and consequently led to annoying omissions in the narrative flow, but those who were paying their money at the drive-ins were rarely concerned with such trivialities.

Friedel's film would have drifted into obscurity if had not been released to video in the UK during the troubled year of 1982. As the crusading tabloid gathered steam, it became another feature to be labelled as a video nasty, on this occasion in September 1984. There it would remain, as one of thirty-nine films deemed too offensive to see release on these shores. The cover to the video made available in the UK became immediately problematic when it alleged that Lisa's age was only thirteen, although this was never actually inferred anywhere in Friedel's movie. This surely can be the only reason why **Lisa, Lisa** caused such a stir, for although its content was undeniably exploitative, the violence occurred away from the camera's gaze. It remained unavailable for over twenty years until its mastering to DVD in 2005. 🐾

The Living Dead at the Manchester Morgue

31	YEAR OF RELEASE: 1974	🕐	RUNTIME: 95 minutes

COUNTRY: Spain/Italy	**CINEMATOGRAPHER:** Francisco Sempere
DIRECTOR: Jorge Grau	
PRODUCTION COMPANY: Star Films S.A., Flaminia Produzioni Cinematografiche	**PRODUCERS:** Edmondo Amati, Manuel Pérez (executive producer)
WRITERS: Juan Cobos, Sandro Continenza, Marcello Coscia, Miguel Rubio	**CERTIFICATE:** Australia: MA (2009); Australia: R; Canada: 13+ (Quebec); UK: 18; UK: X (cut); USA: R
	RECEIPTS: ESP 16,894,971 (Spain)

CAST: Cristina Galbó, Ray Lovelock, Arthur Kennedy, Aldo Massasso, Giorgio Trestini, Roberto Posse, José Lifante, Jeannine Mestre, Gengher Gatti, Fernando Hilbeck, Vera Drudi, Vicente Vega, Francisco Sanz, Paul Benson, Anita Colby, Joaquín Hinojosa, Vito Salier, Isabel Mestres

WHILE RIDING THROUGH the Lake District to escape the madness of London city life, George (Ray Lovelock) becomes stranded when his motorbike accidentally collides with Edna's (Cristina Galbó) car. She is en route to a hospital to have her drug-addicted sister Katie admitted for treatment. Close to the scene of the accident, a group of agricultural scientists are experimenting with ultra-sonic radiation designed to deter the insects in the surrounding area. Their experimentation has a shocking side effect: the recently deceased begin to rise from their graves and shamble through town, slaughtering and then gorging on their victims. George and Edna try to alert the local constabulary but the bigoted sergeant (Arthur Kennedy) appears more interested in arresting the young couple, for little more than their outlandish appearance. While

there are probably no more than a half dozen zombies actually ever seen in the film, the viewer would be unwise to underestimate their murderous potential. This mob proves to be unusually strong and reveals itself eager for blood as one young nurse discovers prior to her breasts being torn off and her stomach ripped to pieces. As their numbers begin to grow, armed with tombstones the zombies try to break down the church door in a nail-biting cemetery sequence before the final bloody showdown, in what purports to be the Manchester Morgue.

In the wake of his Spanish terror **Ceremonia Sangrienta** (1973), released as **Blood Castle**, Jorge Grau was asked to make **The Living Dead at the Manchester Morgue**. Originally entitled **Non si Deve Profanare il Sonno dei Morti**, before going on to be released as **Let Sleeping Corpses**

One of the best zombie films ever made.

Lie, **The Living Dead, Breakfast at the Manchester Morgue, Don't Open the Window** and **Zombi 3**, it was intended to cash in on George A. Romero's unexpected success on **Night of the Living Dead** (1968). Rather than resorting to simple exploitation, Grau carefully considered this premise to create a film that captured both the influence of Hammer's masterpieces and the Italian terrors of the day. Although his zombies were in no way as visually terrifying as those unleashed by Romero and Lucio Fulci, there was no denying the threat in their shambling gait as they staggered with bloodthirsty intent through the English Lake District. This was an unusual collaboration, bringing together an Italian/Spanish team in the countryside of the north west of England, but Grau's crew managed to give this ordinarily picturesque locale a sense of decay that perfectly suited the mood of his film. A black humour would pervade the grisly capers of the zombie horde as it began to go forth and multiply more than twenty-five years before the infected destroyed the entire

country in Danny Boyle's **28 Days Later** (2002). The graphic gore and violence caused problems during the film's initial submission to the BBFC in 1975; one minute and twenty-seven seconds of cuts were demanded before an "X" certification would be issued. When the film appeared on video in 1983, it was bound to invite the attention of the DPP and by October 1983 had been prosecuted and listed as a video nasty. It wouldn't be until the April of 1985 that **The Living Dead at the Manchester Morgue** was removed from the offending list. The VHS release of that year then had to comply with another twenty-six seconds of cuts to those already prescribed in 1975. This meant removing shots of a police officer's mutilated body, a complete cut on all flesh eating, eliminating footage of burning zombies, edits to the entire scene depicting the Doctor's murder by an axe and the excessively gory attack on the nurse. When Grau's film was again considered for release in 2002 all of the previous BBFC cuts were thankfully waived. ❦

The Long Island Cannibal Massacre

📅 YEAR OF RELEASE: 1980	
🕐 RUNTIME: 95 minutes	
🎥 COUNTRY: USA	
🎬 DIRECTOR: Nathan Schiff	

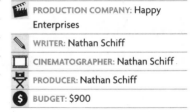

🎬 PRODUCTION COMPANY: Happy Enterprises	
✎ WRITER: Nathan Schiff	
🎞 CINEMATOGRAPHER: Nathan Schiff	
⚱ PRODUCER: Nathan Schiff	
💲 BUDGET: $900	

CAST: John Smihula, Fred Borges, Michael Siegal, Paul Smihula, Richard Stone, Nancy Canberg, Judy Guerevich, Beverly Khazzam, Denise Callabrese, Eddie Battagli, Betty-Jo Melchior

AS SHE LIES in the sun, enjoying an afternoon of peaceful solitude, a young girl is knocked unconscious by a crazy in a mask. He drags her body away, and hides it in the bushes and then ties her up. Sometime later, he returns with a lawn mower to carry out the first of a series of gruesome murders, akin to so much of the exploitation cinema of the period. Inspector James Cameron (John Smihula) is the hard-edged cop assigned to bring the girl's killer to justice. The trail leads him to a woman's decapitated head that has been discarded on a beach. When he fails to get the support he needs from his superiors, he quits the force but very soon finds himself in a descent into a deranged world of torture, slaughter and cannibalism. The masked man and his evil accomplice are chain-sawing and chopping up their victims' bodies, all of whom just happen to be young girls. Their entrails are then sold to a young man, who in turn feeds them to his cannibalistic leprous father and his flesh-eating associates. Cameron had best beware – the father is getting ever stronger by the day.

Nathan Schiff has a reputation for being a next-to-no-budget gore director, shooting his early films on Super 8 mm. To modern eyes, they appear murky, resembling the homemade films of weekend family get-togethers, which is probably all they were ever intended as being. His previous film **Weasels Rip My Flesh** (1979), made at the tender age of sixteen for just $400, was a homage to the B-movie science fiction of the 1950s; its meagre success generated just enough money to allow him to produce **The Long Island Cannibal Massacre**. There was no denying the young Schiff's enthusiasm as he combined many features of the emerging trend for slashers and threw in the splatter of Romero and Fulci's gut munching. The gratuitous gore effects were an exercise in pure imagination, using pig intestines, fish heads, and condoms. Sadly, the acting wasn't to match the director's gusto and the dialogue was at times absurd, but this was a line of horror that honoured the insane tradition of Herschell Gordon Lewis. So much so, his homemade offerings were given midnight screenings in Manhattan, where they garnered a degree of notoriety, which many years later led to his film being released to DVD. ❧

Lucker the Necrophagous

📅 YEAR OF RELEASE: 1986   🕐 RUNTIME: 74 minutes

COUNTRY: Belgium	CINEMATOGRAPHER: John Kupferschmidt
DIRECTOR: Johan Vandewoestijne	PRODUCERS: Filip Beys, André Coppens, Johan Vandewoestijne (executive producer)
PRODUCTION COMPANY: Desert Productions, V.D.S. Films	
WRITERS: Johan Vandewoestijne, John Kupferschmidt	CERTIFICATE: Australia: (Banned); Canada: 18+ (Quebec); USA: Not Rated
	BUDGET: 30,000 Francs Belgium

CAST: Nick Van Suyt, Helga Vandevelde, Let Jotts, Marie Claes, Martine Scherre, Carry Van Middel, John Edwards, Tony Castillo, Veerle Dendooven, Frans Schepens

EIGHT YEARS AGO, John Lucker went on a killing spree, claiming the lives of eight women. Soon after his capture the details of his perverse crimes were revealed, which led to a lifelong sentence in a mental facility. After a failed suicide attempt, he awakes from a coma, rapes and kills two nurses, before fleeing the private clinic in which he has been imprisoned. While on the run, he learns that one of his victims, Cathy Jordan, survived her ordeal. Lucker becomes incensed at her still being alive and the psychotic lust that left eight women for dead all those years ago once again rises to the surface. As he tries to find Cathy, he takes to killing more women, one of whom he keeps for a week before succouring his necrophilic craving. When he finally catches up with Cathy, so begins her psychological torment.

Your death is only the beginning!

Twenty-five-year-old film student Johan Vandewoestijne wasn't overly keen to divulge the true nature of his script when he looked to finance this little venture. It was hardly surprising; the repulsive John Lucker proved to be one of the sickest villains to emerge in a decade that had given birth to so many other perverted maniacs. The prolonged scenes of necrophilia detailing his violation of the putrescent slime-covered corpse were shot a full twelve months before Jörg Buttgereit paraded his hideous spectacle in the lauded **Nekromantik** (1987). Vandewoestijne's direction appeared to have an unholy delight for the maggots and worms that had buried their way into the rotting carcass, which only a week before had been an attractive young woman. This stomach-turning sequence culminated in the now infamous "finger licking good" episode that continues to both shock and amuse its audience. Vandewoestijne's film was always intended as a low-budget piece of exploitation, feverishly endeavouring to disturb with its violence and explicit displays of misogyny. The outrageous content consigned it to the world of underground cinema, a place reserved only for the most audacious in cinematic excess. **Lucker the Necrophagous** could have very easily disappeared without trace, for the producer destroyed virtually all of the negatives once the film had been completed. The original movie was considerably longer, featuring an investigative journalist who got a little too close to the Lucker mythos. Due to its sordid nature, its release to VHS was extremely limited, making it one of the most sought after collector's pieces of the period. When it was recently restored to DVD, the process proved to be extremely problematic, but the final cut has remained true to its grimy underground infamy of twenty-five years past. 🦋

Madhouse

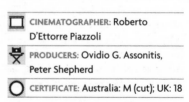

📅	YEAR OF RELEASE: 1981		🎞	CINEMATOGRAPHER: Roberto D'Ettorre Piazzoli
🕐	RUNTIME: 92 minutes			
🌐	COUNTRY: Italy		🏆	PRODUCERS: Ovidio G. Assonitis, Peter Shepherd
🎥	DIRECTOR: Ovidio G. Assonitis			
✒	WRITERS: Ovidio G. Assonitis, Stephen Blakely		⭕	CERTIFICATE: Australia: M (cut); UK: 18

CAST: Trish Everly, Michael MacRae, Dennis Robertson, Morgan Hart, Allison Biggers, Edith Ivey, Richard Baker, Don Devendorf, Jerry Fujikawa, Doug Dillingham, Joe Camp, Janie Baker, Huxsie Scott

J ULIA (TRISH EVERLY) teaches in a school for the deaf in Savannah, Georgia. As she looks forward to her twenty-fifth birthday celebrations, her hideously deformed twin sister Mary (Allison Biggers) resides in the mental ward of the nearby hospital. When they were children, Mary used to take pleasure in inflicting harm on her sister, especially on their birthday. Thankfully, the beautiful Julia has managed to come to terms with this unhappy period of her life and has since gone on to become an adored teacher at the school. With both of their parents now dead, they have only one surviving relative, their uncle, Father James. He appeals to Julia to go to see her sister, but her visit only rekindles Mary's malice and she swears to make Julia "suffer as she had suffered". Upset, Julia returns to her home, a renovated manse that has been converted into apartments. This choice of house was rather interesting, for it was actually supposed to be haunted, thus adding to the film's eerie air. When Mary escapes only days before their birthday, a succession of murders soon ensue. Her choice of weapon was somewhat different from those relished by her contemporaries, but proved just as controversial. She kept at her side a snarling Rottweiler, who gorged his victims' throats and viciously savaged their hands. The evil pet was to receive its just deserts when it burst head-first through a door to be put out of its misery by a handy power drill. The finale is remarkably similar to that observed in **Happy Birthday To Me**, the Canadian slasher released at the same time, but no one has ever been able to determine who exactly copied who.

Egyptian filmmaker Ovidio G. Assonitis's low-budget **There Was A Little Girl** is more commonly known as **Madhouse**, in addition to going by the names **And When She Was Bad** and **Party des Schreckens**, and builds on the poem "There Was a Little Girl" by Henry Wadsworth Longfellow as the premise for its narrative. The director had already acquired a reputation for producing low-budget copies of the

Many people visit … Few ever leave.

far more substantial movies, which included **Beyond the Door** (1974) inspired by **The Exorcist** (1973); similarly **The Visitor** (1979) made ample use of the **The Omen's** (1976) premise and **Tentacoli** (1977) was not unlike the celebrated box office hit **Jaws** (1975). His films may have been highly derivative, but they each saw major theatrical release and rewarded Assonitis with a success that would maintain his position in the industry. With a typically limited budget, he created a well-observed drama, enhanced by the compelling performance of the deaf children in Julia's care. The mood remained sombre and the house atmospheric, allowing Assonitis to conjure with suspense rather than the gore many enthusiasts of the day would have preferred.

Although an improvised dummy was quite often used during the Rottweiler attack scenes, the film made it to the UK list of video nasties, having been released without certification to the home video market. It was released four times on video, originally by Virgin-Label in 1984 in a heavily edited format and then again in 1989. The film's graphic content and seeming cruelty to animals ensured **Madhouse** was not to be passed without cuts in the United Kingdom until 2004. 🐾

Madman

31 YEAR OF RELEASE: 1982	**WRITERS:** Joe Giannone
RUNTIME: 88 minutes	**CINEMATOGRAPHER:** James Lemmo
COUNTRY: USA	**PRODUCERS:** Sam Marion (executive producer), Gary Sales
DIRECTOR: Joe Giannone	
PRODUCTION COMPANY: The Legend Lives Company	**CERTIFICATE:** Australia: R; Canada: 13+ (Québec); Canada: R (Ontario); UK: 18; USA: R

CAST: Gaylen Ross, Tony Fish, Harriet Bass, Seth Jones, Jan Claire, Alexander Murphy Jr., Jimmy Steele, Carl Fredericks, Michael Sullivan, Paul Ehlers, Tom Veilleux, Stephen Clark, Vicki Kenneally, Shelley Mathes, Lori Mathes

O N THE FINAL night of summer camp the counsellors and children gather around the campfire to enjoy the time-honoured practice of telling ghost stories, in a scenario very similar to **The Burning** (1981). Max, the man who runs the camp, talks of Madman Marz, a farmer who was supposed to have lived in the area. In a fit of madness he turned on his family while they slept and butchered them with an axe. After discovering his crime the locals caught up with Marz and hung him. His body, however, disappeared and, so the legend goes, when his name is called he appears armed with his trusty axe. The kids can't resist making fun of the story and call out the psychopath's name. Madman Marz we soon learn

They thought they were alone.

is something more than a legend; his disfigured presence still prowls these woods surrounding the isolated camp. It doesn't take long before counsellors are faced with mutilation and cruel slaughter. Some of the group will meet their end before the hack of his axe, while others have their heads thrust into a car engine and are decapitated by a car bonnet. Director Joe Giannone dared on this occasion to tamper with the rules by having his lead characters fall before the grunting killer, with only the rabble-rouser of the piece, Richie, surviving the grisly onslaught.

This was Joe Gianonne's one and only time in the directorial chair before moving into production. With working titles of "Madman Marz" and "The Legend Lives", he succeeded in making his film a little more than a poor man's **Friday the 13th** in the year when the slasher craze went into overdrive. Under the light of the moon he crafted an air of finality with some commendable night photography and blue-toned lighting that evoked the foreboding in these woods. The chase scene in the kitchen, culminating in a static shot focusing on Ellie's foolish attempt to hide in the fridge, would ensure his audience stayed for the duration and pass the word on so it reached its target audience. This was a low-budget feature with advertising at an absolute premium, but it went on to enjoy a cult status.

The Man From Deep River

 YEAR OF RELEASE: 1972

RUNTIME: 93 minutes

COUNTRY: Italy

DIRECTOR: Umberto Lenzi

PRODUCTION COMPANY: Medusa Produzione, Roas Produzioni

WRITERS: Francesco Barilli, Massimo D'Avak

CINEMATOGRAPHER: Riccardo Pallottini

PRODUCERS: Ovidio G. Assonitis, Giorgio Carlo Rossi (executive producer)

CERTIFICATE: Australia: R; UK: (Banned) (1984–2003); UK: 18 (2003) (heavily cut); USA: Not Rated; UK: X (original rating: 1975)

CAST: Ivan Rassimov, Me Me Lai, Prasitsak Singhara, Sulallewan Suxantat, Ong Ard, Prapas Chindang, Pipop Pupinyo, Tuan Tevan, Chit, Choi, Song Suanhud, Pairach Thaipradit

AFTER KILLING A man in self-defence in a small Thai town, photographer John Bradley (Ivan Rassimov) disappears into the rainforest to capture the wildlife and scenery in his camera's lens. His guide becomes concerned when they appear to be venturing too far up river. His trepidation is borne out when he is killed and, as Bradley awakens, he is captured in the netting of a native tribe. The natives haul him away to their village and string him up, convinced that he is a mythical fish-man. Maraya (Me Me Lai) thinks otherwise; she knows he is only a man and very soon Bradley is reduced to life as a menial slave. After killing Maraya's fiancé, Bradley escapes only to be recaptured, and his punishment begins when he is trussed up on a rotating cross with darts aimed at his exposed body. He survives his ordeal, and eventually gains the tribe's acceptance, marrying Maraya in a rather strange ceremonial ritual. Their happiness is tainted when Maraya falls ill during her pregnancy and Bradley joins the tribesmen to fend off a cannibal attack.

Umberto Lenzi's **Il Paese Del Sesso Selvaggio**, which has also gone by the names **Deep River Savages**, **Mondo Cannibale** and **Sacrifice**, unconsciously pioneered the Italian fascination for cannibal excess. This wasn't the flesh-eating exploitation that was to torment the horror movies of a few years hence; rather, Lenzi presented a well-conceived emotionally charged adventure that only resorted to the gore of cannibalism as the film came to its climactic finale. The human violence was toned down, although it would have been appreciably extreme for the

**See!
The ritual that
frees a woman
to love again!**

audiences of the day; the cruelty forced on the animals, however, would cause Lenzi's film considerable problems. This was the first of the director's trilogy of cannibal features, followed by **Eaten Alive!** (1980) and **Cannibal Ferox** (1981), and even though there was an intensity to its sex scenes it would never have been truly notorious. However, when it was submitted to the BBFC for its 1975 UK cinema release, three minutes and forty-five seconds had to be removed to those scenes involving animal cruelty. When it came uncut to video in the UK in 1982, it survived until March 1984, when it was listed as a video nasty. **The Man from Deep River** remained on the list until September 1985; over forty years after its first release in the UK, the original cuts remain in place. 🦇

Maniac

🦇 🦇 🦇 🦇

📅	YEAR OF RELEASE: 1980	📷	CINEMATOGRAPHER: Robert Lindsay
🕐	RUNTIME: 87 minutes	🎬	PRODUCERS: Andrew W. Garroni, Judd Hamilton (executive producer), William Lustig, John Packard (associate producer), Joe Spinell (executive producer)
🎥	COUNTRY: USA		
🎥	DIRECTOR: William Lustig		
🎬	PRODUCTION COMPANY: Magnum Motion Pictures Inc.		
✏️	WRITERS: C. A. Rosenberg, Joe Spinell	⭕	CERTIFICATE: Australia: (Banned) (original rating); Australia: R (cut) (1982–2004); Australia: R (uncut) (2004); Canada: 16+ (Quebec);

| Canada: 18+ (Quebec) (original rating); New Zealand: R18; UK: (Banned) (original rating); UK: 18 (video rating, cut); USA: R | **BUDGET:** $350,000
 RECEIPTS: $6,000,000 (1981) |

CAST: Joe Spinell, Caroline Munro, Abigail Clayton, Kelly Piper, Rita Montone, Tom Savini, Hyla Marrow, James Brewster, Linda Lee Walter, Tracie Evans, Sharon Mitchell, Carol Henry, Nelia Bacmeister

AN OBSCURED FIGURE watches a young couple as they frolic on the beach. When the young man goes to collect some wood, the voyeur approaches the young woman and without warning takes a razor to her throat. On his return, the young man is attacked by the same killer, who almost decapitates his prey by pulling ever so tightly on the wire that binds his neck.

Hours later, the killer, Frank Zito (Joe Spinell), awakes screaming in his sleep. This overweight Vietnam veteran lives alone in the squalor of a small, one-room apartment located somewhere in New York City. By day, he works as the landlord in a small apartment complex. His tenants have remained oblivious to his fixation for stalking and killing unsuspecting women in the darkened streets of this rundown locale. Having slain his victim, he scalps them in a sequence of vile shots using a razor and then adorns his trophy and their clothing on his bizarre assembly of lifeless mannequins. Once beautified, the mannequins are escorted to his bed, where Frank continues an ongoing conversation with his mother, who was killed in a car accident some years before. She was, in truth, an abusive prostitute whose relentless cruelty scarred her son, turning him into the unhinged killer he has now become. His collection of mannequins never quite satisfies his nonsensical needs, and after only a few nights, boredom sets in and he once again takes to the streets in search of his quarry.

Garbed in hunting gear, Frank places a shotgun in a violin case along with some ammunition and his ever-reliable razor and then steps out into the night. While driving through Brooklyn, he catches sight of an amorous couple leaving a disco to go to their car. The man (Tom Savini) and woman park up in a lot near the Verrazano Bridge and then climb into the back seat for some late-night action. As they kiss, the woman glimpses Frank's shadowed figure at the car window and urges her lover to drive her home. For them it's too late for such concerns; in a series of slow-motion frames, Frank leaps astride the bonnet and blasts the shotgun through the windscreen, blowing the man's head clean apart. The scene carries an additional degree of infamy in that it was believed to have been a simulation of the Son of Sam killings carried out by David Berkowitz between July 1976 and August 1977. With this in mind, the audience knows the woman cowering in the back seat has little chance of survival; Frank mercilessly aims the shotgun and fires. Her disco attire is later put to good use, titivating one of his beloved mannequins.

Several days later while strolling through Central Park, Frank is snapped by a fashion photographer, Anna D'Antoni (Caroline Munro). He manages to locate her address and is so astounded by the quality of her work he asks to take her out to dinner. While attending a photo shoot, Frank catches the eye of one of Anna's models, a girl name Rita. Using a ruse, he later gains entry to her home. Once inside he completely flips, referring to the bound girl as his mother then proclaiming his undying love before stabbing her through the chest. Frank hasn't finished yet; he mutilates her body and as with all of his other female victims hacks off her scalp.

While on their way to the cinema, he offers to take Anna to visit his mother's grave. Within minutes of him standing aside his mother's grave, Frank's mental state becomes a cause for serious concern. He turns and grabs Anna by the throat, but in the ensuing chase, she fights him off with a shovel and duly makes her escape. As he returns to his mother's grave, he finally succumbs to his psychosis. He has become the helpless child he once was, now confronted by his mother's abusive corpse. In a tearful state, he makes his way home only to be set upon by the mannequins who have now embodied the women he has recently murdered. They horde around Frank, clinging onto their weapons of choice and in the film's sickening finale violently stab at his stomach, dismember one of his arms and tear his head from his body, causing a visceral effusion of splatter.

The next morning two police detectives, looking to apprehend a murder suspect, force their way into Frank's apartment. They find him lying on his bed, his stomach covered in blood, the result of what looks to be a self-inflicted knife wound. His silent collection of mannequins give nothing away, giving the detectives a chance to take their leave, at which point Frank's eyes begin to open.

Run from this man!

William Lustig's **Maniac** endorsed both the slasher and splatter phenomena of its day, taking the viewer to a seedy part of New York City witnessed in so many of the period's low-budget features. His grimy take on the Big Apple complimented the degenerate nature of his film; within these seamy environs, the deranged Frank was able to accomplish his killings with unusual finesse, while his director assuredly accentuated the tension leading to the final strike. This adept pacing in those moments before the kill was essential, because this downbeat feature had such an overriding dependency on the precision of its bloodthirsty slaughter. It wasn't until the appearance of Frank's love interest Anna, well over halfway through the story, that **Maniac** at last acquired a much needed element of depth.

With the focus of his film being so reliant on the intensity of the killing, William Lustig did himself a huge favour by securing the services of one of the finest talents in the business, special effects genius Tom Savini, who developed a quite remarkable approach to enhancing the credibility of the scalping scenes. While scalping had been quite commonplace in westerns, it had never before been observed in such close detail in a horror movie. The scalpings were indeed graphic but Savini's crowning moment came with his own grisly death while sitting in the front seat of his car, which proved somewhat ironic considering the film was targeted for its vitriolic attitude towards women. The producers, however, were acutely aware of the film's contentious regard for its female cast and as a result never submitted this feature to the MPAA. They could have got into even more trouble if the crew had been discovered on the streets of New York, as they were staging many scenes guerrilla-style without having paid for the necessary permits. The infamous shotgun

sequence was but one of these scenes and was filmed in the space of a single hour.

Joe Spinell planned a sequel, **Maniac 2: Mr Robbie**, in which he hoped to play the host of a children's television show who had taken to murdering abusive parents. This telling was very similar in concept to **The Psychopath** (1975) and was probably a step too far; production was delayed on the eight-minute-long promotional video until 1986 when the golden age of the slasher movie was sadly at its end. Spinell was unable to secure the necessary financial backing and so moved on to more work. William Lustig's career was far from being over; he would continue as a director with his **Maniac Cop** series and the post-Gulf War slasher **Uncle Sam** (1997). As well as producing a whole string of documentaries, he went on to establish Blue Underground, a company that continues to distribute horror and exploitation cinema. He has never given up hope of remaking his movie, possibly with the help of a French production company. ❧

Maniac Cop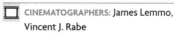

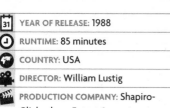

📅 YEAR OF RELEASE: 1988	🎬 CINEMATOGRAPHERS: James Lemmo, Vincent J. Rabe
⏱ RUNTIME: 85 minutes	
🌍 COUNTRY: USA	⚰ PRODUCERS: Larry Cohen, James Glickenhaus (executive producer) Jefferson Richard (co-producer)
🎥 DIRECTOR: William Lustig	
🎬 PRODUCTION COMPANY: Shapiro-Glickenhaus Entertainment	⭕ CERTIFICATE: Australia: R; Canada: 13+ (Quebec); UK: 18; USA: R
✏ WRITER: Larry Cohen	BUDGET: $1,100,000

CAST: Tom Atkins, Bruce Campbell, Laurene Landon, Richard Roundtree, William Smith, Robert Z'Dar, Sheree North, Nina Arvesen, Nick Barbaro, Lou Bonacki, Barry Brenner, Victoria Catlin, James Dixon

SOMETHING HAS GONE seriously wrong on the streets of New York; as a woman chases through the darkened streets tailed by a couple of thugs, she is murdered by the man she had looked to save her. Soon after a driver is pulled over by a policeman for ignoring a red light; his girlfriend watches in horror as his throat is slashed open and his lifeless body is hurled through the windscreen. After another chase, a handcuffed felon is left to die lying face down in wet concrete. The killer then vanishes into the night, leaving a city now in a state of panic. City Hall does all it can to assuage the public outcry by playing down these atrocious crimes and Lieutenant Frank McCrae is put in charge of the investigation. The few witnesses to these killings insist the perpetrator was a policeman and very soon suspicion falls on a young officer. Jack Forrest (Bruce Campbell) is summarily placed under arrest, having been framed by the real killer and a mysterious woman phone-caller. The murders lead to a former officer, Cordell (Robert Z'Dar), but every report shows that he was killed in prison, having been wrongfully jailed by his seniors. Somehow, he has returned to the streets to mete out his revenge, but he is also killing the innocent.

Eight years after directing **Maniac** (1980), Bronx-born William Lustig returned to the gritty streets of New York to unleash **Maniac Cop**, a pulp-styled film that was devoid of any underlying pretension, seeking only to entertain. It had been five years since he had directed his last film **Vigilante** (1983), and by 1988 New York had gone through a major clean up. Lustig, however, in another of his low-budget features presented a city still plagued by the downbeat atmosphere that had been a key element to the success of so many thrillers from the 1970s. His expert direction, particularly in the more violent encounters with Cordell and the prison flashbacks, would ensure **Maniac Cop** became another cult success, one that warranted two sequels, **Maniac Cop 2** (1990) and **Maniac Cop III: Badge of Silence** (1993), with a fourth film in the series, sadly without Robert Z'Dar, now in the planning stage. Lustig's approach perfectly suited Larry Cohen's script, which made clever use of its premise in forcing the urban paranoia that

Sometimes help can be dangerous.

permeated the Big Apple to erupt into frantic hysteria as an officer of the law shamelessly abused his power. Cohen had a considerable track record, having started scripting at the age of seventeen, and had garnered a cult status of his own after working on the hit television series *The Invaders*. Soon after he had worked his way into the director's chair on several low-budget features including **It's Alive** (1974) and **The Stuff** (1985). The imposing figure of Robert Z'Dar had started life as a keyboard player and singer for the Chicago-based rock band Nova Express, a name inspired by the 1964 novel written by William S. Burroughs. Z'Dar has never looked back, and has gone on to enjoy a long career in both film and television. ✿

Mardi Gras Massacre

📅	YEAR OF RELEASE: 1978	🎞	CINEMATOGRAPHERS: Jack McGowan, Don Piel, Jack Weis
🕐	RUNTIME: 97 minutes		
🌐	COUNTRY: USA	👤	PRODUCERS: John Stimac, Jack Weis
🎥	DIRECTOR: Jack Weis	◯	CERTIFICATE: UK: (Banned); USA: X
✎	WRITER: Jack Weis		

CAST: Curt Dawson, Gwen Arment, William Metzo, Laura Misch Owens, Cathryn Lacey, Nancy Dancer, Butch Benit, Wayne Mack, Ronald Tanet

JACK WEIS'S REMAKE of H. G. Lewis's **Blood Feast** (1963) begins with a well-dressed man entering a hip nightclub. He meets up with the most "evil" woman in the place and after a brief conversation escorts her to his apartment. Once in the privacy of his home, this intense-looking individual takes her into a room with a view to engaging in something rather "special". When the viewer gets to see the room, it resembles a temple of satanic worship, but this leaves little impression on his female acquaintance. She still doesn't flinch when he enters the room garbed in an elaborate Aztec-styled mask, and happily strips to lie naked on the bed; in her line of trade she's no doubt seen it all. Her host begins to massage her body, arousing her into a state of ecstasy before tying her down. He then takes hold of a dagger and stabs her in the hand, for it has taken money for evil means; then she is stabbed through the soles of her feet before being finally disembowelled. Shortly after, we meet the detectives who are assigned to bringing this crazed killer to justice. One of them has a thing for prostitutes. It is he who will put an end to these ritualistic murders, as he chases through the New Orleans Mardi Gras in the hope of bringing down this mad man, who offers his victims to an Aztec goddess in the belief she will bequeath him god-like status.

In Weis's telling of Lewis's original story an Aztec high priest takes the place of Fuad, the infamous Egyptian killer, and places the groundbreaking excess of fifteen years past in the unique milieu of low-budget shock movies of the 1970s. The director returned to the Louisiana of his last film, **Crypt of Dark Secrets** (1976), and blended virtually every ingredient of exploitation the decade had to offer: inept acting, the disco beat, exotic dancers, wicked hookers, girl fights, nudity, bondage, torture,

> **Everyone is celebrating; nobody hears the screams of the victims for the sacrifice.**

amusing dialogue and then the requisite blood and guts along with the obligatory disembowelment. While there were killings aplenty, they showed a complete lack of imagination as this sadistic murderer adopted the same routine for each of his victims. **Mardi Gras Massacre** has been understandably accused of being a misogynistic piece of trash in its relish for female mutilation with the cast never given the opportunity to redeem themselves. The sleaze factor typically attracted the attention of the DPP when it was released to video in 1982. While it is widely available in the United States, it is yet to see official distribution in the UK. For Weis this would be his last time in the director's chair, just as the golden age of the slasher was about to dawn.

Martyrs

YEAR OF RELEASE: 2008		**WRITER:** Pascal Laugier	

 RUNTIME: 99 minutes

COUNTRY: France/Canada

CINEMATOGRAPHERS: Stéphane Martin, Nathalie Moliavko-Visotzky, Bruno Philip

 DIRECTOR: Pascal Laugier

PRODUCTION COMPANY: Canal Horizons, Canal+, CinéCinéma, Eskwad, TCB Film, Wild Bunch

PRODUCERS: Frédéric Doniguian (executive producer), Marcel Giroux (executive producer), Richard Grandpierre, Simon Trottier

○ CERTIFICATE: Australia: R; Canada: 18+ (Quebec); Canada: R (Alberta/British Columbia/Manitoba/Nova Scotia/Ontario); New Zealand: R18; UK: 18;

USA: NC-17 (original rating); USA: R (edited version); USA: Unrated (uncut)

$ BUDGET: $6,500,000

CAST: Morjana Alaoui, Mylène Jampanoï, Catherine Bégin, Robert Toupin, Patricia Tulasne, Juliette Gosselin, Xavier Dolan, Isabelle Chasse, Emilie Miskdjian, Mike Chute, Gaëlle Cohen, Anie Pascale, Jessie Pham, Erika Scott

A YOUNG GIRL, LUCIE, is seen escaping from an abandoned warehouse where she has been imprisoned and tortured following her kidnap some time ago. With the authorities unable to identify her captors, she is summarily placed into care. There she meets a young girl named Anna, who learns that Lucie is haunted by the figure of a horribly emaciated woman.

The film jumps forward fifteen years to see Lucie bursting into a family home, brandishing a shotgun, which she engages to send each one of them to the grave. She then contacts Anna to inform her that she has caught up with those who abused her as a child and now needs help to dispose of the bodies. When she meets up with her friend, Anna is plagued by very grave misgivings, fearing that Lucie may have slaughtered a family of innocents. Soon after, Lucie is again accosted by the scarred woman who has tormented her nightmares. Anna watches as her troubled friend fights alone, banging her head against the wall and gashing herself with a knife. Lucie continues in her struggle, pleading with the unseen figure and begging forgiveness for having left her behind all those years ago. Even though she has avenged their

maltreatment, she realizes she will never be free of this anguished image and takes a blade to her own throat.

The following day a distraught Anna sets about cleaning the house and after finding a concealed cellar makes a shocking discovery. Hidden in the shadows is a blindfolded woman with a metal contraption riveted into her head. She attempts to free her and cleanse her wounds, but as she does so she is interrupted by a band of strangers, who arrive and shoot the woman. Anna is then hauled away to meet their leader, an elderly woman they call Mademoiselle. The woman is a member of a covert group seeking to discover the truth about life after death using subjects she terms martyrs. These martyrs are tortured in the mistaken belief that their suffering will provide a view into the next life. However, their cruel experimentation has so far failed. Anna is now imprisoned and brutalized. In her suffering she sees Lucie, who tells her she must "let go"; only then will she be free of the fear of pain and death. Anna has progressed further than those who came before her and after surviving being flayed to the point of near death, she whispers the innermost secrets of her ordeal into the

Mademoiselle's ear. The old woman now summons the members of the society in what will be a shocking finale.

Pascal Laugier wrote the script for this shocking experience while enduring a fit of deep depression; its bleak landscape attests to his troubled state of mind. **Martyrs** has been compared to much of the torture porn of the past ten years, particularly blockbusters such as **Saw** (2004) and **Hostel** (2005). However, this film owes more to the French Extreme Wave of the past decade, which includes cinematic masterpieces such as **Sombre** (1998), **Irreversible** (2002), **13 Tzameti** (2005), **Haute Tension** (2003), **À L'Intérieur** (2007) and **Frontier(s)** (2007), each of which fail to attain the recognition they so truly deserve. These films, along with **Martyrs**, do not intend to seek merely to entertain with their effusion of visceral nastiness; rather, they indeed evoke a gut reaction but frequently appear distanced from their grisly subject matter. In a similar way to his contemporaries, Laugier challenges the existing boundaries of filmmaking and as those before him steadily pushes them further back. The early part of this feature plays out as an extreme tale of revenge set against an unforgiving backdrop while using a ghostly figure to torment an already deeply disturbed lead character. Then Laugier subtly turns his film, edging between nihilism and a paltry chance of salvation. The torture themes of **Saw** and **Hostel** are taken to extremes for these villains are truly detached, seeking only to further their own misguided scientific research. There is nothing in the slightest way of titillation on show here; rather, the lasting impression is one of sadness. As soon as Anna has been introduced to the Mademoiselle, the narrative becomes dispassionate, making it so much more disturbing than its predecessors and as with all contentious filmmaking will continue to divide its audience.

Laugier, a young director who owes so much of his inspiration to Dario Argento, is now looking to build on the success of his controversial **Martyrs** and his earlier terror, **Sainte Ange** (2004), with an American-produced version of this film, which may not be quite as dark as the original.

They did not finish to be alive . . .

Microwave Massacre

31 YEAR OF RELEASE: 1983

RUNTIME: 76 minutes

COUNTRY: USA

DIRECTOR: Wayne Berwick

WRITERS: Craig Muckler (story),
Thomas Singer (screenplay)

CINEMATOGRAPHER: Karen Grossman

PRODUCERS: Craig Muckler, Thomas
Singer

CERTIFICATE: USA: Unrated

CAST: Jackie Vernon, Loren Schein, Al Troupe, Marla Simon, Claire Ginsberg, Lou Ann Webber, Anna Marlowe, Cindy Gant, Susie Grubb, Sarah Alt, Karen Marshall, Phil De Carlo, Aaron Koslow, Ed Thomas, John Harmon, Norman Friedman

BY 1983, THE microwave cooker was becoming increasingly popular in kitchens across the globe; it was only going to be a matter of time before the slasher and splatter generation included them on their inventory of murderous implements. **Microwave Massacre**'s principal selling point has been its assertion to being the worst horror movie of all time, which, given some of the disasters we have all endured in this domain of cinema macabre, makes for quite a claim. Wayne's Berwick's deliberately inept direction introduces Donald (Jackie Vernon), who works by day as a labourer in the construction industry. Poor Donald has had enough of his domineering wife May's (Claire Ginsberg) flamboyant culinary skills, craving only the basic sustenance relished by your ordinary average guy. After a night on the beer, he finally snaps and puts an end to her nagging ways. He sets about chopping her into pieces and then conceals her dismembered, foil-wrapped body parts in the freezer. Sometime later, he helps himself to a snack from the fridge and inadvertently picks up her severed hand. Before he realizes it, he has popped the hand into the over-sized microwave, which was one of his wife's many purchases. It doesn't take long to heat up and as soon as he has savoured his wife's flesh he becomes hooked and his newfound cannibalistic urge comes to the fore. Licking his lips, he goes off in search of something younger and more succulent. It's all too easy; he lures a gamut of hookers and lusty good-time girls back to his place for sex and a spot of microwave home-cooking. He gets such a taste for these juicy morsels he can't resist inviting his pals Philip (Al Troupe) and Roosevelt (Loren Schein) over to share in the fun. As this gastronomic excess comes to an end, Donald's house is shown with a "For Sale" sign, with an electrician busying himself on the much used culinary implement. The camera then draws in to focus on the fridge, revealing May's eyes radiating an incandescent orange.

The voice of Frosty the Snowman was given the chance to return to his comedic roots, as Jackie Vernon savoured every moment of Donald's relentless assault of ridiculous one-liners. Donald has since acquired a cult following thanks to this feature, which was designed solely to reduce its audience into fits of laughter.

There's an eyeful of gratuitous nudity, gore effects that will have you in hysterics along with yet another disco soundtrack. **Microwave Massacre** can certainly lay claim to being so bad it is actually good!

Mortuary

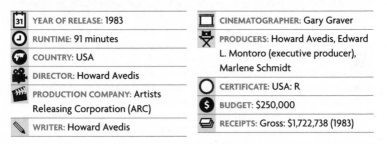

YEAR OF RELEASE: 1983	**CINEMATOGRAPHER:** Gary Graver
RUNTIME: 91 minutes	**PRODUCERS:** Howard Avedis, Edward L. Montoro (executive producer), Marlene Schmidt
COUNTRY: USA	
DIRECTOR: Howard Avedis	**CERTIFICATE:** USA: R
PRODUCTION COMPANY: Artists Releasing Corporation (ARC)	**BUDGET:** $250,000
WRITER: Howard Avedis	**RECEIPTS:** Gross: $1,722,738 (1983)

CAST: Mary Beth McDonough, David Wallace, Bill Paxton, Lynda Day George, Christopher George, Curt Ayers, Bill Conklin, Donna Garrett, Greg Kaye, Denis Mandel, Violet Manes, Alvy Moore, Danny Rogers, Beth Scheffell, Marlene Schmidt

A COUPLE OF TROUBLEMAKERS return to the local mortuary, from where one of them has just been fired. Down in the basement they hear voices and try to find out more, only to stumble upon a black magic ritual arranged by Hank Andrews (Christopher George), the mortuary's owner. In the ensuing panic, they become separated and one of them is killed by a fiend adorned in a long robe, whose make-up would one day resemble the mask in Wes Craven's **Scream** (1996).

Christie Parson (Mary Beth McDonaugh) has been plagued by nightmares and bouts of sleepwalking ever since her father's (Danny Rogers) supposed accidental death. Contrary to her mother Eve's (Lynda Day George) belief, Christie is sure he was murdered. She is also plagued by the image of a figure wearing a cloak bearing an embalming trocar, but in her frantic state of mind no one is prepared to believe her. This changes when her boyfriend (David Wallace), seen entering the mortuary at the beginning of the film, actually catches sight of the imposing figure. The two take it on themselves to investigate further and Christie makes the shocking discovery her mother is implicated in a witches' coven. Their search leads to Hank Andrews' mortuary and his crazed son, Paul (Bill Paxton), who conceals a dark secret. As the killer stalks the town, with his over-sized embalming needle, so the victims begin to fall to the soothing sound of Mozart.

Where nobody rests in peace.

Mortuary was also known as **Embalmed** in the United Kingdom and was one of eleven films directed by Howard Avedis in a fourteen-year run that began in 1972. He had made his reputation as a low-budget exploitation director and on this outing brought the wholesome Mary Beth McDonough, who up until a few years before had been gainfully employed as Erin in the long-running television series **The Waltons**, to his world of sleaze. While **Mortuary** has been accepted as a slasher movie, it didn't quite adhere to the recognized formula; the victims were not directly associated with the heroine and the killer's identity was disclosed halfway through the film. While his feature wasn't to be reliant on gore, it did create a sense of intrigue for the first hour of its running time and true to Avedis's previous work presented plenty of bare-breasted young girls, some of which weren't always alive. His cinematographer for this film was the prolific Gary Graver, who had been a protégé of Orson Wells; his ever-changing career took him from the echelons of high art to the world of shady pornography. He professed he knew "how to make a movie without much money", which made him very good company for Avedis.

Mother's Day

 YEAR OF RELEASE: 1980

 RUNTIME: 90 minutes

 COUNTRY: USA

 DIRECTOR: Charles Kaufman

 PRODUCTION COMPANY: Duty Productions, Saga Films, Troma Entertainment

 WRITERS: Charles Kaufman, Warren Leight

 CINEMATOGRAPHER: Joseph Mangine

PRODUCERS: Alexander Beck (executive producer), Michael Herz (associate producer), Charles Kaufman, Lloyd Kaufman (associate producer), Michael Kravitz

CERTIFICATE: Australia: (Banned) (1985 re-rating) Australia: R (original rating) Canada: R (Manitoba/Ontario) UK: 18 USA: Unrated

 BUDGET: $150,000

CAST: Nancy Hendrickson, Deborah Luce, Tiana Pierce, Frederick Coffin, Michael McCleery, Beatrice Pons, Robert Collins, Peter Fox, Marsella Davidson, Kevin Lowe, Scott Lucas, Ed Battle

THREE YOUNG WOMEN, Abbey (Nancy Hendrickson), Jackie (Deborah Luce) and Trina (Tiana Pierce), get together each year and take off for a weekend of camping, deep in the wilderness. In a series of flashbacks, we are given excerpts of their lives, making the traumatic events that soon follow all the more harrowing. The area is almost deserted, except for one cabin occupied by a domineering mother (Rose Ross) and her halfwit offspring, Ike (Holdem McGuire) and Addley (Billy Ray McQuade). When they are not savouring the oracle of television and modern-day consumer goods, their maniac mother sends her sons into the woods to train for combat, for she lives in fear of her equally twisted sister Queenie, who lives a similarly reclusive life somewhere in the forest. Their way of life thrives on the kidnap of hitchhikers and backpackers with mother inciting her sons into acts of rape, violence and murder. When the girls are captured Jackie is systematically brutalized and doesn't survive for more than a night. Her friends manage to escape and vow a vicious revenge on the dysfunctional family, one that will witness death by television.

After a short spell learning his trade on the periphery of soft-core porn movies, Charles Kaufman turned to the potentially profitable exploitation shocker. **Mother's Day** was a low-budget backwoods rape and revenge movie, which followed in the path of the seminal **Deliverance** (1972) and then used the driving force that impelled the controversial **Last House on the Left** (1972) and Meir Zarchi's **I Spit on Your Grave** (1978) to their violent finales. His movie was made considerably more disturbing by the presence of the deranged mother and his staging of some of the excess away from the prying eyes of his audience, leaving certain more gratuitous scenes to the imagination viewer. There was also an element of very dark satire in its social commentary on consumerism, which was rarely ever ventured in such manipulative features. For what was in essence a sleaze-fuelled horror movie, his film did contain very reasonable character development, which would lead to a successful decade writing for low-budget films

> **I'm so proud of my boys. They never forget their momma.**

and then national television shows. In a remarkable change of career, he established the highly respected bakery and cafe Bread and Cie in San Diego and later joined the Board of the California Restaurant Association.

When **Mother's Day** was presented to the BBFC in December 1980, it was banned from sale in the UK; it has yet to see a certified release on these shores. In 2010, a remake of Kaufman's film starring Rebecca de Mornay was completed and released to cinemas in April 2011; the former director and his associate producer brother Lloyd were invited to make cameo appearances.

Murder-Set-Pieces

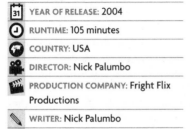

📅 YEAR OF RELEASE: 2004	
🕐 RUNTIME: 105 minutes	
🌐 COUNTRY: USA	
🎥 DIRECTOR: Nick Palumbo	
🎬 PRODUCTION COMPANY: Fright Flix Productions	
✏️ WRITER: Nick Palumbo	
🎞️ CINEMATOGRAPHER: Brendan Flynt	

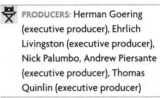

PRODUCERS: Herman Goering (executive producer), Ehrlich Livingston (executive producer), Nick Palumbo, Andrew Piersante (executive producer), Thomas Quinlin (executive producer)

CERTIFICATE: Canada: 18A (Ontario); Ireland: (Banned); UK: (Banned); USA: Unrated (director's cut); USA: R

BUDGET: $2,000,000

CAST: Sven Garrett, Tony Todd, Cerina Vincent, Gunnar Hansen, Edwin Neal, Jade Risser, Valerie Baber, Destiny St Claire, Maria Keough, Renee Sloan, Lauren Palac, Andrea Mitchell, Jessie DeRoock, LeAnn Clinton, Shandee Lang

FLASHBULBS ILLUMINATE THE corpse of a naked woman. We are then introduced to the muscle-bound photographer (Sven Garret) who by day adopts a role as a fashion photographer and spends time with his attractive girlfriend Charlotte (Valerie Baber). However, when night falls he takes to the neon-lit streets of Las Vegas, kidnapping, raping, torturing and murdering naked women, most of them strippers and prostitutes. In a repeat of **Maniac**'s Frank Zito, the photographer also has had a troubled relationship with his mother; this unhappy childhood becomes an excuse for his gratuitous relish for dehumanizing women. Director Nick Palumbo tries to weave the 9/11 psychosis as an added justification for what is nothing more than a sexploitation flick, harking back to the excess of the grindhouse years. The story comes alive when the suspicions of Charlotte's younger sister Jade (Jade Risser) are aroused and so begins a familiar game of cat and mouse.

The film's excessive bloodlust and unrelenting violence towards women would guarantee its ban in many countries across the globe. When submitted for release in the United Kingdom, the BBFC refused to grant it an "18" certificate, thus making it illegal on these shores. They were adamant in their rejection, referencing its sexual violence and violation of UK obscenity laws. In the United States, it saw release to select theatres with an NC-17 certification. When issued on DVD by Lionsgate, it attracted an "R" rating with approximately twenty-two minutes of cuts, removing a series of intense sexually violent and torturous scenes. During filming the police were called out several times for alleged disturbances and Palumbo was almost arrested when one film-processing laboratory became concerned they had in their possession a snuff movie and scenes of child abuse. Three film-processing labs refused to take on this film. Even though surrounded by the kind of controversy that makes such films legendry, and having mustered a two million dollar budget, there are those who would still place Palumbo's misguided effort among the worst splatter films to see the light of day. ❧

The most visceral horror film ever made.

The Mutilator

📅 YEAR OF RELEASE: 1985		🎬 CINEMATOGRAPHER: Peter Schnall	
🕐 RUNTIME: 86 minutes		Producer: Buddy Cooper	
🎥 COUNTRY: USA		⭕ CERTIFICATE: Australia: R (cut); UK: 18 (cut); USA: R	
🎥 DIRECTOR: Buddy Cooper			
✏️ WRITER: Buddy Cooper		💲 BUDGET: $450,000	

CAST: Matt Mitler, Ruth Martinez, Bill Hitchcock, Connie Rogers, Frances Raines, Morey Lampley, Jack Chatham, Ben Moore, Trace Cooper, Pamela Weddle Cooper, Jimmy Guthrie, George Sutton, Steve Davis, Tom Outlaw, Pat Jordon

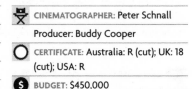

AFTER SEVEN YEARS of constant slash and stalk, the novice Buddy Cooper came up with a highly original premise for his movie. Young Ed is seen diligently working away cleaning his father's rifles; unbeknown to him one of them is loaded and he accidentally fires, killing his mother. When his father arrives home in anticipation of his birthday celebrations, he finds his wife lying dead on the floor and flies into an uncontrollable rage. He picks up one of his shotguns and points it at his terrified son, forcing Ed to flee the family home. The disturbed father takes a bottle of whisky, pours some of it into his wife's mouth and then downs the rest. Ten years later young Ed is a teenage college student and the events that follow adhere very closely to what was by then the firmly established slasher trope. He receives a letter from his father telling him that he needs to go over to their beach house to lock it up for the winter months. Ed thinks this would be a good opportunity for him and his girlfriend, along with two other young couples, to have a few days of fun and relaxation. What Ed doesn't know is just how deranged his heavy breathing father has become, still dreaming of slicing open his son's throat. When the kids get to the beach house, the unforgiving father is lying in wait armed with an axe, pitchfork, chainsaw and numerous fishing hooks. His victims will soon find their heads impaled as trophies as the last girl struggles to get

Their horrifying vacation was no day at the beach!

the car started with daddy descending to remove her head.

Buddy Cooper seemed to take an age in building his characters in a screenplay he admits in hindsight could have done so much better, but his team successfully generated an unsettling atmosphere that would on more than one occasion have their audience jump out of their seats. Cooper was the man who just wouldn't give up; at the time he was practising law and along with a friend came to realize that making a horror movie could be a worthwhile money-spinner. The original estimate for the movie was $84,000, but the costs on what was still a low-budget feature spiralled to $450,000, with Cooper's bank taking a considerable risk in loaning him much of the balance. The shoot took twenty-nine days with an invaluable six months in post-production, which would give this movie a very polished appearance, although Cooper knew nothing about this stage of the editing process. The Mutilator has since been remembered for Mark Shostrom's gruesome effects, particularly the bloody decapitation and one of the girls being impaled by a huge fish hook, which was edited following the film's submission to the BBFC for its release to video in 1993; this would be waived when it was re-submitted ten years later. Only five years into his career, Shostrom would continue to develop as a special effects make-up artist, to make him one of the industry's most sought after creators. ❦

My Bloody Valentine

 **YEAR OF RELEASE:** 1981	**CINEMATOGRAPHER:** Rodney Gibbons
RUNTIME: 90 minutes	**PRODUCERS:** John Dunning, André Link, Stephen A. Miller, Lawrence Nesis (executive producer), Bob Presner (line producer)
COUNTRY: Canada	
DIRECTOR: George Mihalka	
PRODUCTION COMPANY: Canadian Film Development Corporation (CFDC), Famous Players, Paramount Pictures	**CERTIFICATE:** Australia: R; New Zealand: R16; UK: 15 (video re-rating, 2003); UK: 18 (video rating, 1989); UK: X (original rating); USA: R
WRITERS: Stephen A. Miller (story), John Beaird	**BUDGET:** $2,300,000 Canadian
	RECEIPTS: $6,000,000 (1981)

CAST: Paul Kelman, Lori Hallier, Neil Affleck, Keith Knight, Alf Humphreys, Cynthia Dale, Helene Udy, Rob Stein, Thomas Kovacs, Terry Waterland, Carl Marotte, Jim Murchison, Gina Dick, Peter Cowper, Don Francks

ORIGINALLY ENTITLED THE Secret, My Bloody Valentine followed the slasher trend for seasonal holidays, on this occasion beginning in 1961 in the isolated town of Valentine Bluffs. Five miners were trapped in a shaft following a methane gas explosion, doomed by the foremen, who left early to attend the town's Valentine's Day dance. Six weeks later Harry Warden was pulled out alive; having survived on the flesh of his dead colleagues. The torment had driven him to insanity, leading to him being sectioned to a mental institution. Twelve months later, he escaped to attend the Valentine's Day dance. There, he killed the negligent foremen, warning that if

the town ever again held a Valentine's Day dance he would make another return.

Twenty years later with the legend of Harry Warden all but forgotten, some young miners and their girlfriends make plans for a Valentine's Day party. However, as the night of the dance draws near a figure wearing mining gear, pickaxe in hand, creeps into town with bloody murder in mind. The town sheriff and mayor still remember Harry Warden, but are unable to confirm his whereabouts. Finally, on the night of the dance the miner appears and so begins the killing spree. Amidst the mayhem, the party continues into the mine, with the miner in pursuit. It is now we learn that Harry Warden has been dead for more than five years.

When the slaughter begins, it is graphic to say the least, which is why this low-budget cult movie has attracted so much controversy. For the gore-monger it is the rarest of treats, with a misogynistic pickaxe point lunged at a woman's breast and resultant copious flow of blood, along with later shots of a man stabbed up beneath his chin with the pickaxe which then pops out of his eyeball before it projects its socket. Among the many well-handled point-of-view shots, a scalding scene is detailed depicting a face starting to blister while submersed in a pot, in addition to a shocking nail gun to the head. Let's not forget the imaginative impalement scenes using a pointed shower pipe driven through the back of a girl's head and the double death drill bit.

The unmasking of the killer at the finale by the heroine Sarah reveals one of the characters central to the tale: Axel is the deranged killer. A flashback reveals that all those years ago he witnessed Harry Warden's murder of his father, who was one of the offending foremen. When the ceiling collapses, Axel is buried alive. In the restored version, he is shown slicing off his own arm to make his escape before running deeper into the mine calling out to Harry Warden, and warning

This Valentine's Day, romance is DEAD.

that he'll be back. As the screen turns to darkness, the audience can hear the sound of Harry Warden's insane laughter, which abruptly comes to an end as the credits begin to roll.

My Bloody Valentine remains one of the most underrated slasher pictures of the period, although it retains an element of notoriety due to the nine minutes of cuts demanded by the MPAA owing to its violence and gore. This severe editing would inevitably detract from the film's impact, because it was a simple story, which relied heavily on the edits that had been made to its violent excess. There was absolutely nothing unusual about bloodthirsty cinema at this time, but it has been suggested that Paramount Pictures were insistent the footage they deemed to be more extreme should be removed due to the backlash they had already endured with **Friday the 13th**. Director George Mihalka alluded to another reason for the storm that raged over movie violence in general: the murder of John Lennon in December 1980. Rumours were rife that the film had been later issued uncut as a video to the Japanese market. However, Mihalka has always firmly refuted such claims. When Lionsgate secured DVD rights to the film they restored about three and half minutes on its release in early 2009. ❧

The Nail Gun Massacre

📅 YEAR OF RELEASE: 1985	🎞 CINEMATOGRAPHER: Bill Leslie
⏱ RUNTIME: 85 minutes	🎬 PRODUCERS: Linda Bass (executive producer), Joann Hazelbarth (line producer), T. L. Lofton (executive producer), Terry Lofton
🌐 COUNTRY: USA	
📹 Directors: Bill Leslie, Terry Lofton	
🎬 PRODUCTION COMPANY: Futuristic Films	⭕ CERTIFICATE: Australia: R; USA: Not Rated
✎ WRITER: Terry Lofton	💲 BUDGET: $50,000

CAST: Rocky Patterson, Ron Queen, Beau Leland, Michelle Meyer, Sebrina Lawless, Monica Lawless, Jerry Nelson, Mike Coady, Staci Gordon, Randy Hayes, Thom Meyers, John Price, Charles Ladeate, Joann Hazelbarth, Frances Heard

WHEN TERRY LOFTON and Bill Leslie joined forces to create The Nail Gun Massacre, the slasher movie had almost had its day with the sun setting on what had been a veritable golden age of hack and slash. There was, however, an ever-growing video market upon which they could pin their hopes. In the opening shots of their film, whose title is highly evocative of Tobe Hooper's chainsaw-wielding terror, a girl is raped and many years later a killer garbed in a black motorbike helmet and camouflage gear stalks a small town armed with a nail gun and makes his getaways in a gold-coloured hearse. When he speaks his voice sounds robotic and he is prone to the nuances of a Fred Kreuger-styled wit as he readily terminates his victims. As the body count grows (it will reach fifteen before the end of the film), a dismayed Sheriff, Thomas (Ron Queen), sets out to track down the elusive killer and enlists the assistance of his friend Doc James (Rocky Patterson). They learn that those who have suffered at the hands of this nail gun assassin, among whom are a man who takes a nail to the crotch and a couple of girls who have their breasts impaled, have a connection with a reported rape case of many years past. As the sheriff and the doctor

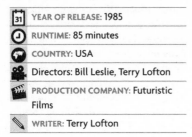

A very penetrating story!

try to keep his potential victims safe from harm, they set themselves up for a surprise when the identity of the killer is revealed just before he literally walks off into the sunset.

Lofton had worked for Warner Brothers on the **Dukes of Hazzard** television show, and while he was eager to make a film, he had precious little in the way of movie-making experience. Bill Leslie already had a production company, so the two got together to work on Lofton's eighty-page script, soon to be reduced to twenty-five. The actors were only given the revised script on the day of the shoot, which meant there was a considerable amount of improvisation. This was seat-of-the-pants low-budget filmmaking with a few porn scenes thrown in for good measure and the killer's two stunt doubles were noticeably of entirely different builds. To keep the expenses down, Lofton brought his grandmother in to play the old dear in the shop and played the part of a truck driver himself. However, he did take his time in hiring the topless girl from a number of gentlemen's clubs in the area. This is far from being a classic of B-cinema, but its haphazard filming continues to attract new viewers.

Nattevagten

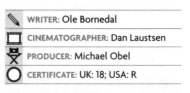

📅 YEAR OF RELEASE: 1994		✏️ WRITER: Ole Bornedal
⏱️ RUNTIME: 107 minutes		🎞️ CINEMATOGRAPHER: Dan Laustsen
🌐 COUNTRY: Denmark		🎬 PRODUCER: Michael Obel
🎥 DIRECTOR: Ole Bornedal		⭕ CERTIFICATE: UK: 18; USA: R
🎞️ PRODUCTION COMPANY: Thura Film		

CAST: Nikolaj Coster-Waldau, Sofie Gråbøl, Kim Bodnia, Lotte Andersen, Ulf Pilgaard, Rikke Louise Andersson, Stig Hoffmeyer, Gyrd Løfquist, Niels Anders Thorn, Leif Adolfsson, Henrik Fiig, Jesper Hyldegaard, Ulrich Thomsen, Christian Friis, Peter Rygaard

MARTIN (NIKOLAJ COSTER-Waldau) couldn't have chosen a worse time to take on the position as a night watchman in the city mortuary, taking on the role to help pay his way through law school. Soon after he begins his new job, the scalped victim of a serial killer is brought in. This will be the first of many young prostitutes under Martin's watch. As the list of victims begins to grow, he continues to endure a troublesome relationship with his girlfriend (Sofie Gråbøl), mostly down to his own shortcomings, and plays a dangerous game of chance with his friend (Kim Bodnia). Alone in the mortuary, the atmosphere becomes more intense as Martin stares at his reflection in a darkened window and he prepares himself to enter the poorly lit room full of corpses and confront a body that keeps moving around. An unusual relationship begins to develop between Martin and the detective investigating these hideous crimes, Peter Wörmer (Ulf Pilgaard), but when one of the victims in the morgue is molested, Martin immediately falls under suspicion. This leads to a shocking twist just before **Nightwatch** meets with its deathly finale.

Humorist, television writer and stage director, Ole Bornedal made quite an impact with his stylish thriller **Nattevagten**, which was later released in the UK as **Nightwatch**. This was an astonishing debut, which was to suggest comparisons with the celebrated work of Alfred Hitchcock. In keeping with one of the grand masters of twentieth-century cinema, Bornedal meticulously elaborated his intricate plot and made use of virtually every single element referenced in the film's opening scenes before expanding upon them and then introducing more than an occasional red herring. In a series of spine-tingling sequences, he heightened the air of suspense and introduced a humour of the darkest kind with cruel intimations of necrophilia. He had at his behest an excellent cast, who may not have been known outside their native Denmark but were revealed as an amiable well-defined bunch, each with their own particular eccentricities of character. Bonedal didn't hurl bucket loads of guts onto his set, but his film's few bloodthirsty moments were quite disturbing and left an impression on the audience. Three years later, he would direct an inferior American remake starring Ewan McGregor before returning to Scandinavian filmmaking, where his unique talent appears most appreciated. 🌟

Nekromantik

📅	YEAR OF RELEASE: 1987	🎞 PHOTOGRAPHER: Uwe Bohrer
⏱	RUNTIME: 75 minutes	⭕ CERTIFICATE: Australia: Refused Classification; Canada: 18+ (Quebec); Canada: (Banned) (Nova Scotia/Ontario); USA: Not Rated
🐗	COUNTRY: Germany	
🎥	DIRECTOR: Jörg Buttgereit	
✎	WRITERS: Jörg Buttgereit, Franz Rodenkirchen	💲 PRODUCER: Manfred O. Jelinski

CAST: Bernd Daktari Lorenz, Beatrice Manowski, Harald Lundt, Colloseo Schulzendorf, Henri Boeck, Clemens Schwender, Jörg Buttgereit, Holger Suhr, Volker Hauptvogel, Harald Weis, Heike Surban, Patricia Leipold, Elke Fuchs, Margit Im Schlaa, Suza Kohlstedt

NEKROMANTIK OPENS WITH a close-up of a woman urinating. Minutes later, the same woman and her husband plough headlong into a fatal crash. The next day the street-cleaning team, among them the surreally deranged Robert Schmadtke, arrive on the scene to wash away their remains. When he arrives home his girlfriend, Betty, is relaxing in the bath, immersed in blood-stained water. As she bathes, Robert amuses himself with his collection of preserved human body parts and daydreams of a rabbit's slaughter, which will become significant in the closing moments of what is an illusory finale.

Elsewhere in another accident, a man is killed by his neighbour, who then seeks to dispose of the evidence. When his body is later uncovered, it is in a terrible state of decay. The same gang of street cleaners are once again summoned, and later on as the crew pack up for the day Robert absconds with the corpse. On his return home, he presents Betty with a hideous homecoming gift, which throws her into absolute delight. The corpse's woeful decomposition is just perfect for this particular couple, who can now take pleasure in their bizarre fantasies and savour the succulence of an eyeball as it reels in its socket. In their sexually charged elation, they hack off a chair leg and Betty sinks it with such gusto

Death is just the beginning!

into the cadaver's crotch. Rolling a condom over the chair leg, she eases herself onto the corpse's magnificent phallus, and then slowly kisses its emaciated face with Robert similarly wrapped in the perverse ecstasy of the moment.

As Betty luxuriates in the arms of her newfound lover, their world of necrophilic nirvana is brought to an unceremonious end when Robert is sacked from his job. The despondent necrophile now has to return home to tell his lover of this appalling state of affairs. Betty is a woman scorned and in her rage takes off with the randy corpse. Alone in the flat Robert takes his frustration out on the cat and is later seen bathing in blood, as a battered furry carcass hangs from the wall. Following an altercation at the cinema, our lovelorn hero attempts to commit suicide with a lethal cocktail of whiskey and pills. Unconscious, he dreams of rebirth from within a plastic bag, and a life as a corpse in which a girl presents him with a severed head.

Aroused by the intensity of his hallucinations, he engages a prostitute, who he escorts to the cemetery. Try as he might, he cannot become sexually aroused, and in the ensuing struggle throttles the life out of her. As the girl lies dead at a graveside, he mounts her and enjoys the sexual gratification he so truly desired. He awakens to find her body at his side and an ageing gravedigger standing over them. Snatching his shovel, he decapitates the old-timer, leaving only his jaw hanging onto his crumpling torso. The scene shifts to reveal the screaming Robert sprinting along the coast, chasing all the way to the finale. Alone in his apartment, he craves that one last thrill and grabbing hold of a knife he thrusts it ever deeper into his bowels, thus intensifying the thrill of his ejaculatory death throes. As he departs this world, he is once again visited by the vision of the slaughter of the rabbit, now shown in reverse. Even in death, Robert will not find peace, for there are plans afoot for his corpse. A shovel is seen removing the soil from his grave, carried by a person wearing lady's slippers.

Jörg Buttgereit's noiresque blend of love, despair and necrophilia came only twelve months after Johan Vandewoestijne's underground **Lucker the Necrophagous**. In a similar way to its Belgian predecessor, its flagrant violation of one of the age-old taboos made it the source of much discord.

Although banned in a number of countries, its outlandish dalliance between art house and gore would acquire a dedicated following which later inspired Buttgereit's documentary **Corpse Fucking Art** and then led to a sequel with **Nekromantik 2: The Return of the Loving Death** in 1991.

The grainy, low-budget tone shot on 8-mm film stock disguised many of the shortcomings with the corpse scenes but combined with a minimalist score to exacerbate the shock content of what was always going to be an underground film. There is a depraved sickness to the proceedings, but there are those who believe that this black comedy carries serious social commentary on the denaturalization and dehumanization of contemporary society. Society is presented as something that is slowly destroying Robert's soul, impelling him to take refuge in this bleak world of perversion as a means of controlling at least part of his life. Sadly in death, Robert finally lost control, but established Buttgereit as a rising force in the world of European horror.

New Year's Evil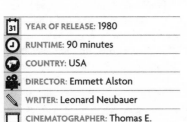

31 YEAR OF RELEASE: 1980		PRODUCERS: Billy Fine (executive producer), Yoram Globus, Menahem Golan, Christopher Pearce (associate producer), Mark L. Rosen (executive producer)	
RUNTIME: 90 minutes			
COUNTRY: USA			
DIRECTOR: Emmett Alston		CERTIFICATE: Australia: R; New Zealand: R18; UK: 18; US: R	
WRITER: Leonard Neubauer			
CINEMATOGRAPHER: Thomas E. Ackerman			

CAST: Roz Kelly, Kip Niven, Chris Wallace, Grant Cramer, Derek Sullivan, Louisa Moritz, Jed Mills, Taaffe O'Connell, Jon Greene, Teri Copley, Anita Crane, Jeannie Anderson, Alicia Dhanifu, Wendy-Sue Rosloff, John London

AS THE CLOCK counts down, Diane Sullivan (Roz Kelly), or Blaze as she likes to be known, hosts a late hour New Wave New Year's television show. The show is in full swing when Diane takes a phone call from a man calling himself Evil, who warns that as the clock strikes midnight over the four time zones he will kill a "Naughty Girl" and Blaze will be the last to die. The team in the studio begin to take precautions, but four hours away on the other side of America, a nurse has already been brutally murdered. In the build up to each of his kills, he appears calm but there is a strange look in his eyes, which turns to vicious malevolence as he trails his prey. While the killer's identity is always known, the story throws in enough red herrings to mislead the audience into believing Blaze's unstable son could be the killer, aggrieved by his mother's indifferent neglect. As Emmett Alston's second film rolled out to an uninspiring climax, Evil took on a gang of bikers. This fracas, however, wouldn't be Blaze's saviour, but would at last disclose the motivation behind this time-driven murderous spree.

New Year's Evil was but one of many films of that year hoping to feed on the success of **Halloween** (1978) and **Friday the 13th** (1980), among them the holiday terrors **Christmas Evil** and **Terror Train** along with the frenzied **Don't Go in the House**, **Prom Night** and **Silent Scream**. These were early days for the emerging slasher craze and the formula that would very soon take shape was still undergoing a process of fine-tuning, which in this instance meant there was a noticeable lack of gore and nudity. However, for all of its failings, Alston's low-budget film certainly entertained as it juxtaposed an eighties rock score with a series of contrived killings, played out to the darkest of unintentional comedy.

> **A celebration of the macabre.**

The New York Ripper

 YEAR OF RELEASE: 1982

 RUNTIME: 91 minutes

 COUNTRY: Italy

DIRECTOR: Lucio Fulci

PRODUCTION COMPANY: Fulvia Film	**CERTIFICATE:** Australia: (Banned, original rating); Australia: R (2005); Canada: 18+ (Quebec); New Zealand: R18; UK: (Banned); UK: 18 (cut); USA: Unrated
WRITERS: Gianfranco Clerici, Lucio Fulci, Vincenzo Mannino, Dardano Sacchetti,	
CINEMATOGRAPHER: Luigi Kuveiller	
PRODUCER: Fabrizio De Angelis,	**RECEIPTS:** ITL 414,859,000 (Italy)

CAST: Jack Hedley, Almanta Suska, Howard Ross, Andrea Occhipinti, Alexandra Delli Colli, Paolo Malco, Cinzia de Ponti, Cosimo Cinieri, Daniela Doria, Babette New, Zora Kerova, Paul E. Guskin, Antone Pagan, Josh Cruze, Marsha MacBride

WHILE ON AN afternoon walk near the Brooklyn Bridge, an elderly man throws a piece of wood for his dog, who returns to his master with a decaying human hand. Lieutenant Fred Williams (Jack Hedley) learns the hand belonged to a call girl by the name of Ann-Lynne, who he discerns had arranged to meet a man whose telephone voice was alleged to have sounded like a cartoon duck, possibly a sly reference to Fulci's earlier giallo, **Don't Torture a Duckling** (1972).

Elsewhere in the city, a young woman (Cinzia De Ponti) heads on her bicycle to the Staten Island Ferry. Before she arrives at the ferry, she gets into an argument with a hot-headed motorist after accidentally scratching his car. When the ferry sets sail, she descends to the car deck to exact her petty revenge but her actions are brought to a halt when, true to the giallo, an unseen figure appears on the scene. He speaks with the same bizarre Donald Duck-styled voice mentioned earlier in the story and then without a word of warning drives a switchblade into her stomach, before graphically disembowelling her. Lt. Williams soon after determines the modus operandi is very similar to that of the killing of Ann-Lynne. He now knows he has a serial killer on his hands.

The scene changes to observe the attractive Jane Lodge (Alexandra Delli Colli) savouring the sleaze of a live sex show, while taping the moans of the two writhing performers. The recording will be later used to stimulate her husband, Dr Lodge (Laurence Welles). As she eases herself into her seat, she is watched by a disconcerting individual who is clearly identified by a missing pair of fingers on his right hand. Once the show is over, the performing girl (Zora Kerova) exits to the darkness of her dressing room. Back stage she hears a noise, but before she is able to call for help she is attacked by a shadowed knifeman, who disembowels her by forcing a broken bottle into her vagina and on into her stomach. At the home of Kitty (Daniela Doria), a prostitute of Lt. Williams' acquaint, the detective receives a threatening phone call from the duck-voiced killer alluding to the murder in the sex club. It may be late but the killer still hasn't finished his work; he trails a young woman through the subway after she has been menaced by the creepy fellow seen in the sex show. Although he stabs her in the leg and cuts into her hands, she manages to survive the ordeal.

As she comes round the next morning in a hospital bed, her waking dreams are of being slashed by a handsome young man who looks very much like her physicist boyfriend Peter Bunch (Andrew Painter). The man the detective is now looking for has a mutilated right hand, but the same individual has just taken the sex-crazed Jane to a sleazy hotel room for a night of prolonged bondage sex.

New York City: it's a nice place to visit, but you wouldn't want to die there!

For thirty years **The New York Ripper**, which has also gone by the names **Lo Squartatore di New York**, **Psycho Ripper** and **The Ripper**, has continued to divide the followers of Lucio Fulci and horror movies alike. It is here, more than anywhere in his entire catalogue of films, he portrayed the human condition at its lowest. This was a downtrodden New York, emphasized by the camera work's tawdry use of colour and grimy locales. Many of the audience had experienced these streets in **The Driller Killer** (1979) and **Maniac** (1980); they were the breeding ground for the extremes of irrational behaviour, this

time directed specifically towards the female cast. The graphic excess would have it labelled as misogynist and it would be subsequently banned in Australia, Germany and Norway. In the UK, it was never registered as a video nasty, solely because the BBFC had the reels to this film escorted from these shores under the guard of Her Majesty's Constabulary. The result of course would make this a highly desirable acquisition. For those who did manage to lay their hands on these forbidden contents, they would discover a level of violence comparable to that of the obscure **Giallo a Venezia** (1979), one of Mario Landi's later films, William Lustig's controversial **Maniac** and Dario Argento's similarly divisive entry for that year, **Tenebre**.

The grindhouse years had always threatened such a feature and Fulci was the man who finally did it. The violence inflicted on the women in this film was imbued with a realism that was to fuel the debate as to whether its existence was nothing more than a showcase of embittered misogyny. The camera's lens was irrefutably voyeuristic as it captured every minute detail of the victims' agonizing torment, with each murder becoming increasingly brutal, leaving the most explicit until the last. In the sadistic finale, the naked Kitty was tied and tortured by the killer, as he expertly engaged a razor blade to slice her body open, seemingly relishing her ear-piercing screams. A series of lengthy close-ups would dwell on the killer as he glided the blade over her breasts before dissecting her nipples, then, in a way that Fulci had mastered, his killer sliced into her eyeballs. The killer's motive would be as bizarre as his blood lust, leaving many of Fulci's fans to believe that this really was a film of misogynistic excess rather than the well-conceived giallo upon which this formidable director had previously built his reputation.

The film remained banned in Britain until 2002 when the BBFC endorsed its submission on the provision that twenty-two seconds were removed from the razor-blade murder and its release came with a minimum of publicity. The film was only issued in the VHS format, as many UK DVD distributors were still reluctant to carry this abominable episode. It wasn't until 2007 that the film was released to DVD by Shameless Films, this time with only nineteen seconds of editing.

Night Ripper

📅	YEAR OF RELEASE: 1986	🎬 CINEMATOGRAPHER: Joe Dinn
🕐	RUNTIME: 86 minutes	👤 PRODUCERS: Phil De Carlo (associate producer), Jeff Hathcock, Paul Herndon (associate producer), John Tomlinson
🌐	COUNTRY: USA	
🎥	DIRECTOR: Jeff Hathcock	
✒	WRITER: Jeff Hathcock	

CAST: James Hansen, April Anne, Larry Thomas, Danielle Louis, Simon de Soto, Suzanne Tegmann, Lawrence Scott, Nick De Santis, Valerie Maddox, Rebecca Nitkin, Brad Thoennes, Tami Tirgrath, Courtney Lercara, Jim Mann, Drew Walker

DAVE, A GLAMOUR photographer, finds himself in dire straits when one of his models is horrifically murdered by a masked knife-wielding killer. Next on the list is his former fiancée. In a series of freeze-frame sequences both have been stabbed in the face and then, off-camera, the killer has taken to disembowelling them. The mutilations are said to resemble the work of Jack the Ripper. It

doesn't take long before Dave becomes the chief suspect in this case. He also fears for the life of his new girlfriend, who until about thirty-six hours before was also modelling before his lens. Murder follows murder as the cast are rolled on screen only to be hacked and slashed by the killer's knife. With the maniac's identity having remained a mystery for the entire film the creepy finale takes place in a mannequin factory, with the final kill being a moment for aficionados of the genre to savour.

Jeff Hathcock's film was shot on video with the VHS generation in mind, appearing at a time when the grindhouse cinemas were beginning to close down in the face of this increasingly successful competition. If he had only been granted a single week's run in these cinemas his audience might have significantly grown. Few people ever had the chance to see **Night Ripper**'s rock-bottom budget killings; in fact only a handful of copies ever made it across the Atlantic. Hathcock's efforts reflect his insignificant budget, and included typically dubious

acting, questionable dialogue, and the editing drawing almost every scene to a close with the shot slowly fading to black. To add to this movie's tragically amateur appearance, an eighties disco vibe was mixed with the sleaze of the porn scores from a decade past. However, for all of its failings there was an enthusiasm at work here, which steered this tale to an effective climax, and to the special effects team's abounding credit it included some rather gory slashings. As with the rest of Hathcock's shot-to-video catalogue, such as the previous year's **Victims**, **Night Ripper** is incredibly difficult to trace and is only available in its original VHS format.

Night of the Bloody Apes

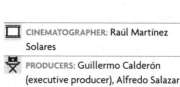

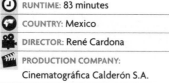

YEAR OF RELEASE: 1969

RUNTIME: 83 minutes

COUNTRY: Mexico

DIRECTOR: René Cardona

PRODUCTION COMPANY: Cinematográfica Calderón S.A.

WRITERS: René Cardona Jr. (story), René Cardona

CINEMATOGRAPHER: Raúl Martínez Solares

PRODUCERS: Guillermo Calderón (executive producer), Alfredo Salazar

CERTIFICATE: UK: X (original rating, cut); UK: (Banned) (1984–99); UK: 18 (re-rating, uncut); USA: R

CAST: José Elías Moreno, Carlos López Moctezuma, Armando Silvestre, Norma Lazareno, Agustín Martínez Solares, Javier Rizo, Gerardo Zepeda, Noelia Noel, Gina Morett

DR KRELLMAN (JOSÉ Elías Moreno) has learned that his teenage son's (Agustín Martínez Solares) leukaemia

is incurable. In a bid to save his life, the doctor transplants the heart of an ape into his son's body, in scenes that depict actual open-heart surgery, which in their day would have been considered unusually graphic. When his son, who had once been so handsome, awakens he has been transformed into a rampaging man ape. Meanwhile, across the city a masked female wrestler is tussling in the ring, with her boyfriend cheering from the crowd. When she badly injures her opponent and leaves the girl in a coma, she begins to have doubts about her future as a wrestler. Her boyfriend works as a detective, and very soon he is on the trail of the psychopathic ape-man, who has escaped his father's laboratory and gone into town to hunt down, strip and rape as many young ladies upon which he can lay his hairy mitts. As he tears into his victims, he rips the flesh from one man's neck, gouges the eyeball of another and then decapitates his next victim in scenes where the blood is washed across the screen by the gallon. When the doctor finally catches up with his wayward son, he performs a second transplant, this time with a heart stolen from the body of the comatose wrestler. His son, however, appears more deranged than ever and it will be up to the police to bring him down in the climactic rooftop sequence, which won't quite be the match of those tragic scenes atop the Empire State Building some fifty or so years before.

Night of the Bloody Apes, which actually featured only one ape, was René Cardona's remake of his B-movie **Doctor of Doom** (1962). For this venture, he looked to spice up his earlier production

An orgy of terror!

with an embarrassment of sex and cheap gore and then in the hope of capitalizing on the Santo phenomenon of the Mexican film industry, he introduced a wresting subplot, with plenty of girl-fight action. This was very loosely interwoven into his film, making for a bizarre hybrid that was originally entitled **Horror y Sexo**. As the film's title suggests, Cardona was hiding absolutely nothing on its Mexican release. This was in many ways a masterpiece of the low-budget exploitation genre, unashamed in its graphic portrayal of violence, gratuitous nudity as well as fake gore, and to cap it all there was a familiarly amusing stream of ridiculous dialogue. With the exception of the grisly heart surgery footage, the effects were very cheap and the ape-man's make-up resembled the kind of mask that would have been at home in rings of the *lucha libre*. For all of its failings, Cardona's movie has engendered a huge following, which was multiplied when it became a surprise addition to the UK's notorious list of video nasties in the November of 1983 following it being made available on video in the January of that year. It had previously seen extensive edits to the rape and murder of the woman in the bedroom along with close-up shots of a stabbing to ensure it had an "X"-rated cinematic release on these shores in 1974. In 1993, an uncut version of the film was mistakenly released by Vipco, but this was withdrawn within days, guaranteeing it to become an almost instantaneous collector's item. 🦋

Night of the Demon

YEAR OF RELEASE: 1980	**WRITERS:** Jim L. Ball, Mike Williams
RUNTIME: 92 minutes	
COUNTRY: USA	**CINEMATOGRAPHER:** John Quick
DIRECTOR: James C. Wasson	**PRODUCER:** Jim L. Ball
PRODUCTION COMPANY: Aldan Company	**CERTIFICATE:** UK: (Banned); UK: 18 (heavily cut); USA: R

CAST: Michael Cutt, Joy Allen, Bob Collins, Jody Lazarus, Rick Fields, Michael Lang, Melanie Graham, Shannon Cooper, Paul Kelleher, Ray Jarris, William F. Nugent, Lynn Eastman-Rossi, Eugene Dow, Don Hurst, Terry Wilson

INSPECTOR HARRIS PREPARES to interview a Professor Nugent, whose face has been bandaged to protect his unsightly mutilations. The traumatized academic is the only survivor of a vicious attack that has occurred deep in the forest. He explains how he became fascinated by reports of a series of grisly murders that seemed to have a connection with a number of Bigfoot sightings in the area. His story is related using a sequence of flashbacks, which tell of how he and a group of young anthropology students set out to lay bare the truth behind the legend. One of the group is determined to discover whether the beast was responsible for the recent death of her father. We learn that he was but one of the many victims, which the flashbacks go on to reveal include a couple of overgrown girl guides, a woodsman, a motorcyclist, a camper and a man who

was making love in the back of his van. The locals eventually allude to a hermit by the name of Crazy Wanda (Melanie Graham) who may know more about the creature. Their trek further into the forest sees them lose their boat and then they come upon a backwoods' ritual in honour of the beast. Soon after, the Bigfoot makes its presence known when it terrorizes one of the party, but on they go, certain that Crazy Wanda can unlock the secret to the beast's existence. When they locate Crazy Wanda they do indeed learn the truth but, in a climactic bloodbath, none of the teenagers will ever make it home.

Well, some of the teenagers would have made it to safety if James C. Wasson had had his way, but the distributors opted for a more downbeat finale. This would be the likeable Wasson's only time in the director's chair as his low-budget gorefest was banned upon entering the UK, Germany and Norway. The scene detailing a urinating motorcyclist having his penis torn off was just a little too much for the scrutiny of the censors in these countries. Such publicity would have duly given his film that key element of notoriety, which was exacerbated as reports of the ever-increasing body count began to spread. Unfortunately, Wasson's budget was so limited it was to undermine his film, hindered further still by only passable acting and his inexperience revealing a novice who still had so much to learn. Michael Cutt, acting in his first feature film, had to supply his own weapons and never saw a penny for his efforts.

Although the gore wasn't entirely realistic, it was there in abundance and the presence of the Bigfoot did make for a series of regular killings, which meant this film was anything but dull. The Bigfoot was admirably played by veteran stuntman Shane Dixon, whose display in certain shots was strangely terrifying. The editing has been the source of much criticism, but the cutaways, dissolves, along with the unsettling flashbacks,

An evil mutation embarks on a wave of brutal butchery.

reveal there was a dedicated talent at work in this film, which climaxed in the claustrophobic finale that has invited comparisons in style to Romero's **Night of the Living Dead** (1968). The plot would be re-hashed several years later in the obscure Bigfoot entry, **Legend of Boggy Creek 2** (1985), which followed from its documentary-styled predecessor of 1972. When **Night of the Demon** was released to video in the UK in June 1982, fans of the film had little over a year to savour its bloodthirsty content before it was banned as a video nasty in October 1983, and there it stayed until the end of the so-called panic. When it was submitted for video release in 1994, a minute and forty-one seconds of cuts were demanded to the arm removal, the castration of the cyclist, the disembowelment and subsequent wounds and a man's face being burned on a stove, before it was granted an official release. Regardless of the limitations in budget, Wasson's film and its beautiful woodland backdrops continue to charm those who stumble across its path.

Night of the Living Dead

📅	YEAR OF RELEASE: 1968	📷	COUNTRY: USA
⏱	RUNTIME: 96 minutes	🎬	DIRECTOR: George A. Romero

PRODUCTION COMPANY: Image Ten, Laurel Group, Market Square Productions, Off Color Films

WRITERS: John A. Russo, George A. Romero

CINEMATOGRAPHER: George A. Romero

PRODUCERS: Karl Hardman, Russell Streiner

CERTIFICATE: Australia: M; Australia: R; Canada: R (Nova Scotia) (original rating); Canada: 14 (Nova Scotia) (DVD rating); Canada: AA (Ontario); Canada: 14A; Canada: 18+ (Quebec) (original rating); Canada: 13+ (Quebec); Canada: R (Manitoba); Ireland: 18; New Zealand: R16; UK: 15 (video rating, 2007); USA: Unrated (1968)

BUDGET: $114,000

RECEIPTS: $30,000,000

CAST: Duane Jones, Judith O'Dea, Karl Hardman, Marilyn Eastman, Keith Wayne, Judith Ridley, Kyra Schon, Charles Craig, S. William Hinzman, George Kosana, Frank Doak

BARBARA (JUDITH O'DEA) and her brother have gone to visit the grave of a family friend but as they walk through the cemetery, they become aware that they are being followed by a dishevelled figure, whom they at first believe is just wanting to pay respect to his departed loved ones. He is joined by more of his unkempt kind and it becomes increasingly obvious the brother and sister are in serious trouble. While Barbara manages to escape from the growing horde, her previously jocular brother is not so fortunate. Alone, she arrives at a rural house, where she meets the calming presence of Ben (Duane Jones). When they enter the house, they find a family hidden away in the basement, whose daughter is obviously in desperate need of a doctor. With the threat of this ravenous zombie plague spiralling out of control, they set to work boarding up

the house in the hope of surviving the night. Occasional broadcasts reveal the extent of the situation. The whole of the US has been besieged by droves of flesh-eating zombies returned from the grave by the radiation emitted from a crashed space probe. The tension among those barricaded in the farmhouse now begins to mount. As the dead begin to descend on this claustrophobic refuge, the isolated survivors learn the zombies can be killed by a blow to the head. Will this knowledge give them the chance to survive or will their own bickering be the death of them?

Inspired by Richard Matheson's tale *I am Legend* written in 1954, George A. Romero scripted his landmark **Night of the Living Dead**, which was originally scheduled to see release as the more provocative **Night of the Flesh Eaters**. It was his very first feature film, and launched him into an incredible career that was to redefine the American horror movie industry and became the model for low-budget filmmakers. As with so many films of its ilk, his feature struggled to raise the necessary capital, which meant he could only afford black and white film stock. This actually enhanced the appeal in his film and made the scenes of murder and zombie cannibalism all the more effective. Unlike so much of its bloodthirsty offspring, **Night of the Living Dead**'s ingeniously ill-lit displays of flesh-eating appeared suggestive, leaving much to the viewer's fetid imagination. When it was released to theatres, its explicit content soon gave considerable cause for concern, but not before the sight of emaciated aunts and uncles rising from their eternal slumber, and then engaging in scenes of gratuitous cannibalism, had been shown at a Saturday afternoon matinee premiere on October 1, 1968, at the Fulton Theatre in Pittsburgh. The youngsters in the theatre were shocked into silence, others reduced to tears; this downbeat portrayal wasn't the kind of entertainment to which they had become accustomed and was a far cry from **Abbot and Costello meet Frankenstein** (1948). A month later, the voluntary MPAA film rating system was introduced, although it should be said this was not as a direct consequence of Romero's endeavours.

Pits the dead against the living in a struggle for survival!

His film eventually did receive the acclaim it was due and was selected for preservation in the National Film Registry as a film acknowledged to be "culturally, historically or aesthetically significant". **Night of the Living Dead**'s initial release in the UK in 1969 came with an "X" certificate and substantial edits to the trowel murder and the removal of all the scenes revelling in the devouring of human flesh. Eleven years later, it was seen in British cinemas as Romero had originally intended and since 1987 has been kept this way for its subsequent releases to video and DVD.

Its significance in relation to the horror movies that emerged during the 1970s cannot be underestimated, for without Romero there may never have been cinema screens awash with shambling flesh-eating zombies. The apocalypse had never been so disturbing, and would continue to be so as a series of directors followed in his cataclysmic path. There are those who insist a considerable part of its legacy is derived from the presentation of a black actor in the lead role at a time when civil rights tensions across the United States were running high. The gunning down of unknown actor Duane Jones' character Ben, after what was apparently the film's climax, has continued to generate much debate, having been cited as a condemnation of American attitudes towards race.

Romero has always insisted Jones was the best actor to audition for the part and it was never his intention to produce a feature with an underlying social commentary. The sequels would follow to complete what appeared to be a "dead trilogy" with the hugely influential **Dawn of the Dead** (1978) and **Day of the Dead** (1985). These were later succeeded by **Land of the Dead** (2005), **Diary of the Dead** (2007) and **Survival of the Dead** (2009). **Night of the Living Dead** has also gone through two remakes; the first in 1990 was directed by special-effects genius Tom Savini and the second was released in 3-D in 2006 but had no affiliation with Romero.

Night School

📅 YEAR OF RELEASE: 1981	🎬 CINEMATOGRAPHER: Mark Irwin
⏱ RUNTIME: 88 minutes	🎬 PRODUCERS: Ruth Avergon, Larry Babb, Marc Gregory Comjcan (executive producer), Bernard Kebadjian (executive producer), Leon Williams (associate producer)
🎥 COUNTRY: USA	
🎥 DIRECTOR: Ken Hughes	
🎬 PRODUCTION COMPANY: Fiducial Resource Industrial, Lorimar Film Entertainment, Paramount Pictures	⭕ CERTIFICATE: Australia: R; UK: 18; USA: R
✎ WRITER: Ruth Avergon	

CAST: Leonard Mann, Rachel Ward, Drew Snyder, Joseph R. Sicari, Nicholas Cairis, Karen MacDonald, Annette Miller, Bill McCann, Margo Skinner, Elizabeth Barnitz, Holly Hardman, Meb Boden, Anne Barron, Leonard Corman, Belle McDonald, Edward C. Higgins

THE CAMERA SETS the mood as the film opens, panning across the night of the Boston skyline. The scene switches to the Jack-n-Jill Day Care Center where the children are heading for home. One of the teachers, Anne Barron (Meb Boden), is waiting on a roundabout when a figure wearing leather motorcycle gear and a blacked-out helmet strides in her direction. A knife is drawn, an arm is raised before her body is slashed and then her head is hacked off; her discarded remains are later found in a back alley. Lieutenant Judd Austin (Leonard Mann) and his partner Detective Taj (Joseph R. Sicari) are promptly assigned to the case. This is the second reported decapitation in the space of a week, the first being found in a duck pond and Anne's head being left in a bucket of water. Anne was also a night student, studying Anthropology at Wendell College, which leads Lieutenant Austin to question Professor Vincent Millett (Drew Snyder), who had been Anne's tutor. He appears to have something of a reputation among his female students and we soon learn from one of Anne's friends, Kim Morrison (Elizabeth Barnitz), that she was rather furtive about a particular liaison. Not long after, Kim's decapitated head is found at the bottom of a fish tank. A waitress (Karen MacDonald) is revealed as the next victim. When the owner of the restaurant where she works arrives the following morning, he finds his eatery in utter chaos. As he tidies the tables and chairs, two builders arrive and ask for something to eat. He warms a large saucepan filled with stew and presents them with his culinary creation. As they tuck into their food, one of the builders finds a hair in his bowl. Another head would later surface in a toilet as the merciless butcher continued in his slaughter of the women of Wendell College, with Austin desperately trying to solve the case.

Night School was filmed in Boston during the fall of 1980, with a small budget and tight production schedule, by Ken Hughes, the director of **Chitty, Chitty, Bang, Bang** (1968). These constraints were of little concern to Hughes, whose feature paid homage to the giallo while exhibiting so many traits of the incumbent slasher that had already begun to emerge. His film played out as a

**A is for Apple,
B is for Bed,
C is for Co-ed,
D is for Dead,
F is for Failing to
keep your Head!**

murder mystery and was not without its moments of humour, yet it was inspired by the legacy of **Psycho** (1960) and dared to include a rather tense shower scene. Cinematographer Mark Irwin's working relationship with Hughes proved vital in creating the chill evident in so many of these set pieces. His bleak outlook would soon attract the attention of David Cronenberg and would lead to an invitation to add his touch to **Scanners** (1981) and then **Videodrome** (1983), before branching out into television, documentaries and substantially more in the way of film. While **Night School** has been criticized for employing a miscellany of styles, certain scenes raised the interest of Dario Argento, who used them to even greater effect in **Tenebrae** (1982). Hughes' movie will also be remembered for the film debut of a young Rachel Ward, who was to return to the genre two years later in the backwoods slasher **The Final Terror**.

The film was released in the United Kingdom as **Terror Eyes** and the unedited video was issued in February 1983. While the decapitations were carried out off screen, the film was still considered a video nasty, largely due to the blood-soaked scenes as the killer hacked through a white tiled room and the girl being threatened by a knife in the restaurant. In June 1985, the film was removed from the banned list when over a minute was cut from two offending scenes. It has, however, yet to see release to DVD. ❦

Night Train Murders

📅 YEAR OF RELEASE: 1975	✏️ WRITERS: Roberto Infascelli, Renato Izzo, Ido Lado, Ettore Sanzò
⏱️ RUNTIME: 94 minutes	
🌍 COUNTRY: Italy	🎬 CINEMATOGRAPHER: Gábor Pogány
🎥 DIRECTOR: Aldo Lado	⭕ CERTIFICATE: Australia: (Banned); Canada: 13+ (Quebec) (re rating); Canada: 18+ (Quebec) (original rating); UK: (Banned); UK: 18 (2008 rating, uncut); USA: R
🎞️ PRODUCTION COMPANY: European Incorporation	

CAST: Flavio Bucci, Macha Méril, Gianfranco De Grassi, Enrico Maria Salerno, Marina Berti, Franco Fabrizi, Irene Miracle, Laura D'Angelo

BLACKIE (FLAVIO BUCCI) and his drug-addicted accomplice Curly (Gianfranco De Grassi) are seen robbing a Santa Claus before embarking on a train travelling south from Germany to Verona. On board they meet a strange but alluring middle-class lady (Macha Méril). Two school friends, Laura (Marina Bertie) and Margaret (Irene Miracle), are also destined for Verona; there they intend to spend Christmas with Margaret's family. When the girls are asked to leave their compartment and take a different train they find themselves trapped in a darkened cabin by the thuggish duo and the woman, who proves the most sadistic of the three. She coerces the girls into confessing to their sexual encounters and then encourages Curly to rape Laura, before the eyes of peeping tom. The virginal young girl is so tight the

frustrated Curly forces a knife between the legs. When he hesitates, the strange woman inflicts the final deathblow. Margaret then manages to break free only to climb from the toilet window before throwing herself to her death.

As the trauma on the train continues, a Christmas Eve party takes place at the house of Margaret's parents. On Christmas morning, they go to the station to meet the girls to see three strangers walking along the platform. One of them, the lady of the group, has badly injured her ankle. The couple invite them to their home to allow her time to recover; it is, after all, the season of good will. The father soon after discovers his daughter should have been arriving on the same train and Curly is wearing a tie that his wife knows was purchased as a Christmas present. The grief-stricken father soon exacts his revenge, repeatedly stabbing and beating the heroin-addicted rapist and then hunting down Blackie with a shotgun. Only the conniving lady survives his revenge-filled carnage, pleading she was at the mercy of these scurrilous villains.

Aldo Lado had debuted four years before with the acclaimed thriller **Short Night of the Glass Dolls** (1971) and then followed with the giallo **Who Saw her Die** (1972). **L'Ultimo Treno della Notte** is a variation on Wes Craven's **Last House on the Left** (1972), moving from a leisurely paced opening to an intense brutality before the final violent confrontation between the distressed father and those who have abused his beloved daughter. Lado, assisted by his cinematographer Gábor Pogány, imbued the train with an insular air that became ever more acute as the girls realize the gravity of their terrifying situation. Craven's violence was appreciably stronger than that observed here, but there is a darker potent evident in Lado's direction. The producers feared his film would be persecuted by the authorities following its rejection by the Italian Board of Censorship and insisted it be burned. Lado wasn't prepared to have his work discarded in such a fashion and offered to cut certain frames, but was careful not to damage the impact of his film. In

Most movies last less than two hours! This is one of everlasting torment!

Italy, the giallo had already cultivated an eager audience, but here Lado chose an exploitative vein with elements of the Eurosleaze that was beginning to arouse the American market; a sleaze attested by the mysterious woman's predilection for pornographic images. It was she who proved the true deviant of this gathering, as Lado has maintained how those of influence and the affluent manipulate the less fortunate in society, invariably to fulfil their own perverse ends. His social commentary failed to impress the UK's licensing body when it was submitted for certification as **Late Night Trains** in 1976. When it was distributed across the country as a video in November 1981, following a previous issue that had almost a minute of violence removed, it survived unscathed until July 1983, when it was then banned as a video nasty. It was later removed from the list in March 1984 to see release without cuts in 2008 when the BBFC announced changes in both media awareness and public knowledge of film styles had reduced the impact and potential for harm from the film's scenes of sexual assault, which to their mind now appeared dated. Lado's film has also gone by the names **Don't Ride on Late Night Trains**, **Last Stop on the Night Train** and **Torture Train**. 🎬

Night Warning

📅 YEAR OF RELEASE: 1983	🎞 CINEMATOGRAPHERS: Robbie Greenberg, Jan de Bont
🕐 RUNTIME: 96 minutes	
🌐 COUNTRY: USA	🎬 PRODUCERS: Stephen F. Breimer, Richard Carrothers (executive producer), Dennis Hennessy (executive producer), Eugene Mazzola (co-producer)
🎥 DIRECTOR: William Asher	
🎬 PRODUCTION COMPANY: S2D Associates, Royal American Pictures	
✎ WRITERS: Stephen F. Breimer, Alan Jay Glueckman	⭕ CERTIFICATE: Australia: R; UK: R; USA: R

CAST: Jimmy McNichol, Susan Tyrrell, Bo Svenson, Marcia Lewis, Julia Duffy, Britt Leach, Steve Eastin, Caskey Swaim, Cooper Neal, Bill Paxton, Kay Kimler, Gary Baxley, Vickie Oleson, Clemente Anchondo, Alex Baker

CARING PARENTS BILL (Gary Baxley) and Anna Lynch (Kay Kimler) have arranged for their three-year-old son Billy to be looked after by his Aunt Cheryl (Susan Tyrrell), while they travel to the west coast on a visit to their parents. As they negotiate a mountain incline, the brakes on their car suddenly fail and they plummet down the mountainside into a fast-flowing river. Director William Asher was very keen to emphasize the severity of these death scenes, which presaged the terrors to come.

Since the death of his parents on that day fourteen years ago, Billy (Jimmy McNichol) has been raised by his Aunt Cheryl. As Billy makes plans for college and dates his teenage girlfriend Julie, he is unaware of his aunt's possessive nature and the lengths to which her incestuous desires will go to keep him

under her wing. She has little time for young Julie and is far from happy about his plans to make a new life in Denver. Billy returns home one afternoon to find Cheryl covered in blood, clutching a kitchen knife. He has no reason to disbelieve her claims that the television repairman, Phil Brody, has tried to rape her. He isn't aware that Brody rejected his aunt's salacious advances and then paid the price.

The police investigation led by the bigoted Lieutenant Joe Carlson (Bo Svenson), ably accompanied by Sergeant Cook (Britt Leach), reveals a homosexual love affair between Brody and Billy's basketball coach Tom Landers (Steve Eastin). This casts increasing doubt on Aunt Cheryl's claims of self-defence, but creates a connection between Billy and Brody. The homophobic Carlson looks to pin the murder on young Billy, convinced that the killing was brought about by the intrigue of a homosexual love triangle. As the lieutenant continues to harass the teenage boy, Cheryl's obsessive nature becomes increasingly volatile and so the violence escalates.

Night Warning, which also went by the names **Butcher, Baker, Nightmare Maker, Momma's Boy, Thrilled to Death** and **The Evil Protégé**, was an uncompromising attempt to examine the delicate issues of incestuous infatuation and homophobia in those unenlightened days when the slasher was enjoying its first wave of blood and guts. William Asher certainly made his mark in creating this cult attraction and would continue to direct in television, but never made another horror movie. As with many creators before him, he had cashed in on the moment but brought together an interesting cast, which saw Bill Bixby at an early point in his career, with the true star of the piece being Susan Tyrrell. In the confines of this dreary little house, she played a part that brought the audience face to face

> **She was lonely.**
> **He was all she had.**
> **No one would**
> **take him from**
> **her – and live . . .**

with an insanity rarely observed in films of the early 1980s. Her role was instrumental in the nomination for the Saturn Awards Best Low Budget Horror Film for 1982, although due to delays in production it didn't see release until the early months of 1983.

While there was a series of gory scenes later on in this film, which involved a tree trunk decapitation and then several stabbings as well as a severed hand, Asher's film has never been considered as being a particularly gruesome affair. However, its gritty cinematography aroused the British tabloids, and following its release to video in April 1983 it was registered as a video nasty. It was eventually dropped from the list in December 1985, but has yet to be granted approval for issue in the United Kingdom. The continuing ban has inherently fuelled the film's cult status, and it is yet to see release to the DVD format. It is, however, accepted that the BBFC would look favourably on any plans to resubmit its content for certification.

Nightmare City

 YEAR OF RELEASE: 1980

 RUNTIME: 92 minutes

 COUNTRY: Italy, Mexico, Spain

 DIRECTOR: Umberto Lenzi

PRODUCTION COMPANY: Dialchi Film, Lotus Films, Televicine S.A. de C.V.

✎ WRITERS: Antonio Cesare Corti, Luis María Delgado

▢ CINEMATOGRAPHER: Hans Burman

⚒ PRODUCERS: Diego Alchimede, Luis Méndez

◯ CERTIFICATE: Australia: R; Canada: 13+ (Quebec); UK: 18 (video rating, cut) (1986); UK:18 (video re-rating, uncut) (2003); USA: R (cut)

CAST: Hugo Stiglitz, Laura Trotter, Maria Rosaria Omaggio, Francisco Rabal, Sonia Viviani, Eduardo Fajardo, Stefania D'Amario, Ugo Bologna, Sara Franchetti, Manuel Zarzo, Tom Felleghy, Pierangelo Civera, Achille Belletti, Mel Ferrer

FILMED OVER AN eight-week period in Italy and Spain, **Nightmare City** was originally entitled **Incubo Sulla Città Contaminate**, and has since gone by the names **City of the Walking Dead** and **Nightmare of a Contaminated City** as well as **Invasion of the Atomic Zombies**. Umberto Lenzi's low-budget zombie movie is a possible precursor to the virus-infected creatures running amok in Danny Boyle's **28 Days Later** (2002) and was certainly an early example of a military backed assault on the zombie host, which for the duration of this film was capable of moving at considerable speed.

While reporter Dean Miller (Hugo Stiglitz) waits at the airport to interview a scientist, he looks on as a Hercules is forced to land. He can't believe his eyes when the disembarking passengers turn out to be a horde of mutated, blood-drinking zombies, akin to the ghouls of horrors past. Only hours ago when their flight took to the skies these were a set of people. Now contaminated by the scientist exposed to radiation, which accounts for their burned faces, they have become a murderous mob. Mass

slaughter ensues as these blood-crazed fiends rampage across the city. In an attempt to escape to safety, Miller and his wife must cross this imperilled region. However, with the military on one side and the contaminants beginning to spread across the other, this is going to be no easy ride. If these ferocious killers are going to survive, they will need as much blood as they can sink their teeth into to replace their damaged red blood cells. For the gore fan, Lenzi's movie is a cheap action-packed zombie flick which, to be fair, contains more than its share of suspense. The violence is typically excessive, although Lenzi has always been keen to extol the social undercurrent to his film, particularly the notion of the psychological impact of a city under siege, torn between a powerless military and its mindless assailants.

The scene in a television studio during the filming of a dance show featuring spandex-clad beauties contains another kind of social relevance, and has been frequently criticized for its misogynistic content. There seems to be a rare delight taken in the exploitative carnage that ensues, which includes an unbelievable breast-gorging sequence. These women, as with the other female victims, are repeatedly stabbed as their blood flows freely across the screen, they have their breasts sliced off, eyes gouged and, if that's not enough, have their clothes torn from their nubile young bodies. When they are not tearing women apart these zombies are shown to have a capacity for guns, knives and any other form of weaponry upon which they can lay their gnarled hands. They then employ

Now they are everywhere! There is no escape!

this arsenal as they lacerate their quarry as an entrée for satiating themselves upon the blood that inevitably spills forth.

The **Groundhog Day** conclusion continues to frustrate many fans of this film. As the couple make their escape clutching onto the helicopter's swaying rope, Miller's wife Anna plunges to her death. Mortified Dean screams in anguish, only to wake up in the safety of his bed. The cycle begins as he journeys to the airport to meet a similar appointment, and a Hercules is again seen to come in to land.

Nightmares in a Damaged Brain

📅	YEAR OF RELEASE: 1981	🎞	CINEMATOGRAPHER: Giovanni Fiore Coltellacci
🕐	RUNTIME: 87 minutes		
🌍	COUNTRY: USA	🎬	PRODUCERS: Christopher Cronyn (associate producer), Bill Milling, William Paul (associate producer), John L. Watkins
🎥	DIRECTOR: Romano Scavolini		
🎬	PRODUCTION COMPANY: Goldmine Productions	⭕	CERTIFICATE: Australia: R; Canada: (Nova Scotia, Banned); UK: 18; USA: R (cut); USA: Unrated
✏️	WRITER: Romano Scavolini		

CAST: Baird Stafford, Sharon Smith, C. J. Cooke, Mik Cribben, Danny Ronan, John L. Watkins, Bill Milling, Scott Praetorius, William Kirksey, Christina Keefe, Tammy Patterson, Kim Patterson, Kathleen Ferguson, William Paul, Tommy Bouvier

GEORGE TATUM HAS only recently been released from the mental institution to which he has been admitted following his dubious doctor's belief he has the cure to his violent bouts of psychosis. His doctor is convinced that a new miracle drug will help Tatum return to a normal life. George's normal way of life takes him to a Times Square sex show where he soon begins to lose his grasp on the sleazy world around him and as his eyes roll and mouth begins to foam; he falls unconscious to the floor. This unnerving episode impels George to a better life in Florida, but he is still very seriously disturbed. Although Florida offers him a far warmer clime, he is still unable to escape the hallucinatory nightmares that have plagued him for so many years. They eventually reveal he murdered his father with an axe when he discovered him cavorting with a prostitute; at the time, he was still only a child. Back at the mental facility, the medical staff have become gravely concerned for they have come to realize they have made a serious error of judgement; the drug will never cure George's deep-rooted psychosis. Far away in Florida George has started to stalk a family, a single mother he looks upon as being neglectful and her young family. One of the children tries to tell his mother he has seen a man loitering around the house, but she refuses to believe him until the phone calls begin,

which leads to a shocking climax, as history is seen to repeat itself.

From the outset former experimental film director Romano Scavolini sought to unsettle his audience using a rather creepy introductory sequence that suggested this would be a psychological terror, but not without a fair degree of violence. In a similar way to John Carpenter's work three years before on **Halloween**, he developed a technique designed to focus at length on a particular object then drawing back to pan around the room, thus creating the impression that there was a malfeasance lurking only just out of sight. In this way, he cleverly augmented the tension without having to rely entirely on cold-blooded brutality, but when it did come, it was truly shocking, culminating in the climatic double axe murder that has become the stuff of slasher legend. Baird Stafford's portrayal of George Tatum has been placed on a par with William Lustig's infamous **Maniac** (1980) and John McNaughton's **Henry: Portrait of a Serial Killer** (1986). When Stafford undertook this role, he was never entirely sure if George's medication was the cure to his psychosis or, as was equally likely, the cause of his problems. This he tried to encapsulate in his interpretation of his director's script, resulting in a rather convincing depiction of a man who had completely lost his mind.

Savolini's film, which has also been entitled **Blood Splash** and **Nightmare**,

Someone left the door to HELL open . . .

343

aroused the attention of the British censors partly owing to the use of several gimmicks, which included a vomit bag being supplied with the video on its release in May 1982 along with a competition to guess the weight of a brain in a jar. In the July of 1983, the film was banned as a video nasty and remained there to become one of the DPP's thirty-nine. In 1984 David Grant of Oppidan, the video company that had first released **Nightmares in a Damaged Brain** prior to the ban, was jailed for eighteen months, although later reduced to twelve, for releasing a version of the film in its uncut form. To this day, the complete brutality originally presented in this film has never been officially made available in the UK. 🐾

Oasis of the Zombies

📅	YEAR OF RELEASE: 1981		🎞	CINEMATOGRAPHER: Max Monteillet
🕐	RUNTIME: 82 minutes		⚒	PRODUCERS: Daniel Lesoeur (associate producer), Marius Lesoeur
🌍	COUNTRY: France		⭕	CERTIFICATE: Canada: 13+ (Quebec); Canada: (Banned) (Ontario); USA: Unrated
🎥	DIRECTOR: Jesus Franco			
🎬	PRODUCTION COMPANY: Eurociné			
✎	WRITER: Jesus Franco			

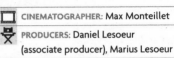

CAST: Manuel Gélin, France Lomay, Jeff Montgomery, Myriam Landson, Eric Viellard, Caroline Audret, Henri Lambert

A COUPLE OF YOUNG girls amble into a remote desert oasis, only to bid a hasty retreat as the living dead begin to rise from the sand. The only survivor of a ferocious World War II desert battle reveals he knows that over $6 million of gold is still buried in the same oasis. His avaricious partner, who wants to keep the booty for himself, then takes a syringe and kills the man who had once been his friend. The veteran's son Robert (Manuel Gélin) soon after reads his father's diaries and learns of the gold bullion. He convinces his friends to journey with him to Africa to retrieve this long-lost treasure trove. Even though they have been warned to stay away from the area, the group set up camp little realizing the gold is guarded by a horde of zombie German soldiers who had been tasked almost forty years before with transporting their cargo by convoy through the desert. When night falls, this putrescent detachment once again rises from their slumber to defend their riches, with the infiltrators forced to stave off an unrelenting attack.

Jesus Franco's mesmeric addition to the zombie craze of the early eighties has been described as one of the worst zombie movies ever made, probably only saved by the battle between the British and German soldiers seen early on in the film. These scenes were spliced from Alfreddo Rizzo's 1971 war film **The Gardens of the Devil**, originally **I Giardini de Diavlo**. For the most part, his pacing appears slow and uneventful, but Franco has a reputation for being a sleaze-monger and a veritable master of exploitation. When the zombies rise from their desert graveyard each one of this desirable cast of young women are subjected to the slavering atrophied hordes in customary Franco style, while their male counterparts are summarily dealt with almost as an afterthought. This band of zombies is not necessarily interested in human brains; their cannibalistic urges will settle for any old blood and guts, which isn't always in copious supply. The make-up used on the lead zombies proved quite effective, particularly the idea of having a worm attached to their emaciated faces. The charred Nazi uniforms added to the final effect as the long-awaited zombie resurrection from the shifting sand dunes supplied a much needed atmospheric menace. Among its many names, Franco's film has been released as **Blood Sucking Nazi Zombies.**

Opera

📅	YEAR OF RELEASE: 1987	🎥	CINEMATOGRAPHER: Ronnie Taylor
⏱️	RUNTIME: 107 minutes	🪑	PRODUCERS: Dario Argento, Ferdinando Caputo (executive producer)
🌐	COUNTRY: Italy		
🎬	DIRECTOR: Dario Argento		
🎞️	PRODUCTION COMPANY: ADC Films, Cecchi Gori Group Tiger Cinematografica	⭕	CERTIFICATE: Australia: R; Canada: R; Canada: 16+ (Quebec); New Zealand: R18; UK: 18; USA: Unrated; USA: R (heavily cut); USA: NC-17 (original rating)
✏️	WRITER: Dario Argento	💲	BUDGET: $8,000,000

CAST: Cristina Marsillach, Ian Charleson, Urbano Barberini, Daria Nicolodi, Coralina Cataldi-Tassoni, Antonella Vitale, William McNamara, Barbara Cupisti, Antonino Iuorio, Carola Stagnaro, Francesca Cassola, Maurizio Garrone, Cristina Giachino, György Gyõriványi, Bjorn Hammer

THE CAMERA TRAINS on the eye of a raven as it reflects the magnificence of an opera house; this will not be the last time the raven is seen in Dario Argento's film. As the cast rehearse for an avant-garde performance of Verdi's opera *Macbeth*, Betty is informed of the death of the lofty lead actress, which gives her the opportunity to step into the limelight in the role of Lady Macbeth. On the opening night, a stagehand is killed when a lighting rig falls to the ground as a shady figure is observed making his way into an empty box in the opera house. As the killer watches Betty from the shadows an attendant insists that he must leave, but is impaled with a coat hook in response. Thankfully, Betty knows nothing of these events and excels to the rapturous applause of the audience. After the performance, she decides to leave the back-stage party to celebrate at the palatial home of her boyfriend's uncle. When her boyfriend, Stefan, leaves her reclining on the bed, Betty is seized from behind by a giallo-inspired masked figure adorned in black leather gloves, who wastes no time in tying her to a pillar, taping her mouth, and then placing needles directly beneath her eyes, making it impossible for her to risk closing them. She has no choice but to watch as the killer drives a blade up into Stefan's throat and on through his mouth. As he falls dead to the floor Betty is untied, but the hooded killer is

**Obsession.
Murder.
Madness.**

far from finished; his sadistic obsession will have her watch more of those who have been close to her die horribly at his hands.

Dario Argento's visually stylish **Opera**, released in the United Sates as **Terror at the Opera**, traversed the line between the traditional giallo and the decade's fading slasher. While the gloved assassin wielded his sharpened knife from the shadows, the customary clues and red herrings of the genre were no longer as prominent. Rather, Argento looked to concentrate on heightening the tension, cleverly using flashbacks and precarious edits to unhinge his audience as Betty's traumatized past gradually came to the fore. As ever, Argento's death scenes were resplendent in their originality, with the slow-motion gunshot to the eye before the keyhole acquiring an immediate notoriety upon the film's release. Throughout the movie, the desire to destroy the eye created an intensity that exceeded anything he and his fellow Italian directors had so far attempted. Many of these graphic images were the work of Sergio Stivaletti and his stomach-churning special effects, which were every bit as shocking as Luis Buñuel's surreal eye-slicing first seen in **Un Chien Andalou** (1929). This intensity appeared to be Argento's response to the frustration he felt at those in his audience who closed their eyes as they sought to avoid the more grisly aspects in his films. In placing needles so close to Betty's eyes, she was never given the chance to take her eyes away from the knifeman as he swiftly slaughtered her beloved Stefan.

Under Argento's experienced direction, Ronnie Taylor's cinematography used point-of-view shots to sweep through the corridors and stairways of the film's various sets, exacerbating the tension as Betty's distressing past began to catch up with her. On its cinematic release in the UK, over thirty seconds of Argento's film had to be removed, which included Santini's skewered tongue, the knife ripping into Stefan's neck and mouth followed by the repeated stabbing, and finally the close-ups detailing the killer forcing a pair of scissors into the wardrobe girl's mouth. 🐾

Peeping Tom

📅	YEAR OF RELEASE: 1960	🎞 CINEMATOGRAPHER: Otto Heller
🕐	RUNTIME: 101 minutes	⚱ PRODUCERS: Albert Fennell (associate producer), Michael Powell
🌐	COUNTRY: UK	
🎥	DIRECTOR: Michael Powell	⭕ CERTIFICATE: Australia: M; UK: X (original rating); UK: 18 (re-rating); UK: 15 (theatrical re-release) (2010); USA: Not Rated
🎬	PRODUCTION COMPANY: Michael Powell (Theatre)	
✎	WRITER: Leo Marks	💲 BUDGET: £135,000

CAST: Karlheinz Böhm (Carl Boehm), Moira Shearer, Anna Massey, Maxine Audley, Brenda Bruce, Miles Malleson, Esmond Knight, Michael Goodliffe, Martin Miller, Jack Watson, Shirley Anne Field, Pamela Green

AS MARK LEWIS (Carl Boehm) attempts to solicit a prostitute, she has no knowledge that he is cunningly filming her using a camera concealed within his coat. The images on screen are detailed from the camera's perspective, a technique pioneered by the cinema of the early 1930s. With the subject captured in such close proximity an unsettling degree of tension is created, which, to Powell's credit, mounts as she escorts Lewis to her home. Even the voyeur of the day would have been shocked by the images of fear-stricken contortions wracking the face of a girl knowing she is about to die. Alone he later savours the film, surrounding himself with the sights and sounds of terror, his fresh-faced shyness concealing the monster within.

The reclusive murderer works with a film crew, with ambitions of making his own films. When he is not at the studio, he is discreetly snapping candid photographs of glamour models, which he trades to a local pornographer. His double life continues at home, where acting as the landlord he rents out part of what once was his father's house, while posing as a tenant. Although withdrawn, he cannot help but be fascinated by the engaging Helen (Anna Massey). He eventually confides in her, describing how his father used him as a psychological guinea pig, wilfully experimenting on the stimuli and effects of fear. Little does she realize Mark is tormented by his father's experimentation, obsessed with the behavioural aspects of fear, specifically the visible impression on the human face.

More horrible than horror! More terrible than terror!

His sordid compulsion remains unabated and a murderous display ensues, this time at the studio. When the body is discovered, the police are quick to link the two killings, each victim having died with a look of stark terror etched into their faces. Mark soon falls under suspicion. Tailed by the police he is traced to the building where he takes photographs of a pin-up model, which ends in her death before his lethal tripod. Two versions of this scene were shot, one of which is credited as being the very first female nude scene in a major British motion feature. The model becomes yet another victim of Mark's macabre fixation.

With the police in hot pursuit, Mark discovers Helen watching one of his self-styled documentaries. He rants about his quest to make movies encapsulating the fear in his victims by using a mirror on his camera. Facing the distinct possibility of a life behind bars, Mark brings his life's work to an appropriate conclusion, killing himself as he did the other girls, impaled by a knife attached to one of the camera's tripod legs. His camera still runs, providing a fitting finale for this gruesome documentary.

While there are those who once considered this a vile piece of voyeurism, which unfortunately led to his demise as an eminent director, Powell's psychological masterpiece has since acquired a huge following. Finally recognized for its true worth, it is lauded as being very much ahead of its time. The camera work is assured throughout, guiding the audience through these sleazy scenes, warranting their eyes never leave the screen. He later noted in his autobiography, "I make a film that nobody wants to see and then, thirty years later, everybody has either seen it or wants to see it." With attitudes becoming more permissive during the 1970s, the critics' view of his film went through a radical transformation. It also attracted the attention of Martin Scorsese, who was very appreciative of its relevance. When it was released on US television it was given the less emotive title of **Face of Fear**.

The sympathetic portrayal would be one of many comparisons drawn with fellow British director, Alfred Hitchcock's **Psycho**, released only a few months later. It would also have an unprecedented effect on some of the more vivid slasher films that terrorized cinemas towards the end of the 1970s. As with the many deranged killers plying their ruthless trade in these films, Powell's lead was twisted by a murderous voyeuristic mania. The point-of-view technique used to such lurid effect in **Peeping Tom** would eventually be popularized by some the more influential slasher movies, principally **Black Christmas** (1974) and **Halloween** (1978), and continued with **Man Bites Dog** (1992), **The Last Horror Movie** (2003) and **Behind the Mask: The Rise of Leslie Vernon** (2006) along with **The Blair Witch Project** (1999).

Philosophy of a Knife

YEAR OF RELEASE: 2008	WRITER: Andrey Iskanov
RUNTIME: 249 minutes	CINEMATOGRAPHER: Andrey Iskanov
COUNTRY: Russia	PRODUCERS: Stephen Biro (producer: Unearthed Films), David Bond (associate producer), Andrey Iskanov
DIRECTOR: Andrey Iskanov	
PRODUCTION COMPANY: Unearthed Films	CERTIFICATE: Canada: R; Canada: 18+ (Quebec); USA: Not Rated

CAST: Yukari Fujimoto, Yumiko Fujiwara, Svyatoslav Iliyasov, Andrey Iskanov, Masaki Kitagava, Tatyana Kopeykina, Vladimir Kucherenko, Veronika Leonova, Victor Ludchenko, Manoush, Reiko Niakawa, Irina Nikitina, Tomoya Okamoto, Elena Probatova, Anatoly Protasov

WHILE THERE ARE those who think Andrey Iskanov created the most graphically violent film ever to see the light of day, he remains resolute in his belief **Philosophy of a Knife** should not be looked upon as a horror movie, and maintains his aversion for the violence seen everyday across the globe. In four hours, much of it shot in black and white, narrated in two, two-hour episodes, he documents the disturbing history of a research laboratory created by the military police of the Imperial Japanese Army based in Harbin, Heilongjiang province, in what was Japanese-occupied China between 1937 and 1945. The facility was developed to research epidemic prevention and weapons of mass destruction. Within the complex, a unit of the chemical and biological warfare research team ascended to notoriety, to become known as the iniquitous Unit 731. The members of this unit conducted torturous and deathly experiments on Soviet, Chinese and, towards the end of the war, American prisoners. They were later prosecuted by the Soviet authorities and convicted of war crimes and crimes against humanity.

God created heaven, man created hell

In this avant-garde terror, Iskanov leaves nothing to the imagination in a four-hour feature that depicts humanity at its most despicable. Such is the sensitivity of this dark moment in history the director was investigated by the Russian Federal Security Service. They carried out a comprehensive search of his residence, removed documents and film footage to determine just how he had learned about biological weaponry, and at the same time identify his source of information. Soon after his arrest, he was imprisoned in a military base. Here he was locked in a cell without a toilet and was forced to endure long periods of intensive interrogation, where he divulged much of his research material had gone back to

the United States. We are left to wonder if the Russian authorities were concerned he knew a little too much, but was saved when he claimed his studies went only as far as 1956. Both those with a historical perspective and the gore mongers will find themselves both fascinated and repulsed by this film, which contains an estimated thirty minutes of contemplative snowfall. This seeming tranquillity, however, is overwhelmed by the horrific onslaught as vivisections and dissections are carried out without anaesthetic, while this butchery carries on a soldier is skinned alive, a foetus torn from its mother's womb, a face burned by X-rays, and one unfortunate has her teeth removed in an agonizing mockery of dentistry. This film's catalogue of atrocities appears to go on and on without end. Such has been the impact of his abominable epic, Iskanov has been the recipient of the highest praise and the most severe criticism for creating a film that is even more explicit than Tun Fei Mou's controversial **Men Behind the Sun** (1988), which had previously recalled this moment from the past that for many should remain dead and buried. 🐾

Pieces

 YEAR OF RELEASE: 1982

 RUNTIME: 85 minutes

COUNTRY: Spain/USA

DIRECTOR: Juan Piquer Simón

PRODUCTION COMPANY: Almena Films, Film Ventures International (FVI), Fort Films, Montoro Productions Ltd

 WRITERS: Dick Randall, John W. Shadow, Juan Piquer Simón

 CINEMATOGRAPHER: Juan Mariné

 PRODUCERS: Stephen Minasian Edward L. Montoro (executive producer US version), Dick Randall

 CERTIFICATE: Australia: R; Canada: 16+ (Quebec); UK: 18; USA: Unrated

 **RECEIPTS:** $2,032,311

CAST: Christopher George, Frank Braña, Lynda Day George, Paul L. Smith, Edmund Purdom, Ian Sera, Jack Taylor, Isabel Luque, Gérard Tichy, Hilda Fuchs, May Heatherly, Roxana Nieto, Cristina Cottrelli, Leticia Marfil, Silvia Gambino, Carmen Aguado, Paco Alvez

WAY BACK IN the 1940s a young boy is caught by his mother as he assembles a puzzle of a naked woman. When she takes his puzzle away, he loses his temper and drives an axe into her head. The film moves forward forty years to a university campus in Boston where a crazy has taken to chain-sawing the body parts of the young female students, before stealing away with certain pieces of their anatomy as he leaves the bloody entrails for the scrutiny of the authorities. Lt. Bracken (Christopher George) has been assigned to the case; he has arranged with the Dean for agent Mary Riggs (Lynda Day George) to work under cover as a tennis coach. Together with a young student, Kendall (Ian Sera), they try to track down the killer, whose audacity extends to stalking a half-naked

student into a lift while trying to hide his over-sized chainsaw.

Juan Piquer Simón was another Spanish master of low-budget exploitative cinema and true to the genre wasted little time in exposing his nubile young cast and throwing in some rather graphic violence and gore, too much of it to the sound of the disco beat! When a girl was stripped naked, you just knew she was lined up for the next kill as this psycho obsessed over their delightfully ripened body parts. There were plenty of suspects, including the creepy looking gardener, the Professor of Anatomy and even the Dean along with numerous red herrings, but **Pieces** has only ever been regarded as a piece of Euro trash produced to cash in on the American slasher market. Its nonsensical script would never elevate it to being a

Pieces ... It's exactly what you think it is!

true horror movie and even the excess of blood failed to convince its eager audience, but Simón's direction did create a sense of sinister atmosphere and a mounting claustrophobic unease as the killer moved in for his prey. Thirty years later, these severed body parts still continue to raise a smile.

Pledge Night

📅 YEAR OF RELEASE: 1990		✎ WRITER: Joyce Snyder	
🕐 RUNTIME: 90 minutes		🎞 CINEMATOGRAPHER: Big Paul Smith	
🌐 COUNTRY: USA		🎬 PRODUCERS: Jerry Landesman (associate producer), Joyce Snyder	
🎥 DIRECTOR: Paul Ziller			
🎬 PRODUCTION COMPANY: Scarlet Productions, Shapiro-Glickenhaus Home Video		◯ CERTIFICATE: USA: R	

CAST: Todd Eastland, Dennis Sullivan, Craig Derrick, David Neal Evans, Robert Lentini, James Davies, Lawton Paseka, Michael T. Henderson, Arthur Lundquist, Steven Christopher Young, Tony Barbieri, Will Kempe, Joey Belladonna, Shannon McMahon, Barbara Summerville

FOR THE FIRST part of Paul Ziller's film, a group of teenage pledges endure endless initiation rituals as they seek to enter a college fraternity during "Hell Week", one of them strictly against his mother's advice. Amidst the scenes of semi-nakedness, there is a series of amusing episodes along with much talk about hazing and the meaning of the college fraternity. The comedic element should have come to a halt when Acid Sid climbed from the toilet to begin killing the cast, but his entrance understandably detracted from what was to follow. Twenty years before in 1968, a young hippie fraternity pledge was accidentally burned to death in a tub of acid. Now his unforgiving corpse returns to savour his revenge on "Hell Week". His retribution begins when his spirit possesses one of the pledges, who appears to have killed one of the fraternity brothers. Minutes later Acid Sid explodes from the stomach of another pledge as the body count once again begins to rise.

As a blizzard raged at Rutgers University,

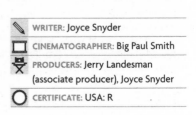

Brothers to the end. The very end.

New Jersey, in the January of 1988, Paul Ziller with very little money attempted to direct a movie that was to take him away from his recent work in pornography, with Anthrax's Joey Belladonna starring as the young Sidney "Acid Sid" Snyder. As with so many cinematic hopefuls, he chose to put together a slasher feature, a phenomenon that by then had run its course. The wind and driving snow were to make the shoot far more difficult than it should have been, but would add to the film's impact, as the cast played out countless scenes in falling temperatures that later felt the wrath of the censors. By the end of the 1980s blood and guts were fine, as were bare breasts, but the two were never to be shown together in the same shot. **Pledge Night** would go on to acquire cult status as Paul Ziller's career ascended to new heights, seeing him move forward to work in both film and television.

Possession

📅 YEAR OF RELEASE: 1981	✏️ WRITER: Andrzej Zulawski
🕐 RUNTIME: 127 minutes	🎞️ CINEMATOGRAPHER: Bruno Nuytten
🌐 COUNTRY: France/West Germany	⏳ PRODUCER: Marie-Laure Reyre
🎥 DIRECTOR: Andrzej Zulawski	⭕ CERTIFICATE: Australia: R; New Zealand: R18; UK: 18; USA: R
🎬 PRODUCTION COMPANY: Gaumont, Oliane Productions, Marianne Productions	💲 RECEIPTS: $1,113,538 (1983) -

CAST: Isabelle Adjani, Sam Neill, Margit Carstensen, Heinz Bennent, Johanna Hofer, Carl Duering, Shaun Lawton, Michael Hogben, Maximilian Rüthlein, Thomas Frey, Leslie Malton

FROM HIS CAR, Mark (Sam Neill) looks out at his home city, a place that we learn, through the imagery of the landscape, has come to trouble him. His wife Anna (Isabelle Adjani) rushes to meet him, but this isn't a joyous reunion. Mark has arrived home too early from an undisclosed trip abroad where cash has been exchanged with a covert government organization. At first, Anna's behaviour appears strange and then Mark discovers that while he has been away his wife has become involved with another man and their son is being cared for by their friend Margie. At first, she will not reveal her lover's identity, but as their incessant rowing escalates into violence in a restaurant, she discloses that for the past year a man named Heinrich (Heinz Bennent) has been her sinister paramour. When the two come face to face in another violent confrontation, Mark realises the two lovers have not seen one another for quite some time. As their marriage steadily deteriorates, the mental states of both Anna and Mark are affected. Anna sees herself as the maker of her own evil and is later seen embraced by the tentacles of a Lovecraftian entity. Mark in turn borders on possessive madness, which manifests itself in the vision of his son's teacher, who is the image of his tormented wife. She embodies the innocent creature she once was. His wife, however, has another nasty surprise in store for her estranged husband as his world of clandestine espionage clashes head on with the horrors of their marital discord.

She created a monster as her secret lover!

While **Possession** contains a series of exceptional gory and violent episodes, in particular, Anna's slicing of her own neck with an electric carving knife and her miscarriage in the underground station, the unsettling surrealism that haunts this film distances it from many accepted perceptions as to the elements that constitute a horror movie. Andrzej Zulawski's film could be interpreted as a reaction to the frustration he endured at seeing his brutal historical feature **Diabel** (1972) censored by his country's government. He left Poland for France and then returned home to have yet another film withdrawn before it had seen completion. His crisis deepened when his own marriage broke down and was captured in the two hours that told the tale of Anna and Mark's torturous separation in the divided city of Cold War Berlin. The bleak landscape that drew Zulawski close to the edge of rationality is reflected in the barbed wire of the Berlin Wall and the encroaching presence of the anonymous security guards. Under his direction, Bruno Nuytten's unnerving camera work appears exceptionally nimble, as it moves from scene to scene in the decaying apartments of this oppressive cityscape.

Zulawski had admired the work of Dario Argento, but now the master of horror cinema returned the compliment, lauding this assault on the senses for its vision and then captured its essence in his next film **Tenebrae** (1982). The performance of Isabelle Adjani was such that she went on to win a Best Actress award at Cannes that year as well as the César Award again for Best Actress and succeeded in re-launching a career which had been tempestuous up until then. Zulawski could also call upon special effects artist Carlo Rambaldi, who had previously worked on **Deep Red** (1975) before moving on to **Close Encounters of the Third Kind** (1977) and then **Alien** (1979), in the creation of the slime-ridden monster. In 1987 when Poland was beginning to shrug off decades of repression, Zulawski was invited back to his homeland to complete his unfinished science fiction film of ten years before,

Na Srebrnym Globie or **The Silver Globe**, which saw release in 1988, although it remains largely unknown in English-speaking countries. Unfortunately, the controversial nature of **Possession** resulted in it being butchered in the United States, reduced to an incomprehensible eighty-one minutes. For a challenging art house movie of this kind, its reception in France was somewhat modest, and on its release to VHS in the UK in the September of 1982 it not surprisingly attracted the wrong kind of attention and was banned as a video nasty in September 1983. Twelve months later, it was cleared by a jury of obscenity in a jury trial and was subsequently removed from the list. It was finally released uncut in the UK in 1999, but still runs to only 119 minutes, unlike its European counterpart which contains an extra four minutes of footage.

The Prey

YEAR OF RELEASE: 1984	**WRITERS:** Edwin Brown, Summer Brown
RUNTIME: 80 minutes	
COUNTRY: USA	**CINEMATOGRAPHER:** Teru Hayashi
DIRECTOR: Edwin Brown	**PRODUCERS:** Edwin Brown, Summer Brown, Frans Rasker (executive producer)
PRODUCTION COMPANY: Essex Productions	
	CERTIFICATE: Australia: R; UK: 18; USA: R

CAST: Debbie Thureson, Steve Bond, Lori Lethin, Robert Wald, Gayle Gannes, Philip Wenckus, Jackson Bostwick, Jackie Coogan, Connie Hunter, Ted Hayden, Garry Goodrow, Carel Struycken

WAY BACK IN the 1940s a forest fire swept through a Colorado forest and burned to death a community of gypsies. One of the children, however, managed to survive. Almost forty years later, a couple of elderly campers become temporarily lost in the vastness of the same forest. While the wife walks down to the lake, her husband takes out an axe and begins to chop firewood. When the wife returns she finds her beloved's decapitated body. Her screams can be heard echoing through the trees as the screen begins to fade.

It's a beautiful day and half a dozen teenagers – you've seen their type before in countless slasher features – arrive in the forest, having travelled for hours in their van. They are welcomed by the Park Sheriff before setting off to enjoy the surrounding woodland. As they head deeper into the overgrown forest, it becomes apparent they are not alone. Point-of-view shots and the sound of someone gasping for breath reveal they are being followed by an unsettling presence. After tracking the group for almost an hour the killer begins to bring them down in scenes that reveal a considerable element of carefully manipulated suspense and culminate in another decapitation by axe, the customary hacking of the throat, and a sleeping bag suffocation. This leads to the slow-motion-styled final girl chase by a hermitic man through the woods, a man who is now in need of company. Only in the final few minutes of this film would the audience get to see the giant gypsy's badly burned features; his appearance was indeed disturbing and the denouement refused to bring the closure for which the viewers would have hoped.

It's not human, and it's got an axe!

The Prey has been criticized, along with many other films of this ilk, for jumping on the **Friday the 13**th bandwagon, but was actually shot during 1978. It wasn't released until June 1984 and lasted a little more than a week in the drive-in theatres across the United States, reaping in its wake rather negative reviews. The pacing proved too slow for the slasher audiences of the day, with an abundance of unnecessary woodland stock footage used as padding. To the director's credit, his use of gore was impressive, but it was strewn just too late in a seemingly prolonged movie. The film was then cut by fifteen minutes, because the distributors felt such a movie could not hold the audience's interest for more than eighty minutes. Rather than edit the unnecessary stock footage, the opening sequence explaining the killer's unfortunate past was left on the cutting room floor. **The Prey** was released to video in 1988 but the original cut has never been seen, nor is it known to exist. Edwin Brown would soon return to a more gainful career in directing porn movies.

Primitive Desires

	YEAR OF RELEASE: 1978		**DIRECTOR:** Sergio Martino
	RUNTIME: 99 minutes		**PRODUCTION COMPANY:** Dania Film, Medusa Produzione
	COUNTRY: Italy		

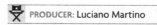

WRITERS: Cesare Frugoni, Sergio Martino

CINEMATOGRAPHER: Giancarlo Ferrando

PRODUCER: Luciano Martino

CAST: Ursula Andress, Stacy Keach, Claudio Cassinelli, Antonio Marsina, Franco Fantasia, Lanfranco Spinola, Carlo Longhi, Luigina Rocchi, Akushula Selayah, Dudley Wanaguru, T. M. Munna, M. Suki, Giovanni Masini

WELL-HEELED SUSAN Stevenson's (Ursula Andress) husband has vanished without trace on an island somewhere off the coast of New Guinea. Accompanied by a respected anthropologist (Stacy Keach) and her scheming brother (Antonio Marsina) they journey to the island to determine his fate. Susan and her brother have only one concern: the location of the uranium deposits that her husband was reported to have found. As the party make their way through the verdant jungles of the island, Susan is saved from a native attack by a newcomer, Manolo (Claudio Cassinelli). It now becomes obvious Susan's husband has abandoned his quest for the uranium and gone in search of a tribe living on a remote mountain called Ra Ra Me, Mountain of the Cannibal God. Manolo has to take the lead when the anthropologist falls into a ravine, but he is unable to save Susan's brother when they are cornered by natives. Manolo and Susan are taken away as prisoners as the natives disembowel her brother's body and cook his carcass over the flames of their fire. The natives believe Susan to be a goddess, and there on the mountain she

would have remained if Manolo hadn't outwitted their captors and killed one of them allowing the pair to make their escape.

Former giallo director Sergio Martino's **La Montagna del dio Cannibale**, also known as **The Mountain of the Cannibal God** and **Slave of the Cannibal God**, resembled a matinee adventure movie of the period, but contained the additional spice of the comely Ursula Andress along with gory scenes of native cannibalism. While the exploits of this cannibal tribe was not as shocking as their counterparts in **Cannibal Holocaust** (1980), the uncut version of this film was not without its share of violence and nudity, which included an exposed brain and the topless Andress. Martino's film acquired a degree of notoriety when it was added to the list of video nasties in November 1983 after being released to video in 1981 as **Prisoner of the Cannibal God**; this was because of many scenes of animal cruelty. It was later removed from the list in May 1985, but its latest release in the UK still has over two minutes of edits to the offending scenes of thirty years past. 🐾

When the price of lust is death . . . !

357

Prom Night

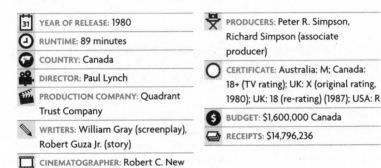

YEAR OF RELEASE: 1980

RUNTIME: 89 minutes

COUNTRY: Canada

DIRECTOR: Paul Lynch

PRODUCTION COMPANY: Quadrant Trust Company

WRITERS: William Gray (screenplay), Robert Guza Jr. (story)

CINEMATOGRAPHER: Robert C. New

PRODUCERS: Peter R. Simpson, Richard Simpson (associate producer)

CERTIFICATE: Australia: M; Canada: 18+ (TV rating); UK: X (original rating, 1980); UK: 18 (re-rating) (1987); USA: R

BUDGET: $1,600,000 Canada

RECEIPTS: $14,796,236

CAST: Leslie Nielsen, Jamie Lee Curtis, Casey Stevens, Anne-Marie Martin, Antoinette Bower, Michael Tough, Robert A. Silverman, Pita Oliver, David Mucci, Jeff Wincott, Mary Beth Rubens, George Touliatos, Melanie Morse MacQuarrie, David Gardner, Joy Thompson

A S FOUR CHILDREN play a game of hide and seek in an abandoned building, young Robin wants to join in. However, the four youngsters have something else in mind and seek to intimidate her. As she is forced against a window ledge to escape their taunts, she loses her balance and falls, plummeting several storeys to her death. The children Wendy, Nick, Jude and Kelly vow solemnly never to tell anyone about what has happened, but someone hidden in the shadows has seen everything. Robin's father (Leslie Nielsen) and the police deduce that Robin was the victim of a known sex offender and they set out to track him down.

Six years later Robin's sister Kim (Jamie Lee Curtis) and her brother Alex (Michael Tough) stand beside their parents at their sister Robin's grave. Shortly afterwards those who had been present when poor Robin fell to her death receive the first of a series of disturbing phone calls, warning of the horrors that will transpire on their forthcoming prom night. The call causes considerable alarm to Kelly, while Jude and Wendy simply laugh it off, believing it to be nothing more than a prank. Unbeknown to them, the man who was arrested that day, Leonard Murch, has escaped the asylum that has kept him from the world for the last six years. His scarred body has never recovered from the burns he received that day as the police pursued his car. Like Michael Myers before him, he heads back to the town where it all happened to mete out his revenge on what will be his victims' prom night, the anniversary of Robin's death. In accordance with the rules being laid down for this emerging genre, Kim will find herself stalked as the final girl, while her friends are slaughtered in the corridors of their school at the hands of a masked machete-wielding maniac.

For Liverpool-born Paul Lynch this was an early episode in what was to become a highly successful directorial career in both film and television. It was also early days for the slasher movie, but his film became an archetype for what followed, embracing so many of the aspects that are now associated with the genre. In the hope of securing extensive distribution, Lynch minimized the gore and, in the spirit of John Carpenter's **Halloween**, chose dimly lit settings in the execution of his murders. In leaving much to the audience's imagination, he kept them hooked until the very last. He had encountered many problems while at the negotiating table as he hoped

to realize sufficient financial backing for this feature; only when Jamie Lee Curtis agreed to take the lead role did the money finally come his way. Paramount had shown an interest in the distribution of **Prom Night**, but were only prepared to put it into 300 theatres, while Avco Embassy Pictures were prepared to open in over 1,200 theatres, which would see Lynch's film go on to generate $14 million. As the consultation continued, Paramount chose instead to release **Friday the 13th**.

Such was the success of the film, three sequels were later released: **Hello Mary Lou: Prom Night II** (1987), **Prom Night III: The Last Kiss** (1990) and **Prom Night IV: Deliver Us from Evil** (1992). A re-imagined **Prom Night** was made for $20 million in 2008, which invited almost universal derision from the critics, yet still went on to make in excess of $43 million.

Psycho

 YEAR OF RELEASE: 1960

 RUNTIME: 104 minutes

 COUNTRY: USA

 DIRECTOR: Alfred Hitchcock

 PRODUCTION COMPANY: Shamley Productions

WRITERS: Joseph Stefano (screenplay), Robert Bloch (novel)

 CINEMATOGRAPHER: John L. Russell

CERTIFICATE: Australia: M; Canada: G (Quebec); Canada: 18A (British Columbia); Canada: 13+ (Quebec); Canada: 18 (Nova Scotia); Canada: PG (Manitoba/Ontario); New Zealand: R16 (2010); UK: 15 (video rating) (1986); UK: X (original rating); USA: Approved (original rating); USA: M (re-rating) (1968); USA: R (re-rating) (1984)

 BUDGET: $806,947

CAST: Anthony Perkins, Vera Miles, John Gavin, Janet Leigh, Martin Balsam, John McIntire, Simon Oakland, Frank Albertson, Patricia Hitchcock, Vaughn Taylor, Lurene Tuttle, John Anderson, Mort Mills

IN A DARKENED Phoenix hotel room, Marion Crane (Janet Leigh) and her lover Sam Loomis (John Gavin) squabble over their future. Marion wants to marry, but Sam does not have the money to support her. On returning to the office where she works, Marion impulsively takes off with $40,000 from a property sale. On the second night of her journey to Sam's hometown, the rain pours heavily making it impossible to see the road clearly. After turning off the highway she spots the Bates Motel, overshadowed by an old house, inspired by Edward Hopper's "The House by the Railroad"; she decides to take shelter for the night. There she is greeted by the reserved proprietor Norman Bates (Anthony Perkins). She signs in under the name Marie Samuels, hoping to avoid attracting the unwanted attention of the police. As she chats with Norman, a man who appears dominated by his ageing mother, she resolves to return to Phoenix with the money. However, she feels it best she spends the night at the motel. Before retiring to bed, she prepares to take a shower. In a lingering moment of voyeuristic perversity, Norman removes a picture from the wall and peers through a peephole, which allows him to watch as Marion undresses. Once she enters the shower, the bathroom door opens. In the film's

pivotal scene, the obscured figure of an old woman pulls back the shower curtain. She reveals a large kitchen knife, and as the blade lifts and strikes so follows one of the most memorable scenes in the history of film, made even more terrifying by composer Bernard Herrmann's fervently screeching string section. Hitchcock had shocked his audience in more ways than one, having killed off his main character and star name at such an early stage in the film.

A week later Marion's sister, Lila, arrives at Sam's store in Fairvale to bring him the bad news that Marion has disappeared. Together with a private detective, Milton Arbogast, they begin searching the area and eventually come across the Bates Motel. Just as he nears the top of the stairs of the house, Arbogast becomes another victim of the old woman's blade. Hitchcock's film now races to its shocking climax. With Lila exploring the house looking for the whereabouts of her murdered sister, Norman heads upstairs. Lila takes the opportunity to slip through the cellar door and makes her way down the steps to a storage room where she sees an old woman sitting in a chair facing away to the wall. When she swings the chair around, she reveals an emaciated corpse dressed in the clothes of an old woman. Hitchcock continues with another highly acclaimed shot, focusing on a single point as a bare light bulb swings from side to side, exposing young Norman dressed in his mother's clothing.

During the epilogue, Lila, Sam and the sheriff wait to hear from a psychiatrist who has been called to examine Norman. The psychiatrist has listened to the whole story, but not from the mouth of Norman, for he no longer exists; rather, it has come from his mother who has assumed complete control of his mind.

Alfred Hitchcock's **Psycho** carried a theatre poster clearly stipulating a "no late admission" policy, for what was billed as a psychological thriller. His film would go on to set a new standard in horror cinema, one that has been much emulated but rarely matched. It has also been considered the first true slasher movie. Adapted from the Robert Bloch's novel of the same name, published in 1959, it was based on the crimes of Wisconsin serial killer Ed Gein. Hitchcock's magnum opus initially garnered mixed reviews, but with subsequent box office success and popular acclaim, it went on to receive four Academy Award nominations.

Executives at Paramount were not pleased with Hitchcock's choice of subject matter, insisting it was "too repulsive" and were categorical in their

**No one ...
BUT NO ONE ...
will be admitted
to the theatre
after the start of
each performance
of Alfred
Hitchcock's
Psycho.**

refusal to advance him the necessary funding. The director decided to film **Psycho** as quickly and cheaply as he could, offering to finance the film himself and shoot it at Universal-International as long as Paramount would act as distributor. He also deferred his director's fee of $250,000 for a 60 per cent ownership of the film negative. This eventually proved acceptable to Paramount. However, he was then confronted by resistance from producer Herbert Coleman and Shamley Productions executive Joan Harrison, who had major doubts as to the viability of such a film. Further budget reductions forced Hitchcock to film in black and white; this would lessen the bloody impact of the shower scene, but would allow him to play with a thematic use of black and white motifs to express the changes in his film's tone. This thematic approach was inspired by George Clouzot's innovative use of black and white in **Les Diaboliques** (1955), a film for which Hitchcock had much admiration, and as with **Psycho** had forbidden late entry.

There were episodes in **Psycho** that proved a direct challenge to the Motion Picture Production Code in the representation of sexuality and violence, with Sam and Marion shown very early in the film sharing the same bed, and Marion wearing only her underwear. The censors claimed they could see one of Leigh's breasts as well as her stand-in's buttocks. Amazingly another cause of concern was Marion's flushing of the toilet, with the torn toilet paper being fully visible. Further criticism came after the film's release, from those who felt it encouraged other filmmakers, as would be evidenced by Herschel G. Lewis and William Castle, who wasted little time in hurling bucket loads of blood and guts across the cinema screen. **Psycho** was to usher in a generation of slashers, none of which, however, would ever be the match of Norman Bates.

Three sequels followed, **Psycho II** (1983), **Psycho III** (1986) and **Psycho IV: The Beginning** (1990), the last being a part-prequel television movie, with a remake of the original in 1998.

Rabid Grannies

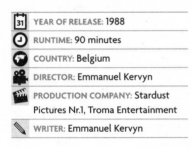

	YEAR OF RELEASE: 1988
	RUNTIME: 90 minutes
	COUNTRY: Belgium
	DIRECTOR: Emmanuel Kervyn
	PRODUCTION COMPANY: Stardust Pictures Nr.1, Troma Entertainment
	WRITER: Emmanuel Kervyn

CINEMATOGRAPHER: Hugo Labye

PRODUCERS: Jean-Bruno Castelain (supervising producer), Pierre Nanta (associate producer), Jonathan Rambert, Johan Vandewoestijne (executive producer)

CERTIFICATE: Australia: M; Canada: R; Canada: (Banned) (Nova Scotia); New Zealand: R16 (cut); UK: 18; USA: R

CAST: Catherine Aymerie, Caroline Braeckman, Richard Cotica, Danielle Daven, Patricia Davia, Robert Du Bois, Florine Elslande, Anne-Marie Fox, Franklin Steward Granvel, Paule Herreman

THE REMINGTON FAMILY members have gathered together at the mansion of their elderly aunts to celebrate their birthday. There is no hiding the fact that they all have a strong dislike of one another, but goodwill ensues because the family fortune is at stake. After the evening meal, the aunts open a present sent by an estranged family member who has an uncanny affiliation with the dark arts. As soon as the aunts open the package, they are possessed by demons and turned into flesh-eating monsters. One of their shocked guests is killed immediately at the table, as the rest scatter to find a place to hide in the mansion's endless rooms and corridors. The cackling aunts begin their search in this bloodthirsty game of hide and seek.

With precious little in the way of money, Emmanuel Kervyn directed a movie that drew upon the slapstick violence of **The Evil Dead** (1981) and pre-empted the visceral craziness of Peter Jackson's **Braindead** by almost four years. As with Jackson's cast, Kervyn made absolutely no attempt to create a likeable crowd, thus there was a delirium to the anticipation of these imaginative kills. Rather than assembling his country's finest actors, the director lavished his funds on the splatter, hacking off one man's limbs before impaling him on a pike, leading to a rotund fellow having his backside chewed off and, in probably the film's most shocking scene, luring

and then sadistically dismembering the aunts' young niece. The torture would continue and in a rather poignant episode, the wicked aunts trap a priest with a shotgun and give him the choice of suicide and eternal damnation or the tortures they will duly inflict on him. As the aunts gleefully tossed their avaricious relatives' body parts around the hallways of their home there was no denying the black humour underlying the bloody carnage. Many versions of Kervyn's film have been heavily censored, but its fans insist the only way to enjoy its content is with the excess remaining entirely intact, as evidenced in the European version.

> **Grandmother, what big teeth you have!**

Re-Animator

🗓 YEAR OF RELEASE: 1985

🕐 RUNTIME: 86 minutes

🌐 COUNTRY: USA

🎥 DIRECTOR: Stuart Gordon

🎬 PRODUCTION COMPANY: Empire Pictures, Re-Animator Productions

✏️ WRITERS: H. P. Lovecraft, Dennis Paoli, William Norris, Stuart Gordon

🎞 CINEMATOGRAPHERS: Mac Ahlberg, Robert Ebinger

🏆 PRODUCERS: Michael Avery (executive producer), Bruce William Curtis (executive producer), Bob Greenberg (associate producer), Charles Donald Storey (associate producer), Brian Yuzna

⭕ CERTIFICATE: Australia: R; Australia: MA (re-rating) (2007); Canada: 13+ (Quebec); New Zealand: R16; UK: 18 (cut); UK: 18 (re-rating uncut, 2007); USA: R (rating surrendered); USA: Unrated

💲 BUDGET: $900,000

🖥 RECEIPTS: $2,023,414

CAST: Jeffrey Combs, Bruce Abbott, Barbara Crampton, David Gale, Robert Sampson, Gerry Black, Carolyn Purdy-Gordon, Peter Kent, Barbara Pieters, Ian Patrick Williams, Bunny Summers, Al Berry, Derek Pendleton, Gene Scherer, James Ellis

WHILE WORKING IN Austria, eccentric medical student Herbert West (Jeffrey Combs) synthesizes a serum with properties that can resurrect the dead. He returns to America and locates in the town of Arkham, Massachusetts, where he takes a place at the Miskatonic University. In the basement of a house that he rents with Dan Cain (Bruce Abbott), he continues in his bizarre experimentation to perfect his eerie green concoction. The girl of Dan's dreams, Megan (Barbara Crampton) cannot shake her sense of disquiet in the presence of the obsessive Herbert, which is compounded when her cat disappears and then turns up dead in his refrigerator. Dan later sees the cat very much alive and in throes of violently sinking its claws into Herbert. The pair are once again forced to kill the shrieking creature. Herbert now recognizes a kindred spirit in Dan and invites him to work alongside him, which takes their research to the town's morgue with typically disastrous consequences. Very soon, with Herbert's helping hand, the dead are seen to rise from the slab, which results in bloody mayhem as the envious Dr Carl Hill (David Gale) attempts to steal West's formula.

Inspired by H. P. Lovecraft's *Herbert West: Re-Animator*, the blend of horror and comedy in Stuart Gordon's film went on to draw favourable comparisons with Sam Raimi's **The Evil Dead** (1981), particularly in its graphic use of comic book-styled excess. While his movie excelled in its craft, the film as a whole refused to take itself too seriously and brought to celluloid the cult figure of Jeffrey Combs playing the most deranged scientist since Victor Frankenstein. Combs' portrayal of the compulsive West has enthralled audiences for more than a quarter of a century and his reckless experimentation gave them just what they wanted as a series of cadavers stumbled out of control to splash 24 gallons of fake blood across the screen. There were many enthusiasts of the time, who considered this one of the goriest films to come out of this visceral decade. Special effects man John Naulin had never had to use so much blood on any of his previous films and found himself a little more involved in the creation of the corpse designs than he would

> **H. P. Lovecraft's classic tale of horror.**

have liked, using photographs of actual cadavers shot in his local mortuary.

Stuart's love of the works of H. P. Lovecraft would see him go on to make several other films featuring the writer's deathly tales, including **From Beyond** (1986), **Castle Freak** (1995) and **Dagon** (2001) along with the **Masters of Horror** episode "**Dreams in the Witch-House**" (2005). The success of **Re-Animator** would be followed by **Bride of Re-Animator** (1990) and over a decade later **Beyond Re-Animator** (2003).

Reeker

31 YEAR OF RELEASE: 2005		🛇 PRODUCERS: Ronnie Apteker (executive producer), Daniel Barone (co-producer), Don Dunn (co-producer and line producer), Tina Illman, David Kitchens (associate producer), Amanda Klein, Dave Payne, Ben Zarai (associate producer)	
⏱ RUNTIME: 90 minutes			
🌐 COUNTRY: USA			
🎥 DIRECTOR: Dave Payne			
🎬 PRODUCTION COMPANY: The Institution, Primal Pictures, Afraid of the Dark			
		◯ CERTIFICATE: Australia: MA; Ireland: 16; UK: 15; USA: Unrated	
✎ WRITER: Dave Payne			
▢ CINEMATOGRAPHER: Mike Mickens			

CAST: Devon Gummersall, Derek Richardson, Tina Illman, Scott Whyte, Arielle Kebbel, Michael Ironside, Eric Mabius, Marcia Strassman, Les Jankey, David Hadinger, Carole Ruggier, Paul Greenstein, Paul Butcher, Steven Zlotnick, Christopher Boyer

A FAMILY DRIVING ACROSS an isolated region of America become immersed in a toxic gas, and its vapours mutilate their dog. When the father goes out to investigate, he returns with half of his face torn away. In a gory sequence, which creates an element of intrigue and would hopefully set the tone for the remainder of the film, something foul then rips into them, leaving them all for dead.

The scene shifts to five students making their way to a festival, driving across a similar desert expanse, with an offended drugs dealer supposedly somewhere on their tail. True to form, their car breaks down, this time in what appears to be a mysteriously deserted diner; I say mysteriously because an hour ago this place was positively thriving. With the highway closed, they have no choice but to stay in the limbo of the aptly named "Halfway Motel". Shortly afterwards the mother from the film's prologue is seen, her mouth now severely disfigured, carving

365

"Tell my son I love him". This is no ordinary motel and there is the distinct impression that they are not alone. Their suspicions are alerted when they run into an awkward individual by the name of Henry (Michael Ironside), who is searching for his wife. For the moment, he is not the one they need to fear, as he is very quickly suffocated by a shrouded figure. It's not long before the kids are afflicted by images of the dead and a cloaked, gas-masked killer with a deadly assortment of fashioned implements begins to chalk up the body count. This particular assassin has the ability to become invisible, but can be traced by his terrible smell, hence the name **Reeker**.

If you can't breathe, then you can't scream.

On the surface this looked like another occasionally amusing teen slasher movie, with a group of likeable,

if not empty-headed youths waiting to be bumped off by a malevolent presence in a desert setting reminiscent of **The Hill Have Eyes** (1977). Dave Payne succeeded in engineering an additional upset at the finale when the protagonists face the cloaked figure of death, with vague echoes of **Final Destination** (2000). On its release, **Reeker** received a reasonably positive reception, but in terms of the development of the genre for a twenty-first century audience, it provided little in the way of progress; but then maybe that was the whole point as it joined a whole raft of films trying to rejuvenate the slasher madness of the 1980s. Sadly, while promising to put the fun back into horror, it lacked much of the necessary pacing that had epitomized so many of its more successful predecessors.

The Return of the Living Dead

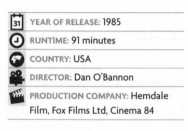

📅 YEAR OF RELEASE: 1985	✏️ WRITERS: Dan O'Bannon, Rudy Ricci, John A. Russo, Russell Streiner
🕐 RUNTIME: 91 minutes	
🌐 COUNTRY: USA	🎬 CINEMATOGRAPHER: Jules Brenner
🎥 DIRECTOR: Dan O'Bannon	🎬 PRODUCERS: John Daly (executive producer), Tom Fox, Derek Gibson (executive producer), Graham Henderson (co-producer)
🎬 PRODUCTION COMPANY: Hemdale Film, Fox Films Ltd, Cinema 84	

CERTIFICATE: Australia: M; Canada: R (Manitoba/Nova Scotia/Ontario); Canada: 13+ (Quebec)

BUDGET: $4,000,000
RECEIPTS: $14,237,000

CAST: Clu Gulager, James Karen, Don Calfa, Thom Mathews, Beverly Randolph, John Philbin, Jewel Shepard, Miguel A. Núñez Jr., Brian Peck, Linnea Quigley

THE PROLOGUE TO The Return of the Living Dead makes a familiar claim, insisting the events in this film are based on something that actually happened and then, in scenes inspired by George A. Romero's **Night of the Living Dead** (1968), reveals several drums containing a discarded experiment once carried out by the armed forces. This experiment had apparently gone hopelessly wrong. The bungling foreman Frank (James Karen), while giving Freddy (Thom Matthews) a tour of the basement to the warehouse where they work, accidentally releases one of the drums and the escaping gas pours into the room giving life to a corpse. In its reanimated state it resorts to type and goes completely wild, before Frank and Freddy finally succeed in its subjugation. They then escort the zombie to the town's mortuary to put an end to its existence in the flames of the cremator.

Meanwhile, Freddy's friends are waiting for him in the town's graveyard. His girlfriend Tina (Beverley Randolph) becomes impatient and decides to return to the warehouse, where she is set upon by a zombie the audience will come to know as Tarman. Over at the mortuary the first zombie

has now been incinerated. However, as the smoke rises from the vents it turns into a deadly gas that contaminates the air and then poisons the rainfall. The scalding rain compels Freddy's friends to take refuge in the warehouse where they find Tina desperately trying to fend off Tarman. As they barricade the basement door, one of the group is killed and very soon they are forced to go back through the cemetery in the hope of finding Freddy. As they make their way through the graveyard, they see the dead beginning to crawl from their graves and in the panic they become separated, making them easy quarry for this flesh-eating horde. Before they can get to Freddy, his situation has taken a turn for the worse; both he and Frank have become infected. They now begin to endure a transformation that will see them join the ranks of the living dead. The finale proved to be cataclysmic and in turn created the seed for yet another movie franchise of the 1980s.

Alien writer Dan O'Bannon noted John Russo's novel written in 1977 for his sequel to **Night of the Living Dead** (1968), and then abandoned the entire plot. In Russo's tale, ten years had passed since the events of the original movie and the zombie contagion had been controlled, that was until a fatal school bus crash. O'Bannon used Russo's premise, but chose to introduce a teenage cast to create a darkly humorous gorefest centred on a group of misfits who had more in common with the living dead than they had with any of their peers. The cult that surrounds **The Return of the Living Dead** regard this movie as a fitting homage to Romero's work, although O'Bannon's zombies differed from their predecessors in being unusually fleet of foot and quite capable of working together as Andrea Bianchi's atrophied creations had been in his doom-ridden **Burial Ground** (1981). The result would be an epic blood bath rife with morbid slapstick and copious nudity where brains and intestines were greedily torn from all and sundry. The studio, however, had major qualms about releasing such an extreme movie and insisted on many cuts before they would consider it for theatrical release. When it did see release there was little in the way of a fanfare and its success at the box office was moderate at best. However, in the years that followed it was to become a cult favourite, which led to a series of sequels, **Return of the Living Dead Part II** (1988), **Return of the Living Dead 3**, (1993), **Necropolis** (2005) and **Rave From the Grave** (2005).

They're back from the grave and ready to party!

Rooms for Tourists

 YEAR OF RELEASE: 2004

RUNTIME: 90 minutes

COUNTRY: Argentina

 DIRECTOR: Adrián García Bogliano

PRODUCTION COMPANY: Mondo Trasho Productions, Roman Porno Eiga

 WRITERS: Adrián García Bogliano, Ramiro García Bogliano

 CINEMATOGRAPHER: Dario Bermeo, Veronica Padron

 PRODUCERS: Sebastian Fretes, Ramiro García Bogliano (associate producer), Hernán Moyano (executive producer), Hernán Moyano (line producer), Rodrigo Ordenes Miro (executive producer), Federico Ricaldoni (associate producer)

 BUDGET: $3,000

CAST: Jimena Krouco, Elena Siritto, Mariela Mujica, Brenda Vera, Victoria Witemburg, Eliana Polonara, Alejandro Lise, Trajano Leydet, Rolf García, Oscar Ponce, Leonardo Menaci, Mariana Pacotti, Liliana Rua, Hernán Sáez

FIVE YOUNG WOMEN travel through an isolated rural region on a coach from Buenos Aires to the Argentine town of Trinidad, one of them seeking an abortion. Images of an unknown girl being beaten after the discovery of a discarded foetus followed by another girl, whose eyes bleed as she stands before a burning woman, plague the guilt-ridden dreams of Theda (Elena Siritto). The bus drops them off in the small town of San Roman, where they find the train scheduled to take them to Trinidad has already departed. They walk through deserted streets to find the townsfolk congregated at the Catholic church, where a local woman is being exorcised in a bizarre ritual conducted by the town's zealous priest (Oscar Ponce). The insane fervour of the ceremony unsettles the girls, but a seemingly kindly local, Nestitor (Rolf García), comes to their rescue, offering rooms for tourists at the large house he owns with his brother. The girls gratefully accept and trek to his secluded home.

The camera work in the house enshrouds it with a disconcerting milieu, which deepens when one of the party is confronted by a figure standing at her window. Theda's terrible visions return;

> **More than what the flesh and bone can stand.**

a masked man now prowls through her nightmares, savagely butchering the women he encounters. When the girls go down to dinner Horacio, the obsessive priest, awaits them. His conversation turns into a sermon on morality and the evil that dwells in the heart of man. The evil becomes manifest in the darkest hours, when one of the girls awakens to be hacked and dismembered by a killer disguised in an ill-defined white mask, very reminiscent of that seen forty years before in Mario Bava's **Blood and Black Lace** (1964). Her piercing screams, the first of many, arouse the other girls, who discover they have been locked in a booby-trapped house with a bloodthirsty psychotic armed with a meat cleaver along with the two untrustworthy brothers. The camera stays close to each as they bid to escape through the surrounding darkness and, one by one, the screaming girls are taken down as the blood begins to flow. Each of them hides a secret and when the reason for their slaughter is finally revealed, it is steeped in an irony that reflects a country still very much in the sway of the Catholic Church.

Filmed twelve months before Eli Roth's **Hostel** (2005), Adrián García Bogliano's **Habitaciones Para**

Turistas belied its modest budget to produce a black and white terror that surpassed so many of its visceral colour counterparts. The grainy monochrome cinematography worked to convey a claustrophobic sense of dread, which didn't detract from the severity of the grisly attacks. Bogliano's aim was to make a slasher movie of substance; this he did with a group of girls the viewer came to care about, set against a town wrapped in the clutches of an ambiguous Catholicism. There was potency to the violence throughout these ninety minutes with scenes of viciousness and a display of bloodletting that looked even more horrific on this deficient stock of film. ✤

Santa Sangre

📅 YEAR OF RELEASE: 1989

🕐 RUNTIME: 123 minutes

🌐 COUNTRY: Mexico/Italy

🎬 DIRECTOR: Alejandro Jodorowsky

🎞 PRODUCTION COMPANY: Produzioni Intersound, Productora Fílmica Real

✎ WRITERS: Alejandro Jodorowsky, Roberto Leoni, Claudio Argento

🎦 CINEMATOGRAPHER: Daniele Nannuzzi

♟ PRODUCERS: Claudio Argento, Anuar Badin (line producer), René Cardona Jr. (executive producer), Angelo Jacono (executive producer)

○ CERTIFICATE: Australia: R; Canada: R (Ontario); Canada: 18+ (Quebec) (uncut version); UK: 18; USA: NC-17 (uncut video version); USA: R (edited version) (1991)

💲 BUDGET: $787,000

CAST: Axel Jodorowsky, Blanca Guerra, Guy Stockwell, Thelma Tixou, Sabrina Dennison, Adan Jodorowsky, Faviola Elenka Tapia, Teo Jodorowsky, María de Jesús Aranzabal, Jesús Juárez, Sergio Bustaman

A YOUNG MAN, FENIX, has been confined to a mental institution; within these walls he has retired to the safety of the upper branches of a tree. Through a series of flashbacks, we see him growing up in the circus in which his parents worked. His mother, Concha, was a trapeze artist, who Fenix watched as she prayed before the image of an armless saint, a deity who was abused as a girl. His father, Olgo, was a knife thrower, who consorted with a seemingly covetous tattooed woman. As the church of the armless saint, Santa Sangre, was bulldozed to the ground, his mother discovered her husband's infidelity and in a fit of jealous rage poured acid over his crotch, prior to him severing her arms and then killing himself. His father's tattooed lover was seen driving away accompanied by Fenix's mute friend.

Fenix returns to the present and is told he has a visitor, his mother. His vision of his mother is of an armless saint who has come to take him away from this domain of madness. On his return to the world beyond the asylum, he meets with his long-lost mute friend Alma, who has grown to become the most grave of women. Against his will, he has to become the arms of his mother. She insists he walks and sits behind her, his arms inserted into the sleeves of her dresses. His hands are forced to do her bidding, which will soon turn to a murderous campaign of revenge. At his mother's request, he will use his father's knives as he struggles to accept his mother has grown to become a spiteful woman whose desires border on the incestuous.

Chilean-born Alejandro Jodorowsky's **Santa Sangre** is a terrifying hallucinatory work of genius. When compared to his previous films it is probably his most coherent piece of cinema, yet remains difficult to define. In its kaleidoscope of vibrant colours and expressive imagery, it is evocative of horror, sensuality, madness and the blackest of humour. With the traumatized Fenix having spent so long away from the world we can never truly be sure if all we see is a product of his deluded imagining or his mother's manipulations. The saddening sight of the elephant's funeral offers the

Forget everything you have ever seen.

grimmest of realities while the mentally challenged children's cocaine snorting reflects on a loss of innocence, all the while in this phantasmagorical dream vision, which just might be locked in Fenix's illusory mindscape. Jodorowsky, a former student of Marcel Marceau, drew upon the more unsettling aspects of Luis Buñuel's surrealism to create a film which broods in its violence and sexuality, and yet portrays a beauty and a tragedy reminiscent of an oedipal Greek tragedy. While many commentators have coupled **Santa Sangre** with Hitchcock's **Psycho** (1960), Georges Franju's **Eyes Without a Face** (1960), the works of Fellini, and that of Claudio Argento's illustrious brother Dario, its artistic merits were overlooked when it was submitted for release in the United States and was originally rated NC-17 due to "several scenes of extremely explicit violence". An edited version of the film was later released for public consumption with an R rating for "bizarre, graphic violence and sensuality, and for drug content". Jodorowsky, who had endured similar criticism for his extreme classic **El Topo** (1970), would never have been distracted by such censure; his was a flamboyant vision that cared little for adhering to popular expectation. **Santa Sangre** was in essence a parody of what had become the self-parodying slasher movies of only a few years before, but its surreal splendour intimated something at variance with this premise. ❦

Saw

📅 YEAR OF RELEASE: 2004

🕐 RUNTIME: 103 minutes

🌏 COUNTRY: Australia/USA

🎥 DIRECTOR: James Wan

🎬 PRODUCTION COMPANY: Evolution Entertainment, Saw Productions Inc., Twisted Pictures

✏️ WRITERS: Leigh Whannell, James Wan

🎞️ CINEMATOGRAPHER: David A. Armstrong

🎬 PRODUCERS: Lark Bernini (associate producer), Peter Block (executive producer), Mark Burg, Jason Constantine (executive producer), Daniel J. Heffner (co-producer), Gregg Hoffman, Oren Koules, Richard H. Prince, Stacey Testro (executive producer)

⭕ CERTIFICATE: Australia: MA; Canada: 18 (Nova Scotia); Canada: 18A (British Columbia/Manitoba/Ontario); Canada: R (Alberta); Canada: R (Nova Scotia) (re-rating); Canada: 18A; Canada: 16+ (Quebec); Ireland: 18; New Zealand: R18; UK: 18; USA: NC-17 (original rating); USA: R (edited for re-rating); USA: Unrated (uncut DVD version)

💲 BUDGET: $1,200,000

🗂️ RECEIPTS: $102,898,683

CAST: Leigh Whannell, Cary Elwes, Danny Glover, Ken Leung, Dina Meyer, Mike Butters, Paul Gutrecht, Michael Emerson, Benito Martinez, Shawnee Smith, Makenzie Vega, Monica Potter, Ned Bellamy, Alexandra Bokyun Chun, Avner Garbi, Tobin Bell

TWO BATTERED AND confused men, a surgeon and a photographer, awaken in what looks to be a grimy, disused public toilet. They are chained by their ankles to quite substantial pipes with a dead man lying between them, his corpse still holding onto a tape player and a gun. After finding cassettes have been placed in their pockets, they learn one must kill the other within the next few hours or their families will lose their lives. The hacksaws they find are not designed to cut into their chains, but it is obvious they can get through flesh and bone. These two unfortunates are the latest victims of the Jigsaw Killer, a predator who thrives on mind games and the slaughter of his victims using the most bizarre contraptions so far seen in a splatter movie. He never actually kills; rather, he traps his prey and creates a scenario where they have to kill to survive. The depravity of the man is highlighted in a series of grisly flashbacks. One in particular shows a girl bound to a chair, her head strapped into a bear-trap mask, which, when the timer goes off, will tear her lower jaw from her face. The key that will save her lies in the stomach of a half-dead man lying partially comatose in the same cell. Her fate rests entirely on her will to survive. As Jigsaw eventually reveals, his victims are not entirely innocent; their questionable morality and disdain for life has brought them to his sickening world. While the men fight to survive, two detectives, Tapp (Danny Glover) and Sing (Ken Leung), discover more of the killer's victims.

Dare you see SAW?

Both James Wan and Leigh Wannell had been involved in the obscure Australian terror **Stygian** (2000), which cultivated a degree of interest at the Melbourne Underground film festival of that same year. However, beyond those Antipodean shores it made precious little impact. Undeterred they produced a nine-minute short in 2003 simply entitled **Saw**; their intention was to get it into the hands of bigger producers who would hopefully listen to their ideas to produce a full-length feature. The short film placed Wannell in the bear-trap mask as he struggled to make his escape. Having been given the go ahead to create a movie,

they shot their film in only eighteen days, but for all of their hard work it was only ever scheduled for release to DVD. There were those who thought its premise bore too many similarities to the highly influential Se7en (1995), and it had all been done before. However, during its pre-screening the merits in Wan's claustrophobic direction attained some recognition and it was decided to give **Saw** a cinematic release, which subsequently attracted a far greater market than this creative team could have ever envisaged. They gave birth to the twenty-first century's first enigmatic serial killer in a complex thriller that cast its audience into the most dismal of settings in a situation of curious plausibility. Such was the movie's success there followed **Saw II** (2005), **Saw III** (2006), **Saw IV** (2007), **Saw V** (2008), **Saw VI** (2009) and **Saw 3D** (2010). Both Wan and Wannell have continued in their respective careers, with Wan directing and Wannell starring in two more horror films beyond the Saw franchise, **Dead Silence** (2007) and **Insidious** (2010).

Scanners

 YEAR OF RELEASE: 1981
RUNTIME: 103 minutes
COUNTRY: Canada
 DIRECTOR: David Cronenberg

 PRODUCTION COMPANY: Canadian Film Development Corporation (CFDC), Filmplan, Victor Solnicki Productions

WRITER: David Cronenberg

CINEMATOGRAPHER: Mark Irwin

PRODUCERS: Pierre David (executive producer), Claude Héroux, Victor Solnicki (executive producer)

 CERTIFICATE: Australia: R; Canada: R; Canada: 13+ (Quebec); New Zealand: R16

BUDGET: $4,100,000 Canadian

RECEIPTS: $14,225,876

CAST: Jennifer O'Neill, Stephen Lack, Patrick McGoohan, Lawrence Dane, Michael Ironside, Robert A. Silverman, Lee Broker, Mavor Moore, Adam Ludwig, Murray Cruchley, Fred Doederlein, Géza Kovács, Sonny Forbes, Jérôme Tiberghien, Denis Lacroix

SCANNERS WAS NEVER intended to be a splatter movie; there was only one instance of effective gore in the entire film, but that one moment was one of the most shocking and most talked about scenes of its day. These shots were very cleverly used in the film's trailer, enhancing David Cronenburg's standing as a horror director of repute and in its wake had the gore fans of that generation queuing in their droves.

In the futuristic year of 1985, Cameron Vale (Stephen Lack) ambles through a shopping mall foraging for leftovers and cigarettes. With one focused stare, he causes a woman to collapse and convulse on the floor, which immediately alerts a couple of undercover agents. In the ensuing chase a tranquilizer dart brings Vale down and he later recovers in a hospital bed funded by ConSec, a weapon and security systems corporation. Here he learns from Dr

> **There are 4 billion people on earth; 237 are Scanners with the most terrifying powers ever created ... and they are winning.**

Ruth (Patrick McGoohan) that he is a Scanner, one of a select group whose mothers were treated with the drug Ephemerol to ease their pregnancies, but instead produced children with mind-reading capabilities and the lethal capacity to blow people's brains apart. The birth defects caused by this fictional drug were a chilling reminder of the tragedy that followed the marketing of Thalidomide, an antiemetic prescribed to pregnant women during the late 1950s and early 1960s.

A covert government operation has been set up to locate the Scanners, designed specifically to subdue their power and prevent a renegade group from taking over the world. While this discussion takes place, the megalomaniac Darryl Revok (Michael Ironside) callously murders ConSec's leading Scanner at a press conference in the infamous exploding head scene.

He escapes from the building, killing five more people. Dr Ruth convinces Vale to infiltrate Revok's Scanners with the intention of putting a halt to their plans for global domination. The film then spirals into one of paranoiac intrigue and the politics of corporate espionage rather than the horror upon which Cronenberg had previously established his reputation.

Up until the release of **The Fly** in 1986, **Scanners** was David Cronenberg's most profitable film, but this nightmare vision was also one of his most problematic undertakings. Due to the rather strange work practices endorsed by the Canadian film industry it was necessary to begin shooting with only two weeks' pre-production; as a consequence there wasn't enough time for the screenplay to be completed, forcing Cronenberg to write his script before shooting between 4 a.m. and 7 a.m. each day. This hampered the production design team, who did not have the necessary time to build sets and there were occasions where the crew had to drive around looking for things to shoot. When it went to the cinemas, the critics didn't take kindly to what some perceived as the foolishness in his dark vision, observing a blandness to this futuristic world and those who inhabited it. They failed to see that in the corporately engineered age that his film envisaged, this was the point he was trying to make. The Academy of Science Fiction, Fantasy & Horror Films took little note of this condemnation and duly awarded the film its Saturn Award in 1981 for "Best International Film".

Four sequels eventually followed; **Scanners II: The New Order** (1990), **Scanners III: The Takeover** (1992), **Scanner Cop** (1994) and **Scanner Cop II: Volkin's Revenge** (1995). Neither David Cronenberg nor any member of his cast from the original film was involved with any of the sequels. For the past four years, a remake has been in discussion but so far there has been little progress in returning it to the big screen. 🍁

School's Out

📅 YEAR OF RELEASE: 1999		✏️ WRITER: Kai Meyer	
🕐 RUNTIME: 93 minutes		🎞️ CINEMATOGRAPHER: Sven Kirsten	
🎬 COUNTRY: Germany		⚙️ PRODUCER: Peter Lohner	
🎥 DIRECTOR: Robert Sigl		⭕ CERTIFICATE: USA: R	
🎬 PRODUCTION COMPANY: RTL		💲 BUDGET: $1,300,000	

CAST: Katharina Wackernagel, Niels-Bruno Schmidt, Marlene Meyer-Dunker, Nils Nelleßen, Rita Lengyel, Urs Remond, Sandra Leonhard, Raphaël Vogt, Michael Habeck, Enie van de Meiklokjes

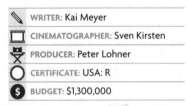

WITH THE SUCCESS of **Scream** (1996), Robert Sigl released his slasher movie to his German homeland. It was his first time directing a full-length feature since his cult horror **Laurin** (1989), a film that had been made for German television. On the last day of school, a group of teenagers get together for their end of year party. While most of the students are there to enjoy the revelry, others have devised a series of shenanigans to upset the teaching staff. Maybe they should have been paying more attention to the radio broadcasts, for a perverted mass murderer has slipped away from the town's mental facility. A teenage girl who had been driving her dad's taxi has already gone missing. The killer has now arrived on the school premises to indulge his most depraved fantasies, and with the students trapped it becomes too easy for him track them down, picking them off one by one until only two remain. As the film builds to its exciting climax, the heroine of the proceedings discovers a clue to the killer's identity, but will she survive to tell the tale?

Schrei – denn ich werde dich töten!, or **School's Out** as it became known in English-speaking countries, was imported into America by the horror film magazine *Fangoria*, and subsequently dubbed into English. The dubbing proved problematic and begged the question as to whether it would have been preferable to subtitle the film, although in *Fangoria*'s defence subtitled features have infrequently deterred many less discerning viewers. It is little wonder the magazine became interested in Sigl's film; with the success of **Scream**, this was a chance to see a return to the slasher fare of the 1980s. The body count was high and was made all the more enticing due to the occasionally imaginative set pieces which led to a steady flow of blood, although the film was never particularly gory, as was the case with many of the more successful eighties slashers. There were facets to this film that made it comparable to Michele Soavi's **Stagefright** (1987), notably its claustrophobic setting and the use of light in the darkened spaces, which were reminiscent of Soavi's mentor Dario Argento. **Schools Out** evinced a menace, which took it beyond the realms of its intended teenage market; so much so, and as with many of its murderous predecessors, it attracted a television sequel, **Das Mädcheninternat – Deine Schreie Wird Niemand Hören**, in 2001.

Schramm: Into the Mind of a Serial Killer

 YEAR OF RELEASE: 1994   RUNTIME: 70 minutes

COUNTRY: Germany	CINEMATOGRAPHER: Manfred O. Jelinski
DIRECTOR: Jörg Buttgereit	
PRODUCTION COMPANY: Jelinski & Buttgereit	PRODUCER: Manfred O. Jelinski
WRITERS: Jörg Buttgereit, Franz Rodenkirchen	CERTIFICATE: New Zealand: R18; USA: Not Rated

CAST: Florian Koerner von Gustorf, Monika M., Micha Brendel, Carolina Harnisch, Xaver Schwarzenberger, Gerd Horvath, Michael Brynntrup, Franz Rodenkirchen, Anne Presting, Eddi Zacharias, Michael Romahn, Volker Hauptvogel

THE SOLITARY LOTHAR Schramm (Florian Koerner von Gustorf) seems like a pleasant fellow; his emotional state, however, is fragile and consequently his psychotic predilections have taken control of his life. As the film begins, he dies following a fall from a ladder while painting over his blood-stained apartment walls. Rather than the pools of blood to which viewers of these films have become accustomed, Schramm lies in a pool of white paint. We learn from a newspaper report that he was the "lipstick murderer" and courtesy of a series of hallucinatory flashbacks there then unfolds this most peculiar tale. When he was alive, Lothar worked as a taxi driver, often escorting a neighbouring prostitute (Monika M.) while she attended to the needs of her undisclosed clientele in a palatial building somewhere close to the centre of the city. He secretly lusts after his exotic neighbour, but his inadequacies make him incapable of expressing his needs before her or any other woman. His only means of communication with women is through violence, although other than the slaying of a couple of door-to-door preachers, his brutality is never shown before the camera. After each of his killings he is revealed savouring his depraved fantasies, for Lothar's world is one dominated by surreal fantasy; to one corpse he applies lipstick, one of his deceased victims is tied up while another's legs are unceremoniously spread-eagled. When this isn't enough, he masturbates with his blow-up doll, gratifying himself with the photographed corpses. His crimes, however, have made him desperately unhappy. Such is Schramm's self-loathing he punishes himself by hammering a nail into his foreskin. This insanity is then tempered

... today I am dirty, but tomorrow I'll be just dirt.

by visions of the beach he knew as a young boy and his dreams of returning to the innocence of childhood.

When he finally gets the chance to engage with the prostitute across the landing he takes her to a restaurant before returning her to his apartment. Here he sedates her by spiking her drink and then removes her clothes to photograph her semi-naked body. The next morning she awakens, oblivious to his unseemly antics. As Lothar passes from this world, the prostitute travels unaccompanied to the building, seen earlier in the film. Here she is left bound and gagged with the murderous taxi driver no longer able to come to her rescue.

Jörg Buttgereit didn't have the money to afford a police car in the making of his film, which is perhaps as well because his feature didn't concern the authorities' efforts to track down this homicidal maniac. Instead, his film guided its viewers on a voyeuristic journey into the delusory vision of a truly unhinged mind. This powerful tale was told using an imaginative time-line as it traversed between the past and present, never truly adopting a sequence of events or the necessity for a linear narrative. While Buttgereit once again sought to disturb

and challenge our everyday perceptions, there was an underlying sub-plot in evidence, relating the frustration of a pathetic individual's unrequited love; one that would make the horror in the bondage epilogue all the more harrowing. Our sympathies came to lie with Florian Koerner von Gustorf and his distant portrayal of this isolated serial killer, for he was never presented as being a wholly inhuman monster; rather, Schramm was a tortured soul trying to return to the lost innocence of his youth.

The film's stock was of the low grade that characterized Buttgereit's filmmaking, which served to reflect his movie's oppressively downbeat tone in a desolate visualization of modern-day Germany. While low budget, Buttgereit's efforts revealed him as an infinitely talented filmmaker, with a touch of the art house auteur manifest in his technique. There were many sequences in **Schramm** observed to echo Luis Buñuel's trademark for the surreal, and the constant juxtaposing of imagery would evoke memories of the work of the esteemed David Lynch during the run of **Twin Peaks** (1990–1) and **Twin Peaks: Fire Walk With Me** (1992) leading to **Lost Highway** (1997).

Scream

YEAR OF RELEASE: 1996		PRODUCTION COMPANY: Dimension Films, Woods Entertainment	
RUNTIME: 111 minutes			
COUNTRY: USA		WRITER: Kevin Williamson	
DIRECTOR: Wes Craven		CINEMATOGRAPHERS: Mark Irwin, Peter Deming	

PRODUCERS: Stuart M. Besser (co-executive producer), Dixie J. Capp, (co-producer), Cathy Konrad, Marianne Maddalena (executive producer), Nicholas Mastandrea (associate producer), Bob Weinstein (executive producer), Harvey Weinstein, Cary Woods

 CERTIFICATE: Australia: MA; Canada: 16+ (Quebec); Canada: 18 (Nova Scotia); Canada: R (Manitoba/Ontario); Canada: 18+ (TV rating); Ireland: 18; New Zealand: R16; UK: 18; USA: TV-MA; USA: R

 BUDGET: $15,000,000

RECEIPTS: $161,600,000

CAST: Drew Barrymore, Roger Jackson, Kevin Patrick Walls, David Booth, Carla Hatley, Neve Campbell, Skeet Ulrich, Lawrence Hecht, Courteney Cox, W. Earl Brown, Rose McGowan, Lois Saunders, David Arquette, Joseph Whipp, Matthew Lillard

THE INTRODUCTION TO Wes Craven's **Scream** was one of the most shocking witnessed on the silver screen in many a year, and while it paid homage to **Psycho** (1960) it also set a new standard for filmmakers treading into the domain of teenage horror. Craven initially focused on the plight of his lead actress (Drew Barrymore) and within minutes had butchered her in a tense sequence as a mysterious voice (Roger L. Jackson) plied her with questions over the telephone. As he forced his way into her home, he was revealed as a man dressed in a ghostly costume; the audience would very soon come to know him as Ghostface.

The murdered girl's classmate, Sydney Prescott (Neve Campbell), whose mother was raped and murdered only twelve months before, is trying to

> **Now everybody is a victim and everybody is a suspect!**

come to terms with all that has gone on in her life. The night after the murder, shown at the beginning of the film, her phone rings and the chilling voice of the killer can once again be heard. He verbally torments her and then assaults her in her home, only to withdraw as he is beaten off. The following night, with her father out of town on business, Sydney is invited to sleep at the house of her friend Tatum (Rose McGowan) and her brother Dwight "Dewey" Riley (David Arquette), who works as a deputy with the sheriff's office. In the seeming safety of Tatum's house, Sydney receives another call from Ghostface, who throws her life into turmoil by telling her the man who was convicted of her mother's murder, one Cotton Weary (Liev Schreiber), is innocent. Suspicion is now thrown on her father (Lawrence Hecht), but no one can seem to locate his whereabouts.

As the killer continues to stalk the fictional town of Woodsboro, California, school is cancelled. Tatum's boyfriend decides it's high time they get their friends together and had a party. As the teenagers gather under one roof, Ghostface quietly enters the scene, providing the perfect opportunity to methodically pick them off one at a time as he works his way to the film's spirited heroine, Sydney Prescott.

Wes Craven returned with an ironic self-awareness for his film **Scream**, to the leafy suburbs that were very similar to those seen around Elm Street, and once again succeeded in popularizing the horror movie for a new generation of cinemagoers. This proved to be the first suspense-driven slasher film to hit major cinemas in almost a decade, as he and scriptwriter Kevin Williamson, of *Dawson's Creek* fame, set about revolutionizing virtually every cliché the genre had for so long relished. Throughout this feature, he liberally

referenced his own film **Nightmare on Elm Street** (1984) and John Carpenter's **Halloween** (1978) as a reminder as to what had gone before. As with the success of **Halloween**, a series of imitators would immediately follow but weren't to detract from **Scream's** monumental impact, principally in the guise of **I Know What You Did Last Summer** (1997), **Halloween H20** (1998), **Urban Legend** (1998) and **Valentine** (2001).

The iconic mask returned in **Scream**, which has since gone on to be of commercially greater significance than those worn by time-served slashers Michael Myers or Jason Vorhees. Craven also looked to dispatch his endearing cast in a variety of bloody and imaginative ways including a throat slitting, a graphic disembowelment, multiple stabbings, a skull crushing by a garage door, an umbrella stabbing and electrocution by television set. Critically the reaction to the film was overwhelming and it was to spawn three sequels in 1997, 2000 and 2011, with a fifth entry now in planning.

Scream Bloody Murder

YEAR OF RELEASE: 1973	**PRODUCTION COMPANY:** Alan Roberts Productions, First American Films, University Film Company
RUNTIME: 90 minutes	
COUNTRY: USA	**WRITERS:** Larry Alexander (screenplay), Marc B. Ray (screenplay)
DIRECTOR: Marc B. Ray	

CINEMATOGRAPHER: Stephen H. Burum

PRODUCERS: Larry Alexander (associate producer), Ron Mitchell (associate producer), Marc B. Ray, Alan Roberts (executive producer)

CERTIFICATE: UK: 15; USA: R

CAST: Fred Holbert, Leigh Mitchell, Robert Knox, Ron Bastone, Suzette Hamilton, Willey Reynolds, A. Maana Tanelah, Florence Lea, Angus Scrimm, Cecil Reddick, Gloria Earl, J. M. Jones

YOUNG MATTHEW'S LOVE for his mother veers out of control when he kills his father with the farm's tractor. His arm, however, becomes trapped in the machinery and he suffers serious injuries. He is soon after taken away to a sanatorium, where they attempt to address his psychological problems, and in due course his lost hand is replaced with a hook. Many years hence, a similar occurrence would happen to one Fred Kreuger. Now aged eighteen, Matthew returns home to find his mother, Daisy, has remarried. When he catches his stepfather becoming amorous with his beloved mother, Matthew seizes an axe and they both fall victim to his maniacal wrath. He journeys to Venice, Los Angeles, leaving a trail of mean-spirited murder, as his deluded state of mind makes it impossible to accept that his mother could ever desire another man. The multiple killings might suggest an inevitable tide of gore, but the film never actually delivered it in the excess promised in the title.

Matthew eventually befriends Vera, who works as a prostitute and has an unusual talent for painting. The poor girl, who due to the limited budget is played by the same actress as his mother, is oblivious to his psychosis and his bizarre interpretation of her canvases. She assumes a motherly role in his life, but gets a horrible shock when he abducts her and holds her hostage in what he claims is his mansion, having already disposed of its previous owner and the maid.

Scream Bloody Murder, also known as **Claw of Terror**, **Matthew** and **Captive Female**, falls into the seventies grindhouse drive-in theatre category of film and is an interesting precursor to the slasher fare of the early 1980s. Marc B. Ray's feature doesn't go along with the last girl scenario although the ending certainly befits the film's depiction of an insane killer on the loose. The intimation of sex and nudity coupled with a maniac with an Oedipal complex who prefers murder with knives, axes and meat cleavers over his hooked hand was the kind of unadulterated exploitative trash made for the drive-in theatres of the day. The deviant Matthew assumed the role of Norman Bates, but now set loose in a world lusting for sleazy excess and he was given licence to go so much further than his schizophrenic predecessor. In the years that followed, Marc moved into television, working on *Ellery Queen* and *The New Mickey Mouse Club*. Stephen H. Burum produced some rather extraordinary camera work for this low-budget feature, warping the perspective during the hallucinatory scenes and helping build the tension in Matthew's mansion. This was the beginning of a highly successful calling, which would see him work in television on *Mork and Mindy* and continue in film on the cult acclaimed

Pray that it never happens to you!

Rumble Fish (1983), *St Elmo's Fire* (1985), *The Untouchables* (1987) and on until his retirement.

Both the DVD and VHS prints of **Scream Bloody Murder** continue to frustrate fans of this and grindhouse cinema as a whole; four minutes were removed from the original cut, but no one has ever been able to identify the differentiation between the original and the edit that exists today.

Sentenced to Hang

📅 YEAR OF RELEASE: 1989		✎ WRITERS: Stephen Shiu, Johnny Mak	
⏱ RUNTIME: 105 minutes		🎞 CINEMATOGRAPHER: Herman Yau	
🎬 COUNTRY: Hong Kong		⚙ PRODUCER: Stephen Shiu	
🎥 DIRECTOR: Taylor Wong		○ CERTIFICATE: Hong Kong: III	

CAST: Kent Cheng, Tony Leung Ka Fai, Carrie Ng, Tin-Ngoh Seung, Feng Tien, Elvis Tsui, Sai-Kit Yung

LI WAI AND his two likeable friends have put up with too much from their boss. They are fed up with being the underdogs of society and so, in an effort to repay their abusive employer, they scheme to kidnap his son. They call themselves The Wolves and as they hatch their desperate plan, they know that one way or another there will be

no going back. As the trio negotiate the ransom the son makes a bid to escape, but in the ensuing struggle is accidentally killed. The Wolves have no choice but to persist in their demands. Their boss refuses to relent and calls in the police. Angered by his actions they scheme to take him as their next victim and then extort money from his family.

In comical scenes so typical of Hong Kong's category III excess, the police appear more interested in wise cracks and beating up potential suspects. The hilarity is soon forgotten as the film takes an inevitably dark turn, leaving these young men behind bars and regretting their chosen path, as the hangman prepares his noose.

Taylor Wong's **Sentenced to Hang** has the notoriety of being the first Hong Kong movie to receive a Category III classification, but is devoid of the excess of the similarly rated films that would follow during the 1990s. There is violence to this film and a solitary scene of full frontal nudity, but this is distanced from the excess that would come to typify the Hong Kong horror industry. Wong's film, however, remains a good fast-paced crime drama where the fear of death is never too far away and contains a poignant narration that recollects an actual series of events from the 1960s, which led to murder and the last hangings in Hong Kong. The director of photography Herman Yau would go on to direct **The Untold Story** (1993), and along with his director has been widely praised for the eerie finale staring down at the noose hanging in the spotlight.

Severance

YEAR OF RELEASE: 2006
RUNTIME: 96 minutes
COUNTRY: UK
DIRECTOR: Christopher Smith
PRODUCTION COMPANY: Qwerty Films, Dan Films, HanWay Films, Isle of Man Film, N1 European Film Produktions GmbH & Co. KG, UK Film Council
WRITERS: James Moran, Christopher Smith
CINEMATOGRAPHER: Ed Wild
PRODUCERS: Alexandra Arlango, Steve Christian (executive producer),

Finola Dwyer (producer: Qwerty Films), Andrew Hildebrand (co-producer: Qwerty Films), Michael Kuhn (executive producer), Jason Newmark, Malcolm Ritchie (co-executive producer), Rosa Romero (line producer), Jill Tandy (co-executive producer), Colleen Woodcock (co-producer: Qwerty Films), Mark Woolley (co-producer: Qwerty Films)

CERTIFICATE: Australia: MA; Canada: 13+ (Quebec); UK: 15; Ireland: 18; New Zealand: R16; USA: R

 BUDGET: £5,000,000

CAST: Toby Stephens, Claudie Blakley, Andy Nyman, Babou Ceesay, Tim McInnerny, Laura Harris, Danny Dyer, David Gilliam, Juli Drajkó, Judit Viktor, Sándor Boros, Levente Törköly, János Oláh, Attila Ferencz, Bela Kasi

ADISHEVELLED GEORGE (DAVID Gilliam) is seen running for his life through the woods with two young girls (Juli Drajkó and Judit Viktor) to the cheer of The Small Faces' "Itchycoo Park". The girls tumble into a concealed pit, while George is soon after trapped in a snare. As he hangs helplessly from the branch of a tree, a masked man appears and without a word swiftly disembowels him with a knife.

The scene then cuts to the events of a few days before, as the European Sales division of Palisade Defence travel to a team-building weekend at a luxury lodge in rural Hungary. Miles away from the nearest town a fallen tree obstructs the road. The agitated driver refuses to take the bus down a rutted track, which Richard (Tim McInnerny) insists will take them directly to the lodge, so the group are left to walk the rest of the way. As they trek through the forest there is an uncomfortable feeling that someone or something is watching their every move. When they arrive at their destination, the lodge falls a long way short of the anticipated luxury; it is in an appalling state of repair. As they attempt to settle in, Harris (Toby Stephens) comes upon a filing cabinet containing company records, all documented in Russian. As they try to make sense of his find over their evening meal, Harris recalls the lodge had once been an asylum, and a century ago a Palisade nerve gas had been deployed to thwart a take-over by the

The company is making cutbacks.

inmates. Jill (Claudie Blakley) had also heard something of its history as a re-education unit for Soviet war criminals. After an escape bid, the same Palisade nerve gas had been used to drive the men from the surrounding buildings. Each of these accounts alluded to a survivor who vowed revenge on the company. The conversation is interrupted when Steve (Danny Dyer) finds a human tooth in the meat pie that the group have been served as their meal. The sense of unease becomes all the more intense. Outside in the forest a group of merciless assassins have now successfully cornered their quarry.

Christopher Smith's feature began life as **P45**, a team-building session where the stereotypical office employees had to pass each of the tests devised for the weekend's itinerary with failure leading to an automatic termination of their contracted employment. His script evolved to become a modern-day translation of the slasher theme, with the final edit producing a blood-thirsty horror comedy intensified by an impending air of doom. **Severance** has invited comparison with Eli Roth's **Hostel** (2005), and is derivative of **The Hills Have Eyes** (1977), **Wrong Turn** (2003) and **Timber Falls** (2007), but unlike its precursors is jollied along for the first hour with a very keen sense of wit, which shouldn't be confused with the puerile antics of the eighties teenage slasher brigade. The death scenes were also admirably handled, with a rather amusing decapitation sequence in addition to an excruciating leg removal in a bear trap.

Severance certainly wasn't found wanting in the shocks department, but it was essentially a dark comedy; however, on its release to DVD it acquired the kind of notoriety Christopher Smith and his crew would have never wanted. In June 2008, seventeen-year-old Simon Everitt, a promising engineering student, was taken against his wishes, to woods near Great Yarmouth in Norfolk. He was then tied up and doused in petrol before being set alight. Although he managed to escape his bonds and stagger a short distance, he collapsed and died. His killers then threw him into a ditch and in an attempt to hide the body, covered him with soil. Jonathan Clarke, nineteen, Jimi-Lee Stewart, twenty-five, and Maria Chandler, forty, were convicted of murder in May 2009. Clarke, Stewart and Mr Everitt had all been involved in a tangled love affair with a young woman in the area. The court was told the idea for the murder came from **Severance**, when Clarke had commented, "Wouldn't it be wicked if you could actually do that to someone in real life?" Clarke was later sentenced to at least twenty-seven years in prison before being considered for parole, with Stewart receiving twenty-two years and Chandler seventeen years. The debate continues as to whether the film should still have its classification raised to "18".

Shaun of the Dead

 YEAR OF RELEASE: 2004

 RUNTIME: 99 minutes

 COUNTRY: UK

 DIRECTOR: Edgar Wright

 PRODUCTION COMPANY: Universal Pictures, Studio Canal, Working Title Films, WT2 Productions, Big Talk Productions, Inside Track 2, FilmFour, De Wolfe Music

 WRITERS: Simon Pegg, Edgar Wright

 CINEMATOGRAPHER: David M. Dunlap

PRODUCERS: Tim Bevan (executive producer), Eric Fellner (executive producer), Mark Hudson (line producer) Alison Owen (executive producer), Nira Park, Ronaldo Vasconcellos (line producer), Natascha Wharton (executive producer), James Wilson (executive producer)

CERTIFICATE: Australia: MA; Canada: 13+ (Quebec); Canada: 18A (British Columbia/Ontario); Ireland: 18; New Zealand: R13; UK: 15; USA: R

 BUDGET: £4,000,000

 RECEIPTS: $13,464,388

CAST: Simon Pegg, Kate Ashfield, Nick Frost, Lucy Davis, Dylan Moran, Nicola Cunningham, Keir Mills, Matt Jaynes, Gavin Ferguson, Peter Serafinowicz, Horton Jupiter, Tim Baggaley, Arvind Doshi, Rafe Spall, Sonnell Dadral, Penelope Wilton

SHAUN (SIMON PEGG) appears to be strolling aimlessly through life with his relationships going steadily downhill. His stepfather seems to delight in hounding him, his girlfriend Liz has become so disillusioned with his ways she has dumped him and, let's face it, life in the electrical shop where he works is dull at best. Shaun is going absolutely nowhere in life. He is so wrapped in his own misery he fails to see the dead have returned from the grave and have one thing in mind: the succulence of human flesh. As he walks to the shops, Shaun remains oblivious to the putrefied host shambling along the streets. The news, however, is full of reports of the increasing atrophied plague, but Shaun continues in his own little world. When he and his idle game-boy friend, Ed, finally realize the events on their own doorstep, Shaun springs into action. First on the list to be saved are his mum (Penelope Wilton) and then his long suffering ex-girlfriend Liz. Armed with a cricket bat, his quest will take him back onto the fear-filled streets of suburban London and a showdown in the lounge bar of his local pub, The Winchester, when it is besieged by these mindless droves.

Bought coffee. Called Mom. Dodged zombies.

Following the success of the television comedy show *Spaced* between 1999 and 2001, Simon Pegg and director Edgar Wright once again joined forces to create **Shaun of the Dead**, returning to many elements of the series' premise and then splattering it with the insanity of **Dawn of the Dead** (1978) and **28 Days Later** (2002). As with these previous zombie classics, the walking dead in this feature weren't without a sense of menace, but thankfully their sluggish nature gave Shaun and his entourage just enough of a chance to dodge between them for a few pints and some well observed one-liners. This wasn't an especially gory movie, but when one unfortunate was ripped to pieces before the camera's lens it did take the audience by complete surprise, thus making it all the more shocking. With so much hilarity and socially relevant humour played out by a cast that included some of the finest cult comedy talent of our times, there were moments when it was very easy to forget this was a bloodthirsty zombie feature. In between the laughter and putrescent mayhem there were certain poignancies to the proceedings, as family, love and friendship in the face of the apocalypse come to the fore, but not before Shaun and his friends have savoured that last pint at The Winchester and dispelled the living dead to the council dump. There was a concern that the comedy in this film wouldn't translate beyond these shores, but it proved a resounding success in the United States with Pegg and Wright being invited by George A. Romero to appear as zombies in **Land of the Dead** (2005).

Silent Night, Deadly Night

📅 YEAR OF RELEASE: 1984	
🕐 RUNTIME: 79 minutes	
🎯 COUNTRY: USA	
🎥 DIRECTOR: Charles E. Sellier Jr.	
🎬 PRODUCTION COMPANY: TriStar Pictures, Slayride	
✒ WRITERS: Paul Caimi (story), Michael Hickey	
🎞 CINEMATOGRAPHER: Henning Schellerup	

🎭 PRODUCERS: Ira Richard Barmak, Scott Schneid (executive producer), Dennis Whitehead (executive producer)

⭕ CERTIFICATE: Australia: R; Canada: R (Manitoba/Nova Scotia/Ontario); Canada: 16+ (Quebec); New Zealand: R18; UK: 18; USA: R

💲 BUDGET: $1,065,000 (estimated)

🗒 RECEIPTS: $2,491,460 (1984)

CAST: Lilyan Chauvin, Gilmer McCormick, Toni Nero, Robert Brian Wilson, Britt Leach, Nancy Borgenicht, H. E. D. Redford, Danny Wagner, Linnea Quigley, Leo Geter, Randy Stumpf, Will Hare, Tara Buckman, Geoff Hansen, Charles Dierkop

ON THE CHRISTMAS Eve of 1971, a young boy watches in horror as his parents are murdered by a crook dressed as Santa. His father was gunned down and his mother raped before having her throat cut. After the trauma of their parents' deaths, both Billy and his brother are sent to a Catholic orphanage, where they spend their formative years enduring the tyranny of the Mother Superior. Billy's drawing of a bloody Santa Claus standing over a decapitated reindeer should have alerted the orphanage to his underlying problems, but the Mother Superior merely punishes him by sending him to his room. He doesn't stay there for long. When he slips away from his room, Billy spies on a couple making love. The Mother Superior catches the couple and beats them with a belt before using it on Billy. The following day he is forced to sit on Santa's lap, but he is scared out of his mind and bolts to his room.

The years roll on; it is now 1984 and Billy is eighteen years old. He now has a job at a local toy store and all seems to be going smoothly until Christmas comes along. In his time at the store, he has developed a liking for Pamela, a very amiable work mate. All, however, is not well, for in a dream he makes love with her, only to be stabbed as their passion begins to heighten. The past then comes back to haunt him when he is instructed to dress as the store's Santa Claus. Later that night as the staff enjoy festive merriment, one of the employees, a young man by the name of Andy, attempts to rape his beloved Pamela. In these fleeting moments, Billy is consumed by a series of flashbacks showing images of his mother's ordeal and the abuse he suffered in the orphanage. It becomes too much; he snaps and hangs Andy with the Christmas lights. When Pamela starts yelling at Billy, he stabs her with a box cutter, repeating the Mother Superior's words, "Punishment is necessary Pamela, punishment is good". The violence escalates as the owner is hit on the head with a hammer and his assistant manager is threatened with an axe before being brought down by a bow and arrow. Love-making couples seem to be his forte; one girl

Santa's here!

is impaled on mounted antlers and her boyfriend thrown from the window. Adorned in the Santa suit he continues on his murderous rampage, with a decapitation and subsequent head-rolling scene. Axe in hand, Billy makes his return to the orphanage to wreak his grisly kind of havoc.

Silent Night, Deadly Night caused considerable concern on its Christmas release in 1984. The controversy focused on the disturbing images of a killer dressed as Santa Claus, which contradicted the seasonal goodwill. Large crowds of incensed families were known to have gathered at cinemas to express their disgust. In the wake of such pressure, the distributor TriStar Pictures removed their advertising for the film only six days after its November release. Shortly afterwards it was withdrawn. However, even though condemned as worthless splatter it went on to cultivate a huge following, adhering to that slasher predilection for the holiday massacre, which has never seemed to die away as recently attested by **Deadly Little Christmas** (2009). It was later re-released by Aquarius Films in spring 1986, replacing the original advertising campaign of "Twas the night before Christmas" with one referencing the controversy surrounding the film and edited close-up shots of Billy armed and ready in his Santa suit. In the United Kingdom, the movie was never submitted for certification and as such was never listed as a video nasty, nor was it privy to any form of official distribution. It wasn't until 2009 when Arrow Films submitted the film to the BBFC for classification that it was passed without cuts with an "18" certificate.

The film was to spawn four sequels: **Silent Night, Deadly Night 2** (1987), **Silent Night, Deadly Night 3: Better Watch Out!** (1989), **Silent Night, Deadly Night 4: Initiation** (1990) and **Silent Night, Deadly Night 5: The Toy Maker** (1991).

Silent Scream

📅 YEAR OF RELEASE: 1980

🕐 RUNTIME: 87 minutes

🎬 COUNTRY: USA

🎥 DIRECTOR: Denny Harris

✎ WRITERS: Ken Wheat, Jim Wheat

🎞 CINEMATOGRAPHERS: Michael D. Murphy, David Shore

🎬 PRODUCERS: Denny Harris (executive producer), Joan Harris (executive producer), Jim Wheat, Ken Wheat, Leslie Zurla (associate producer)

🔘 CERTIFICATE: Australia: R; UK: 18; USA: R

💳 RECEIPTS: grossed $15,800,000

CAST: Rebecca Balding, Cameron Mitchell, Avery Schreiber, Barbara Steele, Steve Doubet, Brad Rearden, John Widelock, Jack Stryker, Thelma Pelish, Tina Tyler, Yvonne De Carlo, Juli Andelman, Annabella Price, Joe Pronto, Jason Zahler

UNABLE TO FIND a room on campus, Scotty Parker (Rebecca Balding) has to look elsewhere for suitable accommodation. She soon makes her choice and moves into Mrs Engels' (Yvonne DeCarlo) creepy old mansion run by her son Mason (Brad Rearden), where three other college students are already boarding. The old house stands away from the town atop a cliff overlooking an eye-catching coastal area. Mrs Engels has her strange son attend to the boarders, as for reasons of her own she rarely leaves the seclusion of her upstairs domicile. As

the evening draws in the students enjoy a few drinks, resulting in some harmless tomfoolery. None of them could have foreseen the murder of fellow student, Peter, who is later found stabbed to death on the deserted beach. A police lieutenant and his partner arrive on the scene to investigate the murder and begin to uncover the family's hidden secret. Victoria (Barbara Steele) is Mason's deranged sister, who was committed to a psychiatric institution fifteen years before. As Scotty nestles away in the seeming safety of the house in the company of Jack, she is unaware that there is a presence creeping around in its passageways.

Filmed in 1977 this would be Denny Harris's only time sat in the directorial chair, while his writers would go onto far greater success with **Pitch Black** (2000) and **The Chronicles of Riddick** (2004). The original cut of this much neglected film was so poorly rendered, the cast had to be called back to endure the trials of a second shoot, which eventually saw release in August 1980 just before the slasher phenomenon seized hold of America's cinemas with the advent of **Friday the 13ᵗʰ**. This typically low-budget affair owed much to **Psycho** (1960) with its unhinged family protagonists and ominous setting, and saw Barbara Steele make her only film appearance of the 1980s. Harris may have had little funding for his film, but he infused a creepy atmosphere to this ageing manse, using the camera to glide through its halls and passageways in a series of suspenseful sequences. With only two murders to its credit, **Silent Scream** was heavily dependent on its adeptness in narrating a simple story, set against the air of gloom permeating the corridors of this mystery-laden abode.

Slaughter Hotel

📅	YEAR OF RELEASE: 1971		✏️	WRITER: Fernando Di Leo
🕐	RUNTIME: 86 minutes		🎞️	CINEMATOGRAPHER: Franco Villa
🐷	COUNTRY: Italy		⚖️	PRODUCERS: Tiziano Longo, Armando Novelli
🎥	DIRECTOR: Fernando Di Leo			
🎬	PRODUCTION COMPANY: Cineproduzioni Daunia 70, Sitoro		⭕	CERTIFICATE: UK: 18 (DVD rating); USA: R (cut)

CAST: Klaus Kinski, Margaret Lee, Rosalba Neri, Jane Garret, John Karlsen, Gioia Desideri, John Ely, Fernando Cerulli, Sandro Rossi, Giulio Baraghini, Ettore Geri, Antonio Radaelli, Monica Strebel, Carla Mancini, Franco Marletta

IN THE OPENING minutes of Fernando Di Leo's film, a masked figure wearing a hood and cape stalks the grounds of a secluded asylum for wealthy women run by Dr Keller (Klaus Kinski), before quietly entering the building. As he advances on his intended victim, she phones for an orderly and without realizing scares him away. We are then introduced to the neurotic cast, one of whom (Rosalba Neri) is an insatiable nymphomaniac; the audience will never be entirely convinced that she is heartfelt in her search of a cure. The masked killers frenzy won't begin until much later in the film, when we become privy to a series of gory and stylish set pieces that would characterize the more sleazy giallo of the day. After a series of highly erotic scenes, the girls are dispatched by the medieval weaponry on display in one of the entrance rooms as the black-gloved killer tries to exact his still undisclosed revenge. The most graphic of these murders details Jane Garret as she pleasures herself just before the killer sneaks upon her, at first stabbing her before slicing her abdomen from her neck down to her pubis. The scene was edited before the film was given a cinematic release in both the United States and the UK, although the uncut version is still thought to be available in France.

Di Leo's **La bestia uccide a sangue freddo**, also known as **Asylum Erotica** and **Cold Blooded Beast**, took complete advantage of the relaxation

The slasher massacre of eight innocent nurses!

in film censorship that came at the end of the 1960s. Any element of credible storyline was sacrificed for the more seamy aspects of sex and bloodthirsty violence as Di Leo unlocked the door for the trashy exploitative cinema of the 1970s. The scenes of simulated sex and masturbation would have fitted perfectly within the context of any soft-core porn movie as some of Europe's horror sex queens, among them Margaret Lee, Rosalba Neri, Jane Garret and Monica Strebel, rolled between the sheets to beguile their slavering audience. In the years that followed both Di Leo and Rosalba Neri would distance themselves from this film, but the director and his cameraman Franco Villa were bold in their experimentation, using the distorted angles and sinuous prowling shots that would become intrinsic to the slasher movies of the next decade. 🍂

The Slayer

📅 YEAR OF RELEASE: 1982	✏️ WRITERS: J. S. Cardone, Bill Ewing
🕐 RUNTIME: 80 minutes	
🎥 COUNTRY: USA	🎞️ CINEMATOGRAPHER: Karen Grossman
🎬 DIRECTOR: J. S. Cardone	🎬 PRODUCERS: J. S. Cardone, Bill Ewing, Anne Kimmel (associate producer), Eric Weston (executive producer)
🎞️ PRODUCTION COMPANY: 21st Century Film Corporation, International Picture Show	
	⭕ CERTIFICATE: Australia: R; UK: 18; USA: R

CAST: Sarah Kendall, Frederick Flynn, Carol Kottenbrook, Alan McRae, Michael Holmes, Paul Gandolfo, Newell Alexander, Ivy Jones, Jennifer Gaffin, Richard Van Brakel, Carl Kraines

SURREAL ARTIST KAY (Sarah Kendall) and her husband David (Alan McRae) are joined by her brother and sister-in-law as they fly out to a remote island off the coast of Georgia to enjoy a family holiday. In her childhood years Kay was plagued by a recurring nightmare, stalked by a malevolent presence she has since called 'the slayer' to face death in the flames of a burning room. The terrors of her sleeping hours have continued and for the past few weeks, their increasingly disturbing nature has started to affect her entire life. Such is their intensity they have become the obsessive inspiration for her latest collection of paintings, each of which reflect an artist bordering on the brink of madness. Her concerned husband is a doctor and is convinced some time away from the pressures of everyday life will ease her troubled state of mind.

The island is a wild and lonely spot and to augment the foreboding air as they make their way to the house, a storm rumbles away beyond the horizon. It doesn't take long before Kay becomes aware that this is the place which has tormented her dreams. Her family do all that they can to calm her, but when night comes and she falls into

Tonight you will meet ...

a fitful sleep something on the island begins to change. In a cleverly conceived stalking sequence, her husband is trailed to the attic and finally decapitated by a presence in the shadows. The following day as the rest of the family try to find him, the unseen killer, now armed with a pitchfork, continues to scour the island. Very soon, Kay's dreams will become a terrifying reality as she fights to stay awake and keep the fiend at bay. With all of her family having been brutally slaughtered at the hands of this monstrous entity, she must now confront a creature of her making.

J. S. Cardone's low-budget **The Slayer**, also known as **Nightmare Island**, would have probably drifted into the periphery of obscurity if it had not later invited interesting comparisons with Wes Craven's dream-laden **Nightmare on Elm Street**, although by this time Craven had already penned his celebrated terror. **The Slayer** observed so much of what had gone before in the slasher fare of the previous two years, but now introduced a new concept in having the heroine come face to face with the horrors of her own psyche. As the storm moved in, so the impending sense of fear became heightened as Robert

Folk's orchestrated score worked to suffuse the ever-building tension. While the pacing was often slow, this was counteracted by the unsettling ambience permeating the house that made for a highly apt setting.

While the gore effects were hindered by the constraint of a limited budget, **The Slayer** has acquired a quite gruesome reputation, particularly in the ingenious decapitation scene, which is yet to be copied. This set piece along with the graphic impalement on a pitchfork detailing the prongs jutting forth from the victim's chest before being snatched back would attract the attention of the British authorities who placed Cardone's film on the list of videos nastiest in October 1983 following its release in June 1982. It was later removed from the offending schedule in April 1985 and was released seven years later with only fourteen seconds of editing to the grisly pitchfork murder. By 2001, the film was passed uncut by the BBFC as it was prepared for issue to DVD. For political science graduate Joseph Cardone, this was but the beginning of a successful career in both writing and directing thrillers along with the occasional horror movie.

Sledgehammer

📅	YEAR OF RELEASE: 1983	🎬	PRODUCERS: Thomas Baldwin (associate producer), Abdalla Itani (executive producer), Nicolas T. Kimaz, Chuck Malouf (executive producer)
🕐	RUNTIME: 87 minutes		
📷	COUNTRY: USA		
🎥	DIRECTOR: David A. Prior		
✏️	WRITER: David A. Prior	⭕	CERTIFICATE: USA: Not Rated
🎞️	CINEMATOGRAPHER: Salim Kimaz	💲	BUDGET: $40,000

CAST: Ted Prior, Linda McGill, John Eastman, Janine Scheer, Tim Aguilar, Sandy Brooke, Stephen Wright, Michael Shanahan, Mary Mendez, Justin Greer, Doug Matley, Ray Lawrence

AFTER AN OVERLY long shot of a rural home, the camera takes us within these four walls to observe a callous mother trying to silence her son, whom she finally locks away in a closet. She then starts to get rather amorous with her lover, unaware that a silhouetted stalker has crept upon them. In an effectively gory scene, that probably drained a substantial part of the film's meagre budget, the lover is whacked on the head with a sledgehammer, with the mother soon to follow.

A crudely made title card informs the audience ten years have passed as a van pulls up outside this now abandoned house. A group of stereotypical eighties college kids have come to party for the whole weekend. It would have remained a fun weekend if one of them hadn't suggested holding a mock séance. In the shadows of their gathering, the house assumes a sinister air and a masked killer armed with knives and the requisite sledgehammer returns from the dead.

While David A. Prior's film contains so many clichés associated with the period, his killer was gifted with paranormal powers that allowed him to change from a hulking murderer to the young child seen in the movie's opening scenes, and then completely disappear from sight. This was Prior's debut in a long career as a low-budget director, which has led to him overseeing more than thirty films. Here, in this shot-on-video feature, he revealed he had the ability to engineer the tension, but there were long moments when his tracking was woefully slow. The goriest scene appeared during the film's opening sequences but, alas, this was not to be matched, even though there was slaughter aplenty. The limitations of the camcorder made much of the filming noticeably blurry and the fadeouts observed a creative team yet to learn their trade, but Prior made perfect use of the light as he worked to create an air of terror in a plot that was guilty of meandering without pace. However, for all of its faults, **Sledgehammer** continues to attract the interest of homemade movie fans and those who wouldn't mind getting behind the camera themselves in the hope of making their own film for next to nothing.

> **Flesh tears – bones shatter – the nightmare has begun.**

Sleepaway Camp

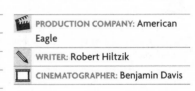

📋 YEAR OF RELEASE: 1983	🎬 PRODUCTION COMPANY: American Eagle
🕐 RUNTIME: 88 minutes	
🎯 COUNTRY: USA	✏️ WRITER: Robert Hiltzik
🎥 DIRECTOR: Robert Hiltzik	⬜ CINEMATOGRAPHER: Benjamin Davis

PRODUCERS: Robert Hiltzik (executive producer), Jerry Silva, Michele Tatosian

CERTIFICATE: Australia: M; Australia: R (DVD rating); Canada: 13+ (Quebec);

Canada: R (Manitoba/Nova Scotia/Ontario); UK: 15 (re-rating) (2004, uncut); UK: 18 (original rating) (cut); USA: R

BUDGET: $350,000

CAST: Felissa Rose, Jonathan Tiersten, Karen Fields, Christopher Collet, Mike Kellin, Katherine Kamhi, Paul DeAngelo, Tom Van Dell, Loris Sallahian, John E. Dunn, Willy Kuskin, Desiree Gould, Owen Hughes, Robert Earl Jones, Susan Glaze

WHEN A GROUP of teenagers cause a boating accident in the middle of a lake, which kills a father and son, the daughter, Angel (Felissa Rose), is taken to live with her peculiar Aunt Martha and cousin Ricky. Eight years later the still traumatized Angela is on her way to her first summer camp with her cousin, who has already made known the feelings he has for her. While at camp, the cook also displays an unhealthy interest in the young Angela. Very quickly, her quiet disposition makes her the butt of her fellow campers' cruel jibes as the buffoonery begins to get out of control. While Ricky is quick to defend her, he cannot stop the bullying campers from being butchered by a mysterious prowler. The hapless Judy is brutally murdered, in a graphic episode, by a curling iron; then follows the slaying of four youngsters in their sleeping bags. Finally, Angela's would-be suitor Paul is decapitated before

"Carrie" meets "Friday the 13th".

the killer is revealed, axe in hand and completely naked.

Robert Hiltzik's **Sleepaway Camp** invites immediate comparisons with **Friday the 13th** (1980) in having a murderer run amok in a remote camp, but its sexual psychology draws from Alfred Hitchcock's **Psycho** (1960) as well as Brian de Palma's **Carrie** (1976), to make this one of the most memorable slasher movies of the early 1980s. Here, the young Hiltzik creates an unnerving atmosphere as an unknown assailant sets about the cast in a series of highly original killings. This isn't a particularly gory movie, but the climax is one of the most shocking screen revelations since Norman Bates' admission some twenty-three years before.

The first-time director had no idea he had created a film which would command such a dedicated following. When he scripted his sequel, it was considered too dark as the film industry sought a deviant villain on a par with the rueful Fred Kreuger. A couple of sequels would eventually come from Michael A. Simpson, **Sleepaway Camp II: Unhappy Campers** (1988) and **Sleepaway Camp III: Teenage Wasteland** (1989). Bruce Springsteen's younger sister, Pamela, played the part of Angela, now a camp counsellor. **Sleepaway Camp IV: The Survivor**, directed by Jim Markovic, was never completed, but the footage that was filmed was released in the Anchor Bay/Starz Entertainment's **Sleepaway Camp** DVD box set. Hiltzik, who had gone on to become a lawyer, scripted and directed **Return to Sleepaway Camp** in 2003, which, after so many setbacks in trying to find a distributor, finally saw release in November 2008. The Hiltzik trilogy will be brought to a close with **Sleepaway Camp Reunion**, which is still in production.

The Slumber Party Massacre

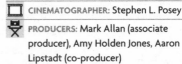

📅 YEAR OF RELEASE: 1982		🎞 CINEMATOGRAPHER: Stephen L. Posey	
🕐 RUNTIME: 77 minutes		🎌 PRODUCERS: Mark Allan (associate producer), Amy Holden Jones, Aaron Lipstadt (co-producer)	
🌍 COUNTRY: USA			
🎥 DIRECTOR: Amy Holden Jones		⭕ CERTIFICATE: Australia: R; New Zealand: R16; UK: 18; USA: R	
✎ WRITER: Amy Holden Jones			
		💲 BUDGET: $250,000	

CAST: Michelle Michaels, Robin Stille, Michael Villella, Debra Deliso, Andree Honore, Jennifer Meyers, Joseph Alan Johnson, David Millbern, Jim Boyce, Pamela Roylance, Brinke Stevens, Rigg Kennedy, Jean Vargas, Anna Patton, Howard Furgason

AMY HOLDEN JONES was observed by many to be a purely feminist writer when she penned her satirical **The Slumber Party Massacre**; she introduces her film with a shower scene along with an ample display of bare breasts. Having grabbed her predominantly male audience's attention she presents a delectable eighteen-year-old high school girl, Trish, who has been left at home in a quiet suburb of Los Angeles while her parents are away on holiday. When she meets up with her girls' basketball team friends she invites them over for a slumber party. The guys in the theatres just couldn't have believed their luck. Valerie, who is new to the group and doesn't quite get on with everyone, decides to stay at home across the street with her annoying younger sister Courtney.

Unknown to them, a maniacal murderer, Russ Thorne, has escaped the asylum. He was incarcerated many years before having slaughtered five people way back in 1969, the same year as the infamous Manson murders. While radio bulletins regularly announce his breakout he cleverly avoids discovery, and then catches sight of Trish and follows her home from school. Prior to arriving at the party, he kills an attractive female electrician and then appropriates her van, which contains the drill that will prove useful later in the evening. Fellow teammate Linda is also disposed when she becomes locked in the school. Hidden away in the darkness Thorne makes his way to the house and gate-crashes the party. Armed with his power drill he begins to terrorize the scantily clad girls for the last twenty minutes of the movie as they run from room to room screaming their heads off. Their only hope of rescue is the estranged new girl who lives across the street.

The highly amusing **Slumber Party Massacre** turned out to be an incredibly successful slasher movie and was the first of four films to see Jones at the director's chair. In the years that followed, she would return to writing considerably more successful screenplays, but who can deny the obvious pleasure she took in lampooning the genre. Here she supplied every facet of the trope with a typically limited budget and left the boys more than satisfied. They couldn't

Close your eyes for a second ... and sleep forever.

have been more delighted in being presented with a cast of hot teenage girls, some nudity and an abundance of splatter as the driller killer armed with his phallic implement ensured the body count began to rise higher and higher. The tension slowly simmered and then arose to boiling point with a devious set of manoeuvres that created innumerable deceptive shocks. It was Valerie, however, who made for the perfect final girl, innocent yet immensely resourceful and leaving the boys only guessing.

The promotional material accompanying this film and the covers to the video and DVD have given this movie an unwarranted reputation for sleaze. It has also been rebuked for its violent stance against women. Jones's detractors have always failed to appreciate her desire to parody rather than exploit. On its 1986 release to video in the UK, the BBFC insisted on a change of name to the **Slumber Party Murders**. It was, however, highly influential and spawned countless inferior copies, notably **The Last Slumber Party** (1988), the **Bikini Bloodbath** (2007–9) series, and all three entries in the **Sorority House Massacre** (1986–91) collection. In its wake, there came three sequels, **Slumber Party Massacre 2** (1987), **Slumber Party Massacre 3** (1990) and **Cheerleader Massacre** (2003) along with the documentary **Sleepless Nights: Revisiting the Slumber Party Massacres** made in 2010. Thirty years later, it remains a great favourite among fans of the genre. 🦇

Snuff

📅 YEAR OF RELEASE: 1976

🕐 RUNTIME: 80 minutes

🌐 COUNTRY: Argentina/Canada/USA

🎥 DIRECTORS: Michael Findlay, Roberta Findlay, Horacio Fredriksson

🎬 PRODUCTION COMPANY: August Films, Selected Pictures

✏️ WRITERS: Michael Findlay, Roberta Findlay A. Bochin

🎞️ CINEMATOGRAPHER: Roberta Findlay

🏆 PRODUCERS: Jack Bravman, Allan Shackleton

CAST: Margarita Amuchástegui, Ana Carro, Liliana Fernández Blanco, Michael Findlay, Roberta Findlay, Alfredo Iglesias, Enrique Larratelli, Mirtha Massa, Aldo Mayo, Clao Villanueva

I T'S 1971, TWO years after the infamous Manson family killings, and a gang of Argentine biker chicks under the control of an uncannily similar character, are relishing their own version of Helter Skelter. As a drugs war rages in the city, an actress is being exploited by her sleazy porn-fuelled producer boyfriend. The leather-clad girls are instructed by their leader Satan (Enrique Larratelli) to slaughter the actress's lover and prepare to make her fit to bear a child for their sacrifice. The tacked on final scene, filmed five years later in 1976, attempts to have the audience believe that they have been privy to the mutilation and real murder of one of the actresses seen in the film. While on set, she is stabbed and dismembered by the film crew, each of whom are then heard escaping the scene as the film runs out.

Filmed in Argentina in 1971, the sleazy exploitation feature **The Slaughter**, written and directed by the husband-and-wife grindhouse filmmaking team of Michael Findlay and Roberta Findlay, drew its sordid inspiration from the Manson family tabloid frenzy of 1969. However, its poor script and dubious acting were never going to turn it into a raging success. Five years later, without the knowledge of the Findlays, independent low-budget distributor Allan Shackleton released the film, which included the now infamous finale. He had read about the allegations surrounding snuff movies being produced in South America

A film that could only be made in South America, where life is CHEAP!

and decided to use **The Slaughter** as his vehicle to exploit this myth. He released his film as **Snuff**, also known as **American Cannibale**, using bogus protesters to picket those cinemas that dared to show the film. Very soon, the radical feminist group Women Against Pornography, who were highly active during the 1970s and 1980s, joined these protests thus exacerbating the film's unsavoury reputation.

Shackleton's publicity campaign certainly worked, for as bad as this film was, it continued to be the focus of much attention. The ending was certainly disturbing, but the effects were largely inspired by the antics of one Herschell Gordon Lewis. Four years before Ruggero Deodato was chastised by the Italian authorities for seemingly making a snuff movie

with **Cannibal Holocaust** (1980), Shackleton faced the wrath of the mayor of New York. He saved himself from a long stretch in prison by presenting the supposedly murdered actress for all to see. In the UK, the uncut video was ready to be released in May 1982, but was cancelled only for bootleg copies to filter into the country. Not surprisingly, **Snuff** found its place on the list of video nasties in July 1983, and there it remained until the crisis came to an end. An uncut version was not approved until 2003. Three years later this lacklustre piece of exploitation would be referenced in the second season of the UK Channel 4's *The Dark Side of Porn*, the episode entitled "Does Snuff Exist?" Unlike so many of the films in this collecton, **Snuff** refuses to be forgotten.

Sorority House Massacre

YEAR OF RELEASE: 1986	**WRITERS:** Carol Frank
RUNTIME: 74 minutes	**CINEMATOGRAPHER:** Marc Reshovsky
COUNTRY: USA	**PRODUCERS:** Ron Diamond, Roger Corman
DIRECTOR: Carol Frank	
PRODUCTION COMPANY: Concorde Pictures	**CERTIFICATE:** Australia: M; UK: 18; USA: R

CAST: Angela O'Neill, Wendy Martel, Pamela Ross, Nicole Rio, John C. Russell, Marcus Vaughter, Vinnie Bilancio, Joe Nassi, Mary Anne, Gillian Frank, Joseph Mansier, Robert Axelrod

LITTLE BETH'S FAMILY were killed by her brother; she only managed to escape by hiding quietly in the basement. He was then committed to an asylum, from which many years later he escapes. Like several mass murderers before him, he then sets off to return to his home town. Beth was brought up by her aunt, who has recently passed away. She has now grown up and is about to settle down in a sorority affiliated to her college. However, although her mind has blocked out the memories of that terrible night from her childhood, she is plagued by nightmares of an ominous figure and a dark house she doesn't recognize. Little does she realize that the sorority house was once her childhood home and her evil brother has sensed her presence. Only when one of her sorority sisters places her under deep hypnosis do the recollections of her traumatic past finally return.

The connections with **Halloween** (1978) were all too obvious, as Carol

A slash course in absolute terror!

Frank for the one and only time in her career sat in the director's chair after working as assistant director on **The Slumber Party Massacre** (1982). Once again, she had the girls chasing around a secluded house wearing only their revealing night attire while a deranged killer prowled around with a sharpened knife. The psychic link had been used elsewhere, but on this occasion it was handled with an element of flair. There were many amusing moments in this film, some of them not intentional, but the stalking sequences did make the audience fall deathly quiet. The kills were far from gory, however, and by 1986 were not considered especially imaginative. This was a slasher done by the numbers as the era slowly came to an end, but Frank's film proved successful enough to generate a couple of sequels, **Sorority House Massacre 2** (1990) and the raunchy **Hard to Die** (1990), also known as **Sorority House Massacre 3**.

Splatter University

 YEAR OF RELEASE: 1984

 RUNTIME: 78 minutes

 COUNTRY: USA

 DIRECTOR: Richard W. Haines

PRODUCTION COMPANY: Aquifilm

WRITERS: Michael Cunningham, Richard W. Haines

CINEMATOGRAPHER: Jim Grib

PRODUCERS: Richard W. Haines, Miljan Peter Ilich (associate producer)

 **CERTIFICATE:** Australia: R; USA: R

CAST: Forbes Riley, Ric Randig, Dick Biel, Kathy LaCommare, Laura Gold, Ken Gerson, Sal Lumetta, Clifford Warren, Noel Stilphen, Mary Ellen David, Jane Doniger Reibel, Dan Eaton, John Elias Michalakis, George Seminara, Joanna Mihalakis

A PATIENT MAKES A bid to escape from a New York City mental hospital, killing one of the orderlies and then donning his clothes. Three years later a University sociology professor is horribly murdered as he works late into the evening. Next semester his replacement Julie (Forbes Riley) is told by Father Perkins (Richard W. Haines) of her predecessor's unfortunate death. It is obvious from the outset that Julie will be severely challenged by her dope-addicted, sex-obsessed students and her views on abortion become the immediate talk of the college.

When their studies are over the class like to party, but their revelry is brought to an unceremonious end when a killer begins to stalk the campus. With the reports of both students and teachers being killed beginning to escalate, Julie becomes enamoured with a fellow lecturer. We learn he was dating a tutor who was only recently murdered, but the colleague who passes this titbit of information is then killed. Fearing the worst, Julie decides to leave her new life, but before she packs her bags her investigations reveal the psychopathic culprit is the escaped mental patient. Together she and her boyfriend try to stop his unforgiving onslaught through the corridors and hallways of the campus with tragic consequences.

The title **Splatter University** typically left nothing to the imagination. As a slasher movie it runs with an air of distinct familiarity, but on this occasion does not observe the motif honoured to the final girl. In a well-crafted sequence the stalker's presence becomes all the more menacing as he strides ever closer to the endearing Julie. There has been criticism of inadequate post-production dubbing, the kids wearing the same clothes and dead bodies that have been observed to move, yet Haines isn't behind the mark when it comes to delivering low-budget blood, as breasts and crotches are sliced open and a disembowelment splurges off screen. Herschell Gordon Lewis would have been proud! Cheap thrills and shots of girls' backsides in tight jeans abound along with an amusing scene where a

Earn a higher degree in terror!

flustered priest when about to meet one of the teaching staff discards his porn magazines. **Splatter University** came at a time when the slasher had been utterly played to death and for all its worth would have found it impossible to bring anything new to the table. Richard W. Haines, having ascended to his first role in the director's chair, continued in a career that would eventually lead into film archiving.

Stagefright: Aquarius

📅 YEAR OF RELEASE: 1987	✏️ WRITERS: George Eastman, Sheila Goldberg
⏱️ RUNTIME: 90 minutes	
🎬 COUNTRY: Italy	🎞️ CINEMATOGRAPHER: Renato Tafuri
🎥 DIRECTOR: Michele Soavi	🎭 PRODUCERS: Joe D'Amato, Donatella Donati,
🎬 PRODUCTION COMPANY: DMV Distribuzione, Filmirage	⭕ CERTIFICATE: Australia: R; Canada: 13+ (Quebec); UK: 18; USA: Unrated
	💲 BUDGET: $1,000,000

CAST: David Brandon, Barbara Cupisti, Domenico Fiore, Robert Gligorov, Mickey Knox, Giovanni Lombardo Radice, Clain Parker, Loredana Parrella, Martin Philips, James Sampson, Ulrike Schwerk, Mary Sellers, Jo Ann Smith, Piero Vida, Richard Barkeley

ALTHOUGH IT IS very late at night, a group of actors are still going through their routine rehearsing for a musical about a crazed killer they call "The Night Owl". When the leading lady, Alicia (Barbara Cupisti), sprains her ankle, she and the wardrobe mistress, Betty (Ulrike Schwerk), quietly leave the theatre to find a doctor. The only hospital in the area is a mental facility, but an amiable psychiatrist is happy to attend to Alicia's injury. Betty notices a patient lying restrained on a bed. He is the former actor Irving Wallace, a man who went wild and slaughtered more than a dozen people. As the girls prepare to return to the theatre, they are unaware Wallace has escaped after killing one of the attendants and is now secreted in the back of Betty's car. On her return, the angered director (David Brandon) dismisses Alicia for having left the rehearsal. She storms out of the building only to find Betty lying prostrate on the floor of the car park, the victim of a cruel murderer.

With two police officers assigned to stand guard over the car park, the pompous director has one of his cast hide the keys so that no one else can slip away from the theatre. He has also changed the script to his play, renaming his "Night Owl" killer "Irving Wallace", and commands his team to continue working through the night so that they can familiarize themselves with the new material. As a thunderstorm rages in the world beyond the theatre, the real Wallace enters the building. He dons the owl-like mask and when mistaken for one of the cast willingly obeys the director's instructions and expertly butchers the girl who has only just hidden the key to the building. In a series of suspense-filled sequences amidst the darkened passageways beneath the theatre, Wallace acts out his grisly fantasies in a succession of gruesome decapitations, a disembowelment and bodily dismemberment. Their only chance to escape this deranged psycho is for one of the cast to find the elusive key.

As the horror industry in Italy continued to struggle, Michele Soavi, who had been Dario Argento's eager protégé, stepped into the director's chair to work alongside two of the most eminent figures from the halcyon days of Italian exploitation, producer Joe D'Amato and writer George Eastman. While learning his trade, Soavi had been assistant director on Argento's **Tenebrae** (1982) and **Phenomena** (1985) along with Lamberto Bava's **A Blade in the Dark** (1983) and **Demons** (1985), in addition to taking minor roles in Lucio Fulci's **City of the Living Dead** (1980) as well as **Tenebrae**, **The New York Ripper** (1982) and **Demons**.

His stylish direction would engender a film worthy of the giallo of a decade past coupled with the slash and hack that had reached its nadir in the United States only a few years before. Eastman's script preferred an accessible linear narrative, but Soavi's adept cinematic approach revealed the apt pupil had ascertained much from his mentor, with imaginative camera work and atmospheric set pieces to distinguish his film with a flair commonly observed in more experienced directors. While there was plenty of blood-letting with the graphic exposition of power drills being forced into yielding flesh, there was also a claustrophobic tension to his film, which would leave his audience clamouring for more. This materialized in **The Church** (1989), **The Sect** (1991) and the acclaimed **Dellamorte Dellamore** (1994). Soavi wouldn't be able to save the Italian cinematic horror, but just for a few more years he ensured it once again became highly entertaining. 🍂

The theatre of death.

Strait-Jacket

📅 YEAR OF RELEASE: 1964

🕐 RUNTIME: 93 minutes

🌐 COUNTRY: USA

🎥 DIRECTOR: William Castle

🎬 PRODUCTION COMPANY: William Castle Productions

✏️ WRITER: Robert Bloch

🎞️ CINEMATOGRAPHER: Arthur E. Arling

PRODUCERS: William Castle, Dona Holloway (associate producer)

⭕ CERTIFICATE: UK: X (theatrical release, cut); USA: Approved; USA: TV-14

CAST: Joan Crawford, Diane Baker, Leif Erickson, Howard St John, John Anthony Hayes, Rochelle Hudson, George Kennedy, Edith Atwater, Mitchell Cox

LUCY HARBIN (JOAN Crawford) returns home one evening to find her husband (Lee Majors) in bed with his former girlfriend. In a blind rage she creeps up to the bed and dispatches them with several blows of a sharpened axe, not realizing her young daughter, Carol, has seen the entire grisly incident. In the days that follow, Lucy is declared mad and sentenced to twenty years in the asylum.

Years later, the cured Lucy is dropped off at the farm where her daughter has gone to stay; Carol appears unaffected by the trauma of that night twenty years ago. She has grown up to become a very popular young lady, engaged to one of the most eligible men in town. The following day Lucy and her daughter spend some time together

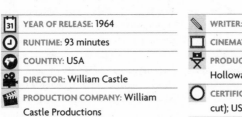

Her husband ... her room ... and another woman!

shopping, which allows her to have a complete makeover that by magic makes her look twenty years younger. However, all is not well for, while in the store, Lucy is convinced she can hear a mocking voice that taunts her with nursery rhymes of her murderous past. During the night, she awakens to the sound of the same goading and then turns to see the shocking sight of two decapitated heads lying beside her. When Carol's Uncle Bill enters the room, the heads are no longer to be seen. This shatters Lucy, who begins to appear increasingly unhinged, just as she had twenty years before. She doesn't help herself when she tries to seduce her future son-in-law and then those who cross her, suspecting she is not entirely sane, soon begin to turn up dead.

William Castle's **Strait-Jacket** was undeniably influenced by **Psycho** (1960) and **Whatever Happened to Baby Jane** (1962), in which Joan Crawford had also had a starring role. Following the success of the Robert Aldrich-directed **Whatever Happened to Baby Jane**, Crawford, now in her sixties, took on the role of a twenty-nine-year-old for **Strait-Jacket**'s prelude. She then played the largest part of the film as a woman of forty-nine, giving a quite remarkable performance as a person unable to escape the catastrophic events of that one night of insanity. Castle, who had always relied on gimmicks to promote his earlier films, was looking to improve his reputation and now had one of Hollywood's greatest stars at his behest. Such was her commitment she supervised the redrafting of the script, made changes to the supporting cast and selected her own wardrobe.

Her presence elevated Castle's direction and, thanks to Robert Bloch's writing, he produced a macabre thriller with a twist ending set in an idyllic farmhouse that was revealed to be a thin veneer for the madness that lurked beneath this seemingly perfect family. When compared to his other movies, this film ran at a fair pace, and in its day those decapitations would have shocked its thrill-seeking audience, even though they offered little in the way of gore. Castle would continue with his B-grade schlock, but sadly the great roles would elude Crawford, whose later work was confined to low-budget features and television.

Strange Behaviour

 YEAR OF RELEASE: 1981

 RUNTIME: 105 minutes

 COUNTRY: Australia/New Zealand

 DIRECTOR: Michael Laughlin

 PRODUCTION COMPANY: Bannon Glen, Endeavour Productions, Fay Richwhite, Hemdale Film, Shadow Lane, South Street Films

WRITERS: Bill Condon, Michael Laughlin

CINEMATOGRAPHER: Louis Horvath

PRODUCERS: John Barnett, Bill Condon, John Daly, William Fayman, Antony I. Ginnane, David Hemmings

CERTIFICATE: Australia: M; New Zealand: R16; UK: 18; USA: R

CAST: Michael Murphy, Louise Fletcher, Dan Shor, Fiona Lewis, Arthur Dignam, Dey Young, Marc McClure, Scott Brady, Charles Lane, Elizabeth Cheshire, Beryl Te Wiata, Jim Boelsen, Billy Al Bengston, Nicole Anderson, Bill Condon

IN THE ONCE quiet college town of Galesberg, Illinois, teenagers are being slaughtered by a group of unknown killers. One of the town's police officers, John Brady (Michael Murphy), is convinced the killings are linked to the behavioural experiments being carried out at the university. In one of the university's lecture theatres the scientist overseeing this shady experimentation, Dr Le Sangel (Arthur Dignam), continues to teach his young pupils via archival film; the doctor passed away from this world some years before. His successor, the aloof Dr Parkinson (Fiona Lewis), now continues with her former mentor's bizarre experiments.

Officer Brady's son Pete (Dan Shor) needs to raise the money to cover his college fees, and the only way he can do this is by volunteering to join the research programme. His girlfriend Caroline (Dey Young) knows nothing of Dr Parkinson's dubious machinations, but it is becoming increasingly obvious those students who enrol in this scheme are turning into mindless creatures with an inclination for slaughter. Brady, however, has a shady past, one connected with the mystifying Le Sangel.

Michael Laughlin's film came as Australian cinema was being revitalized following the success of **Picnic at Hanging Rock** (1975) and **Gallipoli** (1981). One of his producers, Antony

> It's the dead of night and everybody's asleep ... almost everybody.

Ginnane, hoped to begin a wave of low-budget Antipodean horror movies, which started with **Patrick** (1978), and continued with **Thirst** (1979), **The Survivor** (1981) and, that same year, **Dead Kids**, also known as **Strange Behaviour**, **Human Experiments** and **Small Town Massacre**. Filmed in Auckland, New Zealand, with a largely American cast, Laughlin's homage to the horror movies of the 1950s witnessed a painstaking re-creation of the small town atmosphere of the American Mid-West. Co-written with Bill Condon, who went on to script **Gods and Monsters** (1998) and **Chicago** (2002), the imagery in Laughlin's film continues to haunt with the murders seemingly played down to exacerbate the horror at hand. The effect is chillingly surreal as a Tangerine Dream soundscape adds to the heightening paranoia.

After a reasonable reception among the critics, this was the first instalment of the ambitious **Strange Trilogy**, but was cancelled when the second feature **Strange Invaders** (1983) performed rather poorly at the box office. The audience of the day seemingly had little comprehension of such tributes to the nostalgia of 1950s science fiction and horror. When the film was first released in the UK as **Small Town Massacre** in 1986, it passed the scrutiny of the BBFC without being edited. However, subsequent releases saw increasingly more cuts to the suicide scene with the syringe to the eyeball also being slightly edited. **Strange Behaviour**, with its unusual science fiction premise, offers a unique play upon the in-vogue slasher of the early 1980s, one that recalls memories of **The Invasion of the Body Snatchers** (1956).

Streets of Death

YEAR OF RELEASE: 1987		DIRECTOR: Jeff Hathcock	
RUNTIME: 94 minutes		WRITER: Jeff Hathcock	
COUNTRY: USA		PRODUCER: John Tomlinson	

CAST: Simon de Soto, Tommy Kirk, Larry Thomas, Michael N. J. Wright

A COUPLE OF DEPRAVED maniacs, making themselves out to be student filmmakers, kidnap hookers and then place them before the camera before torturing and killing them. While the brutality in the killings is never seen, the body parts are later discovered with the refuse in back alleyways across the city. Their victims' agony is captured on tape and sold to a sleazy character as snuff videos. Officer Kelly Anderson is forced to go undercover in her high heels and stockings to put an end to these wretched crimes.

Jeff Hathcock returns with another piece of shot-on-video slasher misogyny, which once again seems to have vanished from the face of the Earth. Its premise is both graphic and unpleasant with murky photography that works to enhance its unsavoury nature. The acting is typically poor and isn't helped by the unbelievably contrived dialogue. While the bloodthirsty nature of the psycho's activities is kept to a minimum, the level of violence is indeed shocking and adds to the film's notoriety.

Suspiria

YEAR OF RELEASE: 1977		PRODUCTION COMPANY: Seda Spettacoli	
RUNTIME: 98 minutes			
COUNTRY: Italy		WRITERS: Dario Argento, Daria Nicolodi	
DIRECTOR: Dario Argento			

CINEMATOGRAPHER: Luciano Tovoli

PRODUCERS: Claudio Argento, Salvatore Argento (executive producer)

CERTIFICATE: Australia: R; Canada: R; Canada: 13+ (Quebec); Canada: 13+ (Quebec) (Original rating); Canada: 18+ (Quebec) (1977, re-rating); Ireland: 18; New Zealand: R16; UK: 18 (video rating) (1990, uncut); UK: X (original rating, cut); USA: X (original rating); USA: R

CAST: Jessica Harper, Stefania Casini, Flavio Bucci, Miguel Bosé, Barbara Magnolfi, Susanna Javicoli, Eva Axén, Rudolf Schündler, Udo Kier, Alida Valli, Joan Bennett, Margherita Horowitz, Jacopo Mariani, Fulvio Mingozzi, Franca Scagnetti

AS THE RAIN pours down on this stormy night, an American ballet student Suzy Bannion (Jessica Harper) arrives in Freiburg to join an exclusive ballet school. Her taxi journey from the airport seeks from the very outset to unsettle, becoming increasingly claustrophobic and heightening the sense of dread, which rises for the next twenty minutes to a climactic frenzy before culminating in a brutal double murder. When Suzy returns to the school in the warming light of day, she learns that the student seen chasing through the woods the night before fell victim to a vicious murderer. The head of the school, Madame Blanc (Joan Bennett), tries to assuage the novice student's trepidation, but the severity in her assistant Miss Tanner (Alida Valli) puts her very much on edge. This isn't the first student disappearance from the school and as the days go by it becomes glaringly obvious there is something amiss in this esteemed establishment. When Suzy attempts to mingle with her fellow dance students, they are not exactly welcoming, but she eventually befriends Sara (Stefania Casini), who then disappears after being stalked by an unseen malevolence. With her life in jeopardy, Suzy is now forced to uncover the dark secret that lies at the heart of this accursed institution.

The plot to Dario Argento's **Suspiria**, the first of the "Three Mothers Trilogy", is very simple. Although true to the Italian terrors of these years, Argento refuses to adopt an entirely linear narrative; instead he makes an assault on the senses with an intensity of colour, contrasted by deep shadows that threaten and lighting that evokes an air of the surreal as this hellbound institution seeks to haul you asunder. Accompanying this vivid display is a typically disturbing soundtrack from Goblin, which is

The only thing more terrifying than the last twelve minutes of this film are the first eighty-six.

probably the most unsettling score in the history of horror cinema. **Suspiria** is a stylized sensual masterpiece, suggesting menace at almost every turn, yet these lurid hallways and corridors were influenced by the seeming innocence of Walt Disney's **Snow White and the Seven Dwarfs** (1937), a film that made such an impression on Argento as a child. The script to what has been described as a perverse fairy tale was inspired by Thomas De Quincey's drug-induced fantasy, *Confessions of an Opium Eater* or *Suspiria De Profundis*, and was to take place in a children's school, but had to be amended owing to concerns about the controversy it would have undoubtedly caused.

Argento once again proved himself the master of horror cinema and unlike so many of his contemporaries he raised the tension from the film's opening frames, engaging a series of visual shocks before traumatizing the audience with two characteristically elaborate death scenes. Their graphic portrayal was to live on with cinemagoers, but unlike so many of the gialli movies of the period, this excess was only repeated when Sara became encased in razor wire while being pursued through the attic. **Suspiria** allowed Argento to explore his fascination with witches and in so doing he created this multi-layered magnum opus that will invite examination for many years to come.

Tenebrae

📅	**YEAR OF RELEASE:** 1982	📷	**CINEMATOGRAPHER:** Luciano Tovoli
⏱	**RUNTIME:** 110 minutes	⚗	**PRODUCERS:** Claudio Argento, Salvatore Argento (executive producer)
🎞	**COUNTRY:** Italy		
🎥	**DIRECTOR:** Dario Argento	⭕	**CERTIFICATE:** Australia: M; Australia: R; Canada: R; Canada: 16+ (Quebec); New Zealand: R16; UK: 18; USA: X (original rating); USA: R; USA: Unrated (director's cut)
🎬	**PRODUCTION COMPANY:** Sigma Cinematografica Roma		
✏	**WRITER:** Dario Argento		

CAST: Anthony Franciosa, Christian Borromeo, Mirella D'Angelo, Veronica Lario, Ania Pieroni, Eva Robin's, Carola Stagnaro, John Steiner, Lara Wendel, John Saxon, Daria Nicolodi, Giuliano Gemma, Isabella Amadeo

NEW YORK AUTHOR Peter Neal (Anthony Franciosa) flies out to Rome to promote his new murder mystery "Tenebrae". He is met by his agent Bullmer (John Saxon), who has been busy lining up an interview on a talk show. As he arrives in Rome, a woman is caught trying to steal a copy of the book from a shop. Although she convinces the security guard to turn a blind eye, someone is discreetly watching her. When she returns to the comfort of her flat, she is attacked by an assailant who forces the pages of the stolen book into her mouth and then slashes her throat with a razor. The razor is very similar to that which is referenced in Neal's book. Following the discovery of the body, the writer is questioned by Detective Germani (Giuliano Gemma). Soon after he receives a letter and then a grating phone call from the killer, whose mission he reveals is to eliminate those he considers perverts. It's not long before two lesbians are murdered by the black-gloved killer, whose modus operandi again emulates the murders in Neal's latest bestseller. As murder follows upon murder Dario Argento saves his goriest scene until the last, in a stylish sequence that would one day draw comparisons with **Saw** (2004).

When he set out to write **Tenebrae**, which has also gone by the names **Tenebre**, **Unsane**, **Shadow** and **Sotto Gli Occhi dell'Assassino**, Dario Argento put aside his intriguing "Three Mothers Trilogy" to direct one of his most stylish films of the period. His latest movie harked back to a plot device first seen twelve years before in

Unrelenting terror from the maker of DEMONS, CREEPERS and SUSPIRIA!

his landmark giallo **The Bird with the Crystal Plumage** (1970). There would be the customary twists to the tale, along with an abundance of red herrings, which remained true to the format of these vaunted Italian mysteries. Inspired by Andrzej Zulawski's art house terror **Possession** (1981), he combined his visual mastery with the photography of Luciano Tovoli to create a washed-out cityscape with muted colours that were the antithesis of the shadows intimated in the film's title. This bland vision was also very much at odds with the decadent splendour observed in both **Suspiria** (1977) and **Inferno** (1980) and left the impression of an urban sterility lying in a world without soul. Only when the blood began to flow did the audience get a taste of the deep red hues of his previous films. However, even these appeared somewhat restrained until the murder of Veronica Lario just as the film coursed to its suspense-filled denouement. This was a return to the Argento of a few years past, as Veronica lost her arm to the killer's axe and blood spurted freely across her apartment. Tovoli excelled with his long smooth-flowing panoramas, and then moved in to introduce the close-up shots that delivered the visceral shocks Argento fans had come to expect. Goblin returned to write the score and once again captured the atmosphere Argento and his team worked so hard to create.

Their hard work was unfortunately cut by four seconds by the BBFC prior to the film's cinematic release in 1983, specifically to Veronica holding her bloody stump following the arm-chopping scene. Worse was to follow when this cut version was transferred to video later that same year; it was cited as one of the offensive video nasties in March 1984 and remained on the list until the panic was finally forgotten. Poor Veronica's blood bath wasn't to see an unedited release until 2003.

Terror Train

📅 YEAR OF RELEASE: 1980

🕐 RUNTIME: 97 minutes

🌐 COUNTRY: Canada

🎥 DIRECTOR: Roger Spottiswoode

🎬 PRODUCTION COMPANY: Astral Bellevue Pathé, Sandy Howard Productions, Triple T Productions

✎ WRITERS: T. Y. Drake, Daniel Grodnik (story)

🎞 CINEMATOGRAPHER: John Alcott

⚒ PRODUCERS: Lamar Card (executive producer), Don Carmody (line producer), Harold Greenberg, Daniel Grodnik (executive producer)

⭕ CERTIFICATE: Australia: MA (DVD rating); Australia: R; Canada: 13+ (Quebec); UK: X (original rating, 1980); UK: 18 (re-rating) (1989); USA: R

💲 BUDGET: $3,500,000

🗔 RECEIPTS: $8,000,000

CAST: Ben Johnson, Jamie Lee Curtis, Hart Bochner, David Copperfield, Derek McKinnon, Sandee Currie, Timothy Webber, Anthony Sherwood, Howard Busgang, Steve Michaels, Greg Swanson

A COLLEGE FRATERNITY DREAMS up a bizarre initiation game by arranging for one of their girlfriends, Alana (Jamie Lee Curtis), to lure a naive young pledge into bed then switch with a corpse at a New Year's Eve party. Wrapped in the cold embrace of the cadaver, the poor fellow quite literally goes mad and has to be hauled away to a mental institution. Several years later, it is graduation time and, the fraternity holds a fancy dress party on an old steam train. While the wealthy college kids enjoy their masquerade, a killer slips aboard and all too soon embarks upon the slaughter of the revellers, donning their costumes and the accompanying array of masks once he has disposed of them. For Jamie Lee Curtis this will be yet another chase through the shadows and a life or death showdown with a masked killer.

Terror Train was made soon after **Halloween** (1978) and similar to

Carpenter's original relies on building the atmosphere rather than the gore of that same year's **Friday the 13th**. For Canadian director Roger Spottiswoode this was this first of many appearances in the director's chair, having already worked as an editor for Sam Peckinpah, most notably on **Straw Dogs** (1971) and **Pat Garrett and Billy the Kid** (1973). He was lucky enough to have British cinematographer John Alcott on his team, a man who had excelled alongside Stanley Kubrick on **2001: A Space Odyssey** (1968) and **The Shining** (1980). The pair would ensure this was a claustrophobic entry to this fledgling genre, which managed the suspense

A nightmare journey to hell . . .

particularly during the chase sequences and kept much of the bloodshed to the imagination of the assembled audience, although the severed head was still quite graphic for the day. True to slasher lore the killer hid away behind a mask as a series of red herrings were thrown in, amongst them a young David Copperfield who appeared as a menacing magician. For Jamie Lee Curtis this wouldn't quite match the success of **Halloween**, **The Fog** (1980) and **Prom Night** (1980) but it would acquire a recognition as one of the more stylish slasher releases of the period, although the obvious lack of gore almost saw it consigned to obscurity.

The Texas Chain Saw Massacre

 YEAR OF RELEASE: 1974

 RUNTIME: 83 minutes

 COUNTRY: USA

 DIRECTOR: Tobe Hooper

 PRODUCTION COMPANY: Vortex

 WRITERS: Kim Henkel (story), Tobe Hooper (story)

 CINEMATOGRAPHER: Daniel Pearl

PRODUCERS: Kim Henkel (associate producer), Tobe Hooper, Jay Parsley (executive producer) Richard Saenz (associate producer), Louis Peraino

CERTIFICATE: Australia: (Banned) (original rating); Australia: R; Canada: R; Canada: 18+ (Quebec) (original rating: 1974); Canada: 13+ (Quebec) (re-rating: 2004); Ireland: (Banned) (original rating); Ireland: 18; New Zealand: R16 (re-rating: 2007) (uncut); New Zealand: R18; UK: 18 (re-rating: 1999); UK: R (original rating) (1975); UK: (Banned) (original rating); USA: R

 BUDGET: $83,532

 RECEIPTS: $30,859,000

CAST: Marilyn Burns, Allen Danziger, Paul A. Partain, William Vail, Teri McMinn, Edwin Neal, Jim Siedow, Gunnar Hansen, John Dugan, Robert Courtin, William Creamer, John Henry Faulk, Jerry Green, Ed Guinn, Joe Bill Hogan

TOBE HOOPER'S LEGENDARY movie opens in the stifling temperature of a Texas summer. There are reports of graves being violated and corpses assembled as gruesome sculptures in a distant cemetery. Sally Hardesty (Marilyn Burns) and her wheelchair-bound brother, Franklin (Paul A. Partain), take it upon themselves to visit the cemetery to ensure their grandfather's grave has not been desecrated. They travel with three friends, Sally's boyfriend Jerry (Allen Danziger), her best friend Pam (Teri McMinn), and Pam's boyfriend Kirk (William Vail). The grave, they learn, has not been defiled, and safe in this knowledge they decide to continue to the old family homestead.

As they drive deeper into this isolated rural wasteland, Tobe Hooper builds the sense of foreboding with references to an abandoned slaughterhouse, soon after which their van is smeared with blood by a demented hitchhiker. The sense of unease persists when they attempt to fill the van with petrol; the strange attendant issues a warning about returning to their former home. The house, it turns out, was left deserted years ago. Undeterred, the kids explore the area and in the oppressive heat come upon a large farmhouse surrounded by dozens of abandoned vehicles. Kirk walks up to the dismal house with his girlfriend Pam; his

knock, however, goes unanswered. Convinced he can he hear the sound of a distressed animal he enters the ill-kept hallway. Within moments, a huge masked man (Gunnar Hansen) we will come to know as Leatherface stands before him. This masked ogre raises a sledgehammer and slams it into his head. This assault of the senses takes place in mere seconds. Kirk's lifeless body is dragged away into the back room, his fate unknown.

When Kirk fails to return, Pam goes into the house to trace his whereabouts. She screams in terror when she discovers sculptures suspended from the ceiling fashioned with human skulls, furniture decorated with bones and skulls and the floor littered with bones, feathers and traces of blood. She becomes Leatherface's next victim, a meat hook gouged into her back. This scene presented the most brutal slaughter of a female character in a commercially distributed film and significantly altered the boundaries in what was acceptable in relation to cinematic violence. Hanging aloft, she is forced to watch her boyfriend's dismemberment at the hands of this mindless brute and his incessant chainsaw.

When night falls Leatherface's sledgehammer dispatches Jerry as he tries to save Pam, who is barely alive in the freezer. Franklin is the next to meet his maker, this time slaughtered by the psychotic giant's chainsaw. Only Sally is left; frightened for her life she takes flight with Leatherface in hot pursuit. She manages to escape his chainsaw, but is later captured at the petrol station by the outlandish attendant and escorted back to the infernal house. Bound to a chair she once again finds herself in the company of the hitchhiker and now has the pleasure of being introduced to his dysfunctional family, the petrol attendant, an age-old grandpa and the silent figure of Leatherface.

So begins a night of torment, climaxed by a main course of human flesh served by a now feminized Leatherface. Against all odds, Sally escapes by throwing herself through the window. Armed with his noisome chainsaw, Leatherface and the deranged hitchhiker give chase, but the hitchhiker is killed by a truck. When the driver pulls up and tries to help, Leatherface mounts a frenzied assault on the cab. Only when the driver hits him full in the face with a wrench does the pair escape, with Sally narrowly eluding death in the back of a passing pickup truck. Just before the curtain goes down, she is seen laughing at the sight of the aggravated Leatherface, the unremitting buzz of his chainsaw still desperate for human flesh, bathed in the first light of a new dawn. Sally it would appear has completely lost her mind.

Filmed in a gruelling schedule lasting only four weeks, the highly controversial yet hugely influential **The Texas Chain Saw Massacre** was portrayed as a sequence of true events. This brought the sensation

seekers out in their droves and added to the film's success. It was, however, a ruse employed by Tobe Hooper to misinform his audience, just as he felt the American government had when they misled the country over Watergate, the petrol crisis and the atrocities of the Vietnam War. The sensationalism of everyday news reports had come to alarm him; he saw humankind attempting to hide behind a mask, one that obscured the true face of the monster. The grotesque Leatherface was incarcerated in his own mask; this monstrous visage, however, disguised the anguish within and consequently engendered a bizarre sense of pathos. Other observers would later note the underlying commentary in the desolate landscape symbolizing the end of the American dream. As sadistic as the film most certainly was, it was forthright in its use of social commentary, and was the first horror movie to address such concerns.

Wisconsin murderer Ed Gein provided an element of Hooper's inspiration. It was the moral schizophrenia, observed in the case of Houston-based Elmer Wayne Henley, that really caught the director's attention. As a teenager, he had been involved in the abduction, rape and murder of almost thirty teenage boys, some of whom were his friends. When arrested, Henley admitted to the crimes and freely accepted he must be punished; this ethical perversity became the basis for Leatherface and his deranged family, although Henley's lawyers did later appeal against his sentence. The idea for letting a chainsaw loose in his film came to Hooper in the hardware section of a crowded store; it provided the quickest means of getting through the throng. Icelandic–American actor Gunnar Hansen took the preparation for his role as Leatherface a little more seriously; he visited a school for those with learning disabilities, where he could study the pupils first hand and create the character both he and Hooper had discussed.

Hooper struggled to find a distributor for the film. Even though he had minimized the gore, it was still considered far too violent which in turn made it a potential risk. Wes Craven's **Last House on the Left** (1972) had already demonstrated such extremes were viable at the box office, in a film in which he had also engaged a murderous chainsaw. Bryanston Pictures finally took on the distribution; their terms almost resulted in disaster for Hooper, with his cast and crew going through the courts to ensure they were paid. When the company folded in 1976, due to Louis Peraino being convicted on obscenity charges following his involvement with **Deep Throat** four years before, New Line Cinema acquired the distribution rights. They were a little more amenable in agreeing to pay a greater percentage of the gross profits. Hooper's problems, however, were far from being over. The

The idyllic summer's day that became a nightmare of fear and blood . . .

critics were none too pleased with the excess and as a result his film was banned in many countries, including the UK. It did eventually see a limited release owing to the actions of more forward-thinking local councils that were prepared to grant a licence. At the time of the film's banning, the word "chainsaw" was prohibited from the title of any film, resulting in many producers changing the title of their low-budget money earners.

It wasn't until 1999, when the artistic worth of **The Texas Chain Saw Massacre** had been accepted, that the BBFC passed the film uncut. With the tabloid press headlines well in the past, critics now applauded the "bloodless depiction of violence", as they had done with John Carpenter's **Halloween** (1978). Its historical relevance was reappraised, acknowledging its part in laying the foundations for the terrors that had already followed. Hooper's ingenuity originated several key elements in the slasher genre, principally the use of the power tool as a murder weapon and the portrayal of the faceless killer. While the female protagonists were subjected to sadistic violence, the spotlight was thrown to the final girl scenario, the chaste heroine who would become the sole survivor and outlive her male counterparts. Ridley Scott paid tribute to the film in its inspiration for **Alien** (1979), while Alexandre Aja has been keen to extol on its impact during the early years of his career.

Five films would follow, three of which were sequels, **The Texas Chainsaw Massacre II** (1986), **Leatherface: The Texas Chainsaw Massacre III** (1990) and **The Return of the Texas Chainsaw Massacre** (1994), which is also known as **The Texas Chainsaw Massacre: The Next Generation**; and more recently, a reimagining of the original, **The Texas Chainsaw Massacre** (2003), and the prequel **The Texas Chainsaw Massacre:**

The Beginning (2006). A video game was created for the Atari 2600 shortly after the film's release to video in 1982. Its violent nature caused considerable controversy and many stores refused to carry it. It wasn't until 1991, at what was a low point in comic book horror, that Nothstar Comics published "Leatherface". Avatar released their version of a comic inspired by the film in 2005, and in 2006 the DC Comics imprint Wildstorm started publishing a series of stories using Hooper's premise. 🐾

Thirteen Women

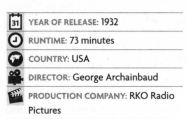

📅	YEAR OF RELEASE: 1932	🎞️	CINEMATOGRAPHER: Leo Tover
🕐	RUNTIME: 73 minutes	⊠	PRODUCERS: David O. Selznick (executive producer)
🎬	COUNTRY: USA		
🎥	DIRECTOR: George Archainbaud	⭘	CERTIFICATE: USA: Approved; USA: Passed (National Board of Review)
🎬	PRODUCTION COMPANY: RKO Radio Pictures		
✏️	WRITERS: Tiffany Thayer (novel), Bartlett Cormack (screenplay)		

CAST: Irene Dunne, Ricardo Cortez, Jill Esmond, Myrna Loy, Mary Duncan, Kay Johnson, Florence Eldridge, C. Henry Gordon, Peg Entwistle, Harriet Hagman, Edward Pawley, Blanche Friderici, Wally Albright

THE THIRTEEN WOMEN were once members of an exclusive girl's college sorority. Although they have gone on to new lives they have kept in touch and now write to a clairvoyant swami (C. Henry Gordon). He sends their horoscopes by mail,

each strangely predicting a terrible death. Little do the women know the clairvoyant is under the hypnotic influence of his secretary, the desirable mixed-race Eurasian Ursula Georgi (Myrna Loy). In the days when she was a student at the college, she was rejected by the sisterhood because of her mixed race. This sensuous creature now plots her revenge. The mysterious letters continue to be delivered, with the women completely unaware they are being manipulated by the person they once wronged. The doom-laden prophesies inevitably begin to become true. Some of the women band together, led by Laura Stanhope (Irene Dunne), to try to stop the sinister swami, not knowing they are the victims of a meticulously crafted plan. There will be those in the group who are deceived into killing themselves or each other. The clairvoyant also falls quite literally into Ursula's grasp; he commits suicide before an oncoming subway train. At the last, only Laura remains alive. She also has fears concerning her horoscope, but hers is somewhat different, as it predicts the death of her son Bobby before his birthday in three days' time. Ursula resorts to more direct measures to ensure Bobby's death comes to pass. With the help of Laura's chauffeur, she tries to kill young Bobby first with poisoned candy and then an explosive ball, but to no avail. Laura realizes someone other than the swami is behind these deaths so she now gets in touch with the local police. Sergeant Barry Clive, who is already familiar with the case, gets involved and is determined to keep Bobby from harm. As the film charges to a climax so befitting these years, the detective catches the dagger-wielding Ursula as she accosts Laura on a train. She flees to the rear carriage before falling to her own death.

George Archainbaud's **Thirteen Women** was also known as **Hypnose**, and sadly only fifty-nine of the original seventy-three minutes are still known to exist of this classic psychological thriller, which contains so many hallmarks of the later sorority slasher. On its release, not even the beautiful art deco design, or the intensity in Max Steiner's score, or the low-cut clinging gowns could assuage the poor reviews. This forced the legendary producer David O. Selznick to take the film out of the theatres and edit fourteen minutes, giving the version that we have today such an unsatisfactorily sudden ending.

This occult-laced feature was based on the scandalous novel of the same name by Tiffany Ellsworth Thayer, who himself had been an actor and was also the co-founder of the Fortean Society in 1931. Archainbaud's film was the **Psycho** (1960) of its day and in its relish to dispatch its cast one by one in a succession of highly stylized death scenes, it provides an interesting precursor to **And Then There Were None** (1945) and the slashers of the 1980s. While the film avoided the lesbianism of the novel, Ursula's sexuality was used to suitable effect, luxuriating in her role as the femme fatale. In the next few years, The Hays Code would soon put an end to such lurid displays along with the story's obvious racist slant. **Thirteen Women** was relatively unique in its exploration of inherent racism, which, given the fact the industry was at this time prone to ridiculous racial stereotypes, was an appreciably bold move. 🐾

Three on a Meathook

YEAR OF RELEASE: 1972	**CINEMATOGRAPHER:** William L. Asman
RUNTIME: 80 minutes	**PRODUCERS:** John Asman, Lee Jones, Joseph Shulten (executive producer)
COUNTRY: USA	
DIRECTOR: William Girdler	**CERTIFICATE:** Australia: R; UK: 18; USA: R
PRODUCTION COMPANY: Studio One	
WRITER: William Girdler	**BUDGET:** $20,000

CAST: Charles Kissinger, James Carroll Pickett, Sherry Steiner, Madelyn Buzzard, John Shaw, Marsha Tarbis, Carolyn Thompson, Kiersten Laine, Linda Thompson, Hugh Smith, Thomas Todd, Smith Haynie, Alice Summers

FOUR ATTRACTIVE YOUNG girls are on their way to a camping holiday in a wooded Lakeland area. After a lengthy skinny dipping session in the lake, they prepare to continue on their journey, but their car breaks down. A young farmer's boy by the name of Billy arrives, and offers to lend a helping hand. He then invites them to stay at the isolated farmhouse where he lives with his father. Little do the girls know, young Billy had interrupted his leisurely day of fishing to spy on them as they splashed around in the cooling lake. His father, who is a butcher famed in the locality for his sausage meat, is furious when he arrives home with the four girls. He reminds his son, "You know what happens to you when you get around women." A little more than twenty minutes into the film, the four girls each meet with

a grisly demise, one in a bath, another stabbed in the back, one shot and the other decapitated by a hatchet.

The following morning Billy is unable to remember anything of his murderous frenzy and this isn't the first time this has happened. His father solemnly lectures him, telling his son he should have listened. In an attempt to appease his anguished son he places some money in Billy's hand and tells him to go and "catch a movie". Strangely, the shot of this troubled young man as he ambles along the neon-lit street is not suggestive of a murderous lunatic, but after what has previously happened, he is still a serious cause for concern. While in town, Billy stops off at a bar and takes in some music. Although he has a little too much to drink, he manages to befriend the barmaid. When he eventually passes out, she offers to take him home. As he awakens at her side in the morning light, the alarm bells begin to ring; she has just noticed the wet patch on his jeans. Surprisingly, Billy calmly takes this in his stride and the two begin to develop a close relationship. When he takes her back to the farm it looks as if history will once again repeat itself; only now does he discover the truth about his father and his long lost cannibalistic mother hidden in the barn.

Who could resist a film by the name of **Three on a Meathook**? William Girdler's film was a gritty low-budget piece of grindhouse exploitation inspired by the tragedy of Ed Gein. Its grainy depiction of brutal murder and

A padlocked shed, hooks of cold steel – a maniac on the loose.

cannibalism predated both **The Texas Chain Saw Massacre** and **Deranged** by almost two years, yet contained very similar themes. While this movie was nowhere near as bloodthirsty as inferred by the title, there were some quite horrific kills, which belied the film's low budget. Such was its grainy appearance, **Three on a Meathook** attracted the plaudit, "it looks like a home movie a serial killer would make". Sadly, Girdler died in a helicopter crash soon after shooting his final feature **Manitou** in 1978. In less than five years he brought nine films to the drive-in theatres of North America, with an unfulfilled promise of so much more. ✒

To All A Goodnight

📅	YEAR OF RELEASE: 1980	✏️ WRITER: Alex Rebar
⏱️	RUNTIME: 90 minutes	🎞️ CINEMATOGRAPHER: Bil Godsey
🌐	COUNTRY: USA	🎬 PRODUCERS: Sandy Cobe, Jay
🎥	DIRECTOR: David Hess	Rasumny, Alex Rebar, Sharyon Reis
🎬	PRODUCTION COMPANY: Four	Cobe, Rick Whitfield
	Features Partners, Intercontinental	⭕ CERTIFICATE: Australia: R; UK: 18;
	Releasing Corporation (IRC)	USA: R

CAST: Jennifer Runyon, Forrest Swanson, Linda Gentile, William Lauer, Judith Bridges, Katherine Herrington, Buck West, Sam Shamshak, Angela Bath, Denise Stearns, Solomon Trager, Jeff Butts, Bill Martin, Jay Rasumny

IT WAS ALMOST time to break up for Christmas at the Calvin Finishing School for Girls, and the students were getting excited about going home. In the joyous hysteria, one of the girls was chased around the dormitory by her friends. When she escaped out onto the balcony, she lost her balance and fell to the floor below.

You'll scream till dawn!

Two years later the Christmas holidays beckon again. Some of the girls have decided to stay on and enjoy a private party. Among them are the shapely Melody (Linda Gentile), the well-spoken Trisha (Angela Bath) from England, the man-mad Leia (Judith Bridges) and the innocent heroine of this tale, Nancy (Jennifer Runyon), who has no desire to be mixed with this bunch. The girls invite a group of young men over, who fly in from wherever, and soon after a psycho dressed as Santa begins killing off the revellers in the empty rooms of the school dormitories. Several of the gang die very early on in the film, but their friends foolishly fail to realize just how serious the situation has become. Although the police offer to track down this lunatic, their efforts prove hopelessly ineffectual.

Whoever is behind his slaughter enjoys using sharp objects that can be turned into weapons; an arrow, a knife, an axe and a propeller are all employed in the murder of these teenagers, with a decapitated head making its way into a shower scene. With most of the cast buried in the school grounds, Nancy finds herself as the last girl leading to the film's customary twist ending.

Last House on the Left's David Hess stepped into the director's chair to create one of the earliest festive slashers that stayed very closely to the formula of the period. **Christmas Evil** appeared around about the same time, but Hess's atmospheric film was to become the lesser known of the two, suffering with poorly lit night photography that obscured so much of Mark Shostrum's gory effects. As would have been expected of Hess, the killings were imaginative, particularly the incident with the propeller, but he struggled with a frustratingly limited budget as many director's did when making these films. Four years later **Silent Night, Deadly Night** caused considerable outrage in having a killer dressed as Santa, but Hess's costumed killer was to attract very little attention.

To Let

YEAR OF RELEASE: 2007	**PRODUCTION COMPANY:** Estudios Picasso, Filmax, Telecinco
RUNTIME: 68 minutes	
COUNTRY: Spain	**WRITERS:** Jaume Balagueró (screenplay), Alberto Marini (screenplay)
DIRECTOR: Jaume Balagueró	

CINEMATOGRAPHER: Pablo Rosso

PRODUCERS: Álvaro Augustín, Carlos Fernández (executive producer), Julio Fernández, Santiago Gimeno (executive producer), Narciso Ibáñez Serrador (executive producer), Aitor Montánchez (executive producer), Goretti Pagès (line producer)

CAST: Macarena Gómez, Nuria González, Adrià Collado, Ruth Díaz, Roberto Romero, David Sandanya

ORIGINALLY ENTITLED PARA entrar a vivir, Jaume Balagueró's short film was made for the Spanish horror television series "Películas para no dormire" (Films to Keep You Awake). Balagueró had already become a director of international repute with his addition to a new generation of cinematic terror, **REC**, in 2007. **To Let** affirmed his eminence as a veritable director of the nail-biting horror rollercoaster ride.

Having just sold their apartment, Mario and his pregnant girlfriend Clara have only fifteen days as they try desperately to find a new abode. Fortune seems to smile on the couple when Mario finds an advertisement for what looks to be the perfect home, folded into his mailbox. He persuades Clara to come along and look the place over. In torrential rain, they journey to what turns out to be a dilapidated building in a neighbourhood that has seen better days. At this point, many couples would have turned around and gone home, but Mario and Clara are on the edge of a domestic crisis. Typically the realtor is a little too keen to make the sale, but in its run-down state they know this is not the right place for them. However, they find it hard to shake the feeling that something hasn't been right since they set foot in the building; their suspicions are confirmed when they enter one of the apartments to find their personal belongings including their photographs. The realtor's psychotic tendencies are now revealed and the two are forced to stay, imprisoned with several other unfortunates, one of whom is not quite what he appears.

The claustrophobia permeating the darkened corridors and stairways of this building is characteristic of Balagueró's work on both **REC** movies. With the restrictions placed on television running time, he has little more than an hour to unfurl this perturbing drama, ensuring that the narrative runs at an adrenalin-injected pace with shocks waiting at each turn. Soon after Mario and Clara have entered the apartment building, the story begins to run in

"6 films to keep you awake".

real time with the tension rising to an unbearable fever pitch taking us through to the film's cruel finale. The gore junkies among you will not be treated to an outrageous body count, and there remains uncertainty as to whether anyone actually dies in this film, but the blood does flow and it will make even the most hardened wince in anguish. In August 2008, Lionsgate released this along with the other episodes in this television series as a box set of horror movies under the name "6 Films to Keep You Awake".

The Toolbox Murders

📅 YEAR OF RELEASE: 1978		🎬 CINEMATOGRAPHER: Gary Graver
🕐 RUNTIME: 93 minutes		⚗ PRODUCERS: Tony DiDio, Jack Kindberg (associate producer), Kenneth Yates (associate producer)
🎥 COUNTRY: USA		
📹 DIRECTOR: Dennis Donnelly		
🎬 PRODUCTION COMPANY: Cal-Am Productions, Tony DiDio Productions		⭕ CERTIFICATE: Australia: Refused Classification; Canada: 18+ (Quebec); Canada: R (Ontario); UK: 18 (video rating) (2000, cut); UK: X (original rating, cut) USA: R
✎ WRITERS: Neva Friedenn, Robert Easter, Ann Kindberg		
		💲 BUDGET: $185,000

CAST: Cameron Mitchell, Pamelyn Ferdin, Wesley Eure, Nicolas Beauvy, Tim Donnelly, Aneta Corsaut, Faith McSwain, Marciee Drake, Evelyn Guerrero, Victoria Perry, Robert Bartlett, Betty Cole, John Hawker, Don Diamond, Alisa Powell

IN A LOS Angeles apartment complex, the young female residents are being stalked and slaughtered by a killer who disguises himself with a ski mask. He uses a variety of tools in the undertaking of his grisly crimes, among them a hammer, a drill, screwdrivers and, in the most graphic killing of them all, a nail gun. For the first twenty-five minutes, the atrocities in this film go a long way to making it a grindhouse classic, but all too soon we learn the man responsible for this trail of death is the complex's owner (Cameron Mitchell). He has taken it on himself to rid the world of immoral women following the death of his daughter in a car crash after falling into a life of sex and drugs. As he continues in his bloody quest, he becomes obsessed with an innocent young girl, Laurie (Pamelyn Ferdin), who lives with her family in the complex. His twisted mind begins to envisage her as surrogate child and, in his unhinged state of mind, he kidnaps her and ties her to his bed, all the while stalking the apartments of the complex. The latter part of the film is almost a eulogy on the fragility of innocence, before the harrowing twist at the finale.

Following the overwhelming success of **The Texas Chain Saw Massacre** (1974), there was a spate of films that sought to capitalize on Tobe Hooper's excess. Among them was television director Dennis Donnelly's **The Toolbox Murders**. As with its illustrious predecessor, Donnelly's film was dogged by controversy, generating anger among feminist groups and getting a spot on the long-running television news magazine *60 Minutes* in a piece on violent misogynist imagery in popular entertainment. This news report conveniently forgot to mention two of the writing team were women. On its initial cinematic release in the UK during 1979, the BBFC insisted on just over two minutes of cuts to Kelly Nichols' bathtub

Bit by bit . . . by bit he carved a nightmare!

masturbation sequence and substantial edits to the murder scenes along with shots of the blood-stained bodies before it was passed with an "X" rating. This version was later released to video in November 1981, but was doomed to become a reviled video nasty in November 1983, even though it had previously had BBFC approval. It wasn't removed from the list until May 1985 when it was accepted it was the same version that had been approved six years before. While **The Toolbox Murders** has never been officially made available in the UK without cuts, it can lay claim to being a major influence on the tool-driven mayhem that soon followed, particularly **The Driller Killer** (1979) and **The Nail Gun Massacre** (1986). It also imitated Tobe Hooper's false claim that the film was based on actual events.

While Donnelly had hoped to follow Tobe Hooper's sensation at the box office, it was Hooper who was asked to direct the remake of his film in 2004. Donnelly would continue an already highly accomplished career in television going on to direct *Charlie's Angels* and *The A-Team*. 🐾

Tormented

YEAR OF RELEASE: 2009	DIRECTOR: Jon Wright
RUNTIME: 87 minutes	PRODUCTION COMPANY: BBC Films, Forward Films, Pathé, Screen West Midlands, Slingshot Productions
COUNTRY: UK	

WRITER: Stephen Prentice

CINEMATOGRAPHER: Trevor Forrest

PRODUCERS: Cavan Ash, Tracy Brimm, Rachel Connors, Arvind Ethan David, Uzma Hasan, François Ivernel, Cameron McCracken, Luke Montagu, Kate Myers, Joe Oppenheimer, Toby Rushton, Jim Spencer, Lee Thomas

CERTIFICATE: Australia: MA; Ireland: 18; UK: 15; USA: R

BUDGET: £700,000

CAST: Alex Pettyfer, April Pearson, Dimitri Leonidas, Calvin Dean, Tuppence Middleton, Georgia King, Mary Nighy, Olly Alexander, James Floyd, Sophie Wu, Hugh Mitchell, Larissa Wilson, Ruby Bentall

JON WRIGHT'S FILM opens at the well-heeled grammar school Fairview High with Oxford-bound head girl Justine (Tuppence Middleton) eulogizing at the funeral of one of her classmates Darren Mullet (Calvin Dean), a boy she barely knew. After her hollow oration, she will learn that the overweight Darren was considered a loser by his tormenting peers and it was their malicious onslaught which finally drove him to suicide. A few days later, Justine is invited by another schoolmate, Alexis (Dimitri Leonidas), to a party at the house of his friend Bradley (Alex Pettyfer). She gets to hear how Darren had a crush on her, and to her horror discovers that he was being bullied by Bradley and his gang of insufferable friends, among them pretty boy Alexis. Not long after, Bradley's reprobate friends receive a series of text messages warning of their impending deaths; the messages are traced to Darren's phone. One by one, this

A new class of terror!

privileged gang of bullies are dragged to their deaths at the hands of an asthmatic zombie who has returned from the dead to mete out the most cruel of revenges. The grave certainly hasn't dulled his imaginative streak as he fervently severs hands with a paper cutter, removes heads with a shovel, strikes another victim with a paddle to propel their eye from its socket, before making use of a screwdriver and crucifix.

Stephen Prentice's screenplay may not have been entirely original, but it was indeed a very British take on the American slasher, created for a new generation set against a suburban backdrop in the West Midlands. The dialogue and characterization possessed an energy that has long been missing from this hack and slash genre, and was not without its sense of humour, albeit at times very dark. Jon Wright was born in 1971, and was lucky enough to be of an age where he grew up with these movies when they were at their peak. Backed by BBC Films, who have a worldwide reputation for tightly budgeted yet exemplary filmmaking, this tale of a bullied schoolboy's revenge contained the finest production values with a cast who, on the international circuit, would have been relatively unknown. This anonymity, combined with their obvious talent, only enhanced the impact of a film that was at times poignant as well as being rather spooky. 🦋

Tourist Trap

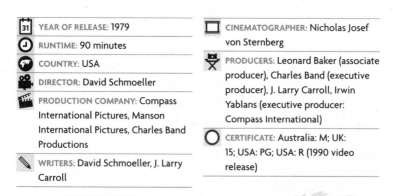

31 YEAR OF RELEASE: 1979

🕐 RUNTIME: 90 minutes

🐷 COUNTRY: USA

🎥 DIRECTOR: David Schmoeller

🎬 PRODUCTION COMPANY: Compass International Pictures, Manson International Pictures, Charles Band Productions

✎ WRITERS: David Schmoeller, J. Larry Carroll

📷 CINEMATOGRAPHER: Nicholas Josef von Sternberg

⚒ PRODUCERS: Leonard Baker (associate producer), Charles Band (executive producer), J. Larry Carroll, Irwin Yablans (executive producer: Compass International)

○ CERTIFICATE: Australia: M; UK: 15; USA: PG; USA: R (1990 video release)

CAST: Chuck Connors, Jocelyn Jones, Jon Van Ness, Robin Sherwood, Tanya Roberts, Dawn Jeffory, Keith McDermott, Shailar Coby, Arlecchino, Victoria Richart, Millie Dill

HAVING DEVELOPED CAR problems, young Woody comes upon a museum filled with wax dummies. He enters in the hope of finding help. He will come to wish he hadn't; objects fly from shelves, and mannequins appear to come alive and poor Woody never gets out alive. His friends, college students Becky, Molly, Eileen and Jerry, set off in a jeep to try to trace his whereabouts. Their trail takes them to "Slausen's Lost Oasis" owned by the reclusive Mr Slausen (Chuck Connors). He agrees to help them out, but against his wishes

some of the girls make their way up to his house hoping to find a telephone. In her search Eileen wanders into a room to be confronted by the creepy mannequins; her sense of unease is heightened when she feels an unseen force around her throat. The sensation begins to tighten and she is left for dead, the victim of a freak with telekinetic powers. As objects are hurled across various rooms and the mannequins again begin to return to life, the teenagers are lured to their deaths by this shady presence. Although the killer's purpose isn't initially clear, he demonstrates an unusual relationship with the mannequins, each of which evinces unsettling human traits. His face remains hidden behind a mask fashioned in the guise of a doll, evoking memories of that worn by Michael Myers twelve months before in **Halloween**. Molly comes to assume the role of the final girl and finds herself the object of the psychopath's affections. In the closing shots she escapes in the jeep, accompanied by four figures that no longer appear to be human.

Tourist Trap was a re-working of a short film David Schmoeller had originally directed three years before, entitled **The Spider Will Kill You**. This low-budget terror proved to be the beginning of a highly successful career that would see him return using a similar premise in **The Puppet Master**, a feature that went straight to video in 1989. There was a perverse pleasure in watching the mannequins come to life, at times laughing in a way that would make your skin run cold, then returning to the silence of this forgotten house.

Every year young people disappear.

Their presence gave this movie an unnerving chill and, along with Chuck Norris's intense portrayal of the unhinged Mr Slausen, made this one of Stephen King's favourite horror movies. It was only the beginning of the slasher's rise as a cult phenomenon, but the creation of a killer with psychic powers was highly original.

Schmoeller was still learning his trade and it is obvious he had taken note of some of the key moments in **Psycho** (1960), **The Texas Chain Saw Massacre** (1974) and **Carrie** (1976). He paced his film, creating the tension that would lead to some quite shocking scenes, including the image of a woman's face being transformed into a plaster mask. On its original American release it was given a "PG" rating, which unfortunately worked against the film's interests, making it a failure at the box office. Several years later, it was re-evaluated and given an "R" rating, which was a fair reflection of the film's disturbing nature. **Tourist Trap** has since gone on to become another cult favourite.

Two Thousand Maniacs!

31 YEAR OF RELEASE: 1964	COUNTRY: USA
RUNTIME: 87 minutes	DIRECTOR: Herschell Gordon Lewis

PRODUCTION COMPANY: Jacqueline Kay, Friedman-Lewis Productions

 PRODUCER: David F. Friedman

 WRITER: Herschell Gordon Lewis

 CERTIFICATE: Australia: R; New Zealand: R16; UK:18; USA: Unrated

 BUDGET: $65,000

CAST: Connie Mason, William Kerwin, Jeffrey Allen White, Shelby Livingston, Ben Moore, Jerome Eden, Gary Bakeman, Mark Douglas, Linda Cochran, Yvonne Gilbert, Michael Korb, Vincent Santo, Andy Wilson, Candi Conder, The Pleasant Valley Boys

HERSCHELL GORDON LEWIS'S film was inspired by the 1947 Lerner and Loewe musical **Brigadoon**. As the residents of Pleasant Valley, Georgia, are joyfully celebrating their centennial, they lure six tourists into the town. All seems well with the group as they are treated as guests of honour. However, things are not what they seem; the centennial in question dates back to the town's annihilation at the hands of a group of Union soldiers during the Civil War. All these years later, the townsfolk still crave revenge. Once separated the tourists are forced to participate in a diversity of horrific games, which result in their blood-splattered deaths. Their grisly demise was considered quite extreme for the mid-1960s: one of the women was dismembered with an axe before being roasted on a barbecue; a mock horse race saw a man torn limb from limb; another victim was rolled downhill in a barrel lined with nails; and finally one of the women was crushed by a boulder

Brutal . . . evil . . . ghastly beyond belief!

in a mechanism reminiscent to a carnival dunk tank. After discovering the townspeople's terrible scheme, the two remaining tourists manage to escape. They soon return with a local sheriff, only to discover the town has disappeared from sight. The film ends with two of the residents looking forward to the next centennial in 2065, when Pleasant Valley will once again rise to resume its vendetta against the hated Yankees.

This low-budget splatter movie marked the second instalment in what became known as "The Blood Trilogy", led by **Blood Feast** (1963) and concluded a year later with **Color Me Blood Red**. Lewis's film has attracted considerable attention among the gore fraternity owing to its bloody and torturous scenes, although it was hampered by B-movie direction and the wooden acting that was to became characteristic of so many of these minor gorefests. The trilogy and its director went on to attract a cult following, largely due to the outrageous portrayal of violence and the flamboyance of the villains. Shot in only fifteen days, early in 1964, **Two Thousand Maniacs!** could boast almost the entire town of St Cloud, Florida, had participated in its production. The film's star was the 1963 Playboy Playmate Connie Mason, in her second appearance in the trilogy. A remake followed in 2005, this time starring Robert Englund.

Un Chien Andalou

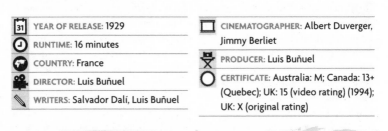

📅 YEAR OF RELEASE: 1929		🎞 CINEMATOGRAPHER: Albert Duverger, Jimmy Berliet
🕐 RUNTIME: 16 minutes		🪑 PRODUCER: Luis Buñuel
🌐 COUNTRY: France		⭕ CERTIFICATE: Australia: M; Canada: 13+ (Quebec); UK: 15 (video rating) (1994); UK: X (original rating)
🎥 DIRECTOR: Luis Buñuel		
✎ WRITERS: Salvador Dalí, Luis Buñuel		

CAST: Simone Mareuil, Pierre Batcheff

THERE HAVE BEEN many attempts to explain Luis Buñuel's collaboration with fellow surrealist Salvador Dalí, all of which have been in vain, for when they first conceived this script, they freely acknowledged one simple rule: "no idea or image that might lend itself to a rational explanation of any kind would be accepted". To their minds, the symbolism in their work could only ever be interpreted by engaging the precepts of deep psychoanalysis and even then any findings would be frustratingly inconclusive. However, as they openly defied convention in their approach to this new art form, their now infamous dreamlike sequence detailing the slitting open of a woman's eye inadvertently had a considerable influence on the visceral excess of the latter years of the twentieth century. This was the first time such an extreme piece of gore had been committed to celluloid, and would act as precedent for directors such as Dario Argento, who applied it in those excruciating scenes from **Opera** (1987), Lucio Fulci notably in **The Beyond** (1981) and **The New York Ripper** (1982) and later still Takashi Miike in the agonizing needle episode from **Audition** (2000). Buñuel, could lay claim to being the cinematic pioneer of this dehumanizing mode of torment, as he set out to shock his audience with the violence in this seminal injury to the eye motif.

This sequence, however, was beset by a strange paradox that proved intrinsic to the subversive nature of this piece. Buñuel was intent on making imagery the focal point of his experimental short feature, wantonly disregarding the recently discovered approach to dialogue and casting aside any notion of plot; yet this same imagery conspired to remove our one chance to behold the dreamlike qualities in his work. When viewed in the context of the next eighty years of cinema, his disturbing vision which was so far ahead of its time, inevitably became the cause of much scandal when it played before the audiences of 1929. Coupled with this violent episode came an intimation of exploitation as male hands were seen to touch a woman's bare breast. Such salacious scenes were not deemed suitable for public consumption in the world of 1929, even though in those clandestine quarters there was already a market for pornographic cinema. Almost a century later **Un Chien Anadalou** contains a powerful legacy with its eternal themes of love, life, sex and death each diffused into Buñuel and Dalí's bizarre vision.

Unhinged

📅	YEAR OF RELEASE: 1982	🎬	CINEMATOGRAPHER: Richard Blakeslee
🕐	RUNTIME: 79 minutes	🎬	PRODUCERS: Dan Biggs (associate producer), Dale Farr (executive producer), Don Gronquist
🌍	COUNTRY: USA		
🎥	DIRECTOR: Don Gronquist	⭕	CERTIFICATE: Australia: R; UK: 18; USA: Unrated
🎬	PRODUCTION COMPANY: Anavisio Productions		
✏️	WRITERS: Don Gronquist, Reagan Ramsey		

CAST: Laurel Munson, Janet Penner, Sara Ansley, Virginia Settle, John Morrison, Barbara Lusch, Bill Simmonds, Francine Molter, Dave Hood

THREE COLLEGE STUDENTS, Terry (Laurel Munson), Nancy (Sara Ansley) and Gloria (Barbara Lusch), are driving through a storm on their way to a music festival. The radio carries an ominous portent, telling of young girls going missing in the area. They take in a little pot and share their hankering for certain young men and then as the rain begins to drive down the car skids out of control and crashes into a ditch. When they climb up to the road they realize they are stranded in a forest and Gloria is badly injured. Thanks to a handyman (John Morrison) they are taken to the sanctuary of a rambling old house owned by two women; they offer to help the girls, but it will be a few days before the girl who has been maimed can leave. The younger of the two women, Marion (Janet Penner), is delighted to see these new faces. Her elderly mother (Virginia Settle) sits in her wheelchair reminiscing about days gone by and warns of the evils that come with the male species, particularly her former husband. As she continues to ramble, she reveals herself unduly disparaging of her seemingly innocuous daughter.

In the confines of the house the tension slowly builds with one of the girls finding a tooth on the floor and then they are both sure they catch sight of someone staring at them through the windows as they undress. As she makes her way through the woods in a bid to find help, Nancy is hacked down by a figure bearing a scythe, in what is a shockingly vivid slaying. When Nancy doesn't return Terry becomes anxious. She is sure she can hear someone breathing heavily and begins wandering around the house. She comes upon a child's room adorned with old black and white pictures of two very young children and observes an old tool belt and a machete. She returns to her room only to see a grimy old man at her window, the same figure she has seen before. The shock of his appearance causes her to start screaming

Get your slice from the reaper. Violence beyond reason. Victims beyond help.

hysterically; Marion comes to comfort her and reveals that the old man is her abandoned brother Carl, whose mind is that of a five year old. The following day Gloria regains consciousness, only to have her head split open with an axe. Only Terry is left; she will soon discover what lies in the shed and confront the twist that would be used again in **April Fool's Day** (1986), which turns **Psycho** on its head and elevates Gronquist's film above so many of its contemporaries.

While the acting in Don Gronquist's feature was not of the highest calibre, he distinguished himself in creating a lingering sense of suspense and shocked his audience with only the use of occasional but effective gore. The body count may not have been particularly high, but the shed, replete with severed bodies and jars of eyeballs, ably made up for this lapse. **Unhinged** retains a typical grainy, ill-lit look, which reflected its minimal budget. This film could have been forgotten if it hadn't been included on the list of the UK's video nasties and during the furore made an appearance on the BBC's news following its release to video in 1983. In the early eighties scenes of girls indulging in soft drugs, full frontal nudity and gore were considered a little too strong for British palates. It was later removed from the list in May 1985, but wasn't submitted by the distributors again until 2005, this time to be passed uncut. ❧

The Untold Story

📅	YEAR OF RELEASE: 1993	
🕐	RUNTIME: 96 minutes	
🎥	COUNTRY: Hong Kong	
🎬	DIRECTOR: Danny Lee, Herman Yau	
🎬	PRODUCTION COMPANY: Cinema City Film Productions	

WRITER: Law Kam Fai

PRODUCER: Danny Lee

CERTIFICATE: Australia: R; Canada: 18+ (Quebec); Canada: R (Manitoba); Canada: R (Ontario) (cut version); Hong Kong: III; USA: Unrated

CAST: Kuang Hsiung, Emily Kwan, Danny Lee, Julie Lee, Fui-On Shing, Anthony Wong Chau-Sang, Parkman Wong

A COUPLE OF GAMBLERS slug it out in a ferocious fight with one of them left for dead; his body is doused in petrol and then set alight. The perpetrator then goes on the run in a bid to escape the investigating detectives. **The Untold Story** moves forward eight years to reveal a number of severed hands lying on a beach. In a change of scene the pitiless murderer witnessed at the beginning of this film, Wong Chi Hang (Anthony Wong), has had a change in lifestyle and is now the owner of the Eight Immortals Restaurant. However, he has fallen under the suspicion of the comedic police authorities, as the family who had until recently owned the restaurant have been reported missing. In his time with the restaurant Wong has built a reputation for serving up the most delicious pork bao, much to the delight of his customers in the neighbourhood. When the disappearances continue

the police have no option but to take him in for questioning and half way through the film in the aftermath of a brutal interrogation he begins to divulge a rather disconcerting story. The grinning Wong was no stranger to rape and murder, and thought nothing of the slaughter of the restaurant owner after a game of cards and then doing the same to his wife. In the most distressing scene in the film, he also took a meat cleaver to the owner's terrified children. He didn't stop there; an innocent woman was brutally violated with chop sticks and then murdered in an unnecessarily protracted sequence, the intensity of which is rarely ever experienced in western filmmaking. His victims' bodies, he discloses, were sliced up to make the tasty pork bao, the delicacy for which he had carved such a standing with his customers. While in police custody, Wong tries to take his own life as, in an about turn,

The Untold Story succeeds in eliciting sympathy for this psychotic felon.

Danny Lee and Herman Yau joined forces to create one of the most notorious Category III films of the decade. Their production was made even more disturbing when they revealed the source of their tale was again based upon an actual occurrence. It was the violence, however, that made this film so shocking, particularly the slaughter of the family, which thrived upon every single grisly detail. The involvement of the young children in these scenes was distressing to say the least and revealed an obvious polarizing of attitude when comparing eastern and western approaches to filmmaking. Lee and Yau sought to immerse their film in an excess of blood and guts in the telling of their story and for the bona fide gore-monger it was manna from heaven, but in the creation of this blood bath they demonstrated a customary callous disregard for human life. As the blood swashed around his kitchen, there was an uncanny disquiet to Anthony Wong's portrayal of this murderous psychopath, with time taken to dwell on his nonchalance as he tossed away the unwanted body parts of his victims and then prepared for his next episode of nastiness. These interludes would be counteracted by a person whose penchant for extreme violence bordered on utter madness and yet the brutal display of the interrogating police officers forced the audience to re-evaluate their opinion of this man, which would add to the impact of Lee and Yau's uncompromising feature. **The Untold Story** would see release under a variety of guises, **Bunman: The Untold Story**, **Human Meat Pies: The Untold Story**, **Human Pork Chop**, **The Eight Immortals Restaurant: The Untold Story** and **The Untold Story: Human Meat Roast Pork Buns**, each of which characterized the unique excess of Hong Kong Category III cinema.

Untraceable

 YEAR OF RELEASE: 2008

 RUNTIME: 101 minutes

COUNTRY: USA

DIRECTOR: Gregory Hoblit

 PRODUCTION COMPANY: Cohen/ Pearl Productions, Lakeshore Entertainment

 WRITERS: Robert Fyvolent, Mark Brinker

 **CINEMATOGRAPHER:** Anastas N. Michos

 PRODUCERS: Andy Cohen, Hawk Koch, Gary Lucchesi, James McQuaide (executive producer), Steven Pearl, Sarah Platt (associate producer), Eric Reid (executive producer), Tom Rosenberg, Harley Tannenbaum (executive producer), Richard S. Wright (executive producer)

CERTIFICATE: Australia: MA; Canada: 16+ (Quebec); Canada: 18A (Alberta/British Columbia/Manitoba/Nova Scotia/Ontario); Ireland: 18; New Zealand: R18; UK: 18; USA: R

BUDGET: $35,000,000

RECEIPTS: $51,800,000

CAST: Diane Lane, Billy Burke, Colin Hanks, Joseph Cross, Mary Beth Hurt, Peter Lewis, Tyrone Giordano, Perla Haney-Jardine, Tim De Zarn, Christopher Cousins, Jesse Tyler Ferguson, Trina Adams, Brynn Baron, John Breen, Dan Callahan

JENNIFER MARSH (DIANE Lane) works in the FBI's cyber-crime division with her colleague Griffin Dowd (Colin Hanks) in the fight to thwart identity theft. An anonymous call takes them to a despicable website calling itself "killwithme.com". The introductory streaming video shows a kitten being horribly tortured and killed. This is only the beginning for in a world aroused by torture porn the site's owner (Joseph Cross) knows those who visit his site will want something a little stronger. He lures his new members with the promise of human quarry. The more people who log onto the website, the quicker and more violently the victim will die.

While Diane Lane was praised for her strong performance, **Untraceable** was criticized for its duplicitous indulgence in the world of torture porn, although it avoided so much of the grisly excess observed in **Saw** (2004) and **Hostel** (2005). The more graphic scenes detail a man slowly bleeding to death, another unfortunate being fatally burned while exposed to deathly heat lamps and a man's skin blistering and peeling as he is submerged in a vat of sulphuric acid.

> **A cyber killer has finally found the perfect accomplice: You.**

Urban Legend

YEAR OF RELEASE: 1998

RUNTIME: 99 minutes

COUNTRY: USA/France

DIRECTOR: Jamie Blanks

PRODUCTION COMPANY: Canal+ Droits Audiovisuels, Original Film, Phoenix Pictures

WRITER: Silvio Horta

CINEMATOGRAPHER: James Chressanthis

PRODUCERS: Brad Luff (executive producer), Gina Matthews, Michael McDonnell, Neal H. Moritz, Brian Leslie Parker (associate producer)

CERTIFICATE: Australia: MA; Canada: 13+ (Quebec); Canada: 14A (Alberta/British Columbia); Canada: AA (Ontario); Canada: PA (Manitoba); Canada: 18 (Nova Scotia); New Zealand: R16; UK: 18; USA: R

$ BUDGET: $14,000,000

RECEIPTS: $72,527,595

CAST: Jared Leto, Alicia Witt, Rebecca Gayheart, Michael Rosenbaum, Loretta Devine, Joshua Jackson, Tara Reid, John Neville, Julian Richings, Robert Englund, Danielle Harris

ON A DARK, rain-soaked new England night, college student Michelle Mancini heads in the direction of a petrol station, unaware that someone is hiding in the back of her car. We never get to see his face, but the tension is shattered by the blow of his axe, which sees Michelle quite literally lose her head. Meanwhile on the campus of nearby Pendleton University, a student gathering hangs onto every word of a disturbing tale going all the way back to 1973 when an aberrant psychology teacher slaughtered six students in one of the university's halls of residence. The following day the whole campus gets to know about Michele's murder; her death is emblazoned across the headlines of the university's student newspaper. In a quiet woodland area, one of the girls from the previous night's discussion, Natalie, confides in

At Pendelton University, urban legends are coming true!

her friend Damon, telling him there was a time when she knew Michelle. Recognizing that Natalie is in need of comfort, Damon comes on a little too strong and is summarily rejected. Annoyed he takes off into the woods; as he urinates in the bushes he falls prey to a shadowed attacker, and is later found hanging from a tree. Although no one will believe her, Natalie is convinced there is a murderer stalking the campus whose unique modus operandi is derived from the tales of urban legend. Very soon, staff and students alike are falling to this cunning killer as a variety of red herrings work to distract the audience, casting suspicion on an ever-changing group of suspects and building to the all-essential twist at the finale.

As he looked to emulate the triumph that had been Wes Craven's **Scream** (1996), Jamie Blanks succeeded in securing a very talented team. These included scriptwriter Silvio Horta, who created a feasible narrative albeit with the inescapable bunch of teenagers, each of them predictably ripe for the ensuing slaughter, and cinematographer James Chressanthis, who made this film visually embody the seventeen million dollars that been made available to terrorize the cinema-going public. This wasn't the first time a good-looking young cast had been butchered on a university campus at the hands of a killer whose strength bordered on being supernatural, but murder by urban legend was a new turn on a formula that had seemingly been exhausted more than a decade before. Banks could be accused of using every cliché in the book as he threw in both the comedy and the splatter, but he created a series of very scary moments and maintained the mystery in his film until the very last moment. His success would lead to a directorial role on a slasher for the new millennia, **Valentine** (2001) with **Urban Legend** being granted a sequel in 2000, **Urban Legends: Final Cut.**

Valentine

📅 YEAR OF RELEASE: 2001	🏆 PRODUCERS: Bruce Berman (executive producer), Grant Rosenberg (executive producer), Jim Rowe (co-producer), Dylan Sellers
🕐 RUNTIME: 96 minutes	
🌐 COUNTRY: USA	
🎥 DIRECTOR: Jamie Banks	
🎬 PRODUCTION COMPANY: Warner Bros. Pictures, Village Roadshow Pictures, NPV Entertainment, Cupid Productions	⭕ CERTIFICATE: Australia: MA; Canada: 13+ (Quebec); Canada: 14 (Nova Scotia); Canada: 14A (Alberta/British Columbia/Manitoba) (Canadian Home Video rating); Canada: AA (Ontario); Ireland: 18; New Zealand: R16; UK: 15; USA: R
✏️ WRITERS: Tom Savage (novel), Donna Powers, Wayne Powers, Gretchen J. Berg, Aaron Harberts	
📷 CINEMATOGRAPHER: Rick Bota	💲 BUDGET: $29,000,000
	💷 RECEIPTS: $36,684,100

CAST: Denise Richards, David Boreanaz, Marley Shelton, Jessica Capshaw, Jessica Cauffiel, Katherine Heigl, Hedy Burress, Fulvio Cecere, Daniel Cosgrove, Johnny Whitworth, Woody Jeffreys

AT THE VALENTINE'S Day dance of 1988, one of the school's nerds, Jeremy Melton, endured a whole series of rejections as he asked four of the most popular girls of his year to dance with him. An insecure slightly overweight girl finally agreed to a dance and sometime later the two were found passionately entwined by a group of the school's bullies. In her embarrassment, the young girl claimed that Jeremy had attacked her, so the gang strip the poor boy and lay into him in front of the entire school. Thirteen years later with Valentine's Day only a matter of days away, the five girls who caused Jeremy so much anguish are now trying to address their ever-fluctuating love lives. One of the girls, whose date goes horribly wrong, falls prey to a killer wearing a Cherub-styled mask. Chillingly, she had been sent a death threat in a Valentine card only days before she was murdered. The rest of the girls then receive similar cards with the killer lying in wait to carry out his deathly threat. With each card being signed J. M., suspicion understandably focuses on the now mature Jeremy, with those around him convinced he is still out to avenge that horrible day from more than a decade past. As one of the girls plays hide and seek with her blind date, she takes an arrow shot to the stomach and so they all become ensnared by this lovelorn assassin.

Having mastered the slasher movie with **Urban Legend** (1998), Jamie

Be my valentine... or else!

Blanks returned with another teenage horror comedy, lampooning the blueprint that had been so successful during the 1980s and, thanks to Wes Craven and writer Kevin Williamson, was beginning to gain popularity at the dawn of this new decade. Blanks' writing team loosely based their tale on Tom Savage's novel, but altered the characters and settings to fit with the basic precepts of their planned slasher. So many of the clichés were in evidence, but this proved to be a well-observed movie, which wanted nothing more than to entertain an audience who were once again becoming excited by this teenage slaughter. There was a lush veneer to the photography that reflected the movie's doting premise and the kills were as inventive as they had been twenty years before and managed to blend the insanity of the eighties with the more polished approach of the twenty-first century. The slasher refused to lie down and die as was evidenced by another killer clown in **Drive Thru** (2007), a return to **Halloween** in **The Pumpkin Karver** (2006) the demonic **Satan's Little Helper** (2004) and Japan's **Slashers** (2001).

Victims

YEAR OF RELEASE: **1985**	COUNTRY: **USA**
RUNTIME: **75 minutes**	DIRECTOR: **Jeff Hathcock**

WRITERS: Jeff Hathcock, Richard Halli (story)

PRODUCERS: Jeff Hathcock, Robert Katz (associate producer)

CINEMATOGRAPHER: David Essex

CAST: Ava Kauffman, Robert Axelrod, Lonny Withers, Ann Richardson, Geri Schlessel, Pam Richards, Janet Walker, Richard Hathcock, Lee Richards, Dee Kwan, Jim Simpson, Ray Gabriel, Phil DeCarlo, Jean Phillips, Don Miller, Chris Hammond, Denize Kazan, Les Reed, Kathy Brothen, Alan Scott, Don Sangil, Ken Blazer, Phil Pierce

AS JEFF HATHCOCK'S descent into misogynistic exploitation begins a woman on a staircase takes an axe to the face, while another is butchered with a machete and then a man in drag thrusts a knife into a woman's back as she leaves her apartment. The scene shifts with an awkward moment of editing to a young couple making love in a forest; they are attacked by a couple of men who have just staged a robbery, with the boyfriend being killed and the girlfriend beaten and raped.

The story doesn't actually get going until four young girls are seen heading into the desert for a weekend of camping and geological study. They encounter a couple of unsavoury individuals while filling up at a petrol station, Peter and Eric, who could have carried out the killings detailed in the movie's first fifteen minutes. The girls quite rightly feel it best to move on. Soon after the viewer is granted a few moments of gratuitous nudity as the girls enjoy themselves in the water,

but this frivolity abruptly ends when they sense someone close by spying on them. As they try to put this incident behind them, Peter and Eric show up, now armed with rifles. They begin to intimidate the defenceless girls before turning to rape and torture. The desert echoes to the sound of the screams of the four girls as they look to escape these sadistic perverts. A series of flashbacks from Vietnam, including an unexplained Asian woman in a darkened room, attempt to temper the villain's despicable crimes, but for them there will be no escape.

Jeff Hathcock's rape revenge feature would be his first entry into the world of the sleazy slasher and would pave the way for a long career in both film as well as cartoons. His movie utilized obvious aspects of plot from **Last House on the Left** (1972), **I Spit On Your Grave** (1978), and **Mother's Day** (1980), but due to his inexperience and lack of funds was devoid of their technical merit. His debut has been lambasted

Four girls alone in the desert. They all became his ... victims!

for being both trashy and hateful; these, however, proved to be the facets that would endear it to the long-time devotees of grindhouse cinema. All these years later we can only wonder if it was originally intended for these fleapit cinemas, as the substandard writing, cinematography and acting suggest this film was made considerably before 1985.

Video Violence

📅 YEAR OF RELEASE: 1987	
⏱ RUNTIME: 90 minutes	
🎥 COUNTRY: USA	
🎬 DIRECTOR: Gary Cohen	

✎ WRITERS: Gary Cohen, Paul Kaye	
🎬 PRODUCERS: Ray Clark, James Golff (executive producer), Salvatore Richichi (executive producer)	
⊙ CERTIFICATE: USA: Unrated	

CAST: Gary Schwartz, Chick Kaplan, Robin Leeds, Paige Lyn Price, Kevin Haver, Art Neill, Bill Biach, Uke, Bart Sumner, Joseph Kordos, Chris Williams, William Toddie, Jackie Neill, Ricky Kotch, Jennifer Biach

STEVEN EMORY AND his wife have recently moved away from New York to start a new life running a video rental store. They are both surprised and delighted to learn nearly everyone in town has a video recorder, even in the video-mad world of 1987, but there is more to this VHS overload. Their customers display an uncomfortable obsession with slasher and splatter movies, along with a sampling of porn. When one of their employees discovers a returned case containing a grisly snuff movie Steven turns to the police for help. When they return to the store the offending video has been replaced and his employee is nowhere to be seen. These crudely produced films, depicting the slow torture and murder of innocents passing through the town, continue to appear in the store. Steven is now forced to carry out his own investigations only to find himself up against a town of psychos.

When renting is not enough ...

Gary Cohen's **Video Violence** remains one of the most widely distributed shot-on-video horror movies of the period and with regard to its technique is considered to be way ahead of its time. Having owned a video store, Cohen created his low-budget feature, made for only a few hundred dollars, to explore the casual viewer's affinity for bloodthirsty violence. When the cable station where he was editing his film became aware of the sordid nature of his film they immediately asked him to leave. His film, however, went on to see release and he unwittingly became one of the pioneers of a new form of home entertainment. While everything about this film is cheap, his story moves at a fast pace, making use of understandably cheap gore effects which are cleverly reserved for the snuff video scenes. **Video Violence** very quickly acquired cult status and sold out, before going on to a second

pressing. That same year the derisive carnage returned in **Video Violence 2**. It didn't end here; the queasy premise of both would surface many years later in the big-budget **Vacancy** (2007).

Cohen is now the Producing Director for Middlesex County, New Jersey's Plays-in-The-Park, having enjoyed a wide-ranging career in both film and theatre. He has also written two books on theatre, *The Community Theater Handbook* and the *The Theater Director's Primer*.

Violent Shit

📅	YEAR OF RELEASE: 1989	📝 WRITER: Andreas Schnaas
🕐	RUNTIME: 75 minutes	🎞 CINEMATOGRAPHER: Steve Aquilina
🎥	COUNTRY: Germany	⚗ PRODUCERS: The Violent Shitters, Andreas Schnaas
🎬	DIRECTOR: Andreas Schnaas	💲 BUDGET: $2,000
🎬	PRODUCTION COMPANY: Reel Gore Productions	

CAST: Andreas Schnaas, Gabi Bäzner, Wolfgang Hinz, Volker Mechter, Christian Biallas, Uwe Boldt, Marco Hegele, Lars Warncke, Werner Knifke, Bettina X., Steve Aquilina, Maren Y.

A CHILD PLAYS WITH his ball and then returns home to be verbally abused by his mother. When the door closes, a scream can be heard from within the house. The blood-stained youngster smiles to the camera, having just killed his mother with a meat cleaver. Twenty years later the adult Karl escapes police custody, having butchered them as they transfer him between prisons. The last of

the policemen is seen at very close proximity falling before the madman's sharpened weapon. Karl, meat cleaver in hand, is now free to return to his murderous ways. His next victim is a woman whose car has broken down in the German countryside; true to the Italian splatter-filled misogyny of this bloodthirsty decade, he thrusts his blade into her breasts. His bloodlust doesn't end here; a man's penis is soon

439

after chopped in half. In a change of weaponry, a gardener is decapitated with a hedge trimmer and so the gorefest continues with bodily dismemberment and a bloody display of intestines. All the while, the killer avers to being plagued by the vision of the devil he saw as a child. In the bizarre finale, his body degenerates to slime, and within minutes we witness his rejuvenation as a baby.

Expect the worst.

As the budget suggests, Andreas Schnaas' first film was an almost amateur project, but could take pride in being Germany's first shot-to-video horror movie. An admirer of Lucio Fulci, Schnaas used what little money he had to pour on as much cheap gore as his bank balance could stand, but offered little in the way of a comprehensible storyline and never appeared concerned with the character development that afforded so many of its contemporaries such credence. Instead, he preferred to linger on the hack and slash of his killer's slaughter, cutting up his victims and ensuring Steve Aquilina's camera was as close as it possibly could be to the bloody display. The title alone would see it banned in many countries, but in the world of underground cinema Schnaas was to go on to gather a dedicated cult following. Against the odds, he continued Karl's low-budget penchant for slaughter less than twelve months later in **Violent Shit 2 – Mother, Hold My Hand** but this wouldn't see release until 1992. He then set to work on a third film hoping to conclude his disreputable series in 1993, but a lack of funds kept the film from release until 1999 when it appeared as **Violent Shit III: Infantry of Doom**, re-titled as **Zombie Doom** for its assault on the US market. With the copyright to these films now lying elsewhere Schnaas has no plans to revive this deranged psychotic.

Visions of Suffering

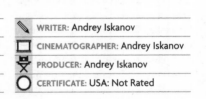

📅 YEAR OF RELEASE: 2006		✎ WRITER: Andrey Iskanov	
🕐 RUNTIME: 120 minutes		🎬 CINEMATOGRAPHER: Andrey Iskanov	
🌐 COUNTRY: Russia		⚖ PRODUCER: Andrey Iskanov	
🎥 DIRECTOR: Andrey Iskanov		◯ CERTIFICATE: USA: Not Rated	

CAST: Igor Anikin, Alexandra Batrumova, Yukari Fujimoto, Svyatoslav Iliyasov, Andrey Iskanov, Alexander Kravchenko, Zoya Makarova, Irina Nikitina, Igor Orlov, Alexander Shevchenko, Victor Silkin, Dmitriy Skripnik

DURING THE MAKING of **Visions of Suffering**, Andrey Iskanov conspired with any accepted notions of surrealism, psychedelia and gore to create a film that remains unique and reflected just how the world of cinematic horror was once again beginning to change. As the opening frames roll onto the screen we are told, "A dream is a reality, rejected by our mind", and so follows a celluloid voyage of visual splendour into a hallucinatory domain of unending nightmare, which at the last defies any attempt at explanation.

Whenever it rains The Man in Glasses (Alexander Shevchenko) is plagued by the hideous nightmare of a person with a misshapen face trudging through dismal swampland grasping at black squid creatures as they descend from the sky. With the intensity of his dreams becoming increasingly alarming, he calls his girlfriend, but damages the phone. The Phone Repairman (Victor Silkin) arrives on the scene, a man whose dominion lies amidst those haunting ghosts who have the power to evoke these terrifying visions. These creatures are known as Vampires, and those who acquire knowledge of their existence are agonizingly punished and then left for slaughter. To ensure word about their activities doesn't get to the ears of mortal man, the Vampires utilize the sadistic skills of The Man in Black (Igor Orlov).

Unaware his life is threatened The Man in Glasses gets through to his girlfriend and arranges to meet her in a bizarre nightclub known as Delirium, an institution with its own set of rules. However, in contacting his girlfriend he has foolishly given the Vampire breed his whereabouts; bloody carnage will inevitably follow. While there is little in the way of dialogue the camera's lens allows us to see addicts with access to mind-bending drugs and the strangest people who freely indulge their inhumane desires. He seeks counsel from The Priest (Andrey Iskanov) only to learn he too is deeply troubled, by his faith and those indescribable dreams that invade his sleep when the rain begins to fall. Demonic creatures conspire to use these nightmares to escape their own hell-borne world and drag the incumbents to the terrors that lie in wait in their unholy realm.

Iskanov's film follows in the path of the Italian masters, preferring to immerse

> **A surreal world you may never wake from.**

the viewer with imagery that seeks to disturb rather than presenting a coherent storyline, taking those who sit before its hypnotic gaze into a vision of drug-induced nightmare. The camera works to heighten the sense of disorientation while assaulting the senses as the dream eventually consumes our sense of reality.

Visiting Hours

YEAR OF RELEASE: 1982		**CINEMATOGRAPHER:** René Verzier
RUNTIME: 105 minutes		**PRODUCERS:** Pierre David, Claude Héroux, Victor Solnicki (executive producer)
COUNTRY: Canada		
DIRECTOR: Jean-Claude Lord		
PRODUCTION COMPANY: Canadian Film Development Corporation (CFDC), Filmplan, Victor Solnicki		**CERTIFICATE:** Australia: R; UK: 18; USA: R
		BUDGET: $5,500,000 Canadian
WRITER: Brian Taggert		**RECEIPTS:** $12,581,713 (1982)

CAST: Michael Ironside, Lee Grant, Linda Purl, William Shatner, Lenore Zann, Harvey Atkin, Helen Hughes, Michael J. Reynolds, Kirsten Bishop, Deborah Kirshenbaum, Elizabeth Leigh-Milne, Maureen McRae, Dustin Waln, Neil Affleck, Damir Andrei

TELEVISION JOURNALIST DEBORAH Ballin's (Lee Grant) strong-willed disposition thrives on controversy. However, her unrestrained defence of a woman accused of murdering her abusive husband leaves one of the studio's cleaning staff seething. An emotional void exists in this man, a trait observed in so many slashers, past and present. As a child, Hawker (Michael Ironside) saw his browbeaten mother throw boiling oil into the face of his abusive father. All these years later, he continues to bear the emotional scars, intimated in a series of vague but unsettling flashbacks. To his twisted way of thinking, this outspoken woman must be silenced, once and for all. After following her home, he wastes no time in disposing of the maid Francine, then bides his time waiting for Ballin before making his vicious assault. Barely surviving the ordeal she is rushed to a hospital and is placed under the care of nurse Sheila Munroe (Linda Purl), whose boundless determination will add her to Hawker's death list.

When he learns Ballin is still alive, Hawker heads to the hospital with murder in mind. The tension mounts as this develops into a taut game of cat and mouse with the murderous psycho shadowing his victims through the deserted wards and corridors of the hospital. There is an insane pleasure insinuated in the terrorizing of his victims before subjecting them to the razor sharpness of his new weapon of choice, a handy scalpel. Hawker doesn't face the customary gaggle of girls associated with the slasher of the last few years, screaming their heads off (literally in some cases) at the first sign of trouble; these women each have an inner strength, which is why they are now in this predicament.

There is no known cure . . . for MURDER.

While there are many gaping holes in the plot, which to some extent detract from this film, Hawker as the silent assassin with his disconcertingly sado-masochistic tendencies is accordingly the creepiest of psychotic killers. As the eerie score seeps into the claustrophobia of the hospital's endless corridors and empty wards, so stalks this misogynistic slayer. Jean Claude Lord's film may resort to so many of the clichés associated with the slasher phenomenon of the period, but it also introduces a cast of strong women who are prepared to fight for their lives rather than the usual stock of teen fodder. **Visiting Hours** couldn't be described as a gory piece, but Lord wasn't averse to lingering over his death scenes and relished getting in as close as possible during the stabbings.

We Are What We Are

YEAR OF RELEASE: 2010		WRITER: Jorge Michel Grau
RUNTIME: 90 minutes		CINEMATOGRAPHER: Santiago Sanchez
COUNTRY: Mexico		
DIRECTOR: Jorge Michel Grau		PRODUCERS: Nicolás Celis, Henner Hoffman (executive producer), Liliana Pardo (executive producer)
PRODUCTION COMPANY: Centro de Capacitación Cinematográfica (CCC), Fondo para la Producción Cinematográfica de Calidad (FOPROCINE)		CERTIFICATE: Australia: MA; Ireland: 16

CAST: Adrián Aguirre, Miriam Balderas, Francisco Barreiro, Carmen Beato, Alan Chávez, Juan Carlos Colombo, Paulina Gaitan, Daniel Giménez Cacho, Miguel Ángel Hoppe, Raúl Kennedy, Octavio Michel, Esteban Soberanes, Humberto Yáñez, Jorge Zárate

THE HEAD OF a family (Humberto Yáñez) shuffles through an affluent shopping centre and falls dead to the floor. The passing shoppers try to ignore his dishevelled presence; he isn't their problem and they know a cleaning crew will be called in to remove his body. In the mortuary, the pathologist finds a finger with a painted fingernail in the father's stomach and reveals him as a cannibal. Up until this revelation, the police had had little interest in the case, but now they know if they can capture his family the headlines would be the making of them.

In another part of the city, the eldest son, Alfredo (Francisco Barreiro) must assume responsibility for the surviving members of the family. He finds it difficult to follow the example set by his father in providing his family with their much-needed ritualistic sacrifice. He fails miserably when he attempts to lure a suitable prostitute on his visit to the red light district, and his attempt to kidnap a homeless child is later thwarted. The family dynamic begins to endure a dramatic change as his mother and sister withdraw from life, dismissing his intended victims,

and his younger brother becomes increasingly psychotic, looking to pick young men up in gay bars and bring them to the family dinner table. As the family return to their all-consuming quest and try to hunt down their prey, the police investigation gets closer to their home, one of the many slums of the city, and leads to a calamitous showdown.

Rather than concerning himself with the bloodthirsty nature of the revived cannibal phenomenon, which had been covered admirably by **Cannibal Hillbillies** (2003) and Germany's **Barricade** (2007), Jorge Michel Grau on his promising directorial debut concentrated on the collapse of an already dysfunctional family in the poverty stricken labyrinthine slums of Mexico City. Unlike the cannibal frenzy of the 1970s and early 1980s, which had very quickly become stale in repeatedly laying emphasis on the plight of its victims, **We Are What We Are** observed the domestic drama of a family of killers as they endeavoured to survive in the ruthless streets of this modern-day city. In what is acknowledged as being the country's

Young. Wild. Hungry.

first cannibal movie, Grau offered a powerful examination of Mexico's corrupt authorities and the country's increasingly divided society, one that appears more inclined to the wealthy and the influx of foreign tourists with money to spend. The poor seem to have been forgotten, which in this instance allowed this family to satiate their craving for human flesh. The reasons for their cannibalism are never fully explained; we can only wonder if their desperate economic circumstances have driven them to this grisly way of life. Theirs is a realistically violent world, a theme Grau wants to return to as he anticipates his next two projects in what should be, given his immense ability, a series of films that match the beauty in this film's cinematography and its compelling storyline. While, as would be expected, there is plenty of gore in this film, the scenes of cannibalism are often shot from a distance and the hand-held close-in shots appear obscured, thus detracting from the grisly delights many fans of this sub-genre would relish, but this ironically makes Grau's film so much more disturbing.

Wedding Slashers

	YEAR OF RELEASE: 2006
	RUNTIME: 80 minutes
	COUNTRY: USA
	DIRECTOR: Carlos Scott
	PRODUCTION COMPANY: The Institution
	WRITERS: Scott Phillips (story), Robert Paul Medrano
	CINEMATOGRAPHER: Richard Griffin

PRODUCERS: Paul Z. Bowles (executive producer), Greta Paola Gallone (associate producer), Greta Paola Gallone (line PRODUCER: Los Angeles), Billy Garberina, Richard Lynch (associate producer)

CERTIFICATE: Canada: 14A (Ontario); Canada: 16+ (Quebec); Canada: R (Manitoba); USA: R

CAST: Barry Adams, Shenoah Allen, Monica Ault, Mark Chavez, Ben Chester, Craig Chrissinger, Dickie Collins, Mark Cumberland, Juliann Dallis, Kerri Daube, Chris L. Dillon, Tanith Fiedler, Maria Ford, Billy Garberina, Paul Greenstein

CARLOS SCOTT'S WEDDING *Slashers* is a highly amusing tribute to the slasher movies of two decades past. In an introductory flashback a young couple are journeying to Vegas, having eloped to get married. They never manage to get there; the love struck couple are killed by a figure wearing a gas mask and cloak, who is not quite on a par with the previous year's **Reeker**. He eulogizes on love and then delivers a blow to the bride's head, splitting it clean open.

Jenna has always dreamed of finding the perfect man and gliding up the aisle. However, whenever she meets the man of her dreams he has a habit of ending up dead. This time she knows it will be different; Alex is just perfect and the wedding date has been set. On the eve before the big day, doubt begins to set in, and who can blame her when the best man is murdered at the bachelor party and some of the girls in the bridal party begin to disappear. Her family, we soon discover, are overly protective of their beloved daughter and

Here comes the blood . . .

will do anything it takes to dispose of her lovers. She was convinced she had escaped their possessive clutches, but they have arrived on the scene to hack their way through the entire wedding party. As you can imagine there's not much in the way of romance and it looks extremely doubtful that the happy couple will make it all of the way to the service.

For these eighty minutes, there are plenty of gory scenes on show, which probably drained the hopelessly diminutive budget. Heads are severed, eyes popped out, throats are cut as the carnage rages out of control. As with its precursors, the acting left much to be desired, but it did give the boys just what they wanted; blood, guts and a plethora of topless shots.

The Werewolf and the Yeti

📅	YEAR OF RELEASE: 1975	✒️ WRITER: Paul Naschy	
🕐	RUNTIME: 94 minutes	🎞️ CINEMATOGRAPHER: Tomàs Pladevall	
🎬	COUNTRY: Spain	🎬 PRODUCERS: José Antonio Pérez Giner, Modesto Pérez Redondo	
🎥	DIRECTOR: Miguel Iglesias		
🎞️	PRODUCTION COMPANY: Profilmes, Profilms	⭕ CERTIFICATE: UK: (Banned); USA: R	
		📚 RECEIPTS: ESP 17,237,197	

CAST: Paul Naschy, Mercedes Molina, Silvia Solar, Gil Vidal, Luis Induni, Josep Castillo Escalona, Ventura Oller, Verónica Miriel, Juan Velilla, Carmen G. Cervera, Pepa Ferrer

ACCOMPANIED BY AN expedition led by Lacombe (Gil Vidal), the Polish count Waldemar Daninsky (Paul Naschy) journeys across the Himalayas in search of the legendary Yeti. Soon after arriving in Katmandu, Waldemar and a scout (Victor Israel) trek into the mountains and come upon a cave. In the confides of the cave Waldemar is captured by two flesh-eating sorceresses who reduce the intrepid adventurer to become little more than their sex slave. Their foul machinations eventually result in his transformation into a werewolf. As the full moon rises, he is set loose to wreak havoc and slaughter anyone or anything that comes into his path. After his disappearance, his fellow explorers attempt to follow his trail, but many of the party are killed by bandits led by Temuljin, and those who survive are incarcerated by a Mongol chief named Sherkan-Kan (Luis Induni). Then we are introduced to the evil Wandesa (Silvia Solar), who tries to cure Waldemar of his lycanthropy, but is unable to prevent the final battle between the werewolf and the Yeti.

The Werewolf and the Yeti has also gone by the names Night of the Howling Beast, La Maldición de la Bestia, Hall of the Mountain King and Horror of the Werewolf and sees the return of Paul Naschy's (born Jacinto Molina Alvarez) heroic

Two bloodthirsty beasts in deadly combat.

adventurer Waldemar Daninsky, who once again falls to the werewolf's curse. The unrelated "Hombre Lobo" movies began life in 1967 with The Mark of the Wolfman and followed with the now lost The Nights of the Wolf Man (1968); this would be the eighth production in this series of twelve films and probably the most ludicrous. Director Miguel Iglesias had acquired a reputation in Spain for his exploitation movies and for the ninety-four-minute running time provided a colourful piece of comic book-styled entertainment, combining terror, action, nudity and a copious flow of blood and guts as members of the expedition suffered beheading and impalement. Horror fans would have to wait until the finale for the battle they craved but those who were in it for the sleaze would see the hero turned into a sex slave by nymphomaniac witches and the cruel flagellation of Waldemar's doe-eyed lover by the perverse Wandesa. The effects were cheap but these scenes still brought this film to the attention of the DPP and the BBFC almost two years after being made available on video in October 1982. It joined the list of video nasties in August 1984 and remained there throughout the hysteria. Its ban under the Video Recordings Act of 1984 has yet to be revoked and the original video is now considered a rare treasure. 🖤

What Have You Done to Solange?

📅	YEAR OF RELEASE: 1972	✏️	WRITERS: Bruno Di Geronimo, Massimo Dallamano, Peter M. Thouet, Edgar Wallace
⏱️	RUNTIME: 103 minutes		
📷	COUNTRY: Italy/West Germany	🎬	CINEMATOGRAPHER: Joe D'Amato
🎥	DIRECTOR: Massimo Dallamano	🏆	PRODUCERS: Leo Pescarolo, Fulvio Lucisano, Horst Wendlandt
🎞️	PRODUCTION COMPANY: Italian International Film, Clodio Cinematografica, Rialto Film Preben-Philipsen	⭕	CERTIFICATE: Canada: 18+ (Quebec); UK: 18; USA: R

CAST: Fabio Testi, Cristina Galbó, Karin Baal, Joachim Fuchsberger, Günther Stoll, Claudia Butenuth, Camille Keaton, Maria Monti, Giancarlo Badessi, Pilar Castel, Giovanna Di Bernardo, Vittorio Fanfoni, Marco Mariani, Antonio Casale, Emilia Wolkowicz, Daniele Micheletti, Antonio Anelli, Rainer Penkert, Carla Mancini

WHILE MARRIED, ENRICO "Henry" Rossini (Fabio Testi) is teaching at a private all girls Catholic school in London; he is also having an affair with one of the students (Christina Galbó). As they drift down the Thames on a romantic outing, his girlfriend suddenly becomes hysterical, insisting she has seen a knife. At first, Henry is dismissive of her claims, but the following day the body of another student is discovered at the same spot. The investigating officers led by Inspector Barth (Joachim Fuchsberger) are faced with a trail of murder, as Enrico becomes the main suspect, owing to his close relationship with several of the girls under his tutelage. When more of the schoolgirls turn up dead at the hands of this black-gloved killer, Enrico and his trusting wife take it on themselves to find the culprit, in the hope of clearing the philandering teacher's name.

While not as stylish as many of the gialli of the period, Massimo Dallamano's **Cosa avete fatto a Solange?** contained all of the elements the genre held so close to its heart: suspense, murder, sex, religion and a series of disturbing flashbacks. Dallamano, who had been the cinematographer on Sergio Leone's **A Fist Full of Dollars** (1964) and **For a Few Dollars More** (1965), based his tale on Edgar Wallace's *The Clue of the New Pin*, first published in 1923. The death scenes were not especially grisly, but Dallamano made up for this with a skilful piece of storytelling, introducing teasing red herrings and carefully laying the clues as he guided this feature on its way towards a series of shocking revelations. His film blended two of the European sub-genres of the period, the giallo and the West German krimi, which had begun life in 1959 under the influence of the Danish movie company Rialto Film, but by 1972 had waned in popularity. As with Mario Bava's **A Bay of Blood** (1971), **What Have You Done to Solange?** was given an extensive release in the United States, which had a major impact on the early years of the following decade's obsession with the slasher. This was also the beginning of the "schoolgirl gialli", which trailed seemingly innocent adolescent girls as a series of deluded predators with strangely moralistic predilections stalked them in the shadows. The outcome would invariably reveal a young girl with a scandalous secret. As

the camera's roving eye caught glimpses of the showering girls, the element of teenage sleaze was diminished when the audience realized the female cast were all at least eighteen years of age. As this new strain of gialli evolved, so too would the sleaze factor; but not in Dallamano's movie.

Alongside Dallamano was his tireless cameraman Joe D'Amato, no more than a dozen films into the two hundred or so features upon which he would come to work. Under the supervision of his experienced director, he assisted in creating the eerie air that has come to characterize this feature, which would later be reproduced in his own creations **Buio Omega** (1979), **Antropophagus** (1980) and **Absurd** (1981). This was augmented by Ennio Morricone's haunting score that suffused the melancholy in the wake of these terrible murders, each of which was left to the audience's imagination. 🦋

The Witch Who Come From the Sea

📅	YEAR OF RELEASE: 1976		🎞️	CINEMATOGRAPHER: Ken Gibb, Dean Cundey
🕐	RUNTIME: 83 minutes			
🌐	COUNTRY: USA		⚱️	PRODUCERS: Matt Cimber, Jefferson Richard (line producer)
🎥	DIRECTOR: Matt Cimber			
✎	WRITER: Robert Thom		⭕	CERTIFICATE: Australia: R; UK: 18; USA: R

CAST: Millie Perkins, Lonny Chapman, Vanessa Brown, Peggy Feury, Jean Pierre Camps, Mark Livingston, Rick Jason, Stafford Morgan, Richard Kennedy, George "Buck" Flower, Roberta Collins, Stan Ross, Lynne Guthrie, Barry Cooper, Gene Rutherford

LONELY MIDDLE-AGED Molly (Millie Perkins) works by night as a barmaid at a seaside bar and spends her days babysitting her nephews, telling them seafaring stories where her father is always portrayed as the hero. Her tales hint at an obsession with the ocean and sailing lore, which seek to fascinate and in time reveal a discernible sense of self-loathing. It becomes obvious that her sister, Cathy (Vanessa Brown), is not entirely at ease with her company, but for the moment we are not sure why. From the beach, she admires the muscular guys as they work out and parade before their on-looking admirers and then drifts into fantasies about their powerful physiques. Her fantasies display violent tendencies as she lures these burly men to her home and in a dreamlike scene has sex with two of them and then ties them up before castrating them off screen, leaving blood pouring over her own naked body. The following morning Molly learns her visions are far more than fantasy when two dead bodies are uncovered. Her friends are aware that she is deeply troubled and are very protective of her. They can't believe she would do such a thing, but Molly is hopelessly tormented by vivid memories of abuse and molestation at the hands of her sea-going father.

Amidst the exploitative excess of the grindhouse years came this almost

Molly really knows how to cut men down to size!

forgotten gem. Shot in 1971, this was a typically low-budget affair which not surprisingly contained some rather dubious acting, but was saved by an intriguing psychological slant to its script and the photography of the aspiring Dean Cundey, who would go on to work with Steven Spielberg. For Matt Cimber, Jane Mansfield's third husband, this was a remarkable change from the exploitative excess with which he had for so long become associated. Robert Thom's script allowed Cimber to pace the development of this disturbed character and then shock his audience with Molly's incestuous past, rather than the bloody display so routinely demanded by the drive-ins and grindhouse cinemas. Her descent into madness would lead to several gory scenes, but the horror in this film concerned Molly, not the men she sliced up in the privacy of her home. Millie Perkins, who assisted with the script, turned in a fine performance as she teetered on the very edge of madness, but this wouldn't save this film when it was handed to the distributors. It took another five years before this feature received a cinematic release and even then it wasn't given an especially long run before disappearing into obscurity. The audience for which it was intended couldn't get to grips with its psychological premise and the lack of sleazy nudity certainly didn't help either, while mainstream cinema was reluctant to handle such a challenging theme. Finally, film historian Walter Olsen and his brother Bill traced the original set of negatives and **The Witch Who Came From the Sea** was granted a deserved reissue, which will afford a new generation of film watchers the chance to savour this hidden treasure.

Its scenes of extreme sexual violence would lead to worldwide bans and further hinder its already problematic distribution. In 1983, the Director of Public Prosecutions included Cimber's film in its list of seventy-two video releases that had avoided BBFC certification and declared it prosecutable for obscenity. It was banned in August 1984 but was removed from the list in the wake of an unsuccessful prosecution in June 1985. However, it wasn't made available in the UK until June 2006. 🐦

The Wizard of Gore

📅 YEAR OF RELEASE: 1970	🎥 CINEMATOGRAPHERS: Alex Ameri, Daniel Krogh
🕐 RUNTIME: 95 minutes	
🌎 COUNTRY: USA	🎬 PRODUCERS: Herschell Gordon Lewis, Fred M. Sandy (executive producer)
👥 DIRECTOR: Herschell Gordon Lewis	
🎬 PRODUCTION COMPANY: Open Sky Entertainment, Sick-A-Scope	⭕ CERTIFICATE: Australia: R; New Zealand: R16; UK: 18; USA: Not Rated
✏️ WRITER: Allen Kahn	💲 BUDGET: $60,000

CAST: Ray Sager, Judy Cler, Wayne Ratay, Phil Laurenson, Jim Rau, Don Alexander, John Elliot, Karin Alexana, Jack Gilbreth, Corinne Kirkin, Monica Blackwell, Sally Brody, Karen Burke, Eric Kelner Raynard, Sheldon Reis

TELEVISION PRESENTER SHELLY Carson (Judy Cler) takes her reluctant boyfriend, sports columnist Jack (Wayne Ratay), along to a magic show staged by Montag the Magnificent (Ray Sager). For his finale, Montag performs his pièce de résistance by sawing a female volunteer in half as she lies helpless in his magic box. The audience gasp in horror, only for the girl to appear completely unharmed to cheers and a hearty round of applause. Days later, when the applause has died, the girl will be found dead, bearing wounds identical to those she would have sustained during the act. The murders continue, with the volunteers' deaths mirroring the endless illusions carried out on stage. In quite graphic scenes a metal spike is hammered into a girl's head, which ruptures her eyeball, swords are eased into their mouths, another is squeezed to death in a press and one poor girl is set ablaze, while another has to endure a drill being driven into her stomach. While the police investigate the crime scenes, they are unable to find any evidence to link the murders to the crafty magician. Shelly asks Montag to consider performing on her show, to which he readily agrees. As her suspicions grow, she prepares to reveal his villainy during his television appearance; only then can the slaughter be brought to an end.

As unconvincing as it may have been, Herschell G. Lewis has considerably more gore on show in this film than was in evidence in his infamous Blood Trilogy. His ambitious but incoherent storyline relies on a series of episodic set pieces, which involve young female volunteers being brutalized during the course of the magician's act. How

Scenes so far beyond any you've ever seen that no description is possible.

could Lewis have known that he was inadvertently paving the way for the torture porn of the twenty-first century, where the premise of the film is to slaughter rather than engage the audience with a well-told tale? The film, it has to be said, did have an interesting conclusion, but the inconsistencies leading to this finale were woeful. The bloodthirsty in the audience would have forgiven the storyline, for this level of gore in **The Wizard of Gore**'s day would have been truly shocking, particularly the eyeball scene. However, it would have been completely over-staged by the ridiculous acting, which ensured these films would only ever be looked upon as camp entries to the genre. For the two weeks of filming, a couple of sheep's carcasses were used to enhance the gory scenes; each had to be kept on the set at all times, making for quite an unpleasant stench. Lewis's film was never forgotten and went on to inspire a remake in 2007, when torture porn had become all the rage.

Wolf Creek

📅	**YEAR OF RELEASE:** 2005	🎬	**PRODUCTION COMPANY:** Dimension Films
🕐	**RUNTIME:** 99 minutes		
🌐	**COUNTRY:** Australia	✏️	**WRITER:** Greg Mclean
🎥	**DIRECTOR:** Greg Mclean	🎞️	**CINEMATOGRAPHER:** Will Gibson

PRODUCERS: George Adams (executive producer), Martin Fabinyi (executive producer), Michael Gudinski (executive producer), Gary Hamilton (executive producer), Matt Hearn (co-producer), Matt Hearn (executive producer), Simon Hewitt (executive producer), David Lightfoot (line producer) David Lightfoot, Greg Mclean, Dale Roberts (post-production producer)

CERTIFICATE: Australia: R; Australia: MA (Cable TV rating); Canada: 18+ (Quebec); Canada: 18A (Alberta/ British Columbia/Manitoba/Nova Scotia/Ontario); Ireland: 18; New Zealand: R18; UK: 18; USA: Unrated (unrated DVD version); USA: R

BUDGET: $1,000,000

RECEIPTS: $16,186,348

CAST: John Jarratt, Cassandra Magrath, Kestie Morassi, Nathan Phillips, Gordon Poole, Guy O'Donnell, Phil Stevenson, Geoff Revell, Andy McPhee, Aaron Sterns, Michael Moody, Andrew Reimer, Vicki Reimer, Isabella Reimer, David Rock

WRITTEN, CO-PRODUCED and directed by Greg McLean on his first outing, the independently produced **Wolf Creek** was inspired by the murder of Peter Falconio and the assault on his girlfriend Joanne in 2001 by Bradley John Murdoch in Australia's Northern Territory. Murdoch's trial was still in session when the film saw release in Australia, which resulted in concern it could influence the proceedings. The Northern Territory court consequently placed an injunction on the film's release across the whole territory. Other killings were later referenced as being intrinsic to the research for McLean's film, including the backpacker serial killer Ivan Milat, but his feature would be maligned in many quarters for using the killing of an innocent to create cinematic entertainment.

The story takes place in 1999, when friends Kristy, Ben and Liz purchase an old car to take them on a dream adventure across Australia's Outback. This likeable bunch travel to the scenic Wolf Creek National Park. While there, they plan to hike to a spectacular meteor crater, which is breathtakingly photographed, as is so much of the terrain in this film. Mclean and his cameraman, Will Gibson, permeate this dreamlike vista with an eerie atmosphere that harks back to the air of **Picnic at Hanging Rock** (1975). Even though swathed in the reverie of this panoramic landscape, danger is never too far away. Their encounters with the locals are appreciably unnerving, some of whom you'd be well wise to stay away from. If you can still recall the oddballs observed on the road to **The Texas Chain Saw Massacre** (1974), **The Hills Have Eyes** (1977) and **Wrong Turn** (2003), then you'll get the picture. As they get closer to Wolf Creek the sense of isolation and the immensity of the Outback, become all the more daunting.

Upon returning from their arduous walk, they are frustrated to find their car will not start. As the rain begins to pour, they have no choice but to spend the night wrapped up on its seats. As they prepare for an uncomfortable few hours of sleep, along comes bushman Mick Taylor, who pulls up his truck and offers to help the stranded trio. After examining the engine, he diagnoses the problem as a faulty coil and in his amiable patter suggests towing them to his camp, where he can then make the repairs. When they accept, the ecstasy of the last few days is cruelly shattered. Unbeknown to them their drink has been drugged and when they awaken, they are plunged into a nightmare world of torture, sexual abuse, grisly dismemberment and death. These are not the obnoxious youth of the halcyon slasher years; these are a set of congenial kids with the rest of their lives lying before them. This ultimately serves to make the horrors to which they are subjected even more real. The audience want them to make it, but Mick Taylor's unhinged tenacity has other ideas.

The epilogue to **Wolf Creek** continues to exasperate so many who endured the torment inflicted on this blighted group of friends, but let's remember McLean was crafting a horror movie and closure is rarely an option in such films. After having spent four months in custody, Ben is finally released due to a complete lack of evidence and is cleared of all suspicion. Silhouetted in the sun, cinema's new monster, Mick Taylor, rifle in hand, ghosts into the dying embers of an unnerving sunset.

Despite the film's commercial success, its reception among the critics was somewhat mixed, many of whom were uneasy with its incessant brutality. There are sequences towards the end of the film that are indeed difficult to watch, principally the shed torture, which is shocking in its realism. During the shooting of Kestie Morassi's torture, the fervour borne in her distressed screams was such that it caused considerable discomfort among the crew. There were reviewers, however, who recognized this movie as a departure from the norm, one that would live on with its audience and force horror cinema to re-evaluate many of its accepted precepts. These were the people who acknowledged McLean's worth as a filmmaker; they weren't alone. **Wolf Creek** was nominated for seven American Film Institute awards, including Best Director.

While on location, one of the settings used during the drive to Wolf Creek had not seen rainfall in over six years. However, once the crew arrived, it rained non-stop for three

Thirty thousand are reported missing in Australia every year. Some are never seen again.

days. McLean and his young cast responded by amending the script to accommodate this unexpected downpour. When filming commenced at the quarry where Mick inflicted his atrocities, the locals vented their rage, as this was the site of a real-life murder. The aggrieved community were convinced the film was exploiting this particular unsavoury episode.

In September 2010 a sequel was announced, returning to the Outback and the monstrous Mick Taylor, with production to commence in 2011. As with its precursor, the story will be partly based on actual events. 🍁

The Woman Eater

📅 YEAR OF RELEASE: 1958		🎬 PRODUCTION COMPANY: Fortress Film Productions Ltd	
🕐 RUNTIME: 70 minutes			
🌍 COUNTRY: UK		✏️ WRITER: Brandon Fleming	
🎥 DIRECTOR: Charles Saunders		🎞️ CINEMATOGRAPHER: Ernest Palmer	
		🎬 PRODUCER: Guido Coen	

CAST: George Coulouris, Vera Day, Peter Wayn, Joyce Gregg, Joy Webster, Jimmy Vaughn, Robert MacKenzie, Norman Claridge, Marpessa Dawn, Sara Leighton, Edward Higgins, Harry Ross, Alexander Field, David Lawton, John A. Tinn

DR JAMES MORAN (George Coulouris) and a business partner embark on a journey to the Amazon jungle in search of a tribe with the power to return the dead to life. They encounter the aforementioned tribe as they become lost in the performance of an unholy ritual, where a woman is sacrificed to a monstrous tree. Moran is later found suffering from the delirium of jungle fever, while his colleague is less fortunate, slain by a native's spear. Several years later Moran returns from his travels to London with a member of the strange tribe, Tanga (Jimmy Vaughan), who he keeps hidden in his creepy basement with the hideous plant seen earlier in the film. Tanga is endowed with the dubious talent of being able to hypnotize buxom women, who are than offered to the constantly hungry plant. Moran savours the delectation of Piccadilly Circus and Soho, having little time for the prostitutes, preferring instead women with a quite specific allure. After he buys a young lady a drink she is escorted to his manse where she falls to the mercy of his despicable tree. Moran looks on, still living in the hope the tree will return these nubile gifts with a serum, which he has been told can rejuvenate the dead.

While there was an absence of blood and guts in this almost forgotten British treasure, **The Woman Eater** bristles with so much of what would, in a few years, become essential to this sanguinary genre. The audience would have had a pretty good idea as to what was going on at Moran's house, but the sight of the carnivorous plant devouring its prey the producers felt should be left to their imagination; such a spectacle would have been far too much in the Britain of 1958. This overlooked B feature pulsed with an underlying lurid sexuality, particularly the "dance of death" and the tearing of one victim's blouse. These scenes will appear tame to modern eyes, but just over half a century ago they were far from commonplace in British cinema. The misogynistic Moran's pursuit of women is a trigger for violence, which culminates in the weird thrill he derives in seeing his murderous plant consume its victims. The film was shown in British theatres as part of a double feature and then exported to the United States before

See the hideous arms devour them in a death-embrace!

being summarily dismissed. This was one of a couple of low-budget horror films, the other being **The Man Without a Body** (1957), made by Guido Coen and Charles Saunders, who had established a reputation for crime thrillers. Saunders would very soon go on to direct Britain's first nudist film, **Nudist Paradise** (1959), and Coen found a lucrative finale to his career producing sex comedies. Their film, as with so many others of this ilk, was poorly financed, but the shots tracing a potential victim through Soho's ill-lit streets would be repeated a couple of years later in Michael Powell's **Peeping Tom** (1960), albeit with considerably more intensity.

In his fifty years in the film industry George Coulouris was a regular in the films of Coen and Saunders, regularly cast as the villain of the piece. He also made appearances in some of the finest films of the twentieth century, including **Citizen Kane** (1941), **For Whom the Bell Tolls** (1943) and **Papillon** (1973), and found work in television, including appearances in **Doctor Who** in 1964 and **Danger Man** (1967). 🎬

Wrong Turn

 YEAR OF RELEASE: 2003

 RUNTIME: 84 minutes

 COUNTRY: USA

 DIRECTOR: Rob Schmidt

PRODUCTION COMPANY: Summit Entertainment, Constantin Film Produktion, Media Cooperation One

 WRITER: Alan B. McElroy

 CINEMATOGRAPHER: John S. Bartley

 PRODUCERS: Hagen Behring (co-executive producer), Don Carmody (executive producer), Don Carmody (line producer), Sven Ebeling (co-executive producer), Erik Feig (producer), Brian J. Gilbert (producer), Mitch Horwits (executive producer), Robert Kulzer (producer), Aaron Ryder (executive producer), Patrick Wachsberger (executive producer), Stan Winston (producer), Jefferson Richard (line producer: additional photography)

 CERTIFICATE: Australia: MA; Canada: 13+ (Quebec); Canada: 18A (Alberta/British Columbia/Manitoba/Ontario); Canada: R (Nova Scotia); Canada: 18A; Ireland: 18; New Zealand: R16; UK: 18; USA: R

 BUDGET: $12,600,000

 RECEIPTS: $28,650,575

CAST: Desmond Harrington, Eliza Dushku, Emmanuelle Chriqui, Jeremy Sisto, Kevin Zegers, Lindy Booth, Julian Richings, Garry Robbins, Ted Clark, Yvonne Gaudry, Joel Harris, David Huband, Wayne Robson, James Downing

TWO COLLEGE STUDENTS, Halley (Yvonne Gaudry) and Rich (Joel Harris), run into trouble on a rock climb in the West Virginia Forest. Rich is thrown from a cliff by an unseen figure then Halley, after trying to escape, trips over a piece of barbed wire and is hauled screaming into the woods, just before her throat is slit.

The scene changes to fresh-out-of-school medical graduate Chris Flynn (Desmond Harrington) driving through the same area to a job interview. He is forced to take a detour due to an accident on the road, and in truth his own impatience. In a scene very reminiscent of Tobe Hooper's **The Texas Chain Saw Massacre** (1974), an old man at a near-derelict petrol station directs him to a dirt track that will bypass the accident. In his haste, he soon after loses control of the car

and ploughs into a stranded Range Rover. The car was carrying a group of young hikers, Jessie (Eliza Dushku), Carly (Emmanuelle Chriqui), her fiancé Scott (Jeremy Sisto) and another couple, Evan and Francine (Kevin Zegers and Lindy Booth). Their tyres have been punctured by a sturdy piece of barbed wire, stretched across the road. Chris, Jessie, Carly and Scott venture into the forest in the hope of finding help, leaving Evan and Francine to attend to the cars. Left alone in the middle of nowhere the two indulge in some sexual foreplay before they hear a sound in the woods. When Evan doesn't return Francine goes into the dense woodland to investigate. She soon discovers her boyfriend's shoes and then his severed ear; it is now she realizes something is seriously wrong. As she staggers from the scene, she is overcome by an obscured figure who binds barbed wire around her mouth.

Chris, Jessie, Carly and Scott come upon a ramshackle mountain cabin, surrounded by vehicles, which again harks back to Tobe Hooper's masterpiece. Within they find an untidy hotchpotch of barbed wire, car keys and, most alarmingly, human body parts. Three disfigured mountain men can now be seen striding towards the cabin, forcing the four to hide in the visceral filth. As they enter, Francine's dead body is unceremoniously hurled onto a table. The friends try to hold back their horror as she is callously butchered in preparation for the family's bloody repast. Theirs will be a bid for survival as they desperately attempt to escape these inbred cannibals; the film follows their efforts to survive as they chase through the darkened woods.

It's the last one you'll ever take.

Wrong Turn was commended for bringing something fresh to the screens on its 2003 release. It is, however, a return to the outlandish families observed in the horror cinema of the 1970s, whose moral perversity freely espoused slaughter and the delicacies of cannibalism. **The Texas Chain Saw Massacre** and **The Hills Have Eyes** (1977) had first introduced these ideas to the big screen, with Andrew Davis's **The Final Terror** returning to the wilds in 1983. Rob Schmidt's film shot in Hamilton, Ontario, attempted to bring these ideas to a new audience. In what is a fast-paced thriller, the group are picked off one by one in a wilderness that captures the spirit of John Boorman's **Deliverance** (1972), with the most annoying being dispatched first. The momentum doesn't relent as the cannibals' arrows bring the hikers down and an axe is thrown in for good measure in an imaginative decapitation scene. The thud of a body can be heard as it falls from a tree through the darkness; the head, unmoving, remaining firmly before the camera's gaze. The closing credits are disrupted by a deputy sheriff being strangled by "Three Finger", who survived the climactic explosion. The scene returns to the credits and the insane laughter heard at the very beginning of the film once again rolls from the screen. The success of this film allowed it to be continued with the 2007 release of the direct-to-video **Wrong Turn 2: Dead End**, which brought a group of celebrities together to fight for their lives in the guise of a real-life television show in these same Virginia backwoods. **Wrong Turn 3: Left for Dead** was released direct-to-video in October 2009. ❦

Xtro

📅	YEAR OF RELEASE: 1982		🎬	PRODUCTION COMPANY: Amalgamated Films
🕐	RUNTIME: 82 minutes		✎	WRITER: Harry Bromley Davenport
🎯	COUNTRY: UK		🎞	CINEMATOGRAPHER: John Metcalfe
🎥	DIRECTOR: Harry Bromley Davenport		⚗	PRODUCERS: Mark Forstater, Bob Shaye

CAST: Maryam d'Abo, Philip Sayer, Bernice Stegers, Simon Nash, Peter Mandell, David Cardy, Anna Wing, Susie Silvey, Katherine Best

SAM (PHILLIP SAYER) and his young son Tony's (Simon Nash) game with the family's pet dog is brought to an abrupt end by the appearance of a huge white light, which abducts Sam. Three years later Tony is still traumatized by his father's inexplicable disappearance; little does he know the white light has returned his father, or rather, what used to be his father. For the moment, Sam has been transformed into a crab-like alien. It doesn't take long before this creature tracks down a lone woman and then attacks her before placing a tentacle deep into her mouth. When she wakens from her ordeal, she sees her dog devouring the body of the alien. Still in shock, she makes her way into the kitchen, and then her stomach begins to swell. Unable to control her body she falls to the floor and in a series of horrific shots gives birth to a fully-grown Sam. It doesn't take long before he finds his way to London where he is reunited with his son and tries to explain to Rachel (Bernice Stegers), his now ex-wife, that he doesn't know where he has been for the past three years. Her new boyfriend is immediately suspicious and although Sam tries to live a normal life, his son very soon learns of his alien powers. Sam makes a gift of them, allowing his son to animate his toys. These powers, however, have a sinister edge, melting telephone boxes, and in time will maim and kill. The hapless babysitter (Maryam d'Abo) soon becomes the object of Sam's desire and finds herself cruelly used as the surrogate for a new generation of alien beings.

Xtro was another successor to Ridley Scott's vaunted **Alien** (1979) and liberally borrowed from John Carpenter's **The Thing** (1982), as director Harry Bromley Davenport crammed a multitude of ideas and influences into his film's strangely atmospheric eighty-two minute run. This low-budget UK feature presented an incoherent narrative held together by a series of episodic accounts, yet remained unusually inventive, throwing in scenes of nudity, an excess of gore and a dwarf dressed as a clown as the schizophrenic alien malevolence conspired to draw upon the audience's compassion. The imaginative set pieces would include a bizarre alien rape scene and a disgusting birth that defied the film's meagre budget, leading to a grotesque finale. This excess would acquire **Xtro** a very unfavourable reputation, which is not entirely in keeping with much of the film's buoyant tone. The UK's DPP, however, were quick to seize on its gruesome content, listing it as yet another loathsome video nasty even though it had been released uncut to cinema with an "18" certificate.

Some extra-terrestrials aren't friendly.

It was later caught up in the tabloid uproar and confiscated in Manchester, Birmingham and Newcastle. The tapes, however, had to be returned when the BBFC indicated that they had previously passed it suitable for cinema release without cuts. When the video was released in 1987 and again in 1992, the ending was altered to make it somewhat downcast when compared to the upbeat spirit of the original.

With his film having become a cult success in the ever-expanding video market of the 1980s, Bromley Davenport returned to direct two sequels **Xtro II: The Second Encounter** (1991) and **Xtro 3: Watch the Skies** (1995) and then in 2010 announced **Xtro 4** was in production, which promises a return to form in being even stranger than the original. 🐾

Your Vice is a Locked Room and Only I Have the Key

📅 YEAR OF RELEASE: 1972	
🕐 RUNTIME: 96 minutes	
🎬 COUNTRY: Italy	
🎥 DIRECTOR: Sergio Martino	
🎞 PRODUCTION COMPANY: Lea Film	

✏️ WRITERS: Adriano Bolzoni, Ernesto Gastaldi, Luciano Martino, Edgar Allan Poe, Sauro Scavolini	
🎞 CINEMATOGRAPHER: Giancarlo Ferrando	
⏳ PRODUCER: Luciano Martino	

CAST: Edwige Fenech, Anita Strindberg, Luigi Pistilli, Ivan Rassimov, Franco Nebbia, Riccardo Salvino, Angela La Vorgna, Enrica Bonaccorti, Daniela Giordano, Ermelinda De Felice, Marco Mariani

IN A BEAUTIFUL locale, very close to Venice, self-destructive Oliviero (Luigi Pistilli) struggles to write his next novel and in his descent into madness he becomes obsessed with the image of Mary, Queen of Scots. His drunken rambling is plagued by the memory of his dead mother and he thinks nothing of publicly demeaning his long-suffering wife Irina (Anita Strindberg). In the privacy of their villa, he also sleeps with his maid Brenda as well as having an adulterous affair with an ex-student who works in the local bookshop. When she is hacked to death by an unseen assailant, Oliviero immediately falls under suspicion, for she was on her way to meet him. Soon after, his maid is butchered as she enjoys herself garbed as the ill-fated Scottish Queen. Even with a killer in their midst, both Oliviero and his submissive wife lie to the authorities, claiming they had to let Brenda go. Then they have the unexpected surprise of having their beautiful niece, Floriana (Edwige Fenech), come to stay with them. She begins to play with the couple's fragile marriage, seducing both and sowing the seeds for their demise as the murders continue and a silver-haired stranger watches in the distance. All the while Oliviero's black cat, Satan, surveys the scene, forever tormenting the downtrodden Irina.

Sergio Martino's bizarrely entitled **Il Tuo Vizio è Una Stanza Chiusa e Solo Io Ne Ho La Chiave** was the fourth in a series of five gialli he worked on between 1970 and 1973. The title followed from his first, **Lo Strano Vizio Della Signora Wardh** also known as **The Strange Vice of Mrs Wardh** (1971), but was never intended as a sequel. This particular entry, which adopted an uncharacteristic experimental approach to the traditional giallo structure, also went by the names **Gently Before She Dies**, **Excite Me** and the highly appropriate, **Eye of the Black Cat**. As Martino's giallo reached its final half hour it drew upon the Gothic elements of Edgar Allan Poe's tale *The Black Cat* and led to a finale that skilfully twisted the great writer's original. This masterfully tense feature was to deliver some rather graphically illustrated murder scenes and immerse them in a sensuous ambience of licentious erotica that was prevalent in Italian cinema at this time. Martino had worked with his cast on many occasions, among them Eurocult actress Edwige Fenech, who was a regular in his films and was no stranger to sex romps and the gialli of the period. She went on to star on chat shows before moving into film production and later made an appearance in **Hostel II** (2007). 🦋

Zombie Bloodbath

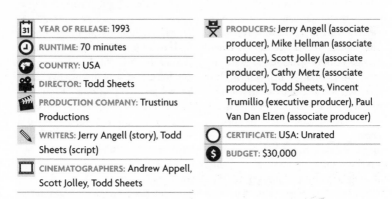

YEAR OF RELEASE: 1993	**PRODUCERS:** Jerry Angell (associate producer), Mike Hellman (associate producer), Scott Jolley (associate producer), Cathy Metz (associate producer), Todd Sheets, Vincent Trumillio (executive producer), Paul Van Dan Elzen (associate producer)
RUNTIME: 70 minutes	
COUNTRY: USA	
DIRECTOR: Todd Sheets	
PRODUCTION COMPANY: Trustinus Productions	
WRITERS: Jerry Angell (story), Todd Sheets (script)	**CERTIFICATE:** USA: Unrated
	BUDGET: $30,000
CINEMATOGRAPHERS: Andrew Appell, Scott Jolley, Todd Sheets	

CAST: Chris Harris, Auggi Alvarez, Frank Dunlay, Jerry Angell, Cathy Metz, Cheryl Metz, T. G. Watkins, Tonia Monahan, Jody Rovick, Kasey Rausch, Kyree King, Jennifer Geigle, Jenny Admire, Julie King, April Davis

SOMEWHERE IN AN outlying region of Kansas City, a nuclear research reactor, which was constructed over an Indian burial ground, is going into melt down. Two years later, the complex has been completely demolished and the network of subterranean tunnels has been secured. The reactor has been replaced by a thriving up-market housing development. While the families above the ground carry on with their day-to-day lives, the atomic zombies bide their time. Their patience is rewarded when some of the youngsters attempt to film in what was once the main access into the reactor complex. When they fall through a damaged section of the passageway into the tunnels below, the growling zombies are presented with a golden opportunity to escape their two years of imprisonment and wreak havoc on the streets above. Three families now band together in a bid to stop the carnage.

Todd Sheets has over thirty films to his name, all produced on a micro-budget, ready to go to video. While his enthusiasm knows no bounds, he been constantly criticized for his ham-fisted

Unearthed! Unstoppable! Undead!

approach to filming and scripting. Thankfully this has never stopped him and he has acquired something of a cult following. Such is his standing that when he set out to make this film, he had over 700 volunteers turn up to play the parts of the zombies. The acting leaves much to be desired, but Sheets makes up for this by pouring on the gore, with intestines constantly being torn out and the unfortunates being dragged away by this mindless horde. His adoration of George Romero's work is there to be seen; it's just a shame no one will give him that little bit of guidance and an ample budget.

This feature would be the first in a trilogy, followed by **Zombie Bloodbath II: Rage of the Undead** (1995) and **Zombie Bloodbath III: Zombie Armageddon** (2000). They were later released as a shot-to-video triple pack, but the first feature still remains the director's favourite. ❦

Zombie Creeping Flesh

📅	YEAR OF RELEASE: 1980	🎬	CINEMATOGRAPHER: John Cabrera
🕐	RUNTIME: 101 minutes	⚱	PRODUCERS: Sergio Cortona, José María Cunillés, Isabel Mulá
🎥	COUNTRY: Italy/Spain		
📹	Directors: Bruno Mattei, Claudio Fraga	⭕	CERTIFICATE: Australia: R; Canada: R; Canada: R (Ontario); Canada: 13+ (Quebec); UK: 18 (re-rating: 2002); UK: (Banned) (1984–2002); UK: X (original rating: 1982); USA: Unrated
🎬	PRODUCTION COMPANY: Beatrice Film, Films Dara		
✎	WRITERS: José María Cunillés, Rossella Drudi, Claudio Fragasso, Bruno Mattei		

CAST: Margit Evelyn Newton, Franco Garofalo, José Gras, Gabriel Renom, Josep Lluís Fonoll, Pietro Fumelli, Bruno Boni, Patrizia Costa, Cesare Di Vito, Sergio Pislar, Bernard Seray, Víctor Israel, Pep Ballester, Joaquín Blanco, Esther Mesina

A CHEMICAL LEAK AT the Hope Centre in Papua New Guinea has started to spread and infect the staff at the plant, turning them into flesh-eating zombies. As these slow-moving zombies begin their mindless rampage, an anti-terrorist team led by Lt. Mike London (José Gras) and including Vincent (Josep Lluís Fonoll), Zantoro (Franco Garofalo) and Osbourne (Gaby Renom) arrives on the island. As they travel across the island, they come upon the news reporting team of Max (Selan Karay) and Lia Rousseau (Margit Evelyn Newton), who are trying to explain a series of attacks on the tribes of the island. The whole country is being overrun by this zombie infestation and the government is on the verge of collapse. When two of the group are consumed by the living dead, the survivors are forced to journey further inland only to face further attacks by this deranged mob. Their investigation reveals the chemical leak wasn't an accident and the zombie plague is about to spread to throw the western world into utter chaos.

Zombie Creeping Flesh started life as **Virus**, a script written by José María Cunillés, that was then turned into a more extravagant venture by Claudio Fragasso and his wife Rossella Drudi. Adolescent cinemagoers had already developed a taste for zombie gut munching following the success of George A. Romero's **Dawn of the Dead** (1978) and Lucio Fulci's **Zombi 2** or **Zombie Flesh Eaters** (1979), and were now craving more. Two studios associated with low-budget horror, Dara Films in Spain and Beatrice Films in Rome, now looked to take advantage of this new demand. The original script set in Africa with entire ships crammed full of zombies was going to be too expensive to produce, so Bruno Mattei,

a master of low-budget sleaze, was brought in as director with Fragasso assigned as his assistant. The project was beset by numerous problems; the filming that had taken place around Barcelona proved virtually unusable. With neither the time nor money available to re-shoot, the movie ultimately bewildered its expectant audience. The feature was further damaged when a series of sets were built to match the stock footage taken from **La Vallée** (1972), none of which were successfully edited into the finished cut.

In keeping with its exploitative roots, **Inferno Dei Morti-Viventi** was to enjoy life under several different names, each designed to cash in on the success of the increasingly lucrative zombie phenomenon. In the United States, it was released as **Hell of the Living Dead** and then came **Cannibal Virus**, **Night of the Zombies**, **Zombie Inferno**, **Zombies of the Savanna**, **Zombi 2: Ultimate Nightmare**, **Zombi 4** and **Zombi 5: Ultimate Nightmare**. No matter which title the distributors used, there was no disguising the fact that this film was a blatant plagiarizing of the critically acclaimed **Dawn of the Dead**. Further to this, Mattei adopted the pseudonym of Vincent Dawn and then garbed his team of anti-terrorists with the same uniforms as Romero's Philadelphia

Pray it will never happen.

SWAT team. As with Romero's film, the only way to take one of this breed down was a gunshot to the head, although this outfit rarely seemed to get this right; but when they did, the head-exploding scenes were a delight for its eager viewers. While it remained true to its low-grade European origins principally with the prerequisite nudity and cannibalism, it also contained some excellent gory flesh ripping which was the match of its putrescent predecessors, splattering a copious supply of blood and guts along with extreme scenes of corpse devouring. The budget, however, didn't always run to effective zombie make-up, with some of the cast looking as if all they had done was rub mud on their faces, while others succeeded in chilling the audience to the very bone.

When the film was submitted to the BBFC prior to its UK release, it had already been edited to safeguard its distribution with an "X" certificate. However, when it was released to video it appeared as the pre-cut cinema release and an uncertified shortened version in October 1982. This would lead to its ban as a video nasty in July 1983 after a successful prosecution in Brighton. It wasn't dropped from the list until July 1985, but then ran into further problems in 1993 following the appalling murder of young Jamie Bulger. It was finally released uncut in 2002.

Zombie Flesh Eaters

 YEAR OF RELEASE: 1979

 RUNTIME: 91 minutes

COUNTRY: Italy

DIRECTOR: Lucio Fulci

PRODUCTION COMPANY: Variety Film Production

WRITER: Elisa Brigan

CINEMATOGRAPHER: Sergio Salvati

PRODUCERS: Fabrizio De Angelis, Ugo Tucci, Gianfranco Couyoumdjian (associate producer)

CERTIFICATE: Australia: R; Canada: R; Canada: 13+ (Quebec); Canada: 18+ (Quebec) (original rating); New Zealand: R16; UK: X (original rating: 1980) (cut); UK: (Banned) (1984–92); UK: 18 (re-rating: 1992) (cut) (re-rating: 2005) (uncut); USA: Unrated

BUDGET: ITL 410,000,000 or $8,000,000

RECEIPTS: ITL 614,000,000 (Italy)

CAST: Tisa Farrow, Ian McCulloch, Richard Johnson, Al Cliver, Auretta Gay, Stefania D'Amario, Olga Karlatos

IN A SCENE that was added to the original footage, a couple of Coast Guards board a deserted boat which has been borne into New York's Hudson River harbour. As they search through the disarray below decks, the zombie captain of the vessel erupts onto the scene. One of the boarders is savaged to death before the shambling monstrosity is brought down by a gunshot; it then collapses seemingly dead. Soon after in the morgue the creature begins to exhibit the faintest signs of life.

The boat, up until recently, had been in the possession of a scientist who was reported missing months ago as he was making his way to the Caribbean. His daughter, Anne Bowles (Tisa Farrow), is determined to find out what happened to him along with a journalist, Peter West (Ian McCollough), who desperately needs a scoop to improve the mood of his demanding editor (Lucio Fulci). When they eventually discover the Island of Matuul, they learn Anne's father had succumbed to a mystifying illness. They become acquainted with Dr David Menard (Richard Johnson) and his scornful wife Paola (Olga Karlatos), who is anxious to depart the secluded island. The zombie attacks that have been reported across the island have left her petrified, but her foolhardy husband is overly eager to undertake research into these macabre occurrences.

Menard should have been mindful of his shrew of a wife; the zombies soon rise from the earth to initiate their vicious assault. The most memorable attack comes from an aquatic zombie, who seizes a scantily clad female crewmember by the throat, then, its frenzy unabated, rips into a Tiger Shark. Paola meets her end as she is dragged by the hair through a closed door by an unseen zombie. In probably the most shocking scene in this bloodthirsty debacle, she is subjected to an impalement to the eye. The survivors are marooned on the island, their boat damaged by an enraged shark. They soon learn the only way to kill these zombies is to shoot them through the head. Only Peter and Anne are able to make an escape. As they enter New York's Harbour, they listen in horror as a radio broadcast warns of a zombie plague that has gripped the entire city. The finale is widely acknowledged as one of Fulci's finest moments, although, as with the prelude, it was added to the original reels following the success of George Romero's **Dawn of the Dead** (1978). The film now turns full circle, training on the droves of walking dead as they mindlessly trudge across the Brooklyn Bridge heading for Manhattan.

Zombie Flesh Eaters has since attracted a multitude of aliases, **Zombie**, **Zombi 2**, **Island of the Living Dead**,

When the Earth spits out the dead . . .

Zombie Island, Gli Ultimi Zombie, Island of the Flesh-Eaters, L'enfer Des Zombies, **Sanguelia** and **Woodoo**, and in its wake bestowed Fulci, whose career had begun to wane, a newfound iconic status. **Dawn of the Dead** was still to see release in Italy and at this point few people had been subjected to hordes of zombies on the rampage since **Night of the Living Dead** (1968) and to a lesser extent in Hammer's **The Plague of the Zombies** (1966). With a very limited budget, effects man Gianatto Di Rossi breathed life into a host of frightening creations, whose sole purpose was to leave the audience quaking in their seats. Fulci's film later saw an Italian release as **Zombi 2**, suggesting it as a sequel to **Zombi**, the country's title for **Dawn of the Dead**. Two more sequels also carried the **Zombi** moniker, neither of which had anything to do with this or Romero's original.

On its 1979, UK release, **Zombie Flesh Eaters** was issued to cinemas on the condition that two minutes of the original footage was removed. This didn't prevent its remaining gory content from being severely criticized; among the disparagers was the recently elected Conservative government. When it went to video, it became a cult favourite, but disappeared from the video stores when it was branded as a video nasty following the introduction of the 1984 Video Recordings Act. It wasn't until 2005 that the UK got the chance to see these grisly proceedings as Fulci had originally intended. 🦋

The Directors:
Blood on their Hands

Dario Argento
(September 7, 1940–)

Dario Argento was born in Rome; his father was a film producer and his mother a photographer. While still at school he worked as a film critic and began writing for various magazines. At the age of twenty he had turned his back on the chance to go to college and opted to become a screenwriter, and in the years that followed worked with Bernardo Bertolucci to write the screenplay for Sergio Leone's western **Once Upon a Time in the West** (1967). His exploits during this period brought him to the attention of Goffredo Lombardo, which led to his directorial debut on the groundbreaking **The Bird with the Crystal Plumage** (1970). His admiration of Alfred Hitchcock was evident during much of this film, which was extraordinarily graphic, but Argento has never been afraid to portray violence although he prefers to use it poetically.

Following this success, he continued to work with the increasingly popular giallo, returning with **The Cat o' Nine Tails** (1971), where he strived for a macabre air to his narrative that mirrored the aura of Edgar Allan Poe, and then resumed with the similarly acclaimed **Four Flies on Grey Velvet** (1972). After an involvement with several television dramas, he returned to film to direct the first of his true masterpieces, **Deep Red** (1975), a work still considered by many critics as the finest giallo ever made. Here he discussed his ideas with the special effects technicians to produce a film that would go on to inspire some of the finest horror directors of the period. For all of the cleverly conceived effects on show in his films he maintained a preference for the careful orchestration of nerve-tingling suspense. This became obvious with the release of his next movie, the almost surreal **Suspiria** (1977), where any notion of plot and characterization became secondary to the atmospherics of sound and vision. This would be the first in his "Three Mothers Trilogy" followed by **Inferno** (1980) and **The Mother of Tears** (2007).

Profoundly impressed by Andrzej Zulawski's **Phenomenon** (1981) he set to work on the giallo-styled **Tenebrae** (1982), which resulted in severe editing across the globe and condemnation from countless censors. He returned to scriptwriting, principally on Lamberto Bava's **Demons** (1985) and **Demons 2** (1986), before directing **Opera** in 1987, set in Parma's Regio Theatre. This was a welcome return to the opulence observed a decade before in **Suspiria** and then **Inferno**, although this was to be a very sad time in his life as his highly influential father passed away.

In 2009 he released the aptly entitled **Giallo** and then prepared to begin work on a remake of his masterpieces from all those years ago, **Deep Red** and **Suspiria**. Dario has spent almost half a century in film, and the enormity of his achievement makes it almost impossible to adequately measure his impact on the genre, having had such a profound influence on so many of his fellow creators and having produced so many works of visionary magnificence. ✤

Mario Bava
(July 31, 1914–April 25, 1980)

Born in San Remo, Liguria, Italy, Mario Bava was the son of Eugenio Bava, a sculptor who ventured into the movie business in 1906 and became one of the most innovative cameramen of the Italian silent era. As a young man Mario had ambitions to be a painter, but found it difficult to make enough money to survive, so in 1934 he followed in his father's footsteps and joined the film industry, working as an assistant to some of the most esteemed cinematographers of the day, among them Massimo Terzano. He was also in the employ of his father, who managed the special effects department at the then Fascist-backed Istituto Luce in Rome.

In less than five years Bava had perfected his skills, so much so he was considered a cinematographer in his own right, although he preferred to be looked upon as cameraman; the idea of being a cinematographer was a little too ostentatious for his liking. After making his debut feature in the early 1940s, his name very quickly became associated with some of the major stars of the era such as Gina Lollobrigida and Aldo Fabrizi as he worked to add his magic to this celluloid world which offered so many possibilities. In 1958 alongside Paolo Heusch, he co-directed a low-budget feature on a single stage that would have gone virtually unnoticed outside his Italian homeland, **Le Morte Viene Dallo Spazio** or **The Day the Sky Exploded**. This was Italy's first venture into science fiction and with very little money his team created an image of a crashed alien spacecraft that would one day be repeated on a far grander scale in Ridley Scott's **Alien** (1979). For the next two years, Bava continued to polish his skills and then sat in the director's chair to create a film that was to become a landmark, **Black Sunday** (1960). This feature would be one of five films released in a year that would have a considerable bearing on the future of cinematic horror. His film opened with probably the most callous scene so far committed to celluloid as Barbara Steele endured the agony of having her face cruelly gouged in a spiked iron mask. The image would alarm censors across the globe, leading to this episode being heavily edited before it was allowed into many countries. It was Bava's artistic manipulation of light and dark, however, amidst a series of Gothic-styled sets filmed in an ominous monochrome, that really defined this feature. When he introduced colour to **I tre volti della paura**, better known as **Black Sabbath** (1963), his expressionistic technique prompted similar acclaim, and was later emulated by Martin Scorsese, who held Bava in such high esteem. Both films were shot in around twelve days and as he departed each set, he already had a clear vision as to how he would edit each feature.

Between 1963 and 1964, he embarked upon two films that would mark the beginning of something new and exciting in Italian cinema, the giallo. **La Ragazza Che Sapeva Troppo**, also known as **The Girl Who Knew Too Much** (1963), and **Sei Donne Per L'Assassino**, provocatively entitled **Blood and Black Lace** (1964), would have a major influence on the stalk and slash movies that became all the rage during the 1980s. Then there came **Terrore Nello Spazio** or **Planet of the Vampires** (1965), which later inspired Dan O'Bannon when he penned the script for **Alien**. Having already given birth to the giallo, Bava created the film that would become the blueprint for the deluge of slasher movies, which started just as the decade came to an end: **Reazione a Catena**, released in the US as **A Bay of Blood** and was also known as **Twitch of the Death Nerve** (1971). His later films were blighted by continual problems with distribution, which led to his retirement in 1978, although he couldn't resist becoming involved with some of the special effects for Dario Argento's **Inferno** before he passed away in 1980 aged 65. His son Lamberto, who had worked as his assistant director, now followed the family tradition and in turn directed several memorable additions to the genre. Lamberto would be the first to admit he could never match his father; few directors ever could, for Mario Bava was a genius whose influence still resonates over thirty years after his death. ❦

Jörg Buttgereit
(December 20, 1963–)

West Berliner Jörg Buttgereit was brought up on films; among them was the excitement of the original Japanese **Godzilla** movies, a subject upon which he would one day put pen to paper to write his own book. He was like so many kids of his age, a monster maniac eagerly collecting the Creature Feature bubble gum cards that were being issued during the early 1970s. His life was transformed on the day of his First Communion when he received a Super-8 camera. From the age of fourteen, he began experimenting with film with his first feature encapsulating so much of his boyhood fascination for the terrors of the silver screen, **Interview With Frankenstein**.

When as an independent filmmaker he set out to create **Nekromantik** in 1987 armed with his Super-8, he had very little money at his disposal. He was, however, gifted with a talented young crew, who were prepared to offer their services free of charge. **Nekromantik** became more than just the most debauched horror movie of its day; it was a challenge to West Germany's implacable attitude towards censorship. Very few extreme horror films ever made it into the country at this time, and those that did were heavily cut. With the images for his creation already being vividly played out in his mind, he set to work on a film that would have major repercussions, not just in West Germany but for the industry as a whole. Ultimately, this vision would play a significant part in breaking down the barriers that divided art and the cinema-going public's attitude towards exploitation, but he was to suffer many years in the wilderness as his film was banned in many parts of the world. It would be the first of several films that confronted his audience's thoughts on death, films that were inevitably driven underground. This would continue with his experimental feature on suicide and violent death in the seven short pieces that made up **Der Todesking**, which saw him step up to 16-mm filming during 1989. It was banned in the US and Australia and is still awaiting release to DVD. Controversy barked at his door once again when **Nekromantik 2** (1991) was finally completed. It was seized by police in Munich following accusations of glorified violence. Buttgereit admits to being alarmed by this turn of events, but it didn't prevent him from returning to make **Schramm** in 1993, the film that was to affirm his place as a visionary auteur.

Recent years have seen the cult director writing books and plays in addition to directing rock videos. He now despairs of so much of his country's horror cinema, feeling there is little to challenge the existing order, although he confesses he has seen almost nothing of the work of Germany's modern-day underground terrors, Olaf Ittenbach and Andreas Schnaas. His back catalogue of films is no longer banned and are now considered to be a veritable form of art, but he laments the film streaming of the Internet and its damaging effect on independent filmmakers. ✤

John Carpenter
(January 16, 1948–)

John Carpenter was born in Carthage, New York, and at the age of five moved to the small farming community of Bowling Green Kentucky. From an early age, he was hooked on going to the movies, at first caught up in the action and excitement of the westerns and then more significantly he was drawn to the B-grade science fiction and weird horror movies of the 1950s. Upon leaving the theatre he wanted to make his own films using his own ideas and soon after began to make his own horror shorts using 8-mm film. Among his early teenage efforts were **Revenge of the Colossal Beasts** (1962) and **Terror From Space** (1963). He boldly took the decision to change course while at university in 1968, leaving Kentucky to go to the University of Southern California's School of Cinematic Arts. Soon immersed in his studies he was tempted by the possibility of making his own features, among which was **The Resurrection of Broncho Billy** (1970), where he contributed to the production as the film's co-writer, editor and composer. It went on to win an Academy Award for Best Live Action Short Film after gaining a theatrical release courtesy of Universal Studios.

After graduating in 1971 he took to the director's chair to make a film that has long since been acknowledged as a cult favourite, the low-budget darkly comedic science fiction spectacle **Dark Star** (1974). Co-written with Dan O'Bannon, Carpenter scored the music and worked on the production over a four-year period, but never saw a penny for his efforts. That same year he wrote the script for **Eyes of Laura Mars** (1978) and was then asked to direct **Assault on Precinct 13** (1976). Again, with little money he wrote the script and put the music together as well as carrying out the post-production editing, effectively launching his career. The film had little impact in the United States, but in Europe it was a box office delight. In 1978 he collaborated with Debra Hill on the film that gave birth to the slasher genre, yet another low-budget production, **Halloween**, written in only two weeks, which went on to become one of the highest grossing independent productions of all time. In its wake came a decade of hack and slash and final girls, each of whom had the strength of mind to overcome their masked assailants. Then followed **The Fog** (1980), where he was so disappointed with the final cut he insisted about a third of the movie had to be re-shot. His commitment was rewarded; the film remains a celebrated entry in the annals of horror cinema, generating a return of over $21 million. Further success followed with **Escape From New York** (1981), which introduced his style of filmmaking to a more mainstream audience. Twelve months later, the same summer that saw **E.T. The Extra-Terrestrial** break the cinema-going public's hearts, he suffered his first commercial failure with **The Thing**. This graphic portrayal with its blood-splattered special effects was a retelling of one of his own favourites from the past, **The Thing from Another World** (1951), although it adhered more closely to John W. Campbell Jr.'s novella, *Who Goes There?* Gore fans loved it, but it was lost on mainstream audiences who preferred the more spiritually uplifting **E.T.** However, this was the dawn of the video market and very soon Carpenter's seeming failure turned to the welcome familiarity of success.

While the mass market was to elude him in the years that followed, the apocalyptic **Prince of Darkness** (1987), featuring Alice Cooper, became another unsettling addition to the world of cinematic terror. Carpenter continued to direct during the 1990s; among his half dozen films of the decade was yet another addition to his occasionally apocalyptic narrative, the psychological terror **In Mouth of Madness** (1994). Recent years have witnessed a preference for scriptwriting, but **Halloween** remains his legacy: the film that he would loved to have seen as a kid! 🍁

Wes Craven
(August 2, 1939–)

Only a handful of horror directors have left their mark on the genre and Wesley Earl Craven is certainly one of them. He was brought up in Cleveland, Ohio, by a family who were from a strict Baptist background and didn't encourage his watching of films, with the notable exception of Walt Disney's family oriented features. Wes can recall his parents being appalled when **Psycho** was released; but their disgust only aroused his interest and would be the inspiration for his unforgettable prelude to **Scream** (1996). He graduated with a combined honours degree in English and Psychology and later attained a Master's degree in Philosophy. He then started teaching English before ascending to become a Professor of Humanities. While he was teaching, he made a short action feature with a student film club in Potsdam, New York, which to his surprise actually made a return. This proved to be a life-changing experience, for it was then that he was ensnared by the bug for filmmaking, and was soon enticed by the more lucrative world of pornographic cinema and the hopes of setting up his own film company. Under a series of pseudonyms, he would learn his craft, which would lead to his first feature film, the bold but notorious **Last House on the Left** (1972). Five years later, he sat in the director's chair, this time for what many consider the second milestone in his career, **The Hills Have Eyes** (1977).

In 1984, when the slasher movie had been quite literally done to death, Wes reinvented the entire genre and at the same time created one of the largest franchises in American cinema with the release of **A Nightmare on Elm Street**. Twelve years later, he repeated this success when **Scream** came to the big screen. With people like Wes lurking behind the scenes, the slasher was never going to be consigned to the grave. Prior to this, in 1988, he had stepped into the domain of George A. Romero and Lucio Fulci, with his acclaimed zombie movie **The Serpent and the Rainbow**. This film, based upon the book by Wade Davis, was a far cry from the excess of their movies; rather, it dwelled on the superstitious rituals and black magic of Haiti at the time of the overthrow of "Baby Doc" Duvalier. Recent years have seen the **Scream** series continue to be a box office revelation and remakes of both **The Hills Have Eyes** (2006) and **Last House on the Left** (2009) have maintained his position as one of horror's most innovative directors. ❧

Sean S. Cunningham
(December 31, 1941–)

Raised in New York, Sean Sexton Cunningham graduated from Stanford University with a Master's degree in Drama and Film. From there he went on to develop a career in managing theatre companies, among which were productions at New York's Lincoln Center, the Oregon Shakespeare Festival and the Mineola Theatre on Long Island. His first film was a semi-documentary entitled **Together** (1971), produced with Wes Craven. He hoped their collaboration would improve on the same idea he had used in his exploitative but unusually gainful "white-coater", **The Art of Marriage** (1970). The film starred Marilyn Chambers, but Cunningham now admits to being embarrassed with his involvement. The return on this venture, however, was enough to allow both Cunningham and Craven to embark upon one of the most controversial films of the decade, **Last House on the Left** (1972). This unrelenting rape revenge tale, based on Ingmar Bergman's **Virgin Spring** (1960), featured one of horror cinema's first chainsaw murders, two years before Tobe Hooper shocked the world with **The Texas Chain Saw Massacre**. More exploitation followed, and then in 1977 he turned to comedy with **Here Come the Tigers**. His efforts weren't to catapult him to stardom, but the transition finally came when, on seeing the success of **Halloween** (1978) and **Alien** (1979), he decided to capitalize on the revitalized craze for horror.

Before he even had a script for **Friday the 13th**, he had gone to *Variety* to announce his film and made sure no one else could use the name. At that point, it was only an idea, but what an idea! Its graphic violence was by no means as mean spirited as that which shocked American audiences in **Last House on the Left**, but it was a bloody showing, which, unlike Carpenter's film, left nothing to the imagination. After **Friday the 13th** there came a whole deluge of carved-up teenagers, and Paramount had an unexpected success on their hands, one that, while occasionally problematic, would generate an immensely lucrative franchise, and would provide Cunningham with plenty of work overseeing the ensuing sequels. Jason wasn't like the other bad guys of the cinema; when he picked up an axe the audience were firmly behind him and with Tom Savini creating the gory effects horror fans were in for the rarest of treats. A series of **House** films would follow during the 1980s, but nothing would compare to the horror spawned by Jason Voorhees. ❧

Lucio Fulci
(June 17, 1927–March 13, 1996)

Born in Rome in 1927, Lucio Fulci began his working life as an art critic and ironically, given the context of the films on show in these pages, opted for a course in medicine. He later moved into scriptwriting with the Experimental Film Studios, which gave him the chance to make several documentaries working under Federico Fellini and Mario Bava. Although he originally intended to pursue a career as a writer for film, Fulci took the opportunity to step into the director's chair with **Il ladri** or **The Thieves** (1959) and so followed a series of comedies. By the mid-1960s, he had expanded his horizons and progressed into adventure films, which included work with Franco Nero. Then in 1969, he directed his first giallo, **Una sull'altra**, which saw release outside Italy as **One On Top of the Other**, and also acquired the emotive title of **Perversion Story**. The content wasn't quite as lurid as that suggested by the title; rather, its premise contained an undercurrent that would become increasingly evident in Fulci's work, the perversity of human nature. This was manifest in his film **Lizard in a Woman's Skin** (1971), which was hugely controversial in its depiction of violence and almost brought charges of animal cruelty owing to Carlo Rambaldi's shocking special effects. However, it also proved to be a resounding success at the Italian box office.

The small town tale of maniacal murder **Non Si Sevizia un Paperino** or **Don't Torture a Duckling** (1972) was to reveal the director's growing predilection for violence of the more graphic kind. While the splatter in this film wasn't the match of his later visceral relish, it paved the way for him to succeed Herschell Gordon Lewis as the "Godfather of Gore". After directing the spaghetti western **Silver Saddle** (1978), so inspired was he by George A. Romero's groundbreaking **Dawn of the Dead** (1978) he set out to emulate this success with a script conceived by Dardano Sacchetti, who for the next few years assisted Fulci in creating some of his most memorable films. Their partnership resulted in a low-budget onslaught of the living dead, **Zombi 2** (1979) as it was known in Italy, which was re-titled as **Zombie Flesh Eaters** in the United Kingdom. It would be later packaged as **Zombie** and **Island of the Living Dead** and was unofficially marketed as the sequel to Romero's flesh-eating frenzy of 1978 with its violent excess making it an instant success. With Sacchetti at his side, he followed with a series of films his fans labelled the Gates of Hell trilogy, each of which was rife with the putrescent creatures that were by then all the rage. Fulci's releases between 1979 and 1983 were described by his critics as being among the most violent and gory films ever made; his fans for quite different reasons weren't too averse to such criticism. **City of the Living Dead** (1980), **The Beyond** (1981), **House by the Cemetery** (1981), **The Black Cat** (1981) and **The New York Ripper** (1982) were among his biggest hits, all of which featured unprecedented levels of on-screen blood and cruelty, with at least one scene of eye gouging in each film. Censors across the world would come down heavily on his efforts with understandable accusations of misogyny. His unrated films went straight to the passion pits of the drive-ins much to the delight of hordes of horror fanatics across the US.

Sadly, for the last ten years of his life Fulci did not enjoy the best of health, constantly plagued by the suicide of his wife in 1969 and the death of his daughter, and then came the acrimonious split with his scriptwriter Dardano Sacchetti. These occurrences were to detract from his later works, with many of his later films being badly written and cheaply produced, although **Aenigma** (1987) and **Voices From Beyond** (1991) hinted at the man who had once almost been on a par with Dario Argento and a creditable mention should be given to **House of Clocks** (1989). The two great Italian horror directors met in 1995 and looked to work together on a new horror feature they called **Wax Mask**, a remake of **House of Wax** (1953), but Fulci died before filming could begin. While his films remain virtually unknown outside the genre, his admirers celebrate his stylish cinematic compositions of extreme gore set against a backdrop of delirious hallucinatory vistas with their seductive images and almost incoherent narrative. Fulci was a man who truly deserved the distinction as the "Godfather of Gore". 🐾

Herschell Gordon Lewis
(June 15, 1929–)

The first "Godfather of Gore" started life in the most innocuous of manners, being brought up in Pennsylvania and after graduating with a degree in Journalism and going on to become a Professor of English Literature. He left his academic life at Mississippi State College to move into managing a radio station, then stepped up to become a director in the same field. A move into advertising in Chicago would see him return to part-time teaching until he began directing commercial adverts. In 1960 Herschell G. Lewis produced his first film, **Prime Time**, shot in the city of Chicago, but from there on in he chose the director's chair, working alongside exploitation producer David F. Friedman. Their collaboration began with **Living Venus** (1961), a fictitious account of Hugh Hefner and his early years with *Playboy*. There followed a series of exploitation movies, many of which contained scenes of soft-core pornography, which would never have made it to a Hollywood feature, owing to the watchful eye of the Hays Office. These films were low-budget ventures, designed to make a fast buck.

When these nude-styled films began to wane in popularity, Lewis and Friedman produced their first horror film and made it available to the drive-in theatres. The gore-ridden **Blood Feast** (1963) shocked its young audience but still had them begging for more. Although considered camp, as many of his movies were, it is now recognized by many as the first splatter movie. **Two Thousand Maniacs!** (1964) and **Color Me Blood Red** (1965) used the same outrageous display of blood-soaked cheap gore effects and set the standard for the horror movies of the next few years as other emerging film companies looked to follow suit. In 1967 Lewis pushed the boundaries by introducing electrical implements to scalp his victims when he let a mad old woman and her mentally challenged son loose in **The Gruesome Twosome**, announcing "The most barbaric humour since the guillotine went out of style". He later resorted to butchering strippers in a sleazy nightclub in the self-parodying ultra-cheap schlock-fest, **The Gore Gore Girls** (1972), before going into semi-retirement from the world of film, although he was occasionally tempted back to stand behind the camera. Away from film he developed a successful career in the areas of copyrighting and marketing, and then after almost thirty years away from directing he returned to begin work in 1999 to make the direct-to-video

Blood Feast 2: All U Can Eat (2002). This movie was as exploitative and sleazy as anything Lewis had previously released, characterized by the same hankering for scantily clad women and copious amounts of blood and guts from over thirty years before. At the age of eighty, Lewis returned to deliver more of his lurid blood-filled madness with **The Uh-Oh Show** (2009), an extreme quiz show that punished the wrong answer with the severing of an arm or a leg; reality TV was never quite like this, well not so far!

His work would influence Tobe Hoper as he embarked on his legendary entry to the world of splatter cinema, and more recent low-budget gore sleaze directors such as Canada's Lee Demarbre, whose **Smash Cut** (2009) combined Lewis's two streams of exploitation, sex and gore, before going on to direct the worthy slasher of the same year, **Summer's Blood**. Lewis has his detractors but among his fans he remains exalted, for without his self-effacing excess we may never had had so many of the excruciating features found in these pages. Herschell Gordon Lewis really was the man "who ought to know better, but don't". 🍁

George Andrew Romero
(February 4, 1940–)

George Romero, like many other directors, will admit to having moments in his professional career where he has become completely fed up with producers, but he has never tired of zombies. So much so, he has been bestowed with the honour as the "Godfather of all Zombies". Without his vision, we may never have seen Lucio Fulci produce his splatter-filled masterpieces and those who have since followed the trail of the walking dead. Inspired by the fantasy elements of Michael Powell and Emeric Pressburger's film **The Tales of Hoffmann** (1951), and having been given an 8-mm camera at the age of fourteen, he looked to a career in media. Soon after graduating Pittsburgh's Carnegie Mellon University in 1960 he went into shooting short films and commercials for The Latent Image, a company he co-founded with friends John Russo and Russell Streiner. The trio soon became bored with commercials and discussed the idea of producing a horror movie, which was no surprise with Romero having been a fan of the legendary Universal features of the 1930s and 1940s as well as the notorious horror comics of the 1950s. They went on to establish Image Ten Productions and between them raised the money to produce **Night of the Living Dead** (1968). Inspired by Richard Matheson's novel *I Am Legend*, Romero's film, co-written with John A. Russo, has became a cult classic and changed the face of modern horror cinema, although, as he has always insisted, none of his flesh-eaters, as they were termed in this film, and his later zombies has ever demonstrated an overwhelming appetite for brains.

The less successful **Season of the Witch** (1972) and **The Crazies** (1973) soon followed, but his next visit to the director's chair produced the critically acclaimed vampire tale **Martin** (1977). Ten years after making his seminal flesh-eating movie, Romero returned with this same atrophied host to breathe life into the highly influential **Dawn of the Dead** (1978). This was the film that was to set the standard for the blood lust of the next three decades and ultimately popularized this flesh-eating breed. In 1982, alongside Stephen King, he returned to the terrors of his youth, directing the comic book inspired **Creepshow**. Romero then made the third entry in his "Dead Series" with **Day of the Dead** (1985), which didn't prosper anywhere near as well as its predecessors at the box office. While Romero has tried to resist the idea that his zombie films have a sociological undercurrent, these films have inadvertently reflected the socio-political climates of three very different decades. Collaborations with his long-time friend Dario Argento on the Edgar Allan Poe adaptation, **Two Evil Eyes** (1990), and Stephen King on **The Dark Half** (1993) have since followed, among many other projects, none of which has captured the cinema-going public's imagination.

It appears he can never escape the walking dead; although he has made other kinds of features he is regarded by both the industry and fans alike as a genre filmmaker. He updated his original screenplay for **Night of the Living Dead** and handed it to special effects maestro Tom Savini, who assumed the role of director for the remake in 1990. Again this film didn't fare too well; it looked as if the dead were about to be returned to the grave. However, having settled down in Toronto he brought a renewed breakdown of society in **Land of the Dead** to his new home city in 2005, followed by a filmmaker's vision of the apocalypse in **Diary of the Dead** (2007). Two years ago, he gave us another insight into how humanity would react to their downfall in **Survival of the Dead** (2009) with a couple more "Dead" movies currently in the planning stage. Recent years have seen Romero become involved with videogames and the writing of DC Comics zombie title "Toe Tags", based on an unused script that was originally intended as a sequel to the original "Dead Trilogy". His favourite zombie movie of the latest batch is Ruben Fleischer's visually stylish **Zombieland** (2009). ❧

Mark Shostrom
(May 13, 1956–)

As a child, Mark was an avid of reader of *Famous Monsters of Filmland* and his introduction to the world of horror movies came with **Bride of Frankenstein** (1935) and the pioneering craft of Jack Pierce. He was later inspired by Dick Smith's book *Do-It Yourself Monster Make-Up Handbook*, from a make-up artist who started with the semi-documentary styled noir **Call Northside 777** (1948) and at the height of his career contributed to the success of **The Exorcist** (1973), **The Taxidriver** (1976) and **Scanners** (1981). At the age of thirteen, Shostrom moved with his parents to Hong Kong where he was exposed to both oriental and European cinema. While living in Hong Kong he also met the widow of Boris Karloff, who became a friend for the next eighteen years.

As with so many kids of his age, Shostrom became addicted to the **Planet of the Apes** films and then later the television series. In 1975 he began corresponding with the acclaimed make-up artist John Chambers, who won an academy award for his work on **Planet of the Apes** (1968). Chambers had started life as a medical technician in World War II, repairing the faces of the injured and building prosthetic limbs. He also created Leonard Nimoy's pointed ears for the original *Star Trek* series. Working from a converted garage next to his house he stayed in touch with the young Shostrom and later appointed him as his mould maker for a film to be made for television. Sadly, this fell through, but a position did come when he was asked to join an aspiring Bart Mixon, although Chambers was still working on his behalf in the background. Shostrom's new partner later went on to create the make-up for the much maligned zombie movie **The Curse of the Screaming Dead** (1982) before going to work on a series of major features, including **A Nightmare on Elm Street Part 2: Freddie's Revenge** (1985), **House of 1,000 Corpses** (2003) and **Pirates of the Caribbean: Dead Man's Chest** (2006).

Thankfully, Shostrom's ingenuity was also recognized; his first major assignment would be the Santa slasher **To All A Goodnight** (1980). Soon after that he found regular engagements, notably on **The Slumber Party Massacre** (1982), **Videodrome** (1983), **A Nightmare on Elm Street** (1984) and the groundbreaking metamorphosis in **A Nightmare on Elm Street Part 2: Freddie's Revenge** (1985). Television also beckoned with placements on prestigious shows such as *Star Trek Deep Space Nine*, *Star Trek Voyager*, *The*

X-Files and *Buffy the Vampire Slayer*, and then he later worked with Tobe Hooper to outdo the CGI effects on his zombie movie **Mortuary** (2005). Shostrom has become one of the genre's greatest heroes and twenty-five years later his imaginative work on **Evil Dead II** (1987) is still lauded by splatter fans across the world. No doubt there will be a youngster reading one of the current selection of monster mags who is inspired by Shostrom's artistic innovation. 🦋

Tom Savini
(November 3, 1946–)

"The more you do, the more you get to do" has remained Tom Savini's philosophy and once he entered film, it certainly paid off. He was born in Pittsburgh, Pennsylvania, six years after his co-conspirator George A. Romero. At the age of twelve, he was inspired when he saw **Man of a Thousand Faces** (1957), which starred James Cagney as the legendary Lon Chaney Sr. He would one day follow his hero, Chaney Sr. to become that rarest of breeds, when he showed himself to be a hugely capable stuntman, actor, make-up artist and director. He was also another make-up artist in the making to be beguiled by the work of Jack Pearce on Universal's **Frankenstein** and was later able to give a fellow creator for whom he had such admiration a call to discuss their techniques: none other than effects wizard Dick Smith. As Savini made his way in the business, he was astounded by the work of his fellow professionals, among them Stuart Freeborn, Rob Bottin, Rick Barker and Stan Winston.

Savini met George Romero while still at school when he was an aspiring actor. Several years later, just as he was about to join Romero on **Night of the Living Dead** (1968), he was drafted and sent to Vietnam as a combat photographer. His wartime experiences between 1969 and 1970 would see him come face to face with the wounded and the dead. For the first time in his life he would encounter something few effects artists would ever see: "anatomically correct gore". When he moved into film and set to creating his gory effects, he strived to achieve the same feeling he had experienced when he was first exposed to these bloody scenes. If his efforts didn't create this same impression, he knew he had not accomplished his goal.

In 1974 he found work with Bob Clark as a special make-up artist and still photographer on his movie **Dead of Night** (1974), which later became known as **Deathdream**. That same year he stepped up to work as the head special make-up artist on Clark's next film, **Deranged**, which was very loosely based on the life of serial killer Ed Gein, and directed by Alan Ormsby. At this time, Savini was working as a freelance photographer by day and as an actor and make-up artist at night doing repertory regional theatre in North Carolina. Here he learned the skills of the trade, both as an actor and in the various areas of production. While teaching and attending Carnegie Mellon University under a fellowship, he finally got the chance to work with Romero on his vampire movie **Martin** (1977). Romero certainly got his money's worth as Savini not only supplied the make-up effects, with one notable wrist-slashing sequence, but also played one of the roles in addition to performing the stunts. The following year he was invited to work on **Dawn of the Dead** (1978). Here Savini came into his own, creating the emaciated creatures that would become his trademark. As this host of zombies rampaged through the shopping mall, they became the inspiration for countless others, including Lucio Fulci, for whose creations Savini would come to have such great respect.

More work as a special-effects man and actor would follow in **Maniac** (1980) and then came another jewel in his crown, **Friday the 13ᵗʰ** (1980). As the years rolled on he would be asked to join two legends of the period, Dario Argento on **Trauma** (1993) and Tobe Hooper for **The Texas Chainsaw Massacre 2** (1986), after having contributed to so many gory masterpieces during the 1980s, among which was the scaled-down **Day of the Dead** (1985). While he readily joined the set on some of the more memorable films of these years, he was not averse to becoming involved in low-budget projects such as his transformation into Jack the Ripper in Christopher Lewis's straight-to-video **The Ripper** (1985). He later played the whip-wielding, vampire-fighting biker 'Sex Machine' in **From Dusk till Dawn** (1996) and only recently fought off an infestation of zombies in **Planet Terror** (2007).

As a director, Savini would come to appreciate George Romero's frustration when the budget on the remake of **Night of the Living Dead** was drastically reduced in 1990. In recent years while still working on many projects he has been running the Special Effects Make-Up and Digital Film Programs at the Douglas Education Center in Monessen, Pennsylvania, as well as writing several books on special effects. It is only in the last decade that Savini's most grisly work has been seen by gore-mongers in the UK and the US following a relaxation in attitudes towards censorship. During the late 1970s and on into the 1980s he endured the frustration of seeing so much of his most accomplished moments end up on the cutting room floor. Now the world can see the true extent of his blood-crazed carnage. ❧

The Video Nasties
They Tried to Ban

Listed below are the seventy-two films that between 1983 and 1985 were registered on the UK Director of Public Prosecutions' offending lists of video nasties. Some of these films only stayed on the list for a matter of months, while thirty-nine of them remained banned until the end of the panic. Most of these films have since been released.

Absurd (1981) also known as *Rosso Sangue*; *Horrible*; *The Monster Hunter*; *Anthropophagus 2*

Anthropophagous: The Beast (1980) also known as *Antropophagus*; *Anthropophagous*; *Antropofago*; *Gomia, Terror en el Mar Egeo*; *Man Beast: Man-Eater*; *The Savage Island*; *The Grim Reaper*

Axe (1974) also known as *Lisa, Lisa*; *California Axe Murder*; *The Axe Murders*

The Beast in Heat (1977) also known as *La Bestia in Calore*; *Horrifying Experiments of S.S. Last Days*

The Beyond (1981) also known as *E Tu Vivrai Nel Terrore – L'aldilà*; *Seven Doors of Death*

Blood Bath (1971) also known as *Reazione a Catena*; *A Bay of Blood*; *Twitch of the Death Nerve*

Blood Feast (1963)

Blood Rites (1968) also known as *The Ghastly Ones*

Bloody Moon (1981) also known as *Die Säge des Todes*

The Bogey Man (1980) also known as *The Boogeyman*

The Burning (1981)

Cannibal Apocalypse (1980) also known as *Apocalypse Domani*

Cannibal Ferox (1981) also known as *Make Them Die Slowly*

Cannibal Holocaust (1980)

The Cannibal Man (1972) also known as original title *La Semana del Asesino*; *The Apartment on the 13th Floor*

Cannibal Terror (1981) also known as *Terreur Cannibale*

Contamination (1980)

Dead & Buried (1981)

Death Trap (1977) also known as *Eaten Alive*

Deep River Savages (1972) also known as *Il paese del sesso selvaggio*; *The Man from Deep River*

Delirium (1979) also known as *Psycho Puppet*

Devil Hunter (1980) also known as *Il cacciatore di uomini*

Don't Go in the House (1980)

Don't Go in the Woods (1982)

Don't Go Near the Park (1981)

Don't Look in the Basement (1973) also known as *The Forgotten*

The Dorm That Dripped Blood (1982) also known as *Pranks*; *Death Dorm*

The Driller Killer (1979)

The Evil Dead (1981)

Evilspeak (1981)

Exposé (1976)

Faces of Death (1980)

Fight For Your Life (1977)

Flesh for Frankenstein (1973) also known as *Andy Warhol's Frankenstein*

Forest of Fear (1980) also known as *Toxic Zombies*; *Bloodeaters*

Frozen Scream (1975)

The Funhouse (1981)

Gestapo's Last Orgy (1977) also known as *L'ultima orgia del III Reich*

The House by the Cemetery (1981) also known as *Quella villa accanto al cimitero*

House on the Edge of the Park (1980) also known as *La casa sperduta nel parco*

Human Experiments (1981) also known as *Strange Behaviour*

I Miss You, Hugs and Kisses (1978) also known as *Drop Dead, Dearest*

I Spit on Your Grave (1978) also known as *Day of the Woman*

Inferno (1980)

Island of Death (1975) also known as *Ta Pedhia tou dhiavolou*

Killer Nun (1978) also known as *Suor Omicidi*

The Last House on the Left (1972)

The Living Dead at the Manchester Morgue (1974) also known as *Non si deve profanare il sonno dei morti*; *The Living Dead*; *Let Sleeping Corpses Lie*; *Don't Open the Window*

Love Camp 7 (1968)

Madhouse (1981) also known as *There Was a Little Girl*

Mardi Gras Massacre (1978)

Night of the Bloody Apes (1969) also known as *La Horripilante bestia humana*

Night of the Demon (1980)

Night School (1981) also known as *Terror Eyes*

Night Train Murders (1975) also known as *L'ultimo treno della note*; *Late Night Trains*

Night Warning (1983) also known as *Butcher, Baker, Nightmare Maker*; *Nightmare Maker*

Nightmares in a Damaged Brain (1981)

Possession (1981)

Primitive Desires (1978) also known as (original title): *La montagna del dio cannibale*; *Prisoner of the Cannibal God*; *Mountain of the Cannibal God*

Return of the Boogeyman (1983) also known as *Boogeyman II*

The Slayer (1982)

Snuff (1976)

SS Experiment Camp (1976) also known as *Lager SSadis Kastrat Kommandantur*

Tenebrae (1982) also known as *Tenebre*

The Toolbox Murders (1978)

Unhinged (1982)

Visiting Hours (1982)

The Werewolf and the Yeti (1975) also known as *La Maldición de la Bestia*

The Witch Who Came From the Sea (1976)

Women Behind Bars (1975) also known as *Des diamants pour l'enfer*

Zombie Creeping Flesh (1980) also known as *Virus*; *Hell of the Living Dead*

Zombie Flesh Eaters (1979) also known as *Zombi 2*; *Zombie*

Chronology
of Movies

Film
Alternative names or remakes

1916
Intolerance

1929
Un Chien Andalou

1932
Thirteen Women
Hypnose

1945
And Then There Were None

1957
The Curse of Frankenstein

1958
Dracula
The Horror of Dracula
The Revenge of Frankenstein

1959
Bucket of Blood
The Woman Eater

1960
Black Sunday
La Maschera del Demonio,
Revenge of the Vampire,
The Mask of Satan
Eyes Without a Face
The Horror Chamber of Dr
Faustus

Jigoku
Peeping Tom
Face of Fear
Psycho

1963
Blood Feast

1964
At Midnight I'll Take Your Soul Away
À Meia-Noite Levarei Sua Alma
Blood and Black Lace
The Evil of Frankenstein
Straight-Jacket
Two Thousand Maniacs!

1965
Color Me Blood Red

1966
Dracula Prince of Darkness

1967
A Taste of Blood
Frankenstein Created Woman
The Gruesome Twosome
This Night I'll Possess Your
    Corpse

1968
Dracula Has Risen From the Grave
The Ghastly Ones
Blood Rites

Night of the Living Dead
The Strange World of Coffin Joe

1969

The Awakening of the Beast
  O Despertar da Besta
Frankenstein Must Be Destroyed
The House that Screamed
  La Residencia, The Boarding School
Night of the Bloody Apes
  Horror y Sexo
One On Top of the Other
  Una sull'altra, Perversion Story

1970

The Bird with the Crystal Plumage
The Horror of Frankenstein
Taste the Blood of Dracula
Wizard of Gore

1971

A Bay of Blood
  Twitch of the Death Nerve,
  Reazione a Catena,
  Ecologia del delitto, Bloodbath,
  Carnage, Last House on the Left II
Lizard in a Woman's Skin
Short Night of the Glass Dolls
  La corta notte delle bambole di vetro,
  Paralyzed
The Slaughter
Slaughter Hotel
  La bestia uccide a sangue freddo,
  Asylum Erotica, Cold Blooded Beast
The Strange Vice of Mrs Wardh
  Lo Strano Vizio Della Signora Wardh
Straw Dogs

1972

Cannibal Man
  Apartment on the 13th Floor
Deliverance

Don't Torture a Duckling
  Non Si Sevizia un Paperino
Dracula A.D. 1972
The Gore Gore Girls
  Blood Orgy
Last House on the Left
The Man From Deep River
  Il Paese Del Sesso Selvaggio, Deep
  River Savages, Mondo Cannibale,
  Sacrifice
Three on a Meat Hook
What Have You Done to Solange?
  Cosa avete fatto a Solange?
Who Saw Her Die
  Chi l'ha vista morire?
Your Vice is a Locked Room and
  Only I have the Key
  Il Tuo Vizio è Una Stanza Chiusa e Solo
  Io Ne Ho La Chiave, Gently Before She
  Dies, Excite Me, Eye of the Black Cat

1973

Death Line
  Raw Meat
Don't Look in the Basement
  Death Ward 13
Flesh for Frankenstein
  Andy Warhol's Flesh for Frankenstein
Frankenstein and the Monster from
  Hell
Satanic Rites of Dracula
Scream Bloody Murder
  Claw of Terror, Matthew,
  The Captive Female

1974

Black Christmas
  Silent Night, Evil Night
Blood for Dracula
Deranged
  Deranged: The Confessions of a
  Necrophile

Frightmare

Island Of Death
*A Craving for Lust, Cruel
Destination, Devils in Mykonos,
Island of Perversion, Psychic Killer 2*

Lisa, Lisa
*Axe, California Axe Massacre, The
Axe Murders, California Axe
Murders, The Virgin Slaughter*

The Living Dead at the Manchester
Morgue
*Non si Deve Profanare il Sonno
dei Morti, Let Sleeping Corpses Lie,
The Living Dead, Breakfast at the
Manchester Morgue, Don't Open the
Window, Zombi 3*

The Texas Chain Saw Massacre

1975

Deep Red
*Profondo Rosso, The Deep Red
Hatchet Murders*

Frozen Scream

Night Train Murders
*L'Ultimo Treno della Notte, Late
Night Trains, Don't Ride on Late
Night Trains, Last Stop on the Night
Train, Torture Train*

The Psychopath

The Werewolf and the Yeti
*Night of the Howling Beast, La
Maldición de la Bestia, Hall of
the Mountain King, Horror of the
Werewolf*

1976

Carrie

Communion
Alice Sweet Alice, Holy Terror

Death Weekend

Expose
Trauma, The House on Straw Hill

The Incredible Torture Show
*Blood Sucking Freaks, Sardu: Master
of the Screaming Virgins*

Savana Violenta

Snuff

The Spider Will Kill You

Who Can Kill a Child?
*Quién Puede Matar a un Niño,
Death is Child's Play, Island of the
Damned*

The Witch that Came in from the Sea

1977

Eaten Alive
*Death Trap, Horror Hotel, Horror
Hotel Massacre, Legend of the Bayou,
Murder on the Bayou, Le Crocodile de
la Mort, Starlight Slaughter*

Haunts

The Hills Have Eyes

Last Cannibal World
Ultimo Mondo Cannibal

The Last House on Dead End Street

Suspiria

1978

Dawn of the Dead
Zombi, Zombie: Dawn of the Dead

Halloween

Hallucinations of a Deranged Mind
Delirios de um Anormal

I Spit on Your Grave
*Day of the Woman, I Hate Your
Guts, The Rape, Revenge of Jennifer
Hills*

Legacy Blood

Mardi Gras Massacre

Primitive Desires
*La Montagna del dio Cannibale, The
Mountain of the Cannibal God, Slave
of the Cannibal God, Prisoner of the
Cannibal God*

The Redeemer Son of Satan
Toolbox Murders
Within the Woods

1979
Alien
Delirium
  Psycho Puppet
Drillerkiller
Giallo a Venezia
Hardcore
Inferno
Jigoku
Tourist Trap
When a Stranger Calls
Zombie Flesh Eaters
  Zombie, Zombi 2, Island of the
  Living Dead, Zombie Island, Gli
  Ultimi Zombie, Island of the Flesh-
  Eaters, L'enfer Des Zombies,
  Sanguelia, Woodoo

1980
Alien 2: On Earth
  Sulla Terra
Antropophagus
The Boogeyman
Cannibal Apocalypse
  Invasion of the Flesh Hunters,
  Apocalypse Domani
Cannibal Holocaust
Christmas Evil
  You Better Watch Out, Terror in
  Toyland
City of the Living Dead
  Paura Nella Citta Dei Morti Viventi,
  Gates of Hell
Contamination
  Alien Contamination,
  Contamination: Alien on Earth,
  Toxic Spawn, Contaminazione,
  Alien 2

Demented
The Devil Hunter
  Sexo Cannibal, The Man Hunter,
  Mandingo Manhunter
Don't Answer the Phone
Don't Go in the House
Eaten Alive
Faces of Death
  The Original Faces of Death
Forest of Fear
  Bloodeaters, Blood Butchers, Toxic
  Zombies
Friday the 13th
He Knows You're Alone
The House on the Edge of the Park
Killer Nun
  Suor Omicidi, Deadly Habit
The Long Island Cannibal Massacre
Maniac
Mondo Cannibale
Mother's Day
New Year's Evil
Night of the Demon
Nightmare City
  Incubo sulla città contaminate, City
  of the Walking Dead, Nightmare of
  a Contaminated City, Invasion of the
  Atomic Zombies
The Prey
Prom Night
Silent Scream
Terror Train
To All A Good Night
Zombie Creeping Flesh
  Inferno Dei Morti-Viventi, Hell
  of the Living Dead, Cannibal Virus,
  Night of the Zombies, Zombie
  Inferno, Zombies of the Savanna,
  Zombi 2: Ultimate Nightmare,
  Zombi 4, Zombi 5: Ultimate
  Nightmare

1981

Absurd
  Rosso Sangue, Anthropophagous 2,
  Horrible, The Grim Reaper 2
The Beyond
Bloody Birthday
Bloody Moon
Burial Ground
  Nights of Terror, The Zombie Dead,
  Zombie Horror, Zombie 3
The Burning
Cannibal Ferox
  Make Them Die Slowly, Woman
  From Deep River
Cannibal Terror
  Terreur Cannibale
Dead and Buried
Don't Go Near the Park
  Curse of the Living Dead,
  Nightstalker, Sanctuary for Evil
The Evil Dead
Evilspeak
  Evilspeaks, Computer Murders
Eyes of a Stranger
Faces of Death II
Final Exam
Friday the 13th 2
The Funhouse
Graduation Day
Halloween II
Happy Birthday to Me
Hell Night
Hospital Massacre
The House by the Cemetery
  Quella Villa Accanto al Cimitero
Just Before Dawn
  Survivance
Madhouse
  There Was A Little Girl, And When
  She Was Bad, Party des Schreckens
Madman
My Bloody Valentine

Night School
  Terror Eyes
Nightmares in a Damaged Brain
  Blood Splash, Nightmare
Oasis of the Zombies
  Blood Sucking Nazi Zombies
Possession
Scanners
Strange Behaviour
  Dead Kids, Human Experiments,
  Small Town Massacre

1982

Alone in the Dark
Basket Case
  House of Freaks
Blood Song
Boarding House
The Curse of the Screaming Dead
Death Screams
  House of Death, Night Screams
Don't Go in the Woods Alone
The Dorm that Dripped Blood
  Pranks
Friday the 13th Part III
Halloween III: Season of the Witch
The New York Ripper
  Lo Squartatore di New York, Psycho
  Ripper, The Ripper
Pieces
The Slayer
  Nightmare Island
The Slumber Party Massacre
  Slumber Party Murders
Tenebrae
  Tenebre, Unsane, Shadow, Sotto Gli
  Occhi dell'Assassino
The Thing
Unhinged
Visiting Hours
Xtro

1983
A Blade in the Dark
A Night to Dismember
American Nightmare
Angst
Blödaren
The Bleeder
The Boogeyman 2
Return of the Boogeyman
Curtains
Fatal Games
Olympic Nightmare
The Final Terror
The Campsite Murders, Forest Primeval
The House on Sorority Row
Microwave Massacre
Mortuary
Embalmed
The Mutilator
Night Warning
Butcher, Baker, Nightmare Maker, Momma's Boy, Thrilled to Death, The Evil Protégé
Psycho II
Sledgehammer
Sleepaway Camp

1984
A Nightmare on Elm Street
Don't Open 'Til Christmas
Friday the 13th: The Final Chapter
Girls Nite Out
The Initiation
Silent Night, Deadly Night
Splatter University

1985
A Nightmare on Elm Street 2: Freddy's Revenge
Amazonia: The Catherine Miles Story
Schiave Bianche: Violenza en Amazzonia, Cannibal Holocaust 2: The Catherine Miles Story
Blood Cult
Blood Tracks
Day of the Dead
Demons
Demons 2
Dèmoni 2 L'Incubo Ritorna
Faces of Death III
Friday the 13th: A New Beginning
The Guard from Underground
Jigoku No Keibiin, Security Guard from Hell
Guinea Pig 2: Flower of Flesh and Blood
Chiniku No Hana
Guinea Pig: The Devil's Experiment
Akumano Jikken, Unabridged Agony
The Hills Have Eyes II
Naked Vengeance
Phenomena
Re-Animator
The Return of the Living Dead
The Ripper
Victims

1986
Aenigma
Aliens
April Fool's Day
Chopping Mall
Friday the 13th Part VI: Jason Lives
Guinea Pig 3: He Never Dies
Senritsu! Shinanai Otoko
Henry: Portrait of a Serial Killer
Killer Party
Lucker the Necrophagous
Nail Gun Massacre
Night Ripper
Psycho III

Sorority House Massacre
The Texas Chainsaw Massacre II

1987

A Nightmare on Elm Street 3:
　Dream Warriors
Angustia
Bad Taste
Evil Dead 2
Hellraiser
Nekromantik
Opera
　Terror at the Opera
Prom Night 2: Hello Mary Lou
Silent Night, Deadly Night 2
The Slumber Party Massacre 2
Stagefright
Streets of Death
Video Violence

1988

555
A Nightmare on Elm Street 4: The
　Dream Master
Amsterdamned
Cannibal Campout
Child's Play
Demons III: The Ogre
　La Casa Dell'Orco or The Ogre House
Edge of the Axe
Evil Dead Trap
Friday the 13th Part VII: The New
　Blood
The Green Inferno
　Natura Contro, Cannibal Holocaust II
Guinea Pig 4: Mermaid in a
　Manhole
　Manhoru no naka no Ningyo
Guinea Pig 5: Android of Notre Dame
　Nôtoru Damu no andoroido
Halloween 4: The Return of Michael
　Myers

Hellbound: Hellraiser II
Il Fantasma di Sodoma
The Last Slumber Party
Maniac Cop
Men Behind the Sun
The Murder Secret
Rabid Grannies
The Return of the Living Dead Part II
Sleepaway Camp 2
Touch of Death
Video Violence 2
The Woodchipper Massacre
Zombi 3

1989

A Nightmare on Elm Street 5: The
　Dream Child
After Death
　*Oltre La Morte, Zombie 4: After
　Death, Zombie Flesh Eaters 3*
Bloody Psycho
The Dead Next Door
Demons 3
　La Chiesa, The Church
Demons 5: The Devil's Veil
　*La Maschera del Demonio, The Mask
　of the Demon*
Demons 6: De Profundis
　*Il Gatto Nero, The Black Cat, From
　The Deep*
Der Todesking
Friday the 13th Part VIII: Jason Takes
　Manhattan
Halloween 5: The Revenge of
　Michael Myers
Hansel and Gretel
House of Clocks
Intruder
Luna di Sangue
Massacre
The Puppet Master
Santa Sangre

Sentenced to Hang
Silent Night, Deadly Night 3: Better Watch Out!
Sleepaway Camp 3: Teenage Wasteland
Violent Shit

1990

Basket Case 2
Bride of Re-Animator
Cat in the Brain
 Un Gatto Nel Cervello, Nightmare Concert, I Volti del Terrore
Child's Play 2
Faces of Death IV
Guinea Pig 6: Devil Doctor Woman
 Pita no akuma no joi-san
Hard to Die
 Sorority House Massacre 3
Leatherface: The Texas Chainsaw Massacre III
Maniac Cop 2
Night of the Living Dead
Pledge Night
Prom Night 3: The Last Kiss
Psycho IV: The Beginning
Scanners II: The New Order
Silent Night, Deadly Night 4: Initiation
The Slumber Party Massacre 3
Sorority House Massacre 2

1991

Basket Case 3: The Progeny
Black Demons
 Dèmoni 3
Child's Play 3
Demons 4: The Devil's Daughter
 La Setta or The Schism
Freddy's Dead: The Final Nightmare
Guinea Pig 7: Slaughter Special
Nekromantik 2: The Return of the Loving Death

The Silence of the Lambs
Silent Night, Deadly Night 5: The Toy Maker
Voices From Beyond
Xtro II: The Second Encounter

1992

Alien 3
Army of Darkness
Brain Dead
 Dead Alive
Candyman
Dr Giggles
Dr Lamb
Hellraiser III: Hell on Earth
Man Bites Dog
Prom Night 4: Deliver us from Evil
Scanners III: The Takeover
Violent Shit 2: Mother, Hold My Hand

1993

Jason Goes to Hell: The Final Friday
Maniac Cop III: Badge of Silence
Return of the Living Dead 3
Trauma
The Untold Story
 Bunman: The Untold Story, Human Meat Pies: The Untold Story, Human Pork Chop, The Eight Immortals Restaurant: The Untold Story, The Untold Story: Human Meat Roast Pork Buns
Zombie Bloodbath

1994

Aftermath
Dellamorte Dellamore
 Cemetery Man
Nightwatch
 Nattevagten
Return of the Boogeyman

The Return of the Texas Chainsaw Massacre
The Texas Chainsaw Massacre: The Next Generation
Scanner Cop
Schramm
Wes Craven's New Nightmare

1995

Candyman: Farewell to Flesh
Der Wag Nach Eden
The Road to Eden
Diary of a Serial Killer
Faces of Death V
Halloween: The Curse of Michael Myers
Scanner Cop II: Volkin's Revenge
Se7en
Xtro 3: Watch the Skies
Zombie Bloodbath II: Rage of the Undead

1996

The Ebola Syndrome
Faces of Death VI
From Dusk till Dawn
Hellraiser: Bloodline
Henry: Portrait of a Serial Killer, Part 2
Scream

1997

Alien 4 Resurrection
I Know What You Did Last Summer
Nightwatch
Scream II
Uncle Sam

1998

Bride of Chucky
Genesis
Halloween H20: 20 Years Later
I Still Know What You Did Last Summer
Psycho
Remake
Return of the Living Dead Part II (1988)
Urban Legend

1999

Anthropophagous 2000
Audition
Camp Blood
Jigoku
School's Out
Schrei – denn ich werde dich töten!
Violent Shit III: Infantry of Doom

2000

American Nightmare
American Psycho
Battle Royale
Final Destination
Hellraiser: Inferno
In the Light of the Moon
Scream III
Urban Legends: Final Cut
Zombie Bloodbath III: Zombie Armageddon (2000)

2001

Ichi the Killer
Jason X
School's Out II
Das Mädcheninternat – Deine Schreie Wird Niemand Hören
Slashers
Valentine
Zombie Chronicles

2002

28 Days Later
American Nightmare
American Psycho 2

Blood Feast 2: All U Can Eat
  Blood Feast 2: Buffet of Blood
Camp Blood 2
Halloween: Resurrection
Hellraiser: Hellseeker
In My Skin
  Dans Ma Peau

2003

Battle Royale II: Requiem,
Beyond Re-Animator
Cabin Fever
Cannibal Hillbillies
Cannibal World
  *Mondo Cannibale, Cannibal
  Holocaust 2: The Beginning*
Cheerleader Massacre
El Tran de la Bruja
  Spook House
Freddy vs. Jason
Haute Tension
  High Tension, Switchblade Romance
House of 1000 Corpses
The Janitor
The Last Horror Movie
Nails
Return to Sleepaway Camp
The Texas Chainsaw Massacre
  Remake
Wrong Turn

2004

2001 Maniacs
  remake of *Two Thousand Maniacs!*
Aliens vs. Predator
Creep
Dawn of the Dead
  Remake
Murder Set Pieces
Rooms for Tourists
  Habitaciones Para Turistas
Satan's Little Helper

Saw
Seed of Chucky
Shaun of the Dead
The Toolbox Murders

2005

Camp Blood 3: Within the Woods
Day of the Dead 2: Contagium
The Devil's Rejects
Evil
The Gingerdead Man
Hellraiser: Deader
Hellraiser: Hellwood
Hostel
Land of the Dead
Mortuary
Necropolis
Rave From the Grave
Reeker
Saw II
Visions of Suffering
Wolf Creek

2006

Behind the Mask: The Rise of Leslie
  Vernon
Bikini Bloodbath
Black Christmas
Cold Prey
  Fritt Vilt
Dead Snow
  Død Snø
Hatchet
The Hills Have Eyes
Night of the Living Dead: 3D
The Pumpkin Karver
Saw III
Severance
The Texas Chainsaw Massacre: The
  Beginning
To Let
  Para entrar a vivir
Wedding Slashers

2007
28 Weeks Later
30 Days of Night
Aliens vs. Predator: Requiem
Barricade
Death Proof
Diary of the Dead
Drive Thru
Halloween
  Remake
The Hills Have Eyes II
Hostel: Part II
Inside
  À L'Intérieur
The Mother of Tears
Planet Terror
Saw IV
Snuff 102
Timber Falls
Vacancy
Wrong Turn 2: Dead End

2008
Embodiment of Evil
Bikini Bloodbath II: Bikini
  Bloodbath Car Wash
Cold Prey 2: Resurrection
Day of the Dead
  Remake
Dying Breed
The Gingerdead Man 2: Passion of
  the Crust
Manhunt
  Rovdyr
Martyrs
Philosopy of a Knife
Prom Night
  Remake
Saw V
Untraceable

2009
Bikini Bloodbath III: Christmas
Cabin Fever 2: Spring Fever
Deadly Little Christmas
Evil – In the Time of Heroes
Friday the 13ᵗʰ
  Remake
Grotesque
Halloween II
  Remake
The Last House on the Left
My Bloody Valentine
  Remake
Saw VI
Skeleton Crew
Smash Cut
Sorority Row
Summer's Blood
Survival of the Dead
The Uh-Oh Show
Tormented
Wrong Turn 3: Left for Dead
Zombieland

2010
A Nightmare on Elm Street
  Remake
Cold Prey 3
Ferozz: The Wild Red Riding Hood
Hatchet 2
I Saw the Devil
I Spit on Your Grave
Saw 3D
We Are What We Are
  Mexican cannibals

2011
Juan de los Muertos
Mother's Day
  Remake
Scream IV

Index
of Directors

Zombie Apocalypse!

created by Stephen Jones

ISBN: 978-1-84901-303-1
Price: £7.99

THE END OF THE WORLD –
WITH FLESH-EATING ZOMBIES!

In the near future, a desperate and ever-more controlling UK government attempts to restore a sense of national pride with a New Festival of Britain. But construction work on the site of an old church in south London releases a centuries-old plague that turns its victims into flesh-hungry ghouls whose bite or scratch passes the contagion – a supernatural virus which has the power to revive the dead – on to others.

'The Death' soon sweeps across London and the whole country descends into chaos. When a drastic attempt to eradicate the outbreak at source fails, the plague spreads quickly to mainland Europe and then across the rest of the world.

Told through a series of interconnected eyewitness narratives – text messages, e-mails, blogs, letters, diaries and transcripts – this is an epic story of a world plunged into chaos as the dead battle the living for total domination.

**Will humanity triumph over the
worldwide zombie plague, or will the
walking dead inherit the Earth?**

Visit www.constablerobinson.com for more information

Zombie Apocalypse! Fightback

created by Stephen Jones

ISBN: 978-1-78033-465-3

Price: £8.99

THERE IS NOTHING TO FEAR BUT FEAR ITSELF . . .
AND ZOMBIES!

Following the outbreak of Human Reanimation Virus – more commonly referred to as 'The Death' – from a hidden crypt beneath a south London church, the centuries-old plague quickly spreads out from its epicentre to engulf the country. But borders are no barrier, and the supernatural disease soon reaches the shores of mainland Europe and is then carried around the rest of the world, turning its victims into flesh-eating zombies and resurrecting the dead as cannibal ghouls.

While we learn more about the mysterious Thomas Moreby – 'Patient Zero' – and track HRV as it reaches out across the globe, the surviving members of the human race begin their fightback against the legions of the walking dead. But even as mankind prepares to battle for its very survival, scientists are attempting to harness the power of the virus for their own requirements, and the Infected themselves are mutating into something . . . *different.*

Told through interconnected eyewitness accounts – emails, text messages, reports, diaries, found video footage and graphic adaptations – the remnants of humanity battle to survive in a world gone mad, as a New Zombie Order discovers that living death is not necessarily the end.

Visit www.constablerobinson.com for more information

The Mammoth Book of
Dracula

edited by Stephen Jones

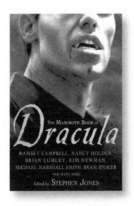

ISBN: 978-1-84901-566-0

Price: £7.99

**"Bram Stoker's courtly, sinister creation is still literature's greatest villain."
Stephen King**

Count Dracula . . . Lord of the Night . . . Prince of Darkness . . . King of the
Vampires! Since his creation more than a century ago, the name of Dracula has
become synonymous with vampire fiction. He is one of the world's most iconic
characters of fiction and film.

Now, this history of the blood-drinking nobleman follows Dracula from his
origins in Transylvania, through his travels down the decades, into a dystopian
twenty-first century where vampires rule the world.

This volume features contributions from acclaimed authors such as **Ramsey
Campbell, Christopher Fowler, Charlaine Harris, Nancy Holder, Nancy
Kilpatrick, Brian Lumley, Graham Masterton, Paul McAuley, Kim Newman,
Michael Marshall Smith, F. Paul Wilson** and many others.

"Here are mysterious strangers with strong, white teeth
aplenty, mystified or mesmerized by the modern world." *The Times*

"An alternate story of Dracula's non-life . . . the overall
standard is excellent." *SFX*

Visit www.constablerobinson.com for more information

The Mammoth Book of
Best New Horror 23
edited by Stephen Jones

ISBN: 978-1-78033-090-7
Price: £7.99

**The latest volume of the world's premier annual showcase
of horror and dark fantasy fiction**

Showcasing the very best, and most terrifying, short stories and novellas of horror and the supernatural by both contemporary masters of horror and exciting newcomers, including **Joan Aitken, Ramsey Campbell, Christopher Fowler, Joe R. Lansdale, John Ajvide Lindqvist, Robert Silverberg, Michael Marshall Smith, Evangeline Walton** and many others.

As ever, the new volume of this long-running and multiple award-winning anthology series also offers a detailed overview of the year in horror, a comprehensive necrology of notable names and a directory of useful contact details for dedicated horror fans and writers.

Now well into its third decade, The Mammoth Book of Best New Horror remains the world's leading annual anthology dedicated solely to showcasing the best in contemporary horror fiction.

'If you want to know what's available, then this is the place to look . . . These stories offer a snapshot of the horror genre.' *Black Static*

'The stories in The Mammoth Book of Best New Horror are proof that horror is still a healthy and viable genre.' *Locus*

Visit www.constablerobinson.com for more information

The Mammoth Book of the
Best of Best New Horror
edited by Stephen Jones

Clive Barker, Harlan Ellison, Neil Gaiman, Stephen King, Peter Straub And Many More

ISBN: 978-1-84901-304-8
Price: £9.99

A twenty year celebration of *Best New Horror*

For the past two decades the annual Mammoth Book of Best New Horror series has been the major showcase for superior short stories and novellas of horror and dark fantasy. This World Fantasy Award, British Fantasy Award and International Horror Guild Award-winning series has published more than 450 stories by around 200 of the genre's most famous and acclaimed authors, as well as many just starting out on their careers.

To celebrate the anthology's twentieth anniversary, the editor has selected from each volume one story that he considers to be the 'best' by some of horror's biggest names, including **Ramsey Campbell, Christopher Fowler, Elizabeth Hand, Joe Hill, Glen Hirshberg, Caitlín R. Kiernan, Terry Lamsley, Tim Lebanon, Brian Lumley, Paul J. Mcauley, Kim Newman, Mark Samuels, Michael Marshall Smith, Lisa Tuttle**, and **Simon Kurt Unsworth**.

"Stephen Jones . . . has a better sense of the genre than almost anyone in this country." Lisa Tuttle, *The Times Books*

Visit www.constablerobinson.com for more information